Under the special patronage of

*President George Bush
of the United States of America*

and

*President Francesco Cossiga
of the Republic of Italy*

TITIAN
Prince of Painters

Marsilio Editori

This exhibition has been organized by
the Comune di Venezia, Assessorato alla Cultura
the Ministero per i Beni Culturali e Ambientali,
the Soprintendenza ai Beni Artistici e Storici di Venezia
and the National Gallery of Art, Washington,
with Galileo Industrie Ottiche, Venezia

An indemnity for this exhibition was granted by
the Federal Council on the Arts and the Humanities

Additional support has been provided by
Silvio Berlusconi Communications

Official Insurance Company
Assicurazioni Generali

Official Air Carrier
Alitalia

EXHIBITION DATES

Palazzo Ducale, Venice
2 June-7 October 1990

National Gallery of Art, Washington
28 October 1990-27 January 1991

ISBN 0-89468-154-0

Cover: Titian, *Venus with a Mirror,*
National Gallery of Art, Washington, Andrew W. Mellon Collection
Back cover: Titian, *Portrait of a Man (Man with a Glove),*
Musée du Louvre, Paris

CONTENTS

COMMITTEE OF HONOR

ENRIQUE BARON CRESPO
Presidente del Parlamento Europeo

NILDE JOTTI
Presidente della Camera dei Deputati

GIOVANNI SPADOLINI
Presidente del Senato

GIULIO ANDREOTTI
Presidente del Consiglio

GIANNI DE MICHELIS
Ministro degli Esteri

CARLO BERNINI
Ministro dei Trasporti

CARLO TOGNOLI
Ministro del Turismo e dello Spettacolo

FERDINANDO FACCHIANO
Ministro per i Beni Culturali e Ambientali

ADVISORY COMMITTEE

NEREO LARONI *President*
J. CARTER BROWN
FRANCESCO CAPOROSSI
FRANCESCO SISINNI

SCIENTIFIC COMMITTEE

FRANCESCO VALCANOVER *President*
DAVID ALAN BROWN
GIOVANNA NEPI SCIRÈ
GIANDOMENICO ROMANELLI

MARCO CHIARINI
GIANVITTORIO DILLON
SYLVIA FERINO
MICHEL LACLOTTE
ANTONIO PAOLUCCI
ALFONSO E. PEREZ SANCHEZ
ANNAMARIA PETRIOLI TOFANI
TERISIO PIGNATTI
LIONELLO PUPPI
PIERRE ROSENBERG
NICOLA SPINOSA
VITALIJ SUSLOV

On 12 October 1989, even with the announcement of Titian, Prince of Painters *at the Gallery in the presence of President Francesco Cossiga of Italy, minister of Foreign Affairs Gianni De Michelis, and Mrs. Bush, the idea of a major international loan exhibition of works by the greatest of all Venetian painters was hard to believe. The last major Titian exhibition, the legendary showing of his work at Ca' Pesaro in Venice, was held more than half a century ago, in 1935.*

Only a particularly close collaboration between the organizers in Venice and Washington, and the extraordinary generosity of the lenders and supporters, have made this exhibition possible. Just one of the paintings, the magnificent Portrait of Doge Andrea Gritti *being lent by the National Gallery of Art to the present exhibition, had also appeared in the earlier show in Venice, when it still belonged to a private Viennese collector. Between 1937 and 1961, the Titian paintings scattered among the Mellon, Widener, and Kress collections came to the National Gallery. Today the most extensive survey of Titian's oeuvre to be found in an American collection can be seen at the Gallery in Washington. We are pleased to lend our six finest Titians to this important exhibition.*

Special thanks are due to our many Italian colleagues and collaborators, among them Professor Francesco Valcanover, head of the Scientific Committee; Giandomenico Romanelli, director of the Musei Civici, Venice; Giovanna Nepi Scirè, Soprintendente ai Beni Artistici e Storici; and Madile Gambier of the Assessorato alla Cultura, Venice. A crucial role in organizing and supporting the show was also taken by Galileo Industrie Ottiche S.p.A., with the leader-

ship and guidance of Dr. Francesco Caporossi. Additional support was provided by Silvio Berlusconi Communications. Indemnification for the exhibition in Washington was provided by the Federal Council on the Arts and the Humanities. David Alan Brown, the Gallery's curator of Italian Renaissance paintings, and his assistant Gretchen Hirschauer were largely responsible for curating the exhibition in Washington.

Numerous art historians contributed to this catalogue, which forms a lasting scholarly tribute to Titian. To all these friends we are grateful for their cooperation in enabling us to present this great exhibition in Washington, its only venue in the United States.

J. CARTER BROWN
Director, National Gallery of Art, Washington

The success of this project has depended largely upon the contributions of numerous individuals from both sides of the Atlantic. At the National Gallery, special thanks are due to Daniel Herrick, Treasurer, and Joseph Krakora, External Affairs Officer; D. Dodge Thompson and his staff in the department of exhibition programs; Gordon Anson, Mark Leithauser, and Gaillard Ravenel, department of installation and design; Mary Yakush, editors office; Mary Suzor and the staff of the office of the registrar; Elizabeth A.C. Weil, corporate relations officer; Robert Echols, Julia Thompson, and Elaine Trigiani, department of Italian Renaissance paintings; and the staff of the library and photographic archives.

This exhibition, which the Ministero per i Beni Culturali e Ambientali, in collaboration with the Assessorato alla Cultura of the City of Venice, with the National Gallery of Art, Washington, and with private enterprise, has brought together on the occasion of the five hundredth anniversary of the birth of Titian, testifies to the importance of collaboration between the public and private sectors, and to the superb results that such a partnership can produce.

The paintings of the great master are dispersed throughout the major museums of the world. To succeed therefore in bringing together paintings, woodcuts and drawings was no simple task. The 1935 exhibition dedicated to Titian, at Ca' Pesaro, which numbered one hundred paintings, included several since removed from Titian's autograph works. Certain works included in 1935 have not returned to Venice, such as the Averoldi polyptych in Brescia, given the greater sensibility in modern times to the potential risks such as those of transport and climate change.

The lending institutions have shown great generosity, and have made possible a carefully selected exhibition of the highest standards of quality and completeness. Those who have contributed with major loans include: the State Hermitage Museum, Leningrad; the Státní Zámek, Kroměříž; the Kunsthistorisches Museum and the Akademie der bildenden Künste, Vienna; the Gemäldegalerie Alte Meister, Kassel; the Museu de Arte, São Paulo, Brazil; the Koninklijk Museum voor Schone Kunsten, Antwerp; the Detroit Institute of Arts; the Thyssen-Bornemisza Collection, Lugano; the Marquess of Bath, Longleat House, Warminster; the Museum Boymans-van Beuningen, Rotterdam; the Musée du Louvre, Paris; and the National Gallery, London.

Particular thanks are due the Museo del Prado, Madrid, for loaning six works, and the National Gallery of Art, Washington, for loaning six paintings including The Feast of the Gods, an extraordinary masterpiece, recently restored, on which the old Giovanni Bellini, the young Titian and others all worked at different times.

The contribution of the major Italian state museums has been no less significant. Important loans have been granted by the Galleria Palatina and the Galleria degli Uffizi, Florence; the Pinacoteca di Brera, Milan; the Gallerie Nazionali di Capodimonte, Naples; the Galleria Borghese, Rome; the Palazzo Ducale, Urbino; and last but not least, the City of Venice.

Since 1974, the Soprintendenza ai Beni Artistici e Storici, Venice, has carried out a program of restorations of Titian's paintings in the Gallerie dell'Accademia and elsewhere in the city. This exhibition did not therefore come as a surprise nor did it cause hasty preparatory conservation. From this point of view the project has been exemplary and stimulating.

The selection of the paintings has been based not only on a plan to illustrate the entire range of themes in Titian's long career and the complex evolution of his style, but has also taken into careful account the state of conservation of the works themselves.

FERDINANDO FACCHIANO
Ministro dei Beni Culturali e Ambientali

Barely two years have passed since, sparked by an idea of Daniele Ferretti's, we launched the organization of this exhibition. For me, then Assessore alla Cultura for the City of Venice, it was by far the most important element in an already crowded exhibition program. The commitment to mount this exhibition depended on a series of crucial factors that would make it possible.

The first was to secure the necessary funding for such an imposing project. We were fortunate indeed to find a Venetian company as sponsor, Galileo Industrie Ottiche, which through its president Francesco Caporossi, took on not only the financial burden but also a considerable number of administrative and promotional tasks, and worked side by side with the other agencies involved. The fact that Galileo Industrie Ottiche has important connections also with Cadore, Titian's birthplace, makes their choice all the more appropriate.

The second sine qua non was the willingness of the principal Italian museums to lend their Titians, necessary to achieve an exhaustive representation of the whole career of the artist as planned by the steering committee. Thanks to the scrupulous and determined assistance of Giovanna Nepi Scirè and to the goodwill and understanding of her colleagues, this goal has been achieved.

A third important condition was the loan of certain masterpieces from abroad, given that Titian's oeuvre is spread throughout the world. Francesco Valcanover and Giandomenico Romanelli, with decisive support from the Italian Foreign Minister Gianni De Michelis, succeeded in obtaining important loans from West and East, indeed wherever this was compatible with the safety and conservation of the work itself.

It is a great pleasure to be able to say that a long list of affirmative responses, those which after all have made the exhibition possible, constitutes proof of the importance accorded to the Assessorato alla Cultura in recent years. Our partnership with the National Gallery of Art, Washington, is a further indication of this.

To have worked with such an enthusiastic and capable team, led by Madile Gambier, even though the caprices of political life have led me elsewhere, for such a fascinating project was for me very gratifying indeed.

NEREO LARONI
President of the Advisory Committee

An exhibition of the art of Titian not only illustrates the work of a supreme artist, who gathers and summarizes in himself, relives, recreates and gives back to history the pictorial culture of Venice, of which he constitutes one of the highest peaks, but also amounts to a celebration of Venice itself, the translation into art of its splendor. In history, the life and work of Titian extend from the League of Cambrai war that saw Venice fighting alone for survival against the whole of Europe, to the Battle of Lepanto at which the whole might of Venice was placed at the service of the defense of European civilization. Titian epitomizes this golden century, which yielded the ripest fruit of the Italian Renaissance, and yet the end of his life and of his career witnessed that dissolution of form, which is like a metaphorical premonition of decadence.

There are many and profound motives for thanking all those who have given their precious collaboration for this show, which in the Palace of the Doges honors both Titian and Venice, and is an incomparable occasion for study, for contemplation and for enjoyment of an art with no equal.

ANTONIO CASELLATI
Mayor of Venice

xii

Contributors to the Catalogue

FILIPPA M. ALIBERTI GAUDIOSO (F.M.A.G.)
LUISA ARRIGONI (L.A.)
IRINA ARTEMIEVA (I.A.)
ADRIANA AUGUSTI (A.A.)
PIETRO MARIA BARDI (P.M.B.)
GIULIANO BRIGANTI (G.B.)
DAVID ALAN BROWN (D.A.B.)
ALESSANDRO CECCHI (A.C.)
M. AGNESE CHIARI MORETTO WIEL (M.A.C.M.W.)
GIANVITTORIO DILLON (G.D.)
ROBERT ECHOLS (R.E.)
SYLVIA FERINO (S.F.)
MARTINA FLEISCHER (M.F.)
JEROEN GILTAIJ (J.G.)
SILVIA GRAMIGNA DIAN (S.G.D.)
JEAN HABERT (J.H.)
RICHARD HARPRATH (R.H.)
KRISTINA HERMANN FIORE (K.H.F.)
JURGEN M. LEHMANN (J.M.L.)
PATRICE MARANDEL (P.M.)
ETTORE MERKEL (E.M.)
ANTONIO NATALI (A.N.)
GIOVANNA NEPI SCIRÈ (G.N.S.)
LOREDANA OLIVATO (L.O.)
SERENA PADOVANI (S.P.)
ANNALISA PERISSA TORRINI (A.P.T.)
TERISIO PIGNATTI (T.P.)
GIUSEPPE MARIA PILO (G.M.P.)
LIONELLO PUPPI (L.P.)
PAOLA ROSSI (P.R.)
FIORELLA SPADAVECCHIA (F.S.)
SANDRO SPONZA (S.S.)
JESUS URREA (J.U.)
FRANCESCO VALCANOVER (F.V.)
ERIK VANDAMME (E.V.)
CATHERINE WHISTLER (C.W.)

Catalogue entries translated by SHARON HECKER, PHILIP RYLANDS, and ELIZABETH WILKINS.
Essay by A. PAOLUCCI translated by JOHN HARPER.
Essays by L. LAZZARINI, V. FASSINA, M. MATTEINI, A. MOLES and G. BORTOLASO translated by SHARON WARRACK.
Essays by G. BENZONI, G. PADOAN, L. PUPPI, and T. PIGNATTI translated by ROBERT ERICH WOLF.
Essays by G. ROMANELLI, F. VALCANOVER, and G. NEPI SCIRÈ, and the chronology by F. VALCANOVER, translated by PHILIP RYLANDS

Lenders to the exhibition

ACCADEMIA CARRARA *Bergamo*

ASHMOLEAN MUSEUM *Oxford*

BIBLIOTECA NAZIONALE MARCIANA *Venice*

THYSSEN-BORNEMISZA COLLECTION *Lugano*

DETROIT INSTITUTE OF ARTS *Detroit*

FONDAZIONE MAGNANI-ROCCA *Corte di Mamiano*

GABINETTO DISEGNI E STAMPE DEGLI
UFFIZI *Florence*

GALLERIA BORGHESE *Rome*

GALLERIA DEGLI UFFIZI *Florence*

GALLERIA GIORGIO FRANCHETTI ALLA CA'
D'ORO *Venice*

GALLERIA NAZIONALE DELLE MARCHE *Urbino*

GALLERIE DELL'ACCADEMIA *Venice*

GEMÄLDEGALERIE DER AKADEMIE DER BILDENDEN
KÜNSTE *Vienna*

KONINKLIJK MUSEUM VOOR SCHONE
KUNSTEN *Antwerp*

KUNSTHISTORISCHES MUSEUM *Vienna*

THE METROPOLITAN MUSEUM OF ART *New York*

MUSÉE DU LOUVRE, DÉPARTEMENT DES
PEINTURES *Paris*

MUSEUM BOYMANS-VAN BEUNINGEN *Rotterdam*

MUSEO CORRER *Venice*

MUSEO DEL PRADO *Madrid*

STATE HERMITAGE MUSEUM *Leningrad*

MUSEU DE ARTE DE SÃO PAULO *São Paulo, Brazil*

MUSEO E GALLERIE NAZIONALI DI
CAPODIMONTE *Naples*

NATIONAL GALLERY OF ART *Washington*

XV

Acknowledgements:

For the Aldermanship of Culture
Alderman of Culture
FULGENZIO LIVIERI
Director of the City Museums
GIANDOMENICO ROMANELLI
Administrative Director
LINO DALLA VALLE
Administrative Office
ANTONIO SERRA, GIOVANNI BUSETTO
SANDRA TAGLIAPIETRA
Press Office
ROBERTA LOMBARDO, STEFANIA ZUIN
Archival Office
FRANCO FLAUTO
Secretariat and Ceremony
PAOLA DE GRANDIS, LORENZA MAZZEGA
Exhibition Office
CHIARA ALESSANDRI, MONICA DA CORTÀ, DANIELA
FERRETTI, MADILE GAMBIER, CLARA URLANDO
School Information Department
STEFANO VERSO
and
MAURIZIO CARLIN, OSCAR D'ANTIGA, GIOVANNI DORIA
GIUSEPPE GUERRA, ELISABETTA MARELLA, MARCO MIZZAN
GIAMPAOLA PATALACCI, MICHELA SCHETTINO
MARIA STELLA VECCHIATI

For Palazzo Ducale
Director
UMBERTO FRANZOI
Scientific Staff
MICHELA KNEZEVICH
Public Relations
IRENEO MANOLI
Technical Assistance
SILVANO BOLDRIN, SERGIO BRUSSA
Archive and Protocol
GIAMPAOLO PEDROCCO, GIANCARLO ZOFFI
and
MARIA BIASIOLI, VITTORIO BASSO, ALCEO D'AMBROSI
GIOVANNI SENIGAGLIA

For the Soprintendenza ai Beni Artistici e Storici
Laboratory of computerized non-destructive analysis
PAOLO SPEZZANI, VIRGINIA VIANELLO
Laboratory and photographic Archive
MARINA AMURO, LORENZO DAL MASO, FERNANDA QUAGLIA
GIANFRANCO SPINAZZI, DINO ZANELLA
School Information Department
ANNALISA PERISSA TORRINI

Administrative Office
ROBERTO DE MARCHI, CESARIO RASO, GRAZIELLA VIANELLO
Export Office
ADRIANA AUGUSTI, GIUSEPPE ZENNARO
Technical Office
ELIO PIO ARMELAO, CARLA CARLISI, LORENZO SIMION
Press Office
ROBERTO FONTANARI
Packing and Moving Staff
LUIGI SANTE SAVIO
and the staff of the Soprintendenza

For Galileo Industrie Ottiche
CLAUDIA BERNA, FEDERICA BRIGGI, PAOLA FRARE

Special thanks to
the Secretary General of the Cabinet of the Mayor
the Ceremonial Office of the Comune of Venezia
the Administrative Direction of the
«Carlo Goldoni» Theatre
the Comitato di Settore and the Divisione VII
of the Ministero per i Beni Culturali e Ambientali
particularly to
ROSETTA MOSCO AGRESTI e MARIA GRAZIA BENINI

ALESSANDRO VATTANI
General Director of the Ministry of Foreign Affairs
GIOVANNI CASTELLANI PASTORIS
Italian Ambassador in Prague
FLAVIO ANDREIS
Director of the Italian Cultural Institute in Prague

A special thank to the Comune and the Soprintendenza
ai Beni Artistici e Storici di Milano for generously lending
the *Maddalena* of the Hermitage

TITIAN

Francesco Valcanover

AN INTRODUCTION TO TITIAN

More than half a century separates the two exhibitions dedicated to Titian. Thumbing through the catalogue of the 1935 exhibition, organized by the City of Venice at Ca' Pesaro and curated by Nino Barbantini and Gino Fogolari, it becomes obvious that several paintings included there are missing from the present exhibition. Some, perhaps ten, have been disqualified by more recent scholarship. The absence of others is justified by the fragility of their supports and grounds, panels mainly, or by their state of conservation, far from ideal given the instability of the materials that jeopardizes many of Titian's works in modern times. These were problems that were, to say the least, underestimated in the 1935 exhibition. Whatismore, the mass of loans from the Pitti, the Uffizi and the Capodimonte museums reflect the authoritarianism that ruled in Italy even in the cultural field in the years before the World War II.

But then again the 1990 exhibition boasts many works absent in 1935. For example, the Palazzo Ducale exhibition will be enhanced by the numerous paintings from the Prado and the National Gallery of Art, Washington, and other works of crucial importance in reconstructing Titian's oeuvre. Among the more important are the fresco fragments from the Fondaco dei Tedeschi, the *sinopia* from the Scuola del Santo, Padua, the *Madonna and Child with Saint Catherine* from the National Gallery, London, the *Portrait of a Gentleman* from Kassel, the *Self-Portrait* from Berlin, the *Young Boy with Dogs* from Rotterdam, and the *Allegory of Prudence* from the National Gallery, London.

The presence of a small number of autograph drawings by Titian, preparatory either to works in the show or to lost paintings, which are interspersed through the exhibition rather than separated in a section of their own, contributes to our understanding of the development of Titian's pictorial ideas.

Compared to the 1935 Ca' Pesaro show, this exhibition offers some as it were unpublished masterpieces – those paintings that have undergone conservative treatment over the past thirty years or in preparation for the exhibition here in the Palazzo Ducale. They can be said now to be more honest witnesses to Titian's genius, and make possible a more accurate understanding of Titian's intentions. Documentation and detailing of this is reserved for the catalogue entries, but it should be mentioned that in Venice particularly the conservation campaign has included every work by the master in the city, with the single exception of the San Salvador *Transfiguration*, which requires a long and meditated campaign of technical and historical documentation before planned conservation can be carried out. It is a highly instructive time, with quantities of new data and insights emerging from the vital and timely conservation work being carried out on an impressive scale, such as is described in Giovanna Nepi Scirè's essay in this catalogue. The results of research with microphotography of paint layers, with x-radiography, infra-red reflectography and the reflectoscope, some of it of exceptional interest, carried out in Venice, in other Italian museums and abroad, have enriched the studies of Titian's entire career, let alone our understanding of single works. For this and other reasons the curatorial committee decided to entrust to the lending institutions the task of writing the catalogue entries, in the certainty that in many instances they would bring to light new data on the still unresolved questions of dating, attribution and meaning in Titian's work. This should in turn stimulate further research, an effect that even the 1935 exhibition had, giving a huge impulse to archival, art historical, socio-economic, and iconographic studies.

The fundamental work by Crowe and Cavalcaselle (1877-78) was followed by monographs by G. Gronau (1904), C. Ricketts (1910) and W. Suida (1935). Among the studies of special aspects of Titian's work those of C. Phillips (1897), L. Hourticq (1919), T. Hetzer (1920, 1929), and R. Longhi (1925, 1927) were of particular importance for their stylistic and critical content, while later monographs by H. Tietze (1936, 1950), T. Hetzer (1948), F. Valcanover (1960), R. Pallucchini (1969) and H.E. Wethey (1969-75), and others no less useful by G.A. Dell'Acqua (1955), A. Morassi (1964), A. Ballarin (1968), D. Rosand (1979) and C. Hope (1980) added significantly to the availability of published images of the work and to Titian's bibliography. Finally it is worth noting some of the general works in which Titian's career is discussed in the context of his time or from different viewpoints: R. Longhi (1946, 1978, 1980), E. Panofsky (1969), S.J. Freedberg (1970), J. Wilde (1974), A. Gentili (1980), D. Rosand (1982), N. Huse and W. Wolters

(1986), M. Lucco and S. Mason Rinaldi (1988) and T. Pignatti (1989).

The bibliography of the present catalogue testifies to the numerous articles and special studies dedicated to Titian in recent decades, concerning especially Titian's beginnings, his putative mannerist period, his extraordinary late style, the hidden meanings of his works, his relations with his patrons and with the culture of his time, historical and political events, and contemporary manners. The bibliography shows how important were the conferences organized for the 400th anniversary of his death in 1976: in Rome the 'Convegno dei Lincei'; in Venice 'Tiziano nel quarto centenario della sua morte' (1977), 'Tiziano ed il Manierismo europeo' (1978), 'Tiziano e Venezia' (1980); in Pieve di Cadore 'Tizianus Cadorinus' (1982); in New York 'Titian, His World and His Legacy' (1982). No less important were the exhibitions organized on the same occasion of Titian's prints in Venice (Muraro and Rosand 1976) and of his drawings in Venice (Oberhuber 1976) and Florence (Meijer 1976 and Rearick 1976). Exhibitions dedicated to Titian took place in Urbino (1976), Milan (1977) and Florence (1978), and Titian has also figured in the wider context of exhibitions dedicated to sixteenth-century Venetian art: 'Giorgione a Venezia' (1978), 'The Golden Century of Venetian Painting' (1979), 'Da Tiziano a el Greco' (1981), 'The Genius of Venice' (1983). Let us not forget that the study of Titian as a draftsman effectively began long after the 1935 exhibition, with Tietze publishing the first *corpus* in 1944, followed by the exhibitions in Venice and Florence mentioned above (1976), W.R. Rearick's study (1977), the catalogues raisonné of T. Pignatti and M.A. Chiari (1979), H.E. Wethey (1987) and M.A. Chiari Moretto Wiel (1980).

New archival research, since the valuable discoveries of the nineteenth and early twentieth centuries, has been conducted above all by Charles Hope, while the fundamental usefulness of such research has been demonstrated by the thorough review of the Archivio General di Simancas (Cloulas 1967, Ferrarino 1975), which filled out the collection of letters between Titian and the Spanish court, by now the most extensive surviving correspondence with regard to the artist (Gandini-Fabbro 1976, 1989).

The essays and entries in this catalogue make further contributions to Titian studies. Quite apart from its ephemeral pretext marking the fifth centenary of the artist's birth, this exhibition stakes its claim firstly as a scholarly and scientific occasion, and secondly as a major cultural event for the greater public, presented in a simple and linear installation intended to make the viewing of Titian's painting as enjoyable as possible, within an exemplary environment for security and conservation.

The exhibition is supplemented by major paintings elsewhere in the city, whose presence in their original locations offers insights into Titian's conception of the relationship between a public work and its architectural and spatial environment: the magnificent altarpieces of *The Assumption of the Virgin* and of the *Pesaro Madonna* in the Church of the Frari, and the *Presentation of the Virgin in the Temple* in the former *albergo* of the Scuola della Carità, now the Gallerie dell'Accademia.

"1513. The last day of May. In the Council of x
The petition copied below was read
Most Illustrious Council of x
I Titian, having since boyhood passed in Cadore onward, Most Serene Prince and Most Excellent Lords, given myself to learning the art of painting not so much for the desire to earn money as for the attempt to acquire a small fame; and being counted among those who currently make a profession of art. And also even as I am presently urgently pressed by His Holiness the Pope and other Lords to go and serve them: So desiring as a most loyal subject to Your Magnificences to leave some mark in this glorious City, I have decided, thinking thus, to be so bold as to offer myself to paint in the Maggior Consiglio and to place all my skill and wit that I have so far gained, beginning, if Your Magnificences deem appopriate, with the large canvas of that battle on the side of the *piazza* which is the most difficult and which a certain man, to this day, has not wanted to take on.
I Most Excellent Lords would be most content to receive in payment for the work whatever fee should be judged proper and much less. But because, as I have said above, I value only my honor, and need only enough to live, would it please Your Magnificences to deign to concede to me for life the first *sansaria* of the Fondaco dei Tedeschi which should become available, notwithstanding others who wait, with the modes, conditions, obligations and exemptions that Giovanni Bellini

1. Titian, "Saint Mark Enthroned," detail. Chiesa della Salute, Venice

has, and two young men that I would take on to help me, to be paid by the Salt Office [Officio del Sal], together with paints and all other necessary things, the same as in the recent months have been conceded by the said Most Illustrious Council to the said Giovanni: That I promise Your Most Excellent Lords to carry out the picture; and with such quickness and excellence that you will be satisfied: to whom I humbly commend myself."

The forthright and determined tone of the petition is interesting. The artist, who was barely twenty-three years of age, first took note of his origins in Cadore and the years of his training in Venice, and then in a tone of firm resolution addressed himself to the Council of Ten, declaring himself ready to paint in the Sala del Maggior Consiglio of the Palazzo Ducale, and to begin with a large canvas to replace the ruined fresco by Guariento of the *Battle of Spoleto* – subtle evidence of his pride, since this had been avoided by the other artists working on the huge project, Gentile and Giovanni Bellini, Alvise Vivarini and Vittore Carpaccio, because it was between two windows in *contre-jour*.

Titian declared his readiness to forego an opportunity to join the Papal court of Leo x in Rome at Pietro Bembo's invitation, and to ignore the invitation of other august patrons, if he were to to work for the Venetian State. This explicit declaration of loyalty to the Republic of Saint Mark was particularly telling in a year in which the fate of the city was far from certain, with the *terraferma* empire invaded by still-rampaging imperial troops. Finally the petition informs us of Titian's self-assurance, as he asks not only to work in the Palazzo Ducale but to benefit from the same sinecure and privileges as Giovanni Bellini.

When in 1513 he offered to replace the eighty-year old Bellini as leading artist of the Republic, not more than fifteen years had passed, if the sources are to be believed, since his arrival in Venice from a remote Alpine corner of the empire, on the threshold of the new century.

Venice was already a city of exceptional splendor, the most glorious and wisely governed of all those visited in 1494 by Philippe de Commynes. It had reached its virtually definitive form, majestically recorded in Jacopo de' Barbari's aerial view, dated 1500. Venice was among the most heavily populated cities in the western world

and its fleet was still a major force in the Mediterranean economy, despite the discovery of the Cape route to India and the ever increasing threat of the Turks. It continued its voluminous maritime trade along the customary sea-lanes and at the same time, not without internal strain, it expanded its mainland territories, where agriculture and the life of the Veneto villa grew side by side. Cultural renewal and growth was no less expansive. Historical, literary and philosophical studies flourished at the Cancelleria di San Marco and at the School of Logic and Natural Philosophy at the Rialto. The printing presses, that of Aldus Manutius particularly, were the busiest in Europe, while Venetian patricians were putting together collections of antiquities, and scientific studies prospered, of which the publication of Luca Pacioli's *Summa de Arithmetica, Geometrica et Proportionalità* was symptomatic.

Artistic style and taste underwent profound changes in this period. The late florid Gothic of the Ca' d'Oro and the Porta della Carta at the Palazzo Ducale was succeeded by the refined architectural forms in marble and Istrian stone of Pietro Lombardo, Mauro Codussi, and Antonio Rizzo. Buildings ancient and modern, public and private, were enriched with sculptures, furnishings, frescoes and paintings that shared the insignia of the Renaissance, all of them imprinted with the traditional mark of the Venetian *Kunstwollen*, color.

At the turn of the century, the time of Titian's training and earliest independent activity, fundamental changes were taking place in Venetian art, only partly explicable by the no-less radical developments in Central Italy. Though brief, Leonardo da Vinci's visit to Venice in 1500 was not without importance for Venetian art. In 1505-06 Albrecht Dürer was in the city. His 'realistic expressionism' stimulated the taste for Northern art among local painters, though this was already a factor in Venice given the diffusion of prints and the presence of Flemish and German paintings in Venetian collections. As early as 1504-05 Giorgione had developed his vision of nature using a novel technique in which he dispensed with preliminary drawings – a revolution to which Giovanni Bellini seems to have responded with his 1505 San Zaccaria *Madonna*, with its new emotive use of color. In the same year Lotto painted his first works, revealing a

2. Titian, "Miracle of the Speaking Babe," fresco detail. Scuola del Santo, Padua

personal and psychologically tense style, which was completely independent of Giorgione's. In 1508 Fra Bartolomeo, preceded by sketches and engravings, drew the attention of Venetian painters to the classicism that Michelangelo and Raphael had developed in Florence and Rome.

Faced by such formidable innovation, the young Titian was perfectly at ease. His childhood is tinted by legend – his spontaneous talent, which prompted him to paint a 'Madonna' from the juices of crushed flowers in his native Pieve di Cadore, or his supposed apprenticeship to Antonio da Cadore, a modest and old-fashioned follower of Bartolomeo Vivarini. Titian's training in Venice, as described by Lodovico Dolce in 1557, also savours of the ideal – with Titian passing from the mosaicist Sebastiano Zuccato to the workshop of Gentile Bellini, which he then quit in favor of Giovanni Bellini and finally Giorgione, indicating thus a precocious discrimination between 'conservative' and 'modern' mentors.

Giovanni Bellini would have seemed to Titian the summation of the Venetian Quattrocento, in the carefully structured responsiveness of his forms and colors, whereas in Giorgione he would have admired the originality, rich with novel senses and significances, of a way of making paint merge in glowing atmospheric transitions, comparable to but linguistically different from Leonardo in this period. But, "urged by nature to greater things," he also looked carefully at the expressive vitality of the *Madonna of the Rose Garlands*, in which Albrecht Dürer revealed "the desire to contribute to the peculiarly Italian genre of the altarpiece and to renew it by projecting the Icon into nature, transforming the *Sacra Conversazione* into an animated debate, with an exaltation of colors" (Chastel 1986). It was this engagement with the 'natural' at first hand that attracted Titian to the numerous paintings by the '*ponentini*,' Northern and especially Flemish artists, which Michiel was to observe in Venetian private collections.

The young Titian was certainly aware of the classical language of Raphael and Michelangelo in Florence and Rome in the opening years of the Cinquecento, which was brought to Venice itself in the person of Fra' Bartolomeo in 1508, and which found in Sebastiano Luciani, like Titian a 'creature' of Giorgione, a second admirer, as his paintings for the churches of San Bartolomeo and San Giovanni Crisostomo make clear. It comes as no surprise to find that in his first secure works, the frescoes of the Fondaco dei Tedeschi finished in 1508-09, Titian showed himself an innovator even with respect to Giorgione, who had completed frescoes at the Fondaco only a few months before. The comparison between the extant fragments of these frescoes, the first visible and public affirmation of the new Venetian art, by the one and by the other, reveals the distance that already separated Titian from Giorgione. Despite the influence that Giorgione exerted over Titian, which all early sources spoke of, their artistic inclinations could hardly have been more different. Giorgione's *Nude*, ensconced in her niche with modulated curves and delicate weight-shift, seems to partake of a poetical dream world. Titian's figures take almost forceful possession of the space around them, with easy confidence, athletically posed with abrupt foreshortenings, addressing themselves to the light in resonating zones of color.

In 1510, at a time of political uncertainty and menace to the Venetian Republic, Titian was commissioned to paint three frescoes of scenes from the life of Saint Anthony at the Scuola del Santo, Padua, completing them the following year. On this occasion Titian's task was not to paint, as at the Fondaco, allusive figures with hidden meanings, but to illustrate for the devout some miracles of this popular Franciscan saint. A *sinopia* by Titian, discovered in the *scuola* in 1969, suggests that his reliance on Giorgione was still a factor, but in the frescoes themselves the narratives, quite unlike Giorgione's, are acted out with strongly felt human emotions, which stop short of rhetoric or religiosity, on an idealized and noble formal plane. Protagonists and witnesses crowd the stage, their grandiose forms and measured gestures combined in slow rhythms that smother even the most dramatic accents. As in the frescoes at the Fondaco and the altarpiece of Santo Spirito in Isola, Titian based his language on the spread of broad colored planes in vivid harmonies, dramatized by a dynamic chiaroscuro. With this spectacle, more intense and vivid than real life, where man and nature come together in an ideal of beauty, classic in its perfection, the young Titian

3. Titian, "Sinopia with Figures, Traces of Landscape," detail.
Arca del Santo, Padua

draws abreast of the achievements of Raphael and Michelangelo.

The maturity of Titian's artistic vocabulary by the time of the Paduan frescoes makes it possible to date the conception of his large woodcut engraving, the *Triumph of Crist* in the same period or soon after. Titian's borrowings from Mantegna, Dürer, Michelangelo and Raphael are transformed into the exceptionally grandiose vitality of the figure style which we later see in the Frari *Assumption*.

There are no other documented works from this period, in which Titian so vigorously matured. Critics have tried in the past, and still try today, to fill out the period on the basis of style, with widely differing views on dating and even attribution. Works which Titian painted prior to the Fondaco commission most likely include the *Flight into Egypt* in the Hermitage, Leningrad, and *Orpheus and Eurydice* in the Accademia Carrara, Bergamo, which share a still archaic description of form. Both reveal a fascination for landscape that Paolo Pino, in 1548, attributed to the young Titian: "I have seen marvelous landscapes by Titian, and far more graceful than those of the Flemings." Again the votive painting of Jacopo Pesaro, in Antwerp has been dated as early as 1503-07, but here, with the exception of the Bellinesque figure of Saint Peter, the confidence evident in both the composition and the technique point to a later date, contemporary with the *Sacre Conversazioni* of the early 1510s.

More convincing instead is the documentation published by Anderson (1976) for a dating in 1508 of the *Christ Carrying the Cross* in the Scuola di San Rocco, which despite the fact that its Giorgione-Titian attribution is still controversial, is most likely to be by Titian, at a time when he was particularly close to Giorgione.

The compositional structure and breadth of form and color that distinguished Titian's Venice and Padua frescoes are shared by a series of other paintings which in the past, and sporadically today, have been attributed to Giorgione, often on account of their subject matter: the so-called 'Ariosto,' the 'Schiavona,' and the *Noli Me Tangere* in London, the *Concert Champêtre* in the Louvre, *Christ and the Adulteress* in Glasgow, the *Madonna and Child with Saints Anthony and Roch* in the Prado, and the Pitti *Concert*. This group even includes the *Saint Mark Enthroned* formerly in Santo Spirito in Isola, of which Vasari (1568) remarked: "many thought it was by Giorgione." Comparison between the *Saint Mark Enthroned* and Giorgione's Castelfranco *Madonna* highlights the tentativeness of Giorgione's composition, however fascinating for its atmospheric quality, whereas Titian, hardly five years later, was composing with monumental forms, bonded in broad areas of color around which the light freely circulates.

During this period when Titian was at work at the Scuola del Santo only Giovanni Bellini rivalled him for primacy in the Venetian school. Giorgione's death in 1510, Sebastiano del Piombo's departure for Rome whence he was drawn by a sense of artistic affinity, Lotto's peregrinations in central and northern Italy, Carpaccio's evolution of a style increasingly archaic and increasingly resistant to change – all this meant that only Giovanni Bellini survived to express with sustained originality the Venetian humanist faith in an ideal world. For Titian this was a time to reflect on the octogenarian 'patriarch,' and on Giorgione, in paintings such as the *Gypsy Madonna* in Vienna and in the *Sacre Conversazioni* of the Marchioness of Bath, of the Fondazione Magnani-Rocca, of Munich, Edinburgh and London – all of them exemplary for both Palma il Vecchio and Paris Bordone – reaching a high point in the *Allegory of the Three Ages of Man* in Edinburgh. Titian shifted the lessons of the 'old masters' away from idealized beauty or internalized dream, toward a joyous sensation of life released by generous form and sumptuous colors in spaces filled by radiant light and atmospheric shadows.

No less endowed with human warmth, and brought alive by the glowing softness of Titian's painting of flesh, are the half-length female portraits, of which the *Flora* in the Uffizi is exemplary. Her sensuous vitality is repeated on a grand scale in the *Sacred and Profane Love* of the Villa Borghese, Rome, full of hidden meanings and among the most felicitous examples of Titian's chromatic classicism. Within this same span of time the ostentatious physical presence of the 'Ariosto' and the 'Schiavona' (National Gallery, London), the earliest examples of the incomparable gallery of portraits we have from Titian's hand, and so provocative compared to Giorgione's portraiture, gives way to a more subtle sensibility and to a more

4. Titian, "The Assumption," detail. Basilica dei Frari, Venice

introspective psychology, expressed in a more delicate relation of form and color, in the two male portraits in Copenhagen and those of the Halifax and Frick collections.

As Titian began to paint his *Sacred and Profane Love* for Nicolò Aurelio and Laura Bagarotto, probably in celebration of their marriage in 1514, he had only recently presented his petition to the Council of Ten of 31 May 1513. His prolific production up to that date justifies his claims and his confidence in drafting his first ideas for the *Battle of Spoleto*. A reflection of these can be seen in the large woodcut of the *Drowning of Pharoah*, which can be identified with that recorded in Besalio's request for a copyright in 1515. The high drama present in this grandiose composition, with its vast open spaces contrasted with dense chiaroscuro, is entirely pictorial in its effects. As Loredana Olivato explains in this catalogue, the miraculous salvation of the Israelites contains a clear political message alluding to the wars following the League of Cambrai in 1508.

Titian's painting for the main altar of the Frari, inaugurated on 19 May 1518, ostensibly narrates the doctrine of the *Assumption of the Virgin Mary*, a doctrine championed by the Franciscan order. It also embodies political meanings similar to those of the woodcut – thanksgiving for the retreating threat to Venice from its League of Cambrai enemies. It had been commissioned in 1516, the year of Giovanni Bellini's death, and established Titian's reputation as the most famous and sought-after painter in Venice.

The structuring of the composition with human architecture, in the absence of any physical indications of setting, and the tangibility of the sculptural figure style, draw for inspiration on Raphael and Michelangelo. Yet, independent of either Raphael's geometric purity or of Michelangelo's obsession with the drama of plastic human form, Titian, in an outburst of impulsive creativity, presented the miraculous event in unity of time and place in an atmosphere drenched with color, as the blazing focal point of the Gothic interior of the church.

At the same time as he was beginning the *Assumption*, Titian came into contact with the Este court of Ferrara. Alfonso I saw Titian as heir to the leadership of the Venetian school after the death of Giovanni Bellini. The latter had painted *The Feast of the Gods* (1514) for a private room in the duke's castle at Ferrara, the *Camerino d'Alabastro*. Bellini's painting was followed by Dosso Dossi's *Bacahanal*, and by commissions, which came to nothing, for works by Fra' Bartolomeo and Raphael.

Titian's first work for Alfonso was most probably the *Tribute Money* in Dresden, which captures sentiments similar to those of the *Christ Carrying the Cross* of the Scuola di San Rocco, translated into a majestic breadth of form and an intense luminosity of color. This was followed in 1519 by three 'bacchanals.'

Titian's expressive freedom was not shackled by a need to render faithfully the written texts, probably set by Alfonso himself, for these mythologies. In his depiction of the legendary rite of the *Venus Worship*, Titian brought to life a classical world made fresh by his sensual naturalism (in contrast to Bellini's ideal vision). The radiant chromatic scale in this evocation of the festive joys of infancy, in the painting now in the Prado, is adapted to religious ardor in the Averoldi *Polyptych*, signed and dated 1522 but begun in 1520, and in the Gozzi *Madonna* of 1520.

The altarpiece in Ancona derived its pyramidal scheme from Raphael's *Madonna of Foligno*. But in place of Raphael's architectonic and imperturbable serenity, Titian painted a vigorous image dramatized by glimmering lights and shadows of an advanced sunset. The figures, human and divine, are presented against a vista vaporous and dense with clouds, closed on its lower edge by the silhouette of Venice.

The contrast of light and darkness unites the different panels of the polyptych that the Papal Legate Altobello Averoldi commissioned to decorate the Brescian church of Santi Nazzaro e Celso. The knowledge of Michelangelo prevails in the *Resurrected Christ* and above all in the *Saint Sebastian*, cramped in his narrow space by the strenuous plasticity with which Titian has conceived him. Soon after the completion of the Brescia altarpiece, painted in the old-fashioned format requested by the patron, Titian was charged with frescoing the new chapel in the Palazzo Ducale for the recently elected Andrea Gritti. The decoration was already complete by 1523, as chronicled by Sanudo. This was probably also the period of the *Saint Christopher*, located on the wall above the

5. Titian, "The Pesaro Madonna," detail. Basilica dei Frari, Venice

staircase to the doge's private apartments and executed in a mere three days of work. This imposing figure, symbol of Venice's domination of the sea, is evidence of Titian's continual awareness of Northern and central Italian art – including Pordenone's proto-mannerist frescoes in the Malchiostro chapel in Treviso, for which Titian himself painted the *Annunciation*. But in his *Deposition* in the Louvre it was Raphael's painting of the same subject, of 1507, that was the inspiration. But the tension and firmness of the Raphael is turned into eloquent naturalness by the felt participation of nature in Titian's version of the sacred drama.

Contemporary with the fresco commissions of the energetic Andrea Gritti, who on his election as doge became the force behind a political strategy that included the arts, bringing about the renewal of the architectural face of Venice, Titian completed two other mythologies, the *Andrians* (Prado, Madrid) and *Bacchus and Ariadne* (National Gallery, London) for Alfonso D'Este's *Camerino* in Ferrara. His presence was documented there in February 1523 and in the last two months of 1524. To an even greater degree than in the *Venus Worship*, Titian's inventive visualization of the relevant passages in the *Imagines* of Philostratus and in Ovid's *Metamorphoses* acquire a dynamic, rhythmic compositional and spatial structure, the figures moving toward sculptural monumentality, while the *chiaroscuro* phrasing is rendered with a glowing palette.

At the time that he was creating in these two Bacchic themes a pictorial harmony balancing truth with nature and classical idealization, Titian also worked on portraits, and with increasing frequency. From the restrained physical energy with its bold color scheme of *Il Bravo* in Vienna to the refined Raphaelism of *Vincenzo Mosti* in the Pitti, Titian moved toward the challenge of representing the sitters's internal humors transformed instantly into the idealization of the *persona* and the depiction of social condition. The most moving examples of this kind of portraiture, which was shortly to bring him clients from among the contemporary aristocracy include the *Man with a Glove* (Louvre), the Solly *Portrait of a Gentleman* (Berlin) and the *Laura dei Dianti* (Germany, private collection), and toward the end of the 1520s, *Federico Gonzaga* in Madrid (1529).

These were not the only paintings that delayed Titian's completion of the altarpiece that Jacopo Pesaro commissioned in 1519 for the altar of the Immaculate Conception in the church of Santa Maria Gloriosa dei Frari. The composition was difficult for Titian, who changed it twice before deciding on one that once more revolutionized the traditional Venetian altarpiece. No longer aligned parallel to the plane defined by the altarframe, the figure groups are disposed according to a scalene triangle converging on the Madonna and Child within the solemn and heavy rhythms of the imposing piers, allusive to the doctrine of the Immaculate Conception, which plunged into depth. In ringing harmonies the pigments change according to the delicate half-shadows or subtle reflections of natural light filtering through the little clouds, stationary against the twin columns which soar unobstructed upwards. This grand theatre is nonetheless modulated by the human dimension, as the holy event accrues to itself the suggestive immediacy of an episode taking place before our very eyes, whereby the hymn to the godhead becomes a celebration of man.

The Bishop of Paphos and his relatives, who with conscious dignity kneel in prayer before the Virgin, are an extraordinarily telling document of contemporary civilization, a role that Titian's portraiture was to emphasize more and more with time.

The mimetic and illusionistic naturalness of the *Pesaro Madonna* is cut through with the figure style of central Italy in Titian's *Death of Saint Peter Martyr* in the Dominican church of Santi Giovanni e Paolo – the Pantheon, like the Frari, where the heroes of the Serenissima were buried. This commission brought the artist into competition with Palma il Vecchio and Pordenone. Perhaps to demonstrate his superiority to Pordenone, who for years had been trying to insinuate himself into Venetian patronage, Titian painted the altarpiece relatively quickly, between 1528 and 27 April 1530. The work, which was lost in a fire on 16 August 1867, was hailed enthusiastically by Aretino as "the most beautiful thing in Italy," while for Vasari (1568) it was "the most finished, the most famous, the greatest and best conceived and executed, which Titian was never to surpass in all his life." More than the innumerable copies and engravings – it is not for the moment possible to

6. Titian, "Madonna and Child with the Infant Baptist and Saint Catherine," detail.
National Gallery, London

pronounce with certainty on two fragments that supposedly survive from the original – it is better to turn to Vasari's description of this work to appreciate the violence intrinsic to the compositional structure of an image marked by a naturalism so intense as to qualify as a stylistic innovation. Vasari, in one of his most evocative passages, given that he identified in the altarpiece traits sympathetic to his own artistic references, wrote:

"[Titian] made the panel with the said martyr, much larger than life in a woodland of enormous trees, fallen to the ground and attacked by the furious pride of a soldier who wounded him in the head and, being only half alive, one sees in his face the horror of death, while in the other monk, who runs ahead fleeing, one perceives the terror and the fear of death; in the sky there are nude angels who issue from a streak of lightning in heaven, which illuminates the landscape, which is very beautiful, and the whole work...."

The illusionistic nexus between figure and landscape, with which Titian captured the cruel drama of Saint Peter's assassination at the edge of the forest, was no less effective for the intimate serenity proper to other paintings of this period such as the *Madonna and Child with Saint Catherine and the Infant Baptist* in London; the *Madonna of the Rabbit* in the Louvre, probably the painting that Titian sent in 1530 to the Duke of Mantua; and the slightly later *Saint Jerome* (Louvre) and the *Adoration of Shepherds* (Pitti Palace), an enchanting night scene – painted in 1532 for Francesco Maria della Rovere and sent two years later to Pesaro – that surely touched the art of Girolamo Savoldo.

The new order of Titian's ideas also produced the lost votive painting of Doge Andrea Gritti of 1531, a majestic composition of figures pulsating with chiaroscuro, as we know from the superb preparatory drawing for *Saint Bernardine* in the Uffizi. In addition there is the *Magdalene* also in the Uffizi, her tremulous nudity bathed in light and scarcely veiled by the fall of her red-blonde hair – an expression of joyous sensuality rather than of pious contrition.

At this period, in which Titian dedicated himself to images of such vitality in the warmth and depth of their tones, Jacopo Sansovino and Pietro Aretino, who had settled in Venice in 1527 following the Sack of Rome, were habitués of Titian's studio in the Biri Grande.

Together they constituted a clique that held sway over artistic matters in the Serenissima through the middle decades of the Cinquecento, in the calmer political climate following the Peace of Bologna in 1529. While Sansovino's sculptural and architectural language corroborated and spurred Titian's artistic progress, Aretino, in his notorious correspondence and his art criticism, immediately became engaged in the cause of promoting Titian. There can be no doubt that however much Aretino's praise accelerated Titian's fame, Aretino benefited to the same degree from the artist's growing success.

The friendship between the two was nourished by an affinity of aesthetic ideals, as the many letters of the "secretary of the world" demonstrate. Exemplary among these is the famous letter Aretino sent to his friend in 1544 and in which the evocative force of the word is woven into the same noble material as a painting by Titian:

"....resting my arms on the windowsill,.... I began to survey the wonderful spectacle of the innumerable boats full of as many foreigners as of countryfolk, which gave a holiday mood to all those floating in them and to the Grand Canal which itself gladdened the hearts of everyone.... And while both the spectators and the boat people began to disperse full of congratulation, and like someone momentarily idle and empty of thoughts, so I turn my eyes to the sky, which was never embellished by so beautiful a painting of lights and shades since God created it. Thus the air was such as those who envy you because they are not like you would wish to depict it. As I describe it, see first the houses which, although of living stone, appear to be of some artificial substance. Then consider the air as I perceived it, in some places clear and vivid, in others cloudy and dull. Observe also my amazement at the clouds made of condensed humidity; in front of me some were almost at the roofs of the houses, and others almost at the horizon, while at the right there was a threatening mass in shades of gray and black. I was truly astonished at the variety of tones which they displayed: the nearest ones burned with the flames of the sun's fire, the more distant glowed less briliantly in tones of red lead. Oh, with what beautiful strokes did Nature's brush push back the air, making it recede from the palaces just as Titian does when he paints a landscape! In some parts there appeared a greeny blue and in others a bluish green truly combined by the whims of Nature, teacher of the masters. With her dark and light tones she pushed into the background and brought to the fore the very things she wished to

7. Titian, "Danäe," detail. Gallerie di Capodimonte, Naples

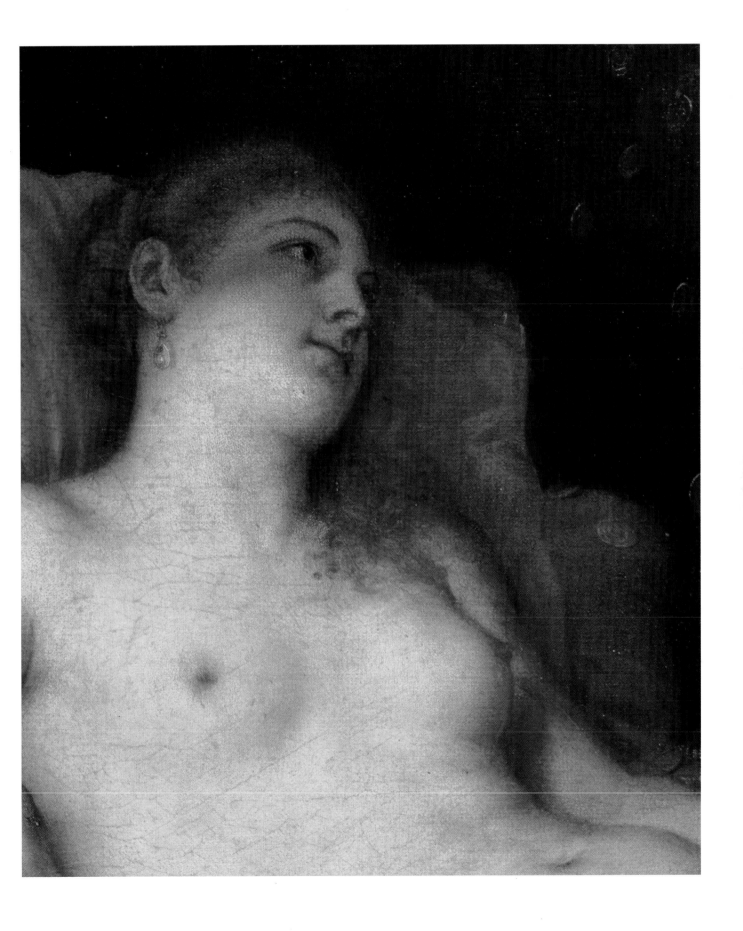

emphasize or to set back, so that I who know that your brush is the essence of her soul exclaimed three or four times, "Oh, Titian, where are you now?'"

Aretino's often flattering but sometimes wicked pen instantly boosted Titian's activity as a portrait painter, beginning with the portrait of Charles V in 1533. That painting brought to the artist a shower of privileges and titles as well as the intimacy of the emperor himself and, consequently, international notoriety.

Titian's portraits in the previous decade had already moved toward a heroic accent, quite different from the tendency to lay bare the psychology, even introspection of Lorenzo Lotto's sitters, or from the rigorous loyalty to observable data in Moroni. Titian in the 30s gave priority to the celebratory and commemorative elements in ideal images, sumptuously and elegantly painted, that responded to the client's dignity and status. Always the "frigidity" of the official portrait is made captivating by the prodigious force of Titian's style, as in those of *Isabella d'Este* (Vienna), *Francesco Maria della Rovere* and *Eleonora Gonzaga* (Uffizi). The latter pair were complete by 1537 when Aretino dedicated a sonnet to them in a letter to Gaspara Stampa on 7 November of that year.

At times, in portraits that were not encumbered by the sitter's status, Titian achieved a particular freshness of conception: the *Girl in a Fur Wrap* (Vienna), for example, or *La Bella* (Palazzo Pitti, Florence), in which the model resembles that of the *Venus* commissioned by Guidobaldo, Francesco Maria della Rovere's son, and which was 'in progress' in 1538. Though modeled on the Dresden *Venus*, Giorgione's ideal beauty contrasts with the earthy sensuality of Titian's nude, luxuriating on her bed in the warmth of a patrician interior.

In a work that looks forward to the imagery of the *poesie* (mythologies) that he was later to paint for the Hapsburgs, Titian at last completed the battle painting for the wall on the piazza side of the Sala del Maggior Consiglio in the Palazzo Ducale, for which he had offered himself back in 1513, substituting the *Battle of Spoleto* by Guariento, and probably representing, as Pallucchini proposed (1969), at Andrea Gritti's behest the Venetian triumph over the imperial troops near Cadore in 1508. Burnt in the disastrous fire in the Palazzo Ducale on 20 December 1577, the battle painting was a highly rhetor-

ical display of violent movements and gestures, as we know from the copy in the Uffizi, from the numerous engravings and above all from the drawing for the entire composition in the Louvre and from the two studies of details in Oxford and Munich. On the basis of the important evidence of these images, it is easy to imagine that at the outset of the project Titian had in mind the famous battles scenes that Leonardo and Michelangelo began in 1503 and 1504 for the Palazzo Vecchio, Florence. Titian would have been exposed to the impetuous inventiveness that marked the cartoons for those projects, through one of Raphael's cartoon for Sistine Chapel, the *Conversion of Saint Paul*, which was in Venice from 1521 in the Grimani collection.

Another lost work shows a comparably exuberant figure style – Titian's *Annunciation*, known from an engraving by Caraglio and painted in competition (unsuccessful this time) with Pordenone in 1537 for the nuns of Santa Maria degli Angeli, Murano. In the same period Titian was working on the *Presentation of the Virgin in the Temple*, begun already in 1539 for the *albergo* of the Scuola Grande di Santa Maria della Carità (now the Gallerie dell'Accademia). This is no less rich in its acceptance of motifs from central Italy as well as in its response to the Romanism of Pordenone's frescoes on the Palazzo D'Anna on the Grand Canal. As never before, the dazzling color works toward an equilibrium of skillfully calculated architectural scenography, glimpses of landscape, and figures, in a classicism close to Serlio's and in sympathy with Doge Andrea Gritti's desire to bestow a classical decorum and dignity on Venice's public face. Jacopo Sansovino had for some time been the chief instrument of this desire, and at the very time that Titian was painting the *Presentation of the Virgin* Sansovino was launching the ambitious remodeling of the Piazza and Piazzetta San Marco with the construction of the Libreria Marciana, effectively creating a single stage-set running uninterrupted from the Mint to the Torre dell'Orologio.

Within the secure realm of Titian's colorism falls also the formal rhetoric of the *Caesars*, painted for the court of Mantua, which was then under the artistic domination of Giulio Romano. Four of the paintings were delivered in 1537.

8. Titian, "Martyrdom of Saint Lawrence," detail. Chiesa dei Gesuiti, Venice

Titian's definitive break with naturalistic illusionism, which was beginning to suffer from academic involution, coincided with the arrival in Venice of the Tuscan artists Francesco Salviati and Giuseppe Porta in 1539, and of Giorgio Vasari in 1541.

Titian was well aware of the shift toward mannerism in the Venetian school of painting, of which he was once again undisputed leader following Pordenone's death in 1539. Lotto's presence was increasingly sporadic, Girolamo Savoldo poetic nocturnes more and more isolated. All were harbingers of early baroque verism, the result of the repatriation of Bonifacio de' Pitati's narratives and Andrea Schiavone's formal elegances to the mainstream of the Venetian tradition, replacing their enthusiasm for Emilian and Central Italian Mannerism. Titian's sympathy for "maniera" was not, however, substantial – it did not include the spiritual world of mannerism but served merely to give greater expressive licence and immediacy in terms of lighting technique, while color would always have the last word. The maturing of this moment in his career was exceptionally quick. In the agitated definition of bombastic form in the *Crowning with Thorns* in the Louvre (executed in 1540 as we now know thanks to the archival research of Binaghi Olivari in a forthcoming publication), in the *Saint John the Baptist* in the Gallerie dell'Accademia, and the ceiling paintings for Santo Spirito in Isola today in the Salute, completed between 1542 and 1544, Titian seems to pitch himself against Michelangelo. But in other contemporary paintings – the *Speech of Alfonso d'Avalos* or the *Ecce Homo* in Vienna (dated 1543) or to a lesser degree the banner in Urbino – the abstracting and programmatic formulae of Tusco-Roman mannerism, the sculptural volumes, the impulsive foreshortening and *contrapposti*, the harsh *chiaroscuro* contrasts, all of these tended to subordinate themselves to the free independence of color.

For Titian the so-called "crisis" of mannerism was definitively wound up in the *Danäe* upon which he was working in 1544 for Cardinal Alessandro Farnese. All plastic tension is here relaxed within the sumptuous preciosity of tints harmonized in calculated combinations of delicately shaded tones. As the first half of the 1540s progressed, Titian put behind him the mannerist expe-

rience, taking up again the translation of the world of the senses into an ideal dimension, even if indelibly marked by the uncertainty that had not previously troubled man's certainty in his own destiny.

In these years in which Titian's development briefly meandered from its course, his incomparable skill in snaring a personality never flagged: *Pietro Bembo's* serene awareness of his intellectual merit (Washington), the freshness of childhood in *Clarice Strozzi* (Berlin) and *Ranuccio Farnese* (Washington), the indomitable will to power of *Paul III* (Naples) and *Andrea Gritti* (Washington), the enigmatic melancholy of the *Young Englishman*, the cynical and irascible temperament of *Aretino* (Florence), the sorrowful beauty that presages the imminent death of *Isabella of Portugal*, wife of Charles v.

In September 1545, Titian abandoned his studio in the Biri Grande for a brief visit to the Marches, as the guest of the Duke of Urbino and reached Rome by October 9. His arrival was met with acclaim at the papal court. Sebastiano del Piombo and Vasari vied to accompany him to see the antiquities and Vasari brought Michelangelo to his studio. Michelangelo's reservations, before the *Danäe*, about Titian's capacity to draw adequately ("disegnare bene") and about Venetian artistic training in general, indicated the basic incomprehension of Roman artists faced by the liberal colorism with which Titian had learned to "counterfeit nature" ("contraffare il vivo"). It was no accident, one would suppose, that Titian was mainly in demand for portraits, of which the most momentous was *Paul III with His Nephews* now at the Capodimonte museum. Exemplary in his conciseness of means, Titian has caught with crude realism the character of each of the three Farnese, who were to prefer from him individual portraits of a more official and less psychological stamp, such as that of *Alessandro Farnese*, also in Naples.

At the end of Titian's stay in Rome he was solemnly awarded the citizenship of Rome on the Campidoglio in March 1546. After a stopover in Florence, he returned to Venice to take up the commissions he had left incomplete the previous year. Among those works completed before his departure for Augsburg in 1548 are most probably the central compartment of the ceiling decoration of the *albergo* of the Scuola di San Giovanni Evangeli-

9. Titian, "Annunciation," detail. Chiesa di San Salvador, Venice

sta (which his assistants were to complete in the lateral compartments); the *Pentecost* for Santo Spirito in Isola, today at the Salute; and the *Votive Portait of the Vendramin Family* in London, in which the conflicting sentiments of the Farnese group yield to the placid serenity of a full awareness of life. By January 1548, accompanied by his son Orazio and Lambert Sustris, Titian was already in Augsburg. Here in this Bavarian city, following his victory at Mühlberg over the Protestant League in 1547, Charles v summoned together all the chief protagonists of the historic events of those years. Titian soon found himself engaged in a series of portraits. Among the first was *Charles v on Horseback*, now in the Prado, a compelling image of royal power elevated to the status of myth. Of the several other portraits carried out, only some have survived, such as the *Antonio Perrenot de Granvelle* in Kansas City, which embodies with unrivalled force the refinement of moral custom.

The Prado *Venus with an Organist*, which critics generally agree is the first version of this theme, also dates from this trip to Augsburg. No longer enclosed by an alcove, as in Guidobaldo of Urbino's painting, Venus reclines languidly on the bed in a broad and pulsating landscape, immersed in the waning light of day that creates soft effects of light in salient chromatic touches. On his return from Augsburg, Titian was faced with the young Jacopo Tintoretto who during the older artist's absence had established his reputation on the Venetian scene. After he briefly frequented Titian's studio, according to the early sources, Tintoretto came of age at the beginning of the 1540s, at a time when mannerist culture constituted the prevalent taste.

He had acheived this with his first public work, in 1548, the *Miracle of the Slave* for the Scuola Grande di San Marco. It was greeted with lavish praise by Aretino, who nevertheless admonished the artist to evolve from "the immediacy of the done, to the patience of doing." After his *Last Supper* for the Church of San Marcuola of 1547, Tintoretto's perfected his talent for violent lighting effects. The dynamic tension of the scene is generated by the sculptural figures in *contrapposto*, by the strenuous contrasts of a miraculous light, and by a palette of non-primary hues, emphasizing the dramatic pathos of Saint Mark's aerial intervention in a language openly narrative in intention and popular in taste, posing a direct challenge to Titian's vision of tonal harmonies of pure color.

The divergent paths of the two artists is also mirrored in their respective patrons – prevalently Venetian (with religious narratives and portraits) for Tintoretto, and prevalently Hapsburg for Titian. This was the case as soon as Titian returned from Augsburg, when he threw himself into painting a series of *The Damned* or of *The Furies* for the Queen of Hungary, sister of Charles v. In the *Sisyphus* and above all in the *Tityus*, in the Prado, the glaring Michelangelism that marked the athletic Old Testament figures of the Santo Spirito ceiling dissolve into a dense texture of almost monochromatic tones, with a grainy impasto that flickers in the light.

Titian's *Saint John the Almsgiver* from the church of San Giovanni Elemosinario belongs to this period. The restrained tension of the composition, still mindful of Pordenone in the complexity of the figure relationships, is conveyed in a highly emotive way by a diffused light, at times insinuating and subtle, at times rapid and dense, which itself condenses and assumes all spatial and formal values. With pictures such as this Titian made a reality of what Paolo Pino, Biondo and Dolci claimed in their polemics with Varchi, Doni, and Vasari himself, of the superiority of color over drawing, of painting over sculpture, and of Venice over Rome.

Early in November 1550 Titian was once more in Augsburg, where Charles v, by this time almost ready to abdicate, had called a Diet. The emperor commissioned a portrait of his son, Prince Philip, already designated his successor to rule the empire and who immediately took his father's place as Titian's principal patron. In the portrait in Madrid, the twenty-four year old prince, encased in his very rich armor, seems carved out of the shadow in an almost heraldic outline, targeted by the light. The likeness is brilliantly evocative of the prince's introverted and diffident personality. Titian's portrait of Johann Friedrich Elector of Saxony, the loser at Mühlberg, is no less penetrating in its expression of a stubborn will.

By August 1551 Titian was back in Venice, which he was never to leave again, excepting brief trips to Brescia and

Pieve di Cadore. He was being pestered with demands from the Hapsburgs, for portraits. Among the few that survive, those in life – size and full-length stand out as of particular interest – the portrait of the Bishop of Trent, *Cristoforo Madruzzo* (1552) in the San Paolo Museum in Brasil, and the no less imposing *Gentleman* in Kassel. As in these, so in the secular and religious history paintings, such as the *Saint Margaret and the Dragon* (Prado), identifiable with a painting mentioned by Titian in a letter to Philip of October 1552, and the *Noli Me Tangere* painted between 1552 and 1554 for Mary of Hapsburg, of which only a fragment remains in the Prado, the formal touches of mannerist drawing are increasingly filtered into structures of densely pigmented colors shattered and dispersed by the light. The cold and distinct distribution of form in the *Adoration of the Holy Trinity* in the Prado, painted for Charles v between 1551 and 1554, certainly reflects the imposition of a counter-Reformationary iconography.

Quite different from this are the first *poesies* that Titian painted for Philip II, between 1553 and 1554, representing *Dänae* and *Venus and Adonis* (Prado), prototypes of numerous versions, as well as the slightly later *Venus with a Mirror* in Washington. The candid sensuality of these themes is realized through a unity of tones tending to underline the expressive rather than the descriptive force of color. Titian's last official portrait of a doge was that of *Francesco Venier*, now in the Thyssen collection, with its rapid evocation of the ducal garments reflecting the dark red of the curtain behind and reaching out to the distant landscape lit up with the blaze of a fire on the lagoon.

At the same that Titian was moving ever further from the the compact form and local surface color of Renaissance painting, he was witness to the establishment of the reputation of Paolo Veronese in Venice. Veronese's altarpiece of the Giustiniani chapel in San Francesco della Vigna was completed slightly later than 1551. Mindful of the compositional scheme of the *Pesaro Madonna*, Paolo obtained a sumptuous chromatic richness by placing limpid metallic colors side by side with the purposeful complexity of the figure arrangement, reminding us that his artistic education in Verona had been in the mannerist orbit of Parmigianino and Giulio

Romano. The mannerist vocabulary served to furnish Paolo, whose art from the beginnings was essentially that of a colorist, with a greater repertoire of figural poses and compositional variety. He quickly found himself engaged in important church commissions as well as governmental ones: the canvases for the ceiling of the Hall of the Council of Ten at the Palazzo Ducale (1553-54) and his first paintings for the church of San Sebastiano (1555-56).

Titian could only have looked on these with nostalgia for the felicitous chromatic classicism of his early career, even while recognizing in them a different order of meaning in which decoration was ascendant. Circumstances offered Titian a way to express his appreciation for the Olympian vision of Paolo, as sympathetic to the architecture of Andrea Palladio as it was antithetic to the tormented and increasingly hallucinatory art of Tintoretto, on the occasion of the competition for the painted ceiling of the main room of the Libreria Marciana. At Titian and Sansovino's invitation a series of artists, the principal Venetian mannerists excluding Tintoretto, participated in the project. According to Ridolfi, the golden chain was awarded by the Procurators at Titian's suggestion to Paolo Veronese, surely for his capacity to embody with vaporous chromatic freedom the dreams and myths of Venice in the later sixteenth century.

Titian's own 'commentary' on Veronese's winning roundels consists of the *Wisdom*, enclosed in the dazzling illusionistic *macchina* of Cristoforo Rosa's *quadratura* ceiling in the *Anti-sala* of the same library.

From the 1550s therefore, let us imagine Titian flanked by these two new protagonists of the Venetian school, Paolo Veronese and Jacopo Tintoretto, each so different in their stylistic habits and preferences – a third, Jacopo Da Ponte, worked his resplendent colors in relative isolation in Bassano. Titian chose to persevere in his insistence on the magical, expressive freedom of the paint itself. Titian's technique as he gave form to his late visions, often on very large canvases, has been authoritatively described by Palma Giovane:

"Titian was truly the most excellent of all painters, since his brushes always gave birth to expressions of life. I was told by Palma il Giovane...., who was himself fortunate enough to enjoy the learned instruction of Titian, that he used to sketch in his pictures with a great mass of colors, which served, as one might say, as a bed or a base for the compositions which he then had to construct; and I too have seen some of these, formed with bold strokes made with brushes laden with colors, sometimes of a pure red earth, which he used, so to speak, for a middle tone, and at other times of white lead; and with the same brush tinted with red, black and yellow he formed a highlight; and observing these principles he made the promise of an exceptional figure appear in four strokes. The most sophisticated connoisseurs found such sketches entirely satisfactory in themselves, and they were greatly in demand since they showed the way to anyone who wished to find the best route into the Ocean of Painting. Having constructed these precious foundations he used to turn his pictures to the wall and leave them there without looking at them, sometimes for several months. When he wanted to apply his brush again he would examine them with the utmost rigor, as if they were his mortal enemies, to see if he could find any faults; and if he discovered anything that did not fully conform to his intentions he would treat his picture like a good surgeon would his patient, reducing if necessary some swelling or excess of flesh, straightening an arm if the bone structure was not exactly right, and if a foot had initially been misplaced correcting it without thinking of the pain it might cost him, and so on. In this way, working on the figures and revising them, he brought them to the most perfect symmetry that the beauty of art and nature can reveal; and after he had done this, while the picture was drying he would turn his hand to another and work on it in the same way. Thus he gradually covered those quintessential forms with living flesh, bringing them by many stages to a state in which they lacked only the breath of life. He never painted a figure all at once and used to say that a man who improvises cannot compose learned or well-constructed verses. But the final stage of his last retouching involved his moderating here and there the brightest highlights by rubbing them with his fingers, reducing the contrast with the middle tones and harmonizing one tone with another; at other times, using his finger he would place a dark stroke in a corner to strengthen it, or a smear of bright red, almost like a drop of blood, which would enliven some subtle refinement; and so he would proceed, bringing his living figures to a state of perfection. And as Palma himself informed me, it is true to say that in the last stages he painted more with his fingers than his brushes."

The novelty of this rapid and abbreviated painting technique, however slow in its gestation of the image, was well understood by Vasari. After seeing the paintings being worked on or being brought to completion in Titian's studio in the Biri Grande in 1566, he wrote:

"But it is true that his method of painting in these late works is very different from the technique he had used as a young man. For the early works are executed with a certain finesse and an incredible diligence, so that they can be seen from close to as well as from a distance; while these last pictures are executed with broad and bold strokes and smudges, so that from nearby nothing can be seen whereas from a distance they seem perfect. This method of painting has caused many artists, who have wished to imitate him and thus display their skill, to produce clumsy pictures. For although many people have thought that they are painted without effort this is not the case, and they deceive themselves, because it is known that these works are much revised and that he went over them so many times with his colors that one can appreciate how much labor is involved. And this method of working, used in this way, is judicious, beautiful and stupendous, because it makes the pictures appear alive and painted with great art, concealing the labor."

Vasari expressed himself in these terms about Titian, however, after having declared before the *Transfiguration* and *The Annunciation* in the church of San Salvador: "these late works, however much good one sees in them, are not esteemed by him, and they do not have that perfection which the other two have."
A certain sector of the public in Vasari's time would have agreed with Vasari. In the same year as his visit to Venice, Agatone guaranteed for Guidobaldo II Duke of Urbino that two paintings of a *Christ* and a *Madonna* were autograph. Two years later the art dealer Niccolò Stoppio wrote to Max Fugger that Titian no longer had good eyesight, and because his hand trembled he never managed to finish anything "and left this concern to his assistants." In 1568 Veit von Bornberg informed Maximilian II that Titian had in his studio seven versions of the fables sent to Philip II, most worthy, according to Jacopo Strada, of the imperial collections. Maximilian replied that he was extremely interested but that he was concerned about Titian's physical capacities to paint given his advanced old age.
Titian was fully aware of the incomprehension that would greet the production of the last phase of a creative evolution born of a searching introspection. In his letter of 22 September informing Philip II of the dispatch of *The Entombment* as well as of the *poesie* of *Diana and*

10. Titian, "Pietà," detail. Gallerie dell'Accademia, Venice

Actaeon and *Diana and Callisto*, Titian reminded his patron that the delays in completing these works was not to be explained by his several commitments but by the cogitation and the protracted process of visualization of his lyrical fantasy that each painting required: "I am never content with my labors, but try always with hardwork to finish them more and to add something." In another letter, of 26 April 1562, Titian expressed his hope that the Spanish king would be pleased by two paintings he had just completed, the *Agony in the Garden* and the *Rape of Europa*, and added: "I will dedicate that space of life left to me to making paintings for Your Most Catholic Majesty, laboring with my brush to give you that satisfaction which I desire and which the greatness of so high a king deserves." To tackle the increasing number of commissions coming to him Titian relied more on his workshop than in the past. Titian himself stated this in a letter of 12 December 1567 in which he notified Philip II of the imminent shipment of the *Martyrdom of Saint Lawrence*, offering to paint a complete cycle of the life of the saint and adding: "and when know your will I will put aside all other work until your wishes are quickly satisfied, as well as using the help of my son Orazio and your servant, and another worthy young man my pupil in order that in that short time that you will command of me, the work will be done...."

In the feverish activity of the studio at the Biri Grande, for some time organized into an efficient workshop, some canvases begun years before were reused. Images that been successful were replicated in copies and versions, such as *The Penitent Magdalen* sent to Philip II in 1561, which is so different in conception from the youthful painting now in the Uffizi. Many works on a large scale were produced such as the several versions of the *Adoration of the Magi* (beginning with the one sent in 1559 to Spain); the large *Last Supper* that on arrival at the Escorial was at once cut down to adapt it to its wall; the three large paintings for the Palazzo Pubblico in Brescia; and the huge votive painting of Doge Antonio Grimani for the Palazzo Ducale, begun in 1555 but still incomplete at Titian's death. One commission that was consigned entirely to the workshop was for the apsidal frescoes of the Archdiaconate church in Pieve di Cadore, carried out in 1566-67 on the basis of drawings by Titian. The

interventions of the workshop are difficult to distinguish from Titian's own hand, given both the efforts of the pupils to imitate the master's own stroke under his direct supervision, and Titian's habit of going over their works during execution with "two sketches of the brush" ("due bozze di pennello") to please the patrons, as remarked by Jacopo Strada, who for business reasons spent a good deal of time in Titian's studio.

In the works carried out by Titian only, the sovereign magic of color is imediately apparent, coming into its own, as Dell'Acqua (1955) has acutely perceived: "in a startling diversity of impasto – now dense and oily, now impalpable and iridescent – and of textures, sometimes light and as if floating... soft and luminous, thick and tumultuously worked over...."

With the deaths in 1556 of Pietro Aretino and in 1558 of Charles v, Titian was alone with his lyrical meditations. Gone from his house wer his sister Orsola and his daughter Lavinia. He returned to some of the themes painted in his youth and maturity, reinterpreting them more and more within the mysterious realm of the "non-finito." He took up the composition of the 1537 *Annunciation* for Santa Maria degli Angeli, Murano, and reworked it for the church of San Domenico, Naples, around 1557, and again in the slightly later version for San Salvador, Venice. In each case the sculptural presence of the figures in the prototype gives way to iridescent apparitions in unison with fictive architectural backdrops and the landscape, fragmented into flashes of light. In the *Crucifixion* placed on the altar of the church of San Domenico in Ancona on 22 July 1558, Christ nailed to the Cross takes form within the murky twilight with razor flashes of light, as if to express the anguished despair of the Virgin, while Saint John spreads his arms in a gesture of wretched incredulity and Saint Dominic clings to the Cross in unutterable grief. The image of this divine mystery assumed an even more despairing pitch in the Escorial version: the solitary Cross presides over a landscape stripped of human life, which shudders with myster as night falls.

To these years, in which Titian was enriching the expressive force of his paint with such dramatic luminous effects, belongs the definitive version of the *Martyrdom of Saint Lawrence*. This composition was first tried in the altarpiece of the same subject in the Gesuiti, Venice, that he had completed in 1558, even though the figure poses and the architectural background, of Roman classical ascendancy, remind us that the painting was begun in the late 1540s. Along the orthogonal line formed by the architecture, each individual is caught by the haunting light in living touches of color vibrating contrappuntally and with sudden echoes in the shadowy atmosphere.

The internalized and profound feeling of reality which drove Titian between the 1550s and 1560s, runs unhindered through the religious paintings and late *poesies* for Philip II. In the 1559 *Entombment* in the Prado and in the versions of *Saint Jerome* in the Thyssen collection and in the Prado, as well as in the *Diana and Actaeon* and *Diana and Callisto* in the National Gallery, Edinburgh, finished between 1556 and 1559, in the *Rape of Europa* in Boston finished by 1562, in the slightly later *Perseus and Andromeda* in the Wallace Collection, London and the Harewood *Diana and Actaeon*, we see an abbreviated descriptive technique, with dragged paint and liquid glazes. In the furious rhythms of the pictorial texture, the Christian and pagan heroes rise to the surface enveloped in a nature unprecedentedly responsive to their sentiments.

This amounts to a cosmic vision in which the regulation of color and form in the Renaissance aesthetic recedes and is even contradicted by the intimate essences of a world of the spirit: man alone with his tragic destiny in the center of the world.

Titian's late portraits, which are marked by an accelerated immediacy and directness of the rapport between artist and sitter, share in this "chromatic alchemy," as Lomazzo (1584) ably put it. In the *Self-Portrait* in Berlin of 1562, densely painted with a rich and delicate palette, the light forcefully highlights the physical features and the temperament of the artist. He still is full of energy, though the face is somewhat hollow his posture stiff, with the hands placed one on the table, the other on his hip. As with his portrait of *Aretino*, it is possible to imagine abandoning the work, ostensibly unfinished, at the time that it seemed to him fulfilled or accomplished. The mood is quite different in the later *Self-Portrait*, in the Prado, and in the self-portrait in the altarpiece of the Archdiaconate church in Pieve di Cadore, which Vasari probably saw in Titian's studio in 1566, given his rather detailed description in the *Lives* (1568). In the two paintings, each painted with a very subtle brushstroke and an almost monochromatic palette, the artist depicts himself in near profile, the gaunt face of the almost octogenarian artist seeming to review the joys and the sadnesses of his long career.

The *Allegory of Prudence* in London, beyond its arcane symbolism, is one of the masterpieces of the aggressive expressionism of Titian's color in these years. The Prado *Entombment*, evoking earlier treatments of the same theme, reaches new heights of anguish in its loosely woven forms within a dark shadows, even compared to the 1559 version that itself dramatically reinterpreted the Louvre version of the 1520s.

Toward the later 1560s, Titian relived the pagan legends and the Christian stories with increasing intensity, as if in a nostalgic farewell laden with the anguish of time irretrievably lost. Under this sign of the awareness of mortality, Titian produced his last great masterpieces, in the silence of a studio no longer bustling with friends and rarely opened to visitors as it was when Giorgio Vasari came in 1566, or when in 1574 Henri de Valois paid him a visit, or whence reached the news of the outbreak of war again with the Turks and of the terrible flaying of Marc'Antonio Bragadin following the ephemeral victory of Lepanto.

Titian's paint at times seems almost transparent, such as in the lyrical spirituality of the *Madonna and Child* in the National Gallery, London, or in the *Nymph and Shepherd* in the Kunsthistorisches Museum, Vienna, the last vestige of a lost Age of Gold. At times he worked his colors in impasto struck through with sparkling light, such as in the *Venus Blindfolding Cupid* in the Borghese Gallery, Rome, a marvelous blend of dabs of paint that slowly dissemble in the fiery sunset; in the *Young Boy with Dogs*, Rotterdam, which it is pleasant to imagine as one of Titian's most informal paintings, since it is complete and not the fragment of a larger work; and in the *Crowning with Thorns* in the Alte Pinakothek, Munich. With the latter Titian transformed the ostentatious sculptural figures of the Louvre prototype into an image of the utmost anguish – a *danse macabre* of forms dissolved in light. Comparable expressive violence, but with occasional preciosities of color, marks the *Flaying of Marsyas*, in Kroměříž, where the cruelty of the mythical fable becomes positively diabolical. Horrifying brutality is the keynote too of the *Tarquin and Lucretia* in the Akademie der bildenden Künste in Vienna, rendered with daubs of paint manipulated even with the fingers on the blood-red of the curtain, which is the only sparing reference to a setting presumably like that of the earlier and full-length version in the Fitzwilliam Museum, Cambridge. The latter was sent to Philip II in 1571, and is a more fulsome but perhaps less expressionistic treatment, perhaps to comply with the tastes of his patron in what amounted to a double late style, as Pallucchini (1969) has defined it: "It is is easy to imagine Titian setting out to describe the episode, in the Cambridge version, with all its descriptive details, desirous of satisfying his patrons, and before such a painting even a Niccolò Stoppio could not have objected; while the Vienna painting, reductive in its subject and its scale, would have enabled Titian to give free rein to his poetic fancy, without other concerns."

Such preoccupations appear no less evident in Titian's last two paintings for Philip II, *Spain Succored by Religion* and the commemorative painting of the Battle of Lepanto today in the Prado, in which the relative finish of the large figures contrasts with the broken colors of the background vistas, the cloudy seascape in the first and the tremendous naval battle in the second.

Any hint of compromise with official taste, such as in the votive painting of Doge Antonio Grimani in the Palazzo Ducale, is dispelled in the late unofficial works that remained in Titian's studio at his death. The *Saint Sebastian* in Leningrad appears to consume himself like a flaring torch in the pathos and the pain echoed by the stabbing lights of the natural setting. No less impressive in this sense is the painting that it is generally thought Titian made for his own tomb in the Frari, the *Pietà* today in the Gallerie dell'Accademia. The mournful solemnity of Christ's compassion here touches its most exalted and memorable note. In the imploring hand that reaches toward the Sibyl, in which both the passion and the resurrection are prophesied, tradition has it that

brushstrokes we see Titian's last brushstrokes as he felt his life draining away from him. The inimitable and unique effect of this image is marred only by one disturbing touch, which is the angel with the torch, whereby Palma il Giovane thought to correct the excessively contorted posture of Titian's putto. This change – apparently the only one – was for the leader of the late mannerist stream that so overwhelmed Venetian art in the last quarter of the century enough to justify placing his signature in the pompous inscription on the lower edge of the panel.

The legacy of Titian, the enormous reserve of ideas that he developed and launched in his long career, was not to pass to his immediate followers, nor even to those who like Padovanino in the mid-seventeenth century tried to revive the chromatic classicism of Titian's early work. His true heirs, who knew how to draw nourishment from the youthful paintings, the mature works, and the "ultima maniera" of Titian, however different the results and altered the meanings, were the great protagonists of the European tradition from the seventeenth to the nineteenth centuries: Nicolas Poussin, Pieter Paul Rubens, Velázquez, Rembrandt, Francisco Goya, Eugène Delacroix, Pierre-Auguste Renoir. These and others were posthumous witnesses to the fulfillment of Titian's claim, expressed in his 31 May 1513 petition to the Council of Ten, that he could be "counted among those who.... make a profession of art."

Gino Benzoni
VENICE IN THE TIME OF TITIAN

If Venice left its mark on Titian, in its turn it was marked and transformed by the artist. The quality we call "Titianesque" has an important part in the image of Venice: think of the *Assumption* in the Chiesa dei Frari with its implied passage from the Virgin to the virgin city and, thus, to the city of the Virgin. Titian's atelier in the Biri Grande came to be imbued with the sense and sensations of Venice, and, at the same time, the city began to blaze with the colors we recognize as Titian's. And those traits, each in its turn, waxed ever more intense, more defined, in the course of the more than three-quarters of a century between the young artist's arrival in Venice at the end of the fifteenth century and his death on 27 August 1576, at the height of the epidemic that ravaged the city.

Jacopo de Barbari's bird's-eye view of Venice of 1500, depicting the city as a maritime fief of Neptune and Mercury, implies that Venice already thought of itself as triumphant. And yet, by 1501 its primacy as a center for importing spices from the East was being eroded, as goods were beginning to be shipped to Lisbon instead, by circumnavigation of Africa. Venice squandered means and energies on efforts at further territorial expansion, or so wrote the diarist Girolamo Priuli, a sort of perennially scolding Savonarola in merchant's clothing. He viewed the fifteenth-century formation of a state extending onto the mainland as a betrayal of a maritime vocation he felt should remain exclusive and unambiguous. The League of Cambrai arose to prevent any further attempts to achieve "monarchy over Italy," and their triumph at Agnadello on 14 May 1509 was a severe blow to the haughty Republic. It was, in fact, faced with total ruin. Yet Venice rose again, thanks to the gifts of its brilliant diplomats and the renewed vigor of its armed forces. With skill and aplomb Venice played its adversaries against each other. Meanwhile, too, the mainland peasantry loyal to Venice terrorized the mainland nobility who were the peasants' neighbors. Though diminished by the loss of its ports in Puglia and its centers in Romagna and Cremona, Chiara d'Adda, Riva, and Rovereto, in time the Serenissima contrived to save itself and to preserve intact the essential traits of its own double physiognomy as a state rooted in both terra firma and sea.

Henceforth aware that the fortunes of Italy would be decided elsewhere, the Venetian ruling class gave up all vain dreams of revival through expansion. It opted instead for a line of conservation and containment, aiming first at slowing down the Spanish absorption of Milan and then, when this became irreparable and was sanctioned in 1559 at Cateau-Cambrésis, settling on neutrality. Its authority was still backed by arms, though, and it kept constantly informed of the situation throughout Europe thanks to the assiduous vigilance of an alert and subtly perceptive diplomatic corps. The Republic was now a state of medium proportions, strong enough to defend itself but also admirably well informed by an almost daily flow of dispatches from its representatives abroad. It could no longer be surprised, and it could easily anticipate other powers' intentions and moves. Besides, this rigorously and even punctiliously pursued neutrality proved highly remunerative.

The Turks devastated Corfu in 1537, triumphed off Prevesa the next year, in 1540 took Nauplia, Malvasia, and the Aegean islands, and disembarked at Cyprus in 1570. The Serenissima put aside its neutrality, adhering to the Holy League, and emerged the victor of the battle of 7 October 1571, off Lepanto. This sensational victory might even be called epochal as it marked the end of Ottoman invincibility. Yet the ultimate outcome for Venice was disappointng: it gained not even a "palm of land." And so, abiding by the dictates of "reason of state" and "civil prudence," Venice detached itself from an all-out war to the bitter end that would have benefited only Philip II of Spain and exhausted Venetian finances and forces. There was the fear too that His Catholic Majesty might take unfair advantage, because Venice, preoccupied by the struggle against the Turks, remained undefended in the West. Venice once again became neutral, abandoning the perfidious ally, on 7 March 1573. "The lesser evil is the spice of good," was the consoling word. Venice, after all, was the city from which one sailed to Constantinople. Traffic in that direction was rejuvenated, and the Venetian patriciate became increasingly convinced that the greatest danger to Venice came from Milan and Madrid.

The Venetians' autonomy, in an Italy either directly or indirectly dominated by the Hapsburgs, was extraordinary. It signified a proud reassertion, with regard to the Holy See, of the city of Saint Mark's jurisdictional tradition *super clericos* and *circa sacra*. Most important, though, was the atmosphere of intellectual freedom. Intellectuals flocked to Venice, as if, in the words of Bernardino Tomitano, to a "haven of liberty." Titian's friend Aretino, with his voracious appetite for pleasure, chose to settle there. Venice was the setting for his *La Venexiana* – "no fable, not a comedy, but a true story" – experiments with all the violence of desire. In a letter of 1579, Francesco Sansovino, who wrote in his guidebook of the city's uniqueness and nobility, would proclaim that "liberty" had established there "its true abode, its temple." Even a king like Henri III of France, when splendidly received in Venice in 1574, took the opportunity while there to shake off the straitjacket of etiquette. He not only paid homage to Titian by visiting the aged master in his home but also, heedless of what gossips might say, passed an entire night in the "humble" dwelling of the courtesan Veronica Franco. In Venice one could find uninhibited freedom of movement, against a background of dazzling beauty. It is easy to understand why Aretino would not leave it, why Titian spent his entire life there. Though he knew its régime to be rigidly aristocratic, Bodin too admired the city that bestowed "la douceur de la liberté" and offered "une grande douceur et liberté de vie".

Venice, radiant *ville lumière* of Cinquecento Europe and magnet for pleasure seekers, intrigues and entangles its visitors. In that sense, it is a city liberated and liberating to the point of being called, and calling itself, "felicitous." Yet, for all its openness, Venice resisted change and even criticism. It insisted upon the accord between those governing and those governed. Rebellious outcries were not tolerated, and even seditious whispers and murmurs were punishable.

It was a duty also of the "excellent government" in Venice to keep watch over religious orthodoxy. Two different professions of faith? Unthinkable. A second, non-Catholic faith – Lutheran, Calvinist, Anabaptist – "would necessarily be against God," Paruta announced. The Venetian government accordingly refused to tolerate heresy, severely and drastically repressing any heretic who may mistakenly have come to Venice trusting he

would not be persecuted there as in the rest of the peninsula. If discovered, he would be punished, although – and in this respect Venice differed from the rest of the peninsula – the state, with its three legal advisers in matters of heresy, did control and moderate the otherwise merciless zeal of the ecclesiastic Inquisition. Two groups were accorded a sort of diplomatic immunity: the German merchants concentrated in their *fontego (fondaco)* in Venice proper, and the students from beyond the Alps enrolled in the nearby University of Padua.

Yet, though Venice walked in the track of Catholicism, it was not blindly obedient to Rome. The bells incessantly ringing in its innumerable churches, the psalms intoned by day and night in its convents and monasteries, its solemn processions, the exaltation of spirit in its devout liturgies, all were evidence of the fusion between *amor Dei* and *amor patriae*. This was eloquently and, indeed, emblematically given visual form in the physical and metaphorical contiguity of the basilica dedicated to Saint Mark and the Palazzo Ducale, as if the former gave sacred sanction to the latter and the palace, in its turn, imprinted the stamp of state on the house of God. It was not by chance that the chief ecclesiastical dignitary and the canons were named by the doge, nor that the patriarch was elected by the senate from a roster of the most qualified members of that political class. The banner bearing the symbol of Saint Mark the Evangelist imputed Christian significance to the worldly glories of Venice, and legitimized also that proudly autonomous strain that counterposed Saint Mark's city to Saint Peter's. The patricians in all their pronouncements claimed a religious motivation for their political stance, though religion itself was subjected to political control. Venetian theologians, however, made themselves heard resoundingly in the early sixteenth century. Paolo Giustinian and Vincenzo Querini, for example, were the authors, in 1513, of the *Libellus ad Leonem X*, perhaps the text most vibrant with renovative thought in the so-called Catholic Reform. In the same context we find Cardinal Gasparo Contarini who, after an exemplary political career in the service of the Serenissima, threw himself body and soul into directing the improvement of the Church in *capite et in membris*. He however would find himself isolated and the target of uncomprehending fury from Rome when he magnanimously urged reconciliation with the Protestant world.

Nor was Venetian spirituality limited to a few elect figures. It expressed itself also through charitable activities. The Scuole was generous toward the widows and orphans of those who had contributed to the industry and commerce of the city, and to those without families – vagabonds, beggars, the wretched and penniless, paupers, all the unfortunate. Even the incurables with their suppurating sores, the syphilitics, even the most despised prostitutes, were not ignored. This was a Christian charity that reached out, with tact and comprehension, also to the hidden, silent, ignored subworld of the poor who, ashamed of their poverty, held themselves aloof in a sort of desperate modesty. It was in Venice, not elsewhere, that the writer Ruzzante let his otherwise forever famished peasant eat his full.

"It is the most beautiful city I have ever seen," Philippe de Commynes said of Venice in 1494, and the Grand Canal, he said, "the most beautiful street in the world." And in the same year the Milanese abbot Pietro Cassola was astounded by the profusion of goods and the "abundance of victuals." City-as-emporium, city-as-market: Venice's mercantile center, the Rialto, was the commercial counterpart to the political center constituted by the Palazzo Ducale. The Rialto was "of the world entire the very wealthiest part," Sanudo exultingly proclaimed. "Nothing whatever originates there," that diarist admitted, yet "everything – whatever one might wish – is found there in abundance." Money flowed freely, though Sanudo exaggerated when he said "everyone is wealthy," as he himself was not monied. The fact is, in the smooth interaction between goods and money the market itself became an authentic producer. "Wherever goods are put on sale, there the goods are," as Sanudo explained in a formula entirely to the point. "The goods arrive continually by way of the sea," he wrote, "from every land and part of the world," thanks to the ways and routes from both East and West.

A conviction widespread in the early sixteenth century was that Venice's appointed task was to "cultivate the sea and leave the land be." And in those same years Machiavelli rightly singled out, as a peculiarity of the city, an anomalous figure found nowhere else: the patrician who buys and sells but also goes to sea. And the idea of Venice as city of and for the sea led, in the mid-1500s, the hydraulic expert Cristoforo Sabbadino to promote his idea of allowing the maximum expansion of the tides, so that the salt water could "rise toward terra firma" unimpeded. This was meant to ensure the healthiness of the air but also to favor the role of Venice as island and port. The city's function as a marine center, to that engineer's mind, was not adequately respected by the insistent propaganda of Alvise Cornaro, apostle of "holy agriculture," who promoted agriculture through grandiose schemes to reclaim the Venetian mainland. With Sabbadino and Cornaro we have two opposite points of view. On the one hand, a Venice that would remain faithful to its marriage with the sea, on the other, a Venetian patrician class ever less interested in navigation, ever more turned toward the mainland and villas graciously adorning that landscape. For Sabbadino the sea remained Venice's true and only friend and ally, while the ruling class was transforming itself from merchants and seafarers to a rural aristocracy living off the land.

Little by little, as the sixteenth century aged, Venice ceased to be a leader as it had been through the middle ages, and no longer derived all its importance from its proximity to the sea. Nor, as in the middle ages, was it in the vanguard. It was not the development of transoceanic navigation in itself that determined this retreat so much as the eruption of newer and fresher energies elsewhere that undermined Venetian primacy in the East as well. Thus it was not Venice's specific weight, so to speak, that diminished in the sixteenth century. That, if anything, increased. Venice reacted not so much by updating and modernizing its marine fleets, which, in the spring of 1570, had been dispatched with feverish speed, and some hundred galleys strong, against the Infidel. But Venice did take steps to convert and diversify an economy that had been bound up fully with the sea. And so, its new character as a manufacturing center came gradually to supersede its traditional role as principal port in exchanges between East and West. And so too was capital diverted to financial speculation, and above all to investments in land.

31

This was the great moment of agriculture: why risk life and goods in a sea infested with pirates, menaced by the Turks, encumbered with competitors, when it is possible to live on land? Although Andrea Calmo's muse carried a strong whiff of fish and brine – poetry for him was the "art of water" and went in fisherman's garb – he recorded with full approval this turn of 180 degrees. The "wise man" allowed the ship to sail and himself remained "on land to live in peace." The ideology of commerce and navigation, once the lifeblood of the diarist Priuli's writings, was now dead and buried. In 1569, in Venice, the Brescian Agostino Gallo published his book on "the twenty days of agriculture and the pleasures of villa life." At that point, almost more than Neptune and Mercury it was Oeres, with Flora and Pomona, that kept watch over the city in the lagoon.

In the thirty years between 1566 and 1595 the percentage of "foreign grains" imported by sea dropped significantly from almost 70 per cent to slightly more than 24 per cent. And whatever wheat did not arrive by boat was a local product from the Venetian mainland. It is calculated that in 1576, the year Titian died, the quantity imported from abroad dropped sharply, to 2.65 per cent, though obviously this was because of the block of traffic due to the plague rampant in the city. "Blessed," then, was the agriculture that brought fertility to the Venetian terra firma now reclaimed and improved: here, as Gallo put it, was the "true alchemy" that multiplied the treasures hidden in the bosom of the earth, and thus "the real understanding of true cultivation of the soil."

Venice, transformed from a maritime state, especially in the latter part of the sixteenth century, dug in its heels, so to speak, planting its feet solidly on earth. This meant a wide-reaching restructuring of the economy and, at the same time, a virtual anthropological mutation in which the nobleman was transformed from merchant into *rentier*. The mainland landscape took on a new look, with villas springing up everywhere. Parallel with this, the patricians' psychology as well as way of life assumed a new configuration as they came to their villas for relaxing and refreshing sojourns but also to supervise first-hand the sowing and reaping. Having become less wedded to the sea than to the land, Venice adapted itself to the loss of its maritime primacy and saw to the development of agriculture as the mainstay of its economy.

On another plane and in other aspects, even the myths by which Venice had once lived were resumed in a new arrangement that appears to be a response to the traumatic defeat at Agnadello in 1509. That confrontation with a world much broader, more dynamic and aggressive, put an end to the medieval era, within which the city-state had first created its political and economic primacy. So that, in a world crowded with more robust and massive state entities, the Venetian Republic, with its modest proportions, was exalted to an *aurea mediocritas*, a golden mean, reinforced by the splendor of an *imago urbis* that conjoined the ever greater number of patrician palace façades along the Grand Canal with the classical cadence of the *renovatio* of Piazza San Marco that Gritti fostered. The patriciate, perhaps in an attempt to overcome its distress at the defeat at Agnadello, set itself up as the embodiment of Good Government.

For the patrician class of Venice to identify itself with perfection was not surprising, as the same idea circulated throughout Europe. An enthusiastic consensus came from abroad that in Venice was to be found "good government" by antonomasia, that it was a fount of "tranquility and universal peace. Venice proposed itself – and was proposed by others – as a model of possible harmony in an agitated, convulsed, clashing, disharmonious world. Even Venetian neutrality, in itself merely a practical choice made in response to an awareness of its own military weakness, became sublimated to the veritable touchstone of superior wisdom. Venice's reputation came to far exceed its true specific and relative weight. No longer itself at the center of a world that had grown too great, it recovered that lost central status through both the dazzling beauty of city and architecture and the fascination of a myth that amplified that beauty.

And so Venice became a city laden with meaning, which best knew how to respond to what the world expected of it, a city that could claim to be a second Rome, second Byzantium, second Athens, virtual Jerusalem, new Jerusalem, true Jerusalem. Not because it was the most powerful city in the world, but because it was a superior city, better, indeed perfect – and therefore unique, above others, exemplary and a model not to be equalled and, at the same time, a model yearned after. And so Venice took its place as center of the universe. A centrality, it should be said, that was ideological, not military, not economic, but not for that any less evident: the city – so it said of itself, so others said of it – "of gold," "of God." And if that was true, then Venice must be the world's true center, the authentic "eye of the world," where humankind best express themselves because from there – from Venice – they can truly gaze on Heaven.

The Palazzo Ducale became the new temple of Solomon. The patriciate deliberating there assumed the semblance of an angelic hierarchy. That presumption was favored by the overwhelmingly powerful deployment of allegory in the art that triumphed in the palace, whose content expressed the idea that the ruling class had of itself, of the mission that earned it special privileges, by divine will, over all others.

City of enigma rife with allusions, with its labyrinth of canals, city of mystery with its nocturnal silences: to a visionary like Postel who sojourned there toward the middle of the sixteenth century, it gleamed and glowed as city of the revelation, the annunciation, the expectation of the universal kingdom, of the hoped-for *restitutio omnium*. Unique among the *civitates* besmirched by the errors and horrors of history, Venice symbolized to Postel the capital of the imminent restoration of God's reign on earth. Venice – not papal Rome – was the *sacrosancta regalitas, veraque Jerusalem*. Thus, as the ideal city, sixteenth-century Venice was elevated to vertiginous heights by extreme hopes. At the same time, though, and precisely because it proposed itself as utopia realized, as perfect magisterium, it was also a city of checkmate and defeat, because of the exaggerated expectation that, though it aroused such hopes, it had to end by disappointing. So, at any rate, we can read Guillaume Postel's experience of the city. But over and beyond the outcome itself, that experience too should be thought of as part of the kaleidoscopic maze and flux of illusions of which Venice is crossroads and crucible.

Venice came, at the same time, to be a center of primary importance in the development, production, and diffusion of culture. Music, the figurative arts, letters, philology, philosophy, science interacted there, intensely, under the impulsion of the exceptional confluence of intellectuals from all over. As publishing center it func-

tioned at an intense rhythm. At the start of the century, Aldo Manuzio was dedicated to the diffusion of ancient literature, Greek in particular, which, thanks to the competent scholars, was being restored to its pristine form. As the Aldine presses were models of excellence, printing became also for Venice a burgeoning industry. It engendered a specialized work force, a vast network of individuals who supported themselves by writing in haste, correcting proofs, translating, plagiarizing, planning entire series of books, organizing anthologies, contributing to miscellanies in verse or prose, seeing to printings and reprintings of the ancient and modern classics. Yet their life was harried and anything but easy. No wonder they envied and admired Titian's pleasure-loving friend Aretino. However little that writer was to be believed when he described himself as the scourge of princes and the master of right and true conduct, by settling in Venice he had nevertheless demonstrated how it was possible to flee the decadence of the courts and live in ease while expressing oneself freely.

In the final analysis, support for that idea came even from Titian himself. For him, Aretino played an important role as loyal and discriminating critic. Titian's brush made an immense contribution to all the many Venices: religious, political, seafaring, even licentious. If Titian belongs to Venice, once his colors had permanently tinged the city Venice belonged to him.

Giandomenico Romanelli

TITIAN'S POLITICS
BETWEEN THE REPUBLIC AND THE EMPIRE

Venetian culture in the middle years of the Cinquecento was punctuated, even sustained and celebrated, by the activity and the authority of a famous art fraternity. Its members' views on historical revisionism and artistic advancement and figurative, literary, rhetorical, and political expression fundamentally redefined the image of Venice – so effectively and so convincingly as to constitute a yardstick for all subsequent centuries. The principal players were Titian and Sansovino (Aretino supplied a steady and sometimes petulant literary element in the form of his letters, but it would be an exaggeration to speak of an art triumvirate composed of Titian, Sansovino, Aretino).[1]

It is in terms of this axis that we can assess a certain group of works of art that amounted to the figurative emanation, the formal and linguistic key to the more general condition of Venetian society in the course of a half century of profound crisis and of radical and revolutionary cultural change.

In Titian's painting (color, light, drawing, composition, technical expedients and rhetorical virtuosities), in the sacred and profane iconography that he adopted, in league with his patrons together with the invenzione and handling of his pagan mythologies, and likewise in Sansovino's Romanism of architecture,[2] we can measure the dazzling process of the creation of an art to celebrate an entire ruling class. It is by this route that we should approach the international dimension of art in this city, which more than ever before or since was to attempt to force the lock of a culture that while not narrow, still responded to the patronage, subject matter and artistic language of the traditional Venetian way. This horizon was to be explicitly ruptured and surpassed: the alluring prospect of imposing, with an imperialistic posture, some kind of artistic primacy of Venice over the competing central Italian culture seems to have been consciously cultivated. Around Titian and Sansovino (with Aretino annexed) the entire system revolved. This system immediately gained ascendancy and therefore officiality, and inserted itself into a more extensive political and cultural strategy.

It is undeniable that the pictorial production of Titian – like the architecture and town planning of Sansovino – in Venice or for Venetian patrons, belonged to a complex semantic field that had in its referents and its institutional and political motivations, precise and inevitable terms of comparison and of interlocution. Titian's debut is exemplary, with the assignment of the sensaria of the Fondaco dei Tedeschi[3] (in addition to the income from the Officio del Sal to pay for two assistants in accordance with a precedent set by Giovanni Bellini), for the highly official Palazzo Ducale paintings, or beyond this with Titian's frescoes for the Fondaco dei Tedeschi, the occasion of his celebrated confronto-scontro with Giorgione. Titian sought this objective – that is to say an official position strongly marked in the ideological sense – long before Sansovino obtained public commissions (he would reside permanently in the city only from 1529 onward). The constitution of the artistic fraternity would seem to have been only the fulfillment of a program initiated some fifteen years earlier by Titian. And yet, although Titian's offer to paint the Battle of Spoleto for the Sala del Maggior Consiglio was accepted as early as 1513, he did not actually carry it out until 1537, "as late as eight years after the Peace of Bologna" as Wolters[4] has pertinently observed, that is to say when "this remote skirmish between imperial and papal troops... had lost the burning topicality which it had had in 1513."

Titian was somewhat less cautious in affirming his political beliefs in the early 1520s, the period of the Saint Christopher on the staircase of the doge's apartments, where it is legitimate to read between the lines the artist's firm public standpoint in the current debate in the Serenissima, which was engaged in a strenuous period of political healing after the lacerating wounds inflicted by the Battle of Agnadello.[5]

Early paintings of no less intentional iconography – from the Judith or Justice of the Fondaco dei Tedeschi, to the Pesaro votive painting in Antwerp and the altarpiece of Saint Mark Enthroned for Santo Spirito in Isola – deal with themes in the civic domain: ex-voto paintings with declared commercial or maritime vocations, or, better still, thanksgiving for a naval victory: we seem to feel Titian's penetration of the hidden well-springs of commissions of this kind, with their revelation of transient situations. He externalized and built upon the intentions of the patron, or at the very least his sympathy made him a sort of outside accomplice.

1. A. Carracci, Portrait of Titian, engraving

TITIANI VECELLII PICTORIS CELEBERRIMI AC FAMOSISSIMI VERA EFFIGIES.

ILL.ᵐᵒ ET Rᵐᵒ D. Dño HENRICO CAETANO S.R.E. CARD. AMPLᵐᵒ Bonᵒ LEGATO
EXIGVVM HOC MVNVS IMAGINIS TITIANI PICT. CVIVS NOMEN ORBIS CONTINERE NON VALET SVBMISSE DICAT SACRATQVE
HVMILL. DEDIT. Q. SERVVS AVGVST. CARRᵈᵉⁿˢ

Leaving aside the *Battle of Spoleto* (left unpainted at the time that it was commissioned), Titian's *presa di coscienza* was most marked in the *Saint Christopher* and above all with *The Assumption* in the Frari; these were followed by the Gozzi altarpiece in Ancona, by that extraordinary *macchina*, the Averoldi polyptych in Brescia; and of course the *Pesaro Madonna* in the Frari.

More or less through the first thirty years of the Cinquecento, Titian worked on a series of portraits (artists, intellectuals, merchants) that describe the physical essence, the form, of a new man, cynical and self-absorbed, the master of his own destiny: in a word, modern. This type was the matrix and the measure upon which Titian was to construct his protagonists down to, effectively, the Peace of Bologna, and his first meeting with Charles V. At this point there was a turning point in the artist's activity, not so much in the linguistic sense, or in the emphasis on some stylistic or formal features at the expense of others. It involved quite simply the artist's entry into the *sancta sanctorum* of the Imperial court, his access to the highest power, adapting his expressive formula to a language capable of communicating with

the non-religious sacrality, terrible and divine, of these great icons.

Titian continued (even if with the delays for which he was notorious and which would always punctuate his activity) to produce official images foreseen in his 1513 contract for works in the Palazzo Ducale. These culminated in the *Votive Painting of Doge Andrea Gritti*, which in 1531 upset the traditional scheme for this kind of votive image. It was a kind of celestial *tableau vivant* that brought together State piety, the consecration of both the ducal office and of the doge himself, the mediatory function of the Virgin or of the protector saints explicitly for the common weal, and the glorification of the Republic and its institutions.

The composition of the Gritti votive painting (destroyed as we know, in the fire of 1574), which is known to us from an engraving and from Tintoretto's variant copy, after 1574, continued that process of the redefinition of the Venetian iconographic universe launched by Titian some time before, and which had in the *Pesaro Madonna* one its highest and most revolutionary moments. (The votive painting of *Doge Antonio Grimani before Faith* was later,

*2. Jacopo Piccini after Titian, "Justice," from the Fondaco dei
Tedeschi, engraving, 1658
3. Nicolò Boldrini after Titian, "Votive Painting of Doge Gritti," destroyed 1572;
woodcut, Francesco Donà substituted for Doge Gritti*

and was the outcome of a changed ideological and historical context.) It is not easy to explain Titian's commitment to the destructuring and re-structuring of an iconographic universe so solidly established in the civic tradition.

Lorenzi,[6] Sinding-Larsen[7] and Wolters[8] have relied on Sanudo's contemporary explanation of the presence of the various saints in this painting for deciphering the meanings of the text ("and the commentary made is very good, of which I have chosen to make a note"). In substance, the dedicatory and congratulatory motives were in the spirit of public acknowledgment for services granted, for example to the artificer of his ducal election (that is to say to Alvise Pisani: "the procurator his mentor, who was in the XLI, and was the cause of making him Doge")[9] to which Saint Louis of Toulouse obviously makes reference in the painting). To these motifs should be added the typical and inevitable signs of Venetianness and the celebration of its symbols: the lion with its wreath of and crown of victory, which constitute (at least in the woodcut version of Boldrini, which we have no reason to consider unfaithful except in the intentional

substitution of doge Gritti with one of his later successors, Francesco Dona [1545-53]), the absolute center of the composition. That this composition and its details were not uninfluential is demonstrated by the variations introduced by Tintoretto in his remake (or copy according to the declared intentions) and were attributable, if one agrees with Wolters, to the "changed conception of the role of the Doge" between the time of Andrea Gritti (1523-38) and the eighth decade of the century. Perhaps the most sensational fact is the changed posture of the doge who is no longer the adoring figure we see in the *Pesaro Madonna* and in the Gritti painting in Titian's version (see also the panel by Vincenzo Catena with Doge Leonardo Loredan in the Correr Museum). The doge becomes, in Tintoretto's work, a kind of grand intercessor and intermediary with the celestial sphere, *pontifex* of a State religion, interpreter of a sacred sublimation of the role of the doge distinct from the heroic and glorious deneanor of Titian's iconographic conception. It was during Andrea Gritti's reign that we witness the final programmatic attempts of radical modification of the institutions of the Republic made

4. Jacopo Tintoretto, "Votive Painting of Doge Andrea Gritti".
Palazzo Ducale, Sala del Collegio, Venice

manifest or transcribed into urban form and architectural language in the great project of *renovatio urbis*, which Gritti himself elaborated and launched, as Manfredo Tafuri has ably shown.[10]

Each of the major players in the new power structure of a Venice always more rigorously aristocratic and oligarchical – Grimani, Pisani, Zeno, Barbaro, Mocenigo, and even Corner – chose the key to his own participation in the construction of the new public, semi-public, and private imagination: the Library of Saint Mark, the Loggetta of the Campanile, the Mint, the redefinition of

San Marco as a whole, of the San Marco-Rialto axis, and of the Calle Larga San Marco; and then again Palazzo Dolfin, the various Corner and Grimani palaces, the *scuole grandi*. Titian was anything but extraneous to this process (it is sufficient to remember how he joined with Francesco Zorzi, Serlio and Fortunio Spira in judging Sansovino's project for the Church of San Francesco della Vigna).[11] As Puppi has shown, Titian incorporated the various architectural influences of the theories and practices of his friends in his paintings (among others, sensationally, the settings of the *Presentation of the*

5. Titian, "Doge Grimani Kneeling before Faith." Palazzo Ducale,
Sala delle Quattro Porte, Venice

Virgin in the Temple, and of the *Pietà*, both in the Accademia, but also of the *Pesaro Madonna*, the *Ecce Homo* in Vienna, the *Crowning with Thorns* in the Louvre and the *Martyrdom of Saint Lawrence* in the Gesuiti). Further, he actively participated in the construction of that classicizing "ideal" environment, official and exalted, which was defined by precise linguistic options: a panorama and a space, attitudes and gestures, allusions and symbolic numbers, no less pregnant and meaningful than the columns and the plinths, the entablatures of the rusticated pilasters, and the arches.

Titian was located where myth and history meet, the classical and the modern, pagan gods and christian allegories, theological virtues and human wisdom.[12] He was once more at Sansovino's side, almost in the role of director, for the decoration of the Marciana library. This was the seam joining past traditions and future horizons; the civic umbilicus capable of giving sense and reason to a sequence of glorious events. The complex web of meanings and allegorical references excuses the old misunderstanding whereby it was believed that Titian's *Wisdom* in the anteroom depicted *History*: it is *History* that speaks from the architecture of the *Presentation*, from the classical altars, the colonnades, the rustication where the entombments of Christ and the last suppers are conducted, or Saint Lawrence martyred, or the pagan fables acted out, or the dazzling counter-Reformationary throng assembled where Doge Grimani worships Faith. This is apparent also in the *reality* of the immediate message – political or devotional – of the painting. It cannot be denied that in the dramatic space of those histories (of Christian salvation as well as in the timeless and almost utopian pagan world), between those spectral figures of men and gods, we are witness to the twilight of Venetian history, to a final curtain-fall.

Titian, who had participated in the building of this world, giving to it word and syntax, perceived already from the 1540s that his production could only take place outside the historical domain: therefore in myth. At this point he abandoned the Venetian dimension (though without leaving his residence in the city), to enter the labyrinth of the imperial court. The experience was to be – beyond the appearances and formalities of the commissions and the high-sounding honors – truly bitter, as

Gentili has shown: the undisputed and even despotic sovereign of Venetian art, Titian was forced to plead with the courts of Charles V and Philip II to obtain payments for works executed and for the sinceures conferred augustly on him or his sons.[13]

Before this Titian participated in the definition of a public image and certainly of a policy of the image subtly played from the summit of the Republic of Venice, without foregoing, as we have seen, substantial formal innovations of his own invention. Although the earliest

works were less than ideological, Titian learned to charge his paintings with meaning, even political, aided by the sensational and formal quality of his style. This was the case with *The Assumption* in the Frari, as David Rosand has convincingly demonstrated.[14]

One can understand how this came about: in the time since the defeat at Agnadello to the Peace of Bologna, Venice suffered years of profound public anxiety and instability, and the most celebrated intellectuals were called upon to that was to give support, direction and perspective to a political strategy in order to respond to a

6. *Vincenzo Catena, "Doge Loredan with the Madonna Enthroned and Saint Mark and John the Baptist." Museo Correr, Venice*

Saint Christopher in the Palazzo Ducale, the Turk in chains in the *Pesaro Madonna* (to which we may add the Pesaro Votive altar in Antwerp), the Gritti votive painting in the Sala del Collegio, the ducal portraits in the Palazzo Ducale, the *Battle of Spoleto* in the Maggior Consiglio, other frescoes and canvases in the Palazzo Ducale now destroyed by fire: these form a corpus of works of notable ideological and political import. These formed Titian's response to Venice's cultural crisis in the crucial years that concluded with the dogeship of Andrea Gritti. Nor is it inappropriate – quite the opposite – to add to these the two woodcuts, the *Triumph of Christ*, and the *Drowning of Pharoah*.[15]

The *Wisdom* in the Marciana is, metaphorically speaking, the seal that closes the chapter, elevating Venice and her history to the dimension of myth within this myth the figure of Wisdom constitutes the "thematic symbol of the whole complex" (Ivanoff).[16] No less eloquent is Titian's profoundly altered participation in the fate of the Republic. Although Venice was no longer physically threatened (or no longer exposed to the same danger of extinction to which Venice had been exposed by the League of Cambrai wars generated by all the Western powers) it was nevertheless moving toward a future of encomiastic literature and tracts, more than of a role on the political chessboard of Europe and the world. Titian seems to have been out of sympathy furthermore with Venice's option for the terraferma. It has been observed that he was totally absent from the world of the villas, which even during Titian's lifetime was passing through one of its best moments. Not only did Titian tend no longer to participate in the Venetian artistic scene or even to include the time-honored symbols that had always been peculiar to Venice, but the pagan fables and the portraits, the Venuses and the Danaës, placed him in the context of international classicism, in which he progressively assumed a prime role.

Nevertheless, at this point – including the dimension of myth – the destinies and the fortunes of the city and the artist were inextricably linked: so much so that the myth of Titian developed parallel to that of the city, his homeland. Titian continued to "make cultural politics" posthumously, constituting a considerable fragment of that belief in the excellency and perfection of Venice

crisis of identity, shattering Venice's sense of cultural, military and diplomatic security and continuity.

Hence Doge Andrea Gritti commissioned Titian to paint frescoes in his chapel in the Palazzo Ducale (today disappeared) as well as a kind political manifesto constituted by the *Saint Christopher*, who, in the Herculean figure of the saintly ferryman put to the test by Jesus himself, affirmed Venice's marine condition, the grand unbeatable bulwark of Faith, the capacity for resistance under pressure, and every other symbolic attribute and moral of Venice as *carrier* of a divine and imperial mission, against the enemies of liberty no less than against the aggressors of Christianity.

The Venice-Virgin in *The Assumption* in the Frari, the

7. Domenico Dalle Greche after Titian, "The Drowning of the Pharoah in the Red Sea." Woodcut, 1549, detail

8. Titian, "Allegory of Wisdom," Libreria Marciana, Venice

which, while its institutions, economy and social harmony showed increasing signs of dilapidation, survived as an ideal of artistic primacy in the name and art of Titian.

[1] On the relations between Titian and Aretino in particular, see M. Gregori, "Tiziano e l'Aretino," in *Tiziano e il Manierismo Europeo*, ed. R. Pallucchini, Florence, 1978, 271-306, 305. Gregori treated the problem in its double nature, both social – including his relations with extremely powerful correspondents – and aesthetic, to the point of claiming that "the writings of Aretino are the most important way of knowing the thoughts of one of the most important painters in the Renaissance."

[2] Concerning Sansovino's parallel role to Titian's, see above all two fundamental publications: M. Tafuri, *Iacopo Sansovino e l'architettura del '500 a Venezia*, Padua, 1969, and D. Howard, *Jacopo Sansovino. Architecture and Patronage in Renaissance Venice*, New Haven and London, 1975. See also: A. Foscari and M. Tafuri, *L'armonia e i conflitti*, Turin, 1983 and M. Tafuri, *Venezia e il Rinascimento*, Turin, 1985. It would be mistaken to limit to this triumvirate the control of that part of Venetian cultural policy formed by the figurative arts. At least Serlio, Francesco Zorzi and perhaps Giulio Camillo Delminio should be included in the first rank of the most influential practitioners and theoreticians; see C. Gould, "Sebastiano Serlio and Venetian Painting," *Journal of the Warburg and Courtauld Institutes*, XXV, 1962, 56-64; C. Pedretti, "Tiziano e il Serlio," in *Tiziano a Venezia*, Vicenza 1980, 243-48; L. Olivato, "Per il Serlio a Venezia; documenti nuovi e documenti rivisitati," *Arte Veneta*, XXVI, 1971, 284-91; F. Yates, *L'arte della memoria* (Italian ed.), Turin, 1972; L. Puppi, "Tiziano e l'architettura," in *Tiziano e il Manierismo europeo, cit.*, 205-30; E. Forssman, *Dorico, ionico, corinzio nell'architettura del Rinascimento*, Bari, 1973.

[3] See most recently, and with references to previous bibliography on the question, C. Hope, *Titian*, London, 1980 and "Titian's role as official painter to the Venetian Republic," in *Tiziano a Venezia, cit.*, 301-05.

[4] W. Wolters, *Storia e politica nei dipinti di Palazzo Ducale* (Italian ed.), Venice, 1987.

[5] Of particular importance in this context is: L. Puppi, "Mito e rappresentazione allegorica in un sogno del luogo di Utopia," in various authors, *Veneto*, Milan, 1977, 346-416 (esp. 387-94). The historic background and description of the Venetian political situation in the period immediately following Agnadello is given in: F. Gilbert, "Venice in the crisis of the League of Cambrai," in *Renaissance Venice*, ed. J. Hale, London, 1973, 274-90. On relations with Gritti, see C. Hope, "Titian's role..."

[6] G. B. Lorenzi, *Monumenti per servire alla storia del Palazzo Ducale di Venezia*, Venice 1868-69.

[7] S. Sinding-Larsen, *Christ in the Council Hall. Studies in the religious iconography of the Venetian Republic*, Rome, 1974.

[8] W. Wolters, *Storia e politica...*

[9] M. Sanudo, *Diarii*, 10.6.1531, ed. R. Fulin, F. Stefani, N. Barozzi, Venice, 1879-1902.

[10] M. Tafuri, ed., *Renovatio Urbis. Venezia nell'età di Andrea Gritti (1523-1535)*, Rome, 1984 (in particular, Tafuri's own essay, "'Renovatio urbis Venetiarum' il problema storiografico, 9-55). M. Tafuri, "Politica, scienza e architettura nella Venezia del '500," in *Cultura e Società nel Rinascimento. Tra riforma e manierismo*, ed. V. Branca and C. Ossola, Florence, 1984, 97-133.

[11] Central to this is: L. Puppi, "Tiziano e l'architettura..." Fundamental also are: U. Vicentini, "Francesco Zorzi, O.F.M. teologo cabalista (1453-1540)," *Le Venezie Francescane*, XXL, 3, 1954, 121-62, 4, 174-226; R. Wittkower, *Architectural Principles in the Age of Humanism*, London, 1949 (Italian ed.

Turin, 1964), 102ff; D. Howard, *Jacopo Sansovino...*; D. Rosand, "Titian's 'Presentation of the Virgin in the Temple' and the Scuola della Carità," *Art Bulletin*, March 1976, 55-84; M. Tafuri, "'Sapienza di Stato' e 'atti mancati': architettura e tecnica urbana nella Venezia del '500," in *Architettura e Utopia nella Venezia del '500* (exhibition catalog), ed. by L. Puppi, Milan, 1980, 16-39; L. Magagnato, *Introduzione e Promemoria di Francesco Giorgi per San Francesco della Vigna architettura di Jacopo Sansovino*, Milan, 1982; A. Foscari, M. Tafuri, *L'armonia...*; M. Tafuri, *Renovatio...*; idem, *Venezia e il Rinascimento...*

[12] See: N. Ivanoff, "Il ciclo allegorico della Libreria sansoviniana," *Arte antica e moderna*, XIII-XVI, 1961, 248-58, and "Il coronamento statuario della Marciana," *Ateneo Veneto*, n.s. II, 1964, no. 1, 100-12, and "Il ciclo dei filosofi della Libreria Marciana a Venezia," *Emporium*, CXI, no. 2, 1964, 207-10, and "I cicli allegorici della Libreria e del Palazzo Ducale di Venezia," in *Rinascimento Europeo e Rinascimento Veneziano*, ed. V. Branca, Florence, 1967, 281-97, and "La Libreria Marciana," *Saggi e Memorie di Storia dell'Arte*, 1968, 37-78; W. Lotz, "La libreria di San Marco e l'urbanistica del Rinascimento," *Bollettino del Centro Internazionale di Studi di Architettura A. Palladio*, 1961, 85-8; Lotz, "Sansovinos Bibliothek von San Marco und die Stadtbaukunst der Renaissance," in *Kunst des Mittelalters in Sachsen*, Festschrift W. Schubert, Weimar, 1967, 336-43; A, Paolucci, "La sala della Libreria e il ciclo pittorico," in *Da Tiziano a El Greco. Per una storia del Manierismo nel Veneto* (exhibition catalog), ed. R. Pallucchini, Milan, 1981, 287-98; G. Romanelli, "Il progetto di Sansovino e lo scalone," in *Da Tiziano a El Greco...*, 277-84; U. Ruggeri, "La decorazione pittorica della Libreria Marciana," in *Cultura e società nel Rinascimento...*, 313-33; M. Tafuri, *Renovatio...*; idem, *Politica, scienza...*; idem, *Venezia e il Rinascimento...*; T. Hirthe, "Die Libreria das Jacopo Sansovino. Studien zu Architektur und Austattung eines offentlichen Geb auds in Venedig," *Münchner Jahrbuch der bildenden Kunst*, 3 Folge, 37, 1986, 131-76; idem, *Il 'Foro all'antico' di Venezia. La trasformazione di Piazza San Marco nel Cinquecento*, Centro tedesco di Studi Veneziani, 35, Venice, 1986.

[13] A. Gentili, *Da Tiziano a Tiziano. Mito e allegoria nella cultura veneziana del Cinquecento*, Milan, 1980.

[14] D. Rosand, *The Meaning of the Mark: Leonardo and Titian* (The Franklin D. Murphy Lectures, Spencer Museum of Art), Lawrence, Kansas, 1980. Concerning this technique, other pertinent and recent writings are: J. Wilde, *Venetian Art from Bellini to Titian*, Oxford, 1974; M. Muraro, "Titien iconographie et politique," in *Symboles de la Renaissance*, Paris, 1976, 31-5; idem, "Tiziano pittore ufficiale della Serenissima," in *Tiziano nel quarto centenario della sua morte...*, Ateneo Veneto, Venice, 1977, 83-100; L. Puppi, *Mito e rappresentazione...*; C. Hope, "Titian's role..."; H. Siebenhüner, "Il 'San Giorgio' Cini," in *Tiziano a Venezia...*, 317-19; P. Fortini Brown, "Painting and History in Renaissance Venice," *Art History*, 1984, no. 3, 263-94; D. Howard, "Giorgione's Tempesta and Titian's Assunta in the context of the Cambrai wars," *Art History*, 1985, no. 3, 271-89; R. Goffen, *Piety and Patronage in Renaissance Venice. Bellini, Titian and the Franciscans*, New Haven and London, 1986.

[15] D. Rosand, Titian's "Presentation..."; M. Muraro and D. Rosand, *Tiziano e la silografia veneziana del Cinquecento*, Venice 1976; L. Olivato, "La submersione di Pharaone," in *Tiziano a Venezia*, 529ff; M. A. Chiari, *Incisioni da Tiziano* (exhibition catalog of the prints and drawings collection of the Museo Correr), Venice, 1982.

[16] N. Ivanoff, "I cicli allegorici...," 286.

Giorgio Padoan
TITIAN'S LETTERS

1 Leonardo da Vinci, though he professed himself a "man without letters," recorded observations that in sharpness of reflection and incisiveness of style have their place among the most memorable writings of those years. Michelangelo Buonarroti composed poems the major poets of his time could envy. In Venice, however, artists seldom committed their thoughts to paper, but seem to have been more attentive to music. The most that can be said of them is that they were conscious of the need to take into account the literary culture of the time, and so, when it came to the choice of themes or iconographic details, they did not disdain the suggestions of freinds or patrons who were men of letters, or they consulted books, illustrated ones in particular, by Latin writers, mostly in vernacular translation.[1] If any conclusion can be drawn from this, it must be that the painters' interests were for the most part (for some almost exclusively) confined to the visual arts. And for that reason we need to repeat loud and clear, however much it may displease some of our own contemporaries and colleagues, that the tendency, still widespread today, to presume that those artists read "elevating" works of exceptional value – rare or philosophical or even hermetic – is a plain and simple distortion of the historical fact.[2] As for Titian, even in the absence of any documentation to enlighten us about his intellectual formation, some writers have not resisted the temptation to trace out for him a compact cultural background.[3]

Titian's name was mentioned by Paolo Giovio[4] around 1525, yet ignored in the roster of praiseworthy painters of the time drawn up by Baldassare Castiglione in *Il Cortegiano*, which was published in 1528 but set in the world of 1507.[5] It appears for the first time in a work of literary importance only in the third edition (1532) of Ariosto's *Orlando Furioso*, though the painter had been in contact since at least 1518 with the poet's patron, Duke Alfonso I d'Este of Ferrara.[6] Tardy recognition indeed,[7] though perhaps not unconnected with Titian's friendship with "the scourge of princes, the divine Pietro Aretino" (he too was mentioned for the first time by Ariosto in that epic poem, Canto XLVI, 14). And even then the reason for mentioning the artist would have been the outline drawing of Ariosto's profile he contributed to that later edition. Besides, the praise is merely generic: "Leonardo, Andrea Mantegna, Gian Bellini, the two Dossi, and he who both sculpts and paints, Michel, more than mortal and truly divine Angelo, Bastian [Sebastiano del Piombo], Raphael, and Titian who brings honor to Cadore no less than the latter two to Venice and Urbino" (Canto XXXIII, 2).

Also significant is the mention in one of the *Dialoghi* by Antonio Brucioli (1.III, Dialogue XIX) in the second edition of 1537,[8] where Sebastiano Serlio and Titian are presented as discussing, in the painter's house, the phenomenon of the rainbow. Titian's part is limited to that of the curious questioner, while the subject itself is treated entirely by Serlio, almost as if alluding to a well-known curiosity of the painter about optical phenomena and his interest in dissertations touching on facts tangentially connected with his art.

Nor is the meaning entirely clear in the dedication of the *Paraphrasi della sesta satira di Giuvenale* "in which are discussed the reasons why married men are miserable – a dialogue which speaks of the sort of wife one should look for and the way she should be treated – The Epithalamium of Catullus on the marriage of Peleus and Thetis," translated into the vernacular by Ludovico Dolce (1538). Ginzburg has discerningly remarked that in the Epithalamio Dolce strays from the Latin text to include images suggested by Titian's painting for Alfonso d'Este, of Ariadne weeping and the procession of Bacchus.[9] Was this meant as homage to the *gentilissimo Tiziano* (as Dolce referred to him in the dedication to Aretino of his translation of 1536 of Horace's *Poetica*)[10] (if the idea for the painting had been suggested by Dolce himself)? Or was this, as Ginzburg suggests, an attempt to demonstrate the superiority of literature over figurative art, as is in fact affirmed in the dedication? Whatever the ease, that dedication, in itself extraordinary, does tell us of the respect with which Titian was regarded by the literati in the 1530s, if not also of the painter's attention to the learned discussions on primacy in the arts.[11] In those colloquies Dolce assumed a position in favor of literature (repeated subsequently in his *Dialogo sulla pittura intitolato l'Aretino*),[12] in implied polemic with the more open-minded views of Titian's friend Aretino, who was rather more knowledgeable about the expressive capacities of the pictorial art ("I take pains to portray the

43

nature of others with the vividness with which the admirable Titian portrays one or another face").[13] In reality, such debate over theoretical questions mirrored changes in taste and habit that many men of letters regarded with unconfessed fear. In the society of the courts, literary and learned writings were traditionally dedicated to the local lord. More and more, however, literary efforts were having to compete other forms of homage that were proving more welcome and, indeed, more pleasing – pictures especially. A painting had the advantage of being more immediately enjoyed and more directly useful in decorating a patrician's dwelling; besides, it was more easily comprehended by the person who received it, as was usually the case with commissioned works, could more nearly satisfy the patron's interest in some particular subject. Most appreciated were portraits and erotic nudes, these being especially useful as pleasing decoration for hall or chamber. With these, it is easy to understand how the better artists could compete with the purveyors of literary works and could not seldom carry the day and undermine the writers' monopoly of the noble lords' hearts and purses. Above all, in the case of the portrait – whether of the patron himself or his familiars or of his own overlord, pope or emperor – the picture could establish a rapport such as no work of literature or learning could match: "The princes," Aretino noted in 1551, "take greater delight in likenesses of faces than in registers of facts, as if the effigy were of greater importance than the eternity of memory."[14]

On less elevated levels of intellectual exchange, the literary man in the High Renaissance could therefore not fail to be aware, however confusedly, that even if his traditional monopoly as purveyor of culture and apologist was not openly questioned, it was becoming increasingly limited by that new reality he had to take into account (though rarely could a painter close down his workshop and live the courtier's life). Disquisitions on the value of figurative art were no longer left exclusively to those directly interested (Leon Battista Alberti, Leonardo, for example), and the man of letters was coming to realize how opportune it was for him to take over the discussion of those questions (obviously so as to end up by proving the superiority of literature), revealing

his implicit if unvoiced fear of finding himself supplanted. Moreover, the fact that the major biographical undertaking of the sixteenth century was Vasari's *Vite* of 1550 – entirely devoted to artists, not writers – is eloquent in this context.

The problem had not posed itself so long as paintings were produced almost exclusively in the service of religious devotion. (Miniatures always remained in some way merely accessory to the primary object, the book.) But once the rapid and constant process of secularization of figurative art was launched, and art was increasingly utilized for political or personal purposes (though without ever becoming exonerated from its traditional task of popularizing religious belief), there was more and more demand for it to broaden that function in the secular field as well. Within the context of religious painting itself, even before Titian's *Assumption of the Virgin* for the church of the Frari was deemed a great artistic achievement, that huge altarpiece was thought of as something exceptional (and was so recorded in Sanudo's diary) and constituted a relevant political factor in the history of the Franciscan order and of its influence in Venice.

Likewise the Pesaro Madonna in the same church had an ulterior purpose: to sanction the result of the effort the friary had made to collect funds for the anti-Turkish crusade, to commemorate the naval victory of Santa Maura, and to exalt the house of Pesaro and its rise to prominence. For even better light on the entire panorama we can recall that, among the subtle threads linking the fortunes of that powerful family with the prestigious Venetian friary, is the fact that its Father Guardian in those same years was himself a Pesaro, Fra Pietro.[15]

For all that the intense friendship between Aretino and Titian[16] (and Sansovino as well) certainly mirrors an accord in tastes and characters, it was rooted also in Aretino's clear awareness of the change afoot. The close bond between Aretino and Titian – whose repute the writer fostered among powerful patrons was mutually advantageous.[17] Thus once he sent a portrait of himself painted by Titian to Francesco Gonzaga; sometimes he sent his own verses along with a painting by Titian, or dedicated one of his works to an individual whose portrait Titian was currently painting (for example, the *Vita di*

Santa Caterina to Marchese Del Vasto). Always Aretino emphasized (even beyond the truth) the two friends' indissoluble union.

Titian drew no small profit from that connection, because Aretino "made his name known as far as his pen reached, and especially to princes of importance" (Vasari). Nor was the writer sparing of his counsel: "Many times," he wrote in 1537, "Raphael and Fra Bastiano (Sebastiano del Piombo) and Titian abided by my judgment, because I know somewhat of the ancient and modern ways."[18] Further, when it came to portraits the writer gave the artist some idea of the aspect that was both artistically more incisive and economically rewarding and urged him to seek commissions from courts well outside the Venetian territory. It was in fact Aretino who induced Titian to renew the connection with the Gonzagas that for some time had been allowed to lapse, and it was his idea to turn to the Farnese for commissions, and the Spanish "initiation" came through him so well. So Mina Gregori is quite right to say that "the writings of Aretino are the most important path in attempting to know what Titian thought."[19]

For his part, the painter was a man of sharp intelligence and aware of his own weakness in literary matters, his profession being "alien to forming words" (as he wrote, with an expression worthy of Aretino himself, in a letter to Ganzaga in 1528). He was open to suggestions from patrons[20] and quick to master the ideas offered him as well as to take advice from his "crony" and to make use of that friend's authoritative status. From Aretino he learned to become his own ever-shrewder "manager." This could mean taking pains to maintain contacts with the most important patrons, or (especially in dealings with the emperor) adopting the criterion favored by Aretino of the "gift in homage" with its implied expectation of due compensation, or not hesitating to request the promised payment, indeed insisting when necessary. Thus the rapport between Aretino and Titian was considerably more than a friendship, and it left its mark unmistakably on all of Titian's correspondence. It involved above all imposing Titian on the attention of the great of the world but also of the literati. It meant also that the painter – by nature courteous and hospitable[21] and a "person likely to season with his pleasantries every

honorable dinner party"[22] was placed in a position to receive in his home intellectuals of varied provenance. Outstanding among these were the architect and treatise writer Serlio,[23] Dolce, the prime translator of classical texts, and the publisher Marcolini. From conversation with these men and others, the master could certainly profit through learning the latest news, acquiring ideas, and attending to their observations when he showed his guests the canvases he was working on, and through them, as well, he made other contacts of no less interest. The description of Titian's garden by the Tuscan grammarian Francesco Priscianese has remained deservedly famous, and it is interesting precisely because it introduces us into one of those discussions that took place during the supper gatherings in the house at San Canciano, enlivened on that particular evening of 15 August, 1540 by Aretino's passionate attack against those who would belittle vernacular Italian in favor of Latin.[24]

From this it is apparent that the main strands in the formation of Titian's personal culture comprised conversations with intellectuals of various persuasions[25] as well as firsthand acquaintance with antique sculptures, drawings, prints, illustrated books of mythology (Ovid in particular) in Italian translation, and, naturally, the paintings of other masters.

II But if such frequentations doubtless enriched our artist's curiosity and interests, and could furnish him with invaluable ideas for his own work, especially for what in the letters are designated as *poesie* (that is, paintings on mythological subjects),[26] they cannot be taken as proof of any solid literary preparation on his own part. Nor, in itself, is there any such evidence in his signature as owner in a copy of Catullus containing the commentary by Alessandro Guarino "Alexandri Guarini expositiones" published in Venice in 1521, which may have been merely a gift he received. It is well known that, in general, painters had little familiarity with Latin – and sometimes even with their own tongue in its literary form. In the case of Titian (who did after all have some antiquarian interests), should it be needed we can rely on the explicit testimony of Dolce who, in dedicating to the painter his translation of Juvenal, wrote: "Now I send it to you so that, not being able to understand it on its own, you can see in mine if the good writers know equally well how to portray with the pen the secrets of the heart,"[27] a passage that undubitably means: since you are not equipped to understand the original Latin, you may be able to see in my translation, etc. And it is no less beyond doubt that, since no one offers something in homage with the intention (or risk) of offending, Dolce quite certainly knew – and most likely from Titian himself – that his dedicatee did not read Latin.

For this reason too there is no reason to dwell on an opuscule of late date titled *Titiani Vecellii equitis pro Cadubriensibus ad Serenissimum Venetiarum Principem Aloysium Mocenicum oratio, habita* VI *kalend. Januariis* MDLXXI, *pro magna navali victoria, Dei gratia, contra Turcos*. This is a Latin oration in which the community of Cadore, Titian's birthplace, officially conveyed to the Doge an expression of its rejoicing over the victory at Lepanto (the date is *more veneto*, so actually 1572). Considering the subject, it would perhaps be more appropriate to think of the painter's homonym who was mayor of Cadore,[28] if the title of "cavaliere" did not speak in favor of our artist. The oration itself, however, is benally pedantic and to all appearances the work of a modest but respectable grammarian who carried out his task by repeating the contribution offered by the woods around Cadore to the building of the victorious fleet. Although the Latin is of a low level, it shows the author to be one who used the language as a tool of his personal profession. If our Tiziano Vecelli were involved, at the age of ninety-two (five) he might at the most have accompanied the Cadore delegation to the presence of the Signoria, leaving it to others to orate the text, and in our context that can assume no significance whatever. It comes down to the fact that the only writings by Titian that can provide some information about his literary culture are his own letters. These make up a corpus so extensive as to be the richest body of correspondence to come down to us from any Renaissance artist. The volume that most recently reprinted them[29] comprises a good 103 letters from Titian (one of which copies another, with variants) and 81 addressed to him. In addition, there are eight petitions to the Venetian authorities (three are public documents connected with them) and a tax declaration of 1566. While there are only

a very few letters we know about but do not have (three from Titian and two addressed to him), it is not hard to suppose that many await discovery in archives not yet explored. The fact is, those known can be grouped, in the overwhelming majority, according to the archives where they were found and which, for various reasons, were methodically explored to the full. If the number of Titian's letters greatly exceeds that of other sixteenth-century artists, there is certainly a valid explanation in the great span of time covered, between 1513 and 1576. But responsible above all if the vast network or international contacts he was able to cultivate, offering, asking, and also protesting when the promise of earned reward for his efforts was not honored. There emerges from all this a rich crop of information of inestimable value for dating paintings, identifying patrons, evaluating earnings, but even more for defining the painter's character, marked as it was with a constant concern to keep all those threads in his own hands and not much disposed to let his concrete interest be scanted.

Highly valuable documentation, then, and it would be very satisfying if we could speak oI Titian as a writer of letters possessed of a secure pen. But as regards the literary valuation of his correspondence, the shadow of doubt lies heavy, and there are strong suspicions that the letters, in the overwhelming majority, may not be altogether attributable to his own hand. This holds even for the petitions and the tax declaration: compiled according to a bureaucratic standard form with little or no leeway for personal expressions, they were customarily left for someone else, familiar with the procedures, to draw up. That such documents were readily subject to rewording on the part of others we know from Titian himself: when in 1549 he sent to Antoine Perrenet de Granvelle, bishop of Arras, "a draft of the *placet* for the benefice of the scala, he asked that, if the present draft is not according to the style of is Majesty's court, will Your Worship please have it corrected and emended wherever necsssary" (no. 108 in the edition cited).

Because such documents are known to us through copies and recopies in public registers (which means that the scribes are likely to have introduced their personal quirks in writing and even errors on their own),[30] we are more likely to find clues to Titian's use of the language in the letters known to us in the original and not as copied into the addresee's register of correspondence. It is a natural supposition, however, that just as he availed himself of an expert for missives concerning juridical matters, so too he followed the practice of the time, at least for letters to personalities of particular importance, and made use of the counsel, if not outright help, of some man of the pen. This is the more likely since, for the actual writing, he often relied on clerks or copyists and limited himself – as is documented in a few specific cases[31] – to signing his name in his own hand or at the most adding a final line. Even the fact that a few letters are clearly in his own hand is not in itself sufficient guarantee of their authorship, because he could have himself merely transcribed the expressions written out or dictated by others (as, for example, in no. 37, of which we shall have more to say below).

Stylistic analysis of the correspondence gives sure evidence of the involvement of others. During the long span of time covered, a number of individuals intervened in

Most Holy Imperial Majesty,
I have consigned to Senor Don Diego de Mendoza the two portraits of Her Serene Highness the Empress, into which I have put all the diligence possible to me. I should have liked to bring them myself, if the length of the voyage and my age would have permitted.

I pray Your Majesty to let me know the faults and deficiencies, sending them (the portraits) back to me so I can correct them, and that Your Majesty won't let anyone else put his hand to them.

For the rest, I refer to what Senor Don Diego will say about my things, and reverently kissing the feet and hands of Your Majesty, I commend myself humbly to your good graces.

Titian's letters to different degrees. Sometimes they entirely reworked what he dictated, sometimes limited themselves to rapidly tidying up the text. In the latter cases, the painter's living voice can still be made out behind the text, but the result is an extravagant hybrid, "poised between artists' jargon and the starchiness of the literati."[32] Consider for example, a letter sent from Venice to Charles v in October 1543 (no. 63) which keeps strictly to the point and in which certain expressions obviously reflect the painter's own speech: "I should have liked to bring these myself," or "Your Majesty won't let anyone else put his hand to them." Compare this with the one that followed (no. 64) which repeats the same message since the first one remained without answer. It is syntactically impeccable, quite differently articulated, and more attentive to the obsequious tone: "the Empress your consort, of blessed memory," "your utterly invincible hand," "without the knowledge of Your Majesty," and the like, and all these elements are indicative of two different hands:

as compared with:
Most Holy Imperial Majesty,
I dispatched some months back to Your Majesty, by the hands of Senor Don Diego your ambassador, the portrait of the Empress your consort, of blessed memory, done by my hand, along with the other that was given to me by you as example.
But because all my wishes in this world are no more then a most ardent desire to serve snd satisfy Your Majesty in whatever I can, I am waiting with infinite devotion to hear if that work of mine has reached you and if it has pleased you or not. Because if I come to know it has been pleasing to you, I will feel that contentment of mind that words do not suffice to say. And if, instead, it should be the contrary, I offer myself to set it to rights in such a way that Your Majesty will be content with it, if Our Lord God will grant me the grace of being able to come and present you with a figure of Venue made by me in your name, which figure, I hope, will be a clear pledge of how much my art may progress if putting itself in Your Majesty's service.
I am presently here in Rome, summoned here by His Holiness, and from these marvelous ancient stones I am learning things thanks to which my art may become worthy of depicting the victories that Our Lord God is preparing for Your Majesty in the East. (Levant)
Meantime I kiss your utterly invincible hand with all the affection and reverence of my heart; and I entreat you to deign to order and see to it that the export permit granted me many years

ago by Your Majesty for grain of the Kingdom of Naples, and the pension of thirty scudi that you ordered should be paid me every year in Milan in compensation for the *Annunciate* I presented to you, be put into effect, because I have had neither one nor the other so far, without the knowledge of Your Majesty.

From Rome on the viii of December MD.XLV
of Your Imperial Majesty, the most humble creature and servitor

TITIANO painter

From Venice, the 5th of October 1545
Most humble and perpetual servant of Your Majesty,
TITIANO

It was already said by Carlo Ridolfi that Titian's official letters were drawn up for him by Bernardino Partenio and Giovanni Maria Verdizotti.[33] For the period prior to Pietro Aretino's arrival in Venice, Erica Tietze-Conrat hypothesized the collaboration of Andrea Navagero and, for the artist's final years, that of his own son Orazio.[34] But besides these, still others will have given their collaboration, even if only from time to time. However, the only personality that emerges with any certainty is Aretino himself, and this beginning with the letter to Federico Gonzaga of June 21, 1527 (the writer had arrived in Venice only three months earlier!). There Aretino's style is immediately recognizable: see, for example, with the initial gerund – one of Pietro's most favorite devices – the allusion to the extraordinary power of Saint Paul as preacher (see Aretino, *Lettere*, ed. Flora, 1:88), the praise of his friend Giulio Romano[35] (*ibid.*, 1:145), and the assertion of the sincerity of Aretino himself (*ibid.*, 1:987), which in this context looks like true and proper self-praise:

Knowing how much Your Excellency loves painting and how much you enhance it, as can be seen in the merits of Messer Giulio Romano; and since I am always desirous of pleasing you, because Messer Pietro Aretino has come here, a Saint Paul indeed in preaching the praises of Your Excellency, I have portrayed him, and knowing how much you love that servitor of yours for his plain-speaking, I am making you a gift of it.

It is obvious that the very idea of both the gift and the letter originated with Aretino, who in that manner was showing Titian the best way (for himself as well) to renew contact with the ruler of Mantua. It is highly significant that a few months later, in October, when Aretino wrote

to Gonzaga to thank him for gifts received, he reminded him of "the promise made to Titian thanks to my portrait that I, in his name, had him present to you," and he even concludes his letter with: "Meanwhile Titian and I kiss your hands."[36] The long succession of letters between the painter and Gonzaga, extending over a full twelve years, shows how much Aretino had seen rightly. Indeed, not seldom in that specific body of correspondence one senses the writer's assiduous presence, if not directly dictating, at least suggesting the most appropriate formulation.

Other letters too are entirely redolent of Aretino. Among those that seem to proclaim his name loudest is, for its particular tonality,[37] one to Messer Vendramo, chamberlain to cardinal Ippolito de' Medici written in December 1534 (no. 37). After having recalled that Messer Pietro Aretino "of a certainty says of Your Most Illustrious Worship what would be said of Christ," Titian adds banteringly: "You will be happy to tell Benedetto, even if no one wishes to hand on bad news nor say things that might offend, that he should be patient because his Mercolina is getting herself laid a bit and seduced and is pregnant." (The modern reader's distaste for Aretino's poisonous tongue should be moderated a bit here, because involved is not a wife but, more probably, a courtesan.)

For its style, one can mention also Titian's letter of March 1544 to Bernardino Maffei, secretary to Cardinal Farnese (no. 57), in which the request of a benefice promised and not yet obtained is enlivened by Aretino's colorful irony:

"I, Signor Bernardino, cast my avid expectations into the arms of your charitable offices: I say avid because, besides the loss it would be to me not to receive such a minimum recompense, there would be the added ignominy that would be heaped upon me because this entire city not only believes that I am about to obtain it but, indeed, have already obtained it. Whence I shall consider it as settled that I shall be paid more than the simple living that I would receive in taking possession of the humble little church promised me on request to our highly illustrious and Most Reverend Lord Master, which is pretty much as if it were requested of the perpetual blessedness of the Pontiff deservedly his ancestor."

Cavalcaselle and Crowe were of the opinion that this letter may have been written under Aretino's dictation,[38] and the hypothesis strikes me as solid. Aretino's voice is plain to hear right from the opening gambit: "Good Sir, the great fame or Cardinal Farnese resounds in such manner in the ears of the world that nothing (no one) is more spoken of and nothing (no one) more praised, so that I, who revere him, not only take comfort in hearing it but as rejuvenated by it." Here there are strokes that could not be more typical had Aretino signed the letter himself. Alongside it can be placed the *incipit* of the letter mentioned earlier: (other letter:) "Most Revered Signor Messer Vendramo, the love you bear me makes you tell me what error abides in me, and you let me know it because it brings me harm and vituperation such as I may not hold and keep those friends and patrons dear to my heart."

Analysis yields similar results in a letter to Prince Philip of Spain of 1554 (no. 130),[39] as in various others, especially in passages where, nothing concrete is said but the scintillating style aims in characteristic Aretinian (Aretino) fashion to create elegant turns of phrases, rhetorical tricks, and, so to speak, verbal winks of the eye. All told, in the corpus of Titian's letters, along with two from himself to Aretino there are fifty-four from Aretino to Titian (of which a full thirty-two in the four years between 1545 and 1548). When we add those that, although signed by Titian, prove in reality to be Pietro's work or at least largely influenced by him, and those in which his intervention is in some way noticeable, if not directly by dictation at least in advice and suggestions, it is clear that Aretino's contribution was of considerable weight, even if what he supplied was nothing of himself

personally but only his innate skill with words. On the other hand, any mentions of Titian in his own letters may have been by explicit agreement between the two.

We have already noted that before and after Aretino's collaboration, but during it as well, thus between 1527 and 1556, others likewise lent a hand in Titian's letter writing, though less extensively and less recognizably, Although the situation is pretty much a tangle, this does not mean we need abandon hope of getting at least an approximate idea of how the painter himself wrote. Obviously variations in stylistic quality, even of considerable breadth, can be found in the writings or one and the same individual in response to different subjects, the different character or social standing of the person addressed, and so on. Aretino himself shifted registers between letters of normal correspondence and those aimed at publication (and which therefore underwent due revision, as doubtless did the two letters Titian wrote to Aretino which were published through the interest of the addressee himself). But if Titian really knew how to write on his own, and with the stylistic rigor that, sometimes more, sometimes less, colors his correspondence, he would certainly not have lapsed into outright slovenlinesses, least of all in letters to personalities of rank. In such cases, because it is impossible to believe that anyone who does know how to write would accept someone else's dictation uncritically if he is capable of himself producing better, the deficiencies in style and language must be attributed to the person signing the letter who, for some reason, must have been unable in the particular case to call on the usual help.

This is so with the letter (judged autograph by the experts) Titian sent to Duke Federico Gonzaga on July 12, 1530 (no. 13). It was written in Bologna where evidently the painter could not make use of the same person who, a year later, would dictate something much more dignified for a letter to the same duke from Venice (no. 18), nor, indeed, of anyone of equal competence (see no. 16). Here is the letter from Bologna (though lacking, in English, its misspellings and Venetianisms):

Most Illustrious Signor Duke,
That Cova or Cornelia is not to be found here in Bologna. Signora Isabella has sent her to stay in Nuvelara for a change of air, she having been ill, and people say that she is pretty much

the worse for the illness, though doing better now. And I, hearing this, doubted I could do anything good, what with her having been ill, and then myself being overcome by the great heat and also a little under the weather, and so as not to fall wholly ill myself, I did not go any farther, thinking to serve Your Excellency for the best in this matter and that you will be satisfied with this.

At first this pleasant lady made such a good impression on me with her features and beauty that I was all afire to paint her in a way that no one knowing her would say I had not portrayed her several times already, and therefore I pray Your Excellency to leave this assignment to me, because at the end of about ten days I will show her to you, if you send to me in Venice the portrait that that other painter made of the said Cornelia, and I will return both to you posthaste, and Your Excellency will know, comparing them, how I desire to serve you.

And I kiss the hand of Your Excellency.

From Bologna the XII July MDXXX.

When Your Excellency has seen the portrait when it is done, if something is lacking I will willingly come to Nuvolara to amend it, but I believe there will be no need of that.

Of Your Most Illustrious Excellency

Servitor TICIAN.

The letter is in Titian's own manner, at least that of around 1530. The haphazard spelling is much influenced by Venetian dialect, especially, naturally enough, in the reduction of double consonants to one: *smarita, esendo, satisfata, fateze,* etc., or the contrary: *carricho*. But note also *sta, conosa, mi, meio, zorni,* etc., as well as such grammatical errors as *l'ano mandata, la stano meio, la son smarita, manchano qualche cosa*. As for the syntax, at various points it is simply pulled to pieces. Nonetheless the concepts are clear and expressed with vigor and come down to this: the mission was not carried through because of inopportune impediments, yet the painter's art will succeed no less in shining just as if, and perhaps even more, he had had the model before his eyes: a deliberately prideful statement, which strikes a typically and instinctively Titianesque note.

It is natural that as the years passed, with the experience he had acquired, Titian should improve his literary style. Not so, however, even as late as September 1539, to judge by a business letter to his sister Doratia (Dorotea) in which he included a note for his cousin Tomà Tito Vecellio (nos. 47, 48). Along with the expected omission of double consonants there is no end of typically Vene-

tian spellings (such as *ziò, maridar, cugnado, nodaro, lezer, zudege,* etc.) but also less frequent errors (like *puplicarla*) and grammatical dialectalisms (like *i dicha* for *essi dicano*). In the note in particular, where he recommends that his cousin follow the business matter closely, the cadence tends to model itself more on speech (for example, "El numero [the amount of Dorotea's dowry] si ben i no se arecorda preciso, el numero non importa" – "The amount, even though I don't recall it exactly, the amount doesn't matter"). The tone likewise is more familiar, to the point of using exceptionally the intimate *tu* (in letters to his sister and in others to the same cousin one finds instead *voi*). But here the syntactical uncertainties and grammatical imprecisions are less harsh, and the concepts are expressed with even more – if possible – exemplary clearness.

If Titian's ability with words was no better than this at the time, then, in the much more fluent letter of 1543 to Cardinal Farnese (no. 55), nothing except the contents can be attributed to him, yet Tietze-Conrat views it as written with that concrete precision to be expected from a letter written by Titian himself.[40]

Another sure point of reference is established by a letter of June 17, 1559, to his son Orazio (no. 140):

Horatio, your delay in writing me has given ne cause for worry. You write me about having four ducats: thus in a letter. As regards that, you are not counting the expense of sending to Milan, or else, out of sheer light-headedness you have made a slip of the pen and, where you wanted to say two thousand, you said four ducats: it suffices that you believe things will go well. I have written to His Majesty that the treasurer of Genoa was not able to pay me. I hope His Majesty will make provision for this. From what you write me, you have in mind going to Genoa. If you think you can get good results, you will do well with the favor of His Excellency. Even if you achieve little that you are on the spot, so can judge it better than I can. Now, going there, be careful not to ride in the heat; if you can make it in two days, take four.

As for my cavalier (horseman), I do not dare write to you before the arrival of that beast of an importunate individual whose mother says she is waiting for him from day to day, that he is in Florence, and she doesn't know in what chest (house) there is the model of the Christ of (Santa Maria sopra) Minerva, so I am very anxious, not being able to serve and satisfy this wish of his, and you should commend me to his courtesy... the patrons. From Venice on June 17 of 1559

Your Father TITIANO V.O

To go by the transcription of this letter (unfortunately the autograph is lost), the dialectalisms would seem reduced to the mostcurrent forms, while the paragraphs are still constructed for the most part in paratactic manner (sequences without connectives). Nevertheless the phrases, in their brevity, very well render the incisiveness of the thought and the ready resort to irony ("out of sheer lightheadedness you have made a slip of the pen") while still showing a willingness to place full confidence in his son, since the person on the spot can valuate better what is happening, and the note of paternal affection is warmhearted ("if you can make it in two days, take four"). One finds a fluent style and substantially secure mastery of the pen likewise in a letter of January 1, 1560, to Tomà Tito Vecellio (no. 145) in which Titian excuses himself for the delay with which his cousin will receive the promised Christmas gift (a *zitornato*, a Venetian sweet). The stylistic level however remains quite elementary, a good distance from the sparkling rhetoric of most of the correspondence, and still retains some dialect forms. As regards the letters of even later years, if Tietze-Conrat's (undocumented) suspicion that they were written by his son Orazio is true, this would rather effectively block acquiring any new evidence though not modify what we already know.

If from the style we move on to the contents, besides providing certain invaluable information the correspondence lets us glimpse close up the artist's vigorous personality, his fatherly affection, his dedication to his work, his proud awareness of his own capacities, and the obstinacy with which, despite the financial ease he enjoyed, he insisted on receiving whatever was due him. What is striking, on the other hand, is the total absence of the slightest allusion to the theoretical aspects of art or even remarks about the technique of painting. References to the artist's travails occur only to stress the long time involved and the hard work (and this, of course, with an eye to the compensation expected). His was the lonely and grand assuredness of the creator: what he produced was given life by his own life in art, and his hand alone, no one else's, could claim the right to retouch any of his pictures (add one brushstroke to any of his pictures). "Although he possessed not much of literature" (Ridolfi), Titian poured all his vast figurative culture into his paintings.

[1] For the importance of translation into the vernacular, see C. Dionisotti, "Tradizione classica e volgarizzamenti," in *Geografia e storia della letteratura italiana*, Turin, 1967, 103-44, and B. Guthmüller, *Studien zu antiken in der italienischen Renaissance*, Weinheim, 1986, and "La Sala dei Giganti nel Palazzo del Te a Mantova," *Quaderni Vaneti*, 8, 1988, 173-91.

[2] In that context, the severe judgment of the major expert on Italian Renaissance literature is entirely correct, that the relations between artists and their literary consultants "is not a terrain on which one can venture with second-hand information. The question would be unavoidable and quite a muddle if, instead of Titian, we had to discuss here Giorgione and the fables that modern scholars have philosophers and scientists, Venetian philosophers and men of letters, and even with the Italo-Greco academy of Aldo Manuzio. Fortunately fables of that sort do not thrive when it comes to Titian's work as a whole. There is the lightning rod of the so-called *Sacred and Profane Love* onto which the excess electrical charge of modern scholarship has spent itself with no great harm. One should recall though, for the humor of it, the marvelous hypothesis that in that work from around 1515 can be recognized the influence of both the *Polifilo* and Bembo, of the devil and the holy water. Such hypotheses are for the most part born outside Italy, out of a total ignorance of the civil and literary history of Italy" (C. Dionisotti, "Tiziano e la letteratura," in *Tiziano e il manierismo europeo*, ed. R. Pallucchini, Florence, 1978, 262). For Giorgione's culture, see G. Padoan, "Il mito di Giorgione intellettuale," in *Giorgione e l'umanesimo veneziano*, ed. R. Pallucchini, Florence, 1981, 425-55.

[3] See, more recently, A. Gentili, *Da Tiziano e Tiziano. Mito e allegoria nella cultura veneziana del Cinquecento*, Milan, 1980, especially part III.

[4] See P. Giovio, "Raphaelis Urbinatis vita" and "Fragmentorum trium dialogorum," in *Scritti d'arte del Cinquecento*, ed. P. Barocchi, Milan and Naples, 1971, I: 16-17, 21; cited by M. Gregori, "Tiziano e l'Aretino," in *Tiziano e il manierismo europeo*, op. cit., 295.

[5] "Those of great excellence in painting are Leonardo da Vinci, Mantegna, Michelangelo, Giorgio da Castel Franco" (B. Castiglione, *Il Libro del Cortegiano*, I, 37).

[6] See G. Campori, "Tiziano e gli Estensi," *Nuova Antologia*, November 1874, 586.

[7] C. Dionisotti, op. cit., 263. For a possible influence of Titian on the depiction of Olimpia in precisely that third edition (*Orlando Furioso*, XI, 33 ff.) see G. Padoan, "'Ut pictura poesis': le 'pitture' di Ariosto, le 'poesie' di Tiziano," in *Momenti del Rinascimento veneto*, Padua, 1978, 356-62. Titian's imprint is detectable also in the later works of Aretino (Ariosto).

[8] C. Dionisotti, op. cit., 268-69, where the fact is stressed that it is in this second edition that Brucioli introduces for the first time two artists as personages in the dialogues (not so in the 1529 edition).

[9] See C. Ginzburg, "Tiziano, Ovidio e i codici della figurazione erotica nel Cinquecento," in *Tiziano e Venezia*, Vicenza, 1980, 130.

[10] From that same year comes Dolce's *Primo libro di Sacripante* in whose preface, along with Michelangelo, he praises only Pordenone (see Dionisotti, op. cit., 270).

[11] See Padoan, "'Ut pictura poesis'," op. cit., and the bibliography there.

[12] For this treatise, see W. Melczer, "L'Aretino' del Dolce e l'estetica veneta nel secondo Cinquecento," in *Tiziano e Venezia*, op. cit., 237-42, and also F. Bernabei, "Tiziano e Ludovico Dolce," in *Tiziano e il manierismo europeo*, op. cit., 307-37, and the bibliography there.

[13] P. Aretino, *Lettere, Il primo e il secondo libro*, ed. F. Flora, Milan, 1960, 393 (this is the dedication to Valdura of the second of the *Ragionamenti*). For the other books of the *Lettere* one still has to use the Parisian edition of 1609, and see *Lettere di, a, su Pietro Areetino nel fondo Bongi dell'Archivio di Stato di Lucca*, ed. 1989. There is also the valuable collection, *Lettere sull'arte, di Pietro Aretino*, with commentary by F. Pettile, ed. E. Camesasca, Milan, 1957.

[14] *Lettere sull'arte*, op. cit., II, 369 (letter DC).

[15] See Padoan, "'Ut pictura poesis'," op. cit., 93.

[16] For which see especially F. Saxl, "Titian and Pietro Aretino," in *Lectures*, London, 1957, 163-73, and M. Gregori, op. cit., 271-306, and the bibliography there.

[17] G. Petrocchi, "Scrittori e poeti nella bottega di Tiziano," in *Tiziano e Venezia*, op. cit., 106, points out that in Aretino's letters "the alphabetical or chronological list of the persons addressed: coincides, in time and in the occasions, with the catalogue of portraits by Titian." The use of poems to accompany statues and paintings caught on very early, and was practised by Castiglione, Bembo, Della Casa, Molza, and others.

[18] *Lettere*, ed. F. Flora, op. cit., I, 163 (no. 133).

[19] M. Gregori, op. cit., 305.

[20] An exemplary document of this is Titian's letter of 1518 to Alfonso I: "The information included seemed to me so fine and ingenious that I do not think (anything better) can be found; and truly the more I thought about it the more I was confirmed in an opinion that the greatness of the art of the ancient painters was in good part, indeed altogether, aided by those great Princes who, with great intelligence, commissioned them" (Titian, *Le Lettere*, from the compendium of Titian documents by Celso Fabbro, presentation by Giuseppe Vecellio, introduction by Ugo Fasola, preface by Clemente Gandini, Belluno, 1977, no. 5).

[21] "His house in Venice has been frequented by whatever princes, men of letters, and fine gentlemen went to or were in Venice in his time, because he, in addition to the excellence of his art, was a gentleman of good breeding and highly refined habits and manners" (G. Vasari, *Le vite*, ed. P. Della Pergola, L. Grassi, G. Previtali, Milan, 1962-66, VII: 338-48).

[22] F. Priscianese, *Della lingua romana*, Venice, 1540 (letter to Ludovico Becci and Luigi Del Riccio in appendix to the text).

[23] See C. Pedretti, "Tiziano e il Serlio," in *Tiziano e Venezia*, op. cit, 243-48.

[24] See G. Padoan, "A casa di Tiziano, una sera d'agosto," in *Momenti del Rinascimento veneto*, op. cit, 371-93.

[25] See A. Chastel, "Titien et les humanistes," in *Tiziano e il manierismo europeo*, op. cit., 106: "Carlo Dionisotti has shown very well the importance of the vernacular translations in the middle of the century. They were produced even in Titian's own entourage (Dolce), and therefore it seems reasonable to suppose that the learned men who frequented his hospitable home sufficed to nourish his culture."

[26] And therefore of pagan subject matter, distinguishing them with perspicuity from subjects of historical and religious character; see Padoan, "'Ut pictura poesis'," op. cit.

[27] See C. Ginzburg, op. cit., 130, and A. Gentili, op. cit., 173-75.

[28] Who in fact in 1534 wrote a letter to the painter in which there are also Latin phrases in "chancellery" style, probably due to the secretary.

[29] Cited in note 20 above, to which can be added *Lettere di artisti italiani ad Antonio Perrenot di Granvelle*, ed. L. Ferrarino, Madrid, 1977, and for an overall view, *Raccolta di lettere sulla pittura, scultura e architettura*, published by C. R. Bottari and S. Ticozzi, Milan, 1822.

[30] There is an example in precisely the first of the documents (op. cit., no. 1), in the petition to the Council of Ten of May 1513 in which the petitioner declares himself, "Io Tician de serviete de Cadore," where the enigmatic "de serviete" – which is not a place name – has been variously interpreted and recently corrected to "dev. servitore," devoted servitor, though placing it before "de Cadore" makes that emendation quite doubtful. Most likely it is merely an error in transcription, probably from "de gr. viecel" – of Gregorio Vecellio – badly written and therefore misread by the copyist. For the form "Viecel" see doc. 146.

[31] See for example nos. 12 and 24 bis.

[32] V. Branca, "Tiziano scrittore inedito," *Corriere della Sera*, March 19, 1968.

[33] See C. Ridolfi, *Le Meraviglie dell'Arte, ovvero le Vite degli illustri pittori veneti e dello stato*, Padua, 1835, I: 272: "It was his familiars and intimate friends Partenio, above-named, and Giovanni Maria Venizzoti (sic)... Who

served him in writing letters to the princes."

[34] See E. Tietze-Conrat, "Titian as Letter Writer," *The Art Bulletin*, XXVI, 2, 1944, 117-23; published also in Italian translation as appendix to Tiziano, (Titian), *Le Lettere*, op. cit., 279-98.

[35] In that same year Aretino sent as gift to Fregoso "the book of sonnets and of lascivious figures" (after drawings by Giulio Romano); see Aretino, *Lettere*, ed. F. Flora, I: 9.

[36] Ed. cit., I: 8; see Gregori, op. cit., 285.

[37] See Tietze-Conrat, op. cit., 282.

[38] A. Crowe and G. B. Cavalcaselle, *Titian: His Life and Times*, London, 1877, II: 97. On the Aretinian theme of "gift," see G. Innamorati, *Tradizione ed invenzione in Pietro Aretino*, Messina and Florence, 1957, 239-41.

[39] See Tietze-Conrat, op. cit., 281.

[40] Ibid., 287.

Lionello Puppi

TITIAN IN THE CRITICAL JUDGMENT OF HIS TIME

Almost from the moment after his appearance on the Venetian art scene Titian enjoyed virtually unstinted critical acclaim, which would become ever more enthusiastic and irreversible as his style developed. For a time this appreciation remained, so to speak, implicit, taking the form of prestigious and renumerative acts of patronage, which, while predicated upon a recognition of the uniqueness of his art, did not take into account any fine distinctions.

When something more explicit was in fact said – as, for example, in the letters of Aretino – it was still a critical exercise taking place within a narrow circle of intellectuals who were as Petrocchi (1980, 108-09) remarked, members of the same learned group to which Titian himself belonged. Even so, the opinions expressed in that circle sometimes exploded into public debate.

Before that happened, however, Paolo Giovio, between 1523 and 1527, had offered vaguely approving statements ("multiplice delicatae artis virtutes"), though these remained unpublished until 1781 (see Barocchi 1977, 17, and 1978, II, 1099). It was Pietro Aretino who praised Titian for his capacity to emulate and indeed surpass Nature by pictorial means. On 8 October 1531, Aretino would write to Massimiliano Stampa: "Concerning the crimson of the garment [of a Saint John] and about the lynx I say nothing because, by comparison, true crimson and the real lynx appear painted and these are living." He isolated the artist's masterly use of color as a decisive factor in his art, writing to Titian himself, on 9 November 1537, that the angel in an Annunciation "has celestial majesty in his countenance, and his cheeks tremble in the gentle softness compounded of milk and blood that the harmonious blend of your coloring counterfeits true to life."

Giulio Camillo Delminio seems to have been thinking along that same line in his small treatise, *Dell'umana deificazione* (cod. 2684, c. 13, Biblioteca Comunale, Udine; see Bolzoni 1985, 10, no. 29), which may date from the early 1530s when he corresponded with Aretino on the subject of Titian (Olivato 1976, 243-44). There he compares the portrait Titian painted of him (now lost) with his own image reflected in a mirror. To explain the superiority of the effect he introduces, among other things, the rather contrived concept of *meraviglia* (mar-vel, amazement, the marvelous and astounding).

Here then are the points of departure for discussion and debate on Titian. Those topics, opportunely developed and framed within a specific set of circumstances, would form the basis for critical judgment of the artist throughout his career.

Serlio, who, in his *Regole generali di architettura* (1537), does not hesitate to assert that "in [Titian's] hands lives the idea of a new nature," while shortly thereafter, in 1537-38, Antonio Brucioli in his *Dialoghi*, in a discussion of "the rainbow" with Serlio and "Titian, that much talked-of painter," proclaims that the latter "with his art makes nature appear more beautiful and, in the proportions of members and coloring of figures, surpasses her as much as nature herself surpasses him in giving him [them] spirit and sense." A marginal note by Dionisotti (1978, 268) remarks that the aim of Brucioli's work was "to test out how subjects concerning natural philosophy could be treated in the vernacular," which assumes a stand taken in the controversy over the relationship between literary expression and figurative expression or, ultimately, between *pictura* and *poesis*. It means also an indirect (and certainly unconscious) reply to a surprising sally of Lodovico Dolce who, in dedicating to one painter one of his ["paraphrases of the sixth Satire of Juvenal"] *Paraphrasi della sesta satira di Giovenale* in 1538, asserts that "if the portraits produced by the perfection of art – which is so with you alone – approach the truth so closely that, with spirit added to them as well, Nature could reside there in vain, still life itself is lacking in them. But in the portrait I am speaking of [Juvenal's verse portrait] one sees only the similitude of that truth and of that life, though it be the same truth and life." Rightly enough, Padoan – who deserves credit for having made that passage known – observes that "Dolce's position is henceforth defensive" (1980, 95) and holds up against it Aretino's "effort" (declared in a letter to Valdura, unfortunately not dated) to "portray the natures of others with the liveliness with which the admirable Titian portrays one face and another." In point of fact, the equivalence Dolce himself admitted soon thereafter (1557) with reference to Ariosto's verses on the beauty of Alcina – "how much the good poets are themselves also painters" – constituted the acceptance among intellectuals of painting as art.

The question was – and had been (with Alberti and Leonardo) and would be – how to establish a properly unified and articulated conceptual definition of painting, and how to identify the system of fundamental and irreducible principles that could guarantee and heighten the predominance of that branch of art over the others, a predominance that could be recognized in its exceptional quality of *artificio*, of suppressing Nature herself by artifice in a dimension both "more beautiful" and "truer." In such an effort to lay down a valid theoretical position – one that must inevitably postulate a quest for and identification of a point of reference – the very existence and acceptance of Titian's art would lead to its examination by a complex, and problematical set of criteria. The resultant conflicts are plain to read in the great leap forward voiced in Aretino's notorious letter of November 1545 in which he harshly criticized Michelangelo's *Last Judgment* for an excess of "licence," subverting precisely those conditions that guarantee the superiority of painting. In that letter, furthermore, he held up Raphael as an exemplary model, though he did allude to or leave room for possible alternatives. Until then, Michelangelo's incomparable excellence had been accepted as beyond question. Thus Aretino's violent attack, accompanied and supported by unstinting re-evaluation of the "pleasing beauty" of Raphael, raised the question of Titian's place in this context: by this time his style and sensational success throughout Europe had made him the leading personality in the realm of painting.

A short time before Aretino's bold sally, Dolce, for better or worse, had recognized in Titian (though with some limitations) the "perfection of art." Then, in a letter to Paolo Crivelli on March 10 of the same year, 1545 (made known by Barocchi 1978, 1:717), Dolce too questioned Michelangelo's predominance, and, though still somewhat condescending toward the Venetians' way of painting ("who is there, in Venice, who knows how to paint?"), he elevated Titian to the veritable height of "another Michelangelo." Here it must be stressed that Aretino's cutting attack and his polemical reinstatement of Raphael to the artistic pantheon meant that greatness could no longer be proclaimed on the basis of an artist's

ability to render "life" more "true" than life. It was now clear that such pronouncements were inevitably meaningless and inexpressive or ambiguous and merely subjective. On the other hand, the "lawfulness" of the procedure and means an artist used would have to be the subject of discourse, which, in the ultimate decisive reckoning, would have to submit the artistic results to verification of just how fully it had obeyed the irreducible principles that sanctioned the superiority of painting and were the *conditio sine qua non* for attaining the utmost in quality.

As regards Titian, again the decisive move was left to Dolce as, step by step, he succeeded in unraveling, developing, and focusing his own reflections. Unfortunately we do not know the chronology of the fundamental pages he addressed to Gasparo Bellini (for which again we are indebted to Barocchi 1978, I:780-91) since they were published only in the collection of *Lettere di diversi eccellentissimi uomini* brought out by Giolito in 1559 but which, all evidence suggests, preceded the *Dialogo della Pittura* Dolce published in 1557. All those "letters" put forth the essential lines and pave the way for the later, more important work, serving as the basis for a sort of "opinion poll" among the intellectuals. In any case, what Dolce wrote to Bellini must have followed his letter of 1545 to Crivelli because it revises the earlier, very severe reservations about Venetian painting. Most likely he decided to sound out the general feeling before coming out publicly and programmatically because of certain events of considerable importance that had occurred in the meantime, most notably the publication of yet another *Dialogo*, this one by Paolo Pino, in 1548. Pino was himself a painter, though his known production is very limited and is only now beginning to be studied *ex professo*. The participants in his dialogue are painters, one Lauro, a Venetian, and Fabio, a Florentine, a factor in itself of no small note. The text is unnecessarily complicated (Schlosser), but at its core is a concern with painting's claim to the status of a liberal art and with reasserting – as a necessary precondition – that "painting is rightfully poetry." In laying out his justifying principles, Pino pursues that ultimate aim by substituting for Alberti's well-known triple division – applying and transposing the ancient rhetorical triad of "disposition, invention, and elocution" Daniello suggested for poetry (Barocchi 1978, II:716) – the relevant categories of drawing, invention, and color. Pino indulges at length in confused subdivisions of those three categories, but does not seem able to come out and say just who had succeeded in embodying that synthesis to the full. But what is most important is that he does raise the figure of Titian to heights that history confirms, admittedly alongside of Michelangelo but with an argument that is both impressive and well argued, unlike the merely exaggeratedly high-flown conclusion Dolce communicated to Crivelli: "If Titian and Michelangelo were a single body, or if Michelangelo's drawing were added to Titian's coloring, he could be said to be the god of painting, since in equal measure they both are truly gods."

In 1549 a capricious and highly gifted author of books on a myriad of subjects, Anton Francesco Doni, a Tuscan transplanted into the Veneto, turned over to Giolito's presses in Venice his opuscule on *Disegno*, this too in dialogue form. It cannot be ascertained if his purpose was to reply to the increasingly anti-Michelangelo tide, but clearly he adopted Pino's theoretical position, without ever expressly citing that little treatise. The discussion is carried on by the author himself and a certain sculptor called Silvio (Cosini?), with Baccio Bandinelli called in later as arbiter. Although two of the three are sculptors, the triple partition of the principal founders of painting is presented hierarchically with drawing – whose supreme practitioner is repeatedly and energetically held to be Michelangelo – at the summit, because only drawing can confer on representation that plastic consistency that renders "truth" more "true."

With a very different perspective and a much broader and more secure battery of arguments, Giorgio Vasari had his say on the subject in the next year with the first edition of his *Vite* published by Torrentino in Florence. To the previous approach he added the idea that *disegno* – drawing, design, and in the largest sense creative conception – is the indispensable guarantee of the translation of an "invention" into a perfect image, and is obviously personified, in its highest and indeed divine expression, by Michelangelo (with justification from Ariosto, *Orlando Furioso* 39:2). The primacy of *disegno* is

well-demonstrated within an historical treatment, which identifies and distributes regional schools (an idea already suggested by Pino) as the patrimony of the Tuscans whose painting, in this way and at the same time, is proclaimed superior and assumed as point of reference for all judgment. Although Vasari recognizes the Venetians' and Titian's, "pleasing and lively manner," he deplores the fact that this is due to a felicitous "coloring" rather than a true knowledge of drawing. Dolce's earlier correspondence with Bellini contained certain points that formed the basis for a response to such provocations as Vasari's and agreed with Aretino's extremely harsh stand of November 1545. These arguments centered on the principle that propriety – *convenevolezza* – must be respected to the full. The "fierceness and *terribilità* in drawing, in which Michelangelo... holds first place among all the painters who ever lived in many ages" does, however, constitute an exception to this principle. *Convenevolezza* is conducive to constructing forms "disdained by that Nature of which painting should be imitator and emulator," and leads also to being "excessively and beyond measure irregular and licentious (*licenzioso*), not to say indecent (*disonesto*)." (I would not ascribe this denunciation of excess to a Counter-Reformation attitude, as some propose.) Dolce, in agreement with Aretino, counters that "the things of Raphael of Urbino" exercise a "temperateness that leaves nothing to be desired," and are nourished by the study of the *bella maniera* of the Ancients and by the will to "contend with Nature" and to seek in "invention" the "truthfulness of the *istoria*" (the subject represented) by harmonizing "beautiful colors" with the "beauty and perfectness of the drawing."

It was precisely this conclusion that made it possible to accord Titian a firm theoretical place outside the narrow limitations of Vasari's judgment. In fact Pino already anticipated this: "They err, those who, wishing to praise the admirable Titian, would say that he colors well; and if he merited no other praise than this," he would be worth little (of little worth). The fact is, on the contrary, that "the utterly excellent Titian, as in every other aspect, is not merely divine in the manner the world holds him to be but utterly divine and without equals, as one in whom perfection of drawing goes along with liveliness of coloring in such a way that his things seem not painted but true."

Thus the universally acknowledged "divinity" of Michelangelo as painter was called into question (though conceded to him as sculptor, for having brought that art "to the excellence of the Ancients"). Whereas Titian was now hailed as *divino* and indeed *divinissimo* (but had not Aretino already declared that in his letter to Giovio of February 1545?), and this because his *maniera* was based on the well-balanced conjugation of the principles that preside over the supremacy of the painting itself. These are precisely those singled out in Pino's expedient rhetoric, and, in fact, accepted by Vasari as well.

When Dolce finally published his personal convictions in dialogue form in 1557, on the presses of Gabriel Giolito in Venice, he left no room for ambiguity. "The entirety of painting," he says, "is divided into three parts: invention, drawing, and coloring." And Titian's way of working, no less than Raphael's, admirably unites these in a figurative order. Not by chance, to hand down such a peremptory judgment, in his *Dialogo della Pittura* Dolce makes Aretino one of his two interlocutors and, in fact, his personal mouthpiece (which can be taken as evidence of their personal exchange and sharing of ideas). To oppose his spokesman, Dolce sets up a Tuscan grammarian, Giovan Francesco Fabrini, who, without dispelling *in toto* the diffidence of his time for the Venetian school, makes so much more explicit the polemic with Vasari. Vasari himself, however, does not seem to have taken up the gauntlet. Dolce made his challenge even more substantial in a subsequent work in 1562, another *Dialogo*, but in which "is discussed the way of improving one's memory" (and which therefore connects up with Camillo's writings on that subject). There the example of Titian's painting is recommended as supreme point of reference for devising the "image" of mythological or any other type of fable or profane or sacred narrative picture. Vasari's expanded edition of his *Vite*, brought out by Giunti in 1568, is irrevocably dogmatic in its assertion of the primacy of the Tuscan school whose triumphal apex is Michelangelo. The Tuscan historiographer repeats his judgment of 1550 concerning Titian and, not without a certain shrewd malice, puts it in the mouth of Michelangelo himself, who is made to say that it is "a pity that in

Venice people are not taught from the start to draw well and that those painters do not have a better method of study," and that "if that man [Titian] were properly backed by art and drawing, as he is by Nature, especially when it comes to copying from life, nothing more nor better could be done."

It was in this way, then, that the fundamental terms of the critical approach to Titian took root in his own time and would remain the point of reference for years to come. Only Lomazzo, writing less than fifteen years after Titian's death, in his *Idea del Tempio* of 1591, would seek to connect the artist's greatness to other categories, proposing that it be recognized in the "demonstration" of the "true practice and logical way of working." Obviously, however, the point of view established by Dolce would be accepted among Venetian intellectuals into and beyond the mid-seventeenth century, when Ridolfi and Boschini made an energetic effort to view the region's art in historical terms. Already with Federico Zuccari's *Lamento della pittura su l'onde venete*, composed during a Venetian sojourn and printed in Mantua in 1605, there was a real concern to consider the artist and his work among those who pursued with intrepid and unshakable determination art that was "true and perfect." And art would be in truth, said Lomazzo, "embellished there [in Venice] in perfect manner by that great Titian, most excellent painter... whose art, in beauty, surpassed almost Nature herself."

David Alan Brown

BELLINI AND TITIAN

Although Titian is one of the most famous and thoroughly studied of all Renaissance artists, his beginnings as a painter remain obscure. He was born at Pieve di Cadore in the Alps north of Venice, probably c. 1488-1490.[1] The scant information we have about his training comes primarily from two early sources, one of which is Vasari's *Vite* (1568). Titian, according to Vasari, was apprenticed to Giovanni Bellini (c. 1430-1516) whose "maniera secca, cruda e stentata" he soon abandoned in favor of Giorgione (c. 1477-1510), the leading master of the younger generation who ushered in the new age in Venetian painting.[2] The second literary source, Lodovico Dolce's *Aretino* of 1557, differs significantly from Vasari.[3] As a friend of Titian, Dolce's detailed account of his formation is no doubt more reliable in claiming that the artist, in Venice by the age of nine (Vasari says ten), was first placed in the shop of a mosaicist and mediocre painter named Sebastiano Zuccato, which he left to work with Gentile Bellini (1429-1507). Subsequently, the young apprentice, "spinto dalla Natura a maggiori grandezze e alla perfettione di quest'arte" (urged by nature to greater things and seeking perfection in art), approached Gentile's more gifted brother Giovanni. The latter's art did not fully satisfy him either, however, so he finally chose Giorgione as his teacher. In Vasari's outline of Titian's training, Giovanni Bellini merely stands for the old manner outmoded by progress; in the *Aretino* he occupies a pivotal place between Gentile Bellini and Giorgione. The distinction Dolce implies between the Bellini brothers is surely one that Titian himself grasped, and it forms the point of departure for evaluating his debt to Giovanni.[4]

As official painter in charge of the decorations in the Palazzo Ducale and as portraitist of the doges, Gentile enjoyed the highest patronage of the Venetian state. He was ennobled by the Emperor in 1469 (as Titian would be later), and he was sent by the Republic to Constantinople in 1479 to work for the Turkish sultan. At home Gentile served the *Serenissima* by meticulously recording his native city, its civic rituals and leading citizens. With the advent of contextual art history, Gentile's work, consisting mainly of large-scale canvases or *teleri* documenting contemporary or historical scenes, is better understood today than in the past,[5] but it

remains artistically poor, as the young Titian quickly discovered.[6] Giovanni also worked extensively for the state, but the narratives he painted were done partly in Gentile's absence and seemingly without much enthusiasm.[7] The two brothers collaborated on one such work, made for a confraternity, the Scuola di San Marco, and the difference between their respective shares is revealing. Unable to finish the *Preaching of Saint Mark in Alexandria* (Brera, Milan) before his death, Gentile induced Giovanni to complete it by bequeathing him an album of their father's drawings.[8] To the artless profusion of detail in Gentile's panoramic crowd scene Giovanni brought a new coherence and luminosity, and a greater variety of pose, gesture and expression.[9] The vital, illusionistic character of Giovanni's changes and additions (Fig. 1) emerges clearly from the recent restoration of the canvas.[10] His updated narrative mode is the ancestor of the *Presentation of the Virgin* (Fig. 2), which Titian painted some thirty years later for the Scuola della Carità (Accademia, Venice).

With his dutiful sibling able to satisfy the demands of state and *scuola*, Giovanni's talents were freed to develop what Venice still lacked in the Quattrocento, a genuinely modern style of painting.[11] In a series of pictorial experiments lasting more than half a century, he absorbed and adapted the innovations of Donatello, Mantegna, Piero della Francesca, and Antonello da Messina. Bellini's achievement shines forth in the famous *Portrait of Doge Leonardo Loredan* (Fig. 3), in the National Gallery, London, painted soon after the sitter's accession in 1501. By contrast to Gentile's static effigies of Loredan's predecessors, seen in profile, Giovanni's portrayal expresses the doge's authority visually in terms of composition, light, and color.[12] If he shared the prevailing conservative taste, Loredan may not have appreciated the difference between Bellini's transcendant likeness and the traditional profile portraits that otherwise defined his image.[13] But connoisseurs, like Sanudo, and practically all of the younger artists, had come to esteem Giovanni over Gentile, as the greatest Venetian painter. Albrecht Dürer, visiting the city in 1505-06, reported that Giovanni, though very old, was "still the best in painting."[14] And Pietro Bembo, a friend of both Bellini and Titian, specified in a letter of 1505 to Isabella d'Este

that it was Giovanni's imaginative freedom – his wish to "vagare a sua voglia nelle pitture" (wander at his will in paintings) – that set him apart from his contemporaries.[15] In this sense of providing inspiration the break in Titian's education came not between Giovanni Bellini and Giorgione but between the two Bellinis: Giovanni was a nonconformist in regard to the tradition in which his brother acquiesced.

While working as Bellini's assistant soon after the turn of the century, Titian may well have witnessed the creation of the London painting, which raised the aesthetically impoverished category of doge portraiture to the highest level of art.[16] Long after his stylistic influence was superseded by that of Giorgione, Giovanni continued to be important for Titian as an examplar of the creative spirit. But while Bellini's broader relevance for Titian seems clear, it is difficult to demonstrate in terms of specific works. Vasari states that Titian abandoned his master's style only after "he had long practiced it," implying the existence of numerous Bellinesque paintings by the young artist, none of which can be identified today. Indeed, so few of Titian's earliest pictures survive that scholarly discussions of his formation tend to become debates over the authorship of works disputed between him and Giorgione. Despite the efforts of generations of scholars, this debate, which has its roots in Titian's own lifetime, still continues.[17] The degree of

confusion may be seen from the fact that while the *Fête Champêtre* in the Louvre, the *Christ and the Adulteress* in Glasgow, the *Madonna with Saints* in the Prado, and the *Female Bust* in the Norton Simon Museum are all attributed to Titian by Terisio Pignatti in his monograph on Giorgione, the same works are given to Giorgione, entirely or in part, by Wethey.[18] Aside from these contested paintings, the number of Titian's early works must be further reduced by eliminating those by artists other than Giorgione.[19] With so little left to represent Titian's juvenilia, it is not surprising that proposals for his youthful activity differ greatly.[20] The works to be discussed here have the merit of confirming Dolce's account of the artist's training, which may have been suggested by Titian himself. In particular, they reveal the nature and extent of the role Bellini took in forming Titian's art.

1. *Giovanni Bellini, Detail of the "Preaching of Saint Mark in Alexandria," Pinacoteca di Brera, Milan.*
2. *Titian, Detail of the "Presentation of the Virgin," Gallerie dell'Accademia, Venice.*

Titian's first generally accepted extant work is the votive picture of *Jacopo Pesaro Presented to Saint Peter by Pope Alexander VI* (cat. no. 4) from Antwerp. The disputed dating of the canvas depends partly upon the event it depicts. Having been appointed admiral of the papal fleet in a war against the Turks, Pesaro commissioned Titian's painting to commemorate his victory at the Battle of Santa Maura in August 1502. While Crowe and Cavalcaselle linked the painting directly with the battle, most subsequent writers have placed it later.[21] The uncertainty about the date arises from the fact that the picture is uneven. While some parts are awkward (the perspective of the pavement), others, seemingly more accomplished – the fictive classical relief, the portraits, the lagoon, the right half – have given rise to the notion that the painting was begun at one time and finished later.[22] Although the proposal that the execution falls into two phases was recently elaborated on the basis of technical evidence, Giles Robertson, following Charles Hope, convincingly argued that it dates from c. 1506, soon after the patron's return to Venice after a three-year absence.[23]

The Antwerp picture, scholars agree, is Titian's most Bellinesque work. Johannes Wilde noted that the color, with red and green repeated throughout the composition, plays a unifying role, as in Bellini's late altarpieces.[24] And Pignatti has aptly compared the painting to Bellini's *Madonna and Child Enthroned with Saints Peter and Paul and a Donor* (Fig. 4), signed and dated 1505, now in Birmingham.[25] This small altarpiece, its kneeling donor and sponsor similar to their counterparts in the Antwerp canvas, epitomizes the style Titian encountered while working as Bellini's assistant, in which forms are subtly evoked, rather than described, by the master's brush. Titian's painting recalls Bellini not only in style but also in details, like the much-discussed relief below the saint's throne, which remains, despite its meaningful relation to the main subject, a prop of the kind Giovanni occasionally introduced into sacred pictures (*Blood of the Redeemer*, London). But it is the figure of Saint Peter (Fig. 5) that is closest to Bellini, so close, in fact, that it has actually been attributed to the older master.[26] The saint's pose, with one leg raised, and his voluminous draperies, cascading over the throne, recall the treatment

of the Virgin in the San Zaccaria altarpiece of 1505, just as his flesh tones are painted in Bellini's manner, thinly on the gesso ground, as revealed by x-rays.[27] In one respect, however, Titian deviates from Bellini's contemporary practice: the lighting of the saint's figure, with his head cast in shadow, recalls the dim illumination of the left compartment, also portraying Peter, in the Frari triptych of 1488. Reflecting Bellinesque models from different periods, the Antwerp picture could not have been executed by Bellini himself.

However indebted to Bellini for its style, the Antwerp painting, in composition and technique, already reveals the young Titian's innate vitality. Earlier Venetian votive pictures had typically balanced the protagonists around the Madonna and Child, as in Bellini's Birmingham altarpiece or his *Pala Barbarigo* of 1488.[28] The asymmetrical grouping in the *Votive Portrait of Doge Giovanni Mocenigo* (Fig. 6) in the National Gallery, London, is closer to Titian, but here, too, the individual figures are

3. Giovanni Bellini, "Portrait of Doge Leonardo Loredan," National Gallery, London.

detached from each other.[29] Rejecting this static formula, Titian's *ex voto* enacts an imagined episode before the battle, in which Saint Peter blesses the banner representing Pesaro's enterprise on behalf of the Church. With the fleet setting sail in the background, the outcome is still uncertain, lending a dramatic note to the scene.[30] The interaction and incipient movement of the figures anticipate the more fluent, unified solutions Titian evolved for the *Madonna and Child with Saints Peter and Paul and a Donor* (cat. no. 4), belonging to the Fondazione Magnani Rocca, and for the Pesaro altarpiece of 1519-26, in the Frari, in which the donor in the Antwerp picture reappears.[31] The use of *chiaroscuro* for Saint Peter marks the beginning of the tonal painting we find more fully developed in Titian's Saint Mark altarpiece of about 1512 in Santa Maria della Salute. The artist's first work is just as innovative in technique: the pope's green and gold brocade cope (Fig. 7) is rendered

with a painterly freedom that was foreign to Bellini. Soon after completing the Antwerp picture, Titian came under Giorgione's spell. The younger artist encountered Giorgione, according to Vasari, in 1507, and he is known to have assisted his mentor in finishing the fresco decoration of the Fondaco dei Tedeschi in 1508. What appears to be Titian's next painting, the *Circumcision* (Fig. 8) in the Yale University Art Gallery, accordingly unites influences from both Bellini and Giorgione, suggesting that Titian, at this stage in his development, did not regard them as incompatible. The ruinous condition of the little panel has caused more than one writer to hesitate before attributing it to Titian, yet the damage has not effaced the grandeur of its design, nor its brilliance of color.[32] And details that are fairly well preserved, like the Virgin's profile and the drapery of the youthful witness holding the jar, are worthy of Titian's brush. He borrowed the composition from a Bellini version of the

4. Giovanni Bellini, "Madonna and Child Enthroned with Saints Peter and Paul and a Donor,"
City Museums and Art Gallery, Birmingham.
Published by permission of Birmingham Museums and Art Gallery.
5. Detail of "Jacopo Pesaro Presented to Saint Peter by Pope Alexander VI,"
attributed to Giovanni Bellini. Koninklijk Museum voor Schone Kunsten, Antwerp.

same subject, now lost but known through innumerable copies and variants, the best of which (Fig. 9) is in the National Gallery, London.[33] Titian has placed his half-length figures, their attitudes practically unchanged from Bellini, in a spacious architectural setting that opens onto a cloud-filled sky. He has also provided a newly dramatic focus for the group in the frightened Christ Child. But if Titian followed a personal impulse in rearranging Bellini's figures to heighten the narrative, his high-keyed colors derive from Giorgione, whose "fiery" hues on the façade of the Fondaco dei Tedeschi Zanetti admired centuries after their creation.[34]

The Antwerp votive picture and the *Circumcision* were painted when Titian had just emerged from Giovanni Bellini's shop. Both works, in effect, critique Bellini's art, which the younger artist, according to the early sources, did not find entirely to his liking. And they look forward, where Titian deviated from his teacher, to his own later

6. Anonymous Fifteenth-Century Venetian, "Doge Giovanni Mocenigo Presented to the Virgin and Child," National Gallery, London.
7. Titian, Detail of "Jacopo Pesaro Presented to Saint Peter by Pope Alexander VI," Koninklijk Museum voor Schone Kunsten, Antwerp.

achievement. The *Circumcision*, moreover, betrays Giorgione's influence, which becomes more striking in the next work belonging to this critical juncture in Titian's career, the so-called *Gypsy Madonna* (Fig. 10) in the Kunsthistorisches Museen, Vienna. Painted on a traditional wood support, the *Madonna* again acknowledges Bellini as the appropriate model for half-length compositions of religious subjects. The x-radiograph of the panel, published by Wilde, reveals that Titian's original design was even closer to Bellini, but it is unclear whether the

Vienna painting similarly features a soldier beneath a tree.

The *Gypsy Madonna* culminates the initial phase of Titian's development, in which Bellini's influence coexisted with that of Giorgione. It also reveals the remarkable individuality stressed by Titian's early biographers. From this picture we can understand why Titian's frescoes at the Fondaco dei Tedeschi were admired by some more highly than Giorgione's. Like the Vienna panel, they incorporate Giorgione's innovations

prototype usually cited in this connection, the *Madonna and Child* (Fig. 11) of 1509, in the Detroit Institute of Arts, is a source for, or a reflection of, the Vienna picture, which is datable to the same time.[35] Titian's figures form an imposing pyramidal group, centering on the motif he favored of a hand emerging from a swirl of drapery. The artist's brilliant hues, particularly the light blue of the Virgin's robe, are indebted to Giorgione, and so is the secular character of the *Gypsy Madonna*, whose title recalls Marcantonio Michiel's reading of Giorgione's *Tempesta* as a gypsy ("cingana") and a soldier in a stormy landscape.[36] The idyllic Giorgionesque landscape in the

and at the same time recall Bellini, still the foremost painter in Venice, and display Titian's own sense of movement and drama. The next stage in Titian's evolution was prompted by Giorgione's untimely death in the late summer of 1510. As Sydney Freedberg has noted, this is the period to which Titian's most Giorgionesque works belong.[37] But if Titian did not appropriate Giorgione's style until after its creator died, he grew impatient for the coveted position Bellini held as state painter. Titian seems to have engaged in a rivalry with Bellini, all the while continuing to recall prototypes, like the San Zaccaria altarpiece, for half-length Madonnas and Holy

8. Titian, "Circumcision of the Christ Child,"
James Jackson Jarves Collection, Yale University Art Gallery, New Haven, Connecticut.

Families he painted in the teens.[38] The conflict between the two artists was generational, not personal.[39] For this reason, when Titian had an opportunity to repaint the *Feast of the Gods* (cat. no. 19), which Bellini had completed in 1514, he limited himself, as we now know from the recent restoration, to cancelling the work of a third hand, leaving what was visible of Bellini's contribution virtually intact, as if out of respect for his old teacher.[40] After Bellini's death in 1516 Titian succeeded him as painter to the Republic. He was in many respects Bellini's heir, and he fulfilled his master's historic mission of bringing Venetian painting into the mainstream of Italian art.

9. Giovanni Bellini Workshop, "Circumcision of the Christ Child,"
National Gallery, London.

10. *Titian, "Madonna and Child (Gypsy Madonna),"*
Kunsthistorisches Museum, Vienna.

*11. Giovanni Bellini and Workshop, "Madonna and Child,"
Detroit Institute of Arts, Detroit.*

[1] About the vexed question of Titian's birthdate see Creighton Gilbert, "Some Findings on Early Works of Titian," in *The Art Bulletin*, vol. LXII, no. 1, March 1980, 70-71. Except notably for Charles Hope (*Titian*, London, 1980, 11-12), most scholars, believing Titian exaggerated his longevity, now opt for the dates given here over the traditional one of about 1480.

[2] Giorgio Vasari, *Vite de' più eccellenti pittori scultori ed architettori*, ed. G. Milanesi, 9 vols., Florence, 1879-1885, vol. VII, 1881, 426-28.

[3] Lodovico Dolce, *Dialogo della pittura... intitolato l'Aretino*, Venice, 1557. See the critical edition by Mark W. Roskill entitled *Dolce's "Aretino" and Venetian Art Theory of the Cinquecento*, New York, 1968, 184-87, 322-24.

[4] Although J.A. Crowe and G.B. Cavalcaselle in their classic biography (*Titian: His Life and Times*, 2 vols., London, 1877, vol. I, 45-46) doubted Dolce's veracity, his paradigm still informs modern analyses of Titian's early career (David Rosand, *Titian*, New York, 1978, 14-15).

[5] See: Jürg Meyer zur Capellen, *Gentile Bellini*, Stuttgart, 1985; and Patricia Fortini Brown, "Painting and History in Renaissance Venice," in *Art History*, vol. VII, no. 3, September 1984, 263-94; and by the same author, *Venetian Narrative Painting in the Age of Carpaccio*, New Haven and London, 1988.

[6] According to Dolce (*Aretino*, ed. Roskill, 1968, 186-87), Titian "non poteva sofferir di seguitar quella via secca e stentata di Gentile," who predicted that his pupil had no future in art! Dolce explicitly affirms that it was Titian's dissatisfaction with Gentile's art which led him to Giovanni.

[7] Rona Goffen, *Giovanni Bellini*, New Haven and London, 1989, 97-98. A document of September 28, 1507 (cited on 269), enjoins Bellini, preoccupied with other commissions, to be more prompt in the service of the Republic.

[8] About this huge canvas and the decorative cycle to which it belonged see most recently: Peter Humfrey, "The Bellinesque Life of St. Mark cycle for the Scuola Grande di San Marco in Venice in its original arrangement," in *Zeitschrift für Kunstgeschichte*, vol. XLVIII, 1985, 225-42; Brown, *Narrative*, 1988, 203, 206-09, 291-95; and Goffen, *Bellini*, 1989, 271-73.

[9] For attempts to distinguish Giovanni's contribution see: Edoardo Arslan, "Studi Belliniani," in *Bollettino d'Arte*, vol. XLVII, no. 1, January-March 1962, 54-55 (40-58), and figs. 5-10; John Pope-Hennessy, *The Portrait in the Renaissance*, New York, 1966, 50-51; and Giles Robertson, *Giovanni Bellini*, Oxford, 1968, 82-83, 124-25; as well as Brown 1988, and Goffen 1989, cited in the previous note.

[10] About the cleaning by Pinin Brambilla Barcilon see Valentina Maderna, "Restauri. La Predica di S. Marco ad Alessandria di Gentile e Giovanni Bellini," in *Brera. Notizie della Pinacoteca*, no. 17, 1988, 1-2.

[11] David Rosand has shown how the system of state patronage constrained artistic creativity ("The Conditions of Painting in Renaissance Venice," in *Painting in Cinquecento Venice: Titian, Veronese, Tintoretto*, New Haven and London, 1982, 4-7).

[12] Goffen, *Bellini*, 1989, 205, 207-12. About doge portraiture see Meyer zur Capellen, "Zum venezianischen Dgenbildnis in der zweiten HClfte des Quattrocento," in *Konsthistorisk Tidskrift*, vol. XLII, 1981, 70-86; and Giandomenico Romanelli, "Ritrattistica dogale: ombre, immagini e volti," in *I Dogi*, ed. Gino Benzoni, Milan, 1982, 125-62.

[13] For a catalogue of portraits of Loredan see Meyer zur Capellen, *Bellini*, 1985, 187-90.

[14] Quoted in Goffen, *Bellini*, 1989, 268.

[15] Quoted in Goffen, *Bellini*, 1989, 268.

[16] Roskill (*Aretino*, 1968, 323) and Rosand (*Titian*, 1978, 15) both date Titian's successive apprenticeships to the Bellini to the period c. 1502-1505.

[17] Vasari (*Vite*, ed. Milanesi, 1881, 428) claimed that if the young Titian had not signed a portrait of a member of the Barbarigo family, it would be taken as Giorgione's. The portrait Vasari describes has been tentatively identified with the *Young Man* in Berlin-Dahlem by Rosand (*Titian*, 1978, 66), who gives it to Titian c. 1506; and with the *Portrait of a Venetian Gentleman* in the National Gallery, Washington, which has been attributed to both Giorgione and Titian

working in collaboration (Fern Rusk Shapley, *Catalogue of the Italian Paintings*, National Gallery of Art, Washington, 1979, vol. I, 213-16), but which may be by Cariani, as the aggressive psychology of the sitter suggests. The *Christ Carrying the Cross* in San Rocco Vasari first assigned to Giorgione and then (apparently correcting himself) to Titian (*Vite*, ed. Milanesi, 1881, 437). Though surely by the latter artist, Rosand's dating, c. 1505-06 (*Titian*, 1978, 64) seems too early. Another contested work is the so-called *Allendale Nativity* in Washington. Although most writers opt for Giorgione (Shapley, *Italian Paintings*, 1979, vol. I, 208-11, and vol. II, pl. 144), S.J. Freedberg (*Painting in Italy 1500 to 1600*, Harmondsworth, 1971, 87) may well be correct in giving the painting to the young Titian. The connection often cited with Giovanni Bellini (commissioned to paint a *Presepio* for Isabella d'Este in 1504) obviously bears on the theme of the present essay, but the attribution problem is too complex to be discussed here. The confusion between Giorgione and Titian is increased by the fact that the younger master is known to have finished certain of Giorgione's works: his share in the *Sleeping Venus* in Dresden is dated to 1507 by Jaynie Anderson ("Giorgione, Titian, and the Sleeping Venus," in *Tiziano e Venezia* [Convegno Internazionale di studi, Venice, 1976] Vicenza, 1980, 337-42).

[18] Terisio Pignatti, *Giorgione*, London, 1971, 121, 122-23, 126-27, and 132-33; and Harold Wethey, *The Paintings of Titian*, 3 vols., London, 1969-1975, vol. I, 1969, 169-70, 174; vol. II, 1971, 159-60; and vol. III, 1975, 167-69.

[19] Mauro Lucco has begun to perform this task by (correctly) reassigning the *Dead Christ* in the Scuola di San Rocco from Titian to the aged Bellini ("Venezia fra Quattro e Cinquecento," in *Storia dell'arte italiana*, part II, vol. I, Turin, 1983, 453 [447-77]) and the *Pastoral Idyll*, formerly at Compton Wynyates, to Titian's fellow pupil of Bellini, Sebastiano del Piombo (*L'opera completa di Sebastiano del Piombo*, Milan, 1980, 91 note 5). A major obstacle to understanding the early Titian lies in the persistent misattribution to him of works which are, in my opinion, by his "shadow," Domenico Mancini. I refer to the already-cited Glasgow *Adulteress*, for which a tentative attribution to Mancini was recently reconsidered (Francis Richardson in *The Genius of Venice 1500-1600*, ed. Jane Martineau and Charles Hope, New York, 1984, cat. no. 35, 169-70), and to other paintings (wrongly) ascribed to Titian, like the *Madonna and Child* in the Metropolitan Museum (Federico Zeri, *Italian Paintings. A Catalogue of the Collection*, New York, 1973, 79-81 [as Titian]) and the *Rest on the Flight into Egypt* in the Hermitage, Leningrad (Rodolfo Pallucchini, *Tiziano*, Florence, 1969, vol. I, 9-10, 234, and vol. II, figs. 22-24 [as Titian]). There is a suggestive resemblance of type and drapery between the Madonna and Child in the Hermitage picture and their counterparts in Mancini's signed and dated (1511) Lendinara altarpiece (Bernard Berenson, *Italian Pictures of the Renaissance. Venetian School*, 2 vols., London, 1957, vol. I, fig. 691). The hypothesis that the angel in this recently-cleaned altarpiece is by Dosso Dossi is untenable (Filippo Trevisani in *Restauri nel Polesine. Dipinti: documentazione e conservazione*, Milan, 1984, 133-66).

[20] Recent reconstructions of Titian's early corpus, differing from each other and from the one proposed here, include the following: Antonio Morassi, "Esordi di Tiziano," in *Arte Veneta*, vol. 8, 1954, 178-98; Freedberg, *Painting in Italy*, 1971, 86-90; Terisio Pignatti, "Giorgione e Tiziano," in *Tiziano e il Manierismo Europeo*, ed. Rodolfo Pallucchini, Florence, 1978, 29-41; Alessandro Ballarin, "Tiziano prima del Fondaco dei Tedeschi," in *Tiziano e Venezia* (Convegno Internazionale di Studi, Venice, 1976), Vicenza, 1980, 493-99, esp. 499 note 7; Hope, *Titian*, 1980, 18-20; and Hillard Goldfarb, "An early masterpiece by Titian rediscovered, and its stylistic implications," in *The Burlington Magazine*, vol. CXXVI, no. 976, July 1984, 419-23.

[21] J.A. Crowe and G.B. Cavalcaselle, *Titian: His Life and Times*, 2 vols., London, 1877, vol. I, 73-79.

[22] Wethey (*Titian*, vol. I, 1969, 152-153) dates the painting c. 1512. William Suida claimed that the portraits and the seascape were not finished until about

1520 (*Tiziano*, Rome, n.d. [1933], 23-24). For similar views see, among others: Hans Tietze, *Titian. The Paintings and Drawings*, London, 1950, 4-5; John Pope-Hennessy, *The Portrait in the Renaissance*, New York, 1966, 277-78; and Pallucchini, *Tiziano*, 1969, 11.

[23] Jürg Meyer zur Capellen, "Beobachtungen zu Jacopo Pesaros Exvoto in Antwerpen," in *Pantheon*, vol. XXXVIII, no. 2, April-June 1980, 144-52. For the contrary view that the style is all of a piece see Giles Robertson in *The Genius of Venice 1500-1600*, ed. Jane Martineau and Charles Hope, New York, 1984, cat. no. 113, 219; and Hope (*Titian*, 1980, 26). Johannes Wilde (*Venetian Art from Bellini to Titian*, Oxford, 1974, 108-109-133), while concurring that this is probably Titian's earliest surviving work, favored a dating of c. 1504.

[24] Wilde, *Venetian Art*, 1974, 109.

[25] Terisio Pignatti, *L'opera completa di Giovanni Bellini*, Milan, 1969, 107 note 184. About Bellini's altarpiece see Peter Cannon-Brooks, *The Cornbury Park Bellini. A contribution towards the study of the late paintings of Giovanni Bellini*, Birmingham, 1977.

[26] Louis Hourticq's theory that Titian completed a painting begun by Bellini by adding the group on the right (*La Jeunesse de Titien*, Paris, 1919, 79-81, 140) was championed by Staale Sinding-Larsen ("Titian's Madonna di Ca' Pesaro and its historical significance," in *Acta archaeologiam et artium historiam pertinentia: Institutum Romanum Norvegiae*, vol. I, 1962, 151 and Appendix I, 159-61), who claimed that the picture was commissioned from Bellini, planned and begun in his shop, and then finished by Titian, possibly after Bellini's death in 1516.

[27] Meyer zur Capellen in *Pantheon*, 1980, figs. 2 and 3.

[28] Goffen, *Bellini*, 1989, 99-107 and fig. 68. The formula becomes even more rigid in the votive painting, signed by Bellini and dated 1510, in the Walters Art Gallery, Baltimore (Goffen, *Bellini*, 1989, 99 and fig. 67).

[29] Lionello Puppi ("La pala votiva Mocenigo della National Gallery di Londra, in *Antichità viva*, vol. VIII, no. 3, 1969, 3-18), after reviewing the various attributions proposed for this intriguing work, favors Gronau's hypothesis of a collaboration between Gentile and Giovanni Bellini. See also Meyer zur Capellen, *Gentile*, 1985, 154-55.

[30] Titian's picture, celebrating Pesaro's victory, was painted against an historical background of disastrous Venetian naval defeats (Frederic Lane, *Venice. A Maritime Republic*, Baltimore, 1973, 241-48).

[31] See: Sinding-Larsen in *Acta archaeolgium*, 1962, 149-52; as well as Pallucchini, *Tiziano*, 1969, 11; and Hope, *Titian*, 1980, 34. About the Magnani painting see Vittorio Sgarbi, *Fondazione Magnani-Rocca. Capolavori della pittura antica*, Milan, 1984, 101-07; and for the Pesaro Madonna, Goffen, *Piety and Patronage in Renaissance Venice. Bellini, Titian, and the Franciscans*, New Haven and London, 1986, 107-37 and plate 3.

[32] The most thorough study of the picture is Charles Seymour, Jr., "A Note on Early Titian: The *Circumcision* Panel at Yale," in *Studies in Late Medieval and Renaissance Painting in Honor of Millard Meiss*, ed. Irving Lavin and John Plummer, New York, 1977, vol. I, 392-98, and vol. II, 130-35, figs. 1-17. Among recent authors it is accepted as Titian's by Francesco Valcanover, *L'opera completa di Tiziano*, Milan, 1969, 92, note 21; Pignatti, *Giorgione*, 1971, cat. no. A33, 129; Pallucchini, *Tiziano*, 1969, 10-11, 232; Freedberg, *Painting*, 1971, 477-57 note 40; and Ballarin in *Tiziano e Venezia*, 1980, 495, note 5, and p. 499, note 7. Dissenting voices include Wethey (*Titian*, vol. I, 1969, cat. no. x-8, p. 171) and Hope (*Titian*, 1980, 40 note 19).

[33] About the Bellini prototype see Goffen, *Bellini*, 1989, 178 and 314-15, notes 77 and 79. It does not seem to have been noticed that the two figures in Titian's painting not accounted for by the first source, namely, the group of the bearded old man (framed in the window), holding the shrinking Child, have a second Bellini model, a shop work representing the analogous theme of the Presentation, (Gertrude Borghero, *Thyssen-Bornemisza Collection. Catalogue Raisonné of the Exhibited Works of Art*, Milan, 1986, cat. no. 26, p. 31).

[34] Anton Maria Zanetti's praise for Giorgione's "tinta sanguina e fiammegian-te" (*Varie pitture a fresco del principali maestri Veneziani*, Venice, 1760, p. IV) echoes Vasari's observation that the mural was "colorito vivacissimamente." Among extant works by Giorgione, the *Three Philosophers* in Vienna is nearest to the *Circumcision* in color.

[35] Wilde's original publication of 1932 is conveniently summarized in his *Venetian Art*, 1974, 113-15 and figs. 95-97. About the Detroit picture see Goffen, *Bellini*, 1989, 63-66. There are several indications that Bellini's painting may follow Titian's and not vice versa: the oblong format is unprecedented in Bellini's Madonnas; and the standing Child is awkward, as is the relation of the figures to their setting, whereas the same elements are improved in the Brera *Madonna and Child* of 1510, in which the cloth of honor reverts to Bellini's habitual symmetry. Although Wethey (*Titian*, vol. I, 1969, cat. no. 47, 98), Rosand (*Titian*, 1978, 70), and Hope (*Titian*, 1980, 22-23) all date Titian's painting c. 1510, it might be earlier by a year or so, as is suggested by the rather primitive landscape and the Bellinesque composition.

[36] Wendy Stedman Sheard, "Giorgione's *Tempesta*: External vs. Internal Texts, in *Italian Culture*, vol. IV, 1983, 145-57.

[37] Freedberg, *Painting*, 1971, 88-90. See also John Shearman, who in attributing the Hampton Court *Shepherd* to Titian, observed that the artist's most Giorgionesque works are "not necessarily the earliest" (*The Early Italian Pictures in the Collection of Her Majesty the Queen*, Cambridge, 1983, cat. no. 271, 253-56 and plate 230).

[38] Compare the *Madonna of the Cherries* in Vienna and the *Sacra Conversazione* in Dresden, both of which contain reminiscences of the tranquil saints in Bellini's *pala*.

[39] Hope downplays any *concorrenza* with Bellini, preferring to identify Carpaccio as Titian's rival ("Titian's Role as Official Painter to the Venetian Republic" in *Tiziano e Venezia* [Convegno Internazionale di Studi, Venice, 1976], Vicenza, 1980, 301-05; and in *Titian*, 1980, 37-39). Yet if Bellini's *senseria* or sinecure at the Fondaco de' Tedeschi was also sought by Carpaccio, who failed to obtain it, Titian's offer to paint in the Sala del Maggior Consiglio in the Ducal Palace seems a direct challenge to Bellini's authority. Jürgen Rapp ("Das Tizian-PortrCt in Kopenhagen: ein Bildnis des Giovanni Bellini," in *Zeitschrift für Kunstgeschichte*, vol. 50, no. 3, 1978, 359-74) argues that Titian's *Portrait of a Man* of c. 1512-14, in Copenhagen, represents Bellini, but the sitter can hardly be an octogenarian.

[40] See the author's entry on the painting in this catalogue (cat. no. 19). The technical evidence is presented in David Bull, "*The Feast of the Gods*: Conservation Treatment and Interpretation," and Joyce Plesters, "*The Feast of the Gods*: Investigation of Material and Techniques" in *Studies in the History of Art*, National Gallery of Art, Washington, vol. 40, 1989, 21-50, 53-103.

Terisio Pignatti
GIORGIONE AND TITIAN

Titian succeeded in becoming part of the Venetian art world before his twentieth birthday, and for a short time he and Giorgione overlapped. The older painter died in 1510, of the plague, while he was still in his early thirties, a circumstance that has given rise to a web of still unresolved scholarly problems.

The two painters first met in the course of the decoration of the recently rebuilt German merchants' quarters, the Fondaco dei Tedeschi. In 1508 Giorgione completed the frescoes on the façade of the building facing the Grand Canal, but no more than a few fragments have survived. The young Titian also executed frescoes for the Fondaco, on the side along the street, probably after Giorgione's time but certainly not simultaneously or in collaboration. Of these, very little remains.[1]

Unfortunately, the few remnants and some engravings Zanetti produced in 1760 are not enough to allow us to discuss Giorgione's frescoes for the Fondaco with any authority. However, they probably were figurative, as Giorgione had executed other outdoor frescoes of this type in Venice. According to early sources, other such figurative frescoes decorated the façades of Giorgione's own house at San Silvestro, the Rettani house at San Canziano, the Grimani houses at the Servi and at San Marcuola, Ca' Soranzo at San Polo, Ca' Gritti at Santa Maria Zobenigo, and various palaces at Santo Stefano as well as the entrance hall of Ca' Loredan (now Vendramin Calergi).[2] We know that the themes Giorgione dipicted on the Fondaco were so novel as to be incomprehensible even to Vasari: large, statuelike figures set into niches, friezes of putti, bands of foliage and garlands, mythologies.[3] Such an iconographic repertory was so unprecedented on Venetian façades as to lead some scholars to suppose that, by channels still very much a mystery to us, Giorgione may have come to know something of the figures within architectural settings that Michelangelo, at the same moment, was painting in the Sistine Chapel.[4]

Aside from the iconographical problem, what struck every writer fortunate enough to see those frescoes when they were still to some extent legible was the extraordinary quality of the color. Little of that can still be made out in the pallid Nude (Fig. 1), which in 1937 was detached from the wall between the windows on the upper story of the Fondaco and is now in the Ca' d'Oro. We can only imagine

the once brilliant coloring of this unusually monumental figure that, in earlier years, could still be described as a "great blaze... within the pronounced shadows and in the predominating reddishness of the colors."[5]

Those traits carried over into Giorgione's work after the Fondaco frescoes. One is in fact struck by the exceptional monumentality of the Three Philosophers he painted for his friend Taddeo Contarini (now Kunsthistorisches Museum, Vienna). Also noteworthy is the essentially physical quality and color: brilliant tints in the foreground melt into the overall setting; natures and figures alike assume a new chromatic consistency that emerges on the surface, palpitates, vibrates in the light.

An even more advanced coloristic sensibility is found in the Sunset Landscape (Fig. 2) once owned by the Donà delle Rose family (now National Gallery, London). It probably represents the culmination and crown of all Giorgione's many series of landscapes, offering the full measure of his cosmic vision of nature. Figure and surroundings enter into a new relationship, while color constitutes the true basis of the picture's impact. The painting also includes an objective reference to an actual landscape in the distant view painted at the right, in all probability the castle at Asolo on the Venetian mainland seen from the west, with the so-called Gate of the Baker, today only in part identifiable near the church of Santa Caterina.[6] Mysterious in subject, as so many of Giorgione's paintings are, the Sunset Landscape constitutes the ultimate step toward a lyrical, contemplative, immobile form. Indeed, one senses that the artist's mind and spirit perhaps were beginning to be troubled by problems of form introduced by other painters of the time, Titian in particular.

The Sunset Landscape was probably followed by the Sleeping Venus now in the Gemäldegalerie, Dresden (Fig. 3). Here again the landscape is connected with the small town of Asolo and yet another view of its castle. However, despite the poor state of conservation of the Venus, there can be no doubt that it is the same picture that the early writer Michiel saw in 1525 in the house of Gerolamo Marcello and explicitly ascribed to Giorgione. In the Venice of 1509 (the likely date for this painting) Giorgione's Sleeping Venus must have appeared absolutely revolutionary, comparable only to the frescoes on the Fondaco. This first totally nude female figure is presented within a landscape. The harmony between human figure and nature melts away into a profundity of spaces that seem to vibrate with music from some unseen source: here is the highest phase of all Giorgione's lyricism. In all likelihood the *Sleeping Venus* was also the first of Giorgione's pictures left unfinished, along with a few others from those last days before he succumbed to the plague of 1510, works such as the *Dead Christ Held up by an Angel*, originally in the Vendramin palace in Venice. According to Michiel, Titian added "the landscape and Cupid" to Giorgione's *Venus*. In point of fact, there once was a small cupid at the feet of the sleeping nude, but it was covered over in a restoration in 1843 and can now be detected only by x-ray. It is possible to identify any contribution by Titian to the landscape, however, given the obvious coherence of the painting as a whole and also its poor state of general conservation. It is true that Titian repeated that same Asolo landscape in such early works as the Lonson *Noli me tangere* (Fig. 4), but obviously that is not a decisive argument for attributing to him the entire background of this *Sleeping Venus*, especially since the same detail had already appeared in the *Sunset Landscape*, which has been firmly ascribed to Giorgione. It is most likely that the very young artist from Cadore painted only the patch of meadow where the cupid once stood, and that what he did in no case encroached on the extraordinary coherence of the background with its hills and rustic village. If anywhere, Titian's hand might be suspected in the almost exuberant flow of drapery on which the Venus lies. We need now to trace the story of Giorgione's last year of life in a small number of pictures. It was then, we believe, that the antipathy between his art and Titian's more than ever came to a head. For confirmation there is the so-called Terris *Portrait of a Man* in the San Diego Fine Arts Gallery (Fig. 5), signed by Giorgione on the back and dated 1510, two facts that make it of exceptional critical importance. The long-haired man in the immediate foreground is viewed from such a close-up vantage point that we see very little other than his face. There can be no doubt that such close-up framing translates into terms of form a deliberate effort to interpret the individual in a more profound and immediate way, almost, one might say, in a Flemish manner. Likewise, color is applied freely to the surface but nevertheless over a base still

1. Giorgione, "Nude," Ca' d'Oro, Venice

graphically precise, assuming naturalistic values and suggesting a rapid, almost summary impression of the sitter. Here then is the product of what was a new pictorial style for Giorgione, one which, in its realistic tendency, approached that of Titian, found, for example, in the latter's Santo Spirito altarpiece (*Saint Mark Enthroned with Saints Cosmas, Damian, Roch, and Sebastian*), probably from 1510 (Fig. 6).

Among other late works by Giorgione, however, some have been attributed to Titian. The latter is sometimes credited with the *Christ Bearing the Cross* in the Scuola Grande di San Rocco in Venice, perhaps because of the elements of realism in the secondary figures.[7] Giorgione's authorship is confirmed, however, by technical and stylistic analysis – despite the notable loss of color caused by successive cleanings and the thinness of the paint itself with its lean oil base. The measured

brushwork characteristic of Giorgione, is, even in x-ray, very different from the already free and aggressive approach of Titian's earliest works, such as the *Concert* in the Palazzo Pitti, Florence.[8]

The *Old Woman* (Fig. 7) with a scroll inscribed *col tempo* (with time) is also given by some to Titian.[9] Such an attribution underestimates Giorgione's own effort at a realistic representation of an old woman lamenting the toll of the years. Besides, everything in that painting is typical of Giorgione: the delicacy of the sign; the gentleness of expression so unlike that *terribilità* found in the young Titian; the calibrated dosage of colors only as absolutely essential and utilizing only a few tonalities (the violet and white of the garment, the brown of the face, the green of the marble parapet), something very different from the more complex palette of the young Titian; and the bland indoor light that permeates the very

2. Giorgione, Detail of the "Sunset Landscape," National Gallery, London
3. Giorgione, Detail of the "Sleeping Venus," Gemäldegalerie, Dresden
4. Titian, Detail of the "Noli me tangere," National Gallery, London

structure of the colors and softens the surface effects. Giorgione's last work, the *Portrait of a Venetian Gentleman* in Washington (Fig. 8), demonstrates that though the older artist had made a real effort to catch up with his young rival, he recognized the considerable distance that separated his art from Titian's: consider, for example, Titian's so-called *Portrait of a Barbarigo* in the National Gallery, London. The Washington portrait should be placed close in time to the *Old Woman*, whose iconographic formula it repeats exactly, and to the portrait of a man in San Diego: the modeling is entirely similar, with surface nuances over a solid, graphic base that comes to the fore in such details as the hand and book or in the strong drawing of the face, which can be made out in x-ray as well.[10] Giorgione's death occurred in the fall of 1510, as proved by the correspondence between Marchesa Isabella d'Este of Mantua and her representative in Venice, Taddeo Albano. His career was cut short at a moment when he was confronting the challenge of Titian, and that may be expressed most fully in the Washington *Portrait of a Venetian Gentleman*. In that work we have some indication of the path Giorgione might have taken had the plague spared him, and it affords grounds for meditating on what path Cinquecento Venetian painting could have taken had both geniuses continued to paint for many years more. We are limited, however, to what Giorgione did in fact create, to works that initiated that vast and poetic phenomenon that goes by the name of "Giorgionism," which proved an essential pole of development in the artistic culture of early sixteenth-century Venice.

Titian was a decidedly independent painter and, one is obliged to recognize, almost the opposite of Giorgione. Typical examples bearing the stamp of his unique genius are his frescoes on the Fondaco (1509?), the Santo Spirito altarpiece (1510?), and the renowned *Concert champêtre* in the Louvre.

It was only a short time after Titian completed his apprenticeship that he made his first bid for fame with the Fondaco frescoes. Yet among the remnants of that early undertaking are few signs of dependence on his presumed masters. Indeed, he appears very much his own man even with respect to Giorgione who, even if he worked only a few yards away, could have appeared cut from the same cloth only to the undiscriminating, tactless

5. Giorgione, "Portrait of a Man," Art Museum, San Diego
6. Titian, Detail of the "Saint Mark Enthroned," Basilica della Salute, Venice

sixteenth century. Recent historians have made much of this contact, viewing it as the basis of a new chapter in the development of Venetian painting. Albrecht Dürer was in Venice in 1505-06, painting the *Madonna of the Rosary* in the church of San Bartolomeo, and Dürer's effect upon the development of the youthful Titian can be inferred from certain drewings executed with vigorous penstrokes that seem more like blows of a gouge or engraving tool. Likwise a sudden interst in landscape (as in the painted cassone fronts in the Museo Civico, Padua) and in the nude figure (the *Lucretia* formerly in the Galerie Fleischmann, Munich) seems to derive not only from Giorgione but also from Dürer's entirely personal approach. Further, Titian's youthful masterpiece, the woodcut *Triumph of Christ*, dated to 1508 by Vasari but more likely 1510, exhibits the influence of the German artist. The incisive linework in the Adam and Eve in Titian's woodcut is comparable to that of examples by Dürer from the same time, for example, the nudes in the *Men's Bath*.[13] Titian was already sensing the sensuous appeal of the human flesh and body and its ability to communicate immediately. Titian had left behind the always hieratical and traditional, humanistic, linear approach of Bellini but also Giorgione's lyrical idealization.

If Dürer contributed to the formation of Titian's temperament, the lesson of Giorgione remains identifiable above all in his Arcadian subject matter and in the way certain landscapes are rendered. Both are notable in the Louvre *Concert champêtre*. However, in that work the connection with the master of Castelfranco remains external and is limited substantially to the subject. Likewise, Giorgione's coloristic influence in the atmospheric impasto of the tones became increasingly feeble, so much so that no more than an echo remains in this particular picture. Titian at twenty, even if he did not join the ranks of Giorgione imitators, was still sufficiently Giorgionesque to confuse art historians several centuries later.[14] Moreover, as we have already noted, as early as the sixteenth century the sources speak of confusion between the last works of the one artist and the first of the other, so that even today some writers continue to question the attribution of the *Concert champêtre*. To my mind, however, there seems no doubt that the work is from Titian's own hand, inspired by Arcadian themes but enriched with that particular tension

individuals who confused his work with that of the much less experienced artist and accorded him praise that must have struck him as the bitterest of offences.[11] If in fact we observe Titian's *Justice* (Fig. 9), which was the cause of the scandal over the highly unfortunate *gaffe*, and compare it with Giorgione's *Nude* from the same building, we see immediately the very different spirit already at work in the younger artist: in the dynamic, vigorous pose of the figure brandishing a sword and treading on a bloody, decapitated head, opposed to Giorgione's nude woman is locked in a stylized elegance; in the incisive symbolism and realistic color, which aims to suggest sensuality even with no more than a bared shoulder; while Giorgione, though proposing a fully nude figure, seems to take refuge in a highly contrived, chromatic abstraction.[12]

When we turn our attention to Titian's frieze from the Fondaco dei Tedeschi and now in the Ca' d'Oro, we readily sense in it a spirit more Northern than classical, one inspired by sources, engravings among them, introduced into Italy by the new European-wide culture of the

7. Giorgione, "Old Woman," Gallerie dell'Accademia, Venice
8. Giorgione, "Portrait of a Venetian Gentleman," National Gallery of Art, Washington

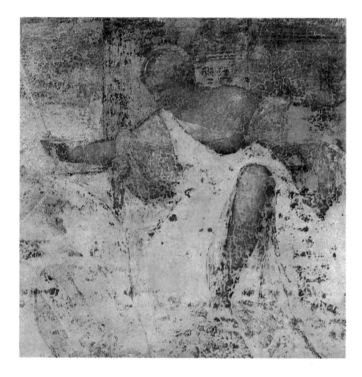

in color and drawing never detectable in the older master's delicate style. In his use of color Titian cannot be confused with the artist from whom some claim he learned so much. In Giorgione we find a thin surface of paint, laid on with short, curving brushstrokes, in glaze after glaze, almost "without making a drawing," as Vasari claimed. But what of all this, can we say, was carried over into Titian's dense, full-bodied palette as seen even in such early works as the Leningrad *Flight into Egypt*, the Glasgow *Christ and the Woman Taken in Adultery*, or the so-called *Gypsy Madonna* in Vienna?

An interior force seems literally to burst through the tense portraits of Titian's *Concert* in the Pitti: a vitality expressed with technical and formal means that are rich in communicativeness, brimming with feeling. All this is inevitably confirmed in the first securely attributed project of Titian's early career, the frescoes in the Scuola del Santo in Padua with the *Miracles of Saint Anthony* painted in 1511. There one grasps virtually first-hand the primordial feelings of the dramatic events represented, the images arising from virtual participation in the mysterious torments of an imagination impelled to create unforgettable images. Youthful enthusiasms intermingle in the young Titian's

creative mind with sudden terrors, the latter perhaps related to the anguish and compassion aroused in him by the events of the war of Cambrai: for example, his own brother Francesco, a soldier, was gravely wounded there. And yet Titian's faith in mankind seems to have been strengthened and renewed, judging from the warrior-saints, Christian miracles, apparitions, and classical myths. The essential masterwork of Titian's early maturity is the altarpiece for the church of Santo Spirito (now in the sacristy of Santa Maria della Salute), marking the end of the plague of 1510. Titian presented the five saints in calm, secure poses, as if in a friendly conversation. Yet the form is classically noble, the implied spirituality elevated, and the colors (recently restored) brightly resounding.[15]

No less grandiosely serene would be the secular images of the *Three Ages of Life* (His Grace the Duke of Edinburgh) and the *Sacred and Profane Love* (Galleria Borghese, Rome). His sense of color likewise was classicizing, over and above the plastic form it clothed. Titian's colors spread resonantly across the surface while his naturalistic imitation was resolved harmoniously into a measured hymn to beauty. It was with such means and in such manner that – Giorgione long since forgotten – Titian early became the uncontested leader of Venetian painting.

[1] G. Nepi Scirè, *Giorgione: Nuda* and F. Valcanover, *Tiziano Vecellio: la Giustizia*, in AA.VV., *Giorgione a Venezia*, Milan, 1978, 117-29 and 130-34.
[2] T. Pignatti, *Giorgione. L'opera completa*, Milan, 1978, 78 ff.
[3] G. Vasari, *Le vite...*, 1550, Florence, 577.
[4] C.H. Smyth, *Michelangelo and Giorgione*, in *Giorgione*, Atti del convegno di studio, Castelfranco Veneto, 1979, 219-20 and B.L. Brown, *Giorgione, Michelangelo and the «maniera moderna»*, in AA.VV., *Renaissance Studies in honor of C.H. Smyth*, Florence, 1985, 97-108.
[5] A.M. Zanetti, *Varie pitture a fresco...*, Venice, 1760, IV.
[6] P. Pellizzari, *Autobiografia dei dipinti di Giorgione*, in *Giorgione*, Atti del convegno di studio, Castelfranco Veneto, 1979, 67-72.
[7] F. Valcanover, *Tiziano Vecellio: Cristo portacroce*, in AA.VV., *Giorgione a Venezia*, Milan, 1978, 149-51.
[8] L. Mucchi, *Caratteri radiografici della pittura di Giorgione*, Florence, 1978.
[9] E. Panofsky, *Problems in Titian, mostly iconographic*, New York, 1969.
[10] L. Mucchi, *Caratteri radiografici*, 1978.
[11] L. Dolce, *Dialogo della pittura intitolato l'Aretino*, Venice, 1557.
[12] T. Pignatti, *Giorgione*, 1978, 156.
[13] T. Pignatti, *The Relationship between German and Venetian Painting in the Late Quattrocento and Early Cinquecento*, in J. Hale, *Renaissance Venice*, London, 1973, 244-73.
[14] T. Pignatti, *Giorgione*, 1978, 133-35.
[15] F. Valcanover, *Tiziano Vecellio: San Marco in trono*, in AA.VV., *Giorgione a Venezia*, Milan, 1978, 163-68.

9. Titian, "Justice." Ca' d'Oro, Venice

Charles Hope

TITIAN AND HIS PATRONS

Titian's immense influence on later painters was due as much to the early spread of his fame and his works as to the excellence of his art. Well before he died in 1576 his name was known to educated people throughout western Europe and his pictures were to be seen in princely collections from Austria to Spain. Titian himself could hardly have anticipated this kind of success, but throughout his life he cultivated wealthy patrons and consistently sought wide public exposure for his paintings. No Italian Renaissance artist handled his career more astutely or with a stronger sense of purpose.

His ambition was evident even in his earliest years in Venice. So far as one can judge, fifteenth-century Venetian artists were praised mainly for their skill, not for their style. This changed with Giorgione, who was probably the first local painter to be admired because his work looked unlike that of other artists, and more specifically because he was able to represent nature in a new way. But it is doubtful whether Giorgione's paintings had a strong direct impact on Venetian taste. He seems to have worked mainly for a small group of private collectors and he showed little interest in the traditional types of Venetian painting – devotional images, whether for private houses or churches, and highly detailed, anecdotal narratives for public buildings. Apart from his frescoes on the exterior of the Fondaco dei Tedeschi, it is

unlikely that any of Giorgione's pictures were on public display in Venice when he died in 1510. Titian, by contrast, seems to have been eager to apply the new ideals in paintings of every kind – in a work for a domestic context such as the *Gypsy Madonna* (Kunsthistorisches Museum, Vienna, c. 1510), in his altarpiece for the monastery of Santo Spirito in Isola (Santa Maria della Salute, Venice, c. 1511-12), or in his narrative frescoes of 1511 in Padua. Even his frescoes at the Fondaco seem to have made more impact than those of Giorgione, and by about 1512 it is likely that three of his oil paintings could be seen in Venetian public buildings. In these early years, doubtless mindful of the example of Dürer, Titian further sought to advertise his ability through large woodcuts which he designed – the *Triumph of Christ* (1508?) and the *Drowning of Pharoah in the Red Sea*. Little is known of Titian's early patrons, but it is clear that from the first he actively cultivated clients prominent in public life. One was Jacopo Pesaro, a leading member of one of the most powerful families in the city, for whom he probably worked as early as 1506. Another was a member of the Barbarigo family, who, Vasari tells us, was so pleased with his portrait that he helped Titian to win his commission for the Fondaco frescoes, in 1508. Yet another was Niccolò Aurelio, a senior civil servant for whom Titian painted the so-called *Sacred and Profane*

1. Titian, "Sacred and Profane Love." Galleria Borghese, Rome

Love (Fig. 1). It can hardly be a coincidence that this major work dates from around 1514, when the artist was engaged in a campaign – in which Aurelio's support must have been invaluable – to establish himself among the painters employed in the redecoration of the Sala del Maggior Consiglio in the Palazzo Ducale.

The project had several obvious attractions for Titian. It offered a regular income in return for relatively little work, a degree of official recognition as one of the leading artists of the city and the opportunity to display his talents in a prominent public location. When he applied to work in the palace, in 1513, he characteristically offered to paint the *Battle of Spoleto*, a subject that not only presented a notable artistic challenge, but which was also destined for the middle of a long wall so far untouched by redecoration. Equally characteristically, once Titian had established himself in the palace, in 1516, he put aside the battle picture for a quarter of a century, having been offered an even more tempting and congenial opportunity to show what he could do.

This was the commission for the huge altarpiece of the *Assumption* for the high altar of the Frari, the largest church in Venice. The painting was probably completed in the unusually short period of two years. Shortly afterward Titian was asked to paint another altarpiece for the Frari, this time for a chapel in the cloister, but this

too he soon put aside in favor of other commissions that offered greater public exposure. The first was from his old patron Jacopo Pesaro, for whom he painted between 1519 and 1526 another altarpiece in the Frari itself, in a particularly prominent and well-lit location in the left aisle. The second was from a lay confraternity which owned a chapel in the other great Venetian church, Santi Giovanni e Paolo. Again this was for an altarpiece, of the *Death of Saint Peter Martyr*, which was painted between 1526 and 1530. Generally regarded as the artist's masterpiece, it was burnt in 1867.

We do not know how much Titian received for the *Assumption*, but it is clear that he painted the other two altarpieces for relatively low fees, no doubt in part because they provided such marvelous advertisements for his skill. By 1530 his position in Venice was secure and thereafter he never exerted himself to the same degree for local patrons. His fees for altarpieces quadrupled in the 1530s, while for the first time he was not above calling on assistants to help in the actual execution. This is not to say that Titian was never prepared to give of his best for Venetian clients. Paintings like the *Presentation of the Virgin* (Accademia, Venice, 1534-38) or the *Vendramin Family* (National Gallery, London; c. 1545) are certainly autograph; and the same was probably true of at least some of the portraits of doges and

2. G. Fontana, "The Battle of Spoleto," engraving detail
3. Titian, "Bacchus and Ariadne." National Gallery, London

votive paintings that he produced for the Palazzo Ducale (all of which were destroyed in 1574 and 1577). But after 1530 he did not seek public exposure for his work in Venice as he had done before: even the *Battle of Spoleto* was completed, in 1538, only after threats of financial penalties from the government (Fig. 2).

Titian had begun to produce important pictures for patrons outside Venice relatively early. Among the most notable early examples were altarpieces for the papal legate Altobello Averoldi (Santi Nazaro e Celso, Brescia), for the canon of Treviso Cathedral, Broccardo Malchiostro (Cathedral, Treviso), and for a merchant resident in Ancona, Alvise Gozzi (Museo Civico, Ancona), all of which date from around 1520. But more significant for the future was his work for the Duke of Ferrara, Alfonso d'Este, who first employed him in 1516, and for whom he painted three Bacchanals between 1518 and 1524 (National Gallery, London; Prado, Madrid) (Fig. 3). Alfonso was one of those rare patrons with a real taste for painting and a shrewd judgment of artistic quality. The pictures that he commissioned – recreations of the kind of masterpieces admired in antiquity – had no close precedents in Venice; he acquired them purely for his own pleasure and he sought the services of the best painters in Italy, first Giovanni Bellini, then Raphael and Fra' Bartolomeo, and finally Titian.

Alfonso's bacchanals had little impact before their removal from Ferrara to Rome in 1598, and none of Titian's other Italian patrons commissioned anything comparable from him. But for Titian himself the artistic opportunity offered by his aristocratic clients.... evidently not always their principal attraction. More important was the fact that they paid very well, particularly in the form of pensions for the artist himself and benefices for his son Pomponio, while allowing him to live in Venice and work at his own pace. Despite the attractions of court patronage, Titian was careful never to become a court painter.

Two factors helped the growth of Titian's reputation outside Venice. The first was personal contact. Through Alfonso d'Este he came to the notice of Federico Gonzaga, the ruler of Mantua, and thanks to Federico he was employed by the emperor Charles v. It was probably through Federico too that he established a relationship with Francesco Maria della Rovere, Duke of Urbino. But scarcely less important in spreading Titian's fame were the efforts first of his friend Pietro Aretino and then of other writers such as Lodovico Dolce. By the later 1550s, through their publications, even those who had never seen his work knew of his reputation as the greatest painter of modern times, just as they knew that Michelangelo was the foremost sculptor.

Until the mid-1550s critical appreciation of Titian's works, at least in print, was of a rather limited kind. He was praised above all for his skill in the application of paint, his *colorito*, and more specifically for his ability to endow his figures with life. These qualities were particularly exemplified in his portraits, and it was mainly as a portraitist that he was in demand among aristocratic patrons. His first works for Federico Gonzaga were portraits, as were those for Charles v, and through his portraiture he came to the attention of the Farnese family of the Pope, Paul iii, for whom he worked in the mid-1540s. An interest in portraiture cannot, of course, be taken as indicative of any more broadly based interest in painting as such. Most of Titian's patrons, indeed, were content to own a few devotional paintings and perhaps a portrait or two, and they employed Titian only because of his high reputation. Even Federico Gonzaga, for example, who had real taste for painting, at first acquired only portraits and religious images from the artist, even though in the second half of the 1530s he exploited his skill in a more imaginative way, commissioning a famous series of eleven paintings of Roman emperors (burnt in 1734). A similar pattern can be seen in the patronage of Francesco Maria della Rovere, for whom Titian painted portraits, small religious pictures and representations of famous rulers of ancient and modern history. Francesco Maria also acquired from the artist the *Woman in a blue dress* in 1536 (Pitti, Florence), a notable example of a genre of picture already popular in Venice that Titian did much to make fashionable elsewhere in Italy, namely depictions of anonymous beautiful women, sometimes clothed, sometimes not. The same model also appears, clad only in a fur wrap, in a painting in Vienna, and again, nude, in the so-called *Venus of Urbino* (Fig. 4) which was acquired by Francesco Maria's son Guidobaldo in 1538. It was probably

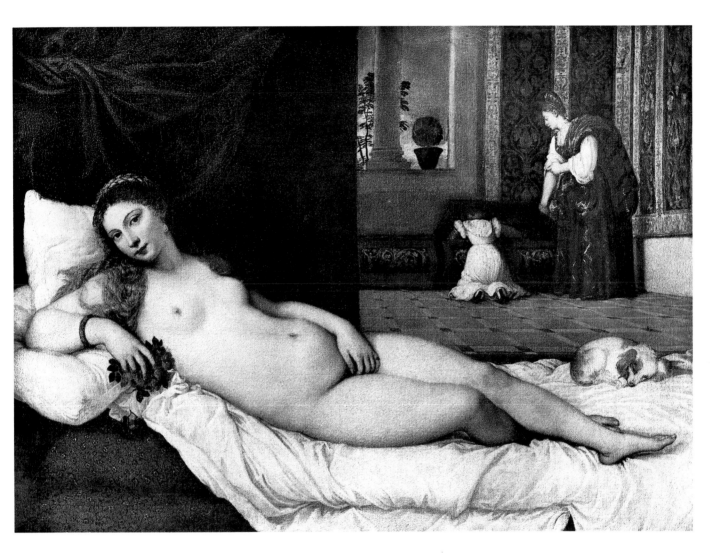

this picture that encouraged Cardinal Alessandro Far-nese in 1543 to commission another painting of a reclining female nude, the *Danae* (Capodimonte, Nap-les), and Titian subsequently produced a number of works of similar character, notably a *Venus* for Charles v and a second *Danäe* (Prado, Madrid), for Charles' son Philip.

Taken as a whole, Titian's output in the 1530s and 1540s was less ambitious and innovative than that of the earlier period, and it certainly does not prepare us for the extraordinary achievements of his later years, which began with his invitation to the Imperial Diet at Augsburg in 1548. From this moment until his death

most of Titian's work was for the Hapsburg family and their associates. Thus in the period 1548-54 alone he is known to have supplied them with at least seventy paintings. Initially his principal patrons were Charles v himself and his sister Mary of Hungary, though he also produced a substantial number of portraits (none of which survive) for Charles' brother Ferdinand, King of the Romans; but increasingly, and especially after 1551, Titian worked for Charles' son Philip II, whom he continued to serve for the rest of his life.

Charles v was rather conventional as a patron. He only commissioned Titian to paint portraits or devotional works of an overt piety. It is true that one of his

4. Titian, "Venus of Urbino." Galleria degli Uffizi, Florence

paintings, the *Equestrian Portrait* (Prado, Madrid; 1548), has no close precedent in scale or subject matter in sixteenth-century painting; but it is by no means clear that Charles himself was responsible for its conception. Of the emperor's devotional paintings the largest and most unusual was the *Trinity* (Prado, Madrid; 1553), which was almost certainly painted according to his general specifications and is as much a reflection of his piety as of his taste. Certainly, there is no reason to believe that he had any very marked appetite for paintings as such. His sister Mary, however, evidently had much more the temperament of a collector. She owned no less than twenty portraits by Titian (including the equestrian portrait), a collection that provided an almost comprehensive visual record of the Hapsburgs of her generation. She also acquired other paintings from Titian, among them a *Noli me Tangere* (Prado, Madrid, fragment; 1554), and three or possibly four large pictures of mythological heroes for her palace at Binche, near Brussels – works that, in their sensational light effects, might have been calculated to demonstrate Titian's mastery of *colore*, just as the heroic male nude figures revealed the power of his *disegno*. This commission, at least, suggests that Mary was aware of the conventions of art criticism then current in Italy; and the unusual nature of the subject matter may indicate that she, not Titian, was responsible for the choice of themes.

Titian first met Philip in Northern Italy in 1549, when he painted a full-length portrait of the prince in armour (Prado, Madrid). A year later the artist revisited Augsburg, this time at the invitation of Philip, and established a relationship with him that was to last a quarter of a century. The arrangement made at Augsburg seems to have been that over the next decade or so Titian would produce about ten large pictures, some mythological and some religious, in return for a generous pension. In 1562 Titian declared that his obligations had been fulfilled, but he continued to supply Philip with new pictures at regular intervals right up until 1576. In all, he sent the king some twenty-five paintings, most of them quite large, making Philip by far the most significant of his patrons; and although he constantly complained about lack of payment, in practice he was very generously rewarded for his efforts.

The most famous of Philip's pictures are the *poesies*, six subjects taken from classical mythology. The first of these, the *Danäe* (Prado, Madrid), was almost certainly painted for Philip even before Titian's second visit to Augsburg (although it is usually dated a few years later). The other five, starting in 1554 with *Venus and Adonis* (Fig. 5) and ending in 1562 with the *Rape of Europa* (Isabella Stewart Gardner Museum, Boston), are slightly larger. It has surprised some historians that a man as straight-laced as Philip should have acquired such overtly sensual pictures. But, as we have seen, several of Titian's other aristocratic patrons – Alfonso d'Este, Alessandro Farnese, Guidobaldo della Rovere and Charles v – had received paintings of a very similar character. Mythology was an established and respectable genre, one that gave artists an opportunity to display their skill by emulating the great poets, in this case Ovid. Nor is it appropriate to argue, as some scholars have done, that Philip's *poesies* were meant to be understood as elaborate allegories, with a profound philosophical or even religious content. It seems from the correspondence between the artist and his patron that the subjects were chosen by Titian; and he never hinted that his pictures should be interpreted in this way.

Philip was equally enthusiastic about Titian's religious paintings. While working on the *poesie* the artist supplied him with several major works of this type, of which the best preserved is the *Entombment* (Prado, Madrid; 1559). In these years the king consistently had the first call on Titian's services, so that even a patron as powerful as Cardinal Ippolito d'Este had to take second place. Thus Titian began an *Adoration of the Magi* (Escorial) for the cardinal, probably in 1556, but when the Spanish ambassador suggested that it might be suitable for Philip, the original was sent to Spain and Ippolito had to make do with a second version of inferior quality (Milan, Ambrosiana). In Titian's last years the pattern remained unchanged. Philip, alone among his patrons, regularly received major autograph paintings, such as the *Martyrdom of Saint Lawrence* (Escorial; 1564-47), *Tarquin and Lucretia* (Fitzwilliam Museum, Cambridge; 1568-71), and the *Saint Jerome* (Escorial, 1575). Other clients usually had to settle for replicas or derivations of earlier compositions, often produced with the help of assistants,

5. Titian, "Venus and Adonis." Museo del Prado, Madrid

for example the *Saint Mary Magdalene* (Capodimonte, Naples) sent to Cardinal Alessandro Farnese in 1567. There are few exceptions, such as the beautiful ceiling-painting of *History* for the Liberia Marciana. But in such cases there was usually a reason why Titian took special pains – in this instance because the building was the work of his great friend Sansovino, and because his picture was displayed in a room next to works by most of the outstanding young painters of Venice.

Titian's work for Philip represents a unique chapter in sixteenth-century patronage. No other patron of the period supported a major painter so enthusiastically over such a long period. None was rewarded with a comparable series of masterpieces. The history of Titian's career after 1551 is to a great extent the history of his work for Philip. And there is little doubt that had he completed the various examples of his so-called late style, such as the *Flaying of Marsyas* (Kroměříž) or the *Nymph and Shepherd* (Kunsthistorisches Museum, Vienna), most of these too would have been sent to Spain. In Philip Titian found his ideal patron, a man who rewarded him royally and gave him the freedom to paint what he wanted, as he wanted.

Rona Goffen

TITIAN, HIS DONORS
AND SACRED SUBJECTS

Titian painted almost every kind of sacred picture – from altarpieces to processional banners – for every kind of patron: princes, prelates, private individuals, religious and secular organizations. One of Titian's earliest works was a sacred subject painted for one of his most eminent Venetian patrons: the votive picture of Jacopo Pesaro, bishop of Paphos, papal legate and a nobleman of considerable wealth. The bishop had commanded the papal fleet in alliance with Venice against the Turks in the battle of Santa Maura (1502), a victory for the Christian forces thanks to Pesaro's efforts – or at least so he himself maintained, in words and in his votive picture by Titian. But how did the young artist come to the attention of such a great man? Perhaps Pesaro first approached Titian's master, Giovanni Bellini. Patriarch of the Venetian school, Bellini had painted an altarpiece for the bishop's cousin and rival, Benedetto Pesaro, Generalissimo da Mar at Santa Maura: the triptych dated 1488, still *in situ* in the generalissimo's funerary chapel in the sacristy of Santa Maria Gloriosa dei Frari, where Jacopo Pesaro's branch of the family also worshiped. Addressing the Collegio shortly after the battle, the bishop expressed his resentment of the credit given his cousin for the victory.[1] Commissioning a work to commemorate his own part at Santa Maura the bishop may well have turned to the generalissimo's artist, hoping to outdo his cousin in this way. If Pesaro did so, Bellini himself may have suggested his young disciple from Cadore – and this might also help explain the strong Bellinesque elements in the Pesaro votive picture, of Titian's works the closest both in style and conception to his old master.

Titian's rise from this point onward was meteoric. Sometime between 1508 and 1516-17, he produced his great woodcut of the *Triumph of Christ*, which became a "bestseller" of the Cinquecento.[2] Even people who could never afford and might never see a painting by him came to know of Titian through this much-published print. By late 1510, Titian was working on a very significant public commission in Padua: frescoes for the *albergo* of the Scuola di Sant'Antonio, a lay confraternity affiliated with the adjacent basilica of the saint (the Santo). Possibly Jacopo Pesaro, a congregant of the Frari, the Conventual Franciscan church of Venice – where there was another

scuola dedicated to Anthony – recommended Titian to the Conventual Franciscans of Padua. In any case, the *scuola* commission was a conspicuous one: to this day, the Santo is one of the most venerated and visited pilgrimage sites in the Christian world. The confraternity shared in that prestige and prominence.

In the *albergo* of the scuola, Titian was required to represent both the terrible physical violence (the *Jealous Husband*, Fig. 1) and scenes of physical stasis that express psychological tension (the *Reattached Foot* and the *Speaking Babe*). These are comparatively rare subjects, but Titian had one conspicuous model near at hand for the latter: the chapel of the saint's tomb in the Santo itself, where the same stories are represented in very similar ways. The *confreres* themselves may have suggested to Titian that his compositions should evoke this sacred site.[3] In any case, thus began Titian's life-long association with the Order of Friars Minor.

While engaged in Padua, or shortly thereafter, Titian was commissioned by the Augustinian Canons to paint his first undisputed surviving altarpiece, *Saint Mark Enthroned with Saints Cosmas and Damian, Roch and Sebastian*, for the church of Santo Spirito in Isola, for which he eventually also produced another altarpiece and a cycle of ceiling paintings.[4] The presence of four plague saints makes the hopeful purpose of the image clear: it was a prayer for deliverance from seemingly endless epidemics.

The Franciscans brought Titian his next ecclesiastical commission – the *Assumption* for the high altar of the Frari, unveiled on 19 May 1518. The individuals who actually paid for this masterpiece remain anonymous: as Mendicants, Fra Germano, *guardian* of the friary, and the other friars had no money of their own, but if the pattern here followed that of other such commissions, members of the parish contributed varying amounts, for the work. The friars themselves would have approved the artist and the subject, the materials to be used (a standard contractual provision), and the scale (another standard provision, and here already determined by the frame in 1516). The friars also presumably guided Titian in his interpretation of the theme.[5] For these reasons, Dolce's much-quoted account of the negative critical reception of the *Assumption* is not credible: his libel

against the convent was evidently motivated by the desire to make Titian's brilliant achievement appear all the more dramatic.[6] But neither Titian nor the *Assumption* has need of such tactics.

Shortly after the installation of the *Assumption*, Titian undertook another work for the same church, the *Pesaro Madonna* (1519-26), commissioned by Bishop Jacopo and his brothers and still *in situ* in the chapel of the Immaculate Conception.[7] The *Madonna* is remarkable for the dignity and prominence accorded the donors, including the bishop's young nephew, through whom the rights and privileges of their patrician lineage can continue. Here one sees the results of collaboration among artist, patron, and clergy: in fulfilling their individual, somewhat idiosyncratic requirements, Titian was inspired to create one of his most original inventions.

While the Pesaro were waiting for the completion of their *pala*, the Franciscans of the Frari returned to Titian for the high altarpiece of the adjacent church of San Nicoletto della Lattuga – another indication that they were pleased with the *Assumption*. First commissioned in 1519, this new work was soon abandoned, at least until Fra Germano approached Titian again about it in 1535.[8] By then Titian had completed another commission for a Franciscan church, the *Madonna in Glory with Saints and Donor*, ordered by the Ragusan merchant Alvise Gozzi for the high altar of San Francesco ad Alto of Ancona in 1520 (Fig. 2). Perhaps the friars themselves were encouraging their patrons to employ Titian? In any case, Gozzi's painting, like the *Pesaro Madonna*, served as a funerary altarpiece.[9] Likewise, the *Stigmatization of Saint Francis* was painted for the funerary chapel of Desiderio Guidone, consecrated in 1561 in San Francesco, Ascoli (and now in the Pinacoteca Civica).

To be sure, the Franciscans did not have a Titian monopoly. For example, in 1519, Altobello Averoldi, the bishop of Pola and Leo x's papal legate in Venice, commissioned the high altarpiece for Santi Nazaro e Celso in Brescia (Fig. 3).[10] Averoldi's patronage may have been inspired by his acrimonious rivalry with the canon Broccardo Malchiostro, for whom Titian was then painting the *Annunciation* for the Duomo of Treviso.[11] The Averoldi altarpiece is a polyptych in accordance with the patron's wishes – Titian's only polyptych, a

1. Titian, "The Miracle of the Jealous Husband," fresco.
Scuola del Santo, Padua

format outmoded in Venice itself by that date. In any case, the panel of *Saint Sebastian* was complete by late 1520 when Alfonso I d'Este, Duke of Ferrara, considered acquiring it for himself.[12] Though these machinations came to nothing, the case reveals something of the way in which Titian's patrons might deal with him: in some instances the primary concern was the authorship and beauty of the image – not its intended use or subject

matter. And by 1520, Alfonso was well-acquainted with Titian's art: the duke was his first great princely patron outside Venice, beginning with the *Tribute Money* of 1516 (Fig. 4).[13] Perhaps Titian "inherited" the duke from Bellini, as he may have inherited Jacopo Pesaro? Just two years earlier, in 1514, Bellini had completed *The Feast of the Gods* for Alfonso – the picture was later altered by Titian – and the cycle for the duke's *studiolo* that began with this work was thereafter completed by Titian's *poesies*. In part through his association with Alfonso, Titian came to the attention of other noble patrons: the duke's sister, Isabella d'Este; her son-in-law, Francesco Maria della Rovere; and her son, Federico Gonzaga – who in turn introduced Titian to Emperor Charles V,[14] the father of Titian's greatest patron, King Philip II of Spain.

Meanwhile, Titian was of course also employed by Venetian patrons, including the *scuola* of Saint Peter Martyr which commissioned an altarpiece for their chapel in the Dominican church of Santi Giovanni e Paolo (Fig. 5). Titian won this commission in a competition against Palma il Vecchio, a member of the confraternity, and it may be that the contest was staged precisely to provide an excuse to employ Titian instead of the older man. Perhaps too the decision was influenced by the longstanding rivalry among the Dominicans and Franciscans, and their habit of attempting to outdo each other in artistic endeavors – a habit of mind also characteristic of *scuole*. In any case, the *scuola* must have been most pleased with the results: unveiled in 1530, the *Saint Peter Martyr* was widely considered Titian's greatest religious work in Venice.[15] Apparently destroyed by fire in 1867, the altarpiece probably resembled the almost contemporary *Saint John The Baptist* (painted for the church of Santa Maria Maggiore) and the San Giovanni Elemosinario altarpiece. And forty-five years after its installation, Titian produced a copy of the *Saint Peter Martyr* for King Philip.[16]

Though the Dominicans of Venice never returned to Titian, their *confreres* elsewhere did employ him: the *Christ Crowned with Thorns* (1540) was painted for the Chapel of the Holy Crown in Santa Maria delle Grazie in Milan,[17] where Titian's work could be compared with one of the icons of Renaissance art, Leonardo's *Last*

2. *Titian, "Madonna in Glory with Saints and Donor," called "the Gozzi Alterpiece."*
Museo Civico, Ancona

3. Titian, "The Resurrection of Christ," called "the Averoldi Alterpiece."
Chiesa dei Santi Nazaro e Celso, Brescia

Supper in the refectory; the *Annunciation* (c. 1557), for San Domenico Maggiore in Naples; and the *Crucified Christ with the Virgin and Saints* (1558), for San Domenico in Ancona (Fig. 6). In Venice itself, for patrons of other religious orders, Titian was producing such works as the *Martyrdom of Saint Lawrence* (1548-59), commissioned by Lorenzo Massolo for his tomb in

S. PETRVS MARTYR A MANICHÆIS INTERFECTVS.
Titianus pinxit Venetiis in templo Dominicanorum.

the church of the Crociferi; and two altarpieces still *in situ* in San Salvatore, the *Transfiguration* and the *Annunciation*.[18]

Since the beginning of his career, Titian had also always painted sacred images for private settings, such as Alfonso's *Tribute Money*. After the completion of the *poesie* for his *studiolo*, Alfonso returned to Titian for another sacred work that may be identified with the *Madonna and Child with Saint Catherine and the Infant*

Baptist, c. 1530. The painting resembles the *Madonna of the Rabbit* commissioned in 1529 by Alfonso's nephew, Federico II Gonzaga, duke of Mantua. Perhaps one duke had requested a version of the other's composition, motivated by a sense of rivalry, as was explicitly the case with the patronage of Federico's nephew, Francesco Maria della Rovere: Gonzaga already has something by Titian, the duke whined, while "we haven't got a thing yet."[19] Gonzaga's *Madonna* includes his portrait in the

4. Titian, "The Tribute Money." Gemäldegalerie, Dresden
5. Engraving after Titian's "Saint Peter Martyr"

guise of a shepherd kneeling in adoration of the Virgin and Child.[20] Meanwhile, Francesco Maria and his consort, Eleonora Gonzaga, had to wait until late 1533 for their first Titian, a *Nativity*: the duke wrote that Eleonora "really wants it for her imminent childbirth," that is, the birth of their son Giulio,[21] 15 April 1533. The eagerness of the mother-to-be was likely based less on collector's zeal than on the hope that the birth of her child would be as painless as pious legend described the Nativity to have been: presumably the duchess shared the common belief of her contemporaries in the miraculous power of images.

Not at the beginning of life but at its end, Charles V also found solace in paintings by Titian. The emperor apparently took the *Dolorosa with Open Hands* with him when he withdrew to Yuste, and on his deathbed contemplated the *Holy Trinity*.[22] Meanwhile, Titian had also established a remarkably cordial relationship with the emperor's son, King Philip, clearly a more compliant – and more generous – patron than the Italians.[23] Two of the king's devotional compositions are included in this exhibition, the *Entombment* and the *Christ Carrying the Cross*; and a third, the *Magdalene*, a lost work, is represented by two variants. Titian himself proposed this last theme as a gift for the monarch: "... a picture of the Magdalene, who approaches with tears in her eyes and supplicating for the needs of her most devoted servant."[24] Vasari and Dolce also emphasized the compassion of such images: however erotic they may seem to modern viewers, it is historically inappropriate to negate this pious emotion.

The *Magdalene* that Titian began for Philip was seen in the artist's house by the Venetian nobleman Silvio Badoer, who obtained it for himself: Philip was sent yet another copy of this popular composition.[25] Clearly Titian sold many works in this way, directly to buyers who came to his studio. The Leningrad *Magdalene*, for example, was in Titian's house at his death, together with numerous other works (for example, *Saint Sebastian*, *Saint Jerome*), some of them painted without a specific contractual agreement, but perhaps to be offered to certain patrons or to be sold to whoever was willing to buy.

Titian himself was the patron of some of his own late religious works, including the *Resurrected Christ Ap-*

pearing to the Virgin, for the church of Santa Maria in Medole (Mantua) (Fig. 7), probably painted c. 1554, when the artist asked the duke of Mantua to transfer the canonry of Medole to a nephew: it seems that Titian conceived the painting as a pious bribe. Some fourteen years later, working with assistance, Titian completed an altarpiece for the Vocellio Chapel in the archdeacon's church of the master's native city, the *Madonna with Saints Titian and Andrew*, in which the artist himself kneels as donor. Finally, the patron of his last great altarpiece was also Titian himself: the *Pietà*, intended for the Chapel of the Crucifix, which was to be his funerary chapel in the Frari.[26] Like other artists who planned depictions of the same subject for their tombs – in-

6. Titian, "Crucified Christ with the Virgin and Saints."
Chiesa di San Domenico, Ancona
7. Titian, "Resurrected Christ Appearing to the Virgin."
Chiesa di Santa Maria, Medole (Mantua)

8. Titian, "Mater Dolorosa with Clasped Hands." Museo del Prado, Madrid

cluding Michelangelo – Titian painted his self-portrait as donor lamenting the death of the Savior, and probably in the guise of Joseph of Arimathea. Emulating Joseph, the artist offers his own tomb to Christ. The *Pietà* is Titian's visual autobiography and artistic testament, a moving commemoration of a great master's genius and a declaration of his personal faith.

[1] M. Sanudo, *Diarii* 4, cols. 460 and 444; and R. Goffen, *Piety and Patronage in Renaissance Venice: Bellini, Titian, and the Franciscans*, New Haven and London, 1986, 116-29, 133-37.

[2] Arguing for the later date: M. Bury, "The 'Triumph of Christ,' after Titian," *Burlington Magazine* 131 (1989): 188-97. Compare D. Rosand and M. Muraro, *Titian and the Venetian Woodcut*, Washington, 1976, 37-54.

[3] S.B. Wilk [McHam], "Titian's Paduan Experience and Its Influence on His Style," *Art Bulletin* 65 (1983), 51-60.

[4] See A. Sambo, "Tiziano davanti ai giudici ecclesiastici," in *Tiziano e Venezia*, Vicenza, 1980, 383-99. Note also the *Christ Carrying the Cross* (Venice, Scuola Grande di San Rocco), painted c. 1508 by Giorgione or by Titian as an altarpiece for the Church of San Rocco; see J. Anderson, "'Christ Carrying the Cross' in San Rocco: Its Commission and Miraculous History," *Arte veneta* 31 (1977), 186-88.

[5] For the iconography, see Goffen, 1977, 73-106, 141-42. For another patron's instructions, see Duke Guidobaldo della Rovere's letter of 5 May 1573; G. Gronau, *Documenti artistici urbinati*, Florence, 1936, 107. Ambient lighting was also considered: see Titian's letter of 6 January 1564, in Gronau, 1936, 101.

[6] *L'Aretino: Dolce's "Aretino" and Venetian Art Theory of the Cinquecento*, ed. M.W. Roskill, New York, 1968, 186-89.

[7]. Goffen, 1977, 107-18, 228-29, no. 30 (a transcription of ASV, Pesaro, *Busta* 102, no. 2).

[8] W. Hood and C. Hope, "Titian's Vatican Altarpiece and the Pictures Underneath," *Art Bulletin* 59 (1977), 534-52.

[9] E. Spadolini, "Dalmatica dall'Archivio Storico di Ancona, Documenti inediti," *Bullettino di archeologia e storia dalmata* 24 (1901), 119.

[10] A. Venturi, *Storia dell'arte italiana*, Milano, 1928, IX, iii, 107.

[11] Hope, 1980, 48.

[12] G. Campori, "Tiziano e gli Estensi," *Nuova antologia* 27 (1874), 591-94. Titian was willing to substitute a replica in the polyptych.

[13] Campori 1874, 584; Gronau, "Tizian und Alfonso d'Este", *Jahrbuch der kunsthistorischen Sammlungen in Wien*, NF 20 (1928), 235; and Modena, Archivio di Stato, Ambasciatori, Florence, *Busta* 23, in Hood and Hope 1977, no. 62.

[14] Dante Bernini, "Tiziano per i Duchi di Urbino," in *Tiziano per i Duchi di Urbino, Mostra didattica*, Urbino, 1976, 17.

[15] For example, on 2 August 1663, the priests found it necessary to "rimediare all'insolenza d'alcuni pietosi quali... andavono copiare il quadro di S. Pietro Martire pretar il piede sopra la pietra sacra"; ASV, Santi Giovanni e Paolo, *Busta* XIV, 57r-v.

[16] A. Cloulas, "Documents concernant Titien conservés aux archives de Simancas," *Mélanges de la Casa de Velazquez* 3 (1967), 281. For the lost version, compare E. Riccòmini, "Il capolavoro di Tiziano non era bruciato," *Giornale dell'arte* (October, 1989), kindly brought to my attention by Dr. Susanna Biadene.

[17] For the date, see M.T. Binaghi Olivari, "Partita doppia milanese per Tiziano," *Arte veneta* 1989 (in press).

[18] Titian varied the composition of the Lawrence (now in the Gesuiti) for Philip II's high altar at the Escorial, 1554-1567. For the *Annunciation*, see Ruggero Maschio, "Una data per l'Annunciazione di Tiziano a S. Salvador," *Arte veneta* 29 (1975), 178-82.

[19] Letter of 16 October 1533 in Gronau, *Documenti*, 88: "...quel S[ignor]re [Gonzaga] ha pur' qualche cosa del suo, che non habbiamo anchora alchuna noi."

[20] Hood and Hope 1977, n. 14.

[21] Gronau, *Documenti*, 87, letter of 6 April 1533: "lo desidera assai per questo suo parto." Augusto Gentili identifies this work with the Pitti *Adoration*; "Due paragrafi per Tiziano e i della Rovere," in *Studi in onore di Giulio Carlo Argan*, ed. S. Marchioni and B. Tavassi La Greca, Rome, 1984, vol. I, 161.

[22] Titian altered a figure in this painting at the emperor's request; see Cloulas 1967, 224 and notes 3, 4.

[23] For the escalating effect of foreign patrons on Titian's prices – not to mention his own financial acumen – see the letter to Francesco Maria della Rovere from his agent, 9 July 1532, in Gronau, 1936, 85-86. On the art market, see Werner L. Gundersheimer, "Patronage in the Renaissance: An Exploratory Approach," in *Patronage in the Renaissance*, ed. G. F. Lytle and S. Orgel, Princeton, 1981, 17 and *passim*.

[24] Letter of 2 April 1561: "...una pitture della *Maddalena*, la quale le si appresenterà innanzi con le lagrime in su gli occhi e supplichevole per li bisogni del suo divotissimo servo." See Luigi Ferrarino, *Tiziano e la corte di Spagna nei documenti dell'Archivio Generale di Simancas*, Madrid, 1975, 61, no. 81.

[25] Vasari-Milanesi, VII: 454.

[26] He later changed his mind, however, and the *Pietà* was never installed there; Goffen 1986, 151-154.

David Rosand
TITIAN AND PICTORIAL SPACE

In realizing the implications of Giorgione's transformation of the art of oil painting on canvas, Titian gave new and powerful expression to the paradox of the art of painting itself. The *pittura di macchia* of his later style in particular – with its rough and broken brushwork, its apparently limited palette operating within a deep toned ground – declares the substantial reality of the painting as pictorial surface; simultaneously, that manner invites active response to its evident incompleteness of formal definition, and the depths implicit in its tonal structure urgently invite the viewer's imaginative projection. Out of such apparent contradiction Titian's painting offers a resolution that unites tactile and visual perception in a wholeness of experience that confirms the fictional truth of the image.

The dialectic relationship between the reality of the flat picture plane and the illusion of space behind it, an inherent condition of all pictorial representation, had became fully theorized in the early Renaissance. Central to the practice of the new mathematically controlled perspective, it received full articulation in Leon Battista Alberti's treatise *De pictura*. The tension between the opacity of the painting's surface and its pretended transparency offered special opportunities for the self-assertion or both the artist and his art. Inscribing his art on that surface, most literally in the geometric operations of perspective construction, the painter nonetheless invites the viewer to see through those surface markings, through the actual traces of the painter's presence, to a fiction beyond their reality. In addition to its purely optical illusion, the commensurability of mathematical perspective afforded rational confirmation of the intellectual as well as physical accessibility of that painted world beyond the picture plane.

In the drawing albums of Jacopo Bellini we find the father of Venetian Renaissance painting exploring the possibilities of the recently established system of pictorial perspective. And his concerns were further developed in the ambitious prospects of his son Gentile's cityscapes and, in still more focused manner, in the monumental altarpieces of Giovanni Bellini. It is in these altarpieces, however, that we sense a major transposition of the values of the Florentine invention: the clarity and commensurability of perspective construction become subject to the penumbra of a different architecture, an architecture founded on the Byzantine experience of the church of San Marco. Although the basic shades may remain the same, the rationality of Brunelleschian geometry, its clear linear articulation, is muted by the irrational glow of golden mosaics and by a tonal envelope that obscures the precision of contours.

In the opening years of the sixteenth century Giorgione's technical revolution of the art of oil painting offered a further challenge to the structural clarity of perspective representation. Shadow and tone assumed the greater role in suggesting space beyond the picture plane, and their invitation to enter a notional world was more subjective, suggestive and evocative rather than demonstrative. Unlike the vectorial indices of perspective orthogonals, shadow offered no clear spatial coordinates but only an absence, an unmarked spatial void. Withholding information, especially at the boundary of proximate forms, such tonal structure required of the viewer a certain projection, an effort of the imagination to fill in the represented reality so obstructed. That participation is of an order different from the reasoned reading of perspective's geometry.

Furthermore, in exploiting the potential of oil painting on canvas Giorgione reversed the traditional sequences of execution and, consequently, of perception. Oil painting on panel, the system perfected by Jan van Eyck and given monumental expression by Giovanni Bellini, built upon a light ground; glazes of translucent color created a depth of luminosity that made light itself the most convincing medium of illusion. Giorgione's painting built instead from dark to light; the brightest areas of his paint structure were applied in a thick impasto of white. Adhering to the woven surface of the canvas, retaining the physicality of its very substance and the traces of its application, such impasto represented an obstacle to the transparency of the picture plane; it threatened the balance between painting's marked surface and its illusionistic pretense.

These, then, are the circumstances and background for Titian's own exploration of pictorial space. Heir to both Giovanni Bellini and Giorgione, the young Titian early demonstrated a keen awareness of the constitutive elements of spatial representation: architectural perspec-

been shifted to the right of the field – a stand of columns serving as syndecdoche for an otherwise indeterminate architectural whole. That shift opens a heavenly backdrop, extending the spatial reach of the image and yet, the massive cumulus clouds filling the sky effectively cause that space, creating a more immediate backdrop for the elevated Mark. Such apparently contradictory impulses, barring deep recession, resolve themselves by establishing a fundamental order close to the controlling picture plane.

More than either of his masters, Titian had an instinctive understanding of the power of the picture plane itself, and his responsiveness to that surface, his respect for it and appropriation of its authority, informs the full range of his painting. We observe in Titian's art a general reluctance to exploit orthogonal recession; rather, deliberately countering the spatial momentum of perspective construction, he favors a shallow foreground stage. More importantly, he acknowledges the picture plane as a major determinant of compositional structure: figures as well as architecture tend either to address that plane frontally or to run parallel to it in profile. It is possible that the experience of his sojourn in Padua (1510-11), where he executed three fresco panels in the Scuola del Santo and where he had ample opportunity to study Giotto's decoration of the Arena Chapel, confirmed his natural tendency toward a classicizing pictorial structure. Certainly his design of the *Miracle of the Speaking Babe* (Fig. 2), the grandest of his frescoes in the Scuola, represents a monumental declaration of such compositional principle.

Although basically committed to a parallelism to the picture plane: Titian was nonetheless flexible enough to respond to the exigencies of particular situations. Responding to the challenge of a specific site, he created compositions that dynamically unite actual and virtual space. The arena in which he most actively explored such possibilities was the church of Santa Maria Gloriosa dei Frari in Venice, where his *Assumption* on the high altar was dedicated in 1518. Scenographically attuning his grand concept to the arch of the quattrocentro choir screen through which it was to be viewed along the axis of the nave, he established the pictorial culmination of the very space of the church – as well as pictorial

tive and luminous landscape, color and tone. But throughout his career there is a certain reluctance to build compositionally upon a consistent and fully realized architectural base.

In his first major altarpiece (Fig. 1), painted for Santo Spirito in Isola about 1509, Titian's immediate Venetian heritage is fully evident, in the gentle pathos of the figures and, especially, in the expressive function of shadow – the gloom enshrouding the patron saint of Venice may well signal the plight of the plague-stricken city.[1] Modifying the traditional composition of the *sacra conversazione*, Titian dissociated the figural and architectural axes: the saints grouped around the enthroned Saint Mark and the perspective of the pavement are centrally focused, but the architecture of the setting has

1. *Titian, "Saint Mark Enthroned," Santa Maria della Salute, Venice*

2. Titian, "Miracle of the Speaking Babe," Scuola del Santo, Padua

affirmation of its dedication to the Virgin.

That sensitivity to spatial experience continued to inspire Titian's next altarpiece in the Frari, painted between 1519 and 1526 for Jacopo Pesaro. Situated on an altar along the left wall of the church, the *Pesaro Madonna* is visible along the length of the nave; the picture must function both as wall painting and as altarpiece, accessible from a diagonal approach as well as frontally. In accommodating this double routing, Titian designed a radically asymmetrical composition. In its several early versions, revealed in x-ray examination, he conceived an ambitious architectural perspective, with the vanishing point well off to the left of the field; the Madonna and Child were enthroned to the right beneath a vaulted canopy that seemed, when viewed on the diagonal from the left, a transept extension of the nave of the Frari itself. The solution may well have appeared too literal to the painter, for he abandoned it in favor of the less rational but more monumental double columns that now soar to heaven. Reorienting the governing spatial axis of his design, from horizontal extension to vertical ascent, Titian thereby elevated the architectural space of the painting to a higher, transcendent level.[2]

Despite his reluctance to exploit the more obvious spatial effects of perspective, Titian's control of architec-

ture was an acknowledged aspect of his achievement. Serlio himself hailed "Il Cavalier Titiano, ne le cui mani vive la idea d'una nuova natura non senza gloria de l'Architettura, la qual è ornamento de la grandezza del suo perfetto Giudicio."[3] But for Titian architecture remained an essentially pictorial element, even when it figured as a dominant determinant of compositional structure. In the *Presentation of the Virgin in the Temple* (Fig. 3), a canvas which still graces the wall for which it was created between 1534 and 1538, the former *sala dell'albergo* of the Scuola Grande di Santa Maria della Carità, it is the strong assertion of the picture plane that brings architectural space under strict pictorial control.[4] As Titian's own style loosens, that control is exercised by more overtly painterly means. A colonnade inspired by the Hadrianeum marches into space at the right of his *Martyrdom of Saint Lawrence*, begun a few years after his return from Rome although not installed until 1559, but its spatial thrust is swallowed by the very darkness in which Titian sets the scene – the example of Giorgione is here raised to a new monumentality. So too in the *Annunciation* for San Salvador (c. 1560-65) the colonnade at the left, its spatial extension already blunted by the radical foreshortening of the low perspective, is thoroughly obliterated by the great glory of heaven that

3. Titian, "Presentation of the Virgin in the Temple,"
Gallerie dell'Accademia, Venice

painted for Santa Maria delle Grazie in Milan in the 1540s, now in the Louvre (Fig. 4), space is created essentially by dynamic figural contrapposto, the violent opposition of limbs and bodies coming to focus on the suffering figure of Christ. Architecture here, massively rusticated and set absolutely parallel to the picture plane, serves as a coordinate field against which is measured the diagonal spatial energy of the dramatic action. As the leading figure at the right initiates the movement into the picture, so the darkness of the imperially crowned opening extends that spatial momentum into the background, a depth reflecting our own space on this side of the plane.

Toward the very end of his career, Titian returned to the composition, in a canvas, today in Munich, that was probably left unfinished in the studio at the time of his death (Fig. 5). Although the basic design is retained, the very manner of execution effectively transposes the theme to another mode. The initial physicality of the conception has been muted; the clearly defined forms of figures and architecture now participate in the larger order of individual marks, a surface network of brush strokes, of broken touches of color. And yet out of that fabric emerges a spatial unity and conviction, an atmospheric space, half-hidden in shadow; out of that darkness the substance itself of thick impasto, highlighting form, is sufficient to declare the materiality of objects only suggestively rendered.

Although the Munich *Crowning with Thorns* is clearly an unfinished canvas, the aesthetic self-sufficiency of such radical painterly expression was evidently fully appreciated in the Cinquecento. There is no more eloquent contemporary witness to this than Giorgio Vasari. In his perceptive distinction between Titian's earlier and later styles, the Aretine critic observes that whereas the early works are painted "with a certain fineness and incredible diligence and can be viewed both from close up and from afar," the later paintings "are executed in bold strokes broadly applied in great patches [macchie], in such a manner that they cannot be looked at closely but from a distance appear perfect." He notes that Titian's pictures are "often repainted, gone over and retouched repeatedly." "Carried out in this way," he concludes, "the method is judicious, beautiful, and magnificent,

explodes above: light itself, realized in the substance of paint, triumphs over rendered architecture. Just such painterly substance – the articulated strokes of Titian's brush, undermining the precision of architectural line – comes increasingly to determine pictorial structure and space in Titian's later work.

That development can be conveniently gauged by following Titian's later modification of his own compositions, such as the *Crowning of Thorns*. In the panel he

4. Titian, *"Crowning with Thorns," Musée du Louvre, Paris*
5. Titian, *"Crowning of Thorns," Alte Pinakothek, Munich*

because the pictures seem to come alive....[5]

It was Pietro Aretino who first celebrated in Titian's brush "the idea of a new nature," and the notion became something of a commonplace in Cinquecento criticism, a ready tag for commenting on the master's painting. Nonetheless, like all such *topoi*, it epitomized a certain truth: Titian's brush did indeed seem to create another nature, a world at once pictorial and substantial.[6]

In the 1530s when the notion began to circulate, Titian's painting was still mimetically referential, that is, its primary goal was to evoke an objective reality beyond itself – our world of solid objects located in coordinated space. By the end of his career, as his painting became more open and suggestive, its mimetic operations assumed a different kind of reality, at once more visually impressionistic and more immediately tactile.[7] The substance of his impasto, the textures of brushwork and woven canvas, the unifying harmony of glazes present a surface of direct sensation. The touch of the brush and, indeed, of the artist's own fingers presents us with a new reality that we readily accept and engage. Just as Giorgione's tonalism had seduced us into participation so, on an infinitely grander scale, Titian's complex surfaces invite us to project our own imagination, to complete their incompleteness.[8] Form and space fuse in a common experience, each confirming the reality of the other – perhaps nowhere more eloquently than in the *Pietà* that the painter evidently intended for his own tomb.

Pictorial space for Titian finally becomes a function of his brush. The continuous fabric of broken touches that run across the most magnificent of his late canvases – the *Flaying of Marsyas*' is the prime example[9] – moves with apparent indiscrimination between solid and void, form and space. But we become sensitive to the inflections of this rugged weave; in our necessarily immediate engagement of this textured surface, we learn to make distinctions, to separate flesh from fur, leaf from bark, to distinguish proximate object and distant horizon. Titian teaches us – as he taught his contemporaries – to read his pictorial language and hence to live in his pictorial space.

[1] For the early dating of the *Saint Mark Altarpiece*, more often assigned to 1511, and the expressive function of shadow in the painting, see D. Rosand, *Titian*, New York, 1978, 68.

[2] Fuller analysis of Titian's Frari altarpieces *in situ* will be found in D. Rosand, *Painting in Cinquecento Venice: Titian, Veronese, Tintoretto*, rev. ed., New Haven and London, 1985, chap. 2: "Titian and the Challenge of the Altarpiece". On the patronage and iconography of this rich complex, see especially Rona Goffan, *Piety and Patronage in Renaissance Venice: Bellini, Titian, and the Franciscans*, New Haven and London, 1986. For the x-radiography of the *Madonna di Ca' Pesaro*: Francesco Valcanover, "La Pala Pesaro" (con note tecniche di Lorenzo Lazzarini), *Quaderni della Soprintendenza ai Beni Artistici e Storici di Venezia*, no. 8, 1979, 57-71.

[3] Sebastiano Serlio, *Regole generali di architetture sopra le cinque maniere de gli edifici*, Venice, 1537, 111.

[4] Rosand, *Painting in Cinquecento Venice*, chap. 3: "Titian's *Presentation of the Virgin in the Temple* and the Scuola della Carità".

[5] Giorgio Vasari, *Le vite de' più eccellenti pittori, scultori ed architettori* (1568), ed. Milanesi, Florence, 1878-1885, VII, 452.

[6] For further references and discussion, see Mina Gregori, "Tiziano e l'Aretino," in *Tiziano a il Manierismo europeo*, ed. Rodolfo Pallucchini, Florence, 1978, 271-306; Franco Bernabei, "Tiziano e Ludovico Dolce," in *ibid.*, 307-37, and David Rosand, "Titian and the Critical Tradition," in *Titian: His World and His Legacy*, ed. D. Rosand, New York, 1982, 1-39.

[7] Reducing Theodor Hetzer's six phase development of Titian's art to three, Erwin Panofsky, *Problems in Titian, Mostly Iconographic*, New York, 1969, 16-26, has suggested a sequence from "object color" to "picture color" to "space color," cf. Hetzer, *Tizian: Geschichte seiner Farbe*, Frankfurt am Main, 1935, esp. 79-83.

[8] I have more fully discussed "The Stroke of the Brush" and its implications in *The Meaning of the Mark: Leonardo and Titian* (The Franklin D. Murphy Lectures: Spencer Museum of Art), Lawrence, Kansas, 1988, 49-93.

[9] Despite the signature and the incredibly fine finish of the crowns, Charles Hope has suggested that this canvas is in fact unfinished: *The Genius of Venice 1500-1600*, exh. cat., ed. Jane Martineau and Charles Hope, London, 1983, 228. For a refutation, see my "Exhibition Review: The Genius of Venice," *Renaissance Quarterly*, XXXVIII, 1985, 196f.

Antonio Paolucci
THE PORTRAITS OF TITIAN

Almost sixty years separate Titian's *Portrait of a Man* (the so-called *Ariosto*) in the National Gallery, London, and his *Jacopo Strada*, now in Vienna, dated 1568. This broad span of time frames Titian's career as a portrait painter. About one hundred portraits are extant, making it possible to follow both the stylistic and human progress of the artist (the development of his art, but also the events, meetings and successes of his life) as well as the course of Italian and European history in the sixteenth century, exemplified through the images of the protagonists of political, religious and cultural power.

This aspect – that of tracking Titian's portraiture as a historical reportage of the century – has always fascinated critics, and with good reason, for as Vasari himself stated "there was almost no famous lord, nor prince, nor great woman, who was not painted by Titian."[1] Doubtless some of Titian's portraits are historical documents in the highest but also concrete sense of the word. The Capodimonte triple portrait of *Pope Paul III Farnese with his Nephews Alessandro and Ottavio* illuminates the personality of that Pope and the politics of the Holy See in the mid-1540s further and better than any document or contemporary account written by some ambassador. In the same way Charles V, mounted on horseback in his armor, alone on the Battlefield of Muhlberg, presents us with a perfect image, eloquent in its frankness, as effective as any political manifesto of the concept of absolute monarchy predominant at that time at the Catholic court of the Hapsburgs.

Behind his extraordinary gift as an historian (as a witness and interpreter of the reality of his time, through the vehicle of his portraiture), lies Titian's sublime ability to penetrate to the real character of his models, which was perhaps his greatest gift.

Aretino wrote of Titian's "sense of things in his brush" (VI, 314). But for Titian the "things" to be understood and represented were not only the physical semblance or the psychological peculiarities of the sitter, nor the various objects and props – clothes, jewels, armor – which had their own role and meaning. One has the impression that for him the "things" to be depicted, to the same degree of intensity, included the social rank, cultural or political standing of the sitter and in a more general sense, the "ideal" persona of the individual, the

collection of all meanings that constituted the sitter's identity for us and also for himself.

Thus Titian's *Pietro Aretino* at the Pitti is more than a veristic or psychological likeness "which breathes, whose pulse throbs and spirit moves in the way I do in life," as Aretino himself wrote to the Grand duke Cosimo de' Medici.[2] It is also "the terrible wonder" of an intellectual and moral temperament implacably revealed: a personality, in this case, of emotional violence, of an irreverent and corrosive intelligence.

Titian's portrait of *Francis I* of France, which he painted without ever having seen his model in real life, reveals a splendid image of pride and bursting vitality, whilst that of Isabella d'Este, painted in homage to a splendor already vanished, records forever the beauty of the Marchioness of Mantua (by then in her old age and certainly no longer beautiful), the "ideal" character of a haughty and intelligent loveliness with which she graced her century. Yet again, in one of the last portraits, that of *Jacopo Strada*, now in the Kunsthistorisches Museum, Vienna, Titian captured the "ideal" character of the antique dealer, "that profession of intrigue, lies and prevarication, which is the high commerce of art." Titian seems truly to have caught his model "in the act of choosing the opportune moment to insinuate himself into his client's trust, with an expression that amounts to an emblem of the trade."[3]

The incredible success of Titian as a portrait painter in the high society of his time can be explained largely by his capacity to divine unerringly and represent vividly the "ideal persona" of his sitters, without, however, distorting either the physical or the psychological likeness of the personage, but rather exalting and emphasizing the one and the other in equal proportion. And so one is justified in the belief that in Titian's portraits the pope and the emperor, the doge and the Marquis of Mantua, recognized themselves not only in the flesh, but also in the guise of all that they represented.

Thus it could happen (and it is one of Titian's merits that he was too objective to flatter his sitters even in the most official circumstances) that the unmasking of the ideal character of the sitter could be so effective and unexpected as to risk brutality and so create some embarrassment. This is the case, for example in the famous canvas

of *Pope Paul III Farnese with his Nephews* and the *Pierluigi Farnese*: the latter is enclosed in his armor, his face devastated by disease but imprinted with fervent resolution, an image full of drama that is "almost Shakespearean in its intensity" (Pallucchini). On no occasion did Titian's portraits fail in verisimilitude, even when pitilessly testifying to a reality not just physical and psychological but also spiritual and ideal.

However to be drawn into the "things," that is inside the skin and even the emotions and thoughts of his sitters, was as nothing compared to Titian's marvelous capacity to place himself at the same time and without contradiction on a place that was completely detached from them.

Indeed we could say that "his exceptionally acute and profound perception" of the upper classes and of high culture, was possible, as Zeri has written, by the fact "that the painter had no illusions about his own status, he was perfectly aware of his position as an outsider." Although his profession obliged him to frequent the great of this earth and even for long periods the court of the Emperor, the culture and habits of such elevated circles remained foreign to his mentality, which was that of a skillful artisan, a pragmatic bourgeois. It should be recalled that we would not have his portrait of *Pope Paul III Farnese with his Nephews*, perhaps the most extraordinary and revealing political document that has come

1. *Titian, "Portrait of a Man (L'Ariosto)." National Gallery, London*
2. *Titian, "Portrait of Federico Gonzaga." Museo del Prado, Madrid*
3. *Titian, "Portrait of Pietro Aretino." Galleria Palatina di Palazzo Pitti, Florence*

ANTONIO PAOLUCCI

down to us in Western art (more important even, as Pallucchini has observed, than Goya's portrait of the *Family of Charles* IV) had Titian not journeyed to Rome. He was attracted there no longer by the fascination of the antique, nor by the fame of the "divine" Michelangelo, but by the hope of obtaining an ecclesiastical benefice for his son Pomponio. And yet it was exactly this sense of being an outsider – in the mediocre and jealously guarded arena of family affections and economic interests, in the diversity of habits and cultural interests – that allowed Titian to observe his sitters with detached curiosity and total objectivity, which allowed him to produce an uninterrupted series of masterpieces.

In fact the qualitative level of Titian's portraits is consistently high. This undisputable fact should serve as a fundamental instrument for those who would try their skills on attributional questions, an understandably crowded and dangerous field. Perhaps the various crises (of mannerism and of the counter-Reformation) that Titian triumphantly overcame in his long life may have caused some moments of uncertainty, some partial relaxing of tension among the many works of his vast catalogue, but this was manifested (if at all) in the history paintings, sacred or profane, and never in his autograph portraits. It is worth repeating that these always maintained an exceptionally high level of expressive felicity whatever cultural influences were in fashion at that time and whatever the consequent changes of style.

If one were to attempt a synthesis (necessarily rapid and touching only upon the salient episodes) of Titian's portraits, it is useful to return to Vasari. After a meeting with the elderly painter in Venice in 1566, Vasari was convinced of two things: that Titian began his career as a portrait painter, and that he was, at the beginning, in this genre, almost a twin of his master Giorgione.

The attribution to Titian of the famous *Concert* in the Pitti (see cat. no. 3) is no longer doubted, nor is the attribution to Giorgione around 1500 of the equally famous Pitti *Three Ages of Man* (an attribution resoundingly confirmed by recent conservation as well as by Mauro Lucco's thorough essay published for the occasion). This lends weight to Vasari's affirmation and illustrates the way Titian opted to break with the Giorgionesque mood.[4]

4. Titian, "Portrait of Charles V on Horseback." Museo del Prado, Madrid
5. Titian, "Portrait of Philip II." Museo del Prado, Madrid

Indeed he did so from the beginning, deploying an extraordinary spiritual energy. It is enough to observe the fervent sensibility and compassion which lights the face of the pianist in the Pitti *Concert* (c. 1510). "In place of Giorgione's pathos, Titian countered with an almost conscious excess of realism."[5] From the first portraits he tended to construct, as Burckhardt claimed, "grandiose beings." If we want to identify the exact point at which the sublime and absorbed vagueness of Giorgione gives way to the fearless affirmation of pure realistic energy, we should refer to the altarpiece of the sacristy of the Salute (c. 1516, see cat. no. 5) and compare the two saints on the right with those on the left – already "natural portraits," as Vasari observed.

The portraits painted by Titian in his youth follow this same pattern: the "modern" protagonists of the frescoes of the Scuola del Santo, the *Ariosto* and the *Schiavona* in the National Gallery, London, up to the *Knight of Malta* in the Uffizi, datable to c. 1515, to the *Violinist* of the Galleria Spada, Rome, the Halifax *Man with a Glove* and the *Officer* in the Frick Collection, New York, the last two datable soon after 1515.

The Giorgionesque composition, together with the psychological and sentimental atmosphere that derives from it, is still substantially present (the *Knight of Malta* illustrates this exactly) but with an increasingly decisive affirmation of the individuality of character and spirit of the sitter.

As Ballarin has noted, Titian, in these early works, was trying to represent a momentary inertia within a movement, offering us the figure with the maximum openness and candor: "the space of the painting is the space created by the expansion of the chromatic planes which compose the human figure, from the breathing of the skin, the folds of a shirt, or the way the hair falls."[6] In this way (we can cite the *Ariosto* or the *Schiavona* in London) the vitality of the sitter becomes the dominant element in the portrait, freed from the romantic Giorgionesque manner and asserting itself with an unashamed authority.

The so-called *Doctor of Parma* in Vienna of c. 1518, "built up from a few gradations of color between the shade and the light shining on the grey plumes, in which the psychological expression is rendered more intense,"[7]

is perhaps the last tribute to the introspective and melancholy mood of the Giorgionesque tradition. Gradually Titian did away with the usual iconographic props (perspective framing, parapets, etcetera), the portrait now takes up the entire field, giving it strength in both a formal plastic sense as well as in a chromatic one.

From the Louvre *Man with a Glove* (c. 1523, see cat. no. 17) to the Pitti *Vincenzo Mosti* (see cat. no. 16), to the *Gentleman with the Falcon* in Omaña, and *Federico Gonzaga* in the Prado (1528), the portraits of the 1520s are evidence of the progressive conquest of what would be the most admired quality of Titian's portraits and the most important reason for his resounding success among the high society of his age. I refer to the splendid *disinvoltura* of his portraits, to the harmonious naturalness with which the figures occupy the space and present themselves to the spectators.

In this sense the portrait of *Federico Gonzaga* constitutes the point of departure for the great production of the following years and decades. In the easy elegance with which the Marquis of Mantua presents himself before our eyes is revealed the ideal character of Federico at that period: the tranquil dominion of legitimate power, a lively yet harmonious nature, an amiable gravity, a promising and pleasure-seeking youth, not, however, without a sense of responsibility and quiet determination.

As we have already noted, the official recognition of the role of Titian as a painter of the powerful dates from 1533 after Charles v, having posed for him at Bologna in a famous canvas that today hangs in the Prado, bestowed on him various honorary titles and above all entrusted him with the political image of himself, his family and his court. How Titian fulfilled this exacting role can be seen in the imperial portraits painted partly in Italy, and partly on his visits to Augsburg in 1548 and 1550-01. From the already mentioned portraits of Charles v and his dog, "the prototype of that series of court portraits that Antonio Moro, after the middle of the century, would preserve forever in his emblematic abstraction"[8] to the *Emperor on Horseback on the Battle Field of Muhlberg* (1548), to *Philip II* in Cincinnatti and in the Prado (1551), the imperial portraits interpret the ideology of power with such vividness that even today we cannot invent an iconography that better explains Catholic authority in Europe in the sixteenth century.

However, it is the same painter who, describing the family of the emperor, or that of the pope (the famous Farnese paintings were executed between 1542 and 1546), knew how to interpret his century with the unflinching objectivity of a great historian who also has that capacity to produce images of his contemporaries which seem almost to have been painted to give him and us pure visual pleasure, something our senses can enjoy. These include the *Cardinal Ippolito de' Medici* (c. 1533) a dandy, elegantly satisfied with himself in his purple velvet Hungarian costume, highlighted with touches of gold and red; the Pitti *La Bella* and the *Young Girl* of Vienna (c. 1533-37) whose poetic flavor lies in the contrast between female nudity, painted with an affectionate naturalness, and the warmth of the fur.

The Pitti *Ippolito Riminaldi* (c. 1545) is a painting whose intensely evocative fascination is more explicit in the various names that the literature has bestowed on it: the *Young Englishman*, the *Gentleman with the Blue-Green Eyes*.[9]

Modern historians cannot refer to the intrigues of Pope Paul III without citing the Capodimonte painting, nor recall the horrors of religious wars without visualizing the tragic figure of Charles V, victorious at the Battle of Muhlberg. Without the Pitti *La Bella*, without *Aretino*, or the *Young Englishman*, or the *Votive Portrait of the Vendramin Family* in London (c. 1550), our aesthetic, intellectual, and spiritual image of this great Italian century would be deprived of its fundamental symbols. We have already stated that all of Titian's portraits were of extremely high quality. The mannerist crisis that caused the uncertainty and unresolved tensions in other genres of his artistic production served only to make his portraits more successful. We can even say that the new language of Titian developed and became more refined in his portraits of the 1540s. In effect, "in the portraits the formal structure of Salviatiesque mannerism is stripped of its ornamental aspects resolving itself into a quality of dynamism which is felt as the spiritual energy of the sitter himself,"[10] while there was an increasing tendency, from the time of the Farnese painting portrait on, to favor "an impressionistic quality of painterliness

effected with rapid and insistent brushstrokes in which the form is devalued in favor of light."[11]

During the 1550s Titian continued with regularity to portray great men; amongst these were *Cardinal Cristoforo Madruzzo* (1552) in the museum of San Paolo, the papal legate *Beccadelli*, today in the Uffizi (1552), *Doge Francesco Venier*, magnificent for the crackling quality of its chromatic impasto (1555, Thyssen-collection, Lugano, Bornemisza, see cat. no. 50). However a new class of sitters began to appear more frequently, requiring a less severe image, lending itself to a more cordial confidentiality, suitable for unconventional presentation.

On the other hand the loose and dramatic paint of Titian's late period, the luminous, coloristic "flagellation" with which he feverishly assaulted the plastic forms, cast in the role of the suffering and the subser-

6. Titian, "Portrait of Jacopo Strada."
Kunsthistorisches Museum, Vienna

vient, were better adapted to a more "impressionistic" portraiture. In these later years Titian painted some of the greatest portraits of all time: *Fabrizio Salvaresio*, Vienna (1558), the *Portrait of a Man* in Baltimore (1561), the *Gentleman with a Flute* in Detroit (1561-62), *Jacopo Strada* (1567-68) in Vienna, the *Self-Portrait* in the Prado (1570, see cat. no. 64) that Adolfo Venturi has described splendidly as "a specter, shadowy and stiffened in his inner life of a seer."[12] These works seem to leap across an entire century and stand comparison with the very best portraits by Rembrandt.

[1] G. Vasari, *Le Vite*, VII (ed. Milanesi 1881), 450.

[2] Taken from Pietro Aretino's letter to Cosimo de' Medici of September 1545. Aretino's comment regarding the realism of the sitters is well known, a comment inspired by cool irony and touch of cynicism typical of him: "e se più fussero stati gli scudi che gliene ho conti, invero i drappi sarieno lucidi, morbidi e rigidi, come il dasegno raso velluto e broccato" (P. Aretino, 1538 ed. Pertile-Camesasca, 1957-60], II, 1957, 107, no. CCLXV). For the *Portrait of Pietro Aretino*, see in particular the exhibition catalogue *Tiziano nelle Gallerie Fiorentine*, Florence, 1978, 31-36.

[3] F. Zeri, *La percezione visiva degli italiani*, Turin 1989, 25.

[4] For the Pitti *Concert* see *Tiziano nelle Gallerie Fiorentine*, 1978, 196-208. For the *Three Ages of Man*, see the recent catalogue published after conservation of the painting by the Soprintendenza per i Beni Artistici e Storici of Florence, and in particular the essay by Mauro Lucco included in the catalogue: "Le cosidette 'Tre età dell'uomo' di Palazzo Pitti," Florence, 1989, 11-28.

[5] R. Pallucchini, *Tiziano*, Florence, 1969, I, 12.

[6] A. Ballarin, *Tiziano*, Florence, 1968, 6-7.

[7] F. Valcanover, *Tutta la pittura di Tiziano*, Milan, 1960, I, 27.

[8] R. Pallucchini, *Tiziano*, 1969, 22-23.

[9] For the critical fortune of this famous portrait and also for the various proposals regarding the identity of the sitter, see the exhaustive entry in *Tiziano nelle Gallerie Fiorentine*, 1978, 285-89, and the relevant entry in this catalogue.

[10] A. Ballarin, *Tiziano*, 1968, 22-3.

[11] R. Pallucchini, *Tiziano*. Lectures held at the Faculty of Letters of the University of Bologna, 1952-53, 1953-54, ed. by O. Fanti and L. Mandelli Puglioli, Bologna, 1954, 211.

[12] A. Venturi, *Storia dell'Arte*, III, IX, Rome 1928, p. IX.

Giovanna Nepi Scirè

RECENT CONSERVATION
OF TITIAN'S PAINTINGS IN VENICE

Between 1970 and 1990 the Soprintendenza ai Beni Artistici e Storici of Venice has carried out a major program of conservation of the paintings of Titian, in addition to the treatment in 1974 of Titian's great panel of the *Assumption* in the Frari, which is extensively described elsewhere.[1] This timely program has safeguarded the masterpieces and endowed them with a new legibility that has opened the way for the revision of our critical assessments. Furthermore, cleaning has frequently brought forward new data concerning the history of the paintings and even thrown light on the creative process itself.

Almost all the key moments in Titian's extraordinary career are represented in this campaign, from the youthful altarpiece of *Saint Mark Enthroned with Saints* now in the Basilica of Santa Maria della Salute, to the lunette of the *Madonna and Child with Two Angels* and *Saint Christopher* in the Palazzo Ducale, the *Pesaro Madonna* in the Frari, the *Annunciation* in the Scuola di San Rocco, the *Presentation of the Virgin* in the Scuola della Carità, the *Pentecost* and the ceiling canvases for Santo Spirito in Isola, the decorative panels from the ceiling of the *albergo* of the Scuola di San Giovanni Evangelista, *Saint John the Baptist* in the Accademia, *Saint James* from San Lio, *Saint John the Almsgiver* in the church of the same name, the *Martyrdom of Saint Lawrence* in the Gesuiti, the *Annunciation* of San Salvador, *Doge Antonio Grimani Kneeling before Faith* from the Sala delle Quattro Porte in the Palazzo Ducale, down to his last work the, *Pietà* in the Accademia, Venice.

The *Saint Mark Enthroned with Saints*, originally in the church of Santo Spirito in Isola, was most probably painted with sound technique. Titian was "accustomed to take care in his paintings and to use good pigments and oils."[2] The latter is especially true of his panels, as testified by a friar of Santo Spirito on 22 March 1545, during the suit brought by Titian against the monastery: "[the altarpiece] has been there quite some time and has not suffered at all from humidity,"[3] not even when, in lieu of the unfinished *Pentecost*, it was temporarily placed on the high altar probably on the north side of the church. The problems must have begun in 1656 with its transfer to a totally different micro-climate (the large Sacristy of the recently completed Basilica della Salute)

and with subsequent clumsy restorations. In a letter to the Provveditore al Sal of 17 August 1787, Pietro Edwards complained of the painting's "extreme disorder" and declined to make any forecast on the outcome of restoration, even if the "sufficient richness" of the original paint gave cause for optimism.[4] The restoration was entrusted to Giuseppe Bertani and Giuseppe Diziani.

In the course of the nineteenth century the altarpiece was restored several more times. On 7 May 1849 it was consigned to Paolo Fabris in view of "the threat of total ruin." The task was seen as particularly arduous both for the "daubing '*all'antico*' that had been given it" and for the general lifting of the paint surface, to the point where the restorer was urged to work with the utmost scrupulousness and without time limits. But even this program was too optimistic, and on 8 June 1851 it had to be admitted that, stripped of its old repainting, the painting required to be "returned to that... harmony which now of necessity it lacks, certain parts being completely without paint which had previously been muddied over by clumsy brushes."[5] The 'painter-restorer,' despite his lack of foresight, was given an additional fee for the reintegration of the surface,[6] and was urged to return the altarpiece, which he did on 8 October of the same year. On 25 January 1882, the Ispettore delle Gallerie, Guglielmo Botti, noted that the painting had "become very opaque, and, in various places the paint had lifted, and under the feet of Saints Cosmas and Damian was even missing entirely."[7] Fabris was charged once again, by the Accademia commission, to consolidate the paint, "replacing it in those parts in which it had fallen off, cleaning lightly the panel of dust, freshening the varnish."[8] The work was to be carried out *in situ* to avoid further paint losses during transport.

The Minister of Education advised furthermore that the restoration should be in conformity with the government circular 'Riparazione ai Dipinti' of 30 January 1877, concealing under an ostensible bureaucratic aloofness a genuine concern for the suitability of previous and subsequent interventions. Indeed already in 1890 Botti observed that the panel was subject to: "such movement as exposed the splitting of the boards,"[9] a condition that worsened the following year, to the point where in 1892

the picture was taken in hand for "the repair of its paint," with carpentry work contracted to Alvise Socal.[10]

The most recent restoration, beyond having taken care of the removal of a thick coat of whitewash on the back, which obstructed the penetration of ultra-violet rays (Fig. 1), saw the elimination of all the rigid struts and cleats, integrating the lacunae with inserts of seasoned poplar. Despite its very damaged condition, above all in the sky, where there were six layers of repaint, the almost total loss of the blue robe of St Mark, with seven layers of repaint, and the irreversible alteration of some of the pigments, the work has regained an unhoped-for reso-

nance of pictorial texture, re-establishing those coloristic qualities that were once perceived by Boschini.[11]

The lunette of the *Madonna and Child with Two Angels* in the Palazzo Ducale, today in the rooms of the Magistrato alle Leggi, was described "at the foot of the stairs of the palace" by Ridolfi who added: "the painting as if super-human has been treated well by time."[12] In 1809 a commission composed of Diedo, Selva, Cicognara, Borsato, the Abbot Morelli, David Rossi and Edwards was given the responsibility of surveying the mural paintings of Venice, following the shocking destruction by French troops of Titian's frescoes in the Chapel of San Nicolò.[13]

Edwards confessed that he was unfamiliar with "those mysterious and secret methods practiced elsewhere whereby fresco paintings are transferred to canvas" and that he had "never witnessed any such experiments." Even so, he knew well the procedure for detaching frescoes whole, and would have done so for *Saint Christopher*, the only surviving fresco by Titian in the Palazzo Ducale other than the *Madonna*, had it not proved too difficult to cut the wall, thus causing the abandonment of the project.[14] It was recommended therefore that those parts of both paintings that were threatening to fall be secured, that the surfaces be cleaned and revived ("rianimare"), that the losses be repaired *a secco*, and finally that the frescoes be protected as necessary with barriers. Giuseppe Baldassini was given the work.

Saint Christopher, narrowly escaping such drastic surgery, is now the only fresco painting by Titian still *in situ* in Venice.[15] During conservation in 1986 some detached fragments of *intonaco* were laid down and the accumulated dust and grime were removed.[16]

Titian painted the head of Saint Christopher and most of the Child in two days, and the body of the Saint and the landscape, in two sessions, during a third *giornata* (fig. 3). He traced the composition directly onto the damp plaster without the aid of cartoons, as one can see from the rounded furrows evident in a raking light; nevertheless, in the execution of the painting he ignored the tracing, testifying once more to his remarkable creative freedom (fig. 4).

The *Madonna and Child* was described in 1853 by

1. *Titian, "Saint Mark Enthroned with Saints." Basilica della Salute, Venice. X-ray reconstruction*

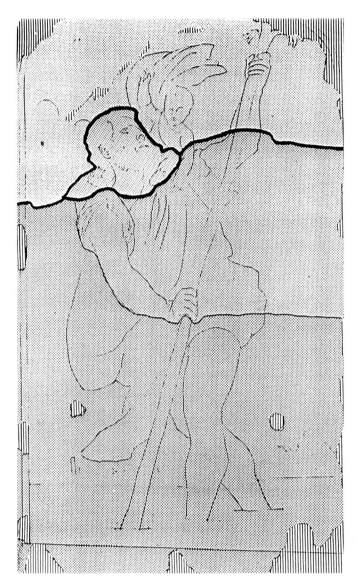

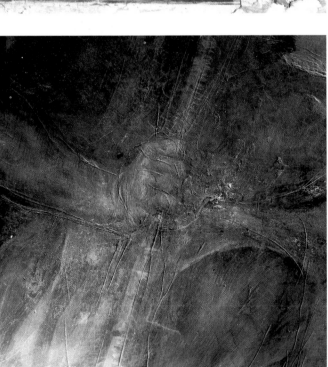

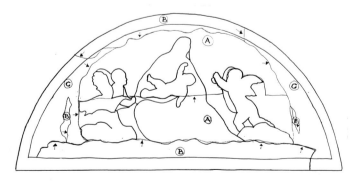

2. Titian, "Saint Christopher." Palazzo Ducale, Venice, detail
showing red threads in the "intonaco"
4. Titian, "Saint Christopher," detail in raking light

3. Graphic-showing the daylines of the fresco of "Saint Christopher"
5. Graphic showing daylines and reconstructed section of the
"Madonna and Child with Two Angels." Palazzo Ducale, Venice
A: original intonaco. B: non-original intonaco. C: old intonaco

Despite its grave deterioration, owed probably to its brutal detachment, the beauty of fresco, refreshed by the most recent cleaning remains.[19]

Although already published, it is worth reproducing here the composite x-radiograph (fig. 6) of the *Pesaro Madonna* in the Frari, carried out by Titian between 1519 and 1526, which documents the laying-in of two different architectural settings, previous to the final one.[20]

The *Annunciation* in the Scuola di San Rocco, oddly, was left untouched by any significant restoration before 1920. In the latter year Luigi Betto lined the work,[21] thus concealing the back of the original canvas on which the drawing of the Virgin could be seen, together with some sketches. Relined in 1935, and again in 1973, the painting was carefully cleaned on the latter occasion.[22] Under a thick blackish layer emerged an unsuspected blue in the sky, while the landscape, the architecture and the wings of the angels became more clearly defined. Unfortunately the mantle of the Virgin, perhaps owing to excessive heat, has suffered an irreversible alteration, from blue to black. Infrared reflectography revealed a *pentimento* in the wing of the angel (figs. 7, 8), and the way in which the cloth had been painted over an already-finished balustrade (figs. 9, 10), itself initially conceived at a lower level (figs. 11, 12), while the sewing box had been added over the pavement (figg. 13, 14). Small *pentimenti* were apparent from close examination of the zone of the columns and of the right-hand building, which must have been shifted. Without its brownish repaints, the painting has acquired a clearer and sharper tonality, which is better suited to a dating late in Titian's youthful period.

The restoration of the large canvas of the *Presentation of the Virgin in the Temple*, painted between 21 August 1534 and 6 March 1539 for the *albergo* of the Scuola di Santa Maria della Carità (today part of the Gallerie dell'Accademia), was of particular importance.[23] Exhaustive examination with infrared and ultraviolet rays was carried out (fig. 15), and these confirmed, together with the analysis of the paint layers, the generally good condition of the painting. However, a zone on the extreme right, running the full height of the painting and 62 cm wide, was very seriously damaged, probably by the

Zanotto as "so degenerated from its original splendour because of the humidity of the place and of the abandonment in which it is left, that it will certainly be lost entirely if the providential hand of he who presently holds the rudder of State does not hasten to rescue it from the damage it has suffered."[17] But the rescue was put off for several decades. Only in 1895 did the regional office for the conservation of monuments turn to Stefanoni of Bergamo to transfer the fresco to canvas and only in 1899 was the work actually carried out.[18]

6. Titian, "Pesaro Madonna." Basilica dei Frari, Venice. X-ray reconstruction
7-14. Titian, "Annunciation." Scuola di San Rocco, Venice.
Infra-red reflectography, details of angel, the drapery over the
balustrade and the basket as compared with painting

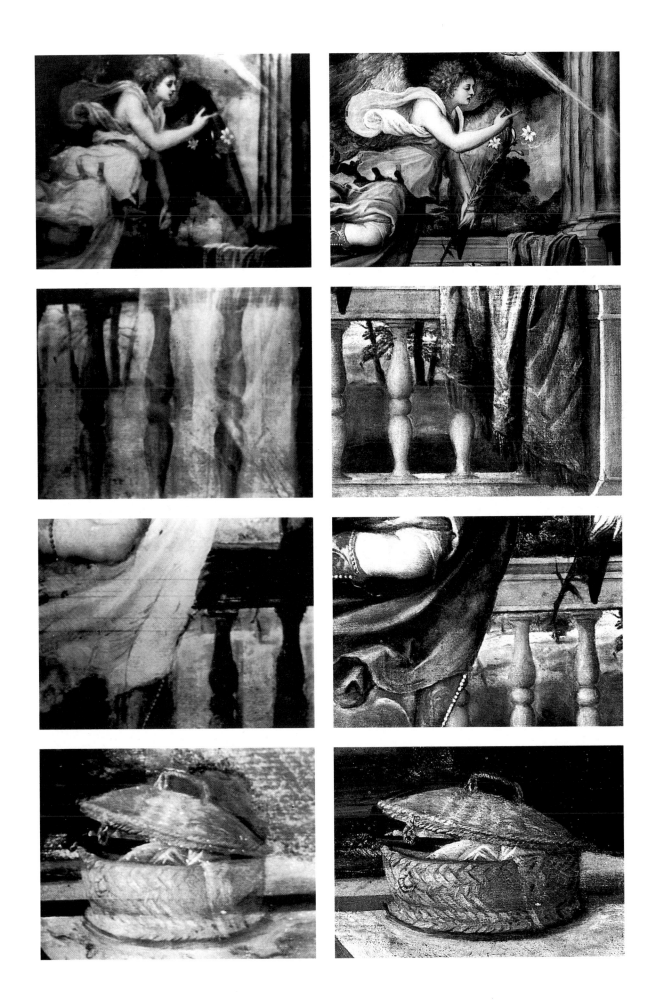

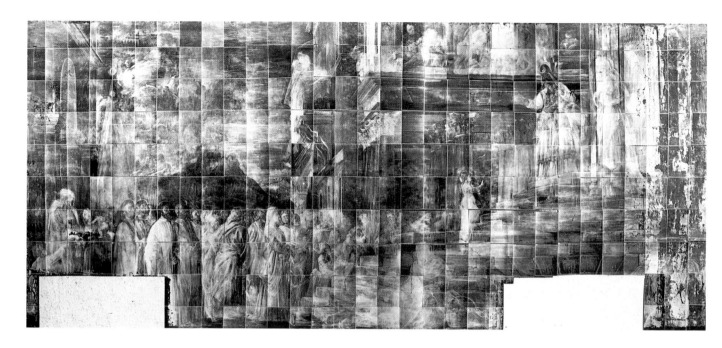

15. Titian, "Presentation of the Virgin in the Temple." Gallerie
dell'Accademia, Venice. X-ray reconstruction
16. Titian, "Presentation of the Virgin in the Temple," x-ray detail,
with pentimento of the first window from the left (a), compared
with the painting (b)

dripping of rainwater. It seems likely that this zone had probably already been ruined at an early date, judging both from the existence of a canvas insert, probably eighteenth-century, on the upper edge, and from its exclusion, together with the torso, from an engraving by Andrea Zucchi of c. 1720. It reappears in its present state in a print by Antonio Viviani of 1833, five years after restoration by Sebastiano Santi. It is rather likely, therefore, that what we see today is non-original. Even so it probably resembles what Titian himself painted and would have shared in the iconography of the painting as a whole.[24] X-rays revealed a different profile of the original borderline. The composite x-radiograph clarified the genesis of the work itself, in which the architectural setting was originally projected about 20 cm lower. The *pentimento* was made by the time the artist had already painted the left window where two completely finished female figures appear (figs. 16 a-b); this was subsequently painted over with two new on-lookers, a man and a woman, at a higher level. In place of the sculptured torso, Titian had foreseen a bas-relief or a mural with centaurs (figs. 18, 19), similar perhaps to his own frescoes on the façade of the Fondaco dei Tedeschi toward the Calle del Buso.

The cleaning revealed the exceptional chromatic quality of the painting, and the perfect balance between the architecture and the landscape and of both with the isocephalic procession. The unity of the work, in which a traditional narrative in the Venetian Quattrocento is given new life, derives above all from the recovery of the resonance of Titian's color.

For the high altar of Santo Spirito in Isola Titian painted a *Pentecost*. This venture was to give him much trouble and would be the cause of litigation with the monastery, as we have seen.[25] Commissioned, as we know from the records of the trial, in 1529 or 1530, the altarpiece was for a long period barely sketched by Titian and only in 1541, following pressure from the monks, was it brought to near-completion and mounted on the altar of the church, where Titian went several times to add finishing touches. Inexplicably, either because of its location on the north side of the church or for inherent technical defects (excessive glue in the gesso ground), toward the end of 1543 "the paint began to flake and crack" and

17. Titian, "Presentation of the Virgin in the Temple," detail
Gallerie dell'Accademia, Venice

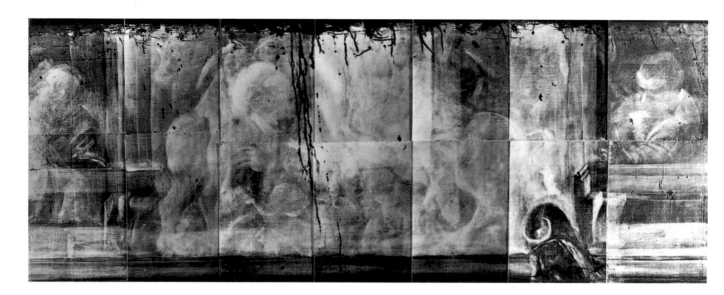

"develop blisters," which Titian attempted to repair *in situ*, scraping down a piece the shape of a "large rhombus" with a knife, then with a handkerchief, and then, infuriated, requesting that it be sent back to his house where he would "sort it out" ("la conzarò"). On 29 May 1545, the lawsuit was in progress, evidently over payment: it is not clear at this point whether the painting was restored, or begun over. As is well known, it was transferred in 1656 to one of the altars of the Basilica of Santa Maria della Salute and enlarged in the lower part with a repetition of the original paving. On 17 August

1787, Edwards, who had removed the picture for restoration, rightly suspected that the lowest part of the pavement was an addition and remarked upon "the harm inflicted on the painting by an old cleaning... the blues which were not bound with white lead are mostly darkened, the greens blackened in the shadows and washed-out in the lights, and the fleshtones undifferentiated and lacklustre, as often can be seen in paintings lacking the final touches. Retouching over abrasion is very frequent... generally speaking this has thoroughly the look of a painting thinly worked originally, consumed

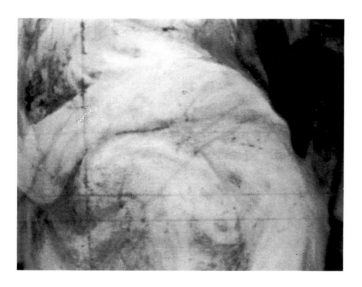

18-19. Titian, "Presentation of the Virgin in the Temple," x-ray detail with pentimento, compared with the painting

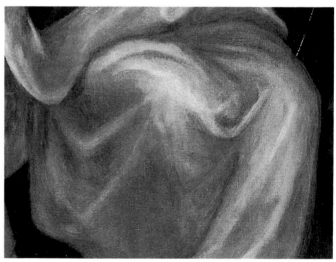

20-21. Titian, "Pentecost." Basilica della Salute, Venice. Infra-red reflectography, detail of the Virgin's dress, compared with the painting

by improper cleanings and oxidised by time... one should not, however, omit to line it even though the original canvas is in very good condition."[26]

Thus we learn that at that time the work had never been lined and the original support was in satisfactory condition. The restoration was conducted by Bertani and Diziani. A century later Crowe and Cavalcaselle complained that the altarpiece was "greatly damaged, especially in the upper part, by repainting."[27] It was lightly cleaned for the 1935 exhibition, while the most recent restoration has left the work in sound condition

and has much improved its appearance and legibility.[28] On this occasion it was possible to document a technique that is rare for Titian: horizontal and vertical lines, revealed by reflectography (figs. 20, 21), used for the purpose of subdividing the pictorial space.

During the trial, it was remarked that "some priors... had had themselves painted on the said altarpiece and others... had had those heads obliterated and had had themselves painted... but when the altarpiece was brought forward none of them were painted thereon."[29] The presence of such *pentimenti* would have confirmed

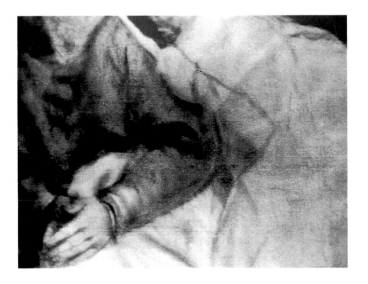

22-23. Titian, "Pentecost," detail of the underdrawing of the arm of the seated apostle to the right of the Virgin, compared with the painting

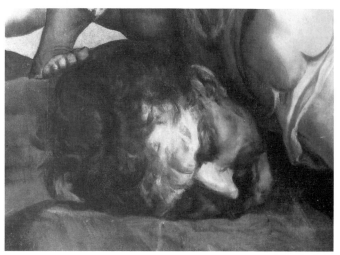

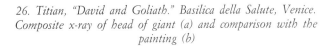

24-25. Titian, "Sacrifice of Abraham" and "Cain Slaying Abel." Basilica della Salute, Venice. Composite x-rays

26. Titian, "David and Goliath." Basilica della Salute, Venice. Composite x-ray of head of giant (a) and comparison with the painting (b)

the identity of the work with the first version, delivered back after repairs. Examination with the reflectography has produced no evidence in this sense, revealing only a change in the profile of the third figure from the left, initially conceived frontally, as well as some scoring (figs. 22, 23). This would tend to favor the hypothesis of a completely new painting. Nevertheless, only a complete composite x-radiograph will settle with certainty this vexed question.[30]

Between 1542 and 1544, Titian also painted the nave ceiling for Santo Spirito, consisting of three large

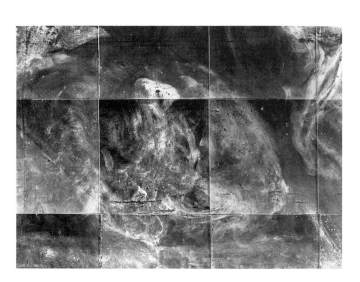

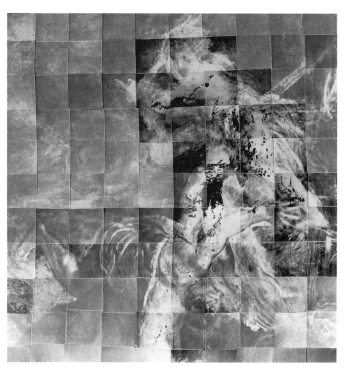

canvases and eight roundels on panel. In 1656 these were shipped together with the others to the Salute. There is no indication that they were restored on this occasion – natural though this might have been. Nevertheless the three central canvases with *David and Goliath*, the *Sacrifice of Abraham*, and *Cain Slaying Abel*, are severely abraded in the skies, which are completely repainted with a non-original configuration of clouds. Traces of Titian's skies are virtually non-existent, as is apparent in the x-rays of the *Sacrifice of Abraham* (fig. 24). Such grave damage all three paintings can be attributed to rainwater or to overzealous cleaning, which has irretrievably altered the azurite, to a much greater degree than is the case for the pigments used for the figures. The fault may be that of a certain Pietro Cardinali, considered disparagingly by Edwards, who on 20 November 1739 completed "the operations on the paintings" of the Salute.[31] Edwards deplored the poor condition of the paintings in 1787.[32] About a century later Crowe and Cavalcaselle denounced the wretched state of the *David and Goliath* in particular, and adding "all the compositions are damaged more or less by old varnishes, which have dimmed and dulled the colours, and taken away their freshness."[33]

The present restoration has secured the adherence of the paint film to the support, reviving the color values of the figures. Work on the eighteenth-century skies was limited to a light cleaning. A consequence of this has

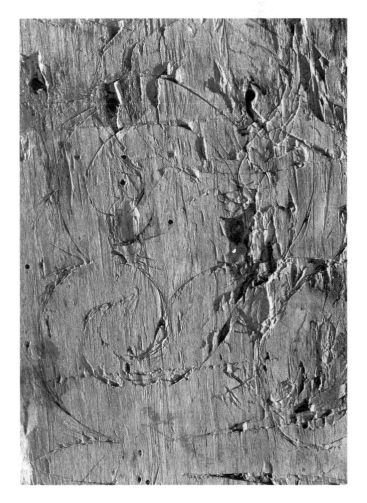

27-28. Titian and workshop, "Symbol of Mark the Evangelist."
Gallerie dell'Accademia, Venice. Composite x-ray, compared with
the painting
29. Titian and workshop, back of the panel "Symbol of Matthew the
Evangelist"

by Titian. The restoration not only made the images more legible but provided interesting details about their gestation. For example, x-rays of the panel with the *Symbol of the Evangelist Mark* show that it was initially conceived with large scrolls of leaves, replaced by a curtain in the completed version (figs. 27, 28). On the verso of the *Evangelist Matthew* a drawing for a frame is engraved (fig. 29), perhaps the same which was to hold the panels in place on the ceiling.

been that the large bodies project unduly toward the spectator, outlined against the formless backgrounds, since the fusion between figure and atmosphere, which so impressed the baroque sensibility, has been irretreivably lost[34] (Figs. 25, 26).

In 1989-90 repairs were also carried out on the panels that once formed part of the decoration the *albergo* of the Scuola di San Giovanni Evangelista, of which the central part was the *Saint John the Evangelist* today in the National Gallery of Art, Washington.[35] These are mainly workshop productions though surely based on a project

In his list of paintings to be consigned to the Gallerie dell'Accademia in 1812 Edwards commented on the *Saint John the Baptist*, formerly in the church of Santa Maria Maggiore: "it has suffered in the past from rubbing and worse still from the changes which were effected by copyists on many occasions." He recalled an excellent restoration of the painting carried out two years previously by Giuseppe Baldassini. Nevertheless it was necessary to intervene again in 1828 when the painting was lined by F. Bianchini,[36] and on 15 April 1846 the Accademia Commission decided that being "darkened

30-31. Titian, "Saint John the Baptist." Gallerie dell'Accademia, Venice. Composite x-ray and infra-red detail of his head

by a yellowish tint, occasioned by poor restoration," it was necessary to proceed "in the era of experience" with its gradual removal. By general consent Giuseppe Gallo Lorenzi was given the work and by 1849 had carried out a "conscientious restoration" ("attento restauro").[37] The recent analysis with ultraviolet light, carried out during the restoration, has identified slight *pentimenti* in the positions of the arms and of the legs (fig. 30), and confirmed the substantially well preserved paint film and

the beauty of Titian's touch, above all in the head of the Saint (fig. 31).[38]

As recorded by Ridolfi, "Titian left in San Leone the Saint James Walking not entirely finished."[39] In 1786, and again in 1793, Giuseppe Mengardi offered to restore the *Saint James*, "making it larger,"[40] but it is not known if this operation can be credited to him or to Gallo Lorenzi who between 1836 and 1838 restored the painting, for a fee of 300 lire.[41] In any case the altarpiece has effectively been enlarged with a new arch, and strips at the bottom and along the left edge, while the original

32-33. Titian, "Saint James." Chiesa di San Lio, Venice.
Composite x-ray and infra-red reflectography, detail of the face
before restoration

arch was lowered so as to suggest that the format of the work was once different (fig. 32). Nevertheless, the intervention seems not to have been particularly successful if Selvatico-Lazari in 1852 described it as "spoiled by restorations" ("guasta dai restauri"). Crowe and Cavalcaselle in 1878 attested to very bad restorations "which have damaged in such a vandalistic way the painting."[42] The painting was lightly cleaned in 1935 for the Titian exhibition, and was radically restored in 1979.[43] Disturbing retouches of the figure and of the landscape were removed, thus confirming, amid the general deterioration, both the unfinished character of the altarpiece and the pictorial quality of the work as a whole, apparent also in the infrared photography carried out prior to the restoration (fig. 33).

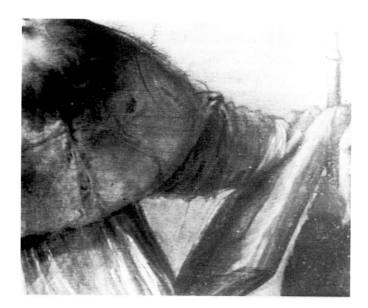

The *Saint John the Almsgiver*, was originally arched. It was presumably made rectangular, with additions on the upper and lower sides, to adapt it to a new high altar erected in 1633.[44] Like the *Saint James*, it was restored by Gallo Lorenzi in 1836-38, for 400 lire.[45] We know of no subsequent restorations and in fact only one type of *stuccatura* and one method of integration with varnish appear on the work.[46] The most recent cleaning reestablished to a surprising degree the integrity of the image and confirmed its very fair state of conservation, notwithstanding its ancient mutilation.[47] What emerged from the cleaning was a vibrant pictorial texture in which the surface begins to fragment itself in light "with soft manner" (Ridolfi: con "tenero modo"), without, however attaining the "disassociated colourism" of his later production. Reflectography, in addition to revealing the fine and rapid drawing (fig. 34), has revealed how initially the artist had painted the Saint wearing his mitre (figs. 35, 36) and another minor *pentimento* in the profile of the pauper.

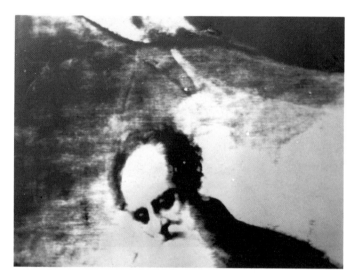

Ridolfi narrated how "in Venice in the Church of the Crociferi Fathers [Titian] painted the Martyrdom of Saint Lawrence... now compromised by some tombs which have been excavated in front of it which bring considerable harm through the stench."[48] A few years later, Scannelli judged it so totally blackened as to be comprehensible solely with the aid of Cornelis Cort's engraving of the subject.[49] On the occasion of their visit to Venice in 1782, the Counts of the North visited the

restoration laboratory at Santi Giovanni e Paolo, whence Edwards had transported the *Martyrdom of Saint Lawrence* so that the archdukes could admire from close-up a masterpiece by Titian, however damaged.[50] Restoration work was planned but Edwards refrained from forecasting the results.[51]

The altarpiece was taken to Paris in 1797, for the Louvre, and underwent heavy-handed restoration, suffering gravely also during the return voyage in 1815.[52] Henceforward the painting encountered a series of misfortunes. In 1834 it was consigned to Gaetano Astolfoni.[53] The provincial commission was unable to decide whether to "remove the repainting carried out in France" and "if it was appropriate to reline it." Following an on-site inspection urged by Astolfoni himself, "one found the lining to be made of many pieces, one overlapping another and applied with such terrible glue that one had to cut the lining in several places to relieve the strenuous shrinking which it induced. One found that all the nudes and the square had been covered over in Paris with the methods of a miniaturist in oil... and from a partial cleaning in a hand of the martyr one is led to hope strongly that under those French daubings one will find sufficient of the original to be able to say with confidence, a Titian is to be worthily restored."[54] The decision was taken to "unline and reline" as well as to "wash a significant portion of the painting."[55] After the cleaning of Saint Laurence, which brought to light the exceptional pictorial quality of the work, and also the extent of its damage, the question arose of just how much intact paint could be found and how complicated and expensive might be the work. Furthermore the Austrian administration and the president of the Accademia itself expressed the just fear that, after restoration, the painting may not "fully retain its own originality" and that in place of one of Titian's finest works "one may not have after vast expense... merely the work of that artist from whom the restoration itself had been commissioned."[56] As the cleaning proceeded, the extensive lacunae became more apparent, even while the beauty of the original parts was revealed.

In a report to the president, Zandomeneghi, Puliti and Lipparini suggested transferring the painting to the Accademia, recommending that the restoration work be entrusted to a skilled painter rather than to "the heavy mechanical hand of a cold restorer."[57] Only Sebastiano Santi, Lattanzio Querena and Astolfoni were considered equal to the situation, and the choice fell on Santi "because more than the others [he was] a capable executor of all manners of painting."[58] Only thus could the painting be restored "to its status as an original and distinguished work by Titian, even superior to that in which the same artist narrated the Martyrdom of Saint Peter, which is to be admired in the Church of SS. Giovanni e Paolo."[59] On 24 April 1835 Santi committed himself, under the watchful eye of the presidency and with the help of the academic body, to the complex task for 1500 lire, as against the 1800 proposed.[60]

But with so many supervisors, disagreements were inevitable: Santi refused to cover over with body color "what was left of the original," against the opinion of the academicians who, perhaps through a misunderstanding of Titian's brushwork, believed the painting to be merely "sketched" and lacking the finish required for legibility and worthiness. Summoned to explain the reasons for his refusal, he firmly countered that the prime duty of every restorer was to conserve "by any means, whatever is original that exists in the painting" and insisted that the repainting should be formally demanded of him "as a guarantee in the event that it does not meet with general approval."[61] Opinions were sought from Zandomeneghi, Politi, Michelangelo Gregoletti, Placido Fabris, and Adeodato Malatesta: all unanimously agreed on the need for the overpainting. Scrupulous and detailed instructions to this effect were given to Santi, recommending him to "make use in this case of the skill practiced by him and by other artists to maximum effect, in other words to deceive even the most expert eye around those parts which it is absolutely indispensable to repaint, making them appear as ancient as the original thanks to the ground soot mixed with starch glue, covering with this all the restored parts, then to clean it and lightly after a quarter of an hour to scrape it with the usual iron instrument until the part returns to the luminosity it had before."[62]

On 20 December 1836, on completion of the work, Santi requested issuance of "the act of approval" ("l'atto di laudo"), in other words certifying that he had perfectly

34-36. Titian "Saint John the Almsgiver." Chiesa di San Giovanni Elemosinario, Venice.
Infra-red reflectography of the arm of the saint showing underdrawing
and infra-red reflectography of the head of the saint, showing a miter on his head,
compared with the painting

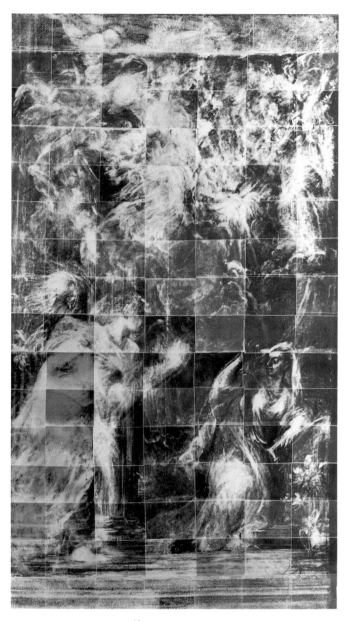

performed his task.[63] But as early as 1856, Zanotto noticed that the *Martyrdom* was "suffering greatly with time."[64]

In August 1877, it was transferred to the sacristy so as to make possible the execution of a copy.[65] In this way Guglielmo Botti, Ispettore delle Gallerie, was enabled to examine it. The canvas was in a deplorable state despite Santi's restoration-repainting and "another restoration or repainting by Lorenzi about twenty years ago, such that

nowadays only the composition, the heads of some soldiers and other small details in the upper part survive of the original painting." The paint film was generally precarious and Botti meticulously counted in one area no fewer than seventy-seven detachments.[66] He suggested "removing the original canvas in order to bring about the adhesion of the old priming and pigments on a new one," but the painting commission, which included the aged Fabris who had followed the three previous restorations, considered it wiser to delay removing the lining canvas.[67] The Ministry authorized the work in 1878, on the basis of Fabris' recommendations, admitting sadly that an outcome "entire and perfect could not be expected."[68] In the end Botti's proposal to transfer the painting to a new canvas was to prevail, and the results could not have been brilliant if, in the same year, Crowe and Cavalcaselle deprecated the numerous restorations inflicted on the work, "one quite modern, which has done much to make earlier injuries irreparable."[69]

Predictably the problems were not over: in 1894 the Academic Commission turned to the Ufficio per la Conservazione dei Monumenti, noting that the painting had fallen more than once in the hands of restorers, who had piled "damage upon damage," repainting it totally, and "then, after transfer from the original canvas to a new one, ended by lavishing a generous layer of varnish, the which twenty years on had turned into a kind of thick black skin which has now completely darkened the painting."[70]

An urgent rescue was needed. The greatest restorer of the time, Luigi Cavenaghi in Milan, was sought out, but Cavenaghi refused, saying that he was too busy with the Caravaggios in San Luigi dei Francesi, Rome. Thus on 24 January 1895, under the close supervision of the Accademia, the work was entrusted to Sidonio Centenari. In 1958-59 the painting was relined once again, by Mauro Pellicioli. This brings us finally to the conservation work carried out in 1981, which served to consolidate the original and nonoriginal paint film, removing the grime and the tinted varnishes of this altarpiece, which despite its tortured history is one of the most remarkable night scenes in Renaissance art.[71]

In 1648 Ridolfi observed of Titian's *Annunciation* in San Salvador, "having been re-managed by an unskilled

37-38. Titian, "Annunciation." Chiesa di San Salvador, Venice.
Composite x-ray and infra-red detail of Virgin

painter, to put in order certain defects of time, [the painting] is compromised in its purity."[72] According to Giuseppe Vedova, editor in 1835 of the second edition of Ridolfi, this painter can be identified as Philip Esengren.[73] In 1733 Zanetti informed us that "now it has been newly repaired."[74] Between 1821 and 1823 it underwent further restoration by Lattanzio Querena, while on 9 February 1896, being muddied with many candle drips, it was cleaned by Giovanni Spoldi.[75]

Recent restoration has significantly augmented our understanding of the work, in addition to improving to an unexpected degree its visible aspect.[76] The composite x-radiograph, which revealed a *pentimento* in the hands of the angel (fig. 37), and other examinations with special rays have confirmed the generally sound conservation of the altarpiece. In the infrared image of the Virgin (fig. 38), the bed behind the curtain is still visible, as documented clearly in Cort's engraving, while reflectography has revealed the reworking of the inscription IGNIS ARDENS NON COMBURENS, perhaps because the original had faded (fig. 39). In addition, it revealed that the famous "fecit fecit" was an old addition above the clearly apparent "faciebat" (fig. 40).[77]

It would have been gratifying on this occasion to tackle the cleaning of the ex-Albertini *Madonna and Child* in the Gallerie dell'Accademia. The excellent x-radiograph (fig. 41) confirms that this is an autograph work by Titian

*39-40. Titian, "Annunciation." Infra-red reflectography detail of
the inscription and the signature
41. Titian. "Madonna and Child." Gallerie dell'Accademia, Venice.
Composite x-ray*

painted over a previous almost-finished, upside-down female figure, perhaps a *Magdalene in Prayer*.[78] Nevertheless it became obvious that, despite the absence of lacunae, the paint film is so consumed and reworked as to render unwise a restoration that would have exposed so impoverished an image.

Doge Antonio Grimani before Faith in the Sala delle Quattro Porte of the Palazzo Ducale was commissioned in 1555 and seen by Vasari during his Venetian visit in 1566 in Titian's house, among other works "sketched and begun." Left incomplete at his death and finished probably by Marco Vecellio, this work was gestated over a long and troublesome period, and this, as in other unfinished works by Titian, is reflected in the numerous, often unfortunate, not to say mimetic restorations.[79]

The first to lay hands on the work, integrating unfinished areas and adding at the sides a prophet and a standard-bearer, both harmonized pictorially with the center of the painting by means of curtains, was Marco Vecellio. Possibly restored in 1739 by Cardinali,[80] on 9 August 1783 Edwards took the painting in hand emphasizing, in a report to the Provveditori al Sal, "the most miserable condition" of the painting "washed once more and superficially put in order."[81] The restoration was carried out by Bertani, Diziani and Baldassini on 28 February 1784. In 1797, as the only surviving canvas by Titian in the Palazzo Ducale, it was taken to Paris where, according to Zanotto, it was damaged by "an uskilled hand," such that "in several places one sees the impasto and the harmony gone and this mainly either by new paint placed

42. Titian, "Pietà." Gallerie dell'Accademia, Venice. Composite x-ray

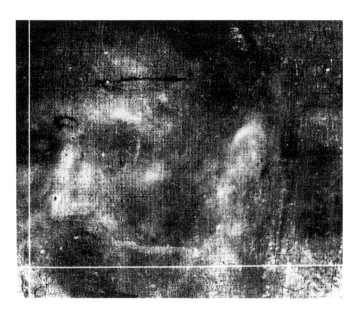

over the old or by ill-matched surface washes; the which altering in only a few years cause here and there nasty and ugly patches...."[82] It was not only the French who perpetuated these crimes since Moschini in 1819 declared: "[the *Annunciation*] is a work which prior to its transfer to Paris and after its return was considerably retouched."[83] On 11 February 1850 the President of the Accademia, Pietro Selvatico, commissioned Tagliapietra "to employ quickly all the means of art to the end that the paint could be prevented from falling," toning down the lacunae with "a general layer of varnish."[84] In 1913 a conservative restoration was carried out by Giuseppe Zennaro.[85]

The most recent restoration, in 1978-79, eliminated the thick layer of repaints, revealing that Titian's share was much larger than previously supposed.[86] The general design is owed to him, as are Saint Mark, the doge, the page boy who holds the crown, the pose of Faith, and unquestionably the distant view. The alteration of the latter detail is the most disturbing of all; nor can Titian's autograph be challenged simply because of the presence of the prisons, built between 1589 and 1602, and therefore clearly not by the artist but simply a clumsy revision.

The x-ray examination of the painting revealed that under the curtain, which is a later addition, the colonnade continues with another column, while in place of the halberd had been painted a lance.

Finally, a careful cleaning has brought to light, under a brownish surface layer, a flag with white and pink stripes, the colors of the Grimani crest, immediately under the head of the soldier with the helmet.

The *Pietà* by Titian had, as is known, its first restoration, to finish certain details and to disguise the seams of the seven canvases of which it is composed, at the hand of Palma il Giovane (fig. 42). Zanotto deplored that a certain Veglio had reduced the painting "almost to its end."[87] If this can be identified with a certain Benedetto Veli (or Veglio) who was born in 1564 in Florence and died in 1634, then the painting underwent extremely early restoration, perhaps at the time it was placed in the church of Sant'Angelo.

In 1828 Sebastiano Santi "restored it to its original splendor," adding, for its adaptation to museum display,

two lateral strips. Several times in this century the picture has required consolidation, above all at the time of the two World Wars, particularly after the second.[88] In 1954 Mauro Pelliccioli discovered, in the course of relining, the sketch of a horse in black chalk on the back of the original canvas.[89] Of this fleeting image no trace was found in the course of the most recent restoration. The x-ray examination carried out in 1954 led to the understanding that the lower part of the Virgin and the legs of Christ were in large part remade, altering the initial posture. New and more sophisticated methods of enquiry during the last restoration, with infra-red and

43-44. Titian, "Pietà." X-ray detail of a male head from the central area, to the right of the Virgin, and an infra-red reflectography detail of the inscription on the votive panel

ultra-violet reflectography, have made it possible to verify that the lower zone, though damaged, is not afflicted by the massive losses that the older and partial x-rays led one to believe.[90] The entire work instead betrays tiny losses of color caused by the fact of being composed of seven canvases of different type and weave; consequently they have different degrees of thickness, probably resulting in the poor adhesion of the paint layer. In the central area Titian went so far as to use an already-painted fragment, in which x-rays have revealed a male face of extraordinary intensity (fig. 43).[91] The infrared reflectograph made it possible to read the dedication on the votive tablet (fig. 44) and documented how the Greek inscriptions above Moses and the Hellespontic Sybil have been several times repainted, only a few original letters surviving. The elimination of the pigmented varnishes used by Pelliccioli has made possible an unhindered visualization of the work, which bears witness to a dramatic conception without precedent, justifying Aretino's hyperbole: "...and now there is Titian, who, as I have mentioned, is enough for all who were there."[92]

I would like to thank Paolo Spezzani who with the invaluable support of his research carried out with the infra-red reflectography and with x-rays (in the latter case assisted by Virginia Vianello), has made possible the discovery of much of the information presented in this essay.

[1] See F. Valcanover, "Il restauro dell'Assunta," in *Tiziano nel quarto centenario della sua morte 1576-1976*, Venice 1977, 41-51. It was unfortunate that at that time the Soprintendenza disposed of neither the equipment nor the financial means for exhaustive x-ray and reflectography documentation. Only two x-ray photographs were taken of the *Assumption*, neither of them instructive.

[2] "[Tiziano era] solito usar diligenza in le sue dipinture e meterge boni coloi et ogli...." See A. Sambo, "Tiziano davanti ai giudici ecclesiastici," in *Tiziano e Venezia* (Convegno internazionale di Studi, Venezia 1976), Venice, 1980, 384ff.

[3] "...è assai tempo che l'è lì et e è stata e non ha patito mai umidità alcuna." Sambo, 1980, 392.

[4] Archivio del Seminario, Venice, *Carte Edwards*, MS 787-7, 17 August 1787: "...otto committiture formavono dapprincipio l'unione di questo pezzo, ma dopo essersi molte volte sconnesse, ed essere state congiunte in varia guisa, sempre però con discapito del dipinto, restarono finalmente legate con istuccature goffissime ed assicurate con chiodi ribattuti sopra la pittura, con ripezzi di tavola, e con grosso colore, ma in modo che volendo adesso gettar in fascio queste tavole per unirle di nuovo a dovere, si arrischierebbe la perdita intiera dell'opera. Alla malconcia materialità del fondo si accompagna la mobilità del dipinto pien di visciche, crepolato, rigido, sobbollito in gran parte, e ridotto in più luoghi come a foggia d'incrostatura disunita ed ineguale.

In grandissimo numero sono li ripezzi di nuova pittura goffissimamente ed in vari tempi applicativi. Alcuni di questi mostrano essere sovrapposti all'originale colore, ed altri servono solo a tingere la tavola scopertasi per le scrostature, dalle quali però sortono sempre molto avanti sul margine dell'antico dipinto. Il San Marco è tutto ricoperto di svelature, e sfregazzi e stucchi e ritocchi che lo sfigurano. Le drapperie degli altri Santi ed il campo sono imbrattati quasi nello stesso modo. Con tutto ciò, siccome la figura del San Sebastiano, su cui si riduce la più spaziosa massa di lume, è per fortuna la meno pregiudicata dell'altre, e la ricchezza sufficiente del colore originale danno un poco di coraggio ai tentativi, io mi lusingo che l'effetto generale di questo laboriosissimo ristauro sara molto aggradevole... – È però conveniente ch'io avveta in anticipazione non essere per alcun modo da tentarsi per questo quadro quegli espedienti che si userebbero in altre circostanze per assicurar in più ragionevol forma la intelaiatura, ed i legami che tengono unite le tavole di tutto il pezzo, e similmente credo di dover ommettere molte delle operazioni tendenti a togliere per l'intiero il sospetto del tarlo." My thanks to the Rector of the Seminary Mons. Giuliano Bertoli and to Mons. Antonio Niero for permission to consult the Seminary archive.

[5] "...riportato a quella... armonia che ora necessariamente gli manca per essere rimaste nude di colore alcune fra le parti imbrattate da prima da imperiti pennelli." Archivio Accademia di Belle Arti, Venice, *Restauro tavola del Tiziano 'San Marco Evangelista e Santi'*, 1849-51. My thanks to Prof. Nedo Fiorentin for his assistance in pursuing this enquiry.

[6] Fabris was originally to be paid 600 lire, of which he had already received in two installments 400 lire on account. The fee was raised to 800 lire, which the painter discounted by 20 lire.

[7] "[Il dipinto era] divenuto molto opaco ed in vari punti il colore è sollevato, e sotti i piedi dei SS. Cosma e Damiano manca in qualche punto." Archivio Accademia di Belle Arti, Venice, *idem*, 1882. In a letter of the Presidency of the Accademia, of 13 February 1882 no. 38, there is a MS note: "fu ristaurata dal Florian poi dal Fabris. La tavola fu in parte abbruciata."

[8] "...rimettendo [il colore] in que' punti in cui è caduto, ripulendo leggermente dalla polvere l'intero dipinto ravvivandone la vernice." This time Fabris was paid 100 lire.

[9] "...movimenti tali che lasciano vedere la fenditura degli assi." Archivio Accademia di Belle Arti, Venice, *Presidenza Collegio Accademico*, letter of 11 January 1890, no. 775.

[10] Archivio Soprintendenza ai Beni Ambientali ed Architettonici, Venice, letter from Botti to Barozzi, 5 September 1891: "Necessita adunque di porre i veli sul dipinto, di procedere al lievo della sprangatura fissa per porre le spranghe a morsetti, onde la tavola sia libera di ristringere e crescere a suo talento senza ostacoli di sorta. Questo è quanto il dovere m'impone di farle conoscere a scanso di qualunque responsabilità, e siccome la commissione permanente di pittura fino al mese di luglio u.d. ebbe a dichiarare, che la rigenerazione pettenkoffer col balsamo di coppale non vi entra per niente, essendo il dipinto benissimo conservato, così fa d'uopo procedere alle operazioni predette e vogliamo salvare questa stupenda opera del Vecellio." On completion of the restoration the painting was definitively located on the altar of the large sacristy of the Salute, despite the opposition of the Commission for Paintings. I am most grateful to Dr. Annalisa Bristot for her generous assistance researching the documents in the Soprintendenza archive.

[11] Conservation was carried out between 1978 and 1985. Alteration affected above all the green pigments. The best preserved figure is that of Saint Roch. The restoration of the support was carried out in large part by Armelao Elio Pio with advice from the Istituto Centrale del Restauro, Rome. The cleaning and integration of the paint surface "a rigatino" was conducted by Alfeo Michieletto and Antonia Sartori Merzagora. For Boschini's remarks, see M. Boschini, *La Carta del navegar pitoresco* (Venice, 1660), ed. A. Pallucchini, Venice and Rome, 1966, 186-87.

[12] "...quale pittura come sopra humana è rispettata dal tempo..." C. Ridolfi,

Le maraviglie dell'arte, Venice, 1648 (ed. Von Hadeln), Berlin 1914-24, I, 49.

[13] Authenticated copy of 6 March 1896 of a document in the Archivio di Stato, Venice, said to be conserved in *fascicolo* 13 of the Monumenti d'antichità, year 1810, *filza* 311. Atti della Prefettura del Dipartimento dell'Adriatico Regno d'Italia (Archivio Soprintendenza ai Beni Ambientali ed Architettonici, Venice).

[14] Restoration work by Vincenzo Cecchi on this painting ("compromised by humidity") is documented in the year 1714 (Archivio di Stato, Venice, *Provveditori al Sal, Parti del Senato, Reg. 28, busta 16,* 24 r and v). See L. Olivato, "Provvedimenti della Repubblica Veneta per la Salvaguardia del patrimonio pittorico nei secoli XVII e XVIII," *Istituto Veneto di Scienze, Lettere ed Arti*, Venice, 1974, 112-13.

[15] F. Berchet considered it "forse l'affresco meglio conservato di Venezia" (*IV Relazione (1896-1897-1898) dell'Ufficio Regionale per la conservazione dei monumenti del Veneto*, Venice, 1899, 26).

[16] The restoration was carried out by O. Nonfarmale. In the lower area red lines traverse horizontally the whole width of the painting (fig. 2). As handed down to us by Cennino Cennini (*Il Libro dell'Arte* [ed. F. Brunello and L. Magagnato], Vicenza, 1971, 214-16), once the *arriccio* was applied, the painter divided the painting surface with at least one centered vertical line, achived with a string soaked in red. Then with the aid of a compass a horizontal line was traced, intersecting orthogonally with the first, at the point where the sight line was to be fixed. In large compositions there may be several lines both vertical and horizontal. It is evident that the thin lines were intended for this purpose, and it is unexplained why they were not covered by paint, as would have been usual.

[17] "...sì scaduta dallo antico splendore a cagione della umidità del luogo e dello abbandono nel quale rimane, per cui verrà tratta a certa ruina, se la man provvidissima di chi regge ora il timon dello stato non accorra tosto a ripararla dai guasti sofferti." F. Zanotto, *Il Palazzo Ducale di Venezia*, I, Venice, 1853, XXXIV.

[18] Berchet, 1899, 27. "Lo Stefanoni si obbligò a farne il trasporto per lire 650, ove avesse dovuto compiere il lavoro a Venezia, e per lire 550 ove gli fosse permesso di terminarlo a Bergamo... la Commissione... accettò il preventivo Stefnaoni alla condizione che il lavoro fosse compiuto a venezia, e il Ministero approvò. I lavori cominciarono in aprile 1899 e furono compiuti col più splendido risultato."

[19] Restored in 1898-90 by O. Nonfarmale. The fresco measures 157×348 cm. It was executed in only two days.

[20] For a lengthy and documented report on this restoration, carried out in 1977 by A. Lazzarin, see: F. Valcanover, "La Pala Pesaro", *Quaderni della Soprintendenza ai Beni Artistici e Storici di Venezia*, 8, Venice, 1979, 57-67.

[21] Archivio della Soprintendenza ai Beni Artistici e Storici di Venezia, *Scuola di San Rocco*, 90a.

[22] See *Tiziano. Catalogo della Mostra*, 1935, 99, no. 42. In 1973 the relining was carried out by A. Lazzarin. The recent cleaning was by Rosa Bagarotto (1989-90).

[23] See G. Nepi Scirè, "Il restauro della 'Presentazione di Maria al Tempio' di Tiziano," *Bolletino d'Arte*, Studi Veneziani, Supplement no. 5, Rome, 1984, 151-64. This last restoration, consisting of the lining and cleaning of the work, was conducted by O. Nonfarmale in 1980.

[24] See: E. Panofsky, *Problems in Titian. Mostly Iconographic*, New York 1969; D. Rosand, "Titian's *Presentation of the Virgin in the Temple* and the Scuola della Carità," *Art Bulletin*, LVII, 1976, 70-73; and Rosand, *Painting in Cinquecento Venice, Titian, Veronese, Tintoretto*, New Haven and London, 1982, 221-38.

[25] Sambo, 1980, 384-85.

[26] "...li pregiudizi inferiti al dipinto con un antico lavacro... gli azzurri che non erano legati con biacca sono in gran parte sfumati, i verdi anneriti negli oscuri e dilavati nei lumi, e le carni sono rimaste molto uniformi e prive di sugo, come

s'incontra bene spesso n e quadri ai quali mancano gl'ultimi finismenti. Li ritocchi di sfregatura sono frequentissimi... generalmente parlando questo quadro ha tutta l'aria d'una pittura scarsissima di colorito nella sua origine, consunta dalle improprie lavature et ossiderata dal tempo... Non si deve però tralasciare di foderarla benché la orginale sia in ottimo stato." Archivio del Seminario, *Carte Edwards*, MS 787-87.

[27] J.A. Crowe and G.B. Cavalcaselle, *The Life and Times of Titian with some account of his family*, 2d ed., London, 1881, II, 72.

[28] *Tiziano. Catalogo della Mostra*, 1935, 159, no. 78. The modern restoration was carried out by A. Lazzarin in 1984 and consisted of lining, cleaning and integration. The non-original area of the pavement, 154 cm [?] high, was retained and hidden with a cloth.

[29] "...alcuni priori... se avevano fatto depenzer sopra la ditta pala, et alcuni altri... fecero depenar quelle teste e si fecero depenzer loro... ma quando la pala portata non li era nessuno di loro depento suso." Sambo, 1980, 390.

[30] This was not done in the 1984 restoration for lack of funds.

[31] Archivio del Seminario, Venice, *Carte Edwards*, MS 87877, 25 February 1788. "...sul quale [Cardinali] congiuntamente alla scarsezza delle nozioni del mestier del ristauro che al suo tempo non era ben conosciuto d'alcuno, si univa tutta con ignoranza, e tutta la temerita di uno sguaiato e vilissimo pittore. Non è possibile discerner subito fin dove da quest'ultimo siasi esteso l'arbitrio degl'impropri redipinti, e quanto inoltrata siasi la imprudente applicazione degli anteriori lavacri." See also: Archivio di Stato, Venice, *Compilazione Leggi, busta* 303, 817r; and L. Olivato, *op. cit.*, 1974, 120-21.

[32] Archivio del Seminario, Venice, MS 787-7, 17 August 1787: "È già lungo tempo che il bisogno di quasi tutti li quadri esistenti nella chiesa e sacrastia della Salute ed il vicino deperimento di alcune fra quelle pitture, hanno esercitato molte private rimostranze ch'io non potei soddisfare fino ad ora...".

[33] Crowe and Cavalcaselle, 1881, II, 73.

[34] The restoration dates from 1989-90. Ferruccio Volpin relined the painting, while Chiara Maida, Alfeo Michieletto, Gloria Tranquilli cleaned and reintegrated the paint surface. The restoration had become urgent in view of the lifting of the original paint film from the support.

[35] Restored 1989-90 by L. Sante Savio. In the 1812 list Edwards noted: "furono tanto dilavate, ritoccate e imbrattate con olio cotto che di poco possono migliorar condizione con nuovo restauro." They were restored by Baldassini in 1817; the panel with the symbol of Saint Matthew again in 1903 by Luigi Betto, and that with the symbol of Saint John in 1904 by G. Bononi (see: S. Moschini Marconi, *Gallerie dell'Accademia di Venezia, Opere d'Arte del secolo XVI*, Rome 1962). They were restored once more by M. Pellicioli for the 1935 Titian exhibition.

[36] See Moschini Marconi, 1962, 259-60.

[37] "...offuscata da una tinta giallastra, a cagione di mal eseguito ristauro." Gallo Lorenzi was paid 250 lire (Archivio Accademia di Belle Arti, Venice [1846-9]). In 1903 and in 1935 the painting was merely revarnished.

[38] Restored in 1981 by O. Nonfarmale, with a double relining, cleaning and a new spring stretcher. The composite x-ray photograph presented here is technically more advanced than that published by F. Valcanover in *Da Tiziano a El Greco. Per la storia del Manierismo a Venezia*, Milan, 1981, 101.

[39] Ridolfi, 1648 (ed. Von Hadeln), I, 205.

[40] See S. Sponza, in *Da Tiziano a el Greco...*, Milan, 1981, no. 21.

[41] Archivio Accademia di Belle Arti, Venice, 20 May 1836-38.

[42] "...i quali hanno danneggiato in modo così vandalico il dipinto." For these quotations see Sponza, 1981, 112.

[43] Restored by A. Lazzarin, who relined and cleaned the painting. See also: Sponza, 1981.

[44] A strip 18 cm in width was added to the upper edge, and 17 cm in width to the lower. Crowe and Cavalcaselle, 1881, I, 381: "...had 'St John the Almsgiver' been left as Titian made it, and had it not been changed from an arched to a square canvas, nothing would prevent us from acknowledging it as

45 Archivio Accademia di Belle Arti, Venice, 1836-38.
46 The stretcher and the lining are in excellent condition and also surely date from the nineteenth century.
47 Restored in 1989-90 by L. Sante Savio.
48 "...in Venezia nella chiesa de' Padri Crociferi dipinse il Martirio di San Lorenzo...or pregiudicato per alcune sepolture che dianzi si cavarono che gli resero molto nocumento per il fetore." Ridolfi, 1648 (ed. Von Hadeln), i, 204.
49 F. Scannelli, Il micorcosmo della pittura, Cesena 1657, 215. Scannelli may on the other hand have misunderstood that this is a night scene, elaborately praised instead by Sandrart in 1675 (Accademiae Nobilissimae Artis Pictoriae, Nuremberg and Frankfurt, 165).
50 Archivio del Seminario, Venice, Carte Edwards, MS 787-7=876-7, 15 February 1781. As Edwards stated, the worst damaged was caused "dal lavoro istituitovi sopra, son già 50 anni, da un certo pittore, che a forza di fregare e rifregare credeva di restituirlo in buon essere, e finalmente dopo averlo ben bene scorticato da tutte le parti, si accinse a ripararlo di sua propria mano."
51 Naturally the restoration work was carried out by colleagues of Edwards: Bertani, Diziani e Baldassini.
52 Archivio Accademia di Belle Arti, Venice, Elenco dei quadri trasportati da Parigi per ordine di Sua Maestà, 1816, no. 13.
53 Archivio Accademia di Belle Arti, Venice, 1834-36. The generous assistance of Prof. Nedo Fiorentin made it possible for me to reconstruct in detail the history of nineteenth century restorations of this painting.
54 "...levarsi li redipinti fattivi in Francia." "...se fosse anche convenienza il rifoderarlo." "...si trovò essere la fodera fatta di molti pezzi a ridosso l'uno dell'altro, ed applicata con cosi pessima colla che dovette spezzarsi in più luoghi per obbedire ad una violenta restrizione a cui fu condotta dalla sua qualità. Si trovò che tutti li nudi ed il campo erano stati ricoperti a Parigi, ove fu con metodi da miniatore ed all'olio... e (per una parziale scoperta fatta in una mano del martire) si giunse a fermamente sperare che sotto quelle francesi impiastratture si doveva trovare tanto di originale da poter dire con sicurezza, sarà lodevolmente restaurato un Tiziano." Letter from Luigi Zandomeneghi to the Presidency of the Accademia, 24 September 1834 no. 490.
55 "...il lavacro di una rilevante porzione del dipinto." Letter from the Presidency of the Accademia to the government, 5 October 1834.
56 "...ritener pienamente la propria originalità." "...non si avesse dopo grave dispendio... se non che un'opera di quell'artista a cui fosse il ristauro medesimo demandato." Letter from the Presidency of the Accademia to the Permanent Commission for Painting, 4 November 1834 no. prot. 554.
57 "...pesante meccanica di un freddissimo restauratore." Letter of 13 November 1834.
58 "...perché più degli altri assiduo esecutore di ogni maniera di dipingere." In 1826 Santi had already restored Titian's Pietà, and the Presentation of the Virgin in Temple, and perhaps also the Martyrdom of Saint Peter Martyr in the church of Santi Giovanni e Paolo.
59 "...il quadro di cui trattasi per opera originale e distinta di Tiziano, ma ancora in grado eguale, ed anzi superiore a quella del medesimo autore esprimente il martirio di S. Pietro che ammirasi nella chiesa de' SS. Giovanni e Paolo." Astolfoni was compensated by being given the restoration of the altarpiece by Pordenone in the church of Susegana.
60 The contract prescribed the removal "in primo luogo con tutta la possibile diligenza e merce [?] i consueti lavacri quegli informi redipinti che vi furono sovrapposti in Francia e scoprendo quindi in ogni sua parte l'originale del Vecellio, che quantunque sommamente danneggiato, pure dalle parziali scoperture fattesi nello stesso eseguire, risulta nella massima parte tuttavia sussistente. Dopo ciò dovrà il Santi procedere con ogni diligenza alla effettuazione, del ristauro, avendo in vista di non ricoprire se non se quella piccola parte che per la sua consunzione assolutamente lo richiedesse e di

conservare tutto il possibile dell'originale. In quanto a quelle porzioni di dipinto che mancano affatto, dovrà il Santi eseguire gli occorrenti studi dal vero, per applicarli alle tracce che tuttora esistono nell'originale; ritenuto però che prima di riportare sul quadro gli studi fatti, dovranno esser questi approvati dalla Commissione accademica di Pittura."
61 "...ond'essere garantito nel caso che ciò non avesse a riportare la comune approvazione." Letter of 17 May 1836.
62 "...far uso in questa circostanza del mezzo da lui e da altri artisti col massimo effetto praticato, quello cioè d'ingannare anche l'occhio più esperto intorno alle parti ch'è assolutamente indispensabile di rimettere, facendole comparire antiche quanto l'originale e ciò mercé la fuligine macinata ed incorporata con la colla d'amito, coprendo con questa tutte le parti ristaurate per detergerle poi e leggermente dopo un quarto d'ora raschiarle col solito mezzo del ferretto fino a che la parte ritorni ad essere luminosa com'era prima." Report of 26 June 1836, no. 587. Santi was also advised that in Saint Lawrence "sia riverberata tutta l'ombra della guancia e del collo... come pure maggiormente riflessata l'orecchia e più decisa nel suo assieme, con dei riflessi composti di tinta aurea." In the torso, in the place of retouching with watercolor Santoi as advised to use a "tinta composta e densa che tendesse piuttosto al dorato, adoperandola con un pennello piatto di capretto a fin di allargare qua e là la luce..." Then again he should "dilatarsi di qualche poco la luce del petto e della spalla diritta, come pure sopra il torace e negli obliqui esterni," and also strengthen the right hand "rendendola almeno di una tinta eguale a quella della sinistra." The figure of the torturer should also be enlivened "con dei lumi riflessi aurei" and the figure supporting the martyr "avrebbe bisogno di piccole correzioni, come il personaggio che attizza il fuoco." To silence Santi's scruples he was reminded that he had had no shyness about repainting when faced with an important work like the Pietà.
63 Work was suspended in the fall of 1836, when Santi was authorized to go to Trieste, at the request of the government, to painting frescoes in the church of Sant'Antonio. For his request for written approval of his work, see the letter of 20 December 1836 no. 722.
64 F. Zanotto, Nuovissima guida di venezia, Venice, 1856, 311.
65 The copy was to be painted by the Austrian Teuchert at the behest of the Emperor (letter of 13 August 1877 no. 385).
66 "...altro restauro o ridipintura del Lorenzi or fa un venti anni circa, dimodoché di originale non rimane oggi che la composizione, qualche testa di alcuni soldati ed altre piccole cose nella parte superiore del dipinto." Letter from Botti to Cecchini secretary of the Accademia on 31 August 1877: "...avendo i detti restauratori applicati dei cattivi glutini e vernici essicative il colore si distacca in alcune parti arricciandosi, ed in molto punti ne ho contati fino a 77. Una forte graffiatura si vede presso la punta della bandiera. Il soldato o manigoldo che con una forca spinge il Santo sulla graticola è in uno stato deplorevole, tanto ha sofferto il colore come in tutta quella parte sinistra del quadro. Presso la face del lato destro del quadro furono praticate dalle cuciture di filo di ferro, vale a dire come legature per sostenere alcune slabbrature della tela vecchia colla tel nuova, rinforzandola nel lato posteriore con sbarre di tela in n. di 5, che furono adese con colla e stucco di gesso. Nella parte inferiore del lato posteriore si vedono tracce di umidità come lo dimostrano le molte macchie o fiori di muffa." Botti recommended insulation of the altarpiece, placing on the altar "una contro fodera di legno ben ricoperto di vernice d'olio di lino e cera fusa in quello e distesa a caldo" and also the repair of the roof which was leaking dangerously.
67 "...levare l'antica tela originale per poter con una nuova meglio afferrare la vecchia mastica ed il colore." Minutes of 7 December 1877 of the Commissione Accademica, composed of Placido Fabris, Pompeo Molmenti, Iacopo d'Andrea, Guglielmo Botti, G.B. Cecchini.
68 "...intero e perfetto ormai non può attendersi." Letter from the Ministry to Botti, 19 December 1878 no. 12706.
69 Crowe and Cavalcaselle, 1881, ii, 26 note 3.

[70] "...indi, trasportato dalla tela originale su altra, finirono col passarvi su un abbondante mano di vernice, la quale a vent'anni circa di distanza s'è mutata in una specie di cotica nera da cui è ora tutto ottenebrato." Archivio della Soprintendenza ai Beni Ambientali e Architettonici, Venice, Ufficio Regionale per la Conservazione dei Monumenti, *San Lorenzo ai Gesuiti*, a11. Letter of 30 September 1894.

[71] The restoration was carried out by O. Nonfarmale.

[72] "...essendo stata racconciata da poco avveduto pittore, per accomodarvi alcuni difetti del tempo, la pregiudicò della sua purità." Ridolfi, 1648 (ed. Von Hadeln), I, 205.

[73] *Le maraviglie dell'arte... descritte dal Cav. Carlo Ridolfi* (2nd edn., corrected and with notes), 2 vols., Padua, 1835, I, 267.

[74] "...ora fu nuovamente aggiustata." A.M. Zanetti, *Descrizione di tutte le pubbliche pitture della Città di Venezia... o sia rinnovazione delle Ricche Minere di Marco Boschini...*, Venice, 1733, 186.

[75] For Querena's restoration, see Archivio Accademia di Belle Arti, Venice, 1821. For Spoldi's restoration, see Archivio della Soprintendenza ai Beni Ambientali e Architettonici, Venice, *Chiesa di S. Salvatore*, A11: "La cera fu levata mediante passaggio di ferro caldo sopra la carta asciugante" and "ripetuti bagni d'essenza di trementina tiepida per levare quella porzione di cera che si era infiltrata fra le trame della tela."

[76] Carried out in 1988-89 by Ottorino Nonfarmale, and consisting of the lining, cleaning, integration and varnishing.

[77] This was reconfirmed, if such was necessary, by x-ray examination.

[78] Turning the image upside down makes the image easier to identify.

[79] "...abbozzate e cominciate". See: G. Nepi Scirè, "'La Fede' di Tiziano", and L. Lazzarini, "Note tecniche," *Quaderni della Soprintendenza ai Beni Artistici e Storici di Venezia*, no. 8, Venice, 1979, pp. 83-94.

[80] Archivio di Stato, Venice, *Compilazione leggi, busta* 303, *carta* 817r. See L. Olivato, 1974, 121.

[81] "...la condizione miserabilissima..." "lavato di nuovo e superficialmente racconciato." Archivio del Seminario, Venezia, *Carte Edwards*, MS 787-7.

[82] "...da imperita mano..." "in piu luoghi si vede tolto l'impasto e l'accordo e ciò precipuamente o da nuove tinte sovrapposte alle antiche, o da male intese velature; le quali alteratasi in pochi anni produssero qui e la sconci e brutture..." F. Zanotto, *Il Palazzo Ducale di Venezia*, Venice, 1858, 8.

[83] "È un'opera che prima che la si portasse a Parigi e dopo che fu riportata, fu considerevolmente ritoccata." G.A. Moschini, *Itinéraire de la ville de Venise,...*, Venice, 1819, 105.

[84] "...d'usar tosto di tutti i mezzi dell'arte a fine di fermare il colore cadente." Archivio Accademia di Belle Arti, Venice, 11 February 1850 no. 64. 216 lire were paid for the work.

[85] Archivio della Soprintendenza ai Beni Ambientali ed Architettonici, Venice, A7, contract no. 139.

[86] The restoration was carried out by Serafino and Ferruccio Volpin, with relining, cleaning and integration.

[87] F. Zanotto, *Pinacoteca della I.R. Accademia di Belle Arti*, Venice 1830, vol. I.

[88] *Ibidem*. See also Moschini-Marconi, *op. cit.*, 1962, 260-1, G. Nepi Scirè, "Tiziano 'la Pietà,'" *Restauri alle Gallerie dell'Accademia (Quaderni della Soprintendenza ai Beni Artistici e Storici di Venezia*, no. 13), Venice 1987, 34, fig. 26.

[89] V. Moschini, "Nuovi ordinamenti e restauri alle Gallerie di Venezia", *Bolletino d'Arte*, XLII, 1957.

[90] Restored between 1984 and 1985 by O. Nonfarmale, who carried out a relining, cleaning and light in-painting with watercolour, a final varnish, and finally its transfer to a new stretcher of wood.

[91] Conceivably a self-portrait, similar to that in the Prado?

[92] "...ed ora ci è Tiziano, il quale, come ho accennato, basta per quanti ci furono." L. Dolce, *Dialogo della Pittura... intitolato l'Aretino*, Venice, 1557, 4.

THE CATALOGUE

I

Frescoes from Fondaco dei Tedeschi

a. *Judith or Justice*

detached fresco, 213×346 cm

b. *Battle between Giants and Monsters*

detached fresco, 158×320.5 cm
Venice, Ca' d'Oro, Galleria Giorgio Franchetti

EXHIBITION   Venice 1978
RESTORATION   1966, L. Tintori

"In the month of August 1508, Tuesday the first. A mass was sung, prepared in the courtyard of the Fondaco dei Tedeschi, just rebuilt...., the Germans begin to enter and perform dances and nevertheless they go on finishing inside and painting outside." Sanudo's valuable testimony in his *Diaries* informs us that by 1 August 1508 the Fondaco dei Tedeschi, the commercial center of the Germans and one of the economic strong points of the Venetian State, was already reconstucted, only a short time after the ruinous fire that, on the night between 27 and 28 January 1505, had destroyed the old building. The works must have been on the way to completion if the German merchants had moved into the building again. It is also clear that, on that date, the frescoing of the external and internal façades of the structure was underway. Giorgione worked on the Grand Canal façade, probably beginning in 1507, since on 8 November 1508 the artist filed a suit against the *Provveditori del Sal* "for the painting of the Fondaco dei Tedeschi." By 11 December of the same year the enterprise was already finished, as on that day Lazzaro Bastiani, Vittore Carpaccio and Vettore di Matteo, by designation of Giovanni Bellini and in the presence of the *Provveditori al Sal*, judged that "the painting made on the façade of the Fondaco dei Tedeschi, made by maestro Zorzi di Castelfranco, and in agreement they gave a judgment and opinion that the above-mentioned maestro merited for said painting 150 [ducats] in total," a sum that, "the said messer Zorzi consenting, was reduced to 130 ducats" (Gualandi 1842). Giorgione's work on the principal façade of the Fondaco dei Tedeschi was well documented, and surely constituted a public manifesto of the Castelfranco master's revolutionary style with which painting, in the modern sense, began.

Titian's name does not appear in the archives. The first to mention his participation in the enterprise was Ludovico Dolce, who in his *Dialogue* of 1557 affirmed that the decor-ation of the walls of the Fondaco toward the Calle del Buso, today 'del Fontego,' had been allotted to Titian who was "not yet twenty," while Giorgione painted "the façade of the Fondaco dei Tedeschi that looks out over the Grand Canal." Nor did Dolce omit reference to the rivalry between Giorgione, by then an affirmed master, and the young Titian, with an episode concerning "a Judith, most wonderful in design and coloring such that, believing commonly when it was unveiled that it was a work by Giorgione, all his friends congratulated him on the best thing by far that he had done. So Giorgione responded with great displeasure that it was by the hand of his pupil, who already demonstrated himself as surpassing the Master, and moreover remained for days at home, being desperate, seeing that the young man knew more than he." The presumed quarrels between the two artists working on the façades of the Fondaco was taken up by Vasari in the second edition of the *Lives* (1568), probably at Titian's prompting. In the life of Titian, his first work was a "portrait of a noble of Ca' Barbarigo, his friend," and following this was the Fondaco project: "Giorgione having done the façade of the Fondaco dei Tedeschi, Barbarigo succeeded in having some scenes on the same building facing the Merceria allotted to Titian.... Many gentlemen not being aware that Giorgione had been replaced, or that Titan was engaged there and that part of his work had been uncovered, met the former and congratulated him on his greater success with the façade toward the Merceria than with that on the Grand Canal. Giorgione felt so mortified at this that, until Titian had finished all the work and it was well known that he had done that section, Giorgione largely refrained from appearing in public, and henceforward he did not want Titian to work anymore, nor did he want to be Titian's friend." From Vasari's description it would seem that Titian took on the execution of the frescoes of the Fondaco after Giorgione had already finished the part entrusted to him, before the autumn of 1508. In this case Titian would have dismantled the scaffolding in the spring of 1509, as Gioseffi suggested (1959). Furthermore the ducal decree of 6 December, in which Leonardo Loredan communicated to the City Council of Nuremburg that the sum of expenses for the Fondaco had reached c. 30,000 ducats against a deposit of 11,250, would lead us to think that by that date all work had been completed (Brunetti 1941).

The subjects treated by Titian on the walls facing the narrow *calle* are known to us primarily through Milesio's description of them in 1715, which is more detailed than all preceding ones. "One sees a Judith with sword in hand, and under her feet the severed head of Prince Holophernes.... located above the door. In the corner toward the Rialto Bridge there is an Eve.... above said figure runs a frieze in chiaroscuro, that girds the entire façade, with animals, arabesques and other fantasies. In the other corner, toward the Calle della Bissa, there is seen a nude Venus, a Levantine, and a Knight of those young men of Venetian noble families called della Calza."

Thus this decoration, which is so important to understanding the art of the youthful Titian, was known to critics until the 1960s exclusively through the early sources and a handful of engravings by Piccini and Zanetti, in the belief that the damaged frescoes remaining on the walls of the Fondaco, (plans to salvage them went back to the mid-1930s) were illegible (Archivio della Soprintendenza ai Monumenti, Venice, 31/10/35, 29/9/36, 1/10 and 1/13/38, 12/5/39).

In 1961 the Soprintendenza had the good fortune to discover a still intelligible and extensive section of the decoration, which was quickly salvaged and restored (Valcanover 1967). This occurred immediatly before the façade of the Fondaco (already mutilated c. 1837 by the elimination of the lateral frescoed turrets), was painted white, transforming it into an anonymous building in place of the original, afire with colors, as can be seen in a detail of a painting by the school of Bonifacio Veronese representing the *Procurator Alvise Grimani Offering Saint Louis of Toulouse Alms for the Poor* (Pinacoteca di Brera, Milan). Thus, today there remain several more or less ruined sections of Titian's frescoes that covered the whole Merceria façade of the Fondaco, 47 meters in length. Together they corroborate the details of Milesio's description (Valcanover 1978).

Although consigned to a site visible only obliquely due to the narrowness of the *calle*, Titian tackled the enterprise with great commitment. He enriched the articulation of the façade by means of a large false moulded cornice that separated the ornamental and figured motifs between and under the windows of the first floor from the large overhead frieze in chiaroscuro, with figures interrupted in the center, above the "Portone di Strada," by the highly colored principal scene, the *Judith*. Even if seen laterally, the façade must surely have given the impression of great chromatic vivacity, by virtue of the intense colors, today mostly gone, of the *Judith*, in contrast to the monochromatic brown of the frieze. Then again the façade would have glowed from the vivid color of the imagery, human and non-human, within large frames of dark red between the single light windows and under their sills. Though controversial (Valcanover 1978, Romano 1981), the iconography of the frescoes must have corresponded to a precise program revolving around the *Judith*, which would have been obligatory for a state building (Muraro 1975). It is most likely that some kind of admonition was intended, at least for the main subjects, aimed at those who might theaten the freedom of Saint Mark, which would have included the Emperor Maximilian, who from the Treaty of Blois of 22 September 1504 to the League of Cambrai of 10 December 1508, vaunted specific territorial claims. From this perspective both the *Judith*, which adumbrates *Justice* (as confirmed by the letters R.A. incribed in the

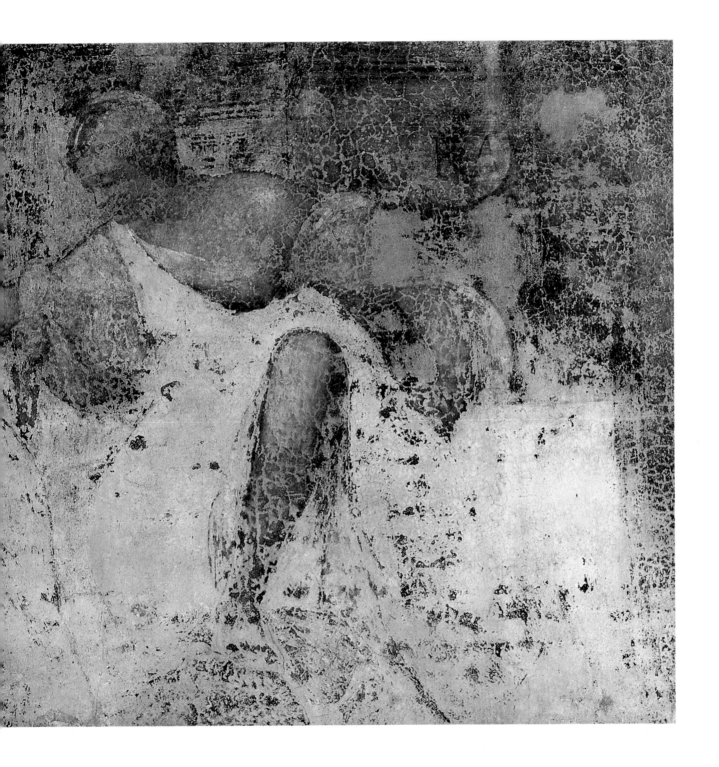

tondo on the architecture to the right, which can be read as *Regum Ars*), and the Peace by Giorgione on the principal façade, known from the engraving by van der Borcht (Nepi Scirè 1978), become loaded allusions to the steadfastness of the Republic, based on peace and justice, specifically in the face of the mortal threat from the great European powers in the years 1508-9.

Zanetti (1760), with his customary modern acuteness of connoisseurship, stressed the distance that separated the young Titian from Giorgione in the shared Fondaco project. In Giorgione's frescoes he noted the very lively chromatic ability, but also the "artificial handling of the shadows, strong, smoky, emphatic," regretting that he "was not able to reproduce.... that sanguine and flaming line" in the engravings that he had made of them. Regarding Titian's *Judith*, he made a direct comparison with Giorgione, observing that Titian "had known with such solid art how to make use of the half-tones, and of the *contrapposti* to bring flesh to that natural tenderness; and moderating the great fire of Giorgione, in the deep shadows; and in the excessive reddening of the tints, forming a style of perfect, very pleasing beauty." Zanetti also gave us his thoughts before another figure, lost today, by Titian: "That female figure.... that seems more like live flesh, in which one

sparkle, but as a shining beacon makes light for he who wishes to follow it. In those by Titian a greater, more tranquil and prudent genius is seen, which, just awakened by the other, walks with him equally and while walking with him surpasses him." Zanetti's acute judgments seem to prefigure the enlightening and sharp definitions of the early Titian by Roberto Longhi, in his *Viatico* of 1946: "The young Titian disencumbers himself fully of Giorgione's timidity."

Today, before the retrieved fragments of Titian's frescoes and the *Nude* by Giorgione, restored as far as possible to the artist's original idea of his artifice (Nepi Scirè 1978), Zanetti's observations and Roberto Longhi's judgment acquire particular merit. Although monumental, Giorgione's *Nude* still partakes, as much in the modulated purity of its construction and form as in the fragrant *sfumato* of color, in the dreamy serenity of contemporary or slightly later works, such as the *Three Philosophers* of the Kunsthistoriches Museum, Vienna, *in primis*, and the *Venus* of the Gemäldegalerie, Dresden. Titian's *Judith* presents itself with more energy of physical and pictorial life. She is poised within a well-defined space, with strongly modeled relief, raising her right arm with the sword and anchoring herself with her left arm on the marble block by pressing her feet down on the head of Holophernes. Somewhat

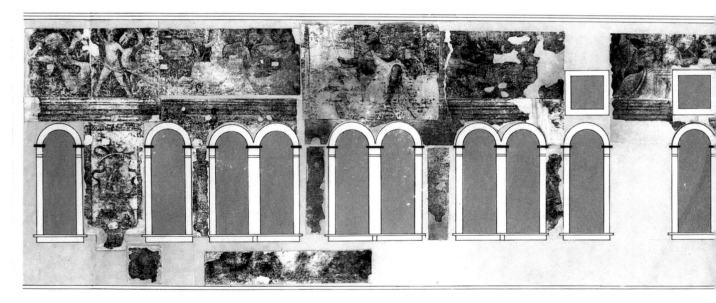

could believe the blood flows, than a painted thing; it shows that Titian had thought of more grandiose forms: he found an impasto that was more joyful in tint with incredible felicity; and had given his figures greater vivacity.... So that in the painting by Giorgione, there is shown a fervid and original genius, that departing or rather flying from the old manner, found another, entirely new and spacious, not like a mere

cramped within the frame, between the architectonic elements on the right and the luminous passage of sky on the left, the image impresses itself immediately on the viewer. Giorgione's treatment of flesh is quite different. While the face of Giorgione's *Nude* is evoked in the dissolving and merging physiognomic features, the face of *Judith*, the best-conserved passage of this extraordinary image, is constructed by thick

Reconstruction of the frescoes from Fondaco dei Tedeschi

dabs, with a process of painting *a macchia* that reappears unchanged in the frescoes of the Scuola del Santo in Padua of 1511. Such a technique allowed Titian, as Morassi observed (1956), "to recompose at a distance the vision of the whole, to obtain not only a complete fusion of the single parts, but also a greater atmospheric depth and a more intense spatial sensation." Even more instructive is Pignatti's comparison between the two images (1978). More than any other critic he focused on Titian's salvaged frescoes and Giorgione's *Nude*, restored in 1967: "If the fascination of Giorgione's painting boils down to the suggestiveness of that paint that catches fire, almost as a formally abstract symbol, Titian instead set out to restore to the figure its plastic structure with a paint laid on in fluent, materially assertive brushstrokes, inscribing it confidently within its architectonic space. The structural elements – the step, the balcony – cease to have that artificiality characteristic of the niche and stair of Giorgione's frescoes; they are structured realistically, and physically accommodate the strongly three-dimensional figure."

The "naturalism" that Titian achieved in the *Judith* has a vitality quite distinct in its figural rhythms, the interlocking color zones, and the plasticity of the modeling, from that of Giorgione's *Nude*. With secure possession of the space Titian sketched out the image in a firm and balaced composition of poses and gestures instantly comprehensible, that generate new expressive possibilities for color and light.

An analogous sense of immediacy, rendered through a rapidity of technique unknown until then in Venice, must have distinguished also the frescoes "of costumes," as Zanetti's engravings, more than the salvaged originals, indicate. It also characterizes the scenes of the frieze, which were more cursively painted, though hardly less forceful, in *chiaroscuro*. In these Titian revealed himself open to various influences. Tablets, coats of arms with fluttering ribbons, antique cuirasses with

139

standards – these were widespread iconographic motifs at the time, in frescoes in Venice and the Veneto, and would certainly have been included in Giorgione's lost frescoes of the Fondaco. But in the larger episodes of the frieze appear recollections of the engraving of the *Battle of the Sea Gods* by Andrea Mantegna, and of a Roman bas-relief of the 1st century A.D. of *Triton and Nereid*, Museo Archeologico, Venice.

The *Battle between Giants and Monsters* has motifs that appear frequently in Northern art, and which we find also in the famous engraving by Jacopo de' Barbari of *A Centaur Chased by Dragons*, and in an early painting by Titian, the *Orpheus and Eurydice* of the Accademia Carrara, Bergamo, testifying to Titian's precocious attention to Flemish painting, of which there were numerous example in Venice, such as the panels by Hieronymus Bosch, still today in the Palazzo Ducale. No less vivid is the reference, in the nude figure in the center of the fresco, to the man with his arms and legs spread wide who brandishes the sword in Antonio Pollaiuolo's engraving of the *Battle of the Nudes*.

The Fondaco frescoes prove Titian's insatiable curiosity for the non-Venetian tradition in order to emancipate himself for the sublime world of Giovanni Bellini and from the intimate dream of Giorgione. Like Sebastiano Luciani, the other artist 'created' by Giorgione, who in the organ shutters of the church of San Bartolomeo in 1509 – the same year in which Titian seems to have finished the frescoes of the Fondaco dei Tedeschi – adapted the 'tonal' lessons of the Master of Castelfranco to the service of a classical monumentality. Together, Sebastiano's four canvases and the murals of the Fondaco dei Tedeschi by Titian thus remain fundamental testimony to the rapid change of taste with respect to Giorgione's 'modern manner.' But while Sebastiano had already abandoned in 1511 the Venetian artistic scene, attracted to Rome by Raphael and Michelangelo, Titian quickly achieved a 'chromatic classicism' of poetic originality in the group of works from between the first and second decade of the century, from the so-called 'Ariosto' of the National Gallery, London, to the *Fête Champêtre* in the Louvre, to the altarpiece formerly in Santo Spirito in Isola and today in the Sacristy of the Salute, to the three *Miracles of Saint Anthony* in Padua, probably begun in 1510 and completed in 1511.

LITERATURE   Sanudo 1496-1533 (ed. 1879), VII; Dolce 1557, 54; Vasari 1568, IV, 563, 566; Milesio 1715; Zanetti 1760, IV, V, VII; Gualandi 1842, 90; Crowe and Cavalcaselle 1877, I, 71; Brunetti 1941, 62-63; Longhi 1946, 22; Morassi 1956; Gioseffi 1959, 55; Valcanover 1967, 267-68; Muraro 1975, 177ff; Valcanover 1978, 130ff (with preceding bibliography); Nepi Scirè 1978, 117ff; Pignatti 1978, 62; Romano 1981, 113ff.

F.V.

2

Christ Carrying the Cross

thin oil on canvas, 70×100 cm
Venice, Scuola di San Rocco

EXHIBITIONS   Venice 1935, Venice 1955, Venice 1978

On 20 December 1520 Sanudo wrote of "the great competition at the Church of San Rocco for an image of Christ being pulled by the Jews, and an altar, where many miracles were and are being performed, to which many many people go, and so many alms are given that the *scuola* will be made beautiful." Lorenzetti (1920) identified the painting with the "Most Holy Crucifix," which according to a deliberation of the board of the Scuola Grande di San Rocco of 22 July 1519 was in a tabernacle known as the "Principio d'altar" in the church of San Rocco on the "pilaster of the large chapel" to the right side of the main altar. The *delibera* goes on to specify that the picture awaited framing in a carved and gilt wood frame costing 30 ducats, and constructed in such a way that "under the crucifix there will be a suitable space to put the Most Holy Sacrament."
The identification of the "Most Holy Crucifix" with *Christ Carrying the Cross* has been doubted by Anderson (1977). However, testimony exists of the rich frame on this painting in woodcuts of the early Cinquecento, going back to an anonymous woodcut of 1520 now in the Museo Correr. The latter shows the tabernacle crowned by a lunette, apparently carved and gilt, representing the Eternal Father blessing, the Holy Spirit and little angels with symbols of the Passion.
The condition of this tabernacle was so fragile by the early 1600s that on 2 January 1621 a project for a new altar was approved (Archivio della Scuola Grande di San Rocco, *Cancelleria, Parti*, IV, *carta* 288), resulting four years later with the transfer of the painting to the apsidal chapel to the right of the chancel (Lorenzetti 1920). In 1955 the *Christ Carrying the Cross* was replaced by an altarpiece by Felice Carena, dedicated to Pius X, and transferred to the Sala dell'Albergo in the Scuola Grande di San Rocco.
The image, apart from the above mentioned engravings, circulated widely through copies, in marble or in paint, in the sixteenth and seventeenth century, listed by Lorenzetti (1920), Richter (1937) and Puppi (1961). Among these is a famous pen sketch in reverse by Van Dyck, dating from his Venetian sojourn of 1622-23, and today preserved in the collection of the Duke of Devonshire (Chatsworth).
Today the *Christ Carrying the Cross* is one of the few paintings whose attribution is still contested between Giorgione and Titian, despite recent studies, which have served to clarify the distance that separates these two artists even from their beginnings. The uncertainty of attribution goes back to the earliest sources. Michiel was probably referring to this famous

and venerated work in a passage describing a painting seen in 1532 at the house of Antonio Pasqualigo: "The head of Saint James with the staff, the hand of Zorzi of Castlefranco or of one of his followers, drawn from the Christ of San Rocco." The ambiguity of this note gave rise to a flat contradiction in Vasari's *Lives*. In the first edition, 1559, he credits it to Giorgione; in the second edition, 1568, after having confirmed this attribution in the "Life" of Giorgione, in Titian's "Life" he observed: "for the church of San Rocco Titian made after the frescoes at the Fondaco dei Tedeschi, the Palazzo Grimani and the Scuola del Santo in Padua a painting of Christ; with the cross on his shoulder and with a cord at his neck pulled by a Jew; this figure, which many have thought to be made by Giorgione, is today the major devotion of Venice, and has had more *scudi* in alms than Titian and Giorgione ever made in their lives." Most of the "definitively attributed literature that followed, based on Vasari's correction, definitively attributed the work to Titian, down to Cavalcaselle (1877) and Morelli (1880). After Wickhoff (1895), who was the first to reattribute the painting to Giorgione, the debate began again between the master of Castelfranco and Titian, this time in the context of several other disputed works: the so-called *Ariosto*, the *Schiavona*, and the *Noli me tangere* of the National Gallery, London, the Pitti *Concert* in Florence (see cat. no. 3), the *Madonna and Child with Saints Anthony and Roch* in the Prado and the *Concert Champêtre* in the Louvre, which most modern critics now assign to the young Titian. Arguing in favor of the attribution to Giorgione are, among others, Cook (1900), Lionello Venturi (1913), Justi (1926), Richter (1937), Coletti (1955), Zampetti (1955, 1968), Robertson (1955), Berenson (1957), Baldass-Heinz (1964), Hornig (1976) and Lattanzi (1981) (with iconological arguments). Meanwhile, the attribution to Titian is sustained by Hourticq (1930), Suida (1935), Morassi (1942), Tietze (1950), Valcanover (1960, 1978), Wethey (1969), Calvesi (1970) and Rosand (1983).
Other critics, such as Gamba (1954) and Pallucchini (1969) following Giuseppe Fiocco (1941), include the painting among those left unfinished by Giorgione and later finished by Titian. Pignatti, after favoring Titian (1955), has now changed his mind to Giorgione (1969, 1989), assigning it to the "realistic phase of the later Giorgione," not without hints of the young Titian.
To complicate the question of attribution, the state of conservation of the work is anything but encouraging. In many parts the thin gray preparation can be seen, owing to the loss or abrasion of the original pigment. The profile of the left figure, neck and beard of the tormentor, the hair of Christ and the beard and cheeks of the old man on the right are altered by retouches of a dark brownish color. The work, however, is unified overall, as testified by x-rays and examination of the paint layers that correspond technically to the *Col Tempo* by

Giorgione at the Gallerie dell'Accademia, Venice (Lazzarini 1978) and to the Pitti *Concert* by Titian in Florence (G. Chiarini 1978, M. Chiarini 1980).

Putting aside the hypothesis of a double intervention by Giorgione and Titian, the attribution problem for this work remains open. As in the Pitti *Concert*, the San Rocco canvas emanates not so much that sensibility grounded in Giorgione's subtle sentimentality, as Titian's immediacy of human contact, based in this case on the dramatic encounter between the scoundrel who stares arrogantly at Christ and Christ himself who turns his face toward the spectator with moving realism. The *Christ Carrying the Cross*, partly on account of the "reticence" of the two Leonardesque lateral figures, may plausibly be one of the works with which Titian made his debut between 1505 and 1510, at a time when he was seeking to master the technique and mood of Giorgione. The figural types, which are original here, would return soon after in Titian's work, rendered with brighter colors and denser impasto. Thus, the Christ turns to offer himself to the light as does the monk in the Pitti *Concert*, while his, face prefigures in its touching expression the Saint Roch of the Salute altarpiece, and again the savage profile of the tormenter prefigures the old man toward whom the handsome boy turns in the *Miracle of the Speaking Babe* at the Scuola del Santo in Padua. As Rosand observes (1983); "Perhaps above all, the physicality of the composition relates it to the art of Titian. At the core of its powerful effect is the physiognomic contrast between the aggressively profiled tormentor and the gentle pathos of Christ; the Savior's face is defined with a linear precision, especially evident along the brow and nose, that is characteristic of Titian's approach and quite unlike the softer mode of Giorgione. Further, the dense impacting of forms within the field, pressed by the frame and proximate to the picture plane, heightens the sense of actuality while constraining the movement of the figures. This density and constraint, reflecting developments in Northern painting, is also alien to the spatial atmosphere of Giorgione's creations. Such motifs as the flanking profiles cut by the frame point in an entirely different direction to the tragic classicism of Mantegna. And such reference allows us to locate the picture with some precision in the early career of Titian, at the moment of his emergence from the workshop of Mantegna's brother-in-law, Gentile Bellini. The manner of execution, dry and reminiscent of a tempera technique further suggests that this is a very early work by the recently graduated master, perhaps his first known painting." While the date proposed by Rosand seems early, the *Christ Carrying the Cross* is surely among some of Titian's earliest works. This is corroborated by Anderson's hypothesis (1977) that this is of the paintings bequeathed by Jacomo de' Zuane, Guardian Grande of the Scuola Grande di San Rocco, for the decoration of the Chapel of the Cross.

However, as Pignatti's essay in this catalogue notes, the Giorgione-Titian problem of attribution for the *Christ Carrying the Cross* remains open. It is one of the few still contested by the many "expansionist" critics of Giorgione's work. Even so, Vasari's decided correction in Titian's favor should not be underestimated (Vasari also credited Giorgione with the frescoes of the Mercerie façade at the Fondaco dei Tedeschi in the 1550 edition of his *Lives*, substituting Titian's name in 1568) – a correction made no doubt after his meeting with Titian in 1566 at the artist's home in the Biri Grande.

LITERATURE Sanudo 1496-1533 (ed. 1896); Michiel 1521-43 (ed. 1884), 180; Vasari 1550, 577; Vasari 1568, III, 568; Crowe and Cavalcaselle 1877, I, 49; Morelli 1880, 200; Wickhoff 1895, 34; Cook 1900, 54; Venturi 1913, 60; Lorenzetti 1920, 181ff; Justi 1926, I, 74; Hourticq 1930, 17; Suida 1935, 35; Richter 1937, 236; Fiocco 1941, 38; Morassi 1942, 141; Tietze 1950, 397; Gamba 1954, 172ff; Coletti 1955, 276; Zampetti 1955, 114; Pignatti 1955, 502; Berenson 1957, 84; Valcanover 1960, I, 42; Puppi 1961, 39; Baldass-Heinz 1964, 156; Zampetti 1968, n.27; Pallucchini 1969, 24; Wethey 1969, 80; Pignatti 1969, 69, 111-12; Calvesi 1970, 184; Hornig 1976, 877ff; Anderson 1977, 203ff; Lazzarini 1978, 49; Pignatti 1978, 115; Valcanover 1978, 149ff; G. Chiarini 1978, 196ff; M. Chiarini 1980, 293; Lattanzi 1981, 108-09; Rosand 1983, 64; Pignatti 1989, 164.

F.V.

3

The Concert

oil on canvas, 86.5×123.5 cm
Florence, Galleria Palatina, Palazzo Pitti

EXHIBITIONS   Venice 1955, Florence 1978
RESTORATION   1976, E. Masini, S. Taiti

The canvas was first cited by Ridolfi (1648) in Venice, in Paolo del Sera's collection, shortly before Cardinal Leopoldo de' Medici acquired it in 1654. From Ridolfi, to Boschini (1660), to the inventory of Leopold's collection (1663-67), it was attributed to Giorgione. The work was universally referred to as such until Morelli (1880) perceived in it instead, despite the unfortunate effect of old repainting, an early work by Titian. The 1976 restoration (M. Chiarini 1980) clarified that the canvas was enlarged by an addition at the top, probably to adapt it to the frame chosen by the Grand Prince Ferdinando, heir to Cosimo III, who, at the beginning of the eighteenth century, coveted the work for his collection in Palazzo Pitti (G. Chiarini 1978). This addition, along with the multiple coats of varnish and heavy repainting, which masked the lacunae but altered the chromatic relations, were cleaned off in 1976, revealing an image that effectively is being seen for the first time in living memory.

For example, during the cleaning it was discovered that the copious garment worn by the central figure, the spinet player with the fur trim at his wrists, was dark blue, not black. This rules out the identification of the player as a cleric, which goes back to Ridolfi ("an Augustinian Friar"), and from which originated the curious Florentine tradition that identified the protagonists as "Luther [once an Augustinian friar], Calvin, and the nun" (that is, Catherine von Bora, ex-nun and Luther's wife from 1525); a tradition that may be partially explained by the mention, in the inventory compiled upon Leopoldo's death in 1675, of the figure with the plumed hat as "a young woman." Even so, at the beginning of the nineteenth century, the iconographic and chronological incongruity between the Reformers and the attribution to Giorgione was noticed. The more plausible title The Concert became fashionable, in accord with a 1663-67 inventory which named it "Tre Musici."

Given the force of their portrait-like individuality, the two figures with instruments have been more or less fantastically identified as this or that musician, including, among others, the famous Obrecht and Verdelot, based on Vasari's description of such a painting by Sebastiano del Piombo, which he saw in Florence (Friedeberg 1917, Hourticq 1930, the inadmissable attribution to Sebastiano was recently reproposed by E.H. Ramsden 1983).

Music, or better, "making music together" (Boehm 1985) is, in effect, the apparent theme of the painting, reminding one how in sixteenth-century Venice music was an integral part of a gentleman's education. It is no accident that the painting makes symbolic reference to the three ages of man. This is more explicit in a second Pitti painting the Three Ages of Man now decisively attributed to Giorgione (Lucco 1989), and it has been argued that the intention was to stress the importance of music in all phases of a civilized life (Wethey 1971, Hoffman 1984).

But as with the Three Ages of Man, this interpretation is not fully satisfactory. The theme of the "concert," a widespread genre in the princely Northern Italian courts in the fifteenth and sixteenth centuries (Lucco 1989), is dominant, and in this case formulated with an intensity that has always fascinated public and critic alike.

The question of attribution has been exhaustively treated by Chiarini (1978). Titian's name, first put forth by Morelli (1880) as an alternative to the traditional attribution to Giorgione, now prevails (Meijer 1979, Rossi 1979, Hope 1980, Gentili 1980 and 1988, Fasolo 1980, Pignatti 1982, Rapp 1987, Chiarini 1988), with the already-noted exception of Ramsden (1983), and of Paronchi (1989), who reverts to Giorgione, adding Sebastiano del Piombo's name for good measure. The youth with the plumed hat has always provoked uncertainty, and continues to vex critics as the "false note" of the composition; such that since Gronau (1904) it has sometimes been considered an insertion by a weak Giorgionesque collaborator (Pallucchini 1969, Valcanover 1969), or even a forgery à la Giorgione by Pietro della Vecchia (Ramsden 1983).

Yet this figure, over whose contours the paint of the central musician's robe is superimposed and which therefore must have been part of the original composition, is not at all incompatible with the group. The face of the figure on the right is similarly abraded and impoverished by past overly-drastic cleanings, the same that flattened the modeling and hardened the features of the youth while, as Pignatti (1969) and Marco Chiarini (1980) have pointed out, the better preserved parts of his clothing show that free handling and rich impasto characteristic of Titian.

In fact, doubts about the attribution to Titian persist less among specialists than in the studies of related fields (Mucchi 1978, Tieri 1982, Boehm 1985). Gloria Chiarini's (1978) argument for "... a complete attribution to Titian in a period within the very early years of the second decade of the century (c. 1510-12)" can be taken as conclusive. The recent juxtaposition of The Concert and the Three Ages of Man in the Galleria Palatina, following the restoration of the latter painting, highlighted both the similarity of culture and subject matter of the two masterpieces, and the profound differences in visual language. Surely it is now possible to dispel forever the confusion, reconfirming the attribution of the Three Ages of Man to the young Giorgione (c. 1500) (Lucco 1989), and of

The Concert entirely to Titian, c. 1510, contemporary with the Salute *Saint Mark Enthroned*, and the frescoes of the Scuola del Santo in Padua (Pignatti 1978).

LITERATURE   Ridolfi 1648 (ed. 1914), I, 99; Boschini 1660 (ed. 1966), 397; Lermolieff (Morelli) 1880 (ed. 1886), 158; Gronau 1904, 291; Friedberg 1917, 169-76; Hourticq 1930, 114-27; Pallucchini 1969, I, 24-25, 241; Valcanover 1969, 95, no. 42; Pignatti 1969, 118; Wethey 1971, II, 91-92; Pignatti 1978, 41, 122-23; G. Chiarini 1978, 196-208; Mucchi 1978, 63; Rossi 1979, 191; Meijer 1979, 106-07; Hope 1980, 77; M. Chiarini 1980, 293-94; Fasolo 1980, 17; Gentili 1980, 43-4; Tieri 1982, 170; Pignatti 1982, 141-42; Ramsden 1983, 5-75; Hoffman 1984, 243-44; Boehm 1985, 131; Gentili 1985, 67; Rapp 1987, 361, 364; M. Chiarini 1988, 13; Lucco 1989, 11-28; Parronchi 1989, 54-56.

S.P.

4.

Jacopo Pesaro Presented to Saint Peter by Pope Alexander VI

oil on canvas, 145×183 cm
Antwerp, Koninklijk Museum voor Schone Kunsten

EXHIBITIONS   Venice 1935, London 1983-84

On 23 August 1502 the allied forces of Spain, Venice and the pope reconquered the Isle of Santa Maura (antique Leucadia) which five years before had fallen into Turkish hands. The commander of the combined fleet was the Venetian Benedetto Pesaro. The papal fleet was led by this kinsman Jacopo Pesaro, bishop of Paphos. From several historic sources it appears that the victory over the Turks was mainly to the credit of the latter. Jacopo Pesaro is clearly the central figure of the painting and the representation is linked to the events just described. This is implied by the later inscription on the tablet at the lower center: RITRATTO DI VNO DI CASA PESARO/ IN VENETIA CHE FV FATTO/ GENERALE DI STA CHIESA./ TITIANO F. Dressed in the gown of the Knights of Malta and carrying the standard of the Borgias, Jacopo Pesaro is kneeling in front of Saint Peter. The latter is enthroned on a marble dais, decorated with a pseudo-antique relief, holding in his left hand the Gospel and with his right hand making the sign of the blessing. At his feet are his attributes, the keys of the Holy Church. Alexander Borgia, with the papal tiara on his head and wearing a magnificent green cope, stands behind Pesaro and presents him to Saint Peter. The background shows the Adriatic Sea, on which several galleys float. From this, two themes emerge: firstly, an homage to papal authority, represented by Saint Peter and Alexander VI, Borgia; second an expression of gratitude, a kind of ex-voto, for the reconquest of Santa Maura.
Although the subject and authorship have always been agreed, upon opinions about the exact date and the context in which the work was painted differ thoroughly. According to one hypothesis the painting must have been executed or at least commissioned before the battle, as no battle scenes are shown (Mather). According to a second theory the work must have been painted before Pope Alexander's death in 1503, since hatred of the Borgias would have prevented a later date for his portrayal (Crowe and Cavalcaselle). On the other hand Hope assumed it must postdate the pope's death) as a living pope would never have been shown standing in the presence of Saint Peter. Since Pesaro was absent from Venice from early 1503 until 1506, the picture would then date from c. 1506-07. All the above theories have in common that they accept the early date: between 1502 and 1507.
A second group of scholars favor a considerably later date. By accepting a later date for Titian's birth (the end of the 1480s) they postpone the execution of the painting at least to c. 1512 (Wethey) or argue that the portrait may even have been finished only c. 1520 (Suida). Orperhaps the portrait may even

have been finished only c. 1520 (Suida). Alternatively Meyer zur Capellen proposed an execution in two distinct phases. Departing from the admittedly archaic composition, reminiscent of the Quattrocento, he distinguishes two hands, an opinion corroborated by x-ray investigation. The first, which would have resulted not only in the painting of Saint Peter's head but the laying-in of the general design of the composition also. This first stage would have been the work of Giovanni Bellini. In 1502-03 Bellini would have received the commission in place of his still-unknown pupil Titian. Circumstances would have restricted his contribution to the above-mentioned parts and the painting would have been completed by Titian c. 1515-20 (the latter period based on stylistic characteristics). From this it is easy to grasp the complexity of the issues. All theories offer more or less interesting points of view, but none provides us with solid evidence and, short of the spectacular discovery of new documentation such as an account or a contract, such evidence will never be forthcoming. Therefore, it seems wisest to accept the least farfetched explanation and reconsider the above-mentioned basic elements: the expression of gratitude to the papacy and the reference to the Battle of Santa Maura. These only make sense at a time when the facts still had topical significance, soon after the battle, which, it must be said, was not an event of historical importance. But for Jacopo Pesaro it was important to stress his personal role in the battle and thus to prevent Benedetto Pesaro, general commander, from taking all credit for the victory. It is also compelling too, that the representation of a member of the Borgia family, considering its reputation, became rather rapidly undesirable, and again that the representation of a standing pope in Saint Peter's company would imply that the former was already dead.
Taking into account these arguments, we conclude that the most plausible dating lies between 1503 and early 1507. Thus the painting may claim to be the earliest Titian, and shows us a painter who, still in search of an individual style, continues the schemes of his master Giovanni Bellini. This compositional insecurity is clearly gone by the time Titian paints once more for Jacopo Pesaro, at the Frari in 1519.

LITERATURE   Crowe and Cavalcaselle 1877, 74-79; Hetzer 1920, 34-35; *Italian Art 1200-1900* 1930, no. 58; Suida 1933, 24-25, 151; *Mostra di Tiziano* 1935, no. 3; Mather 1938, 18-19; Wittkower 1938-39, 202-03; Dell'Acqua 1956, 107; Wethey 1969, 152-53; Tressider 1979, 142-59; Meyer zur Capellen 1980, 144-52; C. Hope 1980, 23-26; *The Genius of Venice* 1983, 219.

E.V.

5

Saint Mark Enthroned and Saints Cosmas and Damian, Roch and Sebastian

oil on canvas, 218×149 cm
Venice, Basilica di Santa Maria della Salute

EXHIBITIONS Venice 1935, Venice 1978
RESTORATION 1978-85, A. Michieletto, A. Sartori, V. Merzagora

This was painted for the altar of Santa Maria in the church of Santo Spirito in Isola, the Venetian headquarters of the Regular Augustinian Canons. Together with other paintings and furniture from the church it was transferred to the Salute after the suppression of the order in 1656. The condition of the painting, which elicited the admiration of Boschini (1660) and Sansovino (1581) for its lively palette, and which according to Vasari was thought by some to be "from Giorgione's hand," must have deteriorated rapidly, giving rise to repeated restoration efforts. In 1787 Edwards pointed to the disfiguring repaints scattered everywhere, especially on Saint Mark. The painting was worked on several times in the nineteenth century, in 1849 and 1882; between 1889 and 1894 the support was reduced in thickness and modified (see Nepi Scirè's essay).

The altarpiece's iconography, with the simultaneous presence of Saint Mark and the four healing saints, clearly indicates its role as an *ex voto* for the cessation of the plague, perhaps commissioned by the state itself in view of the prominence of Venice's patron saint. Only a few years apart, in 1504 and 1509, two plagues befell the city; the first, a very brief one, ended with few victims, while the second was much more violent. If the depiction of Saints Roch and Sebastian was common in paintings that referred to plague episodes, and the presence of Cosmas and Damian, doctor saints and the patrons of physicians, thus reinforced the protection against the disease. By, as it were, placing science alongside faith, one might suppose that the epidemic that occasioned the painting must have been particularly grave and alarming: the second wave of the epidemic, in fact – thus moving the date back to 1510. This is confirmed by stylistic considerations. Most modern historians agree on this date, including Morassi (1966), Pallucchini (1969) who dated it immediately after the Scuola del Santo frescoes, and Valcanover (1960, 1969, 1978), who placed the painting soon after Giorgione's death, late 1510, as does Nepi (1979), while Rosand (1975, 1978) favored an earlier date, c. 1508-09.

The composition is still that of the Quattrocento, of the *Sacra Conversazione* type. The white and red checkered floor generates the architectonic space in which the figures move, and at the same time designates the physical and spiritual level of Saint Mark, who, against an open sky where fleeting light-filled clouds drift by, rises enthroned above the others. He gazes upward not in prayer with the other saints, but in direct conversation with God, as if urged by the other saints who are the direct intermediaries for the prayers of man. Could it be that the presence of the patron saint in this position was intended to symbolize the Republic itself, highlighting its independence from the ecclesiastical hierarchies, its religious faith and also its scientific "rationalism," which was peculiar to the Venetian state? Men's prayers, collected by an absorbed and somewhat absent Sebastian (the only figure facing outward) are conveyed on the rising diagonal of his hands to Saint Mark, who like Sebastian gazes outward but upward, and who partakes in a silent dialogue with the Divinity. This is no longer a prayer, but a firm request, as his solemn and monumental attitude indicates. Even if in the figure of the saint there is a clear relationship to Solomon in the *Judgment of Kingston Lacy* by Sebastiano del Piombo, the spirit with which the two characters are portrayed is quite different. The imposing, serene figure of Solomon, attentive to the emotional dispute and almost ready to descend from the throne, contrasts with the figure of Saint Mark who is compressed and foreshortened by the low viewpoint used here for the first time by Titian – remote from the crowd of saints below, and tense in his encounter with the invisible Divinity. The sky, blue and full of vaporous white clouds, against which the saint is silhouetted, seems to obliterate any possibility of landscape. It is more of a "void," a "non-space" in opposition to the measured space of the foreground.

Even the columns in the shade on the right, insignificant in comparison with the broad and powerful architectonic structure of the later Pesaro altarpiece, eludes any possibility of defining the space behind the figures. It merely highlights the luminous body of Saint Sebastian and the shadow cast over the face and shoulder of Saint Mark, creating a dynamic chiaroscuro accenting his isolation, his "authority" with respect to the other saints, his privileged position as representative of the State. This is quite different from the spirit in which Giovanni Bellini painted the hermit saint somewhat later (probably John Crisostom rather than Jerome) in the altarpiece in San Giovanni Crisostomo. The two lateral saints and the hermit are depicted in separate spaces: Saints Louis and Christopher in a zone defined by architectonic elements and enclosed by the parapet behind them, the hermit on a rock *en plein air* immersed in a celestial landscape with a distant view. Saint John's isolation is complete; he looks neither at the faithful as Saint Louis does, nor at heaven as does Saint Christopher, but only at his tome, while even the hermetic Greek text on the mosaic vault underlines his voluntary solitude, his remoteness (also doctrinal) from the other saints. Instead, the spiritual tension that distanced Titian's Mark from the others is due to their emotional tension. In Titian's altarpiece the vanishing point of the floor, which converges under Mark's feet, defines the space in which the figures move, but also the space proper to Saint Mark, whose recessed throne delimits the background. In this way, the pictorial structure is closer to that of Giorgione's Castelfranco altarpiece, in which the lines of that portion of the floor on which Saints Liberale and Francis stand converge at the feet of the Virgin, while the lines of the flanking portions converge on the Virgin's head. Moreover, the Madonna's throne does not mark the end of the architectonic space, as does that of Saint Mark, but occupies only half of it, clearly measurable in the foreshortened perspective toward the back. And so the elevation of Mark, while enclosing him in the same architectonic space as the other saints, acquires a particular significance. This is not a willed isolation lived in total abstraction from common life, as for Bellini's hermit saint, but rather a different status in which Saint Mark is the voice not only of the faithful but also and above all of the State of which he is the emblem.

All the early historians were in agreement in their praise of the lively palette, the singing intensity of the colors. The contrast between Saint Mark's lacquer-red robe and bright lapis lazuli-blue cloak, the intense reds and yellows of the two doctor saints' clothes, and the dazzling white of the cloth wrapped around Sebastian's waist, appear here for the first time in Titian's work. Only a few years earlier, Giovanni Bellini had painted the altarpiece of San Zaccaria, in which the blue mantle of the Virgin performed as the chromatic and compositional fulcrum, contrasting with the dense red of Saint Jerome's robes.

Perhaps as never before the lesson of Giovanni Bellini emerges in the Salute painting, combined with Titian's meditation on Giorgione, clearly apparent in the heads of Roch and Sebastian. Titian departs from Giorgione precisely in that quest for monumentality which derives from Bellini and which Titian attained in part through the intensity of his chromatic range. It would reach its peak in the fiery painterliness of the *Assumption*, with the dramatic monumentality of the apostles and the Virgin, already far from us in the vortex of little angels. A copy, with some variations, exists in the Church of San Francesco ad Alto in Ancona, and a second, limited to the figures of Roch and Sebastian, in the monastery of Praglia. A 1781 engraving by Wagner represented the altarpiece with the gilt frame which was added before the painting's definitive placement on the altar of the Sacristy of the Salute.

LITERATURE Vasari 1568, VII, 432; Sansovino 1581, 83; Boschini 1660, 186-87; Valcanover 1960, 50; Morassi 1966, 18; Pallucchini 1969, I, 22, 59; Valcanover 1969, 94; Rosand 1975, 58, 59; Valcanover 1978, 163; Rosand 1978, 68; Nepi Scirè 1979, 236ff.

A.A.

6.

Three Seated Figures Reading

sinopia, 233×184 cm
Padua, Presidenza dell'Arca del Santo

EXHIBITION   Padua 1976
RESTORATION   1969, L. Tintori

In 1 December 1510 Titian signed a contract with the Confraternity of Sant'Antonio in Padua for the payment of one of the frescoes with miracles of the saint in the *scuola* next to the Basilica of Saint Anthony, and for the execution of two others. His fee was to be greater than that paid a few months earlier to Gianantonio Requesta, known as "Il Corona," and, in relation to the volume of work, more than that received by Giorgione for the Grand Canal façade of the Fondaco dei Tedeschi. On 23 April 1511 the artist began work again on the three frescoes representing the *Miracle of the Newborn Babe* on the northwest wall, the *Miracle of the Irascible Son* and the *Miracle of the Jealous Husband* on the northeast wall. On 2 December 1511 Titian received payment for "li tre quadri" and signed himself TICIAN DI CADOR (Maschio 1980).

In the three Miracles, Titian's youthful style has fully matured, thereby placing him in the vanguard of the High Renaissance, beside Raphael and Michelangelo. The poetic distance that separates Titian's miracles from those others entrusted to a group of heavy-handed artists, among them Girolamo del Santo, Domenico Campagnola, Benedetto Montagna and possibly even Francesco, Titian's older brother (Morassi 1956), is blatantly apparent.

The *Miracle of the Censer* (Morassi 1956; Pallucchini 1969) has been attributed to Francesco. It was executed in 1511, since on 7 May of that year the foreman Marco Ferrarese was paid to work on the windows the *scuola* and to plaster the wall "outside the miracle of the censer" ("de fuori al miracolo della nave"; Sartori 1955). Of inferior quality, the fresco has also been attributed to Gianmartino Franzapani by Sartori (1955) and to Girolamo del Santo by Grossato (Maschio 1980). Nor has the discovery of the existing *sinopia* under the painted mural, when it was detached for conservation in 1969 (Valcanover 1969), significantly contributed to solving the attributional problem.

The discovery is, however, of exceptional importance, since beneath the gray traces of a *sinopia* evidently related to the three standing figures and to the landscape of the *Miracle of the Censer*, there was a preliminary *sinopia* unmistakably bearing the mark of the youthful Titian's imagination: three seated figures in two tones of red ochre, two females with a bearded male in the middle, and to the left a group of shrubs in sepia.

The cited document of 17 May 1511 attests to the fact that this first *sinopia* dates back to the months in which Titian was working on the three *Miracles*. It is not known, however, what the subject of this fourth fresco for the Scuola del Santo might have been. Maschio (1980) was only speculating when he suggested that it was to have been one of Saint Anthony's several posthumous miracles which failed to satisfy the Confraternity. Conceivably this fresco, begun but not finished, was one of the reasons why Titian interrupted his activity in the Scuola del Santo and left Padua (Puppi 1980). Zampetti (1984) also emphasizes, although from a different perspective, the importance of the *sinopia* in relation to Titian's other work in the Scuola del Santo.

The composition of the three figures intent on reading and conversation is unparalleled by any pictorial or graphic work by Titian up to this time, even if telling comparisons can readily be made with his works at the turn of the first decade. The shrubs for example are rendered with the same lively naturalistic drawing as those lashed by the wind in the *Miracle of the Newborn Babe* and the *Miracle of the Jealous Husband*, or others, no less memorable, such as those in the drawing of the *Edge of the Woods* (Metropolitan Museum of Art, New York), generally dated before 1515, and in Titian's woodcut of the *Sacrifice of Abraham*. His lightning strikes, vibrating with light, delineate the physical and spiritual attitudes of the figures in a scene of intimacy, which evokes the mood of Giorgione with its subtle and still so controversial meanings, also felt in other works by Titian such as the Pitti *Concert*. The young woman on the left bowing her head, in three-quarter length, seems engaged in conversation with the old bearded man, and by the hanging hair seems intent on reading; meanwhile the young woman on the right, rendered in profile, looks straight before her.

The similarity to the figural passages in the three *Miracles* in the *scuola* is clear, particularly in the three faces. The head of the female figure to the left reworks that of the *Judith* of the Fondaco dei Tedeschi. The *sinopia*, of extraordinary freedom in its openness of line but at the same time concise and essential in defining the forms and anticipating the resonant beauty of the color zones to come, is a valuable revelation, pertinent also to his graphic work, of the young Titian's first ideas.

LITERATURE   Sartori 1955, 67; Morassi 1956; Valcanover 1969, 306; Pallucchini 1969, 211; Maschio 1976, 73; Valcanover 1978, 48-49; Maschio 1980, 441ff; Puppi 1980, 545ff; Zampetti 1984, 94-95, 105ff.

F.V.

7

The Triumph of Christ

woodcut, 5 blocks, total c. 38.5×268 cm
inscription: "Gregorius de gregorijs excusit/MDXVII"
Venice, Museo Correr, Gabinetto di Stampe e Disegni (St. PD1195.96.97) I and IV block reproduced in Kristeller, 1906

The grandiose woodcut of *The Triumph of Christ* marks the beginning of Titian's relationship with the world of engraving. Vasari (1568) gave us the first description, dating it 1508. The woodcut is grouped by Vasari with Titian's early works, immediately following the Fondaco frescoes (datable c. 1508) and just before the Saint Anthony frescoes in the Scuola del Santo, Padua (1510-11) and the Santo Spirito altarpiece (*Saint Mark Enthroned with Saints*) now in the Salute (c. 1510).
Vasari justly observed that this was exceptional for its time, for its "verve, beautiful style and its technical achievement." With this Titian established for himself a position as a mature exponent of an expressive means practiced by leading European engravers, from Mantegna to Giulio Campagnola, from Dürer to Marcantonio Raimondi. In addition, that verve (*'fierezza'*) praised by Vasari indicates a profoundly innovative element in the discovery of light and color, which transpire, even from the black and white of the print: a new element, uniquely "Venetian," which prefigures the approaching figurative revolution of which Titian was to be the protagonist. This is what distinguished the *Triumph* from other great engravings of the time, and guaranteed Titian's stylistic singularity. Titian was thoroughly informed of the aesthetic progress of the early Venetian school and at this point goes beyond the accomplishments of Bellini and Giorgione. Clear evidence of a monumentality, a plasticity of Roman origins (Raphael and Michelangelo) moves through the numerous figures of saints and prophets of the *Triumph of Christ*, together with the technical influence of Mantegna and Dürer whose prints would have profoundly impressed the young Titian.

The composition of the friezelike *Triumph of Christ* has justly caused critics to invoke classical sculptural sources. Valcanover wrote (1978): "As in an antique bas-relief, the images parade as in a procession, emerging from the triumphal arch barely alluded to on the left, into a landscape reminiscent of Titian's birth place. Led by Adam and Eve the march of Old Testament figures precedes the two episodes central to the woodcut theme: the Cross, symbol of salvation, and Christ, symbol of power, seated on the globe and holding the scepter. Behind, the apostles, the bishops, the martyrs, the hermits and the saints press forward...." But the majestic woodcut has profound more meanings. It should be related to that singular historical moment when new civil, religious and cultural aspirations crystallized in the city, which seemed the only Italian State capable of defending its liberty against the great European powers and the papacy (Benvenuti 1976).
Whatever the woodcut's true significance may be, Titian was inspired by readily identifiable iconographic, literary and figurative sources. Its close ties to the *Triumph of the Cross* by Girolamo Savonarola, published in 1497, has been noted by several critics as has its relationship to other "Triumphs" of the Medieval and Renaissance literary traditions. For the composition, Titian certainly drew on prints after the *Triumph of Caesar* to which Andrea Mantegna had devoted himself between 1486 and 1492 for the court of the Gonzaga in Mantua and today preserved at Hampton Court.
The structure of the *Triumph of Christ* resembles the religious processions of the time. For example, Muraro and Rosand (1976) published a description of the procession of the Confraternity of the Scuola di San Marcello in Vicenza, 1497, on the day of the Corpus Domini, which has strong affinities with the woodcut.
The complexity and the depth of culture conveyed by the woodcut lead us to doubt Vasari's 1508 dating, although this is still accepted by certain critics (Muraro and Rosand 1976). It is

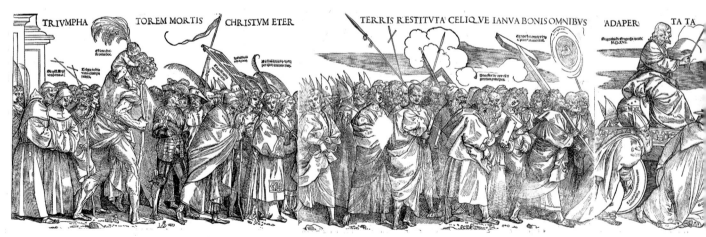

difficult to imagine that the still-youthful Titian could already have been in possession of such a range of visual sources, especially of the Roman School. Several of the figures clearly refer to Michelangelo. The *Good Thief*, for example, who carries the cross in front of Christ, is quoted from the cartoon for the *Battle of Cascina*. Saint Christopher is borrowed from the print of the *Flagbearer* by Agostino Veneziano and Marcantonio Raimondi. The female figure and the putti are generically related to Raphael.

Ridolfi (1648) was the first to suggest that the date of the *Triumph* should be moved back to 1510-11: "Having then moved to Padua, it is said that he portrayed the Triumph of Christ all around a room of the house he took, which can be seen in a woodcut drawn by his own hand, which because it is very well known we shall not trouble to describe." This account, however, has provoked much scepticism. As Sinding-Larsen noted (1975), for Titian to have painted a religious subject of this kind in a private house is unconvincing. Then again, from the stylistic point of view, Pallucchini (1976, XIV) observed that if we wish to give credit to the 1508 date "we must completely re-think the beginnings of Titian's career." It is in fact difficult to believe that the grandiose human theater of the *Triumph* preceded Titian's three *Miracles* in the Scuola del Santo, Padua, completed in the summer of 1511 (Valcanover 1978).

It is not easy to reconstruct the technical history of the woodcut. Several states exist, among which it is difficult to establish an exact relation of chronology (Dreyer 1971; Muraro and Rosand 1976). Unfortunatly, no examples survive of the original state, nor is there any trace of preparatory drawings. Even the engravers of the various editions are anonymous, and we can only guess that Titian employed some of the able German-trained craftsmen active at the time in the Veneto, including perhaps Jacob von Strassburg, who engraved in 1504 the *Triumph of Caesar* as well as a *Roman History*.

In their attempts to identify the first version of the *Triumph*, critics have until now tried to distinguish the various editions on the basis of quality. They attribute to the best of them a higher probability of having derived from the engraving of the original blocks. Until very recently the opinion prevailed that the two editions printed in Flanders by Lambrecht (Ghent 1543) and the widow Liefrink (Antwerp c. 1545) were the best. Even so, there has never been a specific comparative evaluation of the various editions. It is best therefore to stick by incontrovertible facts.

The oldest documented edition is that of 1517, with the signature of the publisher "Gregorius de gregorijs" (Dreyer 1971, i, II). This most probably refers to an application for a *privilegio* on 22 April 1516 (Fulin 1882). The woodcut, in five blocks with Latin inscriptions, is of high quality and was certainly printed in Venice.

The edition in nine blocks with Italian and Latin inscriptions signed "Opus Luce Antonii Uberti in Venetiis impreso" is also dated c. 1517 (Dreyer 1971, 1, IV), and is poorer in quality. Between the de Gregorijs and Uberti editions is another in five blocks with Latin inscriptions that can be attributed to Vavassore (Dreyer 1971, 1, III).

The two Flemish editions do not appear until the 1540s: one signed by Joos Lambrecht of Ghent in 1543, in ten blocks without inscriptions, and another, also in ten blocks with French inscriptions and the signature "par la Vefue Margariete de Corneille Liefrink," and datable soon after the death of Liefrink in 1545 (Dreyer 1971, 1, I).

Critics have tended to judge the Liefrink edition as the closest to Titian's original design (Muraro and Rosand 1976). However, a recent study by Michael Bury (1989) has reopened the entire discussion of the various editions.

Bury convincingly rejected the qualitative methodology, which had favored the Flemish editions of the 1540s, and proposed instead that the de Gregorijs edition of 1517 was the first. In

support of this, he recited a list of figurative connections between the *Triumph* and Titian's works in the years between 1516 and 1519 (the *Assumption*, *The Venus Worship* and others). The Saint Christopher and the Good Thief of the woodcut derive from the *Flagbearer*, after Michelangelo, which was accessible to Titian through the prints of Agostino Veneziano and Raimondi, but apparently not before 1516. Bury concluded that the original drawing by Titian for the *Triumph of Christ* should be dated very close to the 1517 edition by de Gregorijs (at any rate for the part to the right of Christ, whereas the part to the left of Christ may have derived from a drawing of a few years earlier, by Titian or one of his collaborators.)

Bury's new theory poses afresh the question of the place of the woodcut in Titian's artistic development. The precocity, and therefore the importance of the woodcut, would undoubtedly have been greater if Vasari's date could be accepted. Instead Titian was at least twenty-five years of age at the moment of this first experiment with woodcuts, and already had behind him important paintings, such as the altar of *Saint Peter* for Bishop Jacopo Pesaro, or the so-called *Sacred and Profane Love* for Nicolò Aurelio, while he had already begun work on the Frari *Assumption*.

Nonetheless the singularity and autonomy of Titian's graphic style in the *Triumph of Christ* are beyond question, a style that prophesies, with its dazzling counterpoint of light and color "the discovery of the *pittura aperta*, which creates a new era in Venetian art" (Murano and Rosand 1976).

LITERATURE   Vasari 1568 (ed. 1906), VII, 431; Ridolfi 1648 (ed. Von Hadeln 1914), I, 156; Fulin 1882, 188; Kristeller 1906; Mauroner 1941, 25; Dreyer 1971, 32-41; Pignatti 1973, 267-68; Benvenuti 1976, 13-16; Muraro and Rosand 1976, 74-78; Pallucchini 1976, XIV; Valcanover 1978, 170-76; Chiari 1982, 27-28; Bury 1989, 188-97.

T.P.

8.

Rest on the Flight into Egypt

oil on panel, 46.3×61.5 cm
The Marquess of Bath, Longleat House, Warminster,
Wiltshire

EXHIBITION   London 1950

Formerly in the collection of Emporor Rudolf II, Prague, this
passed in 1659 to Archduke Leopold Wilhelm in Vienna and
then, sometime before 1851, to H.A.J. Munro of Novar,
Scotland. It was bought by the Marquess of Bath at Christie's,
London, 1 June 1878.
Attributed to Giorgione by Waagen (1854) and to Beccaruzzi
by Cavalcaselle (1871), it was given to Titian only in 1915, on
the occasion of "The Venetian School" exhibition at the
Burlington Fine Arts Club, London (Wethey 1969). This
attribution, though ignored by Tietze, was accepted by Suida
(1935) and by most recent scholars (Berenson 1957, Valcanover 1960, Pallucchini 1969, Wethey 1969, Pignatti 1981).
Like the *Flight into Egypt* in the Hermitage, Leningrad, which
probably precedes the Fondaco dei Tedeschi frescoes of
1508-09, judging by the rather old-fashioned posing of the
figures (Fomiciova 1967; e Ballarin 1980), the landscape in this
attractive painting is still Giorgionesque in mood, with a
naturalness appropriate to the intimacy of the subject. The
Virgin clasps the Infant closely, and he finds safe haven in His
mother's embrace (as in the Leningrad example, though the
Child's position is reversed). Saint Joseph, to the left, is
absorbed in his own thoughts. Suspended in a common
psychological link, the figures take their place in the space as
isolated units within a common bond of chromatic zones
handled more confidently than in the Leningrad painting. The
figures are prominent in the foreground on the wooded
mound where they have found shelter and which, to the right,
opens toward a steep hill dominated by a round tower just
grazed by light, a motif that, iconographically and pictorially,
evokes the similar scenery in the upper left of the *Miracle of the
Irascible Son* in the Scuola del Santo, Padua. Like the figures,
the landscape is rendered with an extraordinary freshness of
observation, with light variations even in the most delicate and
subtle contrasts.
The inventiveness and the vitality of the "natural" palette
stamp this *Rest on the Flight into Egypt* as one – perhaps the
earliest – of the group of works in which, after the Paduan
frescoes of 1510-11, Titian instilled new life into the meanings
and formulas of the late Quattrocento Venetian *Sacra Conversazione*, formulas to which Giovanni Bellini had remained
faithful up to his last years.
A version of the Longleat painting, larger (91 x 160 cm) and
with some variants, is in the Contini Bonacossi collection,
Florence. This was considered to be from Titian's own hand
by Longhi (1927), Suida (1935), and Berenson (1957) but was
omitted from Tietze's catalogue (1950) and judged by Wethey
(1969) to be a sixteenth-century copy, and by Pallucchini
(1969) a "later workshop repetition of a lost original."

LITERATURE   Waagen 1854, II, 133; Crowe and Cavalcaselle
1871 (ed. 1912), III, 52; Longhi 1927, 220; Suida 1935, 14;
Berenson 1957, 189; Valcanover 1960, I, 51; Fomiciova 1967,
58; Pallucchini 1969, 32; Wethey 1969, 125; Ballarin 1980,
494, 495; Pignatti 1981, 32.

F.V.

9

Madonna and Child with Saints Catherine, Dominic and a Donor

oil on canvas, 138×185 cm
Mamiano (Parma), Fondazione Magnani-Rocca

EXHIBITIONS   Genoa 1946, Genoa 1951, Parma 1984

This grandiose *Sacra Conversazione*, known and admired by Van Dyck who sketched it in reverse (Wethey 1969, Sgarbi 1984), is mentioned with justified admiration in the guides of Genoa by Ratti (1780) and Alizeri (1846) when it was in Palazzo Balbi di Piovera, whence it passed after 1952 to the Luigi Magnani Collection of Reggio Emilia, and thence to that enlightened collector's foundation.

Crowe and Cavalcaselle (1877), Morelli (1892) and Gronau (1900) knew it as a significant work by Titian, but it subsequently disappeared from the critical literature, until Morassi stressed its exceptional quality and importance in his 1946 catalogue of Titian's early works. Morassi speculated that the donor was a member of the Venetian Balbi family, possibly a Domenico, given the presence of the saint. The dating between 1512 and 1514, proposed by Morassi, was accepted by Dell'Acqua (1955), Valcanover (1960) and Pallucchini (1969), while Wethey (1969) proposed a later and less specific date between 1515 and 1520. This is too late, however, given the painting's style and the character of its forms predicated on compositional and chromatic tension, which place it only slightly later than the frescoes of the Scuola del Santo, Padua, and the votive painting of Antwerp (see cat. no. 4). The free and resonant disposition of colored shapes, on the left silhouetted against a shaded backdrop, on the right massed before open, natural vistas, is adapted from the *Miracle of the Speaking Babe* in Padua and from the Antwerp painting.

Brought prominently to the foreground, the large figures take firm possession of the space around them and are composed in a tableau of poses and gestures that mirror the sentimental import of the occasion with particular intensity. The donor is captured in the act of fervent adoration and leans toward the Virgin as does the impassioned Saint Dominic, guarantor of his devotion. The Virgin whose attention is distracted, shifts her body in a "grandiose movement, almost as if inspired by a Michelangelesque Romanism," as Pallucchini observed (1969), to respond to the confident prayer of the faithful worshiper. Saint Catherine is portrayed in profile on the extreme left. Like the Virgin, she is seated on the high fragment of a classical architrave, and bears attentive witness to the sacred meeting. The variety of personality, type, and mood of the protagonists of this *Sacra Conversazione* is ingeniously rendered in the inversion of the two parts into which the composition is divided: greens, lilacs, blues, vibrant reds, in intense and brilliant gradations on the dark brownish tones of the backdrop; whites and blacks of transparent luminosity on the open

landscape, which in its natural measured distances marked by planes of color prefigures the landscape of the Borghese *Sacred and Profane Love.*

There are other reasons why the ex-Balbi *Sacra Conversazione* can be seen as a laboratory of Titian's figurative ideals, adopted immediately and translated into different languages by Paris Bordone and Palma Vecchio: from the broad and monumental figure group conceived in a mood of lively and sincere naturalness, to the details of the faces of the donor and Saint Catherine. The former is a psychological sensitivity portrait of particular and gratifying fidelity, certainly not less so than others of Titian's portraits c. 1515, including the imcomparable male portraits in the collection of the Earl of Halifax, London, and the Frick Collection, New York. The fervid beauty of Saint Catherine, even in this sturdy posture close to Saint Peter of the Antwerp altar, anticipates the splendid female half-lengths later in the second decade, the greatest example of which continues to be the *Flora* in the Uffizi.

The Magnani-Rocca Foundation painting finds an authoritative place among Titian's *Sacre Conversazioni*, which rather before the middle of the second decade tend toward a "chromatic classicism," due to poetic and original absoluteness of the form-color relationship with which Titian, even in this *genre*, distances himself from Giorgione and Giovanni Bellini.

LITERATURE   Ratti 1780, 187; Alizeri 1846, II, 75; Crowe and Cavalcaselle 1877, II, 414; Morelli 1892, 244, no. 4; Gronau 1904, 292; Morassi 1946, 207ff; Dell'Acqua 1955, 60ff; Valcanover 1960, I, 19, 20; Pallucchini 1969, 27ff; Wethey 1969, 109; Sgarbi 1984, 103, 104 (with preceding bibliography).

F.V.

10

The Drowning of Pharoah in the Red Sea

woodcut composed of twelve blocks; second state; 121×221 cm

Venice, private collection

Inscription: "La crudel persecutione del ostinato Re, contro il populo tanto da Dio/ amato. Con la sommersione di esso Pharaone goloso dil inocente/ sangue. Disegnata per mano del grande, et immortal Titiano./ In venetia p[er] domeneco dalle greche depentore Venetiano/ MDXLIX"

The problem of the date of this enormous image by Titian and of the identity of its mysterious publisher has for many years been a subject of debate among scholars. While stylistically there has been general agreement in assigning the engraving to the middle of the second decade, the inscription flatly contradicts this. The impasse was overcome for the first time by Tietze-Conrat (1950), who called attention to a copyright request of February 1515 by Bernardino Benalio, discovered by Mauroner (1941), to reproduce a "drowning of Pharoah," which would have referred to a supposed first state of Titian's woodcut. Tietze-Conrat's discovery did not definitively resolve the complex question. On the contrary it sparked off new theories, such as an ingenious proposal by Pignatti (1973), who placed the overall design in Titian's early years (c. 1510) and the definitive edition in 1549, the date of the inscription. Muraro and Rosand's studies (1976) have been decisive on this subject. They rediscovered a fragment of the first state (Museo Correr, Venice, *Stampe* A. 15, c. 39, no. 48), probably that published by Benalio, which is distinguished from the later and universally known state by the absence of worm holes and especially of "that long hole of a woodworm that disfigures all the successive printings".

A further question that remained unanswered is the matter of "Domenico dalle Greche," whose confused and ill-documented identity contrasts with the fame and prestige of Benalio. More recent research (Olivato 1979) has added considerably to what we know of him. For example, Domenico was the illustrator of a monumental enterprise of the great Venetian naturalist and scholar P.A. Michiel. Through his relationship with Michiel, Dalle Greche frequented Venetian and Paduan intellectual and aristocratic circles to which Michiel, who was appointed director of the Botanical Gardens of Padua in 1551, belonged. This would explain the involvement of an artist of secondary importance in the acquisition of a second version of an engraving by Titian, who at the end of the 1540s was at the peak of his career and social importance. From the stylistic point of view, an early dating is highly plausible. Influenced here and there by non-Venetian sources, its creative approach anticipates Titian's response to subsequent major figurative challenges. As Muraro and Rosand (1976) have observed, the figure of Moses was to serve as a

model for one of the Apostles in the foreground of the *Assumption* of the Frari (see cat. no. 11), just as the horsemen, overwhelmed by the waters, return in the *Battle of Cadore*, judging from the extant preparatory studies (see cat. no. 29). We know that well before 1516, Titian had quoted from Michelangelo's cartoon for the *Battle of Cascina*, from which he has taken the detail of the man seated behind the mother with the suckling babe in the lower right margin of the engraving.

While these considerations enable us to be rather precise about the date and style of the woodcut within Titian's early work, the subject matter itself leads to the definition of a rather precise context for this 'invenzione.' The rendering of the Biblical narrative is nothing if not literal. The Egyptian army is dispatched by Pharoah to pursue the Israelites led by Moses. In attempting to pass through the divide miraculously opened in the Red Sea to allow the Israeli people to cross, the army is overwhelmed by the turbulent waters at a sign from the prophet. Scholars such as Benevenuti, Muraro, and Rosand (1976) have already demonstrated how the miraculous salvation is a transparent allusion to the equally sensational turn of events in the war of the League of Cambrai, when Venice by a miracle saved itself from the European armies set on them by the fury of Pope Julius II. Closer examination of the historic sources and documents of that period, makes it possible to identify with even greater precision the moment that could have given rise to the execution of such an imposing work, which assumed the role of a precise instrument of propaganda for the Venetian government. The most crucial year in the Cambrai crisis of the Serenissima was 1513, despite the Treaty of Blois that removed the French threat, and despite the fact that the Pope was already tending toward compromise, the situation on the battlefields was still desperate. The enemy troops, above all the imperial armies, were devastating the terraferma where the villages along the Brenta were sacked and destroyed and Mestre itself was burned. The overwhelming power of the enemy seemed so absolute and so irresistible that the commander of the Spanish army camped on the shores of the lagoon decided to bombard Venice with cannon. The results were negligible, but the psychological impact on the Venetians must have been tremendous. From the sources (see Merlini, Priuli, Sanudo, cited in Olivato 1979, *passim*), we know that the government had decreed new laws that prohibited pomp, dances and every show of luxury. At the same time rumors were spreading among the people fired by popular sayings and folk tales of dark premonitions of further disasters that were to strike the Republic, which was guilty – according to popular feeling – of the sins of pride and greed, having abandoned the traditional policies of mercantile expansion in order to "attempt new things," that is, the expansion on the terraferma.

In this light the identification of the Venetian populace with the Israelites exiled in Egypt and harshly persecuted for their past sins, does not seem implausible, even at a figurative level. Similarly, the concept of redemption from sin through "humiliation," and the expectation of the ultimate victory of the forces of Good, finds support in the Biblical story and confirmation in the particular circumstances that the Serenissima was experiencing.

It is also worth noting that it was precisely in 1513 that Titian, renouncing a trip to Rome where he had been invited, offered himself as painter of the glorious deeds of the Republic, taking upon himself the honor of representing the Battle of Spoleto, "that is the most difficult and that a certain painter did not want to do," a subject that, with slight alteration, was later transformed into the *Battle of Cadore* (finished only in 1537 and which would perish in the 1577 fire of the Palazzo Ducale) – clear indication of the painter's political commitment. He opted (and certainly it would not have been his decision alone, but probably in response to the clear political will of a specific element of the established Venetian power structure) to abandon a remote episode such as that of Spoleto to refer to a recent and very real armed action, thus more meaningful: the victory in 1508 of the Venetian forces led by Giorgio Cornaro over the imperial army.

In this light the present writer feels that the woodcut of the *Drowning* can be interpreted as Titian's conscious participation in events that so dramatically upset the life of Venice and as his desire to shape his own role as popularizer – even if on the level of the metaphor that reinterprets reality, adapting it to the incontrovertible truths of a Biblical text: the Venetians, equivalent to the Israelites, a people oppressed but ultimately victorious and triumphant over the enemy. This well-defined political plan set out to affirm through the figurative image, specifically because it is so easily comprehensible at all levels, the values upheld by the Serenissima, beyond internal polemic and conflict, as those blessed by God and destined to certain victory.

LITERATURE   Papillon 1776, 160; Heinecken 1778-90, III, 545; Mariette 1851-60, V, 308; Passavant 1860-64, VI, 223; Tietze and Tietze-Conrat 1938, 332, 464; Tietze and Tietze-Conrat 1938, 8, 52; Mauroner 1941, 24; Tietze-Conrat 1950; Richards 1956; Oberhuber 1966, 166; Pallucchini 1969, I, 336; Dreyer 1971, II, 4; Dreyer 1972, 294; Pignatti 1973; Oberhuber 1974, no. 51; Muraro and Rosand 1976, 81-3; Olivato 1979, 529-37.

L.O.

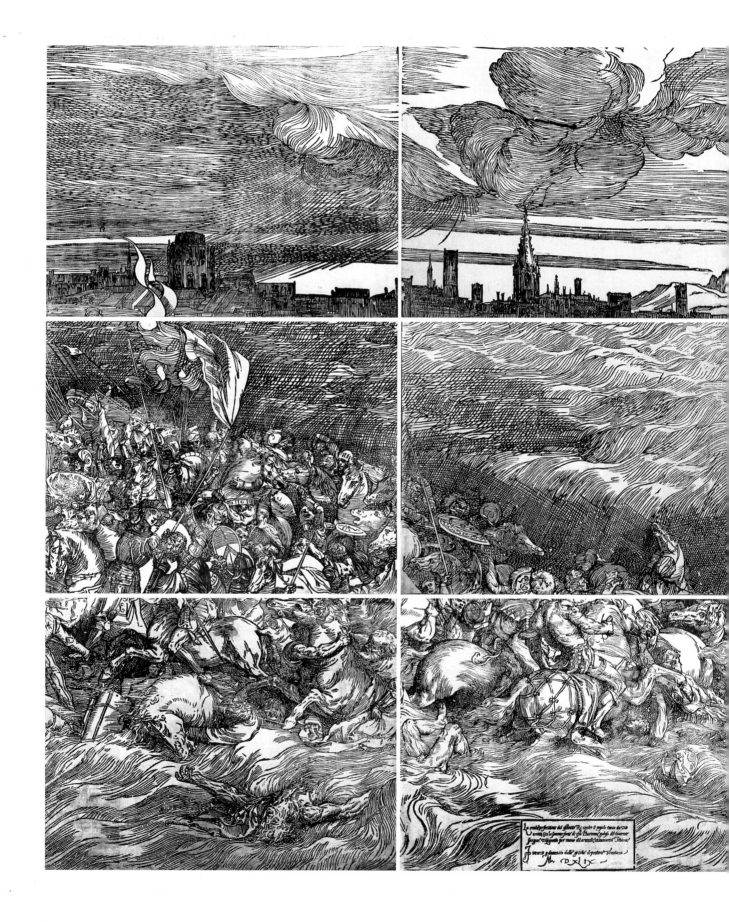

II

The Assumption

oil on panel, 690×360 cm
Venice, Chiesa dei Frari

EXHIBITION   Venice 1935
RESTORATION   1974, A. Lazzarin

Signed on the bottom: TICIANUS.
This majestic panel was inaugurated in its no less monumental marble frame in the main apsidal chapel of the church of Santa Maria Gloriosa dei Frari on 19 May 1518, the day before the Feast of Saint Bernardine, the popular Franciscan preacher elected a patron of the Republic in 1470. The event was recorded with awe by the diarist Marin Sanudo: "The month of May 1518.... the 20th day. It was the day of Saint Bernardine, which is observed following a decision of the Senate, and the offices are closed. And yesterday the large altarpiece of the altar of Santa Maria dei Frati Minori was installed, painted by Titian, and previously there had been a made a frame around it, a grand work of marble at the expense of Maestro Zerman, who is now Guardian."
The *Assumption* was commissioned by the Abbot ("Guardian") of the monastery of the Frari, Germano da Caiole in 1516, the year that appears on the pedestal of the column to the right of the altar: FRATER GERMANUS HANC ARAM ERIGI CVRAVIT MDXVI; while opposite, the inscription records the event of the *Assumption* of Mary: ASSUMPTAE COELUM AETERNI OPIFICI MATRI. The revolutionary novelty of the altarpiece in the context of Venetian painting at the beginning of the sixteenth century was at once perceived by contemporaries such as Lodovico Dolce, who in the *Dialogo* of 1557, after mentioning Titian's frescoes at the Fondaco dei Tedeschi, with his customary subtlety of critical intelligence, commented, "not long after, the execution of a large canvas for the high altar of the Church of the Frati Minori was put into his hands. Here Titian, a young man even now, painted in oils the Virgin ascending to heaven amongst many escorting angels; and above Her he did a figure of God the Father, flanked by a pair of angels. Truly She appears to ascend with humility written all over Her face; and Her drapery flutters delicately. At ground level there are the Apostles, who display gladness and amazement with a variety of poses and are mostly more than life-size. And certainly the grandeur and awesomeness of Michelangelo, the charm and loveliness of Raphael and the coloring proper to nature are incorporated into this painting. It was, nevertheless, the first public commission that Titian carried out in oils; and he did it in the shortest space of time, and in his youth. All of which meant that the clumsy artists and dimwit masses, who had seen up till then nothing but the dead and cold creations of Giovanni Bellini, Gentile and Vivarino (the fact being that Giorgione had not yet received a public commission for a work in oils, and that his creations were mostly limited to half-figures and portraits) – works which had no movement and no projection – grossly maligned this same picture. Later the envy cooled off, and the truth, little by little, opened people's eyes, so that they began to marvel at the new style opened up by Titian in Venice. And from then on all of the artists were at pains to immitate it; but because this took them off their beaten track, they never found their bearings. And certainly one can speak of a miracle at work in the fact that, without as yet having seen the antiquities of Rome, which were a source of enlightenment to all excellent painters, and purely by dint of that little tiny spark which he had uncovered in the works of Giorgione, Titian discerned and apprehended the essence of perfect painting."
Many of the judgments in this passage by Dolce have been incorporated unchanged in modern criticism: on Titian's education, on his early liberation from Giorgione, on the modernizing of his art based on the classicism of Raphael and Michelangelo with the addition of the magic of his color. He also made explicit reference to the reception of the altarpiece by contemporary public opinion, at first far from benevolent, later admiring. Ridolfi (1644) elaborated on the controversies that arose among the monks themselves during the execution of the extraordinary image in the Frari:
"It was said that Titian worked on that panel in the convent of the Frari, that he was annoyed by their frequent visits, and by Fra' Germano, controller of the work who often complained that the Apostles were made too big, and he worked hard to correct their lack of understanding and to make them see that the figures had to be made in proportion to the very vast place where they were to be seen, and that from the viewer's position they would diminish in size; nevertheless, although by the good effect achieved they could have remained satisfied, they did not demonstrate full contentment, until the Imperial Ambassador revealed to them their error (as men do not easily listen to reason, if authority does not intercede) since he considered that painting marvellous, and he tried with generous offers to acquire it, to send it to the Emperor; after which the Fathers, during one of their meetings, agreed on the more prudent decision not to deprive themselves of it to anyone, recognizing that it was not their position, as the knowledge of the Brevario was, to know about painting."
Whether true or not that *The Assumption* came close to being acquired by the Imperial collections, it is sure that after initial difficulties of comprehension, the altarpiece has since enjoyed unstinting admiration.
Remarks on its conservation and visibility began early. In 1566 while in Venice, Vasari (1568) observed that it was "perhaps ill-preserved, one sees little." A century later Boschini (1664) deplored its deterioration, and in particular the figure of the Apostle Peter who was "completely peeled off" ("scrostata").

A hundred years later Zanetti (1771) wrote of the "misty veil, with which time has encumbered this painting." It was fortunately among those paintings omitted from the list of twenty masterpieces drawn up by the French commissioner, which the defeated Venice was to send to Paris for Napoleon's vast museum. In 1816 it was transferred to the Accademia for restoration by Lattanzio Querena. The painter-restorer not only reconstructed the figure of Saint Peter, already seriously damaged by the seventeenth century, as Boschini records, but also worked over in the sky, the hot yellow background in the top, and elsewhere. He then proceeded to finish it with pigmented varnishes in accordance with the aesthetic canon of the time (still not entirely extinct) that was considered the legitimate restitution of a hypothetical golden patina, especially for Venetian paintings (Zeri 1987).

On 24 May 1817 Leopoldo Cicognara, president of the Accademia, wrote to his friend Antonio Canova: "You will see [at the Accademia] an immense gallery of very great old masters and I dare believe it the most beautiful in Europe. The *Assumption* of the Frari takes first place and it was covered in a crust of smoke and incense that made me shudder. Now it is a splendor, it is the only painting to stand up to the *Transfiguration* [of Raphael], even though I, poor devil, think it is more beautiful."

Upon its return to Venice at the end of the World War I, in December 1919, the altarpiece was rightfully restored to its original location. It was subsequently moved again for the 1935 Titian exhibition, and again in 1940 to protect it from damage during World War II. In 1945, the great panel was returned unharmed to its place in the main apse of the Frari. If Titian's masterpiece escaped the violence of man in these wars, it soon began again to show signs of physical deterioration, the consequences in part of its repeated moves in the first half of the century. In 1966, it was treated for worms and in 1974 the panel was brought down from the altar and subjected to careful and thorough conservation carried out in a laboratory set up in the church itself.

The support, flawlessly constructed – with twenty-one boards of a thickness of three centimeters each – and surely supervised by Titian, was disinfested and consolidated. This was followed by the removal of dust and deposits of candle smoke, of the much yellowed non-original paint, and of the repaint dulling the lower part of the Eternal Father, the belt of the angel flying toward him on the left, several of the more hazy heads of the putti on the uppermost limits of the arched part of the panel, the rays of yellow light, the clouds on which the Virgin stands, and the sky streaked with clouds. The work was revealed to be particularly well-preserved with the exception of the Apostle Peter, where Querena's figure has been left intact as so little of the original survives underneath (Valcanover 1977), and of which a preparatory drawing by the artist has come down to us (see cat. no. 12).

Today the *Assumption* is once again as Titian intended it, the focal point of the broad and solemn Gothic spaces of the Frari. For he who enters from the principal entrance, it is visible beyond the marble choir screen, as Zanetti noted in 1771: "At the main altar [of the Frari] is the large panel with the Virgin ascending to the Heavens, the Eternal Father above, and the Apostles on the ground. In spite of the *contre-jour* and of the murky veil with which time has encumbered this painting, one manages to perceive that it is painted with a very grand manner and that there are very beautiful heads; and that it is one of Titian's greatest works made certainly in the fervor of his youth. The equal grandeur of its style, that gave great value to the work and was very well adapted to the vastness of the place in which it was to be positioned, failed to please he who commissioned it; since his eyes were used to seeing figures only as large as nature, or smaller. But he who know its merit offered for it a great price; and changed the mind of he who in error thought badly of it."

The flowing intensity of the color and the stateliness of the forms are today again triumphant over the glare caused by the lateral windows of which Zanetti speaks and upon which Vasari (1568) also remarked. The difficulty of placing the altarpiece against the light was taken into consideration from the beginning, and it is even probable that Titian gave advice for the design of the impressive marble Renaissance frame, which not only harmonizes with the Gothic apse but also tends to isolate the altarpiece from the light that flows intensely from the vast windows (Wilde 1974; Rosand 1982). The iconography of the powerful tabernacle, in its bas-reliefs and sculptural decorations, is bound to the subject of Titian's panel, elaborating the doctrine of the Assumption of Mary into Heaven (Goffen 1986; see also Rosand 1988). Goffen expressed the probable 'political' significance of the project, begun in the same year, 1516, as the Treaty of Noyon, which signified for the Venetian State the definitive end of the mortal danger posed by the League of Cambrai in 1508.

As the sources records, the revolutionary novelties of the *Assumption* are impressive, in the iconography and the language, both of the traditional altarpiece and of this specific theme. In Padua, in the days when he was working at the Scuola del Santo, Titian would have had time to meditate on Mantegna's *Assumption of the Virgin*, frescoed in the Ovetari Chapel at the Eremitani Church. He would also have known the *Immaculate Conception* painted three years earlier by Giovanni Bellini and his assistants for the church of Santa Maria degli Angeli, Murano, today in the church of San Pietro Martire. But the ingenious originality of Titian's *Assumption* emerges precisely in its differences with respect to the compact figurative isolation, almost archaic in its linearity, of the two works by Mantegna and Giovanni Bellini – above all now that

in the latter the grotesque cloud, added in the last century to support the Virgin, has been removed. In the exuberance of his natural forms, Titian presents with dramatic immediacy the miraculous vision whose unity of time and space is accentuated, not diminished, by the different perspectives controlling the earthly and celestial spheres (Hourticq 1919). By the unifying agency of light, the local colors harmonize in polyphonic splendor: from the crowded Apostles, magnificent with their bold foreshortening and emphatic gestures, dispersed against the cold blue sky streaked with clouds; to the Virgin, with her clothes billowing in the wind, spiraling in her gesture of confident adoration, who is raised on high by the adulating host of putti interwoven through the clouds; the lights and the shadows as far as the God the Father, who glides swiftly down from the golden yellow celestial realm.

The majesty of this conception (Venturi 1978; Freedberg 1988) draws Titian close to contemporary Tuscan and Roman figuration. But as Dolce observed as early as 1557, every ascendancy of that culture is absorbed into the beauty (*venustà*) of a palette that appeals to the senses as natural. Titian, specifically in the Frari, in a short span of time, little more than a year, opened a new felicitous chapter of coloristic classicism that was to result in the next few years in the *Bacchanals* for the *Camerino d'Alabastro* of Alfonso I d'Este, and then in the *Pesaro Madonna* in the Frari.

LITERATURE Sanudo 1496-1533 (ed. 1879-1902), xxv, col. 418; Dolce 1557 (ed. Barocchi), 202; Vasari 1568 (ed. Ragghianti), III, 567; Ridolfi 1648 (ed. Von Hadeln), I, 163; Boschini 1664, 297; Zanetti 1771, 110; Crowe and Cavalcaselle 1877, I, 211ff; Hourticq 1919, 180; A. Venturi 1928, 234ff; Pallucchini 1969, 26, 27; Wethey 1969, 74ff; Wilde 1974, 134; Valcanover 1977, 41ff; Rosand 1982, chap. 2; Howard 1985, 271ff; Goffen 1986, 94ff; Zeri 1987, 151; Freedberg 1988, 169, 170; Rosand 1988, 4ff.

F.V.

Study for Saint Peter

black chalk heightened with white chalk, on blue paper, 157×134 mm
London, The Trustees of the British Museum (inv. 1895-9-15-823)

Published for the first time by Robinson (1869) among the drawings of the Malcolm collection, before its acquisition by the British Museum (1895), the drawing was subsequently recognized by Von Hadeln (1924) as a preparatory study for the figure of Saint Peter in Titian's *Assumption* in the Frari (see cat. no. 11).
Titian's authorship of the sheet – whose date, on the basis of that of the altarpiece, can be fixed between 1516 and 1518 or more precisely in the early stages of work on the altarpiece – and its connection to the painting have been unanimously agreed by critics, with the single exception of Hetzer (1940). The *Saint Peter* is now the only extant study for this masterpiece of Titian's early religious production, since recent critics have rightly deleted from the corpus the two pen studies in the Louvre of the *Group of Apostles* (inv. no. 5516) and the *Putti on Clouds* (inv. no. RF479), once believed to be preparatory to the *Assumption*, but now generally attributed to Domenico Campagnola.
In spite of the fact that it is rather worn, this small sketch, of indisputably high quality despite its fragility, constitutes one of the few certain and incontrovertible points of reference for the reconstruction of Titian's development as a draftsman. It is also exemplary of the relationship between Titian's drawings and the creative process of his paintings. Even greater interest derives from the fact that it is the only evidence of the artist's original idea for Saint Peter, profoundly altered by repainting by Lattanzio Querena, who as Sagredo informed us, during the nineteenth-century restoration of the altarpiece "painted the Saint Peter which is still admired today" (Valcanover 1977). This repainting generated the differences that Oberhuber (1976) pointed out when comparing the drawing with the definitive painted version. Not only the drapery and the

inclination of the apostle's head were modified, but also the *chiaroscuro* effects intended to enhance the figure's monumentality. The nineteenth – century over-painting was left intact in the recent restoration, when it was decided instead not to "strip the Saint Peter of Querena's re-working, preferring to consider it an historic overlay, after having verified the substantially incomplete state of the original head by Titian" (Valcanover 1977).
On the *verso* of the London sheet, recent conservation has led to the discovery of two caricatured heads, accepted with doubts by Oberhuber (1976), and also in our opinion not necessarily autograph.
We would like instead to draw attention to the affinity between the *Saint Peter* and the very fine *Head of an Old Man*, in pen and brown ink, in the Teylers Museum, Haarlem (inv. no. KI43; Chiari Moretto Wiel 1989). Despite the difference in medium and despite the general tendency to date the Teylers drawing c. 1510-11, its physical type, sculptural treatment of the planes and dense and constructive painterliness make it possible to shift the Teylers drawing to the period of the *Assumption*, the period that also saw the engraving of Ugo da Carpi's *chiaroscuro* woodcut of *Saint Jerome* possibly before Ugo's departure for Rome (Chiari 1986-7). In the latter, the dynamism and tension of the line, the marked modeling of the vigorously emphatic contours, the movement of the figure, the correspondence of the pose not only to that of the apostles of the *Assumption*, but also to Saint Peter in the Dresden *Tribute Money* and *Saint Sebastian* of the Averoldi polyptych, make of the *Saint Jerome* an invaluable document for understanding Titian's drawing style in the period and for forging the *trait d'union* between the *Assumption* and the Averoldi *Saint Sebastian*.

LITERATURE Robinson 1869, 142, no. 378; Von Hadeln 1924, 52; Fröhlich-Bum 1928, 195; Tietze 1936, i, iii, ii, pl. 33; Tietze and Tietze-Conrat 1936, 184, 191; Popham 1939, 43-44; Hetzer 1940, 167; Tietze 1944; Pallucchini 1969, i, 331; Valcanover 1969, 99; Wethey 1969-75, i, 76; Meijer 1974, 75; Oberhuber 1976, 27, 77; Rearick 1977, 185; Pignatti and Chiari 1979, 8, no. xix; Byam Shaw 1980, 387-88; Rosand 1981, 306; Rosand 1983, fig. 63; Scrase 1983, 291, no. D70; Cocke 1984, 17; Wethey 1987, 143; Chiari Moretto Wiel 1988, 31, 42; Chiari Moretto Wiel 1989, 16, 85.

M.A.C.M.W.

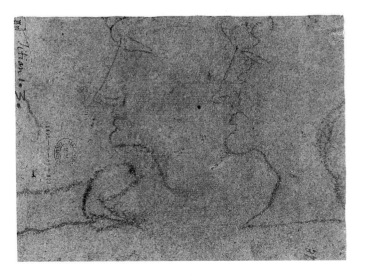

"Caricatures," verso

"Head of an Old Man," drawing in pen and ink. Teylers
Museum, Haarlem

Ugo da Carpi, "Saint Jerome," detail, woodcut

13.

'Il Bravo'

oil on canvas, 75×67 cm (cut on the upper edge and the sides)
Vienna, Kunsthistorisches Museum (inv. no. 64)

EXHIBITIONS   Venice 1955, Versailles 1964, Montreal 1967, Tokyo-Kyoto 1984
RESTORATION   1966, Haijsinek

"The two figures who attack each other were by Titian." This description by Marcantonio Michiel of a painting in the house of Zuanantonio Venier was linked to the painting now in Vienna for the first time by Engerth in his catalogue of 1882. In the seventeenth century Carlo Ridolfi (1648) and Marco Boschini (1660) published exact descriptions and interpretations of this famous painting, which they both attributed to Giorgione. Ridolfi knew the painting in Venice, whereas by Boschini's time it had already passed to the collection of Archduke Leopold Wilhelm in Brussels.

Ridolfi described the scene represented here as follows: "again one saw two half figures, the one representing Caelius Plotius assailed by Claudius, who gripped him by the collar of the jacket, holding the other hand to the side with the dagger, and in the face of the young man apppeared fear and in that of the aggressor cruelty, who in the end was killed by Plotius, whose noble resolution was commended by Caius Imperator, uncle of the dead Claudius." This incident, drawn from Valerius Maximus (VI, i, 12) is based on Plutarch's *Life of Marius* (XIV), in which, however, the aggressor's name is Caius Lusius, not Claudius, and the young man's name is Trebonius, not Plotius. Wind (1969) has reconstructed and amended the critical history of the subject matter.

As for the painting's attributional history, if we assume that this is indeed the painting seen by Michiel, we can say that it was considered to be by Titian in the sixteenth century. In an inventory of the Duke of Hamilton's collection (1639-43) it was described as "a bare arm goeing to kyll a younge man, one more excell't piece of Tyssian or Jorione"; in the *Maraviglie* Ridolfi decisively named Giorgione. In the nineteenth century, by which time the picture was in very poor condition, this attribution was questioned and other names were associated with it such as Cariani (Crowe and Cavalcaselle 1871), Palma Vecchio (Wickhoff 1893) and the Master of the Self-Portraits (Wilde 1933), until Justi (1926), Suida (1927) and Longhi (1927), followed by the majority of critics, once more decided in favor of Titian. The discovery of a drawing depicting the *Entombment of Christ* on the back of the canvas (Oberhammer 1966) tended to confirm this thesis, even though devoted to such drawings on the backs of Titian's paintings, Bert Meijer (1981) felt unable to assert Titian's authorship.

The style of the sleeve of the costume worn by the 'bravo' appeared according to Wethey (1975) for the first time in the Lotto's frescoes for the Suardi chapel in Trescore, begun in 1524; on the basis of this he dated the painting from 1520 to 1525. Previous critics, considering the painting to be Giorgione, dated it accordingly earlier. The theme is unique to this painting: the "virtue of the soldier Trebonius," who defends himself from the indecent, insistent proposals of his superior by killing him. In the court martial he was not only absolved by the general, who was the uncle of the dead officer, but was crowned for his virtue. (That Giorgione's 'Bravo' also in the Kunsthistorisches Museum represents the same theme is unconvincing.) The crown, to which Valerius Maximus makes no reference but which nevertheless here takes on decisive importance, is made (as Justi observed) of interwoven vine tendrils and resembles, even from the pictorial point of view, the thyrsus that appears in Titian's *Bacchanal of the Andrians*.

The variety of ways in which the feelings current in this painting have been interpreted is interesting, depending in part on the subject matter ascribed to it. Boschini, who relied on Ridolfi's interpretation of the virtuous hero, described the scene as follows: "and he who does not see the simplicity of that young man terrified by fear knows not the affliction of the soul nor the fear of death: a sentiment vividly expressed because the assailant seems almost alive, by contrast Claudius so rigid, so cruel, so furious, as to strike terror in the Furies themselves. Two sentiments opposed that form a picturesque conceit that art could do no better." Justi, by contrast, described the facts impartially: "A young man with garland of vines in his blonde curls, and thus just come from a joyful banquet, is gripped by the collar of his coat by a soldier in armor. The assailant grips a dagger with his left hand; the young man draws his sword with his right hand."

Recently Bruce Sutherland has put forward another interpretation of the painting (in a letter to the Kunsthistorisches Museum, 9 October 1989), which refers to an episode described in detail in the *Bacchae* of Euripides and alluded to in Ovid's *Metamorphoses* (III, 515ff): Bacchus' arrest by order of Pentheus, king of Thebes and son of Agave, who intended at all costs to prevent the spreading of the cult of Bacchus in his kingdom and the entry of the God and his entourage. Pentheus shared the fate of other rivals of this peevish divinity who pitilessly wreaked his revenge by inflicting a horrible end on Pentheus, who was torn limb from limb by his own mother and by his sisters, all of them Maenads, Bacchus' followers. If indeed this represents the moment in which Pentheus attempts to arrest Bacchus, the expression of the young God, turned toward us, should no longer be read as frightened by the aggressor but rather as one of astonished and unbridled horror at the presumption of the mortal who has dared to lay hands on a God. The figure of the assailant could then no longer be read as a depraved creature, obsessed by his homosexual longings, but as one who takes a stand against an

'IL BRAVO'

orgiastic and savage cult; gripping the dagger with left hand the king means to parry the sword thrust that his adversary is about to strike.

The representation of this episode is as rare in art as that from Plutarch's life of Marius; the tragic moment of Pentheus' death at the hands of his mother and his sisters, a scene also described in the *Imagines* of Philostratus, was more generally chosen. The fact that Bacchus and his adversary appear in clothing fashionable in the Cinquecento, rather than in classical costume, elicits a certain scepticism. Yet the contrast between the hard, shiny breastplate and the soft garment of the young man brings to mind the passage in the *Metamorphoses* in which Pentheus, whose manly ideals consist of wars, weapons and armor, scoffs at Bacchus, who prefers instead "clothes of purple and gold" and "locks dripping with scents." The blonde curls of the young man are in fact very long, like those of the god depicted in the *Bacchus and Ariadne*, which Titian painted for the *camerino d'alabastro* of Alfonso d'Este. Young men with such long hair appear nowhere else in Titian's work. Furthermore, the expression on the face of the young man does not radiate pure virtue and innocent fear, but has in it something faintly sinister and at the same time magical and bewitching.

In any case this theory can represent at least an alternative to the story of the Wreath of Trebonius, which, though unanimously accepted is not especially convincing. Leaving aside the literary source for the narrative, there is no doubt that the artist has chosen a moment of high drama. Drawing on a tradition effectively developed by Giorgione – that of the half-length figure seen from close up – Titian has created a forceful image of tense conflict. The three-quarter length representation of the protagonist, who is bathed in light, contrasts with the shadowy profile of the other actor: such a contrast is equally effective between the head of Christ and that of Saint Peter in the Dresden *Tribute Money*. However, while the direction of Christ's gaze in the latter painting is parallel to the picture surface, the young man in '*Il Bravo*' has a diagonal address, so that in the act of turning he looks directly at the spectator. The bent arms of the two rivals, distinguished by their contrasting colors and the hands that firmly grip the collar, the sword and the dagger, intensify the drama by cramping it within the narrowest space possible.

In the x-rays of the painting (Wilde 1933) the aggressor is more exactly in profile and wears on his head a kind of emperor's crown. But it is difficult to say whether we are looking at a *pentimento*, that is to say at an earlier version of the same figure later modified, or whether the canvas was initially painted with a different subject.

In Van Dyck's sketch of the painting (Adriani 1940) the aggressor again appears in greater profile; and as a consequence it has been suggested the shadowy *profil perdu* post-

dates Van Dyck's seeing the picture. However, the unity of the paint surface and the free, extemporaneous manner of Van Dyck's sketch undermine this theory.

The exceptionally dramatic and profoundly psychological character of this painting, original in all its details, added to the *bravura* of its technique, amply corroborate Titian's authorship and a dating between 1515 and 1520.

LITERATURE Crowe and Cavalcaselle 1871, ii, 152; Engerth 1884, 168-70; Justi 1926, 279-82; Longhi 1967, 237, 458; Suida 1927, 206-15; Wilde 1933, 121-23; Valcanover 1960, 61, pl. 100; *Gemäldegalerie des Kunsthistorischen Museums* 1966, 54; Garas 1967, 60, 64, 74, 73, 76; *Idem* 1968, 216; Pallucchini 1969, i, 256; Wind 1969; 7-11; Wethey 1975, 130-31, no. 3 (with bibliography); Meijer 1981, 277ff; Rylands 1988, 296-97.

S.F.

14

Six Studies for Saint Sebastian and the Madonna and Child

pen and brown ink, 162×136 mm
Berlin, Staatliche Museen Preussischer Kulturbesitz, Gemäldegalerie (inv. no. K.d.Z. 5962)

This sheet of studies, supported with a backing and slightly stained, entered the museum with the Von Beckerath collection in 1902. It was published for the first time by Von Hadeln (1924), who identified it as preparatory to the *Saint Sebastian* of the Averoldi polyptych (Church of Santi Nazzaro e Celso, Brescia) and it has unanimously been accepted as such by later critics. Von Hadeln (1924) was also the first to relate the splendid drawing in the Stadelsches Kunstinstitut, Frankfurt (pen, brush and dark brown ink on blue paper, inv. no. 5518) as a second preparatory drawing for the same painting (Chiari Moretto Wiel 1989).
The Brescian panel of *Saint Sebastian*, generally understood to be based on Michelangelo's *Rebellious Slave* (Louvre, Paris) of which Titian is thought to have owned a model or drawing, is signed and dated 1522. But the work was seen in Titian's studio at the end of 1520 by Tebaldi, Venetian agent of the Duke of Ferrara. On 1 December of that year Tebaldi sent the court an enthusiastic letter in which he praised the painting and urged the duke to buy it, stealing it away from the papal legate Altobello Averoldi who had commissioned it. From a letter of 23 December, it is clear that although Titian was agreeable, Alfonso d'Este was unwilling because he did not wish to anger the powerful ecclesiastic (Campori 1874).
The final version of the work differs from Tebaldi's description: "the said figure is attached, with one arm raised and the other lowered, to a column and is twisted in such a way that one can see almost his entire back, and each part of his body appears to suffer from one arrow alone, which he has in the middle of his body." This led to a theory (Battisti 1980) that either the painting had been reworked or that Titian, contrary to the evidence of the documents, had after all painted two versions of the work, the first for the Duke of Ferrara and the second for Averoldi. Pending x-radiography of the panel in Brescia, it is not possible to reach a conclusion on the matter. Recently Gilbert (1980), taking his cue from a theory of Tietze's (1954), proposed that the Berlin studies relate not to the Brescia *Saint Sebastian*, but rather to the earlier version of the work seen by Tebaldi. According to Gilbert, Titian at first posed the saint differently and then was struck by Michelangelo's *Slave*, which embodied a superior compositional solution to a figure analagous to his own. He modified the painting, in spite of its already complete state, reworking the leg and the right foot of the saint. Gilbert's argument is based on the disparity between Tebaldi's description and the present appearance of the Brescia painting, consisting of the substitution of a tree for the column, and in the pose of the saint,

described as completely turned, in such a way as to expose his back. These elements Gilbert noted in the Berlin drawing but not in the Brescia panel.
On the one hand it is rather difficult to distinguish between a tree and a column in the summary sketches of the two studies in the upper left of the Berlin sheet, and then again, Tebaldi, who was describing the painting from memory, may easily have been mistaken on this point. On the other hand, the disparity of pose is also inconclusive since it is difficult to judge on the basis of a mere description, however precise and detailed, the greater or lesser torsion of the body.
It is even harder to accept that the saint's pose was modified at a later date, on the basis of Titian's discovery of the *Rebellious Slave*. The Berlin sketches, which can be located at the origin of Titian's idea, are already so close to the final version that is it unthinkable that they could precede Titian's awareness of Michelangelo's sculpture. Titian knew of the *Slave* from the beginning and the Berlin studies document his progress as he adapted the prototype to the definitive painted version, changing the taut muscularity of the *Slave* to the inert limbs of the martyred Sebastian, sustained by ropes that seem to penetrate his body.
A possible reconstruction of the chronology of the four most finished studies for the saint, the upper three of the Berlin sheet and that of Frankfurt, follows. The first study, beginning from the upper left of the Berlin sheet, constitutes in our opinion an initial adaptation of the *Rebellious Slave* in the pose imagined by Titian for the *Saint Sebastian*, perhaps already drafted summarily in the three sketches below (according to Battisti the position of the arm was derived instead from the *Dying Slave*). The second sketch is marked by a more precise definition of the figure in its entirety and a more careful description of the anatomy. In the third, in which the contours of the back correspond almost exactly to those of the painting, the artist's interest was focused on the muscular tension around the spine and shoulders. The latter would have been developed in a series of pen and brush drawings on blue paper, like the sheet in Frankfurt that depicts exactly the same figure as the third study of the Berlin drawing. The emphasis is on the front part of the saint's body, though from a point of view shifted slightly to the right, and with some compositional variants. In this last drawing, the mutilation of the upper part of the sheet precludes an exact understanding of the position of the right arm or the right hand, which hangs inert above the saint's head. The left arm, below which appears a cloth billowing in the wind (eliminated in the painted version), is pushed brusquely back in an unnatural way. This was subsequently changed in favor of the more realistic pose sketched in the Berlin sheet, in which the arm hangs motionless. The different viewpoint explains the different relationship of the saint to the support to which he is bound, whether tree or

column. The position of the legs, similar to that of Michelangelo's *Slave*, is at this point well defined, while the drum of the column on which the right leg is placed, bent and raised even higher than in the Berlin drawing, differs from the painting. Stylistically it is clear that the Frankfurt drawing represents a later phase in Titian's elaboration of the *Saint Sebastian*. If in the Berlin sheet the artist concentrated on the pose of the saint, Titian's concerns were more pictorial in the Städel drawing, evident in the dynamism and tension of the dark, strenuous marks, in the generous use of the brush to create specific chiaroscuro effects and in the use of blue paper.

On the *verso* of the Frankfurt sheet, finally, there are some other sketches: a head in profile, part of a leg and studies of feet. The latter, though modified, carried over to the Brescia painting.

While the function of the *Saint Sebastian* sketches is understood, the purpose of the small *Madonna and Child*, visible in the lower left of the Berlin sheet, is more problematic. Tietze (1936) believed it to be an early idea for the *Madonna* of the Ancona altarpiece, dated 1520. Pallucchini agreed (1969), but as Oberhuber (1976) correctly pointed out, the differences are significant. For certain critics the Virgin's pose is similar to that of Parmigianino's *Madonna of the Rose* (Gemäldegalerie, Dresden), painted in 1529-30, which Titian could have seen in Bologna in January 1530 and then used on the Berlin sheet. The visual parallel is not close enough to be sure of this, and it is in any case difficult to imagine Titian using a sheet ten years old. Furthermore, the rapid, fluid nature of the line points to the character of an annotation, a hastily jotted idea.

Among Titian's works of the early 1520s, one work emerges as a candidate for the painting to which this sketch related: the frescoed lunette of the *Madonna and Child with Two Angels* (Palazzo Ducale, Venice, see cat. no. 20) in which the pose of the principal group is similar.

The numbers in pen in the upper left, in a sixteenth-century hand and apparently a list of payments, are a mystery. According to Hope they are not in Titian's hand.

LITERATURE   Campori 1874, 589; Von Hadeln 1924, 28-29, 47, pl. 6; Von Hadeln 1927, 19, pl. 6; Fröhlich-Bum 1928, 196, no. 11; Tietze 1936, I, 103, II, pl. 56; Tietze and Tietze-Conrat 1936, 191, no. 13; Hetzer 1940, 167; Tietze 1944, no. 1889; Arnolds 1949, 50-54; Tietze 1954, 200; Valcanover 1960, I, 62; Pallucchini 1969, I, 131; Valcanover 1969, 102, no. 105; Wethey 1969, I, 127, no. 92; Karpinski 1976, 261-62; Meijer 1976, 12; Oberhuber 1976, 30, 78, no. 27; Tassi 1976, 11; Meller 1977, 133; Muraro 1978, 219; Oberhuber 1978, 115; Rosand 1978, fig. 64; Dreyer 1979, no. 34; Pignatti and Chiari 1979, 8-9, no. XX; Battisti 1980, 214-16; Byam-Shaw 1980, 387; Dreyer 1980, 510; Furlan 1980, 429; Gilbert 1980, 38-41; Meijer 1981, 286; Rosand 1981, 306, no. 6; Rosand 1983, fig. 64; Wethey 1987, 22, 145, no. 21; Chiari Moretto Wiel 1988, 31, 42, no. 12; Chiari Moretto Wiel 1989, 16, 85, no. 12.

M.A.C.M.W.

*Titian, "Saint Sebastian," recto and verso. Städelsches
Kunstinstitut, Frankfurt*

15

Saint Christopher

fresco, 310×186 cm
Venice, Palazzo Ducale

RESTORATION   1985-86, O. Nonfarmale

The painting is first mentioned by secondary Venetian sources (Ridolfi 1648; Boschini-Zanetti 1797) and was noted by Zanetti (1771) as the only fresco by Titian in the Palazzo Ducale still intact. By virtue of its style and location, the painting can be considered a kind of manifesto of the patron's ducal style. Commissioned by Doge Andrea Gritti (1523-38), probably rather soon after his nomination, such a votive image can readily be interpreted in self-celebrating political terms. Crowe and Cavalcaselle have corroborated, with additional evidence, Rawdon Brown's thesis on this subject: Gritti, who was elected Doge on 20 May 1523, was mindful of the pressure of the French Army in Italy, which according to Guicciardini, was in September 1523 camped in the village of San Cristoforo, one mile from Milan. The iconography of a Saint Christopher placed in the Lagoon of Venice was both an appeal for divine aid from the saint and a firm statement of Venice's readiness to repulse with force any military threat to the Republic. Da Mosto (1966) has drawn attention to what amounted to a prefiguration of the *Saint Christopher* commission. After the liberation of Padua from the forces of the League of Cambrai in 1510, a campaign concluded triumphantly by Andrea Gritti, who was Provveditore Generale in Campo of the Venetian army, the Veronese Giovanni Carotta sent Gritti the gift of an *Atlas Carrying the Heavens* accompanied by the motto: "Sustinet nec fatiscit," an epithet that alluded to the virtues of its receiver. A second iconological precedent for the fresco, in the vicinity of San Marco, consists of an inscription on the underside of an arch of the atrium of the Basilica. The inscription, written in Leonine verses, accompanies a thirteenth-century mosaic of *Saint Christopher* reworked *ex novo* in 1674 from a cartoon by the painter Pietro della Vecchia: "CHRISTOPHORI SANCTI/ FACIEM QUINCU/ MQUE INTUETUR/ ILLE NAMQUE DIE/ NULLO LANG/ UORE TENETUR."
It is hardly necessary to remark how Titian's version of the *Christopher* both shares in and updates the widespread medieval iconography and will from this time be paradigmatic. This is confirmed by the above mentioned mosaic, together with another *Saint Christopher* of 1678, by the mosaicist Giuseppe Paulutti on the exterior of the Basilica, on the "Capitello dell'Annunciata" facing the Piazzetta (Saccardo 1896). Both are indebted to Titian in typology and style. A small *modello* of the *Saint Christopher*, whose location is presently unknown (described as an autograph Titian in a letter from Giulio Cantalamessa to Gino Fogolari dated 28 March 1916, Rome,

in the archives of the Soprintendenza ai Beni Artistici e Storici of Venice) seems likely, from a photographic record, to be an able seventeenth-century exercise based on Titian's original, possibly by Pietro della Vecchia.
Titian worked only three days on the Saint Christopher in the Palazzo Ducale. As in the early frescoes for the Paduan Scuola del Santo, he had recourse to a rapid preparatory drawing, incised on the still-fresh plaster. This drawing, whose traces sometimes coincide and sometimes do not with the lines of the painted image, is apparent thanks to x-radiography along all the main contours of the figure. The graphic morphology here finds its technical and stylistic equivalent in Titian's earlier woodcut of the *Triumph of Christ*.
As for the emphatic plasticity of Christopher's physique and posture, comparison with other frescoes and paintings commissioned by the same doge is less instructive than with mosaics based on cartoons by Titian, interpreted by the meticulously faithful Francesco Zuccato, of *Saints George, Theodore* and *Paul* in the Sacristy of San Marco (Merkel 1980). In these Titian used as models the classical statuary known to him from the Statuario Pubblico of Cardinal Domenico Grimani (also known as the Sala delle Teste) then being installed in the Palazzo Ducale (Perry 1980).
A few years earlier Pordenone had already successfully traveled the fertile road of Roman proto-mannerism in the wake of Raphael and Michelangelo, in frescoes for the Malchiostro Chapel in the Duomo of Treviso (1520) and for the Duomo, Cremona (1521). Titian seems to have painted *Saint Christopher* in a spirit of artistic emulation and rivalry with Pordenone, as affirmed also by documents (Pallucchini 1969).
It has also been observed that the faithful rendering in a morning light of the Bacino San Marco constitutes one of the most precocious "contemporary" narrative passages in Titian's art and in Venetian "vedutismo" as a whole. The view reveals from afar the clear profile of the Campanile and of the Palazzo Ducale, next to the cupolas of the basilica. Topography of this kind appeared for the first time, in the light of a sunset, in *The Gozzi Altarpiece* (1520) of the Museo Civico, Ancona (Zampetti 1988) and later in the *Doge Antonio Grimani before Faith* (post 1555) of the Palazzo Ducale (Nepi Scirè 1979). The *Saint Christopher* is, however, enriched by a wider and more subjectively eloquent vista with, on the right side, the jagged profile of the Dolomites on the horizon.
We still do not know of any studies by Titian for the Palazzo Ducale *Saint Christopher*. One drawing, 330×200 mm, formerly in the Gösta Steuman collection, Stockholm, and now lost, can more appropriately be considered a preparatory study for the same saint in the engraving of *The Triumph of Christ* (Pallucchini 1969).
A copy drawing by Giuseppe Camerata was later used for an

engraving by Andrea Zucchi published by Domenico Lovisa in the *Gran Teatro di Venezia* (1720).

LITERATURE Ridolfi 1648, I, 149; Zanetti 1771, 126; Boschini-Zanetti 1797, 72; Crowe and Cavalcaselle 1877, I, 262-63; Saccardo 1896, 85; Tietze and Tietze-Conrat 1944, n. 1781; Tietze 1949, 178-80; Valcanover 1960, I, 65; Da Mosto 1966, 293; Pallucchini 1969, 56, 258, 330; Wethey 1969, 131; Muraro 1972, 353-54; Merkel 1979, 35; Nepi Scirè 1979, 90; Merkel 1980, 278; Perry 1980, 188-89; Chiari Moretto Wiel 1988, 86; Zampetti 1988, 20-22.

E.M.

16

Portrait of a Gentleman (Tomaso Mosti?)

oil on canvas, 35×67 cm
Florence, Galleria Palatina, Palazzo Pitti

EXHIBITIONS Venice 1935, Stockholm 1962-63, London
1983-84, Moscow and Leningrad 1986
RESTORATION 1909, Vermehren

The back of the canvas is inscribed: "DI THOMASO MOSTI IN
ETÀ DI ANNI XXV L'ANO MDXXVI. THITIANO DA CADORO
PITTORE." Recent investigation has shown (Zecchini 1978) that
the support is original, contrary to the belief of the majority of
critics who have maintained that the painting had been backed
with a new canvas (since Crowe and Cavalcaselle 1877), or
even transferred from panel to canvas. The inscription, then, is
not copied, even if it is probably not contemporary with the
painting.
The work was first mentioned in Florence in the collection of
Cardinal Leopoldo de' Medici (1663-67) who acquired it as a
Titian. Upon the cardinal's death (1675), the painting was
demoted to the status of "copy of Titian, thought to be
original," probably because of the heavy, disfiguring repaint. It
continued to appear regularly in different locations in the
palazzo and the *Guardaroba*, in the eighteenth-and nineteenth-
century inventories, as a copy of Titian (but often also as an
original), as chronicled by Zecchini in the relevant catalogue
entry of *Tiziano nelle gallerie fiorentine* (1978).
Only after the 1909 restoration was the high quality of the
painting, freed from overpainting, revealed, and the attribution to Titian from that moment onward has never been
questioned.
The information given by the inscription is, however, most
problematic. According to this, the painting is a portrait of
Tomaso Mosti at 25 years of age, painted by Titian in 1526.
The date was unconvincing even to Gronau (1904), for stylistic
reasons, and still today critics oscillate between 1520 and 1526.
The identity of the figure constitutes the principal unresolved
problem. The Mosti family, originally from Modena, had
moved to Ferrara at the beginning of the sixteenth century,
and was closely tied to Duke Alfonso I d'Este. The eldest
brother, Tomaso, was appointed rector of the church of San
Leonardo by the Duke in 1524, and later became archpriest of
the Cathedral of Ferrara. The second brother, Vincenzo, was a
favorite courtier of the Duke, who in 1524 gave him a house in
Santa Giustina, and in 1526 invested him with the county of
Rancidoro and Meldolla. After Vincenzo's death, Alfonso
conceded to the surviving son Alfonso the rare privilege of
adding Este to his family name. The third brother, Agostino,
pupil of Ariosto, was a famous man of letters at the court.
Since Titian worked for Alfonso d'Este around the end of the
second decade, the well-informed inscription on the back of

the canvas would seem to be creditable. However, inconsisten-
cies remain. Though it is unlikely that its author mistook the
sitter's Christian name, it still seems questionable whether the
elegant gentleman, between twenty-five and thirty years of age,
could possibly represent the cleric Tomaso Mosti in 1526. In
fact Lazzarini (1952) proposed that this is not Tommaso but
his brother Vincenzo, followed by several scholars including
most recently Boehm (1985). Zecchini suggested that it may
even be the third brother, Agostino, the man of letters.
It remains a fact that if the inscription is contemporary with
the extensive repainting shortly before the work was acquired
by Cardinal Leopoldo, as has been convincingly demonstrated
(Zecchini 1978), its credibility is diminished by the fact that it
was added more than a century after the portrait was painted.
Wethey (1971) left the identity of the figure uncertain between
Tomaso and Vincenzo, but he accepted the date "about 1526,"
followed in this by Zecchini (1978). Rossi (1978) preferred to
leave the subject anonymous, dating it "between 1523 and
1525." Fasolo (1980) accepted without question that it is by
Vincenzo Mosti, but dated it 1520. Hope accepted the identity
as Tomaso and linked the painting with a documented portrait
of an unnamed subject, commissioned by Alfonso d'Este from
Titian in 1520. Robertson, in the catalogue entry of the
exhibition *The Genius of Venice* (1983), agreed with the 1520
dating and speculated that an error of transcription had
changed it to 1526, explicable with the transposition of the 0
to a 6, and in support of the 1520 date stressed its similarity to
the *Man with a Glove* in the Louvre (see cat. no. 17). This
conclusion was reiterated in the catalogue of the exhibition
Rinascimento a Venezia (1986) organized in Leningrad and
Moscow.
The theory of a transcription error strengthens the credibility
of the sitter's identity, which may after all be Tomaso Mosti
before he took orders. But in the absence of more solid
information the question of identity must remain open (Chiari
1982, Chiarini 1988). The dating of the portrait *ca* 1520, which
recent critics have favored (Valcanover 1978, Rearick 1984), is
convincing for the similarities in quality and style to the *Man
with a Glove* in the Louvre, which shares its extraordinarily
modern technique.
Notwithstanding the old damage revealed under the repainting
and mended in the course of the 1909 restoration (there have
been no further restorations since), and notwithstanding the
serious abrasion of the surface, which in certain areas allows
the brownish-red preparation to show through, the delicacy of
the chromatic harmony and the freedom of handling that
animates all the details of the face and clothes can still be fully
appreciated. The frothy, rippling *camicia*, loosely tied at the
neck by a small cord, is trimmed with a thin black line that
enhances its texture and loses itself in a natural way in the fur.
Exceptional passages of stippled grays and whites on the

costume are enriched by an occasional light brown tint echoed below by the brown color of the book. The blue ribbon on the book, barely visible, summarizes with one delicate note of color the silvery tonalities of the whole.

The composition, with in the foreground the swelling sleeve slashed and lined with fur (which has suggested a connection, in reality rather dubious, with Raphael's *Portrait of Baldassare Castiglione*; (Louvre, Paris), successfully avoids showy artifice for expressive immediacy, and the face, formed of vibrant brushstrokes and dense pigments, is made arresting by the casual black beret that completes the figure in a masterly way.

LITERATURE Crowe and Cavalcaselle 1877, I, 271; Gronau 1904, 292; Lazzari 1952, 173-75; Wethey 1971, II, 119-20; Zecchini 1978, 209-16 (with complete bibliography); Valcanover 1978, 66; Rossi 1979, 191; Fasolo 1980, 32; Hope 1980, 62-64, 72 note 12; Chiari 1982, 2099, no. 280; Robertson 1983, 222; Rearick 1984, 64; Boehm 1985, 194; *Rinascimento a Venezia* 1986, no. 14; Chiarini 1988, 65.

S.P.

17

Man with a Glove

oil on canvas, 100×89 cm
Paris, Musée du Louvre (inv. no. 757)

EXHIBITIONS   Venice 1935, Paris 1976, Los Angeles 1979-80
RESTORATION   1789, Martin

Signed "TICIANUS" on the block of marble at bottom right
The work is said to have come from the Gonzaga Collection, Mantua, but contrary to published belief, it is not listed in the inventory made in 1627 at the time of the collection's sale to King Charles I of England (1600-49) with the number 324, which mentions a nude figure (Luzio 1913: "a painting done of a nude youth.... work of Titian"). Subsequently, in the inventories of 1649-51 (no. 235) of the English royal collections and the sale of the king's paintings in 1651 (no. 234), we read indications so vague ("A man by Tytsian" qualified as "Mantua Piece") that Adeline Hulftegger (1955) and Arnauld Brejon (1987) believed that the Louvre painting may as easily have been from the collection of Lord Arundel or from that of the painter Van Dyck. The only certainty is that the painting was part of the collection of Eberhard Jabach (1618-95), a banker from Cologne residing in Paris, who bought paintings from the three collections in London. Louis XIV then bought the portrait from Jabach in 1671, in the second sale of the banker's collection.

Le Brun records the portrait in the 1683 inventory with the number 248: "in the style of Titian." Paillet noted the work in 1695 in the apartment of "Monsieur," brother of the King in Versailles, and also attributed it to the "style of Titian." It was in storage from 1696 onward. It is difficult to explain such discredit of one of the most seductive portraits of Titian's career and one of the most noteworthy works in the royal collection. Bailly returned the portrait to the Master and noted it in Versailles in the Cabinet of paintings of the Superintendent.

The work then appeared in 1715 and 1718 in the gallery of the palace of the Duc d'Antin, director of Royal Buildings, and possibly in Versailles in 1737 in the King's room or the one next to it. It was noted by Lepicie in 1754, and perhaps by Jeaurat in 1760 in the Superintendent's palace, in the salon of the Marquis de Marigny, brother of Madame de Pompadour, and director of Royal Buildings. And finally it was noted by du Rameau in 1784 in the first room of this palace. In 1788 du Rameau noted "a painting badly relined and to be returned to its original form which is smaller." It can be shown in fact that the canvas, considered by Le Brun as pendant to the other *Portrait of a Man* of the collection of Louis XIV preserved at the Louvre (inv. no. 756) and also from Mantua, had – according to the inventory – the same dimensions as this one (100×97 cm) and the same critical fortune up to that time. Today,

however, it has reacquired its original smaller format. The *Man with a Glove* was transferred to the Louvre in 1792.

Hourticq (1919) identified the sitter as the Genoese aristocrat Girolamo Adorno, hired by Charles V in 1522-23 to carry out a mission to Venice. In 1527 Aretino had this portrait by Titian sent, along with his own, to the Marquis of Mantua, Federico II Gonzaga (1500-40). The sending of a portrait of Adorno to the Marquis can be explained by the mutual admiration of the two gentlemen, spoken of in Titian's letters of 1527. But since Adorno died in 1523, one must assume, if one accepts this hypothesis, that the work was only finished four years later. Hourticq also suggested that the portrait of Aretino that accompanied the portrait of the Genoese is Titian's other *Portrait of a Man*, housed at the Louvre and considered until the late 1700s to be its pendant. This identification does not stand up to comparison with the known likenesses of the great man of letters, such as that painted by Titian around 1545 and now in the Pitti Palace, Florence. Wethey (1971) inverted Hourticq's proposal and attempted to identify Adorno in the other Louvre portrait, which presents an older man than that of the *Man with a Glove*, and of the age – c. thirty-three years – of the diplomat when he died in 1523.

Hourticq's identifications have had no following after since Mayer's study (1938), which moved the execution of the painting up to c. 1523, and suggested that the subject was the director of Mantuan affairs in Venice, Giambattista Malatesta. However, though Malatesta mentioned a portrait in letters of 1523 (Crowe and Cavalcaselle 1877), he did not say that it was a portrait of himself. Furthermore, this vague comparison could equally be adapted to the companion piece in the Louvre.

The most recent hypothesis, taken up by Brejon (1987), has been formulated by Charles Hope, who identified it as the portrait of Ferrante Gonzaga, represented in 1523 at age sixteen, upon his return from a stay at the court of Spain. Tietze (1936) limited himself, without seeking an identification, to dating the painting c. 1520, given the style of the portrait, which is still close to that of Giorgione. During the crucial transition period of the 1520s toward an art that was progressively distancing itself from the influence of Giorgione (the models were no longer separated from the spectator by a parapet and instead of being portrayed half-length they were represented to the waist or to the knee), Titian was not yet the universally sought-after portraitist that he was later to become. Up to that time his models, who were friends with whom he maintained close ties, did not present the profound psychological tension of the later official portraits. They were of Titian's own generation, dear to him for their sensibility and fine looks, as is the case with the *Man with a Glove*.

Most critics date the portrait in the early 1520s, c. 1523 (Pallucchini 1969, c. 1523; Wethey 1971, c. 1520-2) a moment

MAN WITH A GLOVE

that saw the beginning of the relationship between Titian and Federico II Gonzaga, and placed the work, along with the other Louvre portrait, immediately after the *Portrait of a Man* of the Alte Pinakothek, Munich, c. 1520. The jacket of the *Man with a Glove*, cut at the neck in a V, and his shirt with the ruffle tightened by a cord around his neck to form a corolla, attest to a fashion that appeared after 1520 and later than the Munich canvas, in which the person's shirt still has a low neckline and no collar.

The figure in the Louvre canvas is shown half-length and slightly turned, his arms gently resting on a block of marble (on which the signature of the painter appears to be engraved) in a manner that gives the pose a relaxed, intimate but sober air, and which defines the space, near the spectator but sufficiently ample, in which the figure moves. The dark, indeterminate background and the black costume permit the painter to insist by contrast on the details that reveal the subject's personality: the face with its transparent skin and lips shaded by a light down, the hands with their "skin raised by the tendons and the blue lines of the veins" (Hourticq), which seem to radiate light, enlivened by the resplendent white of the little collar and the cuffs, an expedient invented by Titian better to express the psychology of the figure. Certain elements symbolize an almost involuntary elegance, such as the gold chain with a medallion decorated by a sapphire and a pearl, the gold ring engraved with an insignia on his extended index finger and above all the gloves lined with fine, light gray leather with hints of yellow. All of these emphasize the austerity implied by the sobriety of Titian's espressive means. They indicate without ostentation the social status of this young twenty year old aristocrat, still a dreamer – in the style of Giorgione – but animated by an "ardent melancholy" (Hourticq) expressed by the same disturbed gaze of the musician in the center of the *Concert* (see cat. no. 3) of the Pitti Palace, Florence. Pallucchini (1969) observed the skillful contrast between the dynamic right hand with the extended finger holding the clothes, and the abandon of the left hand covered by the glove that holds the other glove. This underlines the energetic and sweet nature of the model, implied by the features of his face. The glove was the courtly symbol of humanist elegance of Titian's early youth, among which one needs only cite the *Sacred and Profane Love* of the Galleria Borghese Rome.

The *Man with a Glove*, a true fragment of the Renaissance, presented to us with the warm sympathy that the painter felt for the sitter, began to exert its true charm only in the 1800s, doubtless owing to the nostalgic and romantic beauty of the model, which approaches the modern sensibility. In *La maison du chat-qui-pelote*, Balzac wrote that Titian's portraits seemed to him "endowed with exalted feelings," and at the beginning of our century Hourticq observed that "his portraits express judgments on the men of his time."

LITERATURE *Inventaire de l'hôtel du duc d'Antin* 1715, 9, 1718, 2; F.B. Lepicie, II, 1754, 37, no. XIX; Jeaurat 1760, 29, 2; Villot 1874, II, 270-71, no. 473; I, 282-83, 441-42, II, 421, 425-26; Heath 1879, 87; Both de Tauzia 1883, I, 254, no. 455; Champlin Jr., Perkins, II 1887, 286; Knackfuss 1898, 62, 82; Hurll 1901L, 61-66, Hamel 1903, 81; Gronau 1904, 43-44, 285; Ricketts 1910, 64; Lafenestre, Richtenberger, S.D. (1910), 238; Fischel 1911, XVII, 250, 265; Hourticq 1912, 23-40, 125-46; Luzio 1913, 116; Seymour de Ricci, 1913, 164-65; Raffaelli 1913, 179; Hourticq 1919, 48, 202, 206-14, 216, 267; Von Hadeln 1920, 931-34; Hautecœur 1926, II, 136; Rouches 1929, II, 18-19; Suida 1930, 83-84; Berenson 1932, 574; Suida 1935, 153; Tietze 1936, I, 125, 141, 162, II, 306; Mayer 1938, 289-91; Ozzola 1939, 92; Courvitch 1940, Wulff 1941, 120; Pallucchini 1944, I, XXI; Tietze 1950, 32, 62-64, 390; Hulftegger 1955, 128, 132; Dell'Acqua 1956, 74, 84, 116; Berenson 1957, I, 190; Valcanover 1960, I, 63, pl. 108-9; Chastel, Klein 1963, 330; Von Holst 1957, 129; Bazin 1967, 95; Pallucchini 1969, II, 57, 60, 61, 258-59, 384, 386, 400; Schefer 1969, 98; Bazin 1970, 169; Valcanover, Béguin 1970, 6, 103, no. 114, 142, 144; Judson 1970, 4, 5; Wethey, II 1971, 12, 15, 16, 17, 105, 118, no. 64, 423, III, 1975, 266, no. 64; Goudl 1976, 8; Hours 1976, 7-10, Rossi, Pallucchini, I, 1974, 14; Walther 1978, 36, 37, 45, 71; Hope 1980, 64-68; Brejon, Thiebaut 1981, 247, 281, 312, 333, 334, 390, 401.

J.H.

18

Madonna of the Pesaro Family (Pesaro Madonna)

oil on canvas, 478×266.5 cm
Venice, Chiesa dei Frari

EXHIBITION   Venice 1935
RESTORATION   1977, A. Lazzarin

The Dominican Jacopo Pesaro was elected Bishop of Paphos in 1495 and nominated in 1501 to Papal legate. He commanded the papal fleet allied to a Venetian fleet commanded by his distant cousin Benedetto Pesaro, in the naval battle in which on 30 August 1502 the Turks were defeated at Santa Maura, the ancient Leucadia. It was an ephemeral victory, since the loss of the island was ratified by a treaty signed on 20 May 1503. But Jacopo Pesaro, in commemoration of the military action, entrusted Titian with the execution of a votive painting, today in the Koninklijk Museum voor Schone Kunsten, Antwerp (see cat. no. 4).

The work's date is still uncertain, and some critics place it around 1515 on stylistic grounds. Pesaro seems to have been so pleased with the Antwerp painting that a few years later he commissioned from Titian a painting for the altar of the Immaculate Conception, which he acquired *in perpetuum* on 2 January 1518 for his family in the church of Santa Maria Gloriosa dei Frari. Thus, after the *Assumption*, Titian contracted to paint a second altarpiece on a Marian theme at the Frari. The friars, with the Father Germano at their head, in conceding the altar to Jacopo Pesaro and his successors with the power "*ad habendum, gaudendum, fabricandum, ex ornandum et in ordine ponendum,*" made it a condition that the Pesaros contribute must to the feast in honor of the *Immacolata*, celebrated each 8 December. Sanudo threw light on the involvement of the Pesaro with the cult of the Immaculate Conception when he noted in his diary in 1529 that the commemoration of the victorious battle of Santa Maura did not take place on 30 August, the day of the anniversary, but rather on 8 December. Tietze-Conrat (1953), Tea (1958), Sinding-Larsen (1962), Ettlinger (1979) and Goffen (1986) all stressed that the symbolic significance of the altarpiece is closely connected to the doctrine of the Immaculate Conception. This was understood in the nineteenth century. The parish priest of the Frari on 11 November 1882 informed the president of the Collegio degli Accademici that "since the Pesaro altarpiece is still in the Palazzo Ducale, the function for which it is used cannot take place [the feast of the Immaculate Conception, 8 December] since the altarpiece representing the subject is missing" (Valcanover 1980).

The altarpiece occupied Titian for a long time, from 1519 (the year in which, on 19 April, he was given his first payment) to 27 May 1526, the date of the final payment, as seen in the detailed documents transcribed by Scrinzi (1920). This was among Titian's busiest periods, when he produced, among others the three canvases (1518-23/4) for the *Camerino d'Alabastro* of Alfonso I d'Este in Ferrara; the votive painting of Alvise Gozzi, dated 1520, for the church of San Francesco in Ancona; the Averoldi polyptych, completed in 1522 after three years of work for the church of Santi Nazario e Celso, Brescia; and the frescoes painted in 1523 for Doge Andrea Gritti in the Palazzo Ducale. It was not only the concurrence of such time-consuming commissions that delayed the execution of the Pesaro Madonna. Titian meditated on the composition over a protracted period, as testified by various architectonic *pentimenti* revealed by x-radiography carried out during its recent restoration. Examination of the paint layers with a photomicroscope led to the same conclusion, since paint has been laid over paint at different times and over a long period (Lazzarini 1980). It is probable that Titian began the altarpiece three times, corresponding to the receipts in the documents, in 1519, 1522, and 1525-26, for a comprehensive payment of 102 ducats, including six for the stretcher.

The x-rays showed horizontal traces at the top center, suggesting that in an initial project Titian planned a concave apse as in the panel of *San Nicolò dei Frari* (now in the Pinacoteca Vaticana), on which he may have worked prior to receiving the commission for the *Pesaro Madonna* (Hood and Hope 1977). In the earliest and clearly legible version of the Pesaro Madonna, seen indistinctly by Wolff (1877) and graphically reconstructed by Sinding-Larsen (1962), Titian seems to have intended to unite the fictive architectural setting, consisting of an oblique sequence of pilasters (resembling the setting of the Treviso *Annunciation* reversed) with the real order of the Lombardesque altarframe. In a subsequent change of mind he replaced this with grandiose Corinthian capitals – to be sustained by columns and traversed by a large curtain, which descended on the right toward the ground like the similar motif in the later altarpiece of *Saint John the Almsgiver* (see cat. no. 45). Even this "proto-Baroque" solution failed to satisfy Titian. After some hesitation, he arrived at the definitive version, raising the two columns onto high bases. In their soaring ascent they pierce the clouds and erupt through the physical limits of the altarpiece.

Titian was perhaps advised on the iconography of such a bold conception. For Levi d'Ancona (1957) the columns represent the gates of heaven, for Forsmann (1967), the Jachin and Boar columns of the Temple of Solomon, and for Ettlinger (1979) they were a symbol of the Immaculate Conception insofar as they seem to illustrate the text of *Ecclesiasticus* 24:7: "et tronus meum in columna nubis," a critical text of the liturgy of the Immaculate Conception (Goffen 1986). Only after evolving definitively the architectural setting did Titian apply himself to finishing the figures, probably between 1525 and 1526, as demonstrated by x-radiography and photomicrography of

cross sections of paint samples (Valcanover 1980, Lazzarini 1980).

The revelations afforded by the 1977 conservation have eliminated any possibility that the two grandiose columns are not autograph, as had been suggested by Sinding-Larsen (1962) and Rosand (1971 and 1972). Archival research has been no less fundamental for the comprehension of Titian's revolutionary ideas and of no less importance for the iconological studies. This research, facilitated by Francesca Maria Tiepolo, made it possible to make new identifications of the Pesaros grouped on the right of the altarpiece, replacing the names proposed by Gronau (1904), Sartori (1956) and Fehl (1975). From the registers of the Balla d'Oro in the Archivio di Stato, Venice, we can identify from left to right, Francesco, firstborn son of Leandro Pesaro, already dead in 1528; Antonio and Giovanni, Jacopo's other brothers; and Lunardo and Niccolo, the sons of Antonio Pesaro, born respectively in 1508 and 1515 (Valcanover 1980). The flagbearing warrior is certain not to be Benedetto Pesaro, whose scant friendship with his distant cousin Jacopo was recorded by Sanudo. Fehl's hypothesis (1975) that this is Saint Maurice, rather than Saint George (Vasari 1568) or Saint Theodore (Moschini 1815), is attractive. With the full recovery in 1977 of the splendor of the color, relating in sonorous harmonies and revealed in the free and dynamic "natural" intensity of the light, so admired by Ridolfi (1648) and Zanetti (1774) and which had been obscured by nineteenth-century attempts at restoration (Valcanover 1980), the *Pesaro Madonna* now manifests fully its revolutionary novelty, which Cavalcaselle (1877) could only intuit and which Adolfo Venturi (1928) was the first to stress clearly, recognizing in the painting "the most solemn fulfillment of architectonic rhythm in Titian's art." And "the greatest effect of monumentality obtained by a prodigious equilibrium of zones of shadows and 'light' within a composition where everything is measured in a grave and solemn rhythm," within a composition which "moves the axis from the center, marking with the throne on its very high base reinforced by the pedestal of a column and with the figures grouped around it, the clear diagonal of the canvas." According to Rosand (1971 and 1972), the asymmetry of the altarpiece tends to be oriented toward the viewpoint of those who enter the church from the main door and proceed down the nave. This reading is opposed by Sinding-Larsen (1980) however. In effect, in such a complex diagonal structure, the altarpiece seems to place itself in relation both to the internal and external space of the church (Wilde 1974), creating "a surprisingly realistic window in the dark wall" (Pignatti 1989).

With the *Pesaro Madonna*, only a few years after the *Assumption*, Titian brought to felicitous conclusion the experimentation begun with the *Saint Mark Enthroned with Saints* of Santo Spirito in Isola (see cat. no. 5), achieving the renewal of the Venetian altarpiece and abandoning the traditional frontal centrality of the composition articulated by planes parallel to the frame. In the illusionistic space, rendered dynamic by the interpenetration of oblique and ascending directions, the human and sacred figures form a triangle crowned by the Virgin and Child. Against the two powerful marble shafts, which swell in the light descending from on high and filtered through the cloud, the religious scene assumes a human dimension in the physical and spiritual responses of the protagonists and the secondary figures. To the left, with firm resolution and in proud isolation, Jacopo Pesaro kneels in prayer, while behind him the Turkish prisoner bows his head and the warrior advances, unfolding the banner with the insignia of the Borgia and the Pesaro families. Both figures allude to the battle of Santa Maura. In the center, Saint Peter, distracted from his reading, fixes benevolent eyes on his protegé and seems to reassure him that he will intercede on his behalf with the Virgin. She bends her head to catch the thoughts of Saint Peter and praying Jacopo, controlling with difficulty the restive Child, who in turn is attentive to Saint Francis gesture of impassioned devotion, while behind we catch a glimpse of Saint Anthony in prayer. Below the two Franciscan saints, their intercessors, the members of the Pesaro family, are deep in prayer, each portrayed with stupendous realism in their features and their moods. The youngest Pesaro turns his head toward the spectator as if to catch his attention and to invite his participation in the extraordinary event at which only he and his relatives are present.

A similar freshness of familial sentiment reappeared years later in the *Votive Portrait of the Vendramin Family* of the National Gallery, London, one of Titian's unsurpassed revelations of social history, of which the *Pesaro Madonna* is a first, unforgettable example.

The many copies and engravings of the *Madonna of the Pesaro Family* testify to its popularity (Wethey 1969; Valcanover 1980; Chiari 1982; Catelli Isola 1976).

LITERATURE   Vasari 1568, 567; Ridolfi 1648, 64, 164; Zanetti 1771, 111; Moschini 1815, 194; Crowe and Cavalcaselle 1877, 305; Wolff 1877, 9ff; Gronau 1904, 77ff; Scrinzi 1920, 258, 259; Venturi 1928, 267-68; Tietze-Conrat 1953, 77ff; Bartori 1956, 45; Levi d'Ancona 1957, 70, no. 162; Tea 1958, 605ff; Sinding-Larsen 1962, 139ff; Forsmann 1967, 108ff; Pallucchini 1969, 63; Wethey 1969, 101ff; Rosand 1971, 200ff; Idem 1972, 232; Wilde 1974, 134; Fehl 1975, 75ff; Catelli Isola 1976; Hood and Hope 1977, 545; Ettlinger 1979, 59ff; Lazzarini 1980, figs. 12-19; Sinding-Larsen 1980, 201ff; Valcanover 1980, 57ff; Chiari 1982; Goffen 1986, 107ff; Pignatti 1989, 176-77.

F.V.

19

Feast of the Gods

oil on canvas, 170.2×188 cm
Washington, National Gallery of Art
Widener Collection 1942.9.1 (597)

RESTORATION   1989, D. Bull

The *Feast of the Gods* was the first of an extraordinary series of mythological paintings that Duke Alfonso d'Este commissioned to decorate the *Camerino d'Alabastro* (now destroyed) in his castle at Ferrara. Though the precise location of the *Camerino*, or private study, and the arrangement of its decoration are unclear (Hope 1987), the *Feast of the Gods*, signed by Giovanni Bellini and dated by inscription 1514, was probably not meant to hang alone, as Alfonso solicited further contributions from Raphael and Fra Bartolomeo (Shearman 1987). Influenced no doubt by his sister Isabella d'Este's famous *studiolo* in Mantua, the duke's concept was evidently for a series of bacchanals by the leading masters of Venice, Rome, and Florence. The mythological cycle, as completed, however, differed greatly from Alfonso's original scheme. After the works he ordered from Fra' Bartolomeo and Raphael were interrupted by their untimely deaths in 1517 and 1520, the duke transferred both commissions to Titian, who delivered the *Worship of Venus* (Madrid, Prado), based on Fra' Bartolomeo's sketch, in 1519. During the next half – decade Titian produced two more canvases for the *Camerino* – the *Bacchanal of the Andrians* (Madrid, Prado), and the *Bacchus and Ariadne* (National Gallery, London). Scholars disagree about which of these two works was painted first (Wethey 1975). The decoration was eventually completed by the local court artist Dosso Dossi, who provided a bacchanal (various candidates have been proposed as this work), as well as a painted ceiling and a frieze with ten scenes from the *Aeneid*, of which three are extant (Mezzetti 1965). Unfortunately, less than a century after its creation, the *Camerino* was stripped of its decoration, and the contents were dispersed.

In the second edition of the *Vite* (1568), Vasari claimed that, owing to Bellini's advanced age, Titian finished the *Feast of the Gods*. Although accepted by some later writers, this statement cannot be correct, as Bellini signed and dated the canvas and received a final payment for it in 1514, two years before his death. Vasari's story attempts to account for the fact that much of the present landscape in the painting is manifestly by Titian. Bellini's original landscape background, revealed in the x-radiograph published by John Walker in 1956, consisted of a continuous band of trees behind the figures, a small part of which is still visible on the right. The x-radiographs also betrayed the existence of an intermediate landscape between those of Bellini and Titian, indicating that the original was repainted not once but twice. According to Walker, Titian also

intervened in the figures, adding the identifying attributes of the gods (missing in the x-radiograph) and eroticizing certain of the protagonists' gestures and costumes. Assuming that the gods' attributes were added, Philipp Fehl (1974) proposed a literary source for the painting other than the usually cited *Fasti* by Ovid, namely, an Italian paraphrase of the Roman poet's *Metamorphoses*, in which the revelers who witnessed Priapus' attempted assault on Lotos were mere mortals.

The landscape Titian interpolated in the *Feast of the Gods*, including not only the mountainous view on the left but also most of the foliage in the upper right, has been both admired and deplored. Walker praised the landscape background as "among the most majestic ever created," while Rona Goffen, in a new monograph on Bellini (1989), regards it as a regrettable intrusion. The question remains as to why and when Titian repainted his teacher's masterpiece. Though his intervention is occasionally placed soon after Bellini completed the picture or even before, it is more often and more reasonably stated to have occurred during one of his known visits to Ferrara in 1524, 1525, or 1529. The alteration of the landscape and the presumed changes to the figures are, then, generally explained by the need to bring Bellini's canvas into harmony with Titian's own contributions to the *Camerino*, which, after the failure of the patron's original scheme, dominated the room.

The painstaking cleaning of the *Feast of the Gods*, completed by David Bull, chairman of painting conservation at the National Gallery, in 1989, returned the picture to its former splendor. Freed of discolored varnish and nineteenth-century overpaint, the painting emerged in remarkably good condition with only small, scattered losses. The treatment and concurrent technical examination by Joyce Plesters also shed new light on the complex evolution of the work, particularly on the chronology and significance of the various alterations (1989). The intermediate landscape, for example, which appears to be Ferrarese in style and which may have been executed by Dosso, whose activity in the *Camerino* is recorded, turns out to be much more extensive than was formerly believed. The cleaning and examination further established that the changes to the figures were made in Bellini's distinctive technique and betray his delicate touch, as Giles Robertson (1968) had already intuited, and that the attributes were merely painted on the surface, as was Bellini's custom, and do not point to a change of subject.

Titian's contribution, we can conclude, was limited to the landscape setting for the figures. Previously discolored varnish had reduced the intensity and range of the artist's colors. Now, with the original greens and brilliant ultramarine sky apparent, the landscape has regained its sense of depth and spaciousness. It has also become apparent that the background differs somewhat from those in Titian's bacchanals in London and

Madrid, which retain certain elements of the pastoral mode he adopted from his mentor Giorgione and which set off the foreground trees against a panoramic vista. Rather than seeking to create a harmony with the other bacchanals, Titian seems to have wanted to update the landscape he found in the *Feast of the Gods*, with the result that it marks the beginning of the new and deeper interest in landscape *per se* that characterizes his work in the 1530s (Rosand 1978, 27-29). A practical consideration was that densely painted motifs were needed to cover intermediate landscape. But it is significant that the nearest parallels to his revision of Bellini's painting are offered by works of about 1530, confirming the latest date proposed for Titian's intervention, in 1529 (Hope 1971, 1980). In particular, the mass of foliage in the upper right corner of the painting resembles the leafy boughs in Martino Rota's engraving after Titian's lost altarpiece of the *Death of Saint Peter Martyr*, painted in the late 1520s. Many other motifs added by Titian – the stream, the jagged mountain, the swaying trees – and the same treatment of foliage recur, likewise with diagrammatic clarity, in the woodcut of *Saint*

Jerome in the Wilderness, based on a design dating from the period when he was reworking the *Feast of the Gods* (Rosand 1976, 146-48, and 1978, fig. 86). The result of Titian's experiments with landscape may be seen in the *Madonna and Child with Saint Catherine and the Infant Baptist* in the National Gallery, London, in which a broader, more realistic, rather than idyllic, vision of nature unites the figures with their setting.

LITERATURE   Vasari (1568) (ed. Milanesi, 1881), VI, 474; VII, 433; Wind 1948; Walker 1956, 48-74; Valcanover 1960 (Italian ed.), I, 63-64, pl. 110; and (English ed.) II, 81, pl. 110; Mezzetti 1965, 71-84, figs. 61-64; Robertson 1968, 145-47; Pallucchini 1969, I, 47-48, 250. II, figs. 113-4; Valcanover 1969, 103, no. 107; Hope 1971, 718; Fehl 1974, 37-95; Wethey 1975, 29-41 and cat. nos. 12-15; Rosand 1978, 21; Shapley 1979, 38-47, pls. 26, 26a and b; Hope 1980, 54-55, 60; Hope 1987, 25-42; Shearman 1987, 209-230; Goffen 1989, 246; Bull 1989, 21-50; Plesters 1989, 53-103.

D.A.B.

20

Madonna and Child with Two Angels

fresco, detached in 1899, 157×348 cm
Venice, Palazzo Ducale

EXHIBITION   Venice 1935
RESTORATION   1989-90, O. Nonfarmale

This fresco was painted by Titian in only two days, in a lunette-shaped space at the foot of the Scala dei Senatori toward the courtyard of the same name – today the main access to the Palazzo Ducale – that once led to the palace chapel dedicated to San Nicolò. It was flanked by a *Resurrection* by Francesco Vecellio, a lunette that has also been preserved (Boschini 1664), and from which it was separated according to both Vasari (1568) and Ridolfi (1648), who said it was intact only by a miracle. Later, more precise descriptions of the work eliminate any uncertainty about the original location of Titian's fresco, and indirectly also that of his brother, "... at the foot of the covered stairs, by which the nobility descends to the Church [of San Marco]" (Zanetti 1771) and, "... on the left side..." (Boschini-Zanetti 1797). These references also indicate serious conservation problems by this time, and note the formal similarity between the Virgin and that painted by Titian in the altarpiece of San Nicolò dei Frari (c. 1535), now in the Pinacoteca Vaticana. This observation, which made a purely incidental comparison with one of the few early public works by Titian then in Venice, has prejudiced the critical assessment of the fresco. In the most recent restoration, the fresco has regained a satisfactory state of conservation and legibility, at least with respect to the figures. Crowe and Cavalcaselle (1877), implicitly confusing the two works, inconceivably deduced that the Vatican altarpiece was painted for the church of San Nicolò in the Palazzo Ducale, consequently backdating it to 1523, an error repeated by Berenson (1932) but corrected by Von Hadeln (1914), who also made the first reference to the detached fresco in relation to Titian's other paintings for the church of San Nicolò di Palazzo.

Sanudo (ed. 1892) described on 6 December 1523 the inauguration of the renovated San Nicolò di Palazzo by Doge Andrea Gritti, as follows: "... the new church of San Nicolò... this Doge has had nearly finished, and the Doge, who is well is painted by Titian, even with his dog behind, and other figures, San Nicolò and the four evangelists who write the Gospels; then the gilded altar...." The above-mentioned error of identification of the provenance of the altarpiece of *San Nicolò dei Frari* in the Pinacoteca Vaticana is confirmed beyond doubt by an engraving by Antonio Zatta (1761) that reproduces a section of the Basilica Marciana including the San Nicolò altar and the rough outlines of the lost Titian frescoes mentioned by Sanudo (Hubala 1977).

On the basis of these considerations, the frescoed lunette by Titian on the ramp along the staircase that led to the church of San Nicolò can be dated soon after the election of Doge Andrea Gritti (20 May 1523), thus complementing the frescoes described as executed by Titian in the same year, but "... at a distance ..." from them (Boschini-Zanetti 1797). While most critics have confirmed Titian's authorship, although differing on its date (Valcanover 1960, Pallucchini 1969, Wethey 1969), others erroneously demote it to the status of a workshop production (Tietze 1936) or to Francesco Vecellio (Fiocco 1946).

The present restoration, which has confirmed that it is a fully autograph work by Titian, draws attention to its role as an iconographic precedent to the altarpiece in the Vatican, in the center of which the intimate dialogue between the Virgin and Child reappears hardly varied, and opens up the possibility of

stylistic comparison with other early works such as the *Madonna of the Rabbit* in the Louvre (see cat. no. 23) and the *Marriage of Saint Catherine* in the National Gallery, London (see cat. no. 22). Even the mosaic of the *Madonna Enthroned with Child*, signed by Marco Luciano Rizzo and dated 1530, at the close of the sixteenth-century mosaic cycle of the Sacristy of San Marco – notwithstanding certain Cima-style archaisms – can most readily be explained by the hypothesis of a preparatory cartoon by Titian of the same period as the fresco in question (Merkel 1980).

Of the two praying angels who, supported by little white clouds, converge on the Child, the one to the right is in a three-quarter pose that will be used again in the Vatican altarpiece and elsewhere by Titian. A rarity instead is the other angel, who bears the symbolic red robe of the Child, and whose profile bears the stamp, it seems, of Pordenone's models.

LITERATURE Sanudo 1523 (ed. 1892) xxxv, coll. 254-55; Vasari 1568 (ed. Milanesi 1881), vii, 439; Ridolfi 1648, 149; Boschini 1664, *San Marco*, 71; Zatta 1761, tab. v; Zanetti 1771, 126; Boschini-Zanetti 1797, *San Marco*, 68-69 : Crowe and Cavalcaselle 1877, 172, no. 2; von Hadeln 1914, i, 166-67; Berenson 1932, 575; G. Fogolari 1935, 65; Tietze 1936, 132; Fiocco 1946, 30; Valcanover 1960, i, 60; Pallucchini 1969, 268; Wethey 1969, 100; Hubala 1977, 134.

E.M.

21

Study for Saint Bernardine

charcoal, white chalk, white lead, blue paper; slightly stained; 381×266 mm
Florence, Gabinetto Disegni e Stampe degli Uffizi (inv. no. 1713 F)

On the verso: studies of drapery

The drawing was catalogued by Ferri (1890) with the traditional attribution to Titian, as "study for the figure of Saint Francis in the painting of the Assumption, at the Vatican," and reproduced for the first time by Loeser (1912-21) with the same reference. Von Hadeln (1913) was able to demonstrate that it was instead a preparatory study for the figure of Saint Bernardine in the votive painting of Doge Andrea Gritti, the "new Painting" seen by Sanudo on 6 October 1531 (the day of its official presentation) in the Sala del Collegio in the Palazzo Ducale, destroyed by the 1574 fire.
Titian's composition is known to us through an anonymous woodcut (see Muraro and Rosand 1976, no. 77) in which Doge Andrea Gritti has been replaced by his successor Francesco Donato (Doge 1545-53), but which faithfully reproduces, as Wolters has explained (1983), the lost painting, and also corresponds to the description given by Sanudo and to the copy of the painting executed by Tintoretto's workshop in 1581-82 for the Sala del Collegio. The connection established by Von Hadeln between the study in the Uffizi and the figure of the saint in the foreground to the right in the woodcut leaves no doubt: the drawing corresponds faithfully to the engraved image, not only in the pose, but also in the distribution of the folds of the habit and in the *chiaroscuro* formula.
Von Hadeln (1924) then identified in the studies of drapery on the *verso* two drawings (one in the lower part, the other traced inversely in the upper part of the sheet) for the mantle of the doge, who is on his knees in profile to the left as in the woodcut. Von Hadeln's observations have been accepted by all scholars, with the single exception of Bodmer (1940), who attributed the drawing to Cavedone. However, after Tietze (1944) restored the attribution to Titian, the authorship of these studies and their connection to the Gritti painting were definitively accepted. For this reason the dating of the sheet to 1531 or perhaps the preceding year (Rearick 1975, Pignatti 1979) can also be considered a fact, on the basis of *terminus ante quem* of October 1531.
Among the few studies of draped figures certainly attributable to Titian, either graphite or charcoal, the Saint Bernardine is of particular significance as a document of the formation of an increasingly bold and free language, in which the study of tonal values (characteristic even of pen studies for paintings) finds its natural expressive medium in the softer mediums and in the combination of charcoal and blue paper.

In the most credible reconstruction of Titian's evolution as a draftsman, completed in the wake of the Florence and Venice shows of 1976 (see Pignatti 1979, Chiari Moretto Wiel 1989), this drawing is dated more than a decade later than the small study in the British Museum for the *Saint Peter* in the Frari *Assumption* (see cat. nos. 11, 12) (the earliest analogous study with effects of iridescent light obtained through charcoal highlighted with chalk). Effectively, in the *Saint Bernardine*, "exemplary for the whole of Paris Bordone's , Bonifacio's and Savoldo's generation" (Pignatti), Titian sought through the graphic medium the effects that he wished to obtain in the painted version. Using most probably a model posed in a monk's habit, Titian "succeeds in grasping organically both the form and its coherent illumination" with a few decisive strokes (Rearick). The marks are richly vibrant, tending to dissolve in light until they assume the aspect of applied paint in the shaded areas; in the lower part of the habit the charcoal is rubbed or blurred, perhaps with the fingers, as was also apparently the white chalk.
In the freer sketches on the *verso*, Titian gave a still more dazzling demonstration of the expressive possibilities of this technique, making soft, grainy marks, united by delicate rubbing, and alternating with brilliant applications of white. Contrary to Wethey's belief (1987), the state of conservation of the *verso* is good, excepting some stains. Wethey interpreted both drawings erroneously as a single study of drapery "more similar to a tunic than to a doge's mantle" without taking into account the affinity pointed out by Rearick (1976) between these drawings and the lower border of the doge's mantle in the Tintoretto version of the painting. And this, it would seem, indicates that some parts of the damaged painting remained comprehensible enough to serve as models for the copy by Tintoretto.

LITERATURE Ferri 1890, 256; Loeser 1912-21, no. 4; Von Hadeln 1913, 238; Von Hadeln 1924, 48; Fröhlich-Bum 1928, nos. 26-27; Fogolari 1935, 211, no. 6; Tietze and Tietze-Conrat 1936, 183, 191, nos. 23-24; Bodmer 1940, 14; Mauroner 1941, 46-47; Tietze and Tietze-Conrat 1944, 308, no. 1904; Tietze 1950, 404; Valcanover 1960, 84; Pallucchini 1969, I, 331-32; Valcanover 1969, 107; Dreyer 1972, 231; Wethey 1969-75, III, 258, no. 51; Rearick 1976, no. 22; Oberhuber 1976, no. 36; Muraro and Rosand 1976, no. 77; Rearick 1977, no. 10; Pignatti 1979, 8, no. 225; Wolters 1980, 563-65; Rosand 1981, 306, no. 6; Wethey 1987, 27, 140, no. 14; Wolters 1987, 112; Chiari Moretto Wiel 1988, 32, 48, no. 22; Chiari Moretto Wiel 1989, 20, 89-90, no. 22.

G.D.

"Drapery Studies," verso

22

Madonna and Child with Saint Catherine
and the Infant Baptist in a Landscape

oil on canvas 101×142 cm
London, The Trustees of the National Gallery (no. 635)

RESTORATION 1955

By 1856 the painting was in the Beaucousin Collection, Paris,
from which the National Gallery purchased it in 1860. Prior to
this, it had belonged to the W.C. Coesvelt Collection, London.
It is listed in a catalogue of this collection and in that of two
Christie's auctions in 1837 (2 June) and 1840 (13 June), as
originating from the sacristy of the Escorial. It corresponds in
fact to a description of a painting by Titian that Velázquez, by
order of Philip IV, sent in 1656 to the Escorial, where F. De
Los Santos described it in 1657 in the sacristy (Gould 1959).
As for its earlier history, the most probable hypothesis is that it
belonged to the collection of Cardinal Pietro Aldobrandini
together with other paintings by Titian, which the cardinal had
inherited from the d'Este family. It was no. 78 in an inventory
before 1655 of the paintings of Olimpia Aldobrandini Pam-
phili, with a note that it had been given by Olimpia to Cardinal
Ludovisi in 1621: "a Madonna dressed in turquoise with the
Putto who with its arms raised is playing with a woman on her
knees, who embraces Him, with the Infant Saint John to the
right hand side, to whom the Madonna extends a flower, in a
large painting by the hand of Titian" (D'Onofrio 1964, 159).
The inscription "no. 78 Di Titio," which Gould informs us
(1959) was painted in the lower right corner of the canvas and
which was covered after the 1955 restoration, surely referred
to this inventory.
No. 78 of the Aldobrandini inventory corresponded to the
"*Madonna col Puttino, e San Giouannino, e Santa Catarina alta
pmi sei lunga pmi sette...di mano di Titiano,*" which was no. 44
of a list of paintings belonging to Cardinal Ludovico, compiled
in 1633 after his death (Garas 1967). Together with other
paintings in the Ludovisi estate, the painting was sent to Spain
as a gift to Philip IV from the Duke of Medina de las Torres,
Viceroy of Naples (Garas 1967). Critics agree for the most part
on dating the work c. 1530. Gould is the exception (1959),
postponing the date to the second half of the 1530s and
speculating that there was some workshop intervention.
The date c. 1530, which is convincing, is most clearly sustained
by the stylistic similarity to the *Madonna and Child with Saint
Catherine* (the so-called *Madonna of the Rabbit* of the Louvre,
see cat. no. 23) that can be identified with a painting executed
in 1530 for Federico Gonzaga.
Even the early *Sacre Conversazioni* (c. 1512-15) had revealed
the felicity and expressive originality with which Titian painted
this traditional Venetian theme. The rich and lively flow of the
tonal color, the poses of the figures captured with a sense of
warm humanity, the setting and the landscape vistas so which

characteristic of this expressive novelty, recur in the London canvas with greater maturity. This is apparent in the fullness and intensity of the landscape: a calm and serene nature, the ideal setting for an interpretation in which gestures and glances express sweetness and harmony. The carefully considered responsiveness of the movements and, the beautiful juxtaposition of the yellow and dark blues of Saint Catherine's and the Madonna's robes result from a carefully thought-out composition, eliciting subtle psychological touches of intimate and affectionate naturalness from the poses and gestures. Note for example how the Virgin extends her arm to receive the Infant Baptist's gift without turning her protective gaze away from the Child, and with what tremulous joy the saint inclines her head toward Him.

The painting, for its stylistic qualities and felicitous originality, became one of Titian's most successful prototypes, giving rise to several more or less faithful copies and variants (Pallucchini 1969; Wethey 1969).

LITERATURE   De los Santos 1657 (ed. Sanchez Canton, 1933), 239; Gould 1959, 111-14; Garas 1967, 288; *Idem* 1967, 343; Pallucchini 1969, 72, 264-65; Valcanover 1969, 105-06, no. 136; Wethey 1969, 17, 104-05, no. 59 (with preceding bibliography); Rosand 1983, 104, pl. 22; Christiansen 1987, 196.

P.R.

23

Madonna of the Rabbit

oil on canvas, 71×87 cm
Paris, Musée du Louvre (inv. no. 743)

EXHIBITIONS   Venice 1935, Paris 1945, 1976, 1978-89, Nice
1979, London 1981-82
RESTORATION   1749, Colins and Godefroid

Signed bottom left, on Saint Catherine's wheel: TICIANUS F.
Giambattista Malatesta, the Venetian agent of Federico II
Gonzaga (1550-40), Duke of Mantua and son of Isabella
d'Este, wrote in a letter of 5 February 1530 addressed to his
sovereign that "Titian has shown me the paintings which he is
making for your Highness. That of our Lady with St Catherine
and the other of the nude women are well on. The one of our
Lady he promises to give to your Excellency at the beginning
of Lent and the other at Easter" (Crowe and Cavalcaselle
1877).
From Tietze onward (1936), most critics have agreed that the
painting mentioned by Malatesta can be identified with the
work now in the Louvre and not, as Suida proposed (1934),
with the *Madonna and Child, with Saint Catherine and the
Infant Baptist* painted by Titian in the same years for Alfonso
d'Este, Duke of Ferrara, Federico's maternal uncle. The latter,
now in the National Gallery, London (see cat. no. 22) has
always been compared stylistically with the Paris painting.
Hope (1981) further asserted that the payment Titian received
in March 1530 was specifically for the painting mentioned by
Malatesta.
Hourticq (1919) maintained that Federico II is represented as
a shepherd crowned with laurel leaves, visible on the right of
the painting. This figure, which seems indeed to be a portrait
(as Louis Boullogne the Elder had perceived, discussing it in
his famous lecture on the *Madonna of the Rabbit* held on 12
April 1670 at the Royal Academy, with particular reference to
the portrait and to the distortions of perspective), has an
affinity with the famous portrait of the duke painted by Titian
around 1527-28, now at the Prado. Béguin (1980) accepted
Hourticq's identification and suggested that the crown of
leaves (apparently laurel) on the head of the figure – traditional
attribute of the humanist poet – represents a tribute to the
refined culture of the court of Mantua. The herd of rams could
allude, according to Hope, to the duke's role as head of state.
Hourticq also saw in the figure of Saint Catherine a portrait of
Cecilia, Titian's wife who died in 1530, but this theory was
questioned by Tietze (1936). Malatesta reported in the same
letter that Titian, stricken by the death of his wife, was having
difficulty completing the painting.
The identification of the work cited by the prince's agent with
the painting now in the Louvre, and the probable portrait of
the Duke in the composition, lead us to believe that the

Madonna of the Rabbit was indeed commissioned from Titian
by Federico II, a man who loved nature, and who would have
wanted an image that united devotion with humanism in the
manner of Giorgione's pantheistic ideal, which Titian more
than any other had perpetuated in that decade. This cultured
prince was an *amateur* of Titian's work. He and Titian had first
come into contact around 1523, during Titian's decoration of
the *Camerino d'Alabastro* of Ferrara. Federico had already
obtained from the artist his own portrait, as well as those of
Aretino and Girolamo Adorno.
In 1913 Alessandro Luzio published the inventory of the sale
of the Gonzaga collection in 1627 to Charles I of England. In it
appears a painting of the same subject, number 315 on the list
("The Madonna with the Child in her arms and Saint Catherine.... work of Titian"), but it was omitted from the inventory of Charles I's collection. Claude Ferraton (1949) demonstrated that the Louvre painting came from the collection of
the Duc de Richelieu and not that of Cardinal Mazzarin (as
Cosnac maintained in 1884), nor of Charles I via the banker
Eberhard Jabach (as claimed by Hourticq 1919 and Hautecœur 1926). Wethey (1969) speculated that the canavas
entered the duke's collection through the inheritance of
Cardinal Richelieu, to whom Vincenzo Gonzaga may have
given it c. 1624-47 together with other paintings (among them
the allegories of Mantegna, Lorenzo Costa and Perugino from
the *studiolo* of Isabella d'Este, all now in the Louvre), instead
of selling it to the English king, with the intention of obtaining
the title of Minister to the King of France.
Bernini visited the Duc de Richelieu's collection in 1665
during his visit to France, and Chantelou related how the
sculptor looked closely at the *Madonna of the Rabbit*, "of
which he said that the sky had altered, and that it had
blackened to the point of fading away." According to Loménie
de Brienne, the duke lost his collection in the course of 1665
playing tennis with Louis XIV, who bought twenty-five paintings on 26 December, among them the *Madonna of the Rabbit*
for 50,000 lire (Brejon 1987).
The work was inventoried in 1683 with the number 157 by Le
Brun, and mentioned by Paillet in the gallery at Versailles in
1695. Bailly mentioned it in the Petite Galerie in 1709-10. In
1715 the work was placed in the gallery of the king at
Versailles, and was seen there by Piganiol de la Force in 1738.
Bailly saw it again, in 1757, in the collection of the king at the
Luxembourg palace, while Duplessis noted it in 1785 at the
Louvre, where it was to remain, in the Grande Galerie, until
the creation of the museum in 1793.
X-radiography, published by Hours (1976), has revealed
numerous *pentimenti*, as was normal with Titian. However, a
rabbit, cut in half on the lower right of the painting, seems to
be the result of bad restoration at an unknown date, from a
misunderstood original motif (a pumpkin, if Chataigner de

Lavallée's engraving (1810) is to be believed, even though this print transformed the spiked wheel of Saint Catherine into a *cassone* with handles). Wethey's theory (1969) that the painting was reduced on both sides is unhelpful. The pose of the Virgin was modified, and hence also her dress, which became more stylish, as did that of Saint Catherine. In an earlier version the Virgin turned her face toward the shepherd, which would tend to confirm the elevated status of this figure who from the beginning was crowned with laurel. In addition the basket did not at first have a cover and did not contain fruit. In the final composition, the Virgin restrains a white rabbit, which was added in this phase, becoming a dominant motif. These changes, analysed by Beguin (1980), are important as much for iconographical reasons as for stylistic ones. The representation of the Virgin with rabbits reflects a humanist interest in the *Imagines* of Philostratus, but this literary reference pales before the familial image of a mother who shows her child an animal. This would explain the modifications to the pose of the Virgin. The fruit in the basket (an apple and some grapes) gives the scene, notwithstanding the naturalism of a motif that indicates autumn, a mystical significance of redemption, since these fruits are the symbols of the Passion (original sin redeemed by the wine of the Eucharist). The white rabbit became in Venice, from Dürer and Giovanni Bellini onward, the symbol of the fecundity of Mary without sin (parthenogenesis) and thus of the revelation of the incarnation (Panofsky). The Virgin holds the rabbit with a white cloth which has become almost illegible with time and clumsy restoration, underlining the sacred nature of the animal, symbol of Mary's purity. This symbolic construction is completed by the strawberry plant, plant of Paradise, which grows at the feet of Saint Catherine.

With regard to the style, we find that Titian was loyal to the lyricism of Giorgione (especially in the sumptuous sunset sky layered in orange and blue, recalling the *Pala Gozzi* at the Museo Civic, Ancona), but with mixture of the new classicism coming out of Rome, already apparent in Titian's Averoldi polyptuch of 1522 (Brescia, Chiesa dei Santi Nazaro e Celso). This determined the distribution of the poses of the figures: the shepherd reflects the spectacular *contrapposto* of the Brescia *Saint Sebastian* greatly admired by Titian's contemporaries for its audacious novelty. Freedberg (1971) has observed that the wilfully decentralized and asymmetrical position of the figures, including Saint Catherine who is cut off on the left by the canvas edge, recalls the *Pietà* by Correggio (Galleria Nazionale, Parma).

The changes revealed by x-radiography indicate a slow and careful elaboration of the painting. Béguin (1976) postulated an execution in two periods, with the first idea laid-in at the beginning of the 1520s, then to be completed in a final version in 1530. In effect the composite style characterizes the end of

the transitional period c. 1520. Initally Titian would have conceived the work in the spirit of the *Sacre Conversazioni* which he was producing between 1510 and 1520, dominated by the influence of Giorgione (such as the *Holy Family with John the Baptist*, c. 1510, his Grace the duke of Sutherland, or the *Madonna and Child with Saint Catherine, Saint Dominic and a Donor*, c. 1515-20 of the Fondazione Magnani-Rocca, see cat. no. 9). When he returned to the canvas a few years later, inevitably he altered it to incorporate what he had recently learned. Tietze insisted on the experimental nature of this work, which though small gives the impression of a larger composition reduced, datable c. 1530. The painting belongs then to a group of private paintings, destined for a new class of Italian connoisseurs.

Pallucchini (1969) argued that the principal innovation of the composition consisted in conferring an unprecedentedly active role on the landscape, with the figures "immersed" in the ample spaces instead of filling the foreground with their dominant forms, as in earlier *Sacre Conversazioni*. The genre of the *Sacra Conversazione* lent itself particularly well to this pantheism, given its format of figures pleasantly and harmoniously arranged in a landscape that was one of the most admired aspects of Venetian art: the harmony was achieved through the use of a high horizon line that creates an enveloping landscape through planes that follow one another at regular intervals toward the back and through the diffusion of a warm afternoon light. The careful harmony union of these elements would have suggested the sweet atmosphere of the Veneto pre-Alpine hills in the valley of the Piave, considered the ideal setting for humanist encounters.

The tonalities are more intimate and softer than in the early *Sacre Conversazioni*. The contrast in the central group, of the glowing and refined colors of the light fabrics, the clear skin of the saint, the Child and the Virgin set off against the darker tones of the latter's garments and of the greenery, gives force to the affective sequence of gestures, in a slow and majestic rhythm. The noble shepherd in *contrapposto* on the right is composed of the same hues, diminutively mimicking the main group. The composition seems to balance the Faith incarnate in the Madonna and Child in the foreground with a pagan divinity in the middle distance. The intellectual gravity is emphasized, however in a typically Venetian way, by the domesticity of the fruits in the basket, and of the rabbit that the Virgin grips.

Thus together with the *Sacra Conversazione* in London (see cat. no. 22), which transposes onto a larger scale the new feeling for nature adumbrated by Titian in Federico II Gonzaga's painting, the *Madonna of the Rabbit* constitutes, in spite of its vestigially Giorgionesque character, the prototype of the evolution of Titian's painting at the beginning of the 1530s toward a Roman sense of color. This signalled the beginning of

his definitive break with Giorgione's art. The prototypical aspect of the work was emphasized by Louis Boullogne. In the grand polemics which divided the French artistic scene of the seventeenth century, he claimed that this small canvas symbolized the superiority of color and of the effect of the whole, over drawing.

LITERATURE   Félibien 1666-88, II, 69-70; Bailly 1751, 22, no. 81; Dezallier d'Argenville 1752, 306; Lepicie 1754, II, 19-20; Piganiol de la Force 1764, I, 309-10; Tuetery and Lavallée (Filhol) 1804-28, VII, 1-3; Waagen 1854, 493; Villot 1874, I 282; Crowe and Cavalcaselle 1877, I, 307-08, 336-41, 446; de Cosnac 1884, 198-99, 203, 243; Jouin 1883, 207-14; Lalanne 1885, 233; Champlin and Perkins 1885-1913, III, 135; Luzio 1888, 25; Knackfuss 1898, 56, 74; Engerand 1899, 73; Hamel 1903, 73; Gronau 1904, 86, 283; Guiffrey 1909, 397; Fischel 1911, 54, 218, 251; Luzio 1913, 115, 300-02; de Ricci 1913, I, 157; Hourticq 1919, 214-15; Hautecœur 1926, 132; Washburn Freund 1928, 35-39; Suida (1935), 154; Buscaroli 1935, 171; Tietze 1936, I, 141, 152, 153, 156, 161; II, 305; Frankfurter 1939, 103; Wulff 1941, 120-25; Tietze and Tietze-Conrat 1944, 322; Ferraton 1949, 439, 444; Tietze 1950, 30; Hulftegger 1955, 132, no. 1; Dell'Acqua 1956, 24, 33, 76-77, 118-19; Berenson 1957, I, 189; Bazin 1957, 134; Bazin 1958, 142; Valcanover 1960, I, 66; Hours 1964, 103; Bazin 1967, 151; Pallucchini 1969, I, 57, 71-72, 75, 87, 264, 265, 383, 400, II, pls 196-99; Wethey 1969, I, 17, 104, 105-06, 387, III, 95, 260; Judson 1970, 41; Valcanover and Béguin, 1970, 6, 7, 106, 143, 144; Moussalli 1972, 65; Speck 1976, VI, VII, IX, 1-2, 13-14, 16-18, 40-41, 47, 50-51, 56-57; Rearick 1976, 46; Hours 1976, 12-15; Walther 1978, 39, 53; Germann 1978, 60; Béguin 1980, 480-84; Brejon and Thiebaut 1981, 245, 281, 312, 334, 392, 396, 399, 405; Freedberg 1983, 328, 697; Brejon 1987, 33, 34, 37, 67, 211-12, 477, 486, 487, 489; Chiari Moretto Wiel 1988, 32, 47, 63; Berce and Boubli 1988, 47.

J.H.

24.

The Annunciation

oil on canvas, 166×266 cm
Venice, Scuola Grande di San Rocco

EXHIBITIONS   Venice 1935, Venice 1947
RESTORATION   1989-90, R. Bagarotto

As Zanetti wrote in 1771, he who climbed the grand stairway of the Scuola di San Rocco saw "before ascending the second flight, above, a precious painting by Titian, intact and beautiful, with the Virgin announced by the Angel. It is of the best time of this author; and it possesses all the beauty that was of his most sublime style." All the the early guidebooks and sources described it in this position, faced by Tintoretto's *Visitation*. It was there at least from 1557 (30 October, in *Registro delle pareti*, vol. II, Archivio della Scuola), donated to the *scuola* by the will of 31 October 1555 of the lawyer Melio Cortona, member since 1539: "I will and order that my painting of the Annunciation of the Most Sacred Virgin, by M. Titian's hand, which I have at home, be taken after my death, and given and consigned to the magnificent Guardian and companions of our School of San Rocco, which they must put in the *Albergo* or in the Hall..." (Archivio di Stato, Venice, *Notatorio*, 250, no. 49, published by Cicogna 1834). It is currently placed on the easel near the altar in the Sala del Capitolo. Titian did not execute any paintings for the Scuola di San Rocco as such, even if he was a member from 1551, and in 1553 had offered to "make that large painting of the *albergo* above where there are those of the *Bancha*" (21 September in *Registro delle Parti*, vol. II, Archivio della Scuola, published by Pallucchini and Brunetti 1937), a proposal unanimously accepted but which never materialized.

So the *terminus ante quem* is 1555, but on the basis of style the execution of the painting would seem to be many years earlier, even if it is extremely difficult to establish a precise date, because of the lack of documents or other certain information. Most critics favor 1540, suggested by Gronau (1904), Fischel (1906), Ricketts (1910) and later taken up by Tietze (1936), then Berenson (1957), Pallucchini (1969) and Valcanover (1960), who noted the absence of the mannerist elements peculiar to the works after 1540, while Chiari postponed it to 1542-3, on the basis of a stylistic comparison with the *Madonna and Child with Mary Magdalene*, Leningrad. Cavalcaselle, however, followed by Milanesi, likened it to the *Madonna of the Pesaro Family* (see cat. no. 18), finished in 1526. Only Zanotto anticipated its execution to "shortly after 1515, and when he was about forty years old." Suida, stressing its difference from the *Annunciation* of Naples, considered it to be c. 1530, a date later accepted by Wethey on the grounds that it stylistically precedes the *Annunciation* engraved by Caraglio in 1537.

The recent conservation uncovered an overpainted part of the sky and landscape, giving depth to the vista, and also served to restore the bright and luminous colors. Clearly defined form and limpid color emphasize the calm of the scene, which is scanned with slow and peaceful rhythms. The spatial organization is of a standard Renaissance type, balanced and serene in its classical composure, the only exception being the angel who is caught in mid-air.

Those who date the work around 1540 point to the difference "in the naturalistic description of the setting" from the immediately subsequent works, in which Titian "seems openly to adhere to the mannerist world" (Valcanover 1960). According to Pallucchini (1969) the artist returned, after the lost *Annunciation* for the monastery of Santa Maria degli Angeli, Murano, 1537, "to a more calm, almost archaicizing design," in the same spirit as the *Presentation of the Virgin in the Temple*. But this very archaism of the composition, together with the renewed liveliness of the palette, favors the earlier dating prior to the Santa Maria degli Angeli painting, of 1537. The composition of the latter, known from a sixteenth-century engraving by Caraglio, has a vertical axis centered on the divine rays emanating from the dove and on the swirl of angels rushing toward the miraculous event. The stylistic approach, evident in the *figura serpentinata* of the Angel, develops out of the general sobriety of the *Annunciation* of San Rocco, and is closer to the *Annunciation* in San Domenico, Naples, traditionally dated 1557, in which the Virgin appears similarly posed.

The more relevant comparison in our opinion is with the Virgin and Angel of the upper part of the *Averoldi Polyptych* of 1522 and especially with the Madonna, who inclines forward with her arm on her bosom; in the way her hand is represented, long and tapering; and in the profile of her face. This stylistic similarity is a useful basis for dating, which, in the absence of precise information, we can only approximately locate between the Averoldi polyptych and the lost *Annunciation* of Murano. The state of conservation of the canvas, which has suffered in the past, inhibits a more narrowly defined dating.

Not only is the painting's date controversial, but even its authorship has been questioned, first by Dussler (1935), and then by Suida (1934) who speculated that the angel's drapery had been repainted by Tintoretto. Tietze (1950) followed by Chiari (1982) perceived workshop intervention. However, the latest restoration, which in part recovered the picture's quality, constitutes a confirmation (also in the light of the microexamination of the paint layer) of Titian's autograph. Reflectography has furthermore indicated compositional practices typical of the painter, such as the laying in of the entire architectonic setting even where it was later to be covered (the balustrade, for example, which is visible even where hidden under the red lacquer of the curtain). The base of the column in the right corner is, instead, painted over the extension of the cloak of the Madonna. An interesting *pentimento* is found in the left wing of the angel, which was previously spread wider, occupying the central part of the painting, but was then trimmed back by the landscape.

In the embattled critical history of the San Rocco *Annunciation*, doubts have also arisen over the work's provenance. Milanesi, in his edition of Vasari's *Lives*, wrote: "he made in the church of Santa Maria Nova a panel, an Annunciation," and supposed that it was this that was brought to the Scuola di San Rocco following the closing of the church. Instead, all trace of this "Nunziata," painted according to Vasari after Titian's Roman trip, has gone. An interesting hypothesis has been formulated by Catelli Isola (1976-7) who identified it in an engraving by Enea Vico of 1548 (Gabinetto Nazionale delle Stampe, Rome, inv. no. F.C. 31010), in which the Virgin is placed in an architecture of decidedly Roman classicism, clearly later than the Quattrocentesque San Rocco *Annunci-*

ation. Its details of the cloth, the guinea fowl and the work basket, the symbolic attributes of the Virgin, are also the most successful passages in the painting.

There are no know preparatory studies for this composition. However, some charcoal sketches were discovered on the back of the canvas when in May 1915 it was first detached from the wall of the staircase of the *scuola* to protect it during the war. Fortunately the drawings were seen, described and photographed by Scrinzi before they were hidden under the lining. They represent, on the left, corresponding to the Virgin, a female nude with a cloth hanging from her shoulder, and on her left, a standing male nude, which Scrinzi identified with the *Doryphyos* and claimed that it was obvious in real life but unrecognizable in the photographs, owing to the dark stain of the painted Virgin, which shows through completely due to the thinness of the canvas. On the right, sketched with rapid and rather confused strokes, are two male nudes fighting, one of whom has his left knee on the ground. Scrinzi (1920) maintained that they are of "clear sixteenth-century style" and

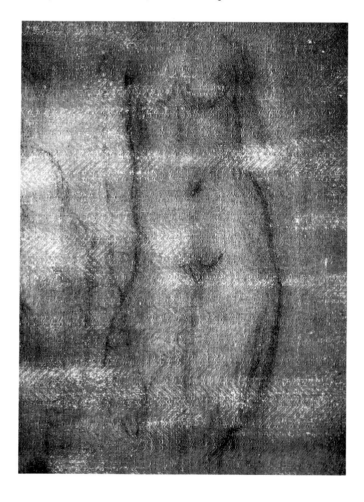

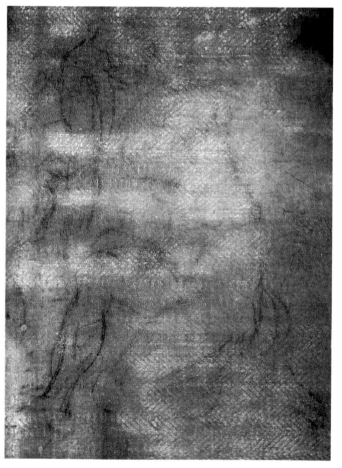

Titian (?), Study in charcoal of a standing female figure, on the back of the canvas (detail)

Titian (?), Study in charcoal of male nudes fighting, on the back of the canvas (detail)

consequently by Titian. Pallucchini limited himself to noting their existence, while Wethey (1960) agreed with Titian's authorship. As far as can be judged from the reproductions, they seem to be traced with the vigorous and secure handling of Titian's charcoal drawings, but in subject or style they are useless for dating the painting.

The work was engraved in the seventeenth century by Valentin Le Febre; an etching exists at the Accademia Carrara, Bergamo (no. 74), another at the Gabinetto Nazionale delle Stampe, Rome (F.N. 6131) and various examples at the Museo Correr, Venice (Gherro 1944, PD 785; St. A8/16, Correr 3608, Molin 2582), and in the nineteenth century Zanotto published it in *Pinacoteca Veneta*.

LITERATURE   Vasari 1568 (ed. Milanesi), VII, 448-49; Boschini 1660, 9th ed., 1965, 98; Boschini 1664, 310-11; Zanetti 1771, ed. 1972; Fossati VI, 30, 1814, 30; Moschini 1815, II, 216-17; Cicogna 1834, IV, 141; Zanotto 1858, I, 87; Crowe and Cavalcaselle 1877, I, 304-5; Gronau 1904, 119-20; Fischel 1906, no. 107; Scrinzi 1920, 257; Suida 1935, 63; Suida 1943, 358; Tietze 1936, I, 151, II, 314; Pallucchini and Brunetti 1937, 8-9; Tietze 398; Berenson 1957, 191; Valcanover 1960, I, 71; Pallucchini 1969, I, 85, 276; Wethey 1969, I, 70; Huse 1989, 354.

A.P.T.

25

Portrait of Isabella d'Este

oil on canvas, 102×64 cm (cut at top and sides)
Vienna, Kunsthistorisches Museum (inv. no. 83)

EXHIBITION Moscow-Leningrad 1980

On the basis of careful research by Luzio (1913) on the numerous portraits of Isabella d'Este by various artists, it has been possible to identify this as the portrait of the young Marchioness painted by Titian in 1534-36. From the correspondence it clearly emerges that Titian, after painting Isabella's portrait aged 56-58, went on to execute a second portrait, showing her in her youth. Rubens copied both works, but only that of the mature Isabella has survived (*Peter Paul Rubens, 1577-1640*, Vienna 1977, no. 5). There exists, however, an engraving by Vorstermann of the Rubens copy of the Vienna painting of the young Isabella. In the engraving, the princess' name clearly appears ("Isabella Estensis Francisci Gonzaga Uxor, a Titiani prototypo P.P. Rubens excudit"). It was this that made it possible to identify the sitter in question (Luzio 1913). From Luzio's documents we deduce that Titian, in order to capture the youthful likeness of Isabella, who was by then sixty years old, may have used another portrait, by Francesco Francia, as a model. This had been given by Isabella to the Ferrarese nobleman Zaninello whose heirs were asked to lend it to Titian for a month. Titian then kept it in his workshop for two years. However, not even the Francia portrait was painted from life. Isabella had already posed for Lorenzo Costa, her court painter, and did not wish to offend him by making herself available to Francia, his rival. Francia was obliged therefore to base himself on yet another portrait and to rely on a description given by Lucrezia Borgia-Bentivoglio. It seems evident that the Titian painting offers us a typical representation of a woman of the highest social level in the flower of her youth, rather than a realistic image of the young Isabella. Indeed, on seeing the work she noted: "The portrait by Titian's hand is of so pleasing a type that we doubt that at the age that he represents we were ever of the beauty it contains."

The noblewoman wears a costume with blue sleeves and white and gold decorations. On her shoulders is a fur stole. Her bodice is black and for this reason the painting is called *Isabella in Black*, to distinguish it from the other portrait (*Isabella in Red*).

Isabella d'Este was born in 1474, the daughter of Ercole I d'Este, Duke of Ferrara and Modena, and of Eleonora d'Aragona, daughter of Ferdinand, King of Naples. She was the wife of Francesco II Gonzaga, Marquis of Mantua, whom she married in 1490. One of the most famous princesses of her time, and among the most important patrons of the Italian Renaissance, Isabella promoted the sciences and made her court a meeting place for some of the most significant personalities of Renaissance culture. She was closely tied to Pietro Bembo and Baldassare Castiglione; artists such as Mantegna, Costa and Bellini worked for her. Nor was she famous only for her promotion of science and art and for her skillful diplomacy; she was admired for her connoisseurship and for her social graces. She had exceptional taste and bodily wore costumes of her own design, hence dictating fashion. She was especially famous for her turbans, similar to the one she wears in this painting, and for her extravagant gold and silver decorations, which are also visible here on the sleeves. These ornaments date back to the Quattrocento and can be seen in works by Pinturicchio and the young Raphael, where they adorn curtains and draperies. Isabella even led the way in cosmetics, creating her own perfumes and creams. Other noblewomen of Italian courts begged to be allowed to use her models, and the Queen of France even requested to be sent a mannequin dressed, from the petticoats to the turban, in the same clothing worn by the Marchesa from Este (Lauts 1952, 326).

Critics have always mentioned this portrait of Isabella (Valcanover, Pallucchini and others) in the company of *La Bella*, originally from Urbino and now at the Pitti Palace. Dated 1536, the latter has erroneously been identified as Isabella's daughter, Eleonora Gonzaga. Comparison between the two paintings hints at the setting of the Vienna *Isabella* before it was cut down. Furthermore, it seems clear that Titian had recourse to *La Bella* for the pose, expression and even costume. As with other paintings that were not from life but based on portraits by other artists – for example those of Charles V by Seisenegger, François I, King of France, Julius II or Sixtus IV – Titian succeeded in strengthening and intensifying the personal characteristics as well as the evidence and air of social status. Here both the young princess' composure and her eccentric way of presenting herself underline her originality and personality. At a time when her age provoked Aretino to mock her, calling her "disonestamente brutta" (dishonestly ugly), and "arcidisonestamente imbellettata" (very dishonestly made up), with "ebony teeth" and "ivory lashes," Titian proposed instead to render homage to the extraordinary personality of the young noblewoman intelligent and cultured and also beautiful, an arbiter of fashion, elegant and sure of herself.

LITERATURE Engerth 1884, 355-7; Luzio 1913, 219-23; Klauner and Oberhammer 1960, 137, 712; Valcanover 1960, pl. 139; Valcanover 1969, no. 174; Pallucchini 1969, 270; Wethey 1971, 95, no. 27 (with preceding bibliography).

S.F.

26.

Portrait of Eleonora Gonzaga della Rovere

oil on canvas, 114×103 cm
Florence, Galleria degli Uffizi (inv. 1890 no. 919)

RESTORATION 1990, E. Masini

The reader is referred to the precise and carefully documented entry by Fausta Paola Squellati in the exhibition catalogue *Tiziano nelle Gallerie Fiorentine*. For this occasion it is possible to add further to our understanding of the iconography, to the history of the commission and to the dating of the portrait in relation to that of the sitter's husband Francesco Maria della Rovere (see cat. no. 28).
The colors of the duchess' dress and headgear, and of that which can be seen under the duke's shining black breastplate, give us a first point of interest. Eleonora wears a dress made of heavy cloth with black and gray lines, enlivened by ornaments in the form of golden bows, while Francesco Maria wears a black outfit under his armor, with slashed sleeves through which gold cloth is pulled. Such similarity in the colors of the clothes of the two sovereigns of Urbino, in a period in which the utmost importance was given to appearance and court ceremony, leads us ask whether this was a specific heraldic reference to the colors of the house of Montefeltro. Supporting evidence comes in a letter from the duchess to Leonardi on 9 January 1539, requesting her "shoulder cover [*spalere*] of yellow satin and black velvet," together with a *Christ* painted by Titian (Gronau 1936).
The supposition is reinforced by earlier portraits of Guidobaldo da Montefeltro and his wife Elisabetta Gonzaga, attributed to Raphael and now also in the Uffizi. Francesco Maria's predecessor is dressed in a black coat and hat both with a small squared pattern of gold thread, while the duchess wears a black dress with rectangles woven in silver and gold thread (Sesti and Baldi 1983, Zecchini 1984).
Both costumes surely derive from the colors of the Montefeltro crest, with the majestic black eagle with a silver crown on a field of gold. It is plausible therefore that Francesco Maria, with his wife Eleonora, would justly dress in the colors of the illustrious family whose greatest representative in the fifteenth century was Federico. Della Rovere was in fact adopted in 1504 by his uncle Guidobaldo, who was without male descendants, and succeeded to the dukedom upon Guidobaldo's death four years later.
In the portrait of Eleonora, for the first time in Titian's portraiture a towerlike clock appears, richly polished and embellished by a statuette placed on the table covered in green velvet, which will later be seen in a series of male portraits, beginning with the *Cristoforo Madruzzo*, probably of 1532 (see cat. no. 47) and ending with the *Portrait of a Gentleman with a Book* in Copenhagen of 1562 (Wethey 1969-75).

For Panofsky (1969), the clock in Eleonora Gonzaga's portrait was an allusion to temperance, either for the regularity of its tick or for the more widespread significance of the *memento mori*. It is worth recalling however that the duke and duchess of Urbino must have been passionate collectors and connoisseurs of these much sought-after and expensive precision instruments. Titian, on at least once occasion, acted as an intermediary between Francesco Maria dell Rovere and the master clockmaker, probably of Augsburg as indicated by the type of the clock in the portrait (see the letters from the duke to Leonardi of 8 October 1532 and late December 1533, in Gronau 1936). As for the circumstances in which the portrait was commissioned and painted, the documents allow us to frame the period in which Titian was working on it.
The *terminus post quem* is known to have been 28 January 1536, when Eleonora wrote to Leonardi, the ducal ambassador in Venice, expressing her desire to be portrayed by Titian if he should find the time to pass through Pesaro, seat of the Urbino court, on his way to Naples to pay homage to Charles v. The artist seems never to have made this trip.
The *terminus ante quem* is supplied by a letter from Aretino to Veronica Gambara of 7 November 1537 (Pertile and Camesasca 1957-60), containing a detailed and laudatory description of the portrait of Francesco Maria, and two sonnets connected to the completed portraits that Aretino had admired in his friend Titian's studio. The tone of the sonnet dedicated to Eleonora's portrait is indicative of his admiration, in which praise for the supreme ability of the artist is united with courtly panegyric: "The union of colors which the style/Of Titian has painted, brings out/The harmony which rules in Leonora/The ministers of her gentle spirit./In her resides modesty in a humble act./Honesty resides in her clothes/Shame in her breast/And her locks veil her and honor her,/Love afflicts her with a noble gaze./Modesty and beauty, eternal enemies/Range in her countenance, and among her lashes/The throne of the graces can be discerned./Prudence looks upon her worth and suggests/In beautiful silence, her other internal virtues/Decorate her forehead with every marvel" (Gregori 1976).
Although the lapse of time between the winter of 1536 and the late autumn of the following year is not great, accustomed as we are to more approximate dates based on style, we can justifiably arrive at greater precision by re-examining the documents relative also to the duke's portrait, the pendant of the duchess' portrait. It will also be useful to note the results of studies made of the male portrait in readiness for conservation prior to this exhibition, more amply discussed in the relevant entry by Antonio Natali.
The first of the two that we hear of, indirectly, is that of Francesco Maria della Rovere, which Titian was planning between the spring and summer of 1536. He needed the

220

duke's armor for this, which was in his possession by 17 July 1536, as we know from the famous letter of the duke to Leonardi in which he urges its retun.

The genesis of the portrait, however, must have been laborious, as the Uffizi drawing indicates (see cat. no. 27). In the latter the armed duke is portrayed full-length within a niche. This solution was later abandoned but its influence endured in the markedly three-dimensional placement of the figure, with his right arm holding his commander's baton pointed on his side, seeming almost to jump from the painting.

In that summer of 1536 Titian was, as usual, working hard to satisfy the demands of the courts of Ferrara, Mantua and the duke and duchess of Urbino for whom he was also painting the portrait of "that woman who wears the blue clothes," most likely the so-called Pitti *Bella* (Valcanover 1969). The question arises whether the artist first painted the portrait of the duke, as the documents seem to indicate, or that of the duchess. The answer possibly rests in the seams around the canvas of the duke's portrait. These had always been faintly visible, but are obvious after the cleaning. The paint is demonstrably autograph and this indicates, as Natali has observed, an enlargement of a smaller canvas already used for another portrait. The *Eleonora Gonzaga* therefore preceded its pendant. Quite possibly Titian kept the duke's armor in his studio long after the July 1536 letter, putting off the beginning of the portrait. At this point the Duchess Eleonora came to Venice, in September 1536, and stayed until early the following year (Valcanover 1969). The artist would thus have given precedence to her portrait, since her presence in the city would have allowed him, in the course ob several sittings, to capture with miniaturistic finesse the details of the hairstyle, the rich clothes and profuse jewelry documenting the wealth and status of the subject. It was certainly more convenient to satisfy the desires of the duchess who was in Venice, rather than the commission of a man of arms who was always busy inspecting his fortesses and troops in defense of the Venetian state when not actually at war, as the biographies and historical texts recount (Leoni 1605, Dennistoun 1909). The duke would have had little time to pose for his own portrait.

The likeness of the armed Francesco Maria probably required the presence of the duke only for the head, so as to capture his "terrible" and vibrant expression. The armor, with the insignia of command, would have been painted at the artist's convenience, worn by a model or a mannequin. This also explains the differences of conception and scale in the two portraits, correctly noticed by Natali. Although they are of the same dimensions, they were conceived at different times and executed successively.

A dating of the portrait of Eleonora Gonzaga in the autumn/winter of 1536-37 becomes even more convincing if we consider the nature of the duchess' clothes, of heavy cloth, with in her right hand a marten's fur muff with a golden head encrusted with pearls and rubies, an accessory reserved for women of high lineage.

The two paintings, finished in November 1537, would have been admired by their patrons in the artists' studio in January of 1538. They would surely have been delighted with the results after the long wait. Eleonora and Francesco Maria were in Venice for the duke's nomination to commander-in-chief of the league of the Emperor, the Pope and Venice to counter the Turkish threat, an honor that signalled on 31 January 1538 the universal recognition of Della Rovere's extraordinary skills (Leoni 1605).

The two portraits were then sent to the *Guardaroba ducale* in Pesaro, where they would have arrived the following 14 April, as we know from the letter of Giovan Maria della Porta to the duchess, who was still in Venice at that time (Gronau 1936).

LITERATURE   Leoni 1605, 435-7; Dennistoun 1909, 68-70; Gronau 1936, 5, 86, 90-4, 139; Pertile-Camesasca 1957-60, I, 1957, 77-8; Panofsky 1969, 88-90, fig. 104; Valcanover 1969, 85, 108-9; Wethey 1969-75, II, 134, II, 249-50; Squellati 1978, no. 29, 121-4 (with preceding bibliography); Gruppo Redazionale 2 1979, no. P 1724; Sesti, Baldi 1983, 248-51; Zecchini 1984, nos. 2-3, 58-70.

A.C.

27

Study for Francesco Maria della Rovere

pen and dark brown ink; traces of sanguine along lower margin, lower left and upper right; squared with pen; on yellowed white paper; laid 237 x 141 mm (maximum dimensions of sheet, arched at the top)
Florence, Gabinetto Disegni e Stampe degli Uffizi (no. 29767 F)

The sheet, has two small inserts made prior to the drawing: one at the top, in correspondence with the peak of the arch, and one at the lower left. In the lower right corner is the mark of the Morelli Collection. On the *verso* of the backing is written in red chalk in an old hand: "2." On the present mat there is a detached slip of paper also bearing the Morelli's mark, and a nineteenth – century transcription of an earlier inscription that must have been on the old support: " – 1693 – Ritratto di Franc.co M.ª p.º della Rovere Duca quarto d'Urbino di man di Titiano Ecc.mo Pittore, quale fu donato a me Giuseppe Coradini dal Sig. Mariano Urbinelli con haverli io fatto fare le cornigie et altro, come qua si vede, Tutto costa grossi tredici in circa, da tenersene gran conto, che cosi desidero. Pregate dio per me." (" – 1693 – Portrait of Francesco Maria p.o della Rovere, fourth Duke of Urbino by the hand of Titian Most Excellent Painter, which was given to me, Giuseppe Coradini by Mr. Mariano Urbinelli with my having the frame made and other, as can be seen here, all at a cost of about 13 *grossi*, to be remembered greatly, that I desire it to be this way. Pray to God for me.")

This drawing was correctly described in the second half of the seventeenth century as the "Portrait of Francesco Maria della Rovere... by Titian's hand" (see inscription above). It belonged in the last century to Giovanni Morelli, who noted its provenance as Urbino (Principe Staccoli Castracani of Urbino), and passed by inheritance to Gustavo Frizzoni. In 1908 it was sold to the Uffizi by the Ginoulhiac family, relatives of Frizzoni (Petrioli Tofani 1983).

The critical history of the sheet begins with a commentary by Frizzoni accompanying its first publication in facsimile (1886). He presented the drawing as "one of the most precious items" of his friend Morelli's collection, and described it as the "first idea" for the portrait of Francesco Maria della Rovere in the Uffizi: "in which one immediately perceives that it is a study from life, done with that energy and security of touch which distinguishes the great Cadorian." Loeser (1922) also described the drawing as a "study in full-length for the portrait," noting that "the pose of the body and the details of the armour are identical in the drawing and the painting." Von Hadeln (1924) sought an explanation for the major difference between the drawing, which is full-length, and the Uffizi portrait, in which the duke is represented in three-quarter length. He proposed that the portrait had originally been conceived full-length and within a niche, as in the drawing, and that the painting was cut at a later date to make it a pendant to the portrait of the duchess (see cat. no. 26). This theory was generally accepted by critics until Rearick (1976) stated decisively that the canvas had never been cut, claiming this on the basis of a technical analysis of the bottom edge. A second theory by Von Hadeln, whereby the drawing was derived from the painting for the purpose of making a woodcut, has never been accepted. Even less convincing is Panofsky's proposal that the Uffizi sheet is a project for a commemorative statue in 1538, the year of the duke's death. All in all the drawing's relation to the painting, as a preparatory study or at least a preliminary idea, is now unanimously accepted. Indeed, as Wethey (1987) has pointed out, it is the "only extant preparatory study for a portrait by Titian"; it is conspicuous also for the squaring, which is original. But the study is only partial and the facial resemblance to the painting is only approximate. The armor instead is the focus of Titian's attention, probably worn by a model, as Rearick explains (1976): "in order to judge the pose, the point of view of the armor and in particular to register the natural position which the armor would have imposed on the subject's anatomy." But also the placement of the figure, determined in the drawing by the two lateral lines of the "niche," corresponds to that which the duke assumes in respect to the red velvet background of the painting. And so the sheet can be said to be one of the rare drawings by Titian classifiable as "preparatory." It is also the closest to the final product, if one takes into account the artist's habit of liberally re-elaborating the composition of even those drawings in which the presence of squaring identifies them as virtual *modelli* (Chiari Moretto Wiel 1989).

The function of this drawing in the genesis of the Uffizi portrait is clarified by the 17 July 1536 letter from Francesco Maria to his agent in Venice, Gian Giacomo Leonardi. The duke urged the return of his "armor," which was "extremely dear" to him. He had lent it to Titian and according to him Titian should already have finished sketching "for his needs" (Gronau 1936). This confirms that Titian must have had the duke's armor at his disposal for some time. It also constitutes a precise point of reference for the dating of the drawing. In the letter, immediately after he requested his armor back, Francesco Maria mentioned his desire to receive a "paper by Titian." Rearick rightly deduced that the duke was speaking of a drawing that would give him some idea of the portrait Titian was working on and that it may well have been this very sheet. Such may also be the explanation for Titian's use of the pen, which, in contrast to the painterly implications of graphite, charcoal or chalk, which Titian seems to have favored in the 1540s, made possible a rather precise description of the details of the armor was more suitable for a presentation drawing.

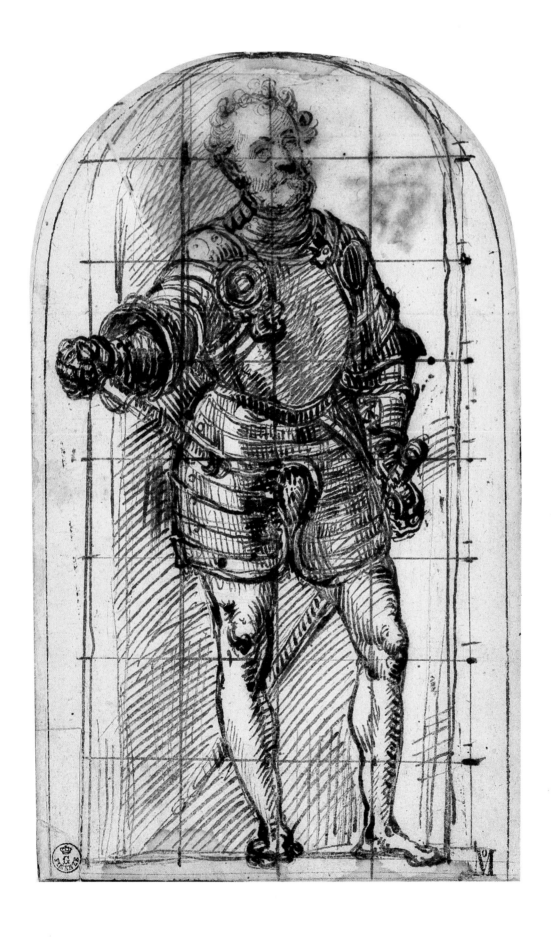

That the use of the pen may have caused Titian to resort to the graphic style and expressive effects of early studies for paintings such as the *Saint Sebastian* (Frankfurt) for the Averoldi Polyptych may seem surprising but testifies to "a substantial coherence" of Titian's vocabulary (Pignatti). Thus Rearick (1976) pointed to the close relationship between this sheet and the Frankfurt study "for the similarly intense and energetic use of the pen," observing that "the muscular definition of the legs, with their strong modelling and emphatic contours, is common to both drawings, as is also the irregular suggestion of the background through abstract parallel lines." Oberhuber (1976) referring to the quest for tonal values that Titian began in the 1520s, observed that "notwithstanding the rather thick pen lines, there is here a full range of tonal gradations, from the deepest shadow to the luminous touches produced by the white paper."

LITERATURE   Frizzoni 1886, pl. xxvii; *Catalogo dei ritratti...* 1911, 41; Loeser 1912-21, series i, fasc. ii, no. 5; Von Hadeln 1924, 30, 49-50; Von Hadeln 1927, pl. 11; Fröhlich-Bum 1928, no. 33; *Exhibition...*, 1930, 313-14, no. 675; Popham 1931, 73, no. 264; Fogolari 1935, no. 9; Tietze and Tietze-Conrat 1936, 175, 191, no. 25; Tietze and Tietze-Conrat 1944, no. 1911; Tietze and Tietze-Conrat 1950, 404; Dell'Acqua 1955, 120; Richter, Morelli 1960, 222; Valcanover 1960, i, 69; Forlani 1961, 42, 61; Valcanover 1969, 110; Pallucchini 1969, i, 332; Panofsky 1969, 88; Wethey 1969-75, ii, 135, no. 89; Rearick 1976, no. 21; Oberhuber 1976, 32; Bernini-Pezzini 1976, 39; Meijer 1976, 11; Rearick 1977, 12, 28, no. 11; Gould 1977, 47; Rosand 1978, fig. 71; Squellati 1979, 118-19; Pignatti 1979, 10, no. 34; Oberhuber 1980, 525, Sunderland-Wethey and Wethey 1980, 76-89; Scrase 1983, 291, no. D71; Dreyer 1980, 510; Petrioli Tofani 1983, 437; Wethey 1987, 15-16, 139-40, no. 13; Bora 1988, 88, 258, no. 18; Chiari Moretti Wiel 1989, 18-19, no. 23.

G.D.

28

Portrait of Francesco Maria della Rovere

oil on canvas, 114×103 cm
Florence, Galleria degli Uffizi (inv. 1890 no. 926)

RESTORATION   1990, E. Masini

Signed: "TITIANUS F"; lower right corner, under the painted surface is written "TICIANUS"

An exhaustive entry for the *Portrait of Francesco Maria della Rovere*, by Fausta Paola Squellati, has been published in the excellent catalogue, *Tiziano nelle Gallerie Fiorentine* (1978, ed. M. Gregori). This entry is fundamental for its exhaustive research of archival documents and inventories, the secondary sources and guides of the Florentine museums, as well as its listing of engravings from the paintings and its updated bibliography. The information so meticulously compiled on that occasion will be summarized here, and an account given of some preliminary results that have emerged from conservation carried out for this exhibition, added to a review of scholarship on the painting since the Florence exhibition.

As we shall see, Titian was probably already planning the painting in 1536, and by April 1538 it had reached Pesaro with its pendant, the portrait of Francesco Maria della Rovere's wife, Eleonora Gonzaga (see cat. no. 26). Giovanni Maria Della Porta, writing to the duchess from Pesaro on 14 April 1538, praised above all the lifelike quality of the portraits, with particular flattery – although admittedly in rather conventional language and not without courtly affectation – reserved for the duchess' likeness (Gronau 1936). The paintings came to Florence with the Della Rovere inheritance (1631) and were sent to the Guardaroba di Vittoria. Squellati's entry (1978) reconstructs their frequent changes of location (within the Medici collections). It is sufficient here to draw attention to one decisive moment for the *Portrait of Francesco Maria della Rovere*: its transfer to the Uffizi on 4 February 1795, where it joined the Venetian school in the picture gallery.

The painting was first mentioned in a letter written by Francesco Maria on 17 July 1536 to Gian Giacomo Leonardi, his agent in Venice, in which he requested the return of his armor, which had been sent to Titian for the purposes of the portrait. The duke at that date assumed that the painter had no more use for it and was anxious that all possible precautions be taken to ensure that the breastplate was returned safely; in the event that the artist still needed the armor, Titian was to be urged to hurry up; in any case, the person charged with the transportation was ordered not to leave without the armor but rather to wait and expedite matters (Gronau 1936). In the same letter, Francesco Maria also asked if "that paper by Titian" could be sent to him as soon as possible. This phrase, which comes directly following the pressure to have the armor back, has plausibly been associated (Rearick 1976) with the

sheet by Titian preserved in the Uffizi (see cat. no. 27) where, in the outline of niche, a model is posed in the identical position to that of the duke in the Uffizi painting. The figure wears a breastplate that is patently Francesco Maria's. According to this theory, which identifies the "paper" mentioned in the letter as the Uffizi sheet, the drawing would have served to convey to the sitter the composition Titian had devised.

Aside from conjecture, the fact remains that this drawing exists (squared, and thus intended for transfer to canvas), and is unquestionably related to the Della Rovere portrait. It is not obviously a preparatory drawing, since the man in armor is full-length, and stands in a niche, like an antique statue, rather than in a room – as is the case with the painting. The background is horizontally divided by a red velvet cloth covering a surface, with a helmet ("borgognotta") and two batons and a branch leaning against the wall, an intended to vaunt his insignia and personal power.

If, then, between the drawing and the painting there exist differences to the point of excluding a direct relationship, the problem remains of deciding – since there are no extant standing portraits of the duke of Urbino by Titian – whether the idea sketched on the sheet was a preliminary idea later rejected (as many critics now hold), or whether it was for a now-lost painting, from which the Uffizi painting was then derived (Bernini Pezzini 1976). Other hypotheses have been advanced: that the drawing was for a monumental posthumous portrait in a niche (Panofsky 1969), or that it was executed after the painting for an engraving (Von Hadeln 1924). Neither of these is convincing.

Direct examination of the painting has discredited the theory that the portrait has been cut down (Von Hadeln 1924; Wethey 1969-75, rectified in Sunderland and Wethey and Wethey 1980), since the paint does not reach the extreme lower edge of the canvas, leaving a margin of white. Before recent conservation the reduction of the painting had seemed a possibility, in view of the more precarious condition (particularly evident in a raking light) of the upper, left and lower sides, to the point where mutilation seemed to be the cause, especially as some stuccoing of old nail holes within the three bands was evident under the paint surface. However, trial cleaning along the borders and in other areas of autograph paint pointed to the homogeneity and continuity of the canvas, thus ruling out the hypothesis of later mutilation and reworking. X-radiography (carried out about ten years ago, see Seracini 1979), revealed a slightly smaller figure of a young man under the image of the duke. Titian had in fact used a previously painted canvas (Sunderland and Wethey and Wethey 1980). When therefore the artist decided to enlarge the format for the portrait of Francesco Maria, he adapted the canvas to a new stretcher, stuccoing the holes that had served to fasten it to the old, smaller stretcher. During the recent operation of re-stretching, it was discovered that the three damaged border areas correspond to three strips of canvas glued onto the large one.) If therefore there is no longer any question that the painting was originally conceived as a full-length figure (such as the preceding *Portrait of Charles v*), there remains the problem of the relationship – which clearly exists – between the squared Uffizi drawing and the canvas. Perhaps, after all, the sheet is simply an early proposal – for submission, if not to close scrutiny, at least to the attention of the sitter – later revised to three-quarter length, retaining, with only slight variations, the pose adopted in the drawing (the pose of the Emperor Claudius in Titian's lost series of *Caesars* for the Palazzo Ducale, Mantua, which we know from Sadeler's engravings). It is not easy to understand the point of this change. It is a fact that the dimensions of the painting are identical to those of the portrait of his wife, to which it is pendant. Yet, the duke and duchess, in their composition and poses, do not seem to have been conceived as pendants. His is a consciously heroic and celebratory pose (complete and autonomous in itself), while the image of the duchess, however elegantly clothed, is more domestic and somewhat smaller in scale.

It is worth noting that the portrait revealed by x-rays under the duke might also be that of a young woman. The images of the plates have been elaborated by Maurizio Seracini with a computer program so as to define more precisely the contours of the overpainted head. The oval-shaped face that emerged is delicate and minute, apparently more consistent with feminine features – which tempt one, without going too far, to compare them to those of *La Bella*, in the Pitti. She, like the hidden face, has arched eyebrows like two spread wings, directly on the septum of a not-so-slender nose. It would, however, be arbitrary to speculate further.

Something about the conception of the duke's portrait remains to be said. His armor is minutely described in Squellati's entry (1978) on the basis of information supplied by Lionello Boccia. Since that time some fresh observations have been made. For example it has been pointed out that the breastplate, of the German type, "recalls those of the workshop of Lorenz and Kolman Helmschmid of Augsburg," of which Francesco Maria was a client (Scalini 1987). It can be compared with a bust attributed to Kolman Helmschmid in the Metropolitan Museum, New York (inv. 38, 143), which also shows sacred figures engraved on the breast, though these are barely visible in the Uffizi portrait. Titian's breastplate differs only in the spiral rather than plain mouldings (Scalini 1989). The helmet, which has no relation to Titian's drawing of a helmet in the Uffizi (see cat. no. 37), has been compared "with a drawing of the lost Thunschen Skizzenbuch, generally referred to as the Helmschmid" (Scalini 1989; but also 1987). Finally, Scalini has suggested that the crouching dragon can be

identified with one in beaten copper in the Carrand Collection at the Bargello, Florence (inv. no. 1639c).

In a letter to Veronica Gambara in late 1537 (Pertile and Camesasca 1957-60), Pietro Aretino praised the pictorial treatment of the armor (in addition to other qualities in the painting). He praised the polish of the metal with its vermilion reflections, emphasizing Titian's mimetic skills and his capacity to express the personality of the duke. Aretino accurately named the various attributes by which Francesco Maria wished to be remembered, mistaking only that the general's batons were of silver ("ariento"). But he correctly identified these as the "staffs" (*verghe*) of "generalship" entrusted to him by Venice (the one the duke holds in his hand), by the Church (the first from the left of the three above), and by Florence (nearest the edge of the canvas). When Aretino spoke of the "staff of fortune" he presumably referred to the oak branch with the motto SE SIBI (Sunderland and Wethey and Wethey 1980). Though he mentioned the helmet, he omitted the crouching dragon, which was not a mere ornament, but a specific allusion to his ties to the house of Aragon (Sunderland and Wethey and Wethey 1980). Aretino's letter perceived the portrait for what it was: a compendium of Francesco Maria's career as a great *condottiere* (Sunderland and Wethey and Wethey 1980), a career to which no further laurels would accrue since the duke died only a few months after the arrival of his portrait in Pesaro.

LITERATURE Von Hadeln 1924, 30, 49-50; Gronau 1936, 92-4; Pertile and Camesasca 1957-60, I, 1957, 77-8; Panofsky 1969, 88-9; Wethey 1969-75, 169-75, II, 1971, 23, 135-6; Bernini and Pezzini 1976, 38-9, 61; Rearick 1976, 46-9; Squellati 1978, 116-21 (with preceding bibliography); Gruppo Redazionale 2 1979, 548; Pignatti 1979, XXXIV; Seracini 1979, 25-6; Sunderland and Wethey and Wethey 1980, 76-89; Hope 1981, 190; Scrase 1983, 291-2; Scalini 1987, 14-18, 38; Wethey 1987, 139-40; Chiari Moretto Wiel 1988, 49-50; Chiari Moretto Wiel 1989, 90; Scalini 1989, 218-19.

A.N.

Studies of Knights

a. *Knight and His Enemy Falling from a Horse*

white and black chalk, partly rubbed, squared in black chalk, on faded blue paper; blackish stains, and some foxing
350×251 mm
Munich, Staatliche Graphische Sammlung (inv. no. 2981)

The drawing has been trimmed on all sides and the lower left corner has been pieced. In the lower left there are traces of an annotation "...toretto," and in the lower center there is an old inventory number "410," both in brown ink. The drawing comes from the collection of the Elector Palatine Karl Theodor.

Erroneously attributed to Tintoretto, this was framed and included in the selection of 556 loose drawings exhibited publicly from 1758 in the engravings gallery at the castle of Mannheim by the Elector Palatine Karl Theodor. In 1794, fearing the possible consequences of the French revolution, he transferred the collection to Munich, where he was by then residing. It was not until 1924 that the keeper, Engelbert Baumeister, recognized Titian's authorship the composition had always exercised particular fascination in view of its dramatic force. Baumeister, and after him other art historians, connected the drawing to the *Knight Falling from His Horse* in the Ashmolean Museum, Oxford (see cat. no. 29b), which Josiah Gilbert (1867) had identified as a study by Titian for the so-called *Battle of Cadore* (Palazzo Ducale, Venice, destroyed by fire in 1577). The latter is known from Giulio Fontana's engraving dated 1569, from a copy in the Uffizi of the 1570s, from an anonymous copper engraving now at the Albertina, Vienna, and finally from a drawing attributed to Peter Paul Rubens in the Museum Plantin-Moretus, Antwerp. In 1948, Erika Tietze-Conrat found in the Cabinet des Dessins of the Louvre an autograph sketch of the entire composition. Vasari in 1568 initiated the confusion over which battle was represented. Until recently it was by most considered, to be the *Battle of Cadore* (1508). Wethey (1975, 1987), however, shed new light on the question. Titian had contracted to execute a painting originally commissioned from Pietro Perugino (1494). The subject was to have formed part of a cycle of (legendary) meetings between Pope Alexander III (1159-81) and the Emperor Frederick Barbarossa (1152-90). According to Wethey, therefore, the subject was the *Battle of Spoleto* (1155), commissioned from Titian in 1513 but executed only in the summer months of 1537 and 1538.
The horseman with a fallen enemy in the Munich drawing does not correspond to any detail in the compositional sketch in the Louvre, nor in any of the copies cited above. Consequently

Hans Tietze and Erika Tietze-Conrat put forward a second theory, that this is a sketch by Titian for a painting by his son Orazio representing *The Battle between Barbarossa and the Romans at the Castel Sant'Angelo*, executed between 1562 and 1564. This was part of the same cycle and was likewise destroyed by fire in 1577. There remains only Vasari's description: "A battle fought in Rome between the Germans of the said Frederick and the Romans near the Castel Sant'Angelo and the Tiber; and in this, among other things, there is a foreshortened horse jumping over an armed soldier, which is very fine; some say that Orazio was helped in this work by his father" (Vasari [Milanesi] VI, 589). If it were true that the Munich drawing is preparatory to Orazio's painting, this would imply a twenty-five year difference with respect to the Oxford drawing. Stylistic considerations force us therefore to exclude this theory.
Pignatti (1973, 1977) suggested that the compositional character of the Munich knight also occurred in the large Titian woodcut of the *Drowning of Pharoah in the Red Sea* (see cat. no. 10). This was probably executed in 1514-15, soon after the commissioning of the *Battle of Spoleto*. However, the figures on horseback in the print do not relate directly to the drawings in question, and Pignatti (1979) has not insisted on this connection.
The two horsemen in the Oxford and Munich sheets differ from those in the Louvre sketch. Nevertheless the Oxford horseman is repeated almost literally in the copies of the *Battle of Spoleto*. Although both drawings are squared, this does not signify that they were necessarily both executed in connection with the mural. The Munich horseman finds its perfect counterpart in horseman at the far left end of the bridge, who rides toward the observer. In the drawing, the horse turns it head to the right, and the rider, depicted bending downward, holds a shield with his left arm while in his fist he holds a short curved sword atop the mane of the animal; the plume and short cloak wave in the wind, while on the ground lies a fallen soldier with his legs bent. Evidently, in the final painting these details were modified or omitted. There can be no doubt regarding the identity of the Munich drawing with the Battle, above all because in both the drawing and the copies the horse and rider are represented from the same viewpoint. The perspective from below and the foreshortening, the vibrant contours and the sharp alternation of light and semi-shadow give the impression that the painter was surely trying to evoke, of the onslaught of a galloping horseman, merciless and sure of victory.

LITERATURE   Von Beckerath 1909, 219-20; Baumeister 1924, 20-5; Hetzer 1926, 158-72, 167; Von Hadeln 1927, pl. 28; Fröhlich-Bum 1928, 164-8, no. 30; Popham 1931, 268, no. 867, pl. CCXXV; Tietze-Conrat 1935-6, 54-7, pl. 54; Tietze

1936, I, 233, pl. 268; Tietze and Tietze-Conrat 1936, 137-97; Dussler 1938, XXI, no. 33, pl. 33; Tietze and Tietze-Conrat 1944, 321, no. 1941, pl. LXVII; Dussler 1948, XXI, no. 33, pl. 33; Tietze 1950, 408; Parker 1956, 384-6, no. 718; Degenhart 1958, 46, pl. I; Ames 1962, no. 212; Schmitt 1927, 79-80, no. 78; Pallucchini 1969, I, 173-4 and 333, II, pl. 573; Pignatti 1970, 82, pl. X, 82; Pignatti 1973, no. 20; Wethey 1975, III, 225-32, no. 3, fig. 61; Oberhuber 1976, 33, 93-5, no. 39, fig. 17; Rearick 1976, 29, 30, no. 12; Pignatti 1977, no. 36; Harprath 1977, 136, 137, no. 93, pl. 68; Pignatti 1979, 10, pl. XXXVII; Chiari 1982, 37-9; Scrase 1983, no. D72, 292-94; Harprath 1983, 41, no. 36; Wethey 1987, 67, 68, 133-4, no. 5b, pl. 132.

R.H.

b. *Knight Falling from His Horse*

Black chalk, on coarse blue paper (now faded to greenish-gray), with faded white chalk heightening, squared for enlargement in red chalk, 274×262 mm
Oxford, Ashmolean Museum

Splashings and rubbings of paint appear on the sheet, especially on the left side, and there are old water-stains particularly around the right and lower edges. An old, partly mutilated inscription in a reddish-brown ink at the lower center reads: *T.an* or possibly *T.mn*. Another, in the lower right corner, *Titiano*, is possibly in the hand of Van Dyck, and besides it is the beginning, *T..*, of a third.

This superb drawing captures a highly-charged moment of energetic movement and imminent collapse; the twisting horse plunges to the ground, its terror vividly conveyed, while the rider strains backward, his tensed calf-muscles clutching the horse's sides, in order to ward off with a lance an attack from above and behind. The black chalk is used in a free, confident manner: it is applied with different pressure on the coarse paper so as to achieve a broad tonal range, within which the sense of muscles moving beneath the flesh in the bodies of both the horse and rider can be conveyed. A little white highlighting was rubbed in parts to sharpen the effect of flexing movement and tension, while some of the details (particularly the horse's hindquarters and neck, and the rider's forehead, left hand and left leg) have been deepened and strengthened, possibly with charcoal or with the black chalk moistened to obtain a more velvety texture, as an indication of the tonal values in the painting. Titian did not study this group

as an isolated element: he very roughly sketched the shape of a rearing horse behind, and he examined the shadow cast by the group on the ground below, while the curved line drawn to the lower right of the group is a further indication of how it was to be placed within a larger composition. The squaring (done with a very sharp piece of red chalk scored through the drawing using a ruler) may indicate that this group was sufficiently well-studied to allow for a progression to the next stage of the enlargement of individual parts into a full-size composition.

This drawing (accepted by all scholars except Crowe and Cavalcaselle in 1877) is almost certainly a preparatory study for Titian's large *Battle* for the Sala del Maggior Consiglio in the Palazzo Ducale, commissioned originally in 1513 but not carried out until mid – 1537-38. There has been much discussion about the possible subject of this picture (which was destroyed by fire in 1577), whether it was the *Battle of Cadore*, when the Venetians defeated the troops of Maximilian I in 1508 (the picture by Francesco Bassano that later replaced Titian's was of that battle) or the *Battle of Spoleto* of 1155, part of the war between Frederick Barbarossa and Alexander III. The latter is the more likely possibility, as the cycle of pictures in the room was mainly concerned with the struggles between the pope and the Holy Roman Emperor (the subjects were altered in the subsequent decoration), and furthermore the *Battle of Spoleto* had originally been commissioned from Perugino in 1494. Titian's lost picture (executed in place of Perugino's) is known through a painted copy now in the Uffizi, an engraving by Giulio Fontana of 1569 (with some additions to the composition) and an anonymous engraving in the Albertina, Vienna. A drawing in the Ashmolean Museum, P.TT 674, inscribed *Rota* and with a suggested attribution to Martino Rota, records the composition of the anonymous print. Wethy (1969-75, III, 225ff) summarized the argument regarding the subject, and included an interesting account of the banners, devices and insignia visible in the copies.

The relationship of this drawing to the lost picture has also been debated (for a summary see Chiari Moretto Wiel 1988, 51) as the group does not correspond precisely with the relevant portion in the final picture. Titian's working methods were such that his designs did not reach a decisively finished stage on paper, unlike the methods of many of his Roman or Florentine contemporaries. He was a vigorous and powerful draftsman from the outset of his career, when as Dolce records he drew 'gagliardamente e con molto prestezza' ('boldly and with much quickness') in Bellini's studio. Despite the fact that relatively few of his drawings survive, we have examples of numerous types of drawings scattered throughout his career, suggesting that drawing has a substantial role to play in the preparation of a commission.

While this arbitrary pattern of survival means that there are no

233

Copy from the Titian's "Battle."
Galleria degli Uffizi, Florence

large sequences of drawings connected with one commission, through which we could follow the development of the master's ideas through different preparatory stages, nevertheless some conclusions can be reached as to Titian's procedures. For instance, a drawing in a similar medium, squared also in red chalk (Ecole des Beaux-Arts, Paris), is clearly a preparatory study for the *Sacrifice of Abraham* of 1542-44, yet it displays numerous variations with respect to the final painting. This type of drawing, like the Oxford sheet, was doubtless achieved on the basis of some preliminary work, and in turn Titian did not put a rein on his invention once he took up the brush. Instead, he often made outline sketches on the canvas itself, clarifying his ideas further, and he was capable of making radical changes in the design of a composition while painting, as we know from the restoration of the *Bacchus and Ariadne* in the National Gallery, London. The Oxford drawing stands first in relation to a vigorous composition study for the entire *Battle* (Musée du Louvre, Paris): there the left foreground includes a horseman charging on a rearing horse with fallen bodies nearby. This idea was transformed into a skirmish of two horseman, of which the new group was explored in the Oxford sheet. By the time he painted the picture, Titian had altered his idea: the horseman was to be seen as a more strongly silhouetted figure, with the horse's head bowed so as to show in full the swelling chest and arching body of its rider as he is dealt a powerful blow. An analogous procedure is seen in another important surviving drawing for the same painting, *Knight and His Enemy Falling from a Horse* in the Staatliche Graphische Sammlung, Munich. The Oxford drawing must date from soon after the Paris compositional study, which was surely made when Titian returned to the *Battle* commission after long delays in the summer of 1537.

LITERATURE *Tiziano nelle Gallerie Fiorentine* 1978, 233; Hope 1980, 96-97, Chiari Moretto Wiel 1988, 51-52, no. 25, pl. 57 (with full bibliography).

C.W.

G. Fontana, engraving from "The Battle," by Titian, (detail)

30

Portrait of Antonio di Porcia e Brugnera

oil on canvas, 115×93 cm
Milan, Pinacoteca di Brera

EXHIBITIONS   Venice 1935, Milan 1977
RESTORATION   1891, L. Cavenaghi

Signed on the right windowsill: TITIANVS
The painting has belonged to the Brera since 1891 when
Eugenia Litta Visconti Arese donated it in memory of her son
Alfonso. The acquisition was immediately given great importance by Giuseppe Bertini, partly on account of the status of
the donor, and was exhibited in the same gallery as the
Marriage of the Virgin by Raphael, the *Dead Christ* by Mantegna, and the *Head of the Redeemer* then attributed to Leonardo, painted by Giovanni Bellini and Carpaccio.
The following year Frizzoni published it for the first time,
comparing it, at Giovanni Morelli's suggestion, to the *Portrait
of Francesco Maria della Rovere* (Florence, Uffizi, see cat. no.
28) and supplying the genealogy of the noble Friulian Porcia
family, as well as precise information about its provenance.
The work had remained in the ancestral castle of the Porcia
near Pordenone until the nineteenth century. Toward the
1830s it was bought by Prince Alfonso Porcia, of Milan, and
from him it passed to his wife Eugenia Vimercati and thence to
their daughter, Duchess Eugenia Litta.
Gronau was the next to write of this painting (1900), dating it
on the basis of its style c. 1540-3. In 1933 Suida, in his
monograph on Titian, backdated it to 1535. On the occasion
of the 1935 exhibition Fogolari assessed the apparent age of
the subject, who it seems was born in 1508, and dated the
portrait 1537-8. All subsequent writers date it between 1535
and 1540, on the basis of its compatibility with the portrait of
the Duke of Urbino and its pendant *Eleonora Gonzaga* (see
cat. nos. 26, 28) documented in 1536-38, and with the *Portrait
of Gabriele Tadino* (Winterthur, private collection), which
bears a non-autograph but probably accurate date of 1538.
In the *Portrait of Antonio di Porcia e Brugnera* Titian employed
the formula of the window opening onto a landscape, adopted
previously in the the *Portrait of a Gentleman with a Beard*
(Alnwick, collection of the Duke of Northumberland), the
Portrait of Baldassare Castiglione (National Gallery of Ireland,
Dublin) in addition to that of *Eleonora Gonzaga*. Although
somewhat neglected in the critical literature, this deserves to
be placed beside other more famous portraits of the 1530s.
Titian was approaching the height of his career as a portraitist,
in terms of volume of commissions, of the status and historical
importance of his sitters, of his renown, and of the quality of
his production at a time when he had departed from the
Giorgionesque vein of his early portraits. Instead, Titian
emphasized the heroic and the ideal aspects of the subject with
eloquent naturalness, but without neglecting individual social
and moral details. He thus arrived at a convincing synthesis of
physical likeness and historic reality.
The color values have suffered with time. The range of blacks
and dark browns, varied with minimal tonal shifts, is today
obscured, such as to make one wish that past restorations had
been more cautious. Still today, however, against the darkness
barely alleviated by the failing light of the landscape, glows the
yellow gold of the heavy knight's chain, the white light of the
camicia at the neck and wrists, the warmth of the fleshtones on
the face and hand, casually placed on the windowsill, and
finally the sparkling metallic reflections of the handle of his
sword.
It should be noted, incidentally, that the x-radiography carried
out for the Milan exhibition *Omaggio a Tiziano* in 1977
revealed a *facture* excepting in the ear, and a fluid technique
with thin paint layers. After Luigi Cavenaghi's 1891 restoration, which brought to light the name of the sitter, 'Ant.
Comes a Porcia' – obviously a later addition and immediately
cleaned off – and which led to the rediscovery of the window
"whence the eye was led to discover a vast tract of landscape
and sky" (Frizzoni 1892), the canvas, "arbitrarily enlarged with
the obvious aim of representing however awkwardly the right
hand entirely, which Titian had painted only partially," has
remained unaltered (the part found by Cavenaghi is now
hidden by the frame) and has not since been restored except
for occasional protective varnishes.
The signature is barely now visible.

LITERATURE   Frizzoni 1892, 20-5; Gronau 1904, 293; Fischel
1907, 80, 234; Malaguzzi Valeri 1908, 104-5, no. 180; Suida
1933, 84 and 166, pl. CLXXX; Tietze 1936, 300; Berenson 1957,
188; Valcanover 1960, 69, no. 146a; Morassi 1966, 24; Valcanover 1969, 110, no. 199; Pallucchini 1969, 82, 273, fig. 248;
Wethey 1971, 133, no. 84, pl. 64.

L.A.

31

Portrait of Cardinal Pietro Bembo

oil on canvas, 94.5×76.5 cm
Washington, National Gallery of Art
Samuel H. Kress Collection 1952.5.28 (826)

RESTORATION   1943, S. Pichetto

The sitter's distinctive aquiline features in this portrait by Titian unmistakably identify him as the artist's friend, the gifted humanist Pietro Bembo (1470-47). The son of a Venetian diplomat, Bembo received a cosmopolitan upbringing, accompanying his father to Florence and other centers of Renaissance culture. His early reputation as a writer was based on *Gli Asolani* (1505), a dialogue on love set at the court of Caterina Cornaro at Asolo and dedicated to Lucrezia Borgia. Like his father, Bembo opted for a career outside Venice. In 1506 he accepted the hospitality of the Duke of Urbino and spent six years at that court, where he was a leading figure in the circle described in Castiglione's *Cortegiano*. In 1513, having taken minor orders, he became secretary to Leo X. After the pope's death in 1521, Bembo settled in Padua, devoting himself to literary pursuits and forming a notable collection of paintings and antiquities. Appointed librarian of Saint Mark's in 1530, he oversaw the construction of Sansovino's *libreria* (Dionisotti 1966).

Vasari reports that Titian was invited to Rome by Bembo, "who was then secretary to Pope Leo X and of whom he had already painted a portrait" (1568). In addition to this early likeness, now lost, Titian painted Bembo again, according to Vasari, after the writer became a cardinal in 1539. A little more than a year later, on 30 May 1540, Bembo wrote to Girolamo Querini asking him to "thank Titian for the gift of my second portrait, which I had intended to write you that I had seen, so that it should be properly paid for. Now that he is so kind as to wish to do me this favor, let it be so and I will some day do something for him in return" (Bembo 1809). Thus Titian is known to have painted Bembo at least twice and probably several times (Coggiola 1914-15). The Washington portrait is clearly one of the two mentioned by Bembo in the letter of 1540. The picture portrays the writer with a relatively short beard. In fact, as Cellini wrote to Benedetto Varchi in 1536, Bembo had begun to grow a beard, which, as it became longer, gave him the appearance of an ancient sage (Bottari 1822). A ruined portrait by Titian at Naples (Valcanover 1969, 116, no. 261; Wethey 1971, 83, pl. 254), showing Bembo with a longer beard, may have been painted during the artist's stay in Rome, a year before Bembo's death at the age of seventy-seven. The earlier Washington painting was probably begun between March 1539, when Bembo was proclaimed cardinal, and October of that year, when he left Venice for Rome. The style of the painting (and the length of the sitter's beard) are consistent with this date.

Titian's dignified portrait is an official likeness, celebrating Bembo's recent elevation. Dressed in the scarlet *biretta* or hat and cape of his office, the sitter's sharp features – the high forehead, gaunt cheeks, and long, thin nose – are idealized to suggest his keen intellect. Titian here ignored the other side of his friend's character, the passionate nature that had involved him in many amorous relationships, including one with "La Morosina," who bore him three sons. But Bembo's countenance, alert despite his years, was not the only means Titian used to characterize his sitter. As a literary theorist, Bembo championed the imitation both of classical models, especially Cicero, and of the Tuscan authors as a guide for writing in the vernacular. As Titian portrayed him, looking to the left and making a rhetorical gesture to the right, Bembo seems to be expounding his linguistic doctrines in a debate about the "questione della lingua" with some imaginary interlocutor. The sinuous contour of the sitter's right arm and hand, joining with the edge of his cape, gives his image the quality of a sculptural portrait bust. The Washington picture may not have been sold by Bernini to his patrons, the Barberini family, as has been claimed, but it was in their collection in the seventeenth century (Lavin 1975), and it would surely have interested their favorite sculptor had he known it.

LITERATURE   Bembo 1809, VI, 316; Bottari 1822, I, 15-16; Vasari (1568) (ed. Milanesi, 1881), VII, 437, 455; Coggiola 1914-15, 484, 493; Valcanover 1960 (Italian ed.), I, 71, pl. 159; and (English ed.), 1960, II, 91, pl. 159; Dionisotti 1966, pp. 133-51; Pallucchini 1969, I, 100-101, 274. II, fig. 25; Valcanover 1969, 111, no. 209; Wethey 1971, 82-83, pl. 90; Lavin 1975, 41, 166, 295, 345, 409; Shapley 1979, 482-83, pl. 343.

D.A.B.

PIETRO BEMBO

32

Saint John the Baptist

oil on canvas, 201×134 cm
Venice, Gallerie dell'Accademia

EXHIBITIONS   Venice 1935, Venice 1946, Venice 1981, London 1983-84
RESTORATION   1981, O. Nonfarmale

The painting, signed TICIANUS on the rock on which the Saint rests his left foot, comes from the church of Santa Maria Maggiore where it hung in the chapel to the right of the presbytery, on the altar of Saint John. Among the numerous and celebrated works of the church (Fulin 1868), this canvas was certainly the most famous, noted and praised by the guides of the city from Sansovino onward. It is curious that the writer of a memorandum in 1807 to the director of the *Demanio* for the Department of the Adriatic, on the occasion of the suppression of the church, omitted it from the list of paintings preserved there, while giving instead a detailed description of what was on the altar: "a Christ, two small panels, two palms with a golden vase, the usual tablecloths, two iron bracelets, a bell, two wooden candles, three *pacteri* of altarpieces, two wooden doors for the interior, three wooden closets" (Archivio di Stato, Venice, 21/33).

The canvas was removed from the building on 30 September 1807 and the danger of its being sent to the Brera was avoided. It was thus among the first paintings consigned to the Accademia. Cicognara recalled in his opening speech on 4 July 1808 "the beautiful painting by Titian which is preserved here as in its own temple, whose possession it pleased our generous prince to secure with a stroke of his most benign generosity" (Moschini Marconi 1972). In the absence of documents specifying the date (the *buste* of the Archivio di Stato have yielded no results), critics have until now advanced widely varying theories, from the beginning of the 1540s (Mayer 1937, and Hope 1980), through the mid-1550s. Crowe and Cavalcaselle (1877-78) considered 1557, the year in which Dolce described it in the *Aretino*, as its *terminus ante quem*.

On the occasion of the 1981 restoration, Valcanover, noting the "...chromatic scale, extraordinarily resplendent, especially in the mountains..." (1981), which compared the style of the work to that of the *Presentation of the Virgin in the Temple* (also recently restored), proposed a dating in the late 1530s, reconfirming this in 1985.

Binaghi Olivari's (1989) dating of the *Crowning with Thorns* in the Louvre to 1540 – a painting frequently compared to the *John the Baptist* for certain physiognomic similarities in the faces – would seem to support Valcanover's point of view. The *Saint John* is a powerful figure of large proportions and well-drawn musculature. The statuesque image, beyond which the landscape opens as a background, precludes any fusion between the two elements, man and nature. The landscape and stony scarp are both backdrop and setting, studied to give the greatest volumetric emphasis to the figure which in its original placement and conditions of light would have been a moving sight.

Called to work for a "...majestic temple... erected... on the model of the Basilica of Santa Maria Maggiore in Rome" (Corner 1758), Titian "...successfully struggled with the 'Etruscan demons' who had rose from every part toward Venice..." (Longhi 1946), clearly felt challenged to measure himself against the Tusco-Roman current that had already taken hold in Venice. It was if he wanted to show the power of his art, capable of creating simultaneously a splendid sculptural figure and an enchanting landscape. With the *John the Baptist*, Titian engaged the debate about art and aesthetics that was evolving in those years in Venice and from which, as the friend of Aretino, Sansovino and the members of the Accademia della Fama (Petrocchi 1976), he could not possibly have disassociated himself.

Ludovico Dolce, who together with Pino (1548) and Biondo (1549), was representative of Venetian painting theorists in the mid Cinquecento, remarked of the *Baptist*: "In the Church of Santa Maria Maggiore [Titian] made a small panel of a Saint John the Baptist in the desert – of which one can believe that there was none so beautiful ever seen, nor better in design or coloring" (1557). Described thus the painting seems to embody a manifesto of the principal themes of what would be published a few years later as Dolce's theory of art: *invenzione, disegno* and *colorito*. Titian demonstrated "invention not without order and ceremony" in this figure, with the attributes that are proper to him, and an allusion to his mission in the limpid cascade of water at his shoulders.

The modeling of the saint's body, full of restrained force, results from several sources: from Titian's knowledge of human anatomy (the *Tabulae Anatomica Sex* of Andrea Vesalius, the first edition of 1538 [Murano 1976]); from Michelangelo (Wilde 1974) (both his works and his human ideal); and from Classical art (Beschi 1976). "The invention is represented in the form, and the form is not other than drawing," wrote Dolce, "...it must then choose the most perfect form by imitating partly nature... and partly the beautiful marble or bronze figures of the ancients...; the painter must be able not only to imitate, but to surpass nature.... This is to demonstrate by means of art in one body only, all that perfection of beauty which nature scarcely ever demonstrates in a thousand."

As to the color, as L. Venturi noted (1964), it seems that not Dolce but Titian himself pronounced his theory of color: "when the painter imitates well the tints and shades and softness of the flesh and the properties of anything, he makes his pictures seem alive, so that only breath is missing from them.... One must always have an eye intent on the hues,

especially of the flesh and the softness..."

It is easy to understand how this programmatic figure, exemplary in its academicism, whose limbs were described by Vasari as "very graceful," was praised both by Titian's contemporaries and by seventeenth – century critics: Boschini (1664), Von Sandrart (1683), and Ridolfi (1648), who admired the beauty of the landscape and (in spite of appearances) the "precursor... emaciated by fasting and long penitence." Zanetti (1771) was enthusiastic because "this single figure contains in it all the beauty of the style of that great painter... and it is most useful to the young professor to study it for its goodness as well as for the setting in which he stands." These same qualities elicit a certain hesitancy in contemporary criticism. Longhi, for example, defined it as "heavy" (1946); Pallucchini (1969) criticized the "blatant academicism" of the painting, stressing how "there is something wearisome in the formulation of this posturing muscular image". "And yet once the 'academicism' is accepted as exemplary and programmatic, and once it is recalled that this is an altarpiece, it is worth drawing attention also to the "resounding fullness of the chromatic impasto" (Valcanover 1985), the intensity of the color, the richness of the pigment, the sureness of Titian's brushstrokes and handling, capable of bringing this image effortlessly into being, even if with some marginal *pentimenti*.

As often happened Titian returned several times to the theme. There is the painting in the Escorial, assigned by the critics to the early 1550s (Valcanover 1978, no. 502a). Although faithful in its iconography to its Venetian prototype, it is quite different in technique, "worked in a pictorial discourse of extremely loose transparency." There is another version from a private collection in Novara, published by Pallucchini (1969, II, 500) and dated in the late 1560s. Finally there is the version known only from Aretino's description in a letter to Count Massimiliano Stampa in 1531. A copy in the National Gallery of Ireland, Dublin, executed for Schulenburg in 1738-39 by Giannantonio Guardi (Morassi 1960), has been cited by Valcanover (1981).

There are no known preparatory drawings for the painting. Numerous engravings testify to the critical success of the work: V. LeFebre (1682); Cochin Noel Robert (1691); M. Comirato (1833) and various nineteenthcentury examples by Buttazon or Buttason, Viviani and an unknown engraver (Biblioteca Museo Correr, Gherro 14/4 [Chiari 1982]). A different iconography is found in the engraving of 1602 in the Gabinetto Nazionale delle Stampe (Catelli Isola 1976) in which, in sympathy with the times, a skull rests in a cavity of the rock next to the *Baptist*, who has an emaciated face.

LITERATURE Dolce 1557 (ed. 1913), 31, 32, 43, 60, 61, 93; Vasari 1568 (ed. Milanesi 1881), VII, 437; Sansovino 1581, 269-70; Ridolfi 1648 (ed. 1835), 216-17; Boschini 1664, 388; Von Sandrart 1683, 161; Corner 1758, 515; Zanetti 1771, 118-19; Cicognara 1808, 22, 1809, 19; Moschini 1815, II, 508; Fulin 1868, 243-6; Crowe and Cavalcaselle 1877, II, 212; Mayer 1937, 178; Longhi 1946, 24; Morassi 1960, 154-5; Venturi 1964, 114; Pallucchini 1969, 97, 281; Wethey 1969, 136, 137; Moschini Marconi 1972, IX, 259-60; Wilde 1974, 168-69; Beschi 1976, 243; Catelli Isola 1976, no. 63; Petrocchi 1976, 103-9; Muraro 1976, 307-8; Valcanover 1978, 112, no. 228 and 135, no. 502; Hope 1980, 69-70; Valcanover 1981, 100-1; Chiari 1982, 88, 93, 258, 275, 315; Valcanover 1985, 179; Binaghi Olivari 1989.

F.S.

33.

Portrait of Ranuccio Farnese

oil on canvas, 89.7×73.6 cm
Washington, National Gallery of Art
Samuel H. Kress Collection 1952.2.11 (1094)

EXHIBITIONS   Leningrad Moscow Kiev Minsk 1976, London 1983-84
RESTORATION   1949-50, M. Modestini

Although the attribution of this splendid life-size portrait to Titian and the identification of the sitter as Ranuccio Farnese (1530-65), son of Pier Luigi Farnese and grandson of Pope Paul III, are now unquestioned, the picture was all but forgotten for two centuries. The date of Titian's painting and the circumstances under which he created it are known from a letter of 22 September, 1542, from the humanist Gianfrancesco Leoni, then in Padua, to Ranuccio's older brother Cardinal Alessandro Farnese (Fabbro 1967). "You undoubtedly know," the letter begins, "that the Bishop of Brescia is preparing to return to Rome, and he will bring with him a portrait of the Prior which he has had done by the divine Titian, for presentation to the Duchess, in which Titian's excellence is to be admired, especially since he executed it partly in the presence of the sitter and partly in his absence." Leoni and the bishop, Andrea Cornaro, were guardians of the twelve-year old Farnese during his stay in Padua, where the boy was studying classics, and Venice, where he had just been made prior of San Giovanni dei Forlani, an important property belonging to the Knights of Malta. The portrait, the letter specifies, was commissioned by Cornaro as a gift for the sitter's mother, Girolama Orsini, who abetted Ranuccio's ecclesiastical career: he was made a cardinal at the age of fifteen, and various bishoprics were also conferred upon him, among them Naples, Ravenna, and Bologna, before his untimely death in 1565.

Titian, engaging Aretino as his sponsor, had offered in 1539 to paint the "principi de la celeberrima stirpe farnese" (*Lettere*, 1957), and when the youngest member of the clan came to Venice two years later, he found his opportunity (Crowe and Cavalcaselle 1877). The portrait, completed in 1542, marks the beginning of his association with the family who became his second-greatest patrons (Wethey 1971, 28-32). Van Dyck copied the painting in his sketchbook of the 1620's, inscribing the drawing "Titianus" (Adriani 1940). The painter's name was again recorded, together with that of the sitter, in an inventory of the Farnese collection in Rome in 1653 (Bertini 1988). Later, the canvas seems to have been transferred first to Parma, where it is listed (without identifying the sitter) in inventories of the Palazzo del Giardino in 1680, 1708, and 1725, and subsequently, with the rest of the Farnese collection, to Naples.

When the portrait reappeared in the Cook Collection in England about 1885, it was widely regarded as a copy (Cook 1905) or a studio work (Ricketts 1910). In the meantime, however, the sitter's identity was re-established (Gronau 1906) on the basis of his age and the white Maltese cross emblazoned on his coat, a distinctive feature noted in the inventories. The identification was confirmed by comparing the portrait with one in a mid-sixteenth-century fresco by Taddeo Zuccaro and assistants in the villa Farnese at Caprarola, which depicts Paul III designating Pier Luigi Farnese commander of the papal forces (Kelly 1939). The frescoed portrait, obviously based on Titian's, represented, according to Vasari (1568), the young Ranuccio Farnese.

After the painting was cleaned and restored, upon entering the Kress Collection, in 1949-50, it was recognized as a masterpiece. Recent technical examination, moreover, confirms that the signature, occasionally doubted in the past, is genuine. Despite some abrasion in the face, the paint surface, particularly the treatment of the costume, displays Titian's own execution. Yet while the painting is a brilliant technical accomplishment, as noted in the 1542 letter, its colors are muted and the light focuses on the head so as not to detract from the artist's perceptive characterization of his subject. In fact, as John Pope-Hennessy has observed (1966), Titian's claim to be the first great portraitist of children is based partly on this picture. The psychology of the portrait involves a poignant contrast between the immature features and shy glance of the sitter and his exalted rank (Rosand 1978), symbolized by the voluminous coat complete with insignia, which rests heavily on his young shoulders. Titian's devotion to his own children may well lie behind his portrait of Ranuccio Farnese, and it was no doubt the sensitive likeness, and not only the demonstration of his skill, which won the artist the patronage he sought.

LITERATURE   Crowe and Cavalcaselle 1877, II, 5-79; Vasari 1568 (ed. Milanesi 1881), VII, 113; Cook 1905, 5-6; Gronau 1906, 3-7; Ricketts 1910, 107; Kelly 1939, 75-77; Adriani 1940, 69; Suida 1952, 38-40; Berenson 1957, I, 192; *Lettere di Aretino*, 1957, I, 129-131; Valcanover 1960 (Italian ed.), I, 73, pl. 167; and (English ed.) II, 93, pl. 167; Pope-Hennessy 1966, 279-80; Fabbro 1967, 3; Pallucchini 1969, I, 99, 107, pls. 264-65, 266; Valcanover 1969, 112-13, no. 224; Wethey 1971, 28, 98-99, cat. no. 31, pls. 109, 113-14; Rosand 1978, 114, pl. 27; Shapley 1979, 483-85, pl. 344; Robertson 1983, 80, 225, cat. no. 121; Bertini 1988, 41, 57, 62, 89.

D.A.B.

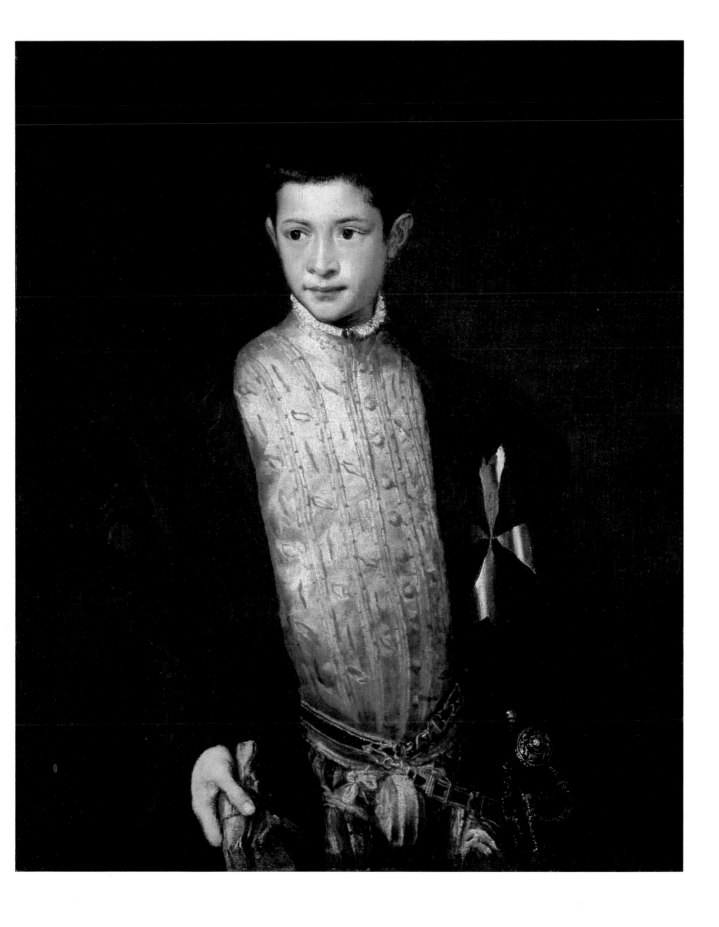

RANUCCIO FARNESE

34

Portrait of Pope Paul III

oil on canvas, 106×85 cm
Naples, Museo e Gallerie Nazionali di Capodimonte (inv. no. 130)

EXHIBITIONS   Venice 1935, San Francisco 1939, Naples 1960, Los Angeles 1979
RESTORATION   1960, L. Tintori

This portrait by Titian, painted in 1543, was recorded in one of Aretino's letters, and by Vasari (1568) who had seen it in the *Guardaroba* of the palace of Cardinal Alessandro Farnese in Rome, from where it originates.

Vasari wrote: "The year that Pope Paul III went to Bologna and thence to Ferrara, Titian accompanied the court, and there painted a portrait of the Pope, and it was a very fine work...." From April of that year (Cittadella 1864, 599) Titian had indeed followed the papal court to Ferrara and Bologna, accompanying Pope Paul III to the meeting of Busseto with Charles V, 21-25 June (Crowe and Cavalcaselle 1878).

The portrait had already been completed in May of 1543 if, as seems logical, the payment of 27 May 1543 to Bernardino della Croce, papal treasurer ("for as much as you have given to M. Titian Venetian painter for having him bring the painting of the portrait of His Holiness that he made") refers to this portrait and not to a different, now lost one, as was once believed (Crowe and Cavalcaselle 1878).

Aretino wrote to Titian from Verona in July 1543: "Fame... takes such great pleasure in publishing the miracle wrought by your brush in the portrait of the Pontiff, that if it were not obliged to announce to the world the generosity demonstrated by your soul in refusing the office of the seal, that as a prize His Holiness thought to give you, it would trumpet how he is alive, how he is now and how he is true." (For Titian's refusal of the office of Keeper of the Papal Seal, previously conferred on Sebastiano Luciani, called 'Del Piombo', see Crowe and Cavalcaselle 1878.)

Pope Paul III Farnese (1468-1549), at the time that Titian portrayed him, was at the height of a pontificate begun in 1534, burdensome but distinguished on the political and religious level as well as artistic. His relations with painters included his patronage of Titian and of Michelangelo (the *Last Judgment* in the Sistine chapel, and the first phase of the frescoes of the Pauline Chapel).

Titian's portrait of 1543 was his first of the Pope and his second for the Farnese family, following his portrait of Ranuccio Farnese the previous year (see cat. no. 33).

As Aretino's letter informs us the portrait was immediately an object of fame and admiration, as confirmed by the large number of copies (Wethey 1971).

Recent critics have agreed on the dating of 1542, and on Titian's autograph, excepting the differing and now discredited opinions of Tietze-Conrat (1946) and of Ortolani (1948). The former believed that the portrait had not been painted from life, but after a prototype by Sebastiano del Piombo, which was believed lost (concerning this, see Ramsden 1969, 1984), questioning further whether the work may not after all be by Sebastiano himself. Ortolani claimed that the portrait was painted during Titian's sojourn in Rome, between 1545-46.

Titian here resorted to a format shared by the portraits of popes and high prelates, established by Raphael and Sebastiano del Piombo, but within this tradition he has worked to such standards of quality and originality of visual language that *Pope Paul III* qualifies as a masterpiece of the genre. The loose spatial definition around the figure, which is structured only by the diagonal point of view, is accompanied by a very lively handling of the paint, vibrating in the rapid strokes of the highlights of the cape. The sitter's facial features have been forcefully and perceptively taken from life, capturing both the physical likeness and the highly intelligent personality of the Pope: his outstretched face thrust forward, lean and wrinkled, the mobile gaze, the slender but still vigorous hands. The image projects a "powerful 'charge' of energy with which the gaunt old man grasps everything, as in a fist" (Ortolani 1948).

LITERATURE   Aretino 1543 (ed. Pertile-Camesasca 1957, II), 8, CLXXI; Vasari 1568 (ed. Milanesi 1881, VII), 442-3; Crowe and Cavalcaselle 1878, II, 9-12; Fogolari 1935, 115; Tietze-Conrat 1946, 73-84; Ortolani 1948, 50-3; Dell'Acqua 1955, 80 123; Ballarin 1968, 23; Pallucchini 1969, 101-2, 107, 278; Ramsden 1969, 430; Valcanover 1969, 113, no. 236; Wethey 1971, 28-9, 122, no. 72 (with preceding bibliography); Pignatti 1979, 74; Hope 1980, 86; Ramsden 1983, 192-3.

P.R.

35

Portrait of a Man (Young Englishman)

oil on canvas, 111×93 cm
Florence, Galleria Palatina, Palazzo Pitti

EXHIBITIONS   Venice 1935, Paris 1935, Belgrade 1938
RESTORATION   1930

Although this is one of Titian's most celebrated paintings, little is known about its provenance, nor is there certainty about the identity of its subject. Gronau's theory (1904), that it represents Guidobaldo della Rovere Duke of Urbino, led to the belief that the work came to Florence with the inheritance of Vittoria, last of the Della Roveres, who married Ferdinando II de' Medici in 1634. However, evidence for this is lacking. The painting was cited for the first time in Florence in an inventory of 1698 as the "Portrait of Pietro Aretino." It was listed as this in the collection of the Grand Prince Ferdinando, by whom, therefore, it was most likely acquired (Allegri 1978). As with Gronau's identification of Guidobaldo, all earlier hypotheses have had a more or less limited following, without any fully supported verification. Pieraccini in his guidebook (ed. 1988) called it Howard, Duke of Norfolk. Venturi (1928) named Ippolito Riminaldi, while Goldsmith-Raggio (1954) suggested Ottavio Farnese. More recently Catelli Isola (1976) has taken up the old listing of the Pitti inventories, believing the painting to be a portrait of the youthful Pietro Aretino that Aretino himself offered to Frederico Gonzaga in a letter of 1527. This however was rejected in the relevant catalogue entry of *Tiziano nelle Gallerie Fiorentine* (Allegri 1978). Accepting the generally agreed date of 1545, Allegri avoided the issue of the sitter's identity, retaining the title traditionally given by the gallery's guidebooks, "The Young Englishman" (or instead "The Man with the Blue-green Eyes").

This seems to be the point reached by present studies (Gould 1976, Fascolo 1980, Hope 1980, Boehm 1985, Chiarini 1988), and to be the most plausible conclusion. In the absence of any point of reference provided by the subject's identity, there remains only the matter of style on which to base the attribution of this masterpiece to Titian and to judge its place in the artist's oeuvre.

The external aspect of the work (enhanced by a light varnish in 1982) is sound, notwithstanding the many old, altered retouches added through the years, which stipple the entire painted surface and which are visible in direct light. On the other hand, the fragile balance of the painting's condition has so far discouraged cleaning and restoration.

Against the vibrant light gray background, to the right of which the hazy shadow of the figure falls, the black silhouette of the subject, whose clothes are adorned by a delicate pattern of horizontal stripes, emerges through subtle tonal transitions. The relaxed gesture of the left arm that rests on his side swells the figure's imposing form while at the same time stressing his slenderness through the subtle glimpse of the gray ground it reveals. The only ornament, the long chain, is now reduced to a shadow of brown with traces of golden glints. Amidst the refined harmony of blacks and grays subtle touches of white stand out such as the lace around the neck and wrists, as does the marvelous head, with its chestnut hair, dark blonde beard and moustache, and blue eyes, the modernity and intensity of which has inspired so much fascinated comment.

The severe monumentality of this image, the "heroic" look, the masterly sureness of touch with a brushstroke either liquid or impastoed, evoking the varied texture of the flesh, the hair, or the fabrics, all confirm the dating c. 1540-45 accepted by the majority of critics. A point of reference is offered, in the same Galleria Palatina, by the portrait commissioned from Titian which Aretino sent to Cosimo I in 1545. This, in its comparable monochromatic symphony of reds, is stylistically slightly more mature and is already influenced by mannerist "anxiety." The "Man with the Blue-green Eyes," with its direct posture and delicacy of touch and tonalities, precedes the Aretino by only a short time.

LITERATURE   Chiavacci-Pieraccini 1888, 51; Gronau 1904, 101; A. Venturi 1928, 325-27; Goldsmith Phillips-Raggio 1954, 233-48; Catelli Isola 1976, 29; Gould 1976, 24; Allegri 1978, 285-89 (with complete bibliography); Fasolo 1980, 53-58; Hope 1980, 76; Boehm 1985, 200; Chiarini 1988, 19.
S.P.

36

Portrait of Benedetto Varchi

oil on canvas, 117×91 cm
Vienna, Kunsthistorisches Museum (inv. no. 91)

EXHIBITIONS   Venice 1935

Signed on right column: TITIANUS F
Given the exceptional quality of this portrait, Titian's authorship has never been doubted. The identity of the figure, however, is more controversial, although Mechel as early as 1783 identified the refined and aristocratic young man as Benedetto Varchi. If we compare the facial features represented with those of Varchi's profile in Domenico Poggini's medal (Hill, fig. XIV, no. 7; Wethey 1971, fig. 84, see also drawing in Steinman 1930, pl. XIV), we notice the same high forehead, domed and somewhat lined, in spite of the different viewpoint. The head, nose and mouth are similar in form, and the hairstyle and cut of the beard are the same. In the Uffizi portrait, attributed to Cristofano dell'Altissimo, and in the painting in the collection of portraits copied from paintings by Giovio – a collection assembled by Roscoe and today housed in the Walker Art Gallery, Liverpool (*Foreign Catalogue* 1977, no. 3310) – Varchi is seen frontally. In spite of the markedly stylized and stereotyped character of these works of scant artistic merit, the roundish form of the head and face recalls the features of the figure portrayed by Titian.
Benedetto Varchi (1503-65) was a celebrated Florentine historian and humanist. He made important contributions to the Tuscan language and, even more, to the aesthetic debate on the *paragone* (Mendelsohn 1982). A large inheritance enabled him to live like an aristocrat, dedicating himself to literature, and to permit himself luxuries such as a portrait by Titian. A crucial factor for this portrait was Varchi's move to Venice together with his patron Filippo Strozzi in 1536. He was tutor to Strozzi's sons until 1540, and had ample opportunity to meet Titian and to befriend him. The age of the figure in the Vienna portrait is surely less than forty years, and thus coincides with that of Varchi, who arrived in Venice at the age of 33 and left four years later to settle in nearby Padua. Many scholars, however, date the painting later, in the 1550s, ten years after Varchi's departure from Venice. Clearly such a conviction jeopardizes the identification of the figure as Varchi. In the present writer's opinion, however, this is beyond questions even supposing that the painter delayed several years before completing the work. In any case this was, for Titian, more the rule than the exception. The traditional dating of 1540 to 1543 (the year in which Varchi returned to Florence) may therefore stand.
The scholar, turned toward the observer in three-quarter length, stands in a relaxed aristocratic pose. The left elbow is poised on the shelf of the column on the right – hand side. The other arm, at his side, holds a small book, which Varchi is apparently engaged in reading, and which he withdraws slightly from view in a gesture that implies modesty and privacy. The head and gaze are deflected to the right. His elegant clothes are black, with a barely perceptible collar trimmed in fur and with red cuffs on the sleeves. The noble column on the right, a glimpse of a wall and a dark curtain in the background to the left characterize the figure's natural environment.
Pentimenti, visible in x-rays, are typical of Titian's creative process. He had initially planned to paint a small handkerchief or glove in Benedetto's left hand, portraying him therefore in the act of holding something (Garberi 1977). He later opted for a more relaxed posture, conferring on the scholar a certain nonchalance and grace. This portrait reflects a genteel and aristocratic spirit, especially apparent in the expression of the pensive and intelligent face, and the faintly interrogative gaze. The open book in his right hand, attribute of the scholar, is the only tangible clue to his personality. The discreet but dignified guise in which Varchi is presented, the few scenic elements marking the aristocratic setting, and his elegant stance make this painting by Titian exemplary for portraitists of the aristocracy in the following centuries, Van Dyck in particular.

LITERATURE   Mechel 1783, 25, no. 28; Engerth 1884, 359-60; Wilde 1938, 176, no. 177; Tietze 1950, 32; Klauner and Oberhammer 1960, I, 139, no. 716; Valcanover 1960, II, pl. 38; Valcanover 1969, no. 340; Pallucchini 1969, 294, fig. 336-7; Wethey 1971, 146, no. 108, pl. 83 (with preceding bibliography); Garberi 1977, 33, no. 14.

S.F.

37

Portrait of Doge Andrea Gritti

oil on canvas, 133.6×103.2 cm
Washington, National Gallery of Art
Samuel H. Kress Collection 1961.9.45 (1408)

EXHIBITION Berne 1947-48
RESTORATION 1955, M. Modestini

This magnificent likeness of Doge Andrea Gritti (1454 or 1455-1538) represents Titian's portraiture at its best. As painter to the *Serenissima*, it was his duty to portray each newly elected doge in a succession portrait, which joined the series of such images in the Sala del Maggior Consiglio, and in a votive painting in the Sala del Collegio (Sansovino 1561). Titian received the customary fee of 25 *ducati* for ther official portrait of Gritti on August 18, 1540, two years after the sitter's death (Hope .... 1980). He also painted the votive picture, which Sanudo described in 1531 (Muraro 1977). Both of these paintings, together with all of Titian's other doge portraits in the Palazzo Ducale, were destroyed in the fire of 1577.

Elsewhere a Titian portrait of Gritti in the Barbarigo collection ("di cui molte copie si veggono") is mentioned by Ridolfi (1648). That painting, now in the Metropolitan Museum in New York, affords a striking contrast to the Washington portrait. The New York picture may only be a product of Titian's studio, where it was found at this death (Valcanover 1969, 112, no. 216; Wethey 1971, 109-10 and fig. 234). Yet it seems to represent Gritti's official image: Domenico Tintoretto's portrait, replacing Titian's lost canvas in the Sala del Maggior Consiglio, adopts the same type (Romanelli 1982, fig. 137), as do many other portraits of the doge. A second group of Gritti portraits, centering on a profile likeness attributed to Catena in the National Gallery, London, also enjoyed a kind of official status: Jacopo Tintoretto's copy after Titian's lost votive painting of Gritti takes over this profile (Valcanover 1969, 139, no. 600; Wethey 1971, 170, cat. no. X-62). These portraits of Gritti, unlike Titian's boldly original Washington portrait, all conform to the staid manner in which doges continued to be portrayed throughout the Cinquecento.

Though inscribed with the names of the artist – TITIANUS E F (Titian, Knight, made it) – and of the patron – ANDREAS GRITI DOGE DI VENETIA – Titian's authorship and the identification of the sitter as Gritti have both occasionally been doubted. Recent technical examination has confirmed the authenticity of the signature, however, and sitter's features are closely similar, and in some cases identical, to those in medals and other portraits that can be firmly identified as Gritti (Puppi 1984). The problem, as Mayer (1937) recognized, is that the style of the painting is not that practiced by Titian during the doge's reign. Dating the work to the end of Gritti's tenure in the late 1530s, as Wethey (1971) and Shapley (1979) have

done, or even to c. 1540, as Tietze proposed (1936), does not account for the strong resemblance the Washington painting bears to certain other portraits that Titian completed between the time of his stay in Rome in 1545-46 and his departure from Venice two years later to join the Emperor in Augsburg. The solution Pallucchini offered must be correct, namely, that Titian's portrait (like the votive painting of 1540) is posthumous (1953, 1969, and 1977).

Pallucchini specifically likened Gritti's portrait to Aretino's in the Pitti Gallery, Florence, a comparison that holds true in each case not only for the massive bulk of the sitter, filling the picture space, but also for Titian's manner of execution, which Aretino complained in a letter of October 1545 was only "sketched rather than finished" (Valcanover 1969, 115, no. 246, pl. 34; Wethey 1971, 75-76, cat. no. 5, pl. 96). The artist's sketchy technique appeared as weel in the unfinished *Pope Paul III and His Grandsons* of 1545-46, in Naples. Like that work, the portrait of Gritti was painted swiftly in vigorous brushstrokes, using the same limited palette of reds and browns, white and gold. The paint application in the Washington picture, on a canvas support that has never been lined, is virtually intact: varying from the transparent layer of the red garment, through which the rough weave of the canvas is visible, to the impasto of the cloak's decorative balls, the handling and color are especially close to those in the *Vendramin Family* of the mid-1540s in the National Gallery, London, (Hope 1980, 106, pl. 20).

Titian's energetic brushwork in the Gritti portrait serves his dynamic conception of the doge, striding forward as if in ceremonial procession. The state portrait thus becomes an action portrait, incorporating not only the style but also the drama of Titian's religious narratives of the 1540s, like the *Ecce Homo* in Vienna or the *Mocking of Christ* in the Louvre. The sweeping movement of the cloak disguises Gritti's corpulence and he appears to be the archetype of the resolute leader. At the same time Titian evidently felt free to characterize his sitter as an individual, because this portrait was not an official one (having been ordered, perhaps, as a memorial by the doge's family). As painter to the doges, he never had a more impressive subject. After distinguishing himself as a military commander and diplomat, Gritti, elected doge in 1523, was no figurehead: he energetically maintained Venice's position between France and the Empire. "Era nato per dominare," Sansovino (1561) said of him, and "... tutte l'età future si ricorderanno di lui." (He was born to rule... and all future generations will remember him.)

Titian's portrait commemorates a doge whose unusually long reign was marked by cultural, as well as political achievement. Gritti presided over a renewal of Venice, welcoming artists and humanists after the Sack of Rome in 1527 ("*Renovatio Urbis.*" *Venezia nell'età di Gritti [1523-1538],* ed. Manfredo

Tafuri, Rome 1984; and Tafuri, *Venezia e il Rinascimento*, Turin 1985). The doge also promoted the Flemish composer Adrian Willaert as choirmaster of San Marco, and he was particularly close to Aretino and Sansovino, who, together with Titian, formed a cultural triumvirate that ruled the city. Soon after his election, Gritti requested Titian to paint a fresco cycle for a chapel in the ducal palace, a commission more suggestive of Rome than Venice. In fact, the way this doge combined a forceful personality with a genuine love for the arts recalls a Roman patron, Pope Julius II, whose own "renovatio" preceded Gritti's. It is in this context that Titian's often-cited borrowing for the Gritti portraits of the massive hand in Michelangelo's *Moses* must be seen. During his Roman sojourn Titian would have encountered this famous work, erected on the pope's tomb early in 1545. It may well be that by quoting Michelangelo's statue in the portrait Titian meant to compare Gritti to his great predecessor. The *Moses* evoked Julius II's "terribilità," and Gritti's own "aspetto terribile" is mentioned in an early biography (quoted in Puppi 1984).

LITERATURE Sansovino 1561, 21v, 42r; Ridolfi 1648, 181; Tietze 1936, 136; Mayer 1937, 308; Pallucchini 1953, 204-05; 1969, 104, 282; 1977, 39 and note to pl. XXVII; Valcanover 1960 (Italian ed.) I, 72, pl. 164a; and (English ed.) II, 92, pl. 164a; Valcanover 1969, I, 103-04, 282; II, figs. 295-97, 31; Wethey 1971, 75-76, 109-10; Muraro 1977, 96; Shapley 1979, 488-90; Hope, *Role*, 1980, 304; Romanelli 1982, 144-45; Puppi 1984, 216-35.

D.A.B.

38

Ceiling of the Church of Santo Spirito in Isola

a. *Cain and Abel*
oil on canvas, 298×282 cm

b. *Sacrifice of Isaac*
oil on canvas, 328×284.5 cm

c. *David and Goliath*
oil on canvas, 300×285 cm
Venice, Basilica di Santa Maria della Salute

EXHIBITIONS   Venice 1935, Venice 1981 (*Cain and Abel*)
RESTORATION   1989-90, F. Volpin, C. Maida, A. Michieletto,
G. Tranquilli

d. *Saint Matthew*
oil on panel, diam. 71 cm

e. *Saint Mark*
oil on panel, diam. 71 cm

f. *Saint Luke*
oil on panel, diam. 71 cm

g. *Saint John*
oil on panel, diam. 71 cm

h. *Saint Jerome*
oil on panel, diam. 71 cm

i. *Saint Augustine*
oil on panel, diam. 71 cm

j. *Saint Ambrose*
oil on panel, diam. 71 cm

k. *Saint Gregory the Great*
oil on panel, diam. 71 cm

EXHIBITION   Venice 1935
RESTORATION   1970, G.B. Tiozzo

In 1541, Giorgio Vasari, who came to Venice to paint a ceiling in Palazzo Cornaro "and a few things for the Compagnia della Calza," presented three drawings for three "large oil paintings" for the ceiling of the Church of Santo Spirito in Isola. Early in 1540 the architect Jacopo Sansovino had rebuilt the façade. In 1542, following Vasari's departure, the ceiling paintings were entrusted instead to Titian, who, as Vasari confirmed, "executed them beautifully, having skillfully been able to foreshorten the figures from below looking up...."

Titian presumably finished the work by 1544, as can be deduced from a letter he wrote to Cardinal Farnese on 11 December: "they [the friars] being evident and ancient debtors for my works" (Crowe and Cavalcaselle 1877). This was confirmed by two witnesses on 22 March 1545, in the course of the suit brought by Titian against the monastery of Santo Spirito, for the altarpiece of the *Pentecost*: "Mr. Tucian has done many paintings in our monastery," and again "Mr. Tucian has done many works for this Church" (Sambo 1980). The Augustinian canons of Santo Spirito called for a pictorial decoration for the church and monastery that would be iconographically unified, based on the prefiguration of the sacrifice of Christ. This included, in addition to Titian's paintings culminating with the Pentecost, the paintings of Giuseppe Porta "Il Salviati": the organ shutters with the *Triumph of David after Slaying Goliath* on the exterior, and the *Revenge of Saul against David* on the interior, and the canvases of the refectory, which were, in addition to the *Last Supper*, three compartments in the ceiling with *Elijah Nourished by the Angel*, the *Fall of Manna*, and the *Prophet Habbakuk Comforts Daniel in the Lair of the Lions*, all of them clearly associated with the Eucharist (Kahr 1966, Niero 1971). The order was abolished in 1656 by Pope Alexander VII, and the furnishings of the church and monastery were assigned to the votive church of Santa Maria della Salute, which was being completed at that time.

The inventory of 25 January 1657 (*more veneto*, 1656) mentioned in addition to the altarpieces of *Saint Mark* and of the *Pentecost* "eleven paintings by Titian, that were on the ceiling of the church," and more precisely "a *David with the Giant Goliath*, a *Sacrifice of Abraham*, an *Abel Killed by His Brother Cain*, four small ovals with the four Doctors of the Church, four similar of the Four Evangelists" (Archivio di Stato, Venice, Santa Maria della Salute, busta 55. See also Pivo 1930). The originals were replaced with copies (Zanetti 1797), while the monastery itself was demolished following the Napoleonic suppressions of 1806.

The eight *tondi* of the *Doctors of the Church* and the *Evangelists* were hung together with Salviati's ceiling painting in the vault of the presbytery, behind the main altar (Zanetti 1733), and were moved to their present position in the sacristy after the 1935 Titian exhibition, adjacent to the altarpiece of *Saint Mark Enthroned*. The three larger paintings were hung on the ceiling of the Sacristy, and arranged according to the Biblical chronology, with the *Sacrifice of Isaac* in the middle, and have remained thus to this day.

In Santo Spirito, the façade of which appears tripartite in an etching by Coronelli, the three paintings would have been located in the vault of the central nave. However, in the sources much confusion surrounds the actual sequence. We owe the first record of their location to Vasari in 1566: "In one is Abraham who sacrifices Isaac; in the other David who cuts the throat of Goliath; and in the third Abel killed by his brother Cain." Sansovino in 1581 did not specify their order, as he was evidently more concerned with the subjects than their placement: "the ceiling, painted in three pictures, in which we see an Abraham who sacrifices, a Cain who kills Abel, and a David who slays Goliath." Borghini (1584) repeated the Vasarian sequence. Stringa, in his additions to Sansovino in 1604, gave a similar version, enriching it with an interesting description of the whole: "The ceiling is very nobly made; being all of very charming work, carvings, frames, and borders decorated with gold, and one sees there, placed in the middle, three large oval spaces." Ridolfi (1648) also agreed with Vasari's text, adding "and in the corners the four doctors of the Church in one of which he depicted himself."

The situation does not change after their transfer to the Salute (although incidentally the inventory of the consignment in 1657 listed the *Sacrifice of Isaac* between *David and Goliath* and *Cain and Abel*), perpetuating the uncertainty and confusion among historians, who often repeated uncritically the descriptions of others. In his *Microcosmo* of 1657, Scannelli gave two different accounts, one with the *Sacrifice of Isaac*, the other with the *David* in the middle. In *La Carta del Navegar pitoresco* of 1660, Marco Boschini who saw the works still in Santo Spirito, already overshadowed by their transfer, noted *David* "as the painting in the middle," while in the two editions of the *Minere*, written after the transfer (1664, 1674), he listed them in their present sequence. This would suggest that the order was altered in their new location in the sacristy of the Salute, except that Martinioni in 1663 followed by Sandrart in 1675 once again noted the *David* in the center.

However, all this confusion should not lead one to suppose that the seventeenth-century arrangement did not correspond to the original. The present order, in addition to respecting the Biblical sequence, is also supported by the fact that the height, of the *Sacrifice of Isaac* is slightly greater (c. 30 cm) than that of the other two canvas. Furthermore, it is also a more complex composition with respect to the lateral panels, which present only two figures (Kahr 1966, Schulz 1968). The theory that the victorious *David* was originally in the center, with its more direct reference to the Holy Spirit to which the church was dedicated (Cocke 1980), must after all be rejected.

Titian's sources for this project, in addition to the preparatory drawings of Vasari which may have influenced him (Tietze and Tietze-Conrat 1944), were Giulio Romano (Hetzer 1935, Kahr 1966), Correggio (Friedlander 1965), Michelangelo – probably via prints – and especially Pordenone who had painted frescoes in the cloister of Santo Stefano between 1532 and 1535 with Old and New Testament stories, including "the Killing of Abel," "the Sacrifice of Abraham" as well as a "David who cuts off the head of a giant shown in rare

foreshortening" (Boschini 1664). These works, as told by Ridolfi, provoked furious rivalry between the two artists.

Though these frescoes are mere shadows after their transfer from the cloister walls, their iconography is known to us through the engravings of Jacopo Piccini. From this Titian captured the violent interlocking of the figures, the powerful musculature and the audacious foreshortenings. As Lomazzo recalled (1590), regarding Titian's perspective, "in this part he studied models made of wood, clay and wax, and from these extracted the postures, but with very short and obtuse distance so that the figures appear larger and more terrible, and the others further back are shorter, creating not merely a right angle, but one nearly obtuse."

The three paintings, in addition to being "decontextualized" today, are gravely compromised in the skies, both the blue backgrounds and the clouds, which are completely lost and repainted. The original tonality, as seen from minuscule surviving fragments, must have been similar to the sky of the *Saint John the Baptist* (Gallerie dell'Accademia, Venice), accentuating in this manner the illusion of "breaking through" to a remote space, the excited emotionality of the attitudes, and in general creating a more unified atmospheric luminosity. It becomes clear how Titian, even before his trip to Rome in October 1545, had come to terms with the artistic culture of Central Italy, though without renouncing the richness of his color and light.

In the *Cain and Abel*, he relegated to the margins the almost-hidden votive altar (*Genesis* 3:24), the object that unleashed Cain's homicidal fury; in this way Titian fused the antecedent and the main event in a synthesis of extraordinary power, where the gestures and the bodies, more than the nearly invisible faces, suggest violent emotion.

In the *Sacrifice of Isaac*, the artist follows the Biblical passage literally (*Genesis* 22:6). There is the ass, the chopped wood and the ram, "with its horns still entangled in a bush," which was to replace Isaac for the sacrifice. *David*, instead, boy-like next to the gigantic dead Goliath, is captured in an unusual pose of prayer, possibly taken from Josephus's *Antichità Giudaiche*, published in Venice in Latin and Italian in 1540 (Kahr 1960).

A preparatory drawing for the *Sacrifice of Isaac* exists at the Ecole des Beaux-Arts, Paris (inv. no. 102; Lavallée 1917), with only the group of the father and son, which corresponded perhaps to a second sheet with the angel (Oberhuber 1976). Even though the drawing is squared for transfer, the variations with respect to the final version attest to the artist's freedom and facility of execution (Cocke 1984).

The enormous critical acclaim of the three canvases, especially in the seventeenth and eighteenth centuries, is documented by numerous engravings by Le Febre, Saiter, Mitelli, Saint Non (Chiari 1982), as well as by copies. Even Tintoretto was drawn

Reconstruction of the ceiling according to J. Schulz

to the invention of *Cain and Abel* in his analogous painting for the Scuola della Trinità (Gallerie dell'Accademia, Venice) (Rossi 1978). Later Gaspare Diziani drew an exact copy of the work (Wiedmann 1988), while Giambattista Piranesi used the figure of Cain in his drawing of the murder scene, in the Ratijen Foundation of Vaduz (Ekserdjian 1989). The young Rubens copied the *Sacrifice of Isaac* on a sheet preserved in the Albertina, Vienna, while according to Boschini (1660), Van Dyck worked hard and long to reproduce the three paintings. The eight tondi with the *Evangelists* and the *Doctors of the Church*, quickly sketched on the almost unprimed wood, were considered autograph by Berenson (1957). For Suida (1933), they were drafted by Titian, but executed by another hand. Recent critics correctly consider them to be mainly workshop (Tietze 1950; Pallucchini, Valcanover, Wethey 1969), as minor parts of the project.

On the basis of Ridolfi, Schulz (1968) has published a convincing reconstruction of the ceiling, with the medallions at the corners of the three main panels.

LITERATURE   Vasari 1568 (ed. Milanesi 1881), VII, 466; Sansovino 1581, c. 83 a; Borghini 1584; Hildescheim 1969, 526; Lomazzo 1590 (ed. Klein 1974), 137; Sansovino-Stringa 1604, 170; Ridolfi 1648 (ed. Von Hadeln), I, 175; Scannelli 1657, 77, 216; Boschini 1660 (ed. Pallucchini), 188ff; Sansovino-Martinioni 1663, 280; Boschini 1664, 351; Boschini 1674, *Dorsoduro*, 28; Sandrart 1675, 164; Zanetti 1797, I, 180; Crowe and Cavalcaselle 1877, I, 490-95; Fröhlich-Bum 1913, 204; Lavallée 1917, 273-74; Pivo 1930, 47ff; Hetzer 1935, 138-39; Tietze 1936, I, 187-89; Tietze and Tietze-Conrat 1944, no. 1962; Berenson 1957, I, 191; Valcanover 1960, I, 26; Friedlander 1965, 118-21; Kahr 1966, 193-205; Schulz 1968, 77-79; Pallucchini 1969, 93-94, 279-80; Panofsky 1969, 30ff; Valcanover 1969, 114, nos. 240 a,b,c,d-k; Wethey 1969, 120-21; Cocke 1971, 734; Niero 1971, 34; Niero 1976, 31; Oberhuber 1976, 95; Rossi 1978, 184; Gioseffi 1980, 230; Battista 1980, 220; Sambo 1980, 383-93; Hope 1980, 101-02; Valcanover 1981, 102-03; Chiari 1982, 104-05, 129, 175-76, 201-34; Rosand 1982, 324; Rosand 1983, fig.77; Chiari Moretto Wiel 1988, 53, 240; Wiedmann 1988, 171; Ekserdjian 1989, 703; Huse and Wolters 1986 (Ital. ed. 1989), 250; Chiari Moretto Wiel 1989, 92.

G.N.S.

39

Last Supper

oil on canvas, 163×104 cm
Urbino, Galleria Nazionale delle Marche (no. 703)

EXHIBITIONS   Venice 1935, Urbino 1973
RESTORATION   1973

The history of the painting has been accurately summarized by
G. Bernini Pezzini (1976). Together with the *Resurrection of
Christ*, it was part of a processional banner, commissioned
from Titian by the Compagnia del Corpus Domini of Urbino.
It was underway in the artist's studio in the winter of 1542, as
the account books of the Compagnia note on 2 December of
that year a payment of 20 gold ducats, sent by messenger to
Titian in Venice. The canvas was complete by 5 February
1544, when the account books record the dispatch to Venice
of 7 gold *scudi* "for the rest of the payment for the banners" by
Titian. Nevertheless, the standard appears to have been still in
Venice on 1 June 1544, the date of an annotation of the
confraternity of the Corpus Domini concerning the disburse-
ment of 25 *bolognini*, the "costs for tbe banner to convey it
from Venice here to Urbino." Bernini Pezzini also specifies on
the basis of the documents that the separation of the two
paintings took place in May 1545 and that by this date the new
stretchers and gilded flagstaff had been made by Pietro Viti,
son of Timoteo. Pietro Viti also attended to the "frieze around
the new banner," for which he collected 50 *bolognini* on 25
June 1546, painting it over the original border. After these
"embellishments," the two canvases were arranged at the sides
of the high altar of the seat of the Compagnia dei Corpus
Domini in Pian di Mercato where they were recorded in 1647
by the Prior Lattanzio Valentini as "placed on the wall with
frames of gilded wood." According to Dolci's testimony in
1775, they were similarly installed when the Compagnia
relocated to the Church of San Francesco in Urbino. In 1866,
the works were transferred to the Instituto di Belle Arti,
whence they reached their present home in 1911.
The *Last Supper* and the *Resurrection* were executed in the
years that saw Titian engaged in numerous important commissions, such as the *Ecce Homo* for the Flemish merchant
Giovanni d'Anna, signed and dated 1543 (Kunsthistorisches
Museum, Vienna); and the ceiling paintings of the Church of
Santo Spirito in Isola, today in the Sacristy of the Salute (see
cat. no. 38), and of the new Sala dell'Albergo of the Scuola
Grande di San Giovanni Evangelista (see cat. no. 42), all of
them marked by a strong a adherence to a Mannerist style.
The two canvases in Urbino fit perfectly in this stylistic period.
In particular, in the *Last Supper*, Titian, exploiting the vertical
format, sets up the composition transversely along the diagonal
created by the table around which the apostles and Christ sit,
captured at the moment in which Christ announces Judas'

betrayal. The event is not represented accordingly to traditional sixteenth-century iconography, for which Leonardo's is
the much admired model, in the refectory of the monastery of
Santa Maria in Milan, and to which Titian himself would revert
in his *Last Suppers* for Philip II and for the refectory of the
convent of San Giovanni e Paolo (D'Argaville 1980). As Gould
has noted (1970), Titian's source was instead Dürer's woodcut
of the *Last Supper* from the *Small Passion*, even if in Titian's
rendering the table is not round nor is John seated next to
Christ but faces him from the other side of the table, while
some other apostles, Judas among them, are merely glimpsed

"Resurrection," oil on canvas, Urbino

in the penumbra. The sense of instability caused by the asymmetry of the composition seems to be reflected in the architecture bathed in light and visible through the openings of the bare setting. For Suida (1935), the building in its central plan evoked Milanese architecture and in particular that of Bramante. Wethey (1969) observed that "the Near Eastern environment of the event explains the round church, which is the Holy Sepulchre, and the Egyptian pyramid (or possibly the pyramid of Cestius in Rome) in the background." For Puppi (1978) "the rotunda and the pyramid, located beyond the interior architectonic frame, is constituted by the montage of heterogeneous elements fused by the knowledge of prints or treatises circulating in the first years of the sixteenth century, but they *work*, ultimately, for their pregnant allusion to the fact of redemption and immortality – the *Resurrection* – represented originally on the other side of the canvas." Pallucchini (1969) accepted Titian's full authorship of the painting, while stressing how "the full-bodied apostles," similar "typologically to those of Giuseppe Salviati," are chromatically subdued by discolored non-original varnishes. The restoration of 1973, briefly described by E. Nanni (1973), has erased the doubts raised by certain critics (Norris 1935, Tietze 1950) about the complete authenticity of the painting and its pendant (Zampetti). It has brought out the delicate freshness of the color notes that palpitate in calculated harmonies in the half light of the enclosed setting around the white glow of the tablecloth, on which each object, such as the glass from the furnaces of Murano, is characterized in its material quality with a careful and memorable touch.

The novelty of the composition of the *Last Supper* of Urbino was to be taken up by Jacopo Tintoretto, though transformed at once in an inventiveness much richer in movement and luministic tension.

LITERATURE   Crowe and Cavalcaselle 1878, II, 361ff.; Suida 1935, 65-66; Norris 1935, no. 128; Tietze 1950, 394; Pallucchini 1969, 96; Wethey 1969, 96; Gould 1970, 170; Nanni 1973, 631; Bernini Pezzini 1976, 68-69; Puppi 1978, 225; Zampetti 1980, 322; D'Argaville 1980, 161ff.

F.V.

40

Danäe

oil on canvas, 120×172 cm
Naples, Museo e Gallerie Nazionali di Capodimonte (inv. no. S 83971)

EXHIBITIONS   Venice 1935, Venice 1981

This painting, a key element in the renewal of Titian's pictorial language after his experiences with mannerism, portrays Danäe, the daughter of Acrisio, King of Argo, who was seduced by Jupiter in the form of a shower of gold while she was held prisoner in the bronze tower, according to Boccaccio's description in the *Genealogia Deorum* based on Ovid's *Metamorphoses* (IV, 607, 113). According to Dolce (1557), Vasari (1568) and Ridolfi (1648), the painting was commissioned by Ottavio Farnese and executed by Titian during his Roman sojourn in 1545-46. When Tietze (1954) published a painting in the Golovin Collection, New York, he claimed that it was the first version, from 1540, of the Capodimonte painting, which he suggested was begun in Venice in 1544. This latter date is supported by Hope (1977), who correctly identified the Capodimonte *Danäe* with the "nude" spoken of by Giovanni della Casa in a letter of 20 September 1544 to Cardinal Alessandro Farnese.

"Messer Titian gave me a portrait of his hand of Our Lord and elegantly convinced me that I would like to be his procurator. But I remind Your Most Reverend Lord of his agreement; that one should find a recompense for that Archbishop, in a way that he can have this benefice, which makes the summit of his happiness. He is ready to paint the portrait of the Illustrious House of Your Most Reverend Lord *in solidum*, everyone including the cats, and if Don Giulio sends him the sketch of the sister-in-law of Signora Camilla, he will enlarge it and surely resembling her, and I, so bound as Your Most Reverend Lordship has made me, am about to burst when the wonderful invention reaches Simon. In addition to this he has almost finished, by commission of Your Most Reverend Lordship, a nude, which would bring the devil upon Cardinal San Silvestro; and that which your Most Reverend Lordship saw in Pesaro in the rooms of the Lord Duke of Urbino [*Venus of Urbino*, Florence, Uffizi] is a Theatine nun next to this one; one could stick on the head of the above-mentioned sister-in-law, if it meant that the benefice would come."

The suggestiveness of the scene is rather clear, even in the detail of the golden rain, "intermingled with sounding coins" in such a way that, as Huse noted (1989), "Titian seems to adhere to a tradition which made of Dan ae a courtesan, not a virtuous heroine."

Giovanni della Casa's letter to Cardinal Farnese is revealing of the desires and demands made of Titian by his august patrons, to which the artist responded with mythologies of a clearly erotic nature, his *poesie*. This is stressed by Ginzburg (1980), who published the unexpurgated letter of Ludovico Dolce to Alessandro Contarini, informing him of the *Venus and Adonis* that Titian promised to send to Philip II in 1553: "The Venus has her back turned, not because of lack of art... but to show a double art. Because thus in turning her face towards Adonis, trying to hold him with both arms, and half seated on a soft peacock-blue piece of cloth, she shows everywhere some sweet and lively sentiments and those also that can only be in her; where it is still more wonderful shrewdness of this divine spirit which in the lower parts one can recognize the dent of the flesh cased by sitting. And so? One can say with truth, that each mark of the brush is one which usually can only be made by Nature's hand.... I swear, My Lord, that there is not to be found a man so acute in vision and judgment, who seeing it would not believe it to be alive; nobody so chilled by the years, or so hard of constitution, would not feel warmed, touched and feel his blood move in his veins. Nor is it a marvel; that if a marble statue could so stimulate with its beauty, penetrating the marrow of a young man, that he left a stain, now what would he do before this which is of flesh, which is beauty itself, which seems to breathe?"

The Roman artistic world could hardly have looked favorably upon such sensual naturalism. Vasari (1568) described just this: "One day, when Michelangelo and Vasari visited Titian at the Belvedere, they saw a painting which he had brought with him of the woman as Danäe with Jupiter in her lap, transformed into a shower of gold, and praised it greatly as was polite. After they had gone, Buonarroti, talking about Titian's work, praised him a good deal, saying he liked his coloring and style, but that it was a pity good design was not taught in Venice from the first, and that her painters did not have a better method of study. Such that if this man, said he, were aided by art and design as he is by Nature, especially in imitating from life, he would not be surpassed, having a very fine wit and a most charming and vivacious style. This is very true, for without design and a study of selected ancient and modern work, skill is useless, and it is impossible by mere drawing from life to impart the grace and perfection of Nature, so that certain parts frequently lack beauty."

If in fact the Danäe was seen by Michelangelo, he would surely have noticed that Titian had revised his figural ideas, such as the *Leda and the Swan*, of which there is a copy in the National Gallery, London, and the *Night* of the Medici Tombs, in favor of a physically illusionistic naturalism, in contrast to Michelangelo's spiritual torment based on the laws of *disegno* and *chiaroscuro*. Titian constructed the Danäe "without preparatory drawing, as indicated by x-radiography" (Mucchi 1977). But that drawings were employed in his workshop, and seriously so, is apparent both from the cited Michelangelo references and from many other cases discerned by critics.

Tietze (1954) and Panofsky (1969) placed the *Danäe* in relation to the same subject painted at Fontainebleau by Primaticcio, which was well – known through engravings. Brendel (1955), resuming in part Crowe and Cavalcaselle's discussion (1877), observes how Cupid derives from the *Throne of Saturn* in the Grimani collection, today in the Museo Archeologico, Venice, and from *Cupid Bending His Bow* of Lysippus, which was widely known in the 1500s through copies. Crowe and Cavalcaselle (1878), Millner Kahr (1979) and Fehl (1980) insisted on the affinity between Titian's painting and the *Danäe* (Galleria Borghese, Rome), which according to Vasari was painted by Correggio together with the *Leda* for Duke Federico Gonzaga, who had commissioned a series of paintings from him depicting the loves of Jupiter. Whatever the source of the invention, it is evident that in the expansive pose with which the female figure emerges from the shadow of the alcove, all trace is gone of the plastic-sculptural effects of slightly earlier paintings, such as the *Baptist* in the Gallerie dell'Accademia or the *Crowning with Thorns* in the Louvre. By this time Titian, with for Alessandro Farnese, had moved toward an original and masterly independence of chromatic language, of exceptional illusionistic freedom, of which the artist would certainly have wished to give a brilliant demonstration in Michelangelo's Rome.

Wethey (1975) gave a detailed list of the many copies of the work, and of the provenance of the *Danäe*. In 1649 it was still in the Palazzo Farnese, Rome, but subsequently traveled to Parma, Naples, Palermo and once more, definitively, to Naples. Wethey also recounted how the painting, stolen by Hermann Goering in World War II, was recovered in the Austrian salt mines of Bad Aussee immediately after the end of the war and returned to the Italian State on 13 August 1947.

LITERATURE   Dolce 1557, 161; Vasari 1568, III, 574-5; Ridolfi 1648, I, 178; Crowe and Cavalcaselle 1878, II, 54ff; Campana 1908, 382ff; Von Hadeln 1926, 78ff; Tietze 1936, II, 302; Tietze 1954, 199ff; Brendel 1955, 121; Valcanover 1960, II, 7-8, 31; Pallucchini 1969, 110-11, 283-4; Panofsky 1969, 23, 144-7; Wethey 1975, 132-3; Hope 1977, 188-9; Mucchi 1977, 300; Millner Kahr 1978, 46-7; Rosand 1978, 122; Fehl 1980, 142; Ginzburg 1980, 125-6; Pallucchini 1980, 402; Hope 1980, 89ff; Valcanover 1981, 109-10; Ost 1983, 129ff; Rosand 1983, Lawner 1988, 151, 122; Huse 1989, 292; Pedrocco 1990, 85ff.

F.V.

Portrait of Cardinal Alessandro Farnese

oil on canvas, 99×79 cm
Naples, Museo e Gallerie Nazionali di Capodimonte (inv. no. 133)

EXHIBITION   Venice 1935
RESTORATION   1960

Recent critics (Pallucchini 1969, Valcanover 1969, Wethey 1971) have included this portrait in their catalogues of Titian's paintings, thrusting aside past hesitations caused by its poor condition (Cavalcaselle and Crowe 1878, Dussler 1935, Serra 1935, Berenson 1957).

Pallucchini's dating, which assigns the work to the artist's Roman sojourn early in 1546, is convincing since it also corresponds nicely to the appearance of the Cardinal (1520-89), who should have been 26 years old. There is undoubtedly a resemblance, as indicated by Pallucchini, to the portrait of the same sitter to the pontiff's right in the *Portrait of Pope Paul III with His Nephews Alessandro and Ottavio* (Gallerie Nazionali di Capodimonte, Naples), another of the Roman works for the Farnese. The portrait of the cardinal alone is a variation of that in the triple portrait and was presumably conceived to satisfy the patron's wish to have a portrait of his own from the great artist's hand. The work he received, however, while of high quality, relies on a relatively conventional formula and a less intense psychological characterization.

Alessandro Farnese, son of Pier Luigi and Girolama Orsini, was made a cardinal at a very young age, on 18 December 1534. During the course of his life he filled several important ecclesiastical offices. He was a man of culture and a generous Maecenas (Von Pastor, 1924, 92-93, 690).

LITERATURE   Cavalcaselle and Crowe 1878 II, 16-17; Dussler 1935, 238; Fogolari 1935, 117; Serra 1935, 561; Berenson 1957 I, 189 no. 133; Pallucchini 1969, 113-4 no. 286; Valcanover 1969, 116 no. 260; Wethey 1971, 32, 97-8 no. 29.

P.R.

"Portrait of Pope Paul III Farnese with His Nephews Alessandro and Ottavio," oil on wood, Naples

42

Ceiling of the Scuola of Saint John the Evangelist

a. *Saint John the Evangelist on Patmos*

oil on canvas, 235×260 cm
Washington, National Gallery of Art
Samuel H. Kress Collection, 1957.14.6 (1484)

RESTORATION   1949, M. Modestini

This exhibition reunites Titian's Saint John the Evangelist on Patmos for the first time with the panels representing cherubs, satyrs, female heads and evangelistic symbols that once surrounded it on the carved and gilded ceiling of the albergo, or board room, of the Scuola Grande di San Giovanni Evangelista in Venice. When the *scuole* were suppressed in the Napoleonic era, the ceiling was dismantled, and the paintings were transferred to the Accademia in 1812. The Saint John, judged to be in ruinous condition, was traded in 1818 to an art dealer named Barbini in Turin and disappeared from sight (Moschini Marconi 1962). Although as late as 1936 it was considered to be lost and known only from an engraving by Andrea Zucchi (Tietze 1936; Suida 1936), the canvas resurfaced on the art market and was acquired by the Kress Foundation in 1954. It proved to be in generally good condition, with serious damage to the original paint only in the area of the head of God the Father and the immediately surrounding angels.

The attribution of the ceiling ensemble to Titian dates back to Sansovino (1581) and is repeated in all the major guidebooks to Venice through the end of the Republic (Schulz 1966). Although no direct evidence concerning the commission has survived, a document of April 1544 mentions that Titian, "painter, man of experience, known to all," was present in the scuola and was asked to give his opinion about whether some existing paintings might be cut to make room for doors into the new albergo, under construction since 1540 and now nearing completion ("reduto a termene") (Schulz 1966). It seems likely that Titian's visit was related to the ceiling commission, especially since in 1543 or 1544 he finished the similarly conceived ceiling paintings for Santo Spirito in Isola, now in Santa Maria della Salute (cat. no. 38). The San Giovanni Evangelista paintings, if commissioned in 1544, may not have been completed until after Titian's stay in Rome from September 1545 through June 1546. Schulz (1966 and 1968) dates the ensemble as late as 1548 on the grounds that the color is richer than in Titian's works of the early 1540s. Wethey (1969) and Pallucchini (1969 and 1980) agree, except that the latter would date the decoration no later than 1547. However, because Titian did use rich color occasionally in the early 1540s, as in the *Ecce Homo* in Vienna of 1543, the

question of whether or not the ensemble was completed before or after the Rome trip cannot be resolved solely on this basis. The Saint John is accepted as an autograph work by Titian, except by Fisher (1977), who proposes that the entire ensemble was executed later in the century after Titian's design, mostly by Palma Giovane. It is true, as Fisher argues, that the Saint John is painted with a degree of looseness and freedom unusual for the 1540s. However, Titian did employ increasingly broad brushwork in these years, and here he may have been inspired to paint even more freely because the work was to be seen on the ceiling, where more detailed execution would have been ineffective. Titian's hand seems evident in the manner in which each brushstroke, however free, always performs a specific descriptive function. In addition, numerous pentimenti, especially in the contours of the forms, show the master's characteristic method of working out the final composition directly on the canvas.

Earlier Venetian *soffitti*, or painted ceilings, by Pordenone and Vasari had begun to suggest the illusion of three-dimensional figures in a unified space beyond the ceiling plane (Schulz 1968). Titian's ceilings at San Giovanni Evangelista and Santo Spirito in Isola built upon Pordenone's and Vasari's achievements, realizing in ceiling painting the emerging Venetian taste for spatial illusionism, movement, and mass. In the mural fresco of Saint Christopher in the Palazzo Ducale in Venice, Titian had already exploited some of the dramatic potential of a monumental figure looming against the sky. His figures in the two soffitti are further dramatized through the use of a very low viewpoint and the consequent foreshortening of the figures. This new approach to the projection of figures in perspective seems to have been inspired by the works of Giulio Romano in Mantua and Correggio in Parma. Titian had been to Mantua several times, and had collaborated with Giulio on the Gabinetto dei Cesari in the Palazzo Ducale there. He would undoubtedly have known Correggio's cupolas as well, probably from a visit to Parma in 1543, if not before (Popham 1959).

Suida and Tietze (both 1936) first noted the similarity of Titian's Saint John to the figure of the same saint in Correggio's cupola at San Giovanni Evangelista. The comparison has been repeated by Popham (1957), Panofsky (1969), Schulz (1966), and Wilde (1974). Other figures, however, are relevant as well. The Elijah and Daniel (possibly Enoch) on the northeast pier in San Giovanni Evangelista and the apostles on the parapet of the Duomo in Parma share certain elements with Titian's saint: the upturned face, bathed in light from above; the arms raised in an awestruck gesture; the exaggerated contrapposto; the bent knees, one lower than the other; the ankles and feet hidden behind the ledge. A counterpart exists in Giulio's works as well. Although he is usually mentioned as an influence on Titian at Santo Spirito in Isola

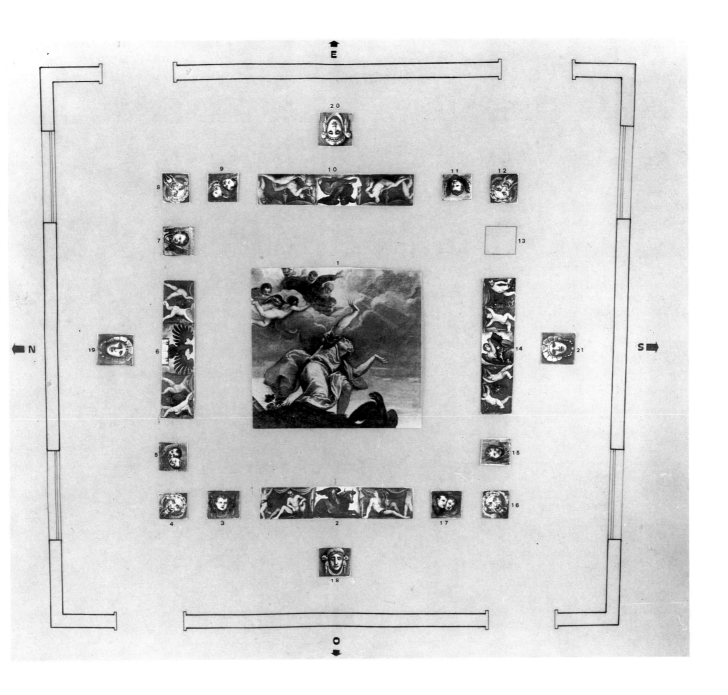

Reconstruction of the ceiling of the Scuola

rather than at San Giovanni Evangelista, Giulio's figure of Saturn in the Sala dei Giganti in the Palazzo del Te is as close to Titian's Saint John as is any individual figure of Correggio's. Unlike Giulio and Correggio, who placed obliquely foreshortened figures of this type in the outer, more vertical parts of their vaults and cupolas as part of a complicated illusionistic system, Titian placed them in the center of a flat ceiling. He eschewed the worm's eye *di sotto in su* viewpoint and, in doing so, provided Veronese and others of that generation with a model for adapting Giulio's and Correggio's elaborate compositions to Venetian soffitti. The shift of the ideal viewpoint from the center to one side permitted the development of convincing illusions without the necessity of employing a succession of different perspective projections. Distortions of form around the periphery and illegibility in the center could be avoided, and the figures could easily be provided with an appropriate stage upon which to enact their drama.

Despite the importance of this innovation, Titian himself seems to have had little interest in the mechanics of illusionism, either to dissolve the entire surface into a fictive space in the manner of Giulio and Correggio, or to suggest a continuum from picture to picture, as in the *soffitti* of Vasari and Pordenone. Instead, he chose to dramatize the visionary experience through one highly expressive figure and a single concentrated burst of light and motion. Illusionism is confined to the centerpiece; the surrounding panels performed the more traditional function of *quadri riportati*, pictures affixed to the ceiling rather than windows into an imaginary reality. The satyr and female heads, in particular, would have reinforced a sense of the solidity of the ceiling plane: they are sculptural in inspiration, *grotteschi* of the type used in architectural decoration by Sansovino, Sanmicheli, and Falconetto. The female heads are especially close to those on the facade of Sansovino's Libreria di San Marco, begun 1537, and Palazzo Corner, begun c. 1545. (Although Popham [1959] proposes Correggio's drawings as a source for the design of the panels with the evangelistic symbols, their playful putti also seem to be inspired by Sansovino: they are close to the paired *putti* on his door for the sacristy of San Marco, also from the mid 1540s, and the *putti* holding garlands on the facade of the Libreria.) The San Giovanni Evangelista ceiling, then, must have resembled a traditional Venetian *soffitto* of the early Cinquecento, decorated with gilded carvings, paintings, and figural reliefs, unexpectedly pierced in the center to reveal the dramatically illusionistic view of Saint John and his miraculous vision.

LITERATURE Sansovino 1581, 101; Ridolfi 1648, 185; Zanetti 1771, 124; Urbani de Ghelthof 1895, 16-17; Tietze 1936, I, 188, pl. 24a. II, 312; Suida 1936, 111; Suida 1956, 74-75, figs. 71-72; Popham 1957, 38-41, fig. 17; Valcanover 1960 (Italian ed.), I pp. 74-75, pl. 178; and (English ed.), II,

95, pl. 178; Moschini Marconi 1962, 262-63; Schulz 1966; Schulz 1968, 3-21, 84-85 pl. 17; Wolters 1968, 56; Panofsky 1969, 35-36, fig. 40; Valcanover 1969, 114 no. 239; Wethey 1969, 137-138, pl. 156; Pallucchini 1969, I, 95, 115, 283, II, pl. 300; Wilde 1974, pp. 168-173, fig. 140; Fisher 1977, 62-67; Shapley 1979, 490-92, pl. 347; Pallucchini 1980, 401; Valcanover 1984, 180, fig. 27.

R.E.

b. *Symbols of the Evangelists, Cherubs, Grotesque Masks and Faces of Women*

oil on panel
Venice, Gallerie dell'Accademia (cat. no. 1035)

EXHIBITION   Venice 1935
RESTORATION   1989, L. Savio

In 1581, Sansovino, described the Scuola di San Giovanni Evangelista: "in the second '*albergo*' inside, the ceiling was made by the always memorable Titian." All the later guides and source spoke of this ceiling as a gem of Venetian painting. This was a complex decoration, made up of twenty-one parts carefully placed in an elegant gilded frame "made from a rare limewood, not subject to woodworm." Unfortunately at the time of the Napoleonic suppressions (1806), when the ceiling was dismantled for transfer to the Regia Accademia di Belle Arti (1812), the frame was destroyed and one of the twelve panels lost. Neither in the archives nor in graphic sources is there an indication of the style of the carvings, which, given the nature of the project, would have been ornate and elaborate, probably designed by Titian himself since the *Notatori* of the *scuola* mention neither architects nor craftsmen in this context. Regarding the lost panel, examination of the survivors makes it obvious that this depicted a pair of little cherubs. Even the dimensions can be deduced from the hypothetical reconstruction of the ceiling oulined below.

The surviving paintings portray: *The Vision of Saint John the Evangelist at Patmos* (see cat. no. 42a) the centerpiece, now at the National Gallery of Art, Washington; *The Symbols of the Evangelists between Pairs of Nudes and Putti; Single Heads of Cherubs; Pairs of Cherub Heads; Masks of Satyrs; and Faces of Women*. These panels, without the central compartment, were exhibited in 1843 in the upper part of the gallery "*delle Riduzioni Accademiche*" (now Sala III of the Gallerie dell'Accademia) and it was on this occasion that a square compart-

ment with a *Cherub* and rectangular compartment with the *Tablets of Law* were painted on canvas by G.A. Lorenzini to complete the cycle. These were subsequently removed. The four main compartments remained on exhibition for a few more years and were restored for the 1935 Titian exhibition, while the minor compartments have since been in storage in the Gallerie dell'Accademia, where they have undergone recent conservation, together with the other four, for this exhibition.

A *terminus post quem* for these works is given by the beginning of the construction of the new *albergo* in 1540 as documented in the *Notatori* of the *scuola* preserved in the Archivio di Stato, Venice. Work dragged on for several years. An interesting document from 16 April 1544 begins: "Since our *albergo* has been brought to the point by the grace of God that at little expense we can finish according to the intention of those whose concern it is, and also because our *scuola* has a great need for this *albergo*...." Later in the same document Tucian seems to be mentioned for the first time, "painter, man of experience known to everyone," as the consulting expert to decide if it was necessary or not to cut the paintings of the Room of the Cross, in order to open two doorways. At this date, therefore, Titian was in contact with the board of the *scuola*, and was much esteemed. So it is quite possible that he had already received the ceiling commission and was already at work. However, this date does not qualify as a *terminus ante quem* since in subsequent documents it is noted that a new chief officer was nominated to supervise the building of the *albergo*, which must have been incomplete. The documents also mention the decision to have "balconies" made facing the inside courtyard (9 April 1545), and these were not finished until 1554. Again in 1552 an artisan was hired to carve the *bancali* along the walls of the room. Keeping in mind that Titian was absent from Venice from September 1544 to June 1546, he would have planned the general disposition of the ceiling immediately following the commission c. 1544, and painted the central compartment and perhaps some heads of putti – those that are stylistically higher in quality. The rest would have been left to the workshop in Titian's absence. Examination with reflectography of the four panels with symbols of the Evangelists has yielded an interesting piece of data: a preliminary composition provided for simple volutes in place of the nude figures and putti. The quality of the nudes and the putti is decisively superior to that of the central part where the symbols of the Evangelists are only roughed in. As early as 1830, Zanotto attributed these parts to Titian himself. Fogolari (1935) pointed to the "passages of noteworthy vigor" that were "not unworthy of Titian" and Schultz (1966) was also convinced of the direct intervention of Titian for these figures. Either Titian, upon returning from Rome, or an able student, improved these four panels, which perhaps appeared too "poor."

There are no documents describing the placement of the twenty-one paintings on the ceiling. We are obliged to rely on historical and artistic considerations drawn from comparisons with other contemporary ceilings, and on technical considerations presented by the panels themselves (see also Schultz's reconstruction of the ceiling, which differs from ours). Floor plans of the *albergo* reveal that it is an irregular quadrilateral, whose sides measure respectively 8.45 meters (west side), 7.95 meters (north and south sides), and 8.65 meters (east side). The difference of length and inclination (the south side is slightly oblique) of the plan of the room is fundamental to the present reconstruction hypothesis. It was noticed that the panels are of slightly different dimensions and shapes, and this information has been related to their position on the longer, shorter, straight and oblique sides of the quadrilateral. The present writer believes that the panels, which are on the average 5 cm narrower than their counterparts, should be placed on the shorter sides (north and south), while their counterparts should be put on the longer side (west and east). The panels that should be put along the shorter sides are those that are 2 and 3 cm higher than their counterparts on the longer sides. The paintings portraying the *Faces of Satyrs* are rhomboid, with different angles according to the corners of the room where they would have been placed. This panel has a more acute angle than the corresponding panel sixteen. Considering that the east wall is 20 cm longer than the west wall, and since on the basis of this hypothesis the sum of the bases of the paintings placed along the east side is 10 cm longer than the corresponding parts on the opposite wall, the difference of 10 cm should be optically corrected from the positioning of the ceiling and the play of the frame. And again: the *Faces of Women*, which would have been placed along the north and south sides (panels nineteen and twenty-one), differ by an average of 10 cm compared to those on the east and west sides (panels eighteen and twenty). Support for this arises from the carving of the numeral xv on the back of the panel portraying a *Face of a Cherub* (panel fifteen) and of the numeral xvII on the back of the panel with *Couple of Cherubs* (panel seventeen). These certainly indicated the sequence of the panels on the ceiling. From this it follows that the *Faces of Women* must have been placed on the outside with respect to the Evangelist symbols and not on the inside, as Schultz suspected, because in that case they would have been included in the numeration. In this way we obtain a precisely calculated geometric composition where the distortion caused by the real space is optically corrected by the form and dimensions of the paintings. Thus, from the center, where the eye converges, one has the impression of a multiplicity and variety of forms and rhythms, which become more and more fragmented toward the outside. If then, from a technical and illusionistic point of view, the composition is consciously structured, it is unlikely

that the iconography was casual or merely decorative either. The text behind this complex portrayal is undoubtedly the *Apocalypse* of Saint John. The discourse begins with the central image where the Evangelist has, at Patmos, the fearful apocalyptic vision and where the mighty conflict between Good (cherubs) and Evil (satyrs) takes place. In chapter four the sky splits and opens (revelation is implied by the drawn curtains) and the four Evangelists before the saint. In the paintings of Saint Luke and Saint Mark, there are male nudes with golden amphorae, which also occur in chapter fifteen, the "golden vials full of the wrath of God," while alongside Mark and Luke appear the two "witnesses" mentioned in chapter eleven who are understood to be Moses and Elias of the Old and New Testaments, or Saints Peter and Paul who spread the gospel of Mark and Luke.

Of the four panels with *Faces of Women*, two have a serene expression, almost contemplative, while the other two seem disturbed and shocked. In chapter twelve of the Apocalypse we read: "And there appeared a great wonder in heaven, a woman clothed with the sun, and the moon under her feet, and upon her head a crown of twelve Stars," understood as the symbolic portrayal of the city of heaven, while further on, in chapter seventeen, another woman, described as "the great whore... decked with gold and precious stones and pearls" would indicate Babylon, the city of earth. In addition, the arrangement of the paintings on the ceiling, as construed in the present hypothesis, seems to have four as its key number. It returns many times in the Revelation as the symbolic number of the four cardinal points and the cross.

The dimensions, which are irregular, are given below for each panel, in millimeters:
1. h 2350×2600 mm
2. h 466×2370×h 456×2370 mm
3. h 389×450×h 388×450 mm
4. h 392×383×h 395×394 mm
5. h 410×418×h 414×415 mm
6. h 492×1982×h 495×1982 mm
7. h 429×405×h 427×409 mm
8. h 411×395×h 416×392 mm
9. h 405×459×h 406×454 mm
10. h 456×2407×h 451×2407 mm
11. h 387×441×h 390×444 mm
12. h 373×390×h 380×395 mm
13.
14. h 485×2030×h 492×2030 mm
15. h 456×398×h 451×400 mm
16. h 430×400×h 427×385 mm
17. h 395×464×h 399×462 mm
18. h 442×477×h 437×475 mm
19. h 520×463×h 524×467 mm
20. h 430×486×h 430×486 mm
21. h 510×440×h 513×442 mm

LITERATURE   Sansovino 1581, 101; Ridolfi 1648, i, 186; Boschini 1664, 295; Martinelli 1705, 378; Zanetti 1733, 294; Zanotto 1830, 174-6; Suida 1933, 67-157; Fogolari 1935, 93; Tietze 1936, i, 188; Suida 1956, 111; Valcanover 1960, i, 103; Moschini-Marconi 1962; Schultz 1966, 89-95; Schultz 1968, 84-5; Pallucchini 1969, 91; Pignatti 1981, 48; Nepi Scirè and Valcanover 1985, 180.

S.G.D.

The Pentecost

oil on canvas, 570×260 cm
Venice, Basilica di Santa Maria della Salute

RESTORATION   1984-85, A. Lazzarin

According to Vasari, Titian painted an altarpiece in 1541 representing the descent of the Holy Ghost on the Apostles "with a God disguised as fire and the Holy Spirit as a dove," for the main altar of the Church of Santo Spirito in Isola in Venice. Vasari continued to relate how the altarpiece quickly deteriorated, causing the friars to refuse the painter's requests for payment. Titian then brought a lawsuit before the ecclesiastical tribunal, which lasted until 1545 and resulted in a new or renewed altarpiece.

Neither the nature nor the possible causes of the deterioration emerge from the records of the proceedings, conserved at the Archivio Patriarcale, Venice (Sambo 1980). On both points the texts, all coming from the monastery, bear confused, reticent and contradictory testimonies. In the spring of 1545 the legal records fall silent, and presumably the suit ended with a settlement, promoted by the Farnese to whom Titian had turned in December 1544, with a petition to Cardinal Alessandro, nephew of Pope Paul III.

As the dossier containing the records of the trial bears two inscriptions: "super confece et pretio" and "super refectione pallae", the greater reliability and veracity of one or the other has been examined (Sambo 1980; Chiari Moretto Wiel 1988), suggesting that either a single painting had been restored, or two versions made. In the latter case, a first painting would have been begun, as noted by the trial records, between 1529 and 1530, delivered, incomplete, in 1541. It deteriorated, was removed and lost, and was replaced by the extant version exhibited here, since 1656 at Santa Maria della Salute. The condition of the first canvas as it was noted in the course of the lawsuit ("rotting and moldy"), assuming the depositions were truthful, necessitates the exclusion of the first hypothesis, that of the single restored version. This tends to be confirmed by the recent conservation of the Salute painting, which, while it restored the brilliant colors, revealed no trace of mold, damage, or *pentimenti* and autograph repainting.

Why would a restoration merit coverage as news, and why would Vasari have written about it? And why the new version? Vasari's account comes in the context of his description of the original altarpiece in which the treatment of the theme is uncanonical, let alone non-traditional in so far as he was aware. In the first version of the *Pentecost*, Titian had adopted a completely symbolic visualization. He had represented "a God" not anthropomorphically but "of fire," as a unitary and primordial principal of energy. With this he had followed to the letter the scriptural story (*Acts of the Apostles* 2: 2-4) and

also those Old Testament prohibitions of the representation of the divinity that, as Supreme Spirit, could have neither form nor image (*Exodus* 20: 4, 32: 8; *Deuteronomy* 4:15-16). These ideas came back into circulation after some of the most radical wings of the Reformation of Zwinglian and Calvinist inspiration had confused many traditional forms of worship with idolatry, bringing the conflict to the point of iconoclasm, in contrast to the ideas more generally held in Reformist circles.

In the first version of the altarpiece the "Spirit in the form of a Dove" could well have been understood both as symbolic and as a visible manifestation – as generation and revelation – of the Father. But such a choice could certainly have caused, in those days in Venice and the Veneto, a renewed debate. Substantial documentation attests to the active presence of an anti-Trinitarian movement in the Veneto between the 1530s and 1540s (Stella 1969). It was in this context of doctrinal tension that connotations of a disciplinary and political nature were quickly assumed. The litigation between Titian and the friars took place between 1544 and 1545. Titian's position would have been particularly difficult if he felt the need to inform the Pope's nephew and to invoke his help (letter of December 1544). But it was most certainly concluded with an honorable compromise, in the form of the execution of a new altarpiece.

A drawing of a *Kneeling Figure Seen from Behind*, now in Leeds the collection of the Earl of Harewood (Von Hadeln 1927, pl. 37; Popham 1931, no. 267), provides further evidence for this. That the Leeds drawing can be traced to Titian's studies for the *Pentecost* seems beyond doubt. The Tietzes (1936), noting how the drawing mirrors the figure of Saint Peter in the painting now at the Salute, saw in it a preparatory study for the first version of the altarpiece, which according to Vasari can be dated 1541, also a plausible date for the drawing, according to the Tietzes.

The Leeds drawing is not only in reverse, but presents striking differences of conception with respect to the extant painting, going beyond the normal relationship between a preparatory study and its final painted presentation. These differences are all the more interesting since Titian in composing the second version, as we suppose, had no reason to distance himself, in this part, from the way the image was conceived and realized in the first version. In fact, he followed the first closely, but with variations that appear significant in the light of the lawsuit that had taken place.

The remaking of the altarpiece was pressing. The sojourn in Rome beginning the following October probably determined what happened. In September 1545 Titian was in Urbino and Pesaro, the guest of Guidobaldo II di Montefeltro. In October he arrived in Rome, where he was the guest of Pope Paul III, summoned there by Cardinal Alessandro Farnese, who in-

formed Vasari of it. He remained there until the beginning of June 1546, staying in rooms in the Belvedere where Michelangelo visited him, and Vasari and Sebastiano del Piombo competed in "leading him to see all the things of Rome." During his stay he painted the celebrated portraits of the Pope and his newphews, and for Ottavio Farnese he painted the *Danäe* now in Naples (see cat. no. 40), so dominated by that renewed feeling for light that was to become typical of Titian in this and the subsequent phase, in which he put behind him the analysis of form prompted by his mannerist experience. The second version of the *Pentecost* is in some ways anomalous in Titian's oeuvre, and is generally regarded as such. This is most easily explained by the internal requirements of the theme itself, of its '*invenzione*' and of the distribution of the elements of which it is composed. It consists of fifteen figures in a group – the Madonna, the Apostles, and the others who were with them in the meeting place at the moment of the descent of the Holy Spirit – distributed canonically in the space on the basis of old iconographic tradition, in a pyramid that has its peak in the dove, symbol of the Spirit. This makes sense in light of the original location of the altarpiece destined to be seen from below looking up. The rays of light radiating from the dove terminate in the tongues of fire on the head of each of the witnesses.

The space within which the event takes place – well over half of the large altarpiece – shows a discipline unusual not only in Titian but in the painting of the Veneto in general, with a highly developed architectonic structure, clearly and incisively delineated. On powerful supporting elements dominated by a prominent cornice rests a barrel-vaulted, coffered ceiling, and in the background is an open window.

Such a conception does not seem casual: such an array of architectonic elements, so lucidly and brilliantly composed, indicates a design tailored to the argument.

Specific elements, such as the clearly defined profiles, and the cast shadows that point to the openings in the two lateral sustaining blocks seem to be drawn from a repertoire accessible in, for example, the *Secondo Libro* of Serlio. But the general ordering of the space and the visual syntax that serves it, and together redefine it, seem based on a global experience requiring circumstances of the greatest moment.

Among "the things of Rome" that Titian saw for the first time were the "structure" *par excellence*, the "monument," the great building of the "new" Saint Peter's.

The state of the building of Saint Peter's is documented by some celebrated drawings by Heemskerck (1532-35) and by others, that record a state of progress that remained substantially unchanged until 1545-46.

The building of Saint Peter's at the time was extremely complex and susceptible to many different influences. What remained of the ancient paleo-Christian basilica greatly emphasized the form of the new building, recent and incomplete. In close contiguity with the old building rose the giant northeastern pillar erected by Bramante; on the opposite side, at the corresponding southeastern pillar, the two piers were connected by the large coffered arch vaulted by Bramante himself. The posthumous testimony of Vasari bore enthusiastic witness to the latter's technical skill. Beyond the great crossing space, to be covered by the cupola, rose the "doric wall" built provisionally by Bramante; behind it were the other two giant piers and the corresponding coffered arch on the north-south axis that gave access to "Bramante's choir." The motif of the coffers is fully evident in a drawing (Uffizi 1848A) that seems to be a plan and documents a primary visual aspect of the work (Thoenes 1937). Two drawings of the Uffizi (4Av. and 5Ar.), among others, document it, showing also, at the planning stage, the image of the tripartite windows of the Bramante choir, which were only partially realized. The sight of the new Saint Peter's, which was under construction in 1545-46 and above all that which remained... of Bramante, must have made an enormous impression on Titian. The clarity, the masterly balance of mass, the grand arches connnecting the crossing and the choir undoubtedly left their mark. An echo is probably found in Titian's brilliantly modelled architecture in the *Pentecost*. It proves how much importance the painter gave to this aspect of the painting (Pilo 1989).

Saint Peter's was the mother church of Christianity. Its reconstruction in progress signified the reaffirmation of the central and indisputable role that the Catholic Church claimed for itself. The Pentecost was the presupposition of every visible manifestation of the Church in the world.

In the wake of the opening of the Council of Trent begun in December 1545, the ideal solution for resolving the urgent problem of the remaking of the altarpiece for Santo Spirito could have been to borrow the central theme of the "new" basilica of Saint Peter.

If this hypothesis is true, this prior fact, the immediate influence of the Roman experience, would justify the dating soon after 1546, which other internal references in the altarpiece offer seem to favor on their own account, supported by the evidence of works such as the *Crowning with Thorns* for Santa Maria delle Grazie (Louvre; 1540; see Binaghi Olivari in the forthcoming *Arte Veneta*) and the above-mentioned *Danäe* for Ottavio Farnese. This dating would also comply with a careful rereading of the encomiastic – but, as always in these cases, pertinent – quatrains by Boschini.

LITERATURE Vasari 1568 (ed. Milanesi 1881), VII, 444; Van Dyck ff 96v.-97; Ridolfi 1648 (ed. Von Hadeln), I, 175; Boschini 1660, 163; Boschini 1664, 348; Boschini 1674, *D.D.*, 25; Martinelli 1684, 389; Ganessa 1705, 440; Zanetti 1733 (ed. 1797), 26; Zanetti 1771, 106-07; Crowe and Cavalcaselle 1877,

II, 68-73; Phillips 1898; Gronau 1900; Fischel 1904, XXVII; Fischel 1907, XXXVIII, 192, 320, 336; Lorenzetti 1926, 530; Fogolari 1935, 158-59, no. 78; Suida 1935, 134, 178; Tietze 1936, I, 208-09; Tietze and Tietze-Conrat 1936, 137-92; Tietze 1949, 399, pl. 237; Tietze 1950, 398, pl. 237; Pallucchini 1953-54, I, 195-96; Berenson 1957, I, 191; Valcanover 1960, II, pl. 70; Pallucchini 1969, I, 93, 148, 303; Wethey 1969, I, 121-22; Valcanover 1969, 125; Niero 1980, 25-26; Sambo 1980, 383-93; Ruggeri Augusti 1986, 119; Chiari Moretto Wiel 1988, 52-53; Pilo 1989, 152-67.

G.M.P.

44

Tityus

oil on canvas, 253×217 cm
Madrid, Museo del Prado (inv. no. 427)

RESTORATION 1969

According to the description of Calveta del Estrella, official chronicler of Philip II, on the occasion of the celebrations at the castle of Binche for the visit that Charles V and his heir made to Flanders in 1549, the painting was part of the decoration of the main hall and was placed over the windows with three other paintings.

It was Mary of Hungary, sister of the Emperor and governor of the Low Countries, who commissioned from Titian the series of paintings of "the damned," also known as "the furies." This is confirmed in 1557 by Ludovico Dolce, the artist's friend, who recalled that Titian had painted the canvases of *Tityus* and *Sisyphus* between 1548 and June 1549, at the time when Cardinal Granvella wrote to the painter to tell him that he had received two of the "four damned." Again in 1553, the *Tantalus*, promised by Titian, never reached Mary of Hungary, as we learn from the Imperial Ambassador's expressions of disappointment, and was substituted with a work by the Flemish artist Michiel van Coxie. The fourth canvas, which portrayed *Ixion*, appeared in an inventory of the paintings of Mary of Hungary, which was made upon her death in 1568, and was lost in the Alcázar fire of 1734 along with the *Tantalus* canvas, once the entire series had become the property of the Spanish monarch and had been transferred to Madrid before 1566.

The choice of theme was not casual, considering the symbolic weight of the mythological figures chosen to decorate the residence of the representative of the Spanish Sovereign. The large dimensions of the paintings would have also emphasized the moral significance of their subjects.

The story of Tityus and his companions was taken from Ovid's *Metamorphoses* (Book IV) in which Juno, after having entered the doors of Hell, arrives in the place of the damned where Sisyphus pushes his sandstone, Tityus lies chained while a vulture tears at his internal organs, Ixion is tied to a wheel in perpetual motion and Tantalus tries vainly to quench his thirst. The reasons for the tortures inflicted on the damned vary according to the interpreters of Ovid: Juan Perez de Moya, in his *Filosofía Secreta* (1585) written soon after Philip II received the series of paintings, attributed the punishment inflicted on Tityus to the fact that "having tried to use violence against Latona, he provoked the anger of Apollo and Diana who shot him with thunderbolts and condemned him to Hell where he remained bound; here the vultures devoured his internal organs which continued to grow again and in this way they never stop being eaten nor does Tityus ever stop suffering."

Perez de Moya also recalled how Lucretius (Book III) considered Tityus a symbol of sexual depravity. Strabo mentioned that he was "a tyrant and a cruel and degenerate man in his sexual behaviour, that Apollo killed with his arrows." Other interpreters explained that Apollo had imprisoned him in the depths of the earth because he had tried to take possession of the Oracle of Delphi or that the myth demonstrated how human strength, however great, could be punished by divine justice. So Tityus' torment could have been the consequence of his sexual appetite for a mother with children or of the insolent pride led led him to compete with a divinity for the sacred oracle. Titian's canvas, whose meaning is completed by the others of the same series, placed the emphasis on the perils of infidelity, which were a threat to the Sovereign, on moderation in the expansionism that could have threatened the property of the Crown, and on the divine origin of the power of the monarch to whom fearful respect should always be shown. Titian portrayed a subject of colossal dimensions, belonging to the tradition of pictorial gigantism of Michelangelo. Situated in the foreground and occupying the entire surface of the painting, Tityus lies chained to a mass of rocks and tree trunks, arms open, while he struggles in vain to free himself from the voracity of an eagle, portrayed here instead of a vulture, the predatory bird that feeds on live prey. The unstable position of the corpulent figure and the drama of the event create a mood of intense agitation, accentuated by murky tonalities that reveal a mannerist handling of colors.

The paintings were greatly admired by the Spanish sovereigns and had a special place in their principal Madrid residence, giving their name to one of the rooms ("Hall of the Furies"). They were later placed in the "Hall of the Mirrors" where they suffered the consequences of the 1734 fire. The surviving paintings, *Tityus* and *Sisyphus*, passed to the Palacio del Buen Retiro and later decorated the "antechamber" of the new Palacio Real until they entered the Prado in 1828.

LITERATURE Dolce 1557, 192, 333-36; Vasari 1558 (ed. Milanesi 1881) II, 451; Ridolfi 1648 (Von Hadeln 1914), I, 192; Palomino 1724 (ed. 1947), 804; Ponz 1776, VI, 28; Clea Bermúdez 1800, V, 39; Madrazo 1843, 162, no. 756; Crowe and Cavalcaselle 1877, II, 197; Justi 1889, 183; Gronau 1921, 156; Beroqui 1926, 155-6, 248-53, 305; Suida 1935, 95, 100, 176, 177, fig. 229; Tietze 1936, II, 298-9; Panofsky 1939, 217; Berenson 1957, 188; Valcanover 1970, II, 55; *Catologo Museo del Prado* 1969, no. 427; Pallucchini 1969, 126, 127, 291, fig. 341; Panofsky 1969, no. 320; Laufuente Ferrari 1970, 159; Bremejo de la Rica 1974, 278; Wethey 1975, III, 157-60; Rosand 1978, 40, fig. 53; Angulo Iñíguez 1979, 146-50; López Torrijos 1985; Bosque 1985, 43; Orso 1986, 45, 70-9, 82, 83, 95, 96, 162, 181, fig. 22.

J.U.

45

Saint John the Almsgiver

oil on canvas, 229×156 cm
Venice, Chiesa di San Giovanni Elemosinario

EXHIBITIONS   Venice 1935, Lausanne 1947, Venice 1981,
Moscow-Leningrad 1986, Sidney 1988
RESTORATION   1989-90, L. Savio

The altarpiece has always decorated the main altar of the
church of San Giovanni Elemosinario, Venice. It has been
returned as far as possible to its original dimensions for this
exhibition. The results of the restoration and of the related
technical and scientific examinations are recounted by Giovanna Nepi Scirè in her essay in this catalog.
After recording that Titian had executed in 1530 (actually
1532-33) in Bologna a portrait of Charles v "completely
armed," through the mediation of Pietro Aretino and Cardinal
Ippolito de' Medici, Giorgio Vasari (1568) continued: "On
returning to Venice Titian found many nobles had taken up
Pordenone, loudly praising his works on the ceiling of the hall
of the Pregadi and elsewhere. They had obtained for him a
commission to execute a panel in San Giovanni Elemosinario,
to be done in competition with Titian, who shortly before had
done Saint John the Almsgiver there dressed as a bishop." This
chronology for the painting, reiterated by Ridolfi (1648), and
apparently supported by the 1533 date on the altar frame, has
been accepted above all by earlier critics. Fogolari (1935), even
if he separates the altarpiece from the date of 1533, evidently
that of the construction of the altar (Tietze 1950), places it
between 1530 and 1535. Friedländer (1965) instead proposed
a dating between 1535 and 1537, given the connections of the
figure type of the saint in the altarpiece with the drawing of
Saint Augustine by Pordenone in Windsor (no. 5458), datable
c. 1529 and supposedly preparatory for one of the frescoes
executed by Pordenone in the cupola of San Giovanni Elemosinario, of which some fragments have recently been
recovered.
Furlan (1981) mentioned that the pose of the saint in the
Windsor drawing, which is related to the composition in
Piacenza, was reworked in another drawing, in Oxford, which
in turn is similar to that of Saint John the Almsgiver by Titian,
"who on more than one occasion seems to have taken cues or
stimuli from the works of his dangerous rival." This may have
been the case with the altarpiece of Saint John the Almsgiver,
which is later than both the frescoes and the altarpiece with
Saints Sebastian, Roch and Catherine, painted by Pordenone
most likely between 1530 and 1535, and was probably painted
by Titian after Pordenone's death in 1539. Roberto Longhi
(1946) also dropped the early dating of the Titian altarpiece,
after Tietze (1950) who proposed the 1540s (1540/45). Longhi
elaborated in his sharp prose on his view that the Titian should

be dated c. 1545, at the end of Titian's "mannerist crisis":
"Compared to the innocent candor of the Saint Mark that,
amber-colored, shines in the early altar of the Salute, what
moral pride, what stubborn authority! Florence and Rome
have by now convinced Titian that humanity, even as a beggar,
cannot act but be invested with dignity and power; but the
more the gesture is guarded violence (and here of a pre-
meditated contrast between reading and charity), the more
Titian tackles and consumes it, attacking every part with his
lashes of air and light, loaded and streaked in a kind, I would
say, of chromatic flagellation."
The date of the altarpiece, proposed for reasons of style by
Roberto Longhi, should today be revised now that the painting's visible aspect has been freed from repainting and encrust-
ation of non-original, altered varnishes. The brushwork and
handling so similar to those of the Tityus (see cat. no. 44) and
Sisyphus in the Prado, and above all to the Santa Maria Nuova
Saint Jerome, today in the Brera, locate the Saint John rather
before 1550, the date assigned to it by Wethey (1969).
Bracketed between shade and light, like Saint Mark in the
early altarpiece of Santo Spirito in Isola, Saint John, Patriarch
of Alexandria, sits astride a diagonal axis leading from the
beggar in the lower left to the bishop's crosier held by the
young assistant on the right. Thus Titian repeated the compositional plan of the the Pesaro Madonna (see cat. no. 18),
turning however from a sumptuous variety of dense color to
low-keyed colors, varying the subdued tonalities within the
narrow range of ambers that reflect the disquiet that by this
time distances Titian from that certainty in the fate of man that
nourished the images of his first maturity.
The forms are articulated with complexity, but each plastic
tension is described within the sensuous preciosity of a tinted
and dense atmosphere. Against the dark blue sky variegated by
clouds, and under the curtain that falls to the left, a device that
Titian had tried and abandoned in the Pesaro Madonna, the
saint, holding the large open book with his left hand and
twisting his torso, addresses himself to the beggar, offering him
alms. The grainy pigments in the chiaroscuro harmonize
marvelously in simplified relationships: the violet-brown of the
cope, the iridescent white in the gray of the surplice, the wine
red of the robe, as unprecedented as the greens and dark
browns with which the mendicant and the assistant emerge
from the deep gulfs of shadow.
The brushwork is of irrepressible strength, in rapid and broad
phrasing, whose crossed and superimposed strokes generate
an ineffable expressiveness. Such extraordinary dynamism of
handling, with its crescendo of touches creating a design
susceptible to an interactive exchange of color and light,
affirms how Titian, having adopted the matter of paint as the
main protaganist of his art, in the altarpiece of Saint John the
Almsgiver, initiated the magic "impressionism" with which he

would express with ever greater desperation the tragedy and anguish of human existence.

LITERATURE   Vasari 1568, III, 570; Ridolfi 1648, I, 123, 171, 417; Crowe and Cavalcaselle 1877, I, 354; Fogolari 1935, no. 24; Longhi 1946, 24; Tietze 1950, 397; Friedländer 1965, 120-21; Wethey 1969, 138; Gould 1972, 109ff; Furlan 1980, 74; Valcanover 1981, 106.

F.V.

46.

Portrait of a Captain with a Cupid and a Dog

oil on canvas, 229×155.5 cm
Kassel, Staatliche Kunstsammlungen Gemäldegalerie Alte Meister (cat. no. 488)

EXHIBITION Vienna, Kassel 1955-56
RESTORATION 1956-61, S. von Reden

Originally in the collection of the Duc de Tallard, Paris, the painting was purchased in 1756 in Paris by Wilhelm VIII of Hesse-Kassel.
Not cited by Vasari and unknown to the other sources, the portrait was first mentioned in Paris by Mariette (1720), to whom it seemed "déplaisant." Not even the critics of the nineteenth and early twentieth centuries fully appreciated this masterpiece: Morelli (1890-93), Berenson (1894, 1906) and Gronau (1900, 1904) did not associate it with Titian at all. Only after Justi (1894) identified the portrait as that of Giovanni Francesco Acquaviva, Duke of Atri, did critics begin to take seriously the question of the identity of the portrayed figure: "Dieudonne de Gozon, Grand Master of the Malta Order" according to the eighteenth – century French inventories, and "Alfonso d'Avalos, Marchese del Vasto," in the nineteenth – century catalogues of Kassel. All these names were rejected first by Suida (1933) and then by Von Hadeln (1934), who published another portrait of Acquaviva, at that time and still today in a private collection. The portrait remained anonymous until 1977 when Wethey, unconvincingly, returned to the person of Acquaviva. In 1977 Siebenhüner put forward Emanuele Filiberto of Savoy (1528-80), while Ost (1982) suggested Gabriele Serbelloni (1509-80), soldier of fortune who fought with Charles V and Captain of Pope Pius IV until 1559 when he switched to the service of Philip II. Hope (1983), however, was dubious. Whereas opinions continue to differ about the officer's identity, the consensus on the particular importance of the portrait, both for its iconographic complexity and for its outsize dimensions, is unanimous (Pallucchini 1969; Wethey 1971). There is general agreement too about its date. Crowe and Cavalcaselle (1878) suggested 1550-52 onward for the figure, and shifted the date of the landscape background back to c. 1560-70.
The dimensions, surpassing those of all other full-length portraits by Titian (excluding the equestrian portrait of Charles V in the Prado), imply the elevated social, political and economic status of the bearded man, sumptuously and eccentrically dressed. Certainly he must have held a prestigious military post. Indeed, apart from this Titian represented in full-length only Charles V, Philip II and the Prince Bishop of Trento, Cristoforo Madruzzo, who was very close to Charles V after the Council of Trent. Men who qualified for such "imperial" portraits were generally also men who would receive a public monument. In the Kassel painting the figure is represented as Mars, god of war. The artist may have been inspired by the Capitoline *Mars*, which he would have seen during his Roman sojourn of 1545-46.
Who then was this "New Mars" of 1550-52? Since Titian in this period had no contact with France, excepting a proposed portrait of the French ambassador Bonnivit referred to by Aretino in one of his letters, our man must be sought in the sphere of Charles V's military commanders or his noblest and most powerful allies, such as the Estes, the Della Rovere, the Medici or the Gonzaga. Gabriele Serbelloni can be rejected on historical grounds. Though esteemed as a man of arms by Charles V, and one of his "100 Illustrious Captains" as described by contemporary chroniclers, he was not a member of a sufficiently illustrious family. His political career began only in 1559 with Pope Pius VI, but by that time the Kassel portrait was already complete or nearly complete, at least in the figurative part.
The mysterious unknown soldier could instead be Ferrante Gonzaga (1507-57), third son of the Marchesi Francesco and Isabella di Este, sent by his father to the court of Charles V in Madrid. In 1546 he succeeded Alfonso d'Avalos as governor of Milan. As early as 1534 he was in contact with Titian, through his brother Federico, who was by 1530 Duke of Mantua. In the following years Titian executed various works for Ferrante who acquired as governor of Milan a key role for the payment of pensions assigned to Titian by Charles V and payable from the city treasury. The letters between them were numerous, from 1548 to 1551, concerning paintings but above all the pension. In April 1549 Pietro Aretino wrote to Ferrante, dedicating a sonnet to him, in which he eulogized him as the "New Mars," "God of Wisdom and Valor," "unconquered Duke," "Italian hero, divine Ferrante" (Aretino, *Lettere*, 1609). It is perfectly possible either that Gonzaga commissioned a portrait of himself from Titian at this time or more likely that Titian himself made the portrait on his own initiative, in order to secure a pension. This theory is strengthened by the strong resemblance between the painting and the monument erected to Ferrante Gonzaga in Guastalla by Leone Leoni in 1594.
It is not easy to reconstruct the painting's movements after its completion. There is no trace of it in the inventories of Mantua and Guastalla, nor is it known how and when it reached France, from whence in the eighteenth century it found its way to Kassel.

LITERATURE Mariette 1858-9, V, 329; Lehmann 1980, 256-9 (with preceding bibliography); Sunderland-Wethey and Wethey 1980, 89-96; Ost 1982, *passim*; Hornig 1982, 359ff; Pochat 1984, 145ff; Schleier 1985, 627; Lehmann 1986, 37-40.

J.M.L.

47

Portrait of Cristoforo Madruzzo

oil on canvas, 210×109 cm
São Paulo, Collection Museu de Arte de São Paolo

EXHIBITIONS   Trento 1987, Milan 1988
RESTORATION   1956

The inscription visible today on the painting are as follows: in the background at the top right: ANNO MDLII AETATIS/SUAE XXXVIII/TICIAN... FECIT; on the clock: 1552. Other inscriptions existed on the pages under the clock and possibly on the step in the lower left. The painting was last restored by Picchetto in New York before its acquisition by the São Paolo Museum. However, even during restoration it was not possible to decipher more of the inscriptions.

Originally in the Castello del Buonconsiglio in Trento, where Cristoforo Madruzzo was prince-bishop, the painting remained there when his nephew Ludovico succeeded to this office in 1567 (Camesasca 1987). A 1559 inventory of the castle (Innsbruck, *Archivio Imperiale della Luogotenenza, Tient*, Cat. C.M. no. 105; Camesasca 1987) recorded it in the "'stua' of the Bishops." In 1648 Ridolfi noted that Titian "upon his return to Italy" – most likely after his second sojourn in Germany in August 1551 – "visited the Cardinal of Trento who wanted to be portrayed by him."

Vasari (1568), however, cited the "Portrait of the Cardinal of Trento, then a young man," just after that of Don Diego Mendoza, which he claimed was of 1541. The work reappeared in an inventory of 1682, among the possessions of the Roccabruna of Trento. After the family's extinction in 1735, the painting passed by inheritance to the Guadenti della Torre barons (Emert 1939), from whom Valentino Salvatori of Trento inherited it in 1855 (Oberzinner 1900-01). The Salvatoris sold it around 1905 to Mme Trotti of Paris, who gave it to J. Stillmann, causing a heated polemic in the September 1906 *Gazzetta di Venezia* about its clandestine exportation. The heirs of the new owner transferred it to New York in 1907. At this time, possibly before leaving Italy, the work underwent a misleading repainting that fused the stockings and the edges of the clothes into one, giving the mistaken impression of a pair of breeches. This effect does not appear in Fischel's 1920 monograph and thus must have been eliminated before that date (Camesasca 1987). The painting was bought by Avery Rockefeller in 1942, then by Knoedler's in 1950. In the same year it became part of the collections of the museum of São Paolo.

The figure represented is Cristoforo Madruzzo, born to a noble family of Trento on 5 July 1511. His father's prestige permitted him to obtain canonry in Trento and the parishes of Merano and Lienz at a very young age. He became deacon of the Duomo of Trento and Canon of Augsburg, Salzburg and Bressanone. Between 1532 and 1537 he studied law in Bologna. In 1539, upon the death of Clesio, he became prince-bishop of Trento. In 1542 became bishop of Bressanone as well, and in 1545 was nominated cardinal. An eminent figure at the Council of Trent, he frequently took a courageous stance between empire and papacy. He died in Tivoli in 1577, as stated on his epitaph in the Roman church of Sant'Onofrio (Forcella 1979).

The chronological placement of the painting between 1542 and 1552 has been greatly debated owing to differing interpretations of the sources, beginning with Vasari's equivocal citation immediately following the portrait of Mendoza, dated 1541, but including certain letters. For example, in a letter of 10 July 1542 a correspondent informed the Prince-Bishop that Titian had finished his portrait (Oberziner 1900-01). But when Titian went to Augsburg for the first time in 1548 he stopped in Ceneda, where Count Girolamo della Torre introduced him to Madruzzo, at that time with Charles V and his court (Crowe and Cavalcaselle 1877). Thus, if the artist had already executed a portrait of the prince-bishop, it would have been unnecessary in 1548 to have needed an introduction by way of a hired person (Wethey 1971).

Discussion also revolves around the dates legible on the work itself. The indication of the subject's age (thirty-eight years), the portrait's similarity to Titian's *Philip in Armor* (Prado, Madrid), begun in 1551, or that of Capodimonte of 1553, in addition to the 1552 date repeated in the inscription and on the clock, support Camesasca's (1987), Dell'Acqua's (1955) and Morassi's (1966) assumptions either that the portrait "documented" in 1542 was finished ten years later, or that this is a second portrait of Madruzzo. On the 1552 dating Pallucchini (1969) and Wethey (1971) agree.

LITERATURE   Wethey 1971, 116-17, no. 62; Camesasca 1987, (with full bibliography).

P.M.B.

48

Venus with an Organist and Dog

oil on canvas, 136×220 cm
Madrid, Museo del Prado (inv. no. 420)

EXHIBITION   Tokyo 1987
RESTORATION   1965

Painted for the Venetian Francesco Assonica, this *Venus* was later acquired by King Charles I of England, upon whose death in 1649 it was bought by the Spanish ambassador for the royal collections. The painting is listed in the 1666 inventory of the paintings of the Alcázar of Madrid.

This was not Titian's first canvas of this theme, since in 1548 he delivered to the Emperor visiting Hamburg a painting identical to that of the Museo del Prado (inv. no. 421) and signed by the artist. In addition to being of higher quality, it presents a figure of Cupid instead of the little dog, and the young musician is differently posed. The splendid body of Venus dominates the scene, adding to the sensuousness of her graces a sense of quiet and repose disturbed only by the playful instincts of the little animal. The red velvet on which the nude goddess lies, and the pink curtain set off the feminine body and small head with its blonde hair held up with clips and a string of pearls.

The presence of the organist, dressed, armed with a sword and attracted by the nudity of Venus, contributes to the high-keyed eroticism of the scene. Sensuality is expressed even by the perfect Renaissance garden that appears in the background: a pair of lovers on the left, fawns in amorous combat and the satyr of the fountain on which a peacock perches.

The richness of the tonalities unites the sense of visual beauty, underlined by the unabashed female nude and by the natural setting, with the pleasure of hearing the music played by the young organist. Venus thus becomes the goddess of beautiful sounds and the synthesis of a notion of beauty with clear Neoplatonic connotations.

Titian's interest in this theme was constant and he painted at least five versions. Its originality derives from the inclusion of the musician in the representation of Venus. The artist, who knew Petrarch's madrigal poetry, made music one of his favorite pastimes, thanks in part to an instrument received as a gift from Alessandro degli Organi.

The painting suffered serious damage in the area of the abdomen and the legs of Venus during the Napoleonic wars and was restored before its return to Spain in 1816. This, together with the existence of several versions of this subject, attenuates the value of a work which probably involved workshop collaboration. Dateable to c. 1550, the painting was acquired by the Prado in 1827.

LITERATURE Ridolfi 1648 (ed. Von Hadeln 1914), I, 194; Ponz 1793 (ed. 192), V, 57; Madrazo 1843, no. 459; Crowe and Cavalcaselle 1877, II, 158; Madrazo 1884, 130; Gronau 1904; Beroqui 1925, 84; Suida 1935, 118, 175; Tietze 1930, II, 296; Beroqui 1946, 78-84; Berenson 1957, 187; Bottineau 1958, 319; Valcanover 1960, II, fig. 33; *Catalogo Museo del Prado* 1963, no. 420; Panofsky 1969, fig. 137; Pallucchini 1969, 293; Lafuente Ferrari 1970, 169; Aguilera 1972, 146; Sarfatti 1973, fig. 66; Wethey 1975, III, 63-8, 199, 201, no. 50; Angulo Iñígues 1979, 141; Clark 1980, 18; Goodman 1983, 178-86; Praz 1986, fig. XXV; Studdert and Kennedy 1987, 27-40.

J.U.

49

Portrait of Daniele Barbaro

oil on canvas, 81×69 cm
Madrid, Museo del Prado (cat. no. 414)

RESTORATION 1951

Daniele Matteo Alvise Barbaro was born in Venice on 8 February 1514 to an important noble Venetian family. He began his schooling in Verona, where his family lived, and then continued his studies at the University of Padua, where he studied with Benedetto Lampridio, a commentator on Aristotle and a great authority on ancient texts. Barbaro studied philosophy at the courses of Marcantonio de Passeri and Vincenzo Maggi, as well as mathematics, astronomy, natural sciences, medicine and optics, demonstrating a wide variety of interests.

In the course of his university studies, he was intimate with personalities such as Domenico Morosini, Ludovico Beccadelli and Bernardo Navagero, and frequented the company of Benedetto Varchi and Sperone Speroni. He knew Pietro Bembo and in 1540 he participated in the foundation of the Accademia degli Infiammati. In the same year he received his doctorate in Arts. In 1545 the Republic nominated him Superintendent of the construction of the Botanical Garden of Padua, which was intended to promote medical studies. Three years later he was nominated "Provveditore di Comune," a position that acquainted him with the condition of the poorest classes. His career in the service of the Serenissima culminated in 1549, with his nomination as ambassador to the Court of Saint James, residing in London until 1551, the year in which he became Patriarch of Aquileia, succeeding Giovanni Grimani.

Barbaro took part in the Council of Trent and in 1561 established his residence there, contributing among other things to the debate on the inclusion of books on the Index with notable prudence and good sense. In 1563 he returned to Verona, although meanwhile in Rome repeated, but unsuccessful, attempts were made to raise him to the cardinalate. There can be no doubt that his career took second place to his philosophical and literary interests. In 1556 he translated and edited Vitruvius' *Dieci Libri dell'Architettura* and in 1569 wrote an original work, *La Pratica della Prospettiva*, which attracted considerable interest and was widely influential. Barbaro died in Verona on 13 April 1570.

In the Madrid painting Barbaro looks about forty years old. He is portrayed in three-quarter length, with a book in his left hand. He gazes into the middle distance while his closed lips denote tension. The light that falls on his head and clenched hand conveys his penetrating and intellectual mind.

This is probably the painting that in 1650 belonged to J. van Uffel, Antwerp, in whose collection it was engraved by Hollar, and replicates, in a tighter composition, the portrait mentioned in a letter by Aretino in 1545 in Paolo Giovio's collection in Como, and now in the National Gallery of Canada, Ottawa. The latter work, in contrast to the Prado portrait, bears an inscription naming the sitter.

In 1666 the *Daniele Barbaro* was mentioned for the first time in Spain, in an inventory of the Alcazar, Madrid, and was included in the inventories of 1686 and 1734 of the same palace, correctly attributed to Titian. Before 1843 it was acquired by the Prado from the Spanish Royal Collections.

LITERATURE   Madrazo 1843, 143, no. 682; Crowe and Caval-caselle 1877, II, 446; Allende Balazar, Sanchez Canton 1919, 64-5; Beroqui 1926, 245-6; Idem 1946, 99-101; Venturi 1932, 482; Suida 1935, 89, 172; Tietze 1936, II, 299; Berenson 1957, 187; Valcanover 1960, I, 191; *Catalogo Museo del Prado* 1963, no. 414; Valcanover 1969, no. 336; Pallucchini 1969, 283, fig. 298-9; Wethey 1971, II, 81; Angulo Iñíguez 1979, 179.

J.U.

DANIELE BARBARO

50

Portrait of Doge Francesco Venier

oil on canvas, 113×99 cm
Lugano, Thyssen-Bornemisza Collection

EXHIBITIONS London 1964-65, Washington-Detroit-Minneapolis-Cleveland, Los Angeles-Denver-Forthworth-New York 1979-81, Paris 1982, Moscow-Leningrad Kiev 1983-84

Francesco Venier, who was elected doge on 11 June 1564 and died two years later on 2 June 1656, was the last doge whose portrait Titian painted for the Palazzo Ducale, in his role as official painter to the State. In 1517, less than a year after the death of Giovanni Bellini, Titian had succeeded to the coveted 'sensaria del Fondaco dei Tedeschi,' a traditional sinecure for the official painters to the Republic who apart from being exempt from paying taxes were entitled to 100 *scudi* annually and to an additional 25 *scudi* for each ducal portrait or votive painting of the doge kneeling before the Virgin and surrounded by saints for public installation in the Palazzo Ducale. Venier commissioned his portrait from Titian, together with a votive painting of his predecessor Marcantonio Trevisan, soon after his election. The portrait was completed at the beginning of 1555 (Titian received payment on March of that year) and placed in the Sala del Maggior Consiglio where it was later destroyed, together with Titian's other portraits and innumerable priceless treasures, in the disastrous fire of 1577. Venier also commissioned from Titian the votive painting of Doge Antonio Grimani (d. 1523) as if to atone for the unjust condemnation of Grimani in 1499 when he was 'Capitan da Mar' and was severely defeated by the Turks at the Battle of Zonchio. The Grimani painting remained in Titian's studio at his death, probably because it was unfinished, thus escaping destruction in the 1577 fire. After Venier's death Titian ceased to portray further doges: the two succeeding doges, Lorenzo and Girolamo Priuli, relieved him of the task and contracted Girolamo di Tiziano and Jacopo Tintoretto instead. This extremely fine portrait, together with the very few other extant ducal portraits by Titian (not more than three, including this one, can be considered securely autograph), compensates for the loss of the others destroyed by fire. It was surely painted from life, before the summer of 1556. The vitality of the sitter's glance and posture, and the strong sense of personality that emanates from this painting, exclude the possibility that this might be a posthumous image. The expression of the lean face, the eyes shining like those of a sick man, seems to project an inner pensiveness, an unrelieved anxiety, and while the aquiline nose, the veins prominent on the temples, the hollowed cheeks and the thinned beard, project physical infirmity and premature aging, the tight lips and the erect head with a remnant of pride, conscious of status, express self-confidence and determination. The thin body seems yet more fragile and oppressed by suffering, suggested by the way the left hand grips almost fiercely at the rich gold mantle as if to relieve him of its weight, while the right reaches forward in a delicate gesture of peace, but also of fearful concern. Francesco Venier was by this time close to death. We know that he suffered chronic ill-health, and during his reign was so enfeebled that he could walk only when sustained by two servants. But we also know that he lived a severe and frugal life and was a skilled administrator.
The landscape glimpsed through the window, with a fire on the lagoon and a sailboat blown by the same winds that fan the distant flames and draw the smoke toward the low clouds of the last light of evening, is one of Titian's finest, perhaps the most beautiful among those fleeting and sparkling visions that, beginning in this period, appear behind his portraits and his religious and secular works and accentuate the vital immediacy of his technique.
This portrait was likely to have been painted in 1555, the same year as the official portrait made for the Palazzo Ducale, a dating that matches perfectly the stylistic features of the piece. It was formerly in the collection of Prince Trivulzio, and was published by Von Hadeln for the first time soon after it entered the Thyssen collection, in 1930. It has been unanimously accepted by all subsequent writers.

LITERATURE Von Hadeln 1930, 489, 492; Hanfstaengl 1930, 18; Suida 1933, 108-09, 168; Idem 1933[2], 106-07, 187; Tietze 1936, 207; Pallucchini 1969, I, 159, 303, 341, II, pls. 400, 401; Valcanover 1969, I, 124-25, no. 381; Pallucchini 1977, 44; Walter 1978, 81; Pignatti 1981, II no. 363, 4-26.

G.B.

51

Venus with a Mirror

oil on canvas, 124.5×104.1 cm
Washington, National Gallery of Art
Andrew W. Mellon Collection 1937.1.34 (34)

EXHIBITIONS   Los Angeles 1979

The earliest mention of a "Venus looking into a mirror" painted by Titian occurs in the list of his works delivered to King Philip II, of 1574: "Venus con Amor gli tiene il specchio." Early writers (Crowe and Cavalcaselle 1877) assumed that this lost picture was a replica of the celebrated *Venus with a Mirror*, then in the Hermitage and now in the National Gallery in Washington. Other known treatments of the theme were likewise thought to derive from the same painting. But, as a comprehensive study by Poglayen-Neuwall (1934) demonstrated, the various copies and variants, together with written sources, indicate that there were formerly at least two major compositions by the master, in addition to the extant version in Washington. One of these was the picture for Philip II, while the second, described by Ridolfi (1648), belonged to the jurist Niccolò Crasso. Crasso's picture showed two attendant cupids, one of whom supported the mirror, whereas in the Washington example the second cupid holds a wreath. Philip's painting featured only one cupid and, unlike the other two autograph versions, portrayed the goddess clothed (*Venus Genetrix*) rather than nude (*Venus Pudica*). More recent studies (Wethey 1975, and Fomiciova 1977) suggest that the problem is even more complex than hitherto suspected. And it is not merely one of sorting out the innumerable copies and replicas, in order to establish the Titian prototypes, but also of determining how they were produced in his studio and afterwards (Hope 1980).

The x-radiograph published by Shapley (1971-72) sheds light on the evolution of the Washington painting. It reveals that the *Venus* was painted on a canvas Titian had previously used in a horizontal direction to depict two three-quarter length figures of a man and woman, standing side by side. Then, discarding that fine double portrait for some unknown reason, the artist turned the canvas to a vertical axis and painted a Venus similar in pose to the final version but differing in the details of her clothing. The nude goddess we see today was dressed initially in a white chemise, a more decorous arrangement also found in Rubens' copy after Titian at Lugano. But the importance of the x-radiograph is not limited to the portrait or the differently clothed Venus. A recent technical examination, carried out by Paula De Cristofaro of the Gallery's conservation department, revealed that one motif in the underpainted portrait, visible in the x-radiograph, was not covered over. The artist left exposed the man's coat (not armor, as sometimes stated) to form the velvet wrap encircling the lower part of Venus' body. This improvisation, typical of Titian, suggests that the Washington *Venus* may have preceded the other versions in which the wrap recurs. Another *pentimento* disclosed by the x-radiograph – the change in position of cupid's legs – also suggests that the Washington picture preceded those which adopt the final attitude.

Whether or not it was the first of Titian's depictions of *Venus with a Mirror*, the Washington painting has a unique status. Among the extant versions, it is the only one that is fully accepted as an autograph work by the master's own hand. Further, the picture has a history of ownership that goes back directly to his studio. Like the Hermitage *Magdalene*, which shares the same provenance, the *Venus with a Mirror* seems to have been kept by Titian until his death in 1576, perhaps because he was particularly fond of it or intended it to serve as a model for making replicas. In 1581 the canvas was sold by the master's son Pomponio Vecellio, together with the house and its other contents, to Cristoforo Barbarigo. Then, having been praised by Ridolfi (1648), Boschini (1660), and in Sansovino (1663), the picture was acquired from the Barbarigo heirs by Czar Nicholas I in 1850. Andrew Mellon finally purchased it from the Hermitage in 1931 and donated it to the National Gallery of Art six years later.

The iconography of the *Venus with a Mirror* is rich but not arcane. The protagonists and some of their accessories, like the wrap, reappear in a series of paintings of Venus with a musician that occupied Titian and his studio intermittently in the decades after 1548. In these works, Venus reclines, nude and bejeweled, on a couch accompanied by Cupid, who, in two cases, crowns his mother with a floral wreath. The principal cupid in the Washington picture holds up the mirror in which the goddess studies her reflection, so that the subject might be called Venus at her toilet. The motif of the mirror links the painting, in turn, with another, earlier series of half-length female figures by Titian representing comely mortals, most likely courtesans, of which a well-known example is the *Young Woman at Her Toilet* in the Louvre (Goodman-Soellner 1983). In the Washington picture Venus is seated on the couch, her hands held to her breast and lap in a modest gesture recalling that of the famous Roman statue of the goddess that later belonged to the Medici (Uffizi, Florence). Titian might have seen the antique (or a copy) in Rome during his sojourn of 1545-46, when, as he wrote, he was "learning from the marvelous ancient stones" being unearthed in the city.

Though recalling a classical prototype, Titian's Venus is, nevertheless, a flesh and blood creature who vividly expresses a contemporary ideal of beauty defined by the master (Rosand 1978). Titian's brush exploits the potential of the oil medium to convey textural effects: the goddess of love and beauty reveals as much as conceals her pliant flesh, as she pulls about

her the wrap of wine-colored velvet, trimmed with gold and silver and lined in fur, evoking the sense of touch, while pearls adorn the braids of her blond hair. Comparably opulent figures grace the mythologies Titian painted for Philip II in the 1550s. The Washington picture probably dates from the middle of the decade, between the *Venus and Adonis* of 1553-54 in the Prado and the *Diana and Actaeon* of 1556-59 in Edinburgh.

LITERATURE Ridolfi 1648, 181, 194; Boschini 1660, pp. 664-5; Sansovino 1663, 370; Crowe and Cavalcaselle 1877, II, 334-36; Poglayen-Neuwall 1934, 358-94; Valcanover 1960 (Italian ed.), II, 39-40, pl. 62; and (English ed.) 1960, III, 41, pl. 62; Pallucchini 1969, I, 143, 302. II, figs. 396-397, pl. XLIII; Valcanover 1969, 124-25, no. 384; Shapley 1971-72, 93-106; Wethey 1975, 200-3, 242-45, pls. 126-33; Fomiciova 1977, 195-9; Rosand 1978, 33-4, pl. 1; Pignatti 1979, 76-78, cat. no. 21; Shapley 1979, 476-80, pls. 341, 341a, b, c; Hope 1980, 158-60; Goodman-Soellner 1983, 426-42.

D.A.B.

Composite x-ray of the painting

52

Study of Legs for the Martyrdom
of Saint Lawrence

charcoal, white chalk, faded blue paper, 409×252 mm
Florence, Gabinetto Disegni e Stampe degli Uffizi
(no. 12907 F)

Inscribed in the bottom at center in pen, in a seventeenth-century (?) hand, "T^an". Cut along the lower edge. Worn along the traces of a horizontal crease in the center. The top left corner, cut, has been reintegrated with restoration. On the verso: sketches of figures.

The provenance of this sheet, from the collection of Cardinal Leopoldo de' Medici, is documented by a letter dated 20 November 1671, in which Paolo Del Sera, agent and trusted expert of Leopoldo in Venice, expresses his opinion on a group of drawings sent from Florence for his viewing. Among these, Del Sera wrote of having recognized a few "very beautiful" sheets by Titian and noted in particular a study of legs for the *Martyrdom of Saint Lawrence* in the Church of the Jesuits, clearly identifiable with the exhibited drawing (see Petrioli Tofani 1976).

After its publication by Von Hadeln (1924), who accepted as autograph only the recto but without perceiving its relationship to the Gesuiti altarpiece, the drawing was published again by Fröhlich-Bum (1928) as a late work by Titian, datable 1550-60, and by Popham (1931), who argued that it was a preliminary study for the *Saint Christopher* fresco in the Palazzo Ducale. Its connection with the Gesuiti altarpiece was established by Eugene von Rothschild (1931), who recognized in the drawing on the recto a preparatory study for the torturer on the right of the *Martyrdom of Saint Lawrence*. The upper part of this figure is barely sketched in a simple outline, while the legs, upon which the artist concentrated, spring energetically in a dynamic foreshortening, enhanced by darting lines and vibrant chiaroscuro rendered in charcoal smears and glowing chalk highlights partially worked with the brush. At the lower right Titian examined in detail the left foot, cut off by the lower margin of the sheet. The graphic style of this marvelous study reflects the transition from Titian's "mannerist experiences" to "that cursive and abbreviated pictorial structure, where the light rises with the pigments themselves" (Valcanover 1981), two stylistic phases represented among Titian's drawings in the 1550s by the *Horsemen* of Oxford and Munich, and by the study for the *Sacrifice of Abraham* of the Ecole des Beaux-Arts, Paris, on the one hand, and by the study for the *Agony in the Garden* of the Uffizi on the other. With respect to the years 1548 and 1559, between which the *Martyrdom of Saint Lawrence* was executed, the date of the drawing oscillates between that proposed by Rearick and Wethey at the beginning of the painting, c. 1548 (for Rosand c. 1547-48), and that preferred by Oberhuber and Pignatti

toward the end of the 50s. The latter seems, however, too advanced with respect to the style of the drawing, which is still tied to a "constructive sculptural" character (Chiari Moretto Weil 1989) proper to the drawings executed between the fourth and fifth decades.

The drawings on the verso of the sheet have given rise to contrasting views. Opinions range from a full acceptance of the sketches as Titian's (Rearick 1976), to a sweeping rejection by Wethey, who even attributed the upper torso sketched on the recto to another hand. The prevailing tendency, however, is to distinguish the interventions of a dilettante responsible at least for the profile at the center (Tietze and Tietze-Conrat 1944) from other possibly autograph sketches. The reclining half-length male is based on an antique model, the so-called *Bed of Polyclitus* (Rosand 1975) which, according to Rearick, would later have served as a point of departure for the *Entombment of Christ* (Prado, Madrid, no. 441).

LITERATURE Von Hadeln 1924, no. 31; Fröhlich-Bum 1928, 198, no. 38; *Exhibition...*1930, 311; 663; Popham 1931, 72, no. 263; Von Rothschild 1931, 205; Fogolari 1935, 213, no. 16; Tietze and Tietze-Conrat 1936, 186, 192, no. 34; Tietze 1937, 351; Tietze and Tietze-Conrat 1944, no. 1906; Tietze 1950, 38, 404; Valcanover 1960, 41; Forlani 1961, 42, no. 62; Valcanover 1969, 126; Pallucchini 1969, I, 333; Wethey 1969-75, I, 139-40; Rosand 1975, 242-45; Petrioli-Tofani 1981, 107; Rosand 1981, 306, no. 6; Valcanover 1981, 110; Wethey 1987, 40, 142, no. 17; Chiari Moretto Weil 1988, 33, 54, no. 29; Chiari Moretto Weil 1989, 20, 93, no. 29.

G.D.

Figure Sketches, verso

53

Martyrdom of Saint Lawrence

oil on canvas, 493×277 cm
Venice, Chiesa dei Gesuiti

EXHIBITIONS   Venice 1935, Venice 1971, Venice 1981
RESTORATION   1981, O. Nonfarmale.

The first to inform us of the patron of this altarpiece, which bears Titian's signature (possibly non-original), was the often-overlooked Zanotto (1860). He correctly named Lorenzo Massolo, and on the basis of Zanetti (1771), stated that the work preceded the version for Philip II by a few years. He also observed that none of the literary sources (Surius, Vettorius, Prudentius, Baronius, etc.) mentioned that the saint was forced to pray to the idols.

The vast collection of documents gathered by Gallo (1935) reveals that the altarpiece took several years to complete, which was not unusual for Titian. On 18 November 1548, Massolo, in making out his will, ordered that, besides himself, his wife and his daughter (who had died very young), "...no other should be placed in the said tomb, which is in the church of the Crosechieri in front of my altar...." This was the second chapel on the right side of the nave, evidently already erected even if not entirely finished. Massolo also arranged that some details of the tomb and the chapel be completed and noted that the altarpiece had still to be finished.

Massolo's exclusion of others from burial in his tomb was presumably motivated by the fact that his wife Elisabetta almost certainly had at about the age of fifty a son, Quirino, by Monsignor Giovanni della Casa. Upon Massolo's death, 25 January 1557, the widow pressed the executor of her will: "if the arch and altarpiece of the Crosechieri are not finished, have them finish it with the greatest speed possible...." This will (Biblioteca Museo Correr, Cod. Cic. 3423/17) followed one of ten years earlier (25 May 1547), probably drawn up at the time of her pregnancy and the above-mentioned birth, in which she requested "to be buried in the Church of the Crosichieri of Venice in *our tomb*...." Gallo concluded, and all subsequent critics have concurred, that the altarpiece was begun by Titian immediately after his return from Rome, where, it should be noted, the painter had gone on the insistence of Senator Girolamo Querini, Elisabetta's uncle. Even so, it is fair to remark (Gallo himself involuntarily hints at this, stressing the ties of friendship between Titian and the commissioning family and their willingness not to rush the painter) that some time may have elapsed between the commissioning of the work and its execution. Thus while the commission would date from after Titian's return from Rome and before Massolo's will (1546-47), work may not have begun until after his sojourn in Augsburg, from late 1547 to the final months of the following year. For reasons which we shall come

to later this seems to be the likeliest date for the laying – in of the composition. Evidently, this also applies to the study of the legs of the figure on the right, in the Uffizi (see cat. no. 52), which would confirm the theory of Chiari Moretto Wiel (1988), who has also recently published an updated bibliography (1989) on this painting.

While the references to classical architecture and borrowings from Roman sculpture are numerous, they are difficult to pin down precisely, and they seem more to be suggestive interpretations than precise citations. Even so, the latter are present, inevitably, since they constituted necessary working tools for any painting *atelier* of that time, above all Titian's, as aptly illustrated by Zanowsky (1938). Such models were easily available, both in Venice (the *Dying Gaul* of the Grimani Collection that inspired the saint is an incontrovertible example); (Beschi 1976), in the interpretative treatises of the period (Serlio *in primis*), and in Rome, in the meditation on "modern texts," above all those of Michelangelo and the late Raphael, considered the most authoritative interpreters of the antique. An example of the latter is the torturer who grips the body of Lawrence (Briganti 1981), who more nearly derives from Raphael's Baglioni *Entombment* in the Borghese Gallery than from the similar figure in Mantegna's engraving of the same subject (as proposed by Kennedy, 1956, 1958).

The subject has been amply discussed by Brendel (1955), Kennedy (1958), Pallucchini (1969), Beschi (1976), Battisti (1980, 1976), and summarized by Valcanover (1981). We shall limit ourselves to quoting Gentili (1980) who remarked that in Titian it is enough to evoke his immense "culture of images assembled piece by piece and uninterruptedly through his long career, to the point that even the written sources were respected as a repertoire of absolute value..." (1980), and from this to note how Saxl's "transmigration of images" (1957, Italian ed. 1965) are difficult to define with complete certainty. The female statue, apparently an invention of Titian's, which stands over a classical altar, holds a small winged figure with her right hand, like the Athena Parthenos. Unquestionably she represents a pagan idol, which though standard in scenes of martyrdoms, is unprecedented and anomalous for Saint Lawrence. It would have been more comprehensible if it had been an emperor's bust or a pagan divinity or a male nude such as Mars, Hercules or Apollo, all of them more obvious because richer in meanings and more iconographically relevant (Panofsky 1969).

The solution proposed by the present writer, as an alternative to that of Kennedy (1963) who thought the statue to be the goddess Roma, is that it represents Vesta, explicitly recalled by Prudentius in the *Passio Sancti Laurenti*, the only text from which Titian would have drawn. The significance of this image would be its reference to the passage from Paganism to Christianity, which, with the martyrdom of Lawrence, signaled

the fall of that religion (*Mors ills sancti martyris/Mors vera templorum fuit*) and the triumph of the new faith. This theory is supported by the presence of the same small statue in the subsequent version for Philip II (which was ready for dispatch to the Escorial at the end of 1567), as well as in Cort's 1571 engraving, which refers to both versions (1982) and which was authorized by Titian. On the base of the statue in the Escorial version is written "Invictissimo Philippo Hispaniorum Regi," defender *par excellence* of the Catholic faith.

The essay by Gaston (1974) tends to confirm this interpretation. In it he traced the iconographic sources of the subject to some coins of Galba, taken from a volume of Enea Vico published in Venice in 1548. This is the principal reason for believing (with reserve, since these coins were certainly known in Venice before this date), that this was the year in which Titian began the execution of the work.

This solution however does not exhaust all the iconographic problems. It leaves untouched that which is the most intriguing aspect of the work's patronage, trup by brought to light Gallo's discoveries. There were too many clues for Gallo to escape the conviction that the work was commissioned, or at least desired, not just by Lorenzo Massolo but also by his wife, a woman who was extolled by Aretino, Bembo and obviously della Casa, as beautiful, cultured and gifted with great intelligence and every rare quality. She lived in the same house as Girolamo Querini, one of the most influential Venetians of his time. Girolamo played a key role in the culture of his time. Titian executed two portraits of Elisabetta and she was the first to inform us of that which was to become the tomb of the two spouses (*archa nostra*).

It is legitimate then to assert that this painting could not have been executed without Elisabetta's participating or influencing it in some way, and that Titian would have been duty-bound or at least logically would have included her in the painting.

A scene of this kind would seem to argue against such an inclusion, however. It does not allow for women who console Lawrence in his martyrdom or pray for him. Nor could this

Page from Enea Vico, 1548 edition.

"Hieroglyph of Virtue" playing card from the book of Giovanni Palazzi.

impasse be resolved with heraldry, which would have favored the role of the man, whose name saint was in any case the subject of the narrative. Nor objectively would it have been appropriate to imply that Elisabetta had commissioned the work.

No canonical solution presented itself, but even so, the matter had to be confronted in some way. The only possibility, given the cultural climate of the time, lay in the cryptic, hermeneutic language ("hieroglyphics") that was were well-suited to the personality of Elisabetta Quierini as well as to Titian's approach to his works, especially the *poesie*.

The company of Pietro Bembo and his circle could have led in just this direction. Titian may have intended the female figure, who is veiled (the only iconographic touch alluding to Elisabetta's name-saint), as an allusion to his patron. He represented her here as an antique classical idol, probably Vesta, who was also veiled and who was the least compromised in the pagan Olympus with respect to the new faith. On the contrary, Vesta was the guardian of familial virtues, which in a painting commemorating two deceased could not omit reference to those of the bride, especially if Elisabetta was a paragon of *gravitas* as suggested by contemporary descriptions and references.

To substantiate this, let us consult a small book entitled *Le Virtu' in giocco, ovvero Dame Patritie di Venetia . . .*, published in Venice in 1681 by the "bookseller at the sign of Fortune," Giovanni Parè. For Gallo (1935) the author was anonymous, but it was in fact Giovanni Palazzi, who initialled the introduction G.P. The appendix included a deck of playing cards. (The Biblioteca Correr has an example of a beautiful deck separated from the text.) The five of spades is dedicated to "Elisabetta Querini, with the hieroglyph of Virtue, invented by her, who scorns lightning bolts and fears not the dark." This would explain the setting of Titian's altarpiece as a *nocturne*. It is significant that the "lightning" mentioned by Vasari (1568) in the Gesuiti painting would be substituted by moonlight in the version executed for Philip II.

The playing card is practically identical to the allegory of *Virtue* engraved by Ripa (1630) and must have been Ripa's source. It is so similar to the small sculpture held by the veiled goddess in the *Martyrdom* that there has to be a connection; indeed it is the almost over-obvious explanation for an element that is otherwise inexplicable. It is this among Ripa's *figure ad intaglio* in the *Iconologia* that most resembles the statuette, and not other allegories no less appropriate such as Victory, Strength and so on. The fact that the winged figure is in profile also has an explanation that eluded Gaston: the links that connected the Querini family to the Emperor Galba, the former claiming descent from the Gens Galbana (Barbaro). This then must have induced Elisabetta Querini to "invent" that "hieroglyph" and to give it the form that three copper

coins of her august ancestor inspired and legitimated.

The Roman *Victory* thus assumed for Elisabetta the conceptual and formal significance of *Virtue* and with this symbol she could present herself as a Roman matron, and at another level of interpretation, which does not exclude but rather completes the preceding one, as a Roman divinity.

It is curious how this double reading of the iconography is matched by a double reading in the formal sense. This painting, on account of the circumstances of commission, as well as for incidental reasons (the trip to Rome) and because of its cultural context, could be considered the most philologically Roman among Titian's works. Consequently, this more than any other was susceptible to the fascination of the taste and culture that looked to Rome as its most natural and coherent reference point. Yet – and one of the motives was surely the long gestation of the work in the artist's studio – it cannot only be understood in this objectively restrictive view, as became clear in the Venetian "mannerism" exhibition in 1981. On that occasion, Giuliano Briganti wrote authoritatively: "to speak of 'mannerism,' even of 'Venetian mannerism,' before a painting such as the *Martyrdom of Saint Lawrence* seems to me an insult." Similarly Giovanni Testori drew attention to the absence of "self-sufficient mannerisms," at least in the light of the relevant definitions of the most recent historiography. To these "the great Venetian tradition – and the concept is meaningful because here we speak of that painter and that painting – responds by going to the place... seeing and conquering."

Alas it is not possible to be sure that Elisabetta ever saw the painting raised into position. We know that she died one or two days before 1 February 1559 (Gallo 1935). From Ridolfi (1648) we learn that in this same year the painting, copied by Palma il Giovane, was already *in situ*, where it was expressly mentioned for the first time by García Hernandez in a letter of 9 October 1564 to the minister of Philip II, Gonzalo Perez (1975). In it he proposed to his Sovereign the possibility of obtaining a copy of the Gesuiti canvas, for a very good price, to be painted by Girolamo Dente. The interesting annotation of the king in the margin of this document ("that [Girolamo] make them so that one is different from the other, so that in this manner [Hernandez] can have two") seems to confirm the existence of a replica of this canvas, which was to be different from both the Gesuiti work and the version for Philip II, which Titian was then painting. Thus it is possible that Cort's engraving replicated this third version. This, however, in the absence of any documentation, is merely hypothetical. The Gesuiti canvas remained in its original location until 1730 (Zanetti 1733) when it was moved to the first altar on the left side of the same church, rebuilt in great part by the Jesuits, who bought the complex of the Crociferi in 1657.

LITERATURE   Biblioteca Museo Correr, Cod. Cic., 3423/17; Biblioteca Museo Correr, ms. Barbaro, *ad vocem*; Vico 1548; Vasari 1568 (ed. Milanesi 1881), VII, 453; Ripa 1630, III, 176-77; Ridolfi 1648 (ed. Von Hadeln) 1914, II, 172; G.P. (G. Palazzi), 1681, 45-47; Zanetti 1733, 383; Zanetti 1771, 122; Zanotto 1860, II, no. 90; Gallo 1935, 155-74; Zarnowski 1938, 3-26; Brendel 1955, 113-25; Kennedy 1958, 237-43; *Idem*, 196326; Saxl 1965; Pallucchini 1969, 150; Panofsky 1969, 54; Gaston 1974, 358-67; Ferrarino 1975, 92-94; Beschi 1976, 2-43; Battisti 1980, 213-25; Gentili 1980, 191; Valcanover 1981, 110; Briganti 1981; Testori 1981; Chiari 1982, 56, no. 11, fig. p. 57; Chiari Moretto Wiel 1988, 54, no. 29; *Idem* 1989, 93, no. 29.

S.S.

54

Allegory of Wisdom

oil on canvas, 177×177 cm
Venice, Libreria Marciana, Antisala

Jacopo Sansovino, who came to Venice in 1527 following the Sack of Rome and soon after was to become architect of the State, began in 1537 the construction of the Libreria Marciana. This was one of the building projects that formed part of the radical renovation of the Piazza and Piazzetta of San Marco. It was entrusted to the Tuscan architect by the Procuratori di Supra, in the certainty that he and only he could give a triumphal and modern aspect, in terms of the classical ideal, to the principal setting for state ceremonial in the Republic (Romanelli 1981). Perhaps the richest and most ornate building that has been built since the ancients, as it was enthusiastically described by Andrea Palladio in 1570, it was built up to the sixteenth arch by Sansovino, and completed by Scamozzi in 1591.

The interior decorations, marked by the mannerist Tusco-Roman taste prevalent in Venice during the 1550s, correspond to the concepts of formal dignity in the architecture and the external sculpture. The room to be decorated was the Sala Grande with a sumptuous ceiling *alla Romana*. Between the fall of 1556 and spring of 1557 seven artists chosen by Sansovino on the advice of his friend Titian (Giovanni De Mio, Giuseppe Porta "Il Salviati," Battista Franco, Giulio Licinio, Giambattista Zelotti, Paolo Veronese and Andrea Schiavone) each painted three *tondi* of allegories of human knowledge in its various disciplines (Paolucci 1981, Ruggeri 1984, Valcanover 1988). Conspicuous among those artists omitted from the project was Tintoretto, presumably at Titian's behest (mentioned also in early sources; see Ridolfi 1648, Pignatti 1976). Even so the diversity of styles represented by this group constitutes a kind of visual "manifesto" of Venetian Mannerism. Titian reserved for himself the octagon in the center of the vault of the vestibule or antechamber. The ceiling decoration, carried out in 1559-60 by the Brescian Cristoforo Rosa with the assistance of his brother Stefano, consists of a quadrangle of coupled spiral columns crowned by a large, deep, and very richly carved gilded frame and embellished by a veritable palimpset of balconies, friezes and arcane classical mouldings foreshortened in the most ostentatious perspective-illusionism (Perry 1972). It was valued by Titian and Sansovino at 30 gold ducats, on 22 April 1560 (Von Hadeln 1911).

Since the relevant document specifies that "the figure which goes in the middle" was excluded from the payment, it seems probable that Titian's painting was still unfinished at that date, even if it is logical to suppose that the work was underway. For Ridolfi (1648) the painting represented "History," according to Boschini (1674), "a little woman with a letter in her hand... by Titian", "Wisdom" for Moschini (1815), and then a whole variety of interpretations (Schulz 1961). The most likely title for this octagon is "Divine Wisdom," in view of Ivanoff's (1968) observation that the object in the right hand of the female figure is not, as is generally believed, a book, but a rectangular mirror (with a wooden frame typical of the period as can be seen in Titian's *poesie* in Edinburgh, the *Diana and Acteon* of 1556-59), an attribute of Wisdom, or rather Divine Providence." In this case, the *putto* bearing the mirror would be Eros, "who embodies, according to the Neoplatonic doctrine, the Mystery of creation...." In effect, Titian's octagon is emblematic of the iconographic plan of the entire Libreria. Although Tietze, even in the French edition of his Titian monograph (1940), judges the painting "in view of its decorative superficial style essentially a workshop piece," it is correctly considered autograph by recent critics. Although at the summit of the abnormal, vertiginous enframement, which Vasari recalled as "highly praised" by his contemporaries, the image of *Wisdom* is contained by the small space without any perspective illusion. On the thick blanket of clouds, the female form unwinds in the rhythms, as she looks intently at herself in the mirror that the *putto* struggles to hold up for her. In the dense and dynamic dialectic of those parts in full light with those in penumbra the hues refract in a refined iridescence of ineffable vitality. It is almost as if his association with the ceiling competition for the principal room, a tribute to mannerist precepts, provoked Titian to declaring his loyalty to that world in the vestibule, even though from the 1540s he was already giving a new meaning to color that would characterize the main stream of his late work.

LITERATURE   Ridolfi 1648 (ed. 1914), II, 202; Boschini 1674, *San Marco*, 67; Moschini 1815, II, 490; Crowe and Cavalcaselle 1878, II, 264; Tietze 1950, 385; Schulz 1961, 95; Ivanoff 1968, 65; Pallucchini 1969, 95-96; Perry 1972, 75ff; Wethey 1975, 204-05; Pignatti 1976, I, 49ff; Paolucci 1981, 287ff; Romanelli 1981, 277ff; Ruggeri 1984, 313ff; Zorzi 1987, 161; Valcanover 1988, 37ff.

F.V.

55

Archangel Gabriel

charcoal, white chalk, cerulean paper; worn and stained on the front, 422×279 mm

Florence, Gabinetto Disegni e Stampe degli Uffizi (no. 12903F)

Verso: Study of separate draped figure, and other studies.

Charles Loeser was the first to publish this drawing, in a collection of facsimiles of the drawings of the Uffizi (1912-21) as "Study for the Angel in the Annunciation of San Salvatore," noting at the same time the differences with respect to the painted version: "the arms are not crossed on the chest, as in the painting; Titian's first thought being to extend the angel's right hand to offer a lily and greet Mary, as in the Annunciation of Treviso. Thus, in the painting the movement of the step, that in the drawing is of the left leg almost counterbalancing the action of the arm, is altered."

The connection with the Venetian altarpiece was accepted by later critics though at first doubtfully by Fröhlich-Bum (1928) and then by the Tietzes (1936) and the majority of scholars (Valcanover 1969; Pallucchini 1969; Wethey 1969-75), with some reserve by Wilde (1975) and Rearick (1976). The latter noted that the drawing is still nearer, in the pose of the angel, to the polyptych of Dubrovnik, a workshop collaboration based on drawings by Titian, datable to a later period. Rearick supposed that it could be a "revision" of the study for the Angel of Dubrovnik in preparation for the *Annunciation* of San Domenico Maggiore, Naples, 1557. Most recently Wethey (1987) reiterated the more likely connection with the altarpiece of San Salvador. In effect the relationship of this Angel with those of Dubrovnik and Naples is superficial. More significant than the mere pose of the Angel (the position of the arm and leg) is the way he affects the space around him, giving a sense of that reverberation provoked by his luminous apparition, which is already suggested by the drawing: the twisting of the shoulders toward the observer with respect to the head, seen in profile, the arrangement of the drapery and the belt, and above all the incidence of the light with the same emphatic underlining of shadows on the neck and waist. The connection with the altarpiece of San Salvador allows us to date the drawing 1559-60, at the end of a stylistic development during which Titian was expressing himself on paper, with the most appropriate materials to hand – graphite, charcoal, chalk – in purely pictorial terms. If, as has been observed (see Chiari Moretti Wiel 1989), preparatory drawings that seem finished to a fairly advanced stage of definition were modified again by Titian during the execution of his paintings, one can also say that the creative process begins with the drawings themselves.

In this study for the Angel, which Oberhuber has considered the most extraordinary of the late drawings, Titian "painted with charcoal, evoking tenebrous darkness and transparent lights that aspire to transform action into color" (1976). Describing the figure with fluent marks and rapid, broken strokes, and rubbing the charcoal and chalk on the cerulean paper as if to dissolve the colors or expand the shadows, he gave life to a palpitating image, rich in tonal vibrations.

The *verso* of the sheet, also certainly autograph and of exceptional quality, in addition to a state of preservation that allows full appreciation of its dazzling luministic effects, was published only in 1937, after the detachment of the backing by A.L. Mayer who sees in the splendid draped figure an *Annunciatory Virgin* corresponding to the *Angel*. The most convincing interpretation of this and other studies on the *verso* is by Rearick, who recognized in the barely perceptible sketch on the lower left a figure with hands outstretched, very close to that of the Madonna in the *Crucifixion* of San Domenico in Ancona. If this is so, then it is easy to suppose that the main figure is a preliminary study for the Saint John the Evangelist in the same painting. Confirmation for this theory rests, as Agnese Chiari Moretto Wiel (1989) noted, with the fact that the patron of the altarpiece of Ancona was the same Antonio Cornovì della Vecchia who commissioned Titian's *Annunciation* in San Salvador (Meschio 1975). The fact that the two paintings shared a single patron and virtually contemporary dates – the first finished in 1558 and the second started perhaps at the end of May 1559 – strengthens the ties between the *recto* and *verso* of the Uffizi sheet and validates the relationship of the *Annunciatory Angel* to the San Salvador altar piece.

LITERATURE Loeser 1922, no. 11; Von Hadeln 1924, no. 35; Von Hadeln 1927, no. 41; Fröhlich-Bum 1928, no. 44; *Exhibition...* 1930. 312, no. 670; Popham 1931, 74, no. 269; Fogolari 1935, 213, no. 17; Tietze and Tietze-Conrat 1936, 186, 192, no. 37; Mayer 1937, 311; Tietze and Tietze-Conrat 1944, 310, no. 1905; Dell'Acqua 1956, 135; Valcanover 1960, 47; Valcanover 1969, 131; Pallucchini 1969, I, 333; Wethey 1969-75, I, 72, III, 257, no. 11; Wilde 1974, 194; Rearick 1976, no. 27; Oberhuber 1976, 34-5; Rearick 1977, no. 16; Rosand 1978, fig. 78; Pignatti 1979, 11, no. 48; Scrasse 1983, 295, no. D74; Wethey 1987, 29-30, 128, no. 3; Chiari Moretto Wiel 1988, 34, 59, no. 37; Chiari Moretto Wiel 1989, 21, 96, no. 37.

G.D.

Draped Figure, verso

56

The Annunciation

oil on canvas, 403×235 cm
Venice, Chiesa di San Salvador

EXHIBITION   Venice, 1935
RESTORATION   1988-89, O. Nonfarmale

On 7 May 1559 Antonio Cornovì della Vecchia dictated his will to the notary Giovan Battista Benzoni. He belonged to one of the richest merchant families in Venice, whence he had moved from his native Ancona. In his will he requested to be buried in the church of San Salvador together with his father Venturino in the chapel of Augustine, which he had recently purchased for this purpose. 300 ducats were to be allocated to the "Reverend Fathers" for this purpose. Moreover, the altar was to be "made of pietra viva according to the design and the agreement made with the stonecutter to whom I have given money on account for said work, similarly, also to Mr. Titian to make the altarpiece of the Incarnation of our Lord....." These works were to be finished within six months of Cornovì's death (Maschio 1975). Thus by 1559 the Augustinian Canons of San Salvador had sold the chapel of Saint Augustine to the Cornovì as a family shrine, and there existed already a plan for a new altar and for the execution of an altarpiece by Titian. The purchaser was not to die until 1572, as a second will confirms. However, in the meantime his father Venturino, brother of that Antonio who had commissioned from Titian the *Crucifixion* of San Domenico of Ancona (completed in 1558), was buried in front of the altar. On the tombstone the epigraph can still be read: VENTURINI CORNOVÌ AVETULA/ANT. FILIUS ET SIBI MCLIX P. /OBIIT ANNO SALUTIS MDXLIX/AETATIS VERO SUAE/LXIII. It is probable, therefore, that at the end of 1559 or at least by the beginning of 1560, Antonio, who was still alive, personally supervised the work on the altar in Istrian stone with gilding (generally attributed to Jacopo Sansovino, though he is not expressly mentioned in the will) and Titian's painting. In the arch above the tympanum traces of frescoes have reappeared depicting two angels, part of the entire decorative scheme that had already vanished by Zanetti's time (1733), and which included in the cupola "little angels in the corners in chiaroscuro," painted according to Boschini (1644) by Francesco Vecellio, who died in 1560. These works, then, also formed part of Cornovì's project.
Vasari (1568) was the first to write, albeit somewhat negatively, of the work, which he saw during his visit to Venice in 1566. Consequently this date long stood as a *terminus ante quem* prior to the discovery of Antonio Cornovì's will. Nevertheless Pallucchini (1969), observing that the monopoly accorded to Titian on 5 March 1566 by the Council of Ten did not include the print by Cornelis Cort, narrowed the dating to between 1564 and 1565. Meanwhile Fiocco (1953-54) argued that 1560

was the latest date for the frescoing of the cupola of the chapel by Francesco Vecellio since he died in that year.
According to Ridolfi (1648) "seeming to the Fathers that that painting was not, in respect to his others, brought to perfection, the artist, in order to make them realize their little understanding, wrote these two genuine verbs: Titinus Fecit Fecit." Since then the legend of Titian wishing to place emphasis on his supreme artistic work, repeating twice the miracle of his creativity, has been accepted blindly by all critics with the single exception of Tietze (1936), who doubted the authenticity at least of the second *Fecit*, believing it an addition of a restorer. In reality, the two words, though old, are repaints, perhaps by that same "not very skilled painter" who "set right some defects of time, compromising the painting's purity," as noted by Ridolfi. Under the two *Fecit*, as reflectograph and x-radiograph analyses have revealed, there is instead a clear *faciebat*, the same verb applied to the earlier Averoldi polyptych in Brescia. The inscription "Ignis Ardens non comburens" seems also to have been reworked, perhaps because the original had faded. Traced under the flower vase, this is an allusion to Mary's virginity, perpetual like Mose's burning bush (*Exodus* 3:2; see also, *Officium Beatae Marie Virginis*: "rubem quem viderat Moyses in combustum conservata agnovimus Tuam laudabilem virginitatem"), and appears often in Titian's Marian paintings. In this case, it has been symbolized in an unusual manner by the bouquet of red flowers, which, though they resemble roses, are upon closer examination, botanically unidentifiable. Indeed, in Cornelis Cort's engraving they have been transformed into flames. On the book that Mary has closed at the appearance of the angel, we read instead the word "signu" (signum), perhaps derived from the Gospel of Saint Luke (2:12): "et hoc vobis signum." Titian treated the theme of the Annunciation many times in his long career, from the *Annunciation* in Treviso, to that of San Rocco, to the two lost versions of Santa Maria Nova and Santa Maria degli Angeli of Murano (later in Aranjuez), to the *Annunciation* for San Domenico Maggiore, Naples, which is the closest to the San Salvador version in date. But the process of formal dissolution is much advanced in the latter. With extraordinary nonconformism, Titian transforms the traditional frightened maiden into a serene and aware creature. While it is normally the Virgin who folds her hands on her breast, Titian has transferred this gesture to the Angel, originally conceived with its arms extended and hands clasped (see the x-radiographic recomposition).
It has been observed (Kennedy 1956) that the gesture of the Virgin who lifts her veil is taken from a fourth-century relief in the Grimani collection. Nevertheless, unlike the Grimani funerary *stele*, or other similar images, the woman does not attempt to hide her face or even, as in Simone Martini's *Annunciation*, to withdraw instinctively behind the mantle.

Mary does not cover her face, she uncovers it. Distancing the veil, she exposes her face to the flood of divine light, in an attitude of complete acceptance of the event. It was not by chance that Antonio specified in his will an "altarpiece of the Incarnation of our Lord...." With its jubilant angels around the dove, symbol of the Holy Spirit, the iconic significance of the work is not limited to the Annunciation. It is both the Annunciation and the realization itself of the announcement through the mystery of Incarnation, recognized in Mary by the angel, who lacks the usual attribute of the lily, in the reverent act of crossing his arms.

In Cornelis Cort's engraving (reversed) a bed is clearly visible to the left of the Virgin behind the hangings. In the painting today, the bed is hardly visible, although apparent in the infrared photograph (p. 127). An *Annunciate Angel* in the Uffizi (cat. no. 55), with a standing draped figure on the verso, was published for the first time by Loeser (1920-21) as a study for the angel of this altarpiece. More recently Rearick (1976) noticed links between the Madonna of the *Crucifixion* of San Domenico in Ancona and a semi-erased image of the lower part of the verso, for which the draped figure could be a first idea (Chiari 1988). Although the first version of the painting showed the angel with its hands joined, as in the Uffizi drawing, the clothing, the sleeves, the drapery, and the profile are all differently disposed. It would seem therefore more correct to speak not of a preparatory drawing, but of a contemporary sketch for the figure of Gabriel, then painted with notable freedom.

Ludovico Dolce's words perfectly suit this late work by Titian, in which "the flesh trembles," "the lights fight and play with the shadows," while in the swirling *impasto* of the paint the "desperate greatness" of the artist, so singular as to defy the comprehension of his contemporaries, is once again made visible.

LITERATURE   Vasari 1568 (ed. Milanesi 1881), VII, 499; Sansovino 1581, 121; Sansovino-Stringa 1604, 121; Ridolfi 1648 (ed. Von Hadeln 1914), I, 205; Sansovino-Martinioni 1663, 94; Boschini 1664, 134; Zanetti 1733, 186; Crowe and Cavalcaselle 1877, II, 352-4; Loeser 1912-21, series I, fasc. II, no. 11; *Mostra di Tiziano* 1935, no. 87; Tietze 1936, I, 237, 240, II, 313; Fiocco 1953-54, 197; Kennedy 1956, 237; Valcanover 1960, II, 108-09; Pallucchini 1969, 319; Valcanover 1969, 131, no. 445; Wethey 1969, 71-72; Maschio 1975, 178-82; Ivanoff 1977, 189-91; Dell'Acqua 1978, *passim*; Hope 1980, 141; Bergstein 1986, 34-35; Chiari Moretto Weil 1988, 53-60; Hope 1988, 66; Chiari Moretto Weil 1989, 96-97.

G.N.S.

57.

Helmet

charcoal and white chalk, slightly worn sky-blue paper, 452×358 mm Florence, Gabinetto Disegni e Stampe degli Uffizi (no. 566 Orn.)

Signed at bottom left, in charcoal, in the artist's hand "24 [0?] and in the center, in a seventeenth-century hand (?), TIZIAN. On the *verso*, sketches of figures.

This is undoubtedly the most eloquent example of a way of perceiving drawing in essentially pictorial terms, which characterized above all Titian's graphite and charcoal studies from his early years. One can truly say that here Titian used charcoal "as if it were a brush... to cover the paper with highlights and deep shadows that bring images to life by their reciprocal action" (Oberhuber). The dimensions of this sheet, the largest that has come down to us, give the drawing the semblance of a painting, in which the solitary helmet, studied from life, impresses by its extraordinary sculptural and luministic qualities with a singular monumentality. The technique contributes to this effect, since no other drawing by Titian is "so exuberant, decisive and uncompromising in the use of materials" (Rearick), in the study of a range of tonal gradations that move from an intense and velvety black of the charcoal to the dazzling highlights of the chalk, with a variety and richness of transitions that can rival, as Wethey (1978) noted, those of any oil painting by Titian.

The exceptional character of this sheet within the extant corpus of Titian's drawings explains why it was not initially accepted by scholars. Published by P.N. Ferri in his catalogue of the drawings of the Uffizi (1890) with a traditional attribution to Titian, it was then rejected by Ricketts (1910), who gave it instead to Tintoretto, and by Fröhlich-Bum, who named Veronese. Ferri even specified it as the "study of a large-size helmet, for the portrait of the Duke of Urbino, in the Uffizi," and even if this was not in fact the case and was denied by Loeser (1912-21), the latter argued nevertheless that it was similar in date to the portrait, and Von Hadeln (1924), who also rejected the links to the Urbino portrait, authoritatively asserted that it was autograph. Following its exhibition at the Titian show in 1935, Suida (1935) associated the drawing with the *Battle* in the Palazzo Ducale, with a dating *c.* 1537. This was accepted by several critics with few variations (Pallucchini 1969, Rosand 1975, Wethey 1987). The Tietzes (1944), however, post dated the drawing to the decade 1550-60, an opinion shared by Oberhuber (1976), Pignatti (1979) and Chiari Moretto Wiel (1989) who argued for the early 60s. The most attentive study of the sheet is that of Rearick (1876) who, after abandoning the search for the painting for which the drawing may have been preliminary, noted that the helmet seemed to belong to a rare and secret chivalric type produced by the Augsburg manufacturers in the second half of the

sixteenth century and that a similar helmet appears in copies of Titian's lost portrait of Emperor Ferdinand I, painted in 1548. This argument remains unsubstantiated, and has even been questioned by Stuart Pyhrr, according to whom it was not possible to establish with certainty if this is a German or a North Italian helmet (see Wethey 1987, 17). In any case it is likely that the drawing was related to a history painting of some kind, unless in the end it was simply a life study without any particular relationship to a commissioned painting.

The sketches on the verso of the sheet, which were attributed by the Tietzes (1944) to Palma il Giovane, were returned to Titian by Rearick on the basis of comparison with "the aspects of his freer style" exemplified in the upper part of the *Study of Legs for the Martyrdom of Saint Lawrence* and its *verso*, which, it must be said, are not universally accepted as Titian's. Several figures have bows and arrows, leading Rearick to speculate that the artist had in mind a mythological subject such as the killing of Niobe, although there is no evidence that Titian ever worked on such a theme.

LITERATURE Ferri 1890, 257, no. 566; Ricketts 1910, 161; Loeser 1912-21, no. 6; Von Hadeln 1924, no. 25, Fröhlich-Bum 1928, 195, note 51; Fogolari 1935, 212, no. 12; Suida 1935, 77; Tietze and Tietze-Conrat 1944, 310, no. 1897; *Mostra di disegni...*1960, 19, no. 100; Valcanover 1960, I, 68-69; Valcanover 1969, 110; Pallucchini 1969, I, 332; Petrioli Tofani 1972, no. 65; Rearick 1976, 24; Oberhuber 1976, 44; Pignatti 1976, 267; Rosand 1978, fig. 70; Muraro 1978, 132; Pignatti 1979, no. 47; Wethey 1987, 16-17, 136, no. 10; Chiari Moretto Wiel 1988, 33, 54, no. 30; Chiari Moretto Wiel 1989, 19, 93, no. 30.

G.D.

Figure Sketches, verso

Tizian

58

Madonna and Child

oil on canvas, 124×96 cm
Venice, Galleria dell'Accademia, Collection Albertini (cat. 1359)

EXHIBITIONS   London 1930, Tokyo 1985, Sydney 1988

In 1981, the Gallerie dell'Accademia acquired this work by testamentary bequest of Leonardo Albertini. It was listed in the collection of the Marchesi Mazenta of Milan, attributed to Titian, in an inventory of 1616 (Castello Sforzesco, Milan). In 1628, an appraisal of some paintings of the family by "Giambattista Cerrano, illustrious painter, before the brothers left their effects to Signor Godonio Mazenta," included Titian's *Madonna and Child* "of two *braccia*," roughly corresponding to the painting's present dimensions. It was cited once more in the inventory compiled by the brothers Ludovico and Alessandro Mazenta on 30 December 1678. It remained with the family until 1879 when it passed to their descendants, the Pinetti di Martinengo (Bergamo), and was then acquired in 1960 by Luigi Albertini, father of Leonardo.

Recognized as Titian's by Suida (1930, 1935), Wittgens (1930), Modigliani (1942), Berenson (1956), Wethey (1969) and Valcanover, but with doubts (1969), and as such exhibited in London in 1930, it was ignored by Tietze and Pallucchini, while Longhi (1946) tended toward Jacopo Bassano, as one of many copies of a famous lost Titian prototype. Numerous replicas testify to the enormous success of this devotional image: from the engraving in reverse in the second half of the seventeenth century, published by Pietro Daret (Modigliani 1942), to the canvas with slight variations attributed to Padovanino in the sacristy of the Duomo, Padua, and to numerous others listed by Wethey. To those we can add that which recently appeared in a Christie's auction (New York, 5/31/89) assigned to Alessandro Turchi "l'Orbetto," as well as a hasty version by a seventeenth-century Venetian (Bruno Vianello Collection).

The painting is indeed by Titian, as confirmed by reflectographic and radiographic studies. These revealed the build-up of the composition through the use of rapid, superimposed brushstrokes, typical of other works by the artist during the 1560s. It is related to the signed *Madonna and Child* in the Alte Pinakothek, Munich, and the *Annunciation* of San Salvador, but in contrast to these the colors are rather worn and certain areas reworked, clouding the surface and causing the hesitancy of certain critics.

Notwithstanding this filter, the figures of the Virgin and Child are realized in a vibrant burst of sudden dazzling light in the burning bush, symbol of the perennial Virginity of Mary (*Exodus*, 3:2; *Officium Beatae Mariae Virginis*: "Rubum quem viderat Moyses in combustum conservatam agnovimus tuam laudabilem virginitatem"), which appears on the left and is present also in the virtually contemporary altarpiece of San Salvador. Ultraviolet analysis reveals that the artist had used a canvas upon which a previous subject had already been painted, probably a praying *Saint*, perhaps a *Magdalene*.

LITERATURE   Suida 1930, 45; *Id.* 1935, 138, 181; Wittgens 1930, XI, 73, 88; Modigliani 1942, V; Longhi 1946, 65; Berenson 1957, 190; Valcanover 1960, II, 71; *Id.* 1969, 130, no. 431; Wethey 1969, I, 100, no. 52; *Riflettoscopia...* 1984, 34-41; Nepi Scirè, Valcanover 1985, 179; Nepi Scirè 1988, 50-51.

G.N.S.

Composite x-ray of the painting, upside down

59

Self-Portrait

oil on canvas, 96×75 cm
Berlin, Staatliche Museen, Gemäldegalerie (no. 163)

EXHIBITIONS Washington 1948, Detroit, Cleveland, Minneapolis, San Francisco, Los Angeles, St. Louis, Pittsburgh, Toledo 1948-49, Wiesbaden 1949, Berlin 1950-51, Wiesbaden 1953, Los Angeles 1979

This was acquired in Venice from the Sant' Angelo Raffaele branch of the Barbarigo family by L. Cicognara, and sold by him to E. Solly of Berlin (Malamani, 1988). In 1821 it came with the Solly collection to the Berlin museum.

Together with the Prado canvas (no. 407), this is one of only two extant autograph portraits in which Titian recorded for us his own likeness, recognizable also in several other extant paintings.

There are disagreements regarding the date, which oscillates between 1550 and c. 1562. Wethey (1971) took up the earlier date, sustained previously by Gronau (1904) and others, and argued that the painting is contemporary with the *Self-Portrait* engraved by Giovanni Britto datable to 1550 (Muraro-Rosand 1976). That the beard is not gray and the face of the subject still vigorous would seem to confirm this. The earlier dating, c. 1562, advanced by Pallucchini (1969), Valcanover (1969) (with a margin of doubt) and Pignatti (1979), is supported by the identification of this with the self-portrait seen by Vasari in 1566, in the painter's home, recorded (1568) in these terms: "his self portrait finished by him four years ago, very fine and natural." Though other evidence is lacking, the handling of the paint belongs stylistically to the period of the early 60s: an impasto of color in the clothing applied with rapid streaks of light that bring the painting close to the artist's late style. As has been noted, the portrait does not exhibit the same degree of finish in all areas (see, for example, the left hand), but the wonderful strength and expressive completeness of the painting make this an irrelevant consideration.

In contrast to the two other self-portraits, the Prado canvas and Britto's woodcut, this portrait lacks reference to the tools of the artist's trade. The only biographical touch is the chain on his front, the insignia of the Knight of the Golden Spur bestowed upon him in 1533 by Charles v (Crowe Cavalcaselle 1877, II, 344).

As in other masterly portraits by Titian, it is the particular pose adopted for capturing the model that underlines its internal characterization. In this case, the figure majestically dominates the space, by the broad curve of his shoulders and arms, while his attitude, with willful tension expressed by the face bathed in light, and by the hands, bestows a sense of energy and pride constituting the existential measure of the subject. In this manner, Titian presents his image of himself using the same language with which he had painted that of other protagonists of his time. In this visual translation of the "myth of the self," the artist has achieved a vehement sense of the living human document.

LITERATURE Vasari 1568 (ed. Milanesi 1881), VII, 458; Crowe and Cavalcaselle 1877, I, 481-83; Malamani 1888, II, 112ff, 126, 132; Gronau 1904, 170-71, 247, 286; Pallucchini 1969, 173, 313; Valcanover 1969, 130 no. 443; Wethey 1971, 49-50, 143-44 no. 104 (with preceding bibliography); Pignatti 1979, pp. 78, 162; Rosand 1983, pl. I.

P.R.

60

Venus and Adonis

oil on canvas, 106.7×133.3 cm
New York, The Metropolitan Museum of Art, Jules S. Bache
Collection, 1949

EXHIBITIONS   San Francisco 1938; New York 1939; Stockholm 1962-63
RESTORATION   1976, Brealey

Among Titian's *poesie* or mythological narratives are several
portrayals of the subject of Venus and Adonis, which became
so popular that more than thirty painted and engraved copies
are known. The principal treatments, those by or closely
associated with the master, can be divided into two groups
(Wethey 1975). The first group centers on the picture in the
Prado, which Titian completed in 1554 for Philip II of Spain.
This nearly square canvas and its derivatives differ in size and
format, as well as in certain compositional details, from the
second group, designated the Farnese type after a lost painting
of 'Venus and Adonis' that Titian made for that family
(Wethey 1975). Examples of the so-called Farnese type include
those in the Metropolitan Museum, New York, and in the
National Gallery of Art, Washington. These two paintings are
smaller than the Prado version and oblong in format, which
has the effect of reducing the landscape setting. They also
show Cupid awake, clutching a dove (not asleep, as in the
Prado type), and Adonis holding two (not three) hounds.
Other differences further distinguish the two groups: Venus'
chariot in the Prado painting is replaced by a burst of light,
and an overturned urn is omitted. The New York picture
retains the motif of Cupid's bow and quiver of arrows hanging
in the tree, which is missing in the Washington version.
Though the lost original may go back to the time of Titian's
association with the Farnese in 1545-46, the New York and
Washington paintings postdate the Prado version in style. The
two canvases, nearly identical in size and composition, have
generally been dated to the same period, c. 1560-65 (Wethey
1975, Shapley 1979). While the New York version has often
been paired with that in Washington, sometimes to the
disadvantage of the former (Tietze 1950), Pallucchini (1969)
nevertheless argued that the Metropolitan Museum painting
was superior to the one in Washington, and Federico Zeri
(1973) likewise claimed that it was substantially autograph.
After the cleaning by John Brealey in 1976, it has become
strikingly evident, in fact, that the Metropolitan Museum
picture was executed in great part by Titian himself. By
contrast to the Washington painting, with its somber cast
(caused by the dark ground showing through the abraded
paint layers), the rich but restrained palette of the New York
canvas is typical of the master in the 1560s: the reds and golds

of the figures (repeated in the rainbow) are set off by the green, blue and brown of their setting.

The compact format of the Metropolitan Museum picture and its Washington analogue centers attention on the protagonists. As in many of his other *poesies*, Titian's source was Ovid's *Metamorphoses*, which relates how the goddess Venus fell in love with a mortal youth, the hunter Adonis, who, heedless of her warnings, pursued and fell prey to a boar. Titian portrays the dramatic incident, not found in his literary source, when Venus vainly attempts to restrain her handsome young lover from departing for the hunt. Though Titian's choice of Adonis' flight was criticized by Borghini (*Il Riposo*, 1584), precedents for his interpretation are found in ancient art. The friezelike grouping of figures suggests a source in Roman sarcophagus reliefs that the painter could have seen during his Roman sojourn of 1545-56. Venus' pose in particular can be traced to a famous series of reliefs, representing Cupid and Psyche, known in the Renaissance as the *Bed of Polyclitus* (Rosand 1975). In the sculpted prototypes, as in the painting, the female figure is shown from the back, seated and turning in a contrapposto position. In Titian's case, however, the twisted pose has a poignant and not merely formal character, as Venus clings to Adonis, who strides away from her. Their intertwined movements and exchanged glances underscore the tragic irony of the scene.

LITERATURE   Tietze 1950, 402; Valcanover (Italian ed.) 1960, II, 44-5; Valcanover (English ed.) 1960, III, 47; Pallucchini 1969, 142, 315; Panofsky 1969, 150-1; Valcanover 1969, 128, no. 428; Rosand 1972, 535-40; Zeri and Gardner 1973, 81-82; Rosand 1975, 242-45; Wethey, 1975, III, 188-94, 241-42; Shapley 1979, I, 492-95, II, pl. 348; Gentili 1988, 178.

D.A.B.

61

Saint James Major

oil on canvas, 231×137 cm
Venice, Chiesa di San Lio

EXHIBITION   Venice 1935; Venice 1981, Rome 1986-87
RESTORATION   1979, A. Lazzarin

Stringa (1604) was the first to remark that Titian painted, in the church of San Lio, Venice, a "Saint James of notable beauty" but he does not say on which altar, or even where. The painting was subsequently mentioned by Verdizotti (1622), and the saint himself was drawn by Van Dyck in the same year (Adriani 1965). As already noted (1981), Saint James Major was the patron of the milliner's guild, which was based at the church of San Lio. According to Zanotto (1858), "on the removal of the panel of Saint Michael by Jacopo Tintoretto," this painting took its place after 1604, following the transfer of the altar to the milliners thirty years earlier.

Zanotto's essay was neglected by all subsequent critics or historians of this painting, and the present writer was unaware of it at the time of the Venice exhibition in 1981. However, apart from some inaccuracies such as the claim that Stringa had failed to record the painting, and other insufficiently documented information such as the date of acquisition of the altar by the milliners' guild, unknown also to Micconi-Finamore in I mestieri, 1988, Zanotto concords with the date now generally given to this altarpiece, and was even aware of minor details such as the brief existence on the same altar of Tintoretto's painting which was substituted by the Titian.

That Zampetti (1985) has tried to replace Tintoretto with Lotto, in spite of the fact that Tintoretto was still alive when Sansovino was writing (1581), and that Stringa made no amendment, is a problem that is marginal to this subject. One can only say that "evident" errors (1985) are not attributable to this writer, but to Sansovino himself, to Stringa and to all others who followed them, writing about Tintoretto. Nor can the mistakes be blamed on the compilers of the Pastoral Visits of Priuli and Zane, whose job certainly was not to make attributions. Perhaps the error is actually Zampetti's, who recorded, correctly, that in April of 1545 Lotto made a note of an expense of 1 lira and 6 soldi to convey a Saint Michael to Treviso (1969), but who seems to ignore the fact that, two months later he bought "a stretcher for the other Saint Michael," a canvas that according to him would already have been executed in Venice. From this it is clear that, unless there were three paintings of this subject, the Saint Michael sent to Treviso was precisely that executed for San Lio and that, at least until that moment, had never been placed in the church. It also escaped Zampetti (because it had been omitted from the indices of the Libro delle spese diverse), that the purchase of the canvas, stretcher, etcetera, for the Saint Michael of San

Lio was recorded on 10 February 1542 (1969), and that therefore the two paintings by Lotto of this subject are documented to an equal degree. It is, therefore, rather probable that the same scholar's previous hypothesis was at least in part the true one, that the painting "was never exhibited" (1985), even if, once an agreement had been reached on the fee, the painting would have been consigned to the priest (though we do not know what he did with it). Besides, that the painting did not please the patron is obvious, nor should we underestimate Tintoretto's ruthlessness in procuring commissions.

The critical literature concerning Titian's Saint James, above all during the last century, focused upon its damaged condition and unintelligibility. Nevertheless it was unanimously considered among Titian's last paintings, probably on the basis of a passage by Ridolfi (1648), who stated that it was incomplete. This would have led, at the time of its placement on the milliners' altar, to its adaptation by some other painter, who according to Zanotto was Marco Vecellio, who also completed the Doge Antonio Grimani before Faith (see cat. no. 74). The two works, for Zanotto, would have had similar histories. This altarpiece, in particular, would have remained in Titian's studio whence, after the known events surrounding his inheritance, it would have been retrieved by the proprietors, and placed over the altar in that church, "completely renovated, restored and brought back to beautiful form" (Stringa). Surely, it should be added, in that very year of 1604, if one takes into account both Stringa's remark and the argumentum ex silentio of the minute of Zane's Pastoral Visit.

Of the later vicissitudes of this work, the most traumatic was its enlargement, still visible and no longer reversible owing to the changed dimensions of the altar. It has already been observed (Sponza 1981 and 1986), and should be stressed again, that this has upset the formal relations within the work, making the figure appear more withdrawn, thus proportionately smaller with respect to that of the original composition and, consequently, more immersed in the landscape. Finally, the enlargement of the upper portion and the different point from which the light originates generate a different compositional balance, accentuated also by the addition, if only of a few centimeters, on the left side.

Together with all this must be considered the need of the restorers of the last century to harmonize the original parts with the additions, and last but not least the need to reinterpret the work according to the taste of the period. This relegated Titian's late activity to an inferior qualitative level than that of his youth or maturity, and it is no wonder that, on the occasion of the 1935 show, Fogolari dated the work to the 1540s and that all later critics followed, tending, however, to move the execution to the second half of the decade, between 1547 and 1548 for Valcanover (1969) and Pallucchini (1969), close to 1550 for Wethey (1969).

Only after the last complete restoration, on the occasion of the Venetian mannerism exhibition (1981), did the canvas acquire a different aspect and, thus initiate a process of revision of all that had seemed agreed and certain.

Nevertheless, specifically because it was alien to the theme of that exhibition, the painting was not discussed. It is irrelevant to a debate Titian's controversial mannerism, of which the *Saint James* betrays only a faded memory, however important the mannerist episode may have been for his subsequent development. It should not be forgotten that this was evident to several critics, including Pallucchini (oral communication), who were in agreement. For Rearick, "the *San Giacomo Maggiore* is fascinating as an unfinished relic of the master's very old age..." (1981), while for Dell'Acqua "the *San Giacomo Maggiore* of the church of San Lio goes back to a much later moment, for its full reabsorption of the formal schemes of mannerism in the leavened material density of the old Titian" (1981), while for Mascherpa, who did not deal specifically with problems of dating, "the *San Giacomo Maggiore* of San Lio [is] characterized by the touch of the brushstroke that cuts like a razor to the narrative essence and at the same time harvests the reality of the soul, the glistening eyes... lost in the sunset and in the vision of things that are only conceded to him" (1981). This implies that Mascherpa had taken note of the later dating, and was in agreement with it.

Zampetti too accedes to these conclusions, accepting "a dating much later than that currently proposed by critics" (1985) and that, in the writer's view, should be approximately the mid-1560s.

LITERATURE   Sansovino 1581, 12; Sansovino, Stringa 1604, f. 110r; Verdizotti 1622 (ed. 1809); Ridolfi 1648 (ed. Hadeln 1914), I, 205; Zanotto 1858, I, inc. 25; Fogolari 1935, no. 17; Adriani 1965, f. 10v; Zampetti ed. 1969, 255; 1969, 238; Pallucchini 1969, I, 287; Valcanover 1969, 118, no. 288; Wethey 1969, 133, no. 103; Dell'Acqua 1981, 289-97; Mascherpa 1981; Pallucchini 1981; Rearick 1981, 700; Sponza 1981, 112; Zampetti 1985, 30-7, 1985, 34; Sponza 1986, 244-47; Micconi-Finamore in *I mestieri* 1988, 320.

S.S.

62

Penitent Magdalene

oil on canvas, 118×97 cm
Leningrad, The State Hermitage Museum (Inv. 117)

EXHIBITIONS   Venice 1935, Moscow 1962, USA 1979
RESTORATION   1978, E. Gherasimov

On the left above the amphora is the signature: TITIANUS P. Titian produced numerous versions of the *Penitent Magdalene* with minor variations. Ridolfi (1648) noted six although only two of these can be identified with extant works. The first is now in Naples at the Galleria Nazionale di Capodimonte (cat. no. 63) and is most likely a studio work sent to Alessandro Farnese in 1567. The second is at the Hermitage, and is superior in quality. Titian was especially fond of this painting, such that he kept it in his house until his death. In 1581 Pomponio Vecellio sold the family house with all its contents, including the *Magdalene*, to the Venetian patrician Cristoforo Barbarigo. Subsequently Bevilacqua (1845) erroneously associated the Barbarigo painting with Vasari's tale of the *Magdalene* destined for Philip II and bought for 100 *scudi* by the Venetian gentleman Silvio Badoer.

The various replicas and copies have been studied in detail by Wethey (1969), who identified four different compositional models. There are two versions of the "Hermitage" type. According to Wethey, one of them is in Paolo Candiani's Collection (Busto Arsizio, Varese), considered by the majority of scholars a late autograph work; the other, that of the Staatsgalerie in Stuttgart, is believed autograph by Berenson (1957) and Pallucchini (1969), notwithstanding the existence of the Hermitage painting (presently at the J. Paul Getty Museum in Malibu, California).

Most scholars are unanimous in dating the Leningrad *Magdalene* to c. 1565. Mayer (1930) noted that the engraving by Cornelis Cort (Le Blanc 1855, II, 120) executed in 1566, was made from both the Naples canvas and the Hermitage variant. Braunfels (1976-80, 409) wrote of the Leningrad painting: "... as for the 'Magdalene' we do not know if the version in the house in the Biri Grande was the first or the best." The former possibility seems most dubious, while the latter appears very likely, taking into account that Vasari, visiting Titian in 1566, could not have seen the painting sent to Philip II five years earlier. It is also improbable that he visited Silvio Badoer. It is possible that the *Magdalene* described by Vasari in the "Life" of Titian is the painting Titian kept in his Studio. "He then did a dishevelled Magdalene with her hair falling over her shoulders, throat and breast, to send to the Catholic king. She raises her eyes to heaven, showing her penitence in the redness of her eyes and her tears for her sin. This picture, therefore, greatly moves those who behold it, and what is more, although very beautiful, it moves not to lust but to compassion."

Comparison between the Hermitage painting and the Palazzo Pitti version reveals how Titian changed and enriched the composition, how he adjusted its style, completely transforming the image of the saint. Without recourse to strong light effects, Titian captured the drama of the scene. The muted light cloaks Mary Magdalene's body and contrasts with the gloomy twilight of the setting sun; an opaque and sepulchral light reflects on the smooth surface of the forehead, and cold white lights shine on the glass of the chalice with the myrrh. The heroine's emotions are human and sincere, and Titian's brushwork underlines the materiality of each detail with perfect mastery: the warmth of her body, the full and fine red hair, the folds of her mantle and of her silk shawl. For Ridolfi (189) Mary Magdalene's pose, in all the analogous compositions derived from an antique sculpture, "... The idea of which was taken from an antique marble of a woman, that can be seen in the studios...." This was also stressed by Rothschild (1931). The *Penitent Magdalene* was judged the finest work in the Barbarigo Collection. The acquisition of the painting together with the rest of the famous Venetian collection was an event of exceptional importance in the Hermitage's history. Bruni (director of the Hermitage from 1849 to 1863) noted that "for this painting alone one could have paid the sum of 600,000 francs; instead, this was the amount paid for the entire Barbarigo collection of paintings in 1850" (Levinson-Lessing 1986).

LITERATURE   Vasari 1568 (ed. Milanesi 1881), VII; Ridolfi 1648 (ed. 1914), I; Sansovino 1663, 174; Cochin 1769, 141-42; Bevilacqua 1845, no. 79; Waagen 1864, 409; Crowe and Cavalcaselle 1878, II, 314; Bode 1882, 33; Penther 1886, 30; Von Tschudi 1897, 5; Levi 1900, 286; Fischel 1907, 170; Venturi 1912, 146; Von Hadeln 1926, 78; Mayer 1930, 102; Rothschild 1931, 207; Suida 1933, 133; Serra 1934-45, 551; Tietze 1936, 291, 325; Lazarev 1939, 56; Gurvic 1940, 44; Luzio 1940, 596-98; Arslan 1952, 525; Zeri 1957, 24; Berenson 1957, I, 186, II, no. 1003; Bazin 1958, 62; Valcanover 1960, II, 20, 48; Fomiciova 1967, 65; Valcanover 1969, no. 448; Pallucchini 1969, 318; Wethey 1969, 146, cat. 123; Fomiciova 1974, 469, 471; Fahy 1979, 97; Pignatti 1980, no. 392; Braunfels 1976-80, 409; Vsevolozhskaya 1981, 275; Siebenhüner 1981, 28, 31; Levinson-Lessing 1986, 293.

I.A.

63

Penitent Magdalene

oil on canvas, 128×103 cm
Naples, Museo e Gallerie Nazionali di Capodimonte (inv. no. 136)

EXHIBITION Tokyo 1980

Signed on the left: TITIANUS P.
According to Wethey (1969) this was painted by Titian in 1567 and sent as a gift the following year to Cardinal Alessandro Farnese in Rome. In 1680 the painting was in Parma with the Farnese Collection in the Palazzo del Giardino (Campori 1870). After various moves, it went to Naples in the second half of the eighteenth century, then to Rome (1800), once more to Naples, to Palermo (1806), and, after the defeat of Napoleon, it returned definitively to Capodimonte in 1815. The painting typifies the problems pertaining to workshop intervention in Titian's production, particularly regarding the many versions depicting themes that were in great demand among Titian's patrons. This was the case with the *Penitent Magdalene*. The subject was first tackled by Titian at the beginning of the 1530s in the famous canvas, now in the Uffizi, Florence, with a religiosity anything but void of sensuality. In the early 1560s Titian returned to the theme, modifying it iconographically and stylistically in accordance with Counter-Reformation morality. The first version was painted for Philip II. A reference to it appears in a letter of 1561, in which, among other things, the august patron urged his ambassador to Venice, Garcia Hernandez, to take the necessary precautions for shipment to Spain, which took place at the end of December.
The painting at once met with general approval in Venetian circles, since, as Vasari records (1568), it was immediately requested by a "Venetian the gentleman." Following his remarks on the *Martyrdom of Saint Lawrence* in the Gesuiti, of 1548-59, and on the *Saint Nicholas of Bari* in San Sebastiano, Vasari wrote: "He then did a dishevelled Magdalene with her hair falling over her shoulders, throat and breast, to send to the Catholic king. She raises her eyes to heaven, showing her penitence in the redness of her eyes and her tears for her sin. This picture, therefore, greatly moves those who behold it, and what is more, although very beautiful, it moves not to lust but to compassion. When finished, it so pleased Silvio, a Venetian noble, that he gave Titian 100 crowns for it, so that the artist was forced to do another of equal beauty for the Catholic King."
A copy of this "dishevelled Saint Mary Magdalene" by Luca Giordano exists in the Escorial, where Titian's work (lost in a fire in Great Britain in 1783) was once kept (Inglesia Vieja). Several versions exist in which the participation of Titian's workshop is more or less evident, as well as numerous copies both contemporary and later. Wethey (1969) subdivided them into three types: of the Escorial, of Naples and of the Hermitage, depending upon even modest variations in the landscape, the hair and the clothes, the presence or absence of the small unguent vase, its different material, and in the position of the skull. In the Naples painting Wethey praised the high quality, although the majority of critics (prior to its restoration in 1960) deplored the intervention of the workshop. According to Causa (1960), in the wake of its cleaning the most plausible attribution continued to be "Titian and workshop."
Direct comparison in the present exhibition between the Naples version and that in the Hermitage, believed to be the best of the known late versions of the 1561 *Magdalene*, partly because it entered the Saint Petersburg Collection with other paintings from Titian's estate, should provide the occasion for judging the relative merits of the two works.

LITERATURE Burckhard 1855, 1057ff; Campori 1870, 227; Crowe and Cavalcaselle 1878, II, 290; Gronau 1904, 189; Fischel 1907, 178, 255; de Rinaldis 1911, 154-6 (ed. 1928), 338-40; Suida 1940, 591ff; Arslan 1952, 327; Berenson 1957, 189; Zeri 1957, 19; Molaioli 1960, 48; Valcanover 1960, II, 72; Pallucchini 1969, no. 503; Wethey 1969, 145-51; Braunfels 1980, 407ff; Petrelli 1980, no. 10; Igenhoff Danhäuser 1984, 44ff; Mosco 1986, 192ff.

F.V.

64

Self-Portrait

oil on canvas, 86×69 cm
Madrid, Museo del Prado (inv. no. 407)

RESTORATION   1966

The figure is portrayed in profile, dressed in black with a cap of the same color. In his hand he holds a paint brush alluding to his art, while the double golden chain that adorns his chest expresses the sober refinement of one who knows the emptiness of ostentation. The chromatic synthesis, based on tones of black, gray, white and red in soft brushstrokes, gives rise to a strong sense of abstraction within a strongly realistic image. In this introspective self-portrait Titian seems to summarize his own long career. The painter meditates back on memories of his life passed in the proud knowledge of his craft: Count Palatine, Knight of the Golden Spur, admired by the emperor, by kings and princes, friend of the most famous artists – many of whom had already passed away – citizen of Rome, concerned about collecting the sums owed to him by the Spanish monarch. While residing in the Biri Grande in San Canciano during the years when he executed this self-portrait, he dedicated himself to the sale of lumber, with the help of his favorite son Orazio; nor did he miss the opportunity to act as intermediary between the Spanish and Turkish ambassadors; and he was gratified too by his nomination to the Florentine Academy, together with Palladio and Tintoretto.
An earlier self-portrait was sent by Titian to Spain in 1550. Two years later he sent a second in which he portrayed himself with the image of the then – prince Philip.
In this painting now in the Prado, which was probably acquired by Philip IV with the sale of the Rubens' collection, Titian's pale, thin and tired face appears without that expressive power that marks the self-portrait of the Staatliche Museen, Berlin (see cat. no. 59), painted, according to Vasari, in 1562. Nor can the serenity of this figure, seen in profile, be compared to the provocative arrogance that characterizes the other self-portrait in London. This portrait of the Prado is rather similar to the image of Titian in the engraving of 1567 of Cornelis Cort, of the *Adoration of the Holy Trinity*, in which the Flemish artist introduced a few variations with respect to the original. It is also similar to the self-portrait in the *Allegory of Prudence* of the National Gallery of London (see cat. no. 67) which seems to have been executed c. 1565. The Prado canvas can be placed between the two dates.

LITERATURE   Madrazo 1843, 147, no. 695; Crowe and Cavalcaselle 1877, II, 62-3; Allende-Salazar and Sanches Cantón 1919, 80-81; Foscari 1935, 18; Suida 1935, 113, 155; Tietze 1936, II, 299; Baloqui 1946, 171-72; Pallucchini 1954, II, 128; *Catalogo Museo del Prado* 1963, no. 407; Valcanover 1969, no. 476; Pallucchini 1969, 328, fig. 516-17; Pérez Sanchéz 1974, 155; Wilde 1974, 242; Sutton 1976, 202, 403; Angulo Iñíguez 1979, 180; Fasolo 1980, 87; Creighton 1980, 65-6; Birr, Diéz 1982, 70; Rosand 1982, 9, fig. 1-(8).

J.U.

65

Madonna and Child with Saints Titian
and Andrew

oil on canvas, 102.3×137 cm
Pieve di Cadore, Chiesa Arcidiaconale

EXHIBITION   Venice 1935, Belluno 1951
RESTORATION   1974, A. Lazzarini

"Titian made in Cadore, his birthplace, a panel in which is Our Lady and Saint Tiziano Bishop, and he himself is portrayed on his knees." Thus Vasari described in 1568 Titian's painting for the chapel of the Vecellio family in his old parish. In 1622 the Anonimo del Tizianello recorded Titian's picture, "in which he painted himself kneeling behind Saint Tiziano, who is adoring the Madonna and on the other side Saint Andrew the Apostle, in which he portrayed his brother Francesco so naturally that they seem alive and breathing." Again in 1648 Ridolfi wrote that Titian "wanted to leave a record of himself in his homeland in his family chapel... in the panel of Tiziano the Bishop with Saint Andrew adoring the Queen of Heaven with his own portrait." The painting has been engraved, as Titian, by LeFebre in 1682, and there are other later prints. The Pieve di Cadore altarpiece corresponds precisely to the description given it by the sources, with the only difference being that it is painted on a canvas rather than a panel support: a detail that has never been given importance, even when the authorship of the painting itself was being questioned.
Cavalcaselle (1877-88) was the first to propose that this was begun by Titian in 1560 and finished by his son Orazio "in view of a certain emptiness of color, a certain deficiency in the modeling and drawing... a thick and diaphanous tint..." Cavalcaselle cautioned however that the work had "suffered injuries" and had been "cleaned and also restored."
Indeed the canvas was cut in the center during an attempted theft before 1729-32 (Fabbro 1963) and recomposed immediately after. The cut is perfectly visible in a raking light. This was probably the occasion of the first restoration, to which we can attribute the damage caused by cleaning, by retouches and by the "complete reworking of the blue cloak of the Virgin," which Cavalcaselle noted. The cut of the canvas' central part has certainly been the most serious trauma suffered by the painting, but not the only one. With the demolition of the old parish church in 1764, prior to the construction of the existing archdiaconate consecrated in 1819, the painting became the object of dispute among the Vecellio descendants. After changing hands many times it went to the Casa Jacobi, where it remained from 1817 to 1847. In the latter year it was returned to the church and placed on the altar of San Tiziano, commissioned by Taddeo Jacobi and Alessandro Vecellio (Fabbro 1963), as attested by the commemorative plaque placed next to the altar.
In contrast to Cavalcaselle, in 1927 Adolfo Venturi reat-tributed the work to Titian, pointing to its compositional and chromatic virtues and in particular to its relationship to the *Mond Madonna* in the National Gallery, London. In Venturi's wake, critics divided into two groups: on one side Fogolari (1935), Norris (1935), Pallucchini (1935), De Logu (1950) and Fiocco (1951) judged the Pieve di Cadore picture to be an autograph Titian, while on the other side Suida (1936) and Tietze (1936) believed it to be a collaborative and workshop production. When Venturi saw the work it must have been in better condition than at present, prior to the restorations of 1935, 1951 and finally following the theft in 1971.
We know, thanks to the records of the Soprintendenza ai Beni Artistici e Storici of the Veneto, that in the 1935 restoration a double lining was applied, the stretcher replaced, and the picture given "a new varnish with a very light glaze... integrating the tonal equilibrium of the painting (letter from the Superintendent to the Ispettore Onorario of Pieve di Cadore, 27 August 1935). In 1951 the altarpiece was again restored on the occasion of the exhibition of the Vecellios. In the catalogue (Bellini 1951), Valcanover, on the basis of the results of the restoration (consisting of relining, cleaning, stuccoing and retouching) returned to A. Venturi's reading of the work. Titian's authorship was reconfirmed later by Valcanover (1960) and Pallucchini (1969), and in general by most critics after 1951, with Wethey (1961) as the only dissenter, maintaining that the painting was by the workshop. In 1971 the painting was stolen again, and removed from its stretcher by cutting along its perimeter. It was recovered immediately, and subjected once more to conservation: it was again relined and the standard operations of cleaning and pictorial reintegration were performed.
Today the votive altarpiece, painted on canvas with an extremely thin, almost non-existent layer of priming, is severely abraded and extensively retouched. The stale varnish is probably the cause for the green tone of the Virgin's originally blue cloak, already greenish when Venturi saw it. On this basis it would seem rather rash to doubt the authenticity of a painting that has suffered such surface loss and falsification of its chromatic-formal values, without taking into account the sources that agree in their attribution of the work to Titian, and all those factors that have negatively influenced its state of conservation.
Close in date to the *Mond Madonna* but certainly earlier than 1568, the date of the second edition of Vasari's *Lives*, the Pieve di Cadore altarpiece belongs to the years in which Titian "alone with his poetic imaginings, was to take up again his melancholy meditation in the safe harbor of his memories" (Valcanover 1960). Thus in the figure of the Madonna suckling the Child, Titian returned with a touch of sadness to the tender relationship between Mother and Son that he had expressed with such feeling in small works of the 20s and 30s, such as the

Rest on the Flight into Egypt, Marquess of Bath (see cat. no. 8), the *Madonna and Child* in the Thyssen collection, Lugano, and the *Madonna and Child with Saint Catherine and the Infant Baptist* in the National Gallery, London (see cat. no. 22). Scientific examination has corroborated the painting's autograph status. Reflectography and x-radiography have revealed *pentimenti*, such as a shorter beard in the self-portrait, the tips of Saint Tiziano's miter displaced to the left, the different solution to the background drapery and other details modified in the final version. Thanks to Borghini, we know that this was standard practice with Titian. Above all one wonders who among his collaborators would have dared to take the liberty of modifying the master's composition. X-radiography has also shown that the handling of the paint corresponds to that of other works by Titian (see the catalogues of the Milan [1978] and Venice [1981] exhibitions; also Valcanover 1979; Nepi Scirè 1979, 1983, 1987). Examination of the paint layers of a fragment of the green curtain has given similar results to those of analogous analyses carried out on micro-samples from some of Titian's Venetian paintings (Nepi Scirè 1979; Lazzarini 1983).

The bishop's miter is conspicuous among the best preserved parts of the painting, showing still a silky luminosity similar to that of the miter of Saint Louis in the Ancona altarpiece, with golden embroidery and inset jewels, notably the large ruby, which gleams against the background of green drapery. It is hard to imagine that Titian, who remained tied emotionally and financially to his birthplace, would not have painted personally a work destined for his family chapel, especially as it would not have caused problems of either time or place. This was the case with the now-lost frescoes of the choir of the old church, which the documents explicitly attribute to students working from the master's drawings. Finally the self-portrait in the background, which resembles the Prado self-portrait, is the visual equivalent of the author's signature.

The critical history of the painting seems to typify the attributional vagaries of works that have sustained damage.

LITERATURE   Vasari 1568 (ed. Milanesi 1906), VII; Anonimo del Tizianello (ed. Verdizotti) 1622; Ridolfi 1648 (ed. Von Hadeln 1914), I, 203; Crowe and Cavalcaselle 1877-88, II, 266ff; A. Venturi 1928, III, 297ff; Fogolari 1935, 165; Norris 1935, II, 127; Pallucchini 1935, XIII, 119, no. 3; Suida 1936, 102; Tietze 1936, 245-47; Delogu 1950, 54; Fiocco 1951, II, 99; Fabbro and Valcanover 1951, 63, 65; Valcanover 1960, 25, 49, no. 125; Fabbro 1963, 6-13; Wethey 1969, 103, no. 57; Pallucchini 1969, I, 183, 198; Valcanover 1969, 489.

F.M.A.G.

X-ray reconstruction of the painting made by Soprintendenza ai Beni Artistici e Storici di Venezia

66

Venus Blindfolding Cupid

oil on canvas, 118×185 cm
Rome, Galleria Borghese (inv. no. 170)

EXHIBITIONS   Vienna 1935, Tokyo 1980, Rome 1985, Moscow-Leningrad 1986
RESTORATION   1921, T. Venturini Papari

Datable c. 1565 (Hetzer 1935, Tietze 1936, Della Pergola 1956, Valcanover 1969; Wethey 1975; 1565-58 for Fischel 1907; and 1566-68 for Pallucchini 1964), the painting is mentioned in neither primary nor secondary sources of the period. Even the purpose of the work is unknown. It is worth noting only that the mountains in the background have been recognized as those of Cadore (Putelli 1966), Titian's birthplace, where he was working in 1565.
In 1608 the painting was probably sold by Cardinal Sfrondato to Cardinal Scipione Borghese together with other works of art (Della Pergola 1955). A document of 1613 recorded a payment of 10 *scudi* to the gilder Annibale Durante "for a frame gilded with foliage in relief... for the painting by Titian...." The measurements of the document had been interpreted as referred to the (present) seventeenth-century frame of the painting (Della Pergola 1955), even though it is not a frame of foliage, but of a sequence of winged heads of putti alternating with sea shells, appropriate to the theme of Venus.
The first important text about the painting is a poetic work of 1613 entitled *La Galleria dell'Illustrissimo e Reverendissimo Signor Scipione Cardinale Borghese cantata da Scipione Francucci*: eleven pages of verse dedicated to the description of the painting from the viewpoint of Cardinal Borghese's period. After an homage to Titian, "sublime painter, brightest sun which gives light to colors and makes nature grow pale," the poet presents Venus as "lavish show of Divine beauty." Francucci identified the subject as *Venus Blindfolding Cupid* and asked if the goddess was perhaps attempting to prevent Cupid from drawing his bow. The poet stressed the futility of Venus' action, claiming "blind Cupid becomes blind passion." The dominant feelings of the other putto, according to Francucci, are compassion for the blindfolded one and doubt about his own behavior. The two "beautiful, lovely and proud" nymphs are identified as "Dori, modest and beautiful nymph" (who holds the bow) and "Armilla, glory of honesty and Goddess of Beauty." They are described as foes uselessly armed against Cupid: "Fools, you don't know that Cupid is never blind / whenever you open your beautiful eyes, o he is with you."
In the first systematic description of the Borghese collection in 1650 Giacomo Manilli recorded: "The Venus with Two Nymphs is by Titian." In his *Vite degli illustri pittori veneti* (1648) Ridolfi described the painting as "Three Graces with Cupid and some shepherdesses" – shepherdesses who evidently do not exist. In subsequent inventories and guides it was indifferently cited as "Venus with Two Nymphs" or "The Three Graces." The 1693 inventory specified: "A large painting, The Three Graces by Titian with two Putti with a Crystal in front" (Della Pergola 1964). The same title recurs in the guide *Mercurio Errante* of 1760, while *Roma antica e moderna* (1775) designated it as "Venus with Two Nymphs, Titian." In the *Nota dei quadri... che ritornaron in Roma nel settembre 1816*, from Paris whence they had been transported by Napoleon, "The Three Graces of Titian" appears among other works of art owned by Prince Camillo Borghese.
The alternating interpretations as *Venus* or as *The Three Graces* were based on an ancient notion referred to by Claudian still taken up by J. von Sandrart in *Iconologia Deorum* (1680), that Venus was one of the Three Graces. The painting constitutes a rare instance of a mythology of the pagan gods painted by Titian "after" the conclusion of the Council of Trent in 1563.
Venus Blindfolding Cupid hints at diverse iconographic readings, and eludes precise classification in this sense. Most modern critics have favored a pedagogical explanation, more moralistic in tone than would have been customary in Cardinal Borghese's time, adopting the title "The Education of Cupid" (Valentiner 1930; Hetzer 1935; Tietze 1936; Panofsky 1969; Friedländer 1967). Suida instead called it "The Apprenticeship of Cupid" (1933).
Venus' behavior toward her children expresses a sense of the dramatic force of destiny. A fiery sky and the movement of the drapery of the nymph who hurries to bring the bow (more suited in size to Apollo than to Cupid) create the drama of the occasion. The seeing Cupid is afflicted by sadness, while he leans pensively on his mother's shoulder. The prevalent red contrasts with the blue tints of Venus' mantle, the seeing putto's wing and the turquoise mountains.
In Petrarch's *Trionfi* and in the figurative tradition widespread through fifteenth-century woodcuts, Cupid is blind. On tarot cards or in Baccio Baldini's engraving (Bartsch 1980) the planet Venus is accompanied by a blindfolded Cupid and by the Three Graces.
The presence of two Cupids in Titian's painting could be interpreted as an expression of "reciprocal love" according to classical usage described by Cartari (1571). But as Panofsky explained, a Neoplatonic interpretation is also possible, whereby the seeing Cupid (Anteros) refers to Divine Love, which elevates the human soul to the contemplation of God, and blindfolded Cupid (Eros) refers to Earthly Love. Panofsky believed that the nymphs were allegories of Marital Love and Chastity (1939) or of Pleasure and Chastity (1969). He concluded that this is a wedding painting, even though the dramatic character of the picture seems to make this unlikely.

For Wind (1986) it was instead an allegorical initiation of Cupid personified by Venus in the double guise of clear perception and blind passion.

Tietze, basing himself on a theory put forward by Lionello Venturi (1933), considered the *Golden Ass* of Apuleius in Firenzuola's 1550 translation as the source of the theme. In this case, Venus intends to punish Cupid for his adventures with Psyche, consigning his weapons to a brother. For Friedländer (1967) the central divinity would have been Vesta who, in the presence of her priestesses, disarms love; but in the canvas in question the Vestals appear to bring rather than to carry away Cupid's weapons.

In this oblong composition, Titian re-elaborated elements already inserted in the supposed allegory of the Marchese del Vasto (c. 1532, Paris, Louvre), creating greater space around the figures.

Engraved reproductions of *Venus Blindfolding Cupid* were not made in Titian's time, even though he promoted the diffusion in prints of others of his works. In the seventeenth century it was reproduced in an etching by Louis de Boulogne, in the eighteenth century by Robert Strange, and in the nineteenth cenury by Domenico Marchetti (cat. Gabinetto Nazionale delle Stampe, 1977).

The painting was copied by various painters, particularly in the early seventeenth century when Venetian painting, and Titian's in particular, contributed to the birth of classical baroque art. The beauty of the chromatic texture of the painting, created by large vibrant touches, inspired Francucci in his description of "Titian, who tempered his color in the foaming waves in which Venus, goddess of beauty, was born" (1613). The harmonies of the golden lights of the reds, blues and fleshtones are characterized by a luminosity evoking the amber light that distinguishes the coloring of Titian's late works.

The copies listed by Wethey (1975) include those of Genoa, ex Palazzo Balbi; Karlstadt, Landresidenset; Museo de Bellas Artes, Seville, before 1686; National Gallery of Art, Washington, c. 1570, attributed to L. Sustris; formerly in the house of Van Dyck, a copy by Van Dyck, who also drew the entire composition in his Italian sketchbook of 1622-27; a partial copy of Venus and the two Cupids, whereabouts unknown; a copy of the seeing Cupid by A. Varotari, and a similar copy, both in the Alte Pinakothek, Munich. To this list may be added the copies of the blindfolded Cupid attributed to Velàzquez by Mayer, formerly Contini-Bonacossi collection, Florence (Bardi 1979) and one owned by the Borghese family in 1700 mentioned in the guide of the Galleria Borghese by Domenico Montelatici.

LITERATURE Apuleio (ed. 1550), 64; Cartari 1571, 500; Francucci 1613, 107-17; Ridolfi 1648 (ed. 1835), 257; Manilli 1650, 64; Von Sandrart 1680, 194; Montelatici 1700, 257; Mercurio... 1760, 38; *Roma antica e moderna* 1775, 158; *Nota dei Quadri...* 1816, 11; Fischel 1907, 180; Valentiner 1930, I, 25; Suida 1933, 119; L. Venturi 1933, III, 525; Hetzer 1935, 169; Tietze 1936, 241; Panofsky 1939, 155-69; Della Pergola 1955, no. 235; Della Pergola 1964, 456; Pallucchini 1964, 321; Putelli 1966, 339; Friedländer 1967, 50-52; Panofsky 1969, 129-36; Valcanover 1969, no. 450; Wethey 1975, III, no. 4, 85; Catelli Isola 1977, nos. 155, 318, 334; *The Illustrated Bartsch* 1980, XXXIV, 192, 300; Bardi 1981, no. 169.

K.H.F.

67

Allegory of Time Governed by Prudence

oil on canvas, 75.6×68.6 cm
London, The Trustees of the National Gallery

RESTORATION 1966

The painting bears in the upper part the inscription: EX PRAETE/RITO (to the left) PRAESENS PRUDEN/TER AGIT (in the center) NI FUTURU[M]/ ACTIONE[M] DE/TURPET (to the right) ("From the past, the present acts prudently lest it spoil future action").

The *Allegory of Prudence* passed to the National Gallery in 1966, the gift of David Koetser. Since 1955, when it appeared at Christie's on 22 November, it had been lost from view. Its provenance before this has been painstakingly traced by Wethey (1971) who nevertheless was unable to establish its location before 1740 when the work was inventoried in the Crozat collection, Paris (Stuffman 1968). It is sufficient to note here that the work was in the sale of the collection of the Duc de Tallard, Paris, in 1756, as an autograph Titian – and only Wind (1976) has ever contested this. Ten years later, it was still in Paris, in the possession of Chevalier Menabuoni, and was described as a triple portrait of Pope Julius II on the left, Duke Alfonso d'Este in the center, and Emperor Charles V on the right (Duvaux 1873). This approach to its subject was revived when, it was exhibited in 1828 by the British Institute (no. 14) with Pope Paul III as the old man on the left. By this time it was in the collection of the Earl of Aberdeen.

In 1924, Von Hadeln examined the enigmatic subject matter. The canvas was then in the collection of Francis Howard, London, where it was to remain until 1955, and was published for the first time. Von Hadeln proposed that the work was an allegory of the three ages of man, with the heads of the animals – wolf, lion and dog – portrayed under the three faces, representing "a symbolical expansion" of that idea. He also speculated that the painting was originally the cover for another portrait. We owe to Panofsky and Saxl and Panofsky (1926, 1930, 1963, 1955, 1969) a convincing and illuminating interpretation of the image. The key rests with the inscription, which establishes the three divisions of *Time* (past, present and future); subordinates them to the morality and discipline of *Prudentia*, which in turn results from the triple and connected scanning of "Memoria," "Intelligentia", and "Providentia." This is precisely the same as in a tradition established by the *Liber de moribus* of the Pseudoseneca and by the *Repertorium morale* of Petrus Berehorius ("in praeteritum recordatione, in praesentium ordinatione, in futurorum meditatione"), two texts whose compilation dates back to the fourteenth century. On the iconographic level, Panofsky and Saxl and Panofsky traced a long way back the triplicate image of Prudence (for example in the floor of the Cathedral of Siena, in the relief

assigned to the circle of Antonio Rossellino in the Victoria and Albert Museum, London, etcetera). Together they noticed of Time the allegory as a youth, mature man, and old man (as in the drawing by Baccio Bandinelli in the Metropolitan Museum, New York) and of a three-headed monster – a wolf, the past that devours; a lion, the present that acts; and a dog, the future that flatters. The latter originally was associated with the representation in the form of a serpent of Serapis-Apollo-Sol based on a passage of the *Saturnalia* (20, 133ff) by Macrobius (as in sheet iv of the Cod. Reg. Lat. 1290 in the Vatican, or in an engraving by Jan Collaert from Giovanni Stradano but, also, and of most interest to us, in the woodcut on folio Y1 of the Aldine Press's *Hypnerotomachia Poliphili* of 1499). The adoption of the Macrobian animals to symbolize Prudence is attributed to Pierio Valeriano, ambiguously since in the *Hieroglyphica* – first published in 1556, a repertoire of immense importance for the figurative arts – he admitted that the tripartite monster could also allude to Time, while still emphasizing Prudence. In the relevant entry in his repertoire Valeriano claimed that the serpent indicated Prudence, since it "non praesentia tantum examinet, verum et lapsa et futura meditatur" ("not only does it look at present things, but in truth also reflects on the past and future ones"). But, as the revelatory image is that of "capita ea, Canis unum, Lupi alterum, tertium Leonis" ("those heads, one of Dog, another of Wolf, the third of Lion") as in Macrobius, he allows that it could easily be the attribute of Serapis (Apollo, Sol), to which it was appropriate, because. Prudence governs time.

There can be no doubt that Pierio Valeriano gives us the iconological source of Titian's painting, together with the woodcut of the *Polifilo*. Not only could Titian have known Valeriano's text, given its popularity with painters, but even less could he have ignored it given his broad and cultivated circle of friends and his literary interests (Padoan 1980, twice, and Petrocchi 1980). It was written by a scholar who had a close friendship with Alvise Cornaro, who had previously acted on Titian's behalf, as we have discussed elsewhere (Puppi 1980). Nor should we overlook a detail of the sculptural decoration of the Cornaro Odeon in Padua, of the tripartite symbol within a general context inspired by the ideal of the "sober life," in other words of "prudence" (Bresciani Alvarez 1980, 198). Titian was probably familiar with the carved image of the triple head (but as human faces, implying the three ages of man) on the coat of arms of the Zacco family, visible on the façade of their Paduan residence rebuilt between 1555 and 1556 (Puppi 1980).

The London painting links the heads of the wolf, the lion and the dog to the superimposed heads of three human faces in which Panofsky (1955, 1962, 1969) convincingly recognized, from the left, the features of Titian (compare the Madrid *Self-Portrait*, cat. no. 64), his son Orazio (1525-76) and his nephew Marco (1545-161?). Hill's theory (1956), that the faces in the center and right represent Cardinal Ippolito de'Medici, in adolescence and maturity, is fanciful.

Panofsky acutely noted that the central images (the present) are the most sculptural – clearly delineated in prominent relief and carefully balanced – while those on the left (the past) withdraw into the penumbra, and those on the right (the future) shine in the light. In spite of this, Arasse (1980) correctly saw in the vertical and horizontal *concatenatio* of the images and in the relationship of these to the inscription, not only Titian's participation in the iconographic debate (see Olivato 1979, 245) but also a sort of conscious ambiguity, explicit in the exact coincidence of form and content, and prohibiting a single or definitive interpretation of at least three codes as emblem, allegory, and self-portrait. We find ourselves in the presence of a most unusual figurative testament, as a reflection on Time (the time of life that, in in its final hours finds fullness and hope in the "living generations" in accordance with the mercantile "ethics of the Venetians" [Padoan 1980, 94]), governed by Prudence. The linguistic and formal order, at a very high pitch and tied to the late and sensational period of the *poesie*, suggests a dating of this masterpiece around 1565, as proposed by Tietze (1950) and accepted by the majority of scholars (Valcanover, Pallucchini etcetera), with the exception of Wethey who preferred 1570. 1565 is all the more credible considering that Titian was concerned at this time with providing for the financial future of his family (Panofsky 1969) and hence this painting, obviously for private use, may be understood both as testimony and pledge of that commitment.

LITERATURE   Duvaux 1873, CCXCI-CCXCII; Von Hadeln 1924, 179-80; Panofsky and Saxl 1926, 177-81; Panofsky 1930, 1-35; Suida 1935, 89; Tietze 1950, 378; Hill 1956, 40-41; Valcanover 1960, 49, no. 120; Panofsky 1962, 1955, 147ff; Wind 1967, 260; Stuffman 1968, 76; Pallucchini 1969, 317; Panofsky 1969, 102-08; Valcanover 1969, 131, no. 449; Wethey 1969, 50, 145-46, no. 107; Arasse 1980, 155-58, 159-60; Puppi 1980, 555-56.

L.P.

68

Saint Jerome

oil on canvas, 137.5×97 cm
Lugano, Thyssen-Bornemisza Collection

EXHIBITIONS   Rotterdam 1959-60, Essen 1960, London 1961, Stuttgart 1988-89

This penitent *Saint Jerome*, unanimously dated 1570 and 1575, is one of the few works that can be assigned with certainty to the last years of Titian's activity. These works are few in number, but all are of sublime quality and supreme poetic suggestiveness. The *Saint Jerome* takes up a theme that recurs several times in Titian's work, beginning with the *Penitent Saint Jerome* cited in a letter of 1531 from Titian to Federico Gonzaga and identified by the majority of scholars with the painting of this subject now in the Louvre. The final appearance of the theme is in with the painting sent in 1575 to Philip II, documented by a letter of 24 September of that year to the King from the Spanish ambassador to Venice Guzmán de Silva, now exhibited in the Nuevos Museos del Escorial.
The Thyssen painting is a later version of the altarpiece executed by Titian in 1555 for the Church of Santa Maria Nuova in Venice and now in the Pinacoteca di Brera, Milan. A miniature version of this altarpiece exists, probably a workshop production if not actually a copy, at the Accademia di San Luca, Rome. Fewer than twenty years later, Titian returned to the Santa Maria Nuova altarpiece in a version of greatly reduced dimensions. That painting is now in the Thyssen collection. The composition is notably simplified, eliminating the saint's attributes to the left: the books, skull and hourglass. Titian also accentuated the sense of verticality that in the Brera painting had been dictated by the format demand of its function as an altarpiece. But the change of style in Titian from the 1560s, with that optical and technical innovation that carried him on the wave of a pressing creative surge to the "magic impressionism" (Longhi's phrase) of his last years, manifests itself fully and felicitously in this painting. The landscape, less detailed than that of the Brera altarpiece, resembles a luminous and ill-defined dazzle, where earth and sky, trees, rocks, and clouds mingle in a kind of whirlwind of light and shade, in which the figure is also confounded: a perception of form as totally subject to the materiality of light. The figure of the saint has lost that clear physical definition that in the Brera painting was a reflex of the mannerist poetic ideal, and is disbanded and absorbed by the landscape surrounding him, to be revealed only by the light that generates the colors.
When in 1965 the painting was relined, a preparatory drawing for the figure of Saint Jerome, in reverse, was discovered on the back of the canvas. While the position of the arm laid on the book looks forward to the finished painting on the front,

the drapery resembles instead that of the Brera prototype. In the eighteenth century, a *Saint Jerome* by Titian was recorded in the Palazzo Balbi, Genoa (Ratti 1780, 189). On 3 November 1805 this was purchased by Andrew Wilson and sold in London (Peter Coxe, 6 May 1810, lot no. 8); it was sold then at the Rendelsham sale (23 May 1810, lot no. 8). (This information was supplied by E.K. Waterhouse to H.E. Wethey.) Since the Thyssen painting came from England, where it was first recorded in the collection S.E.W. Browne, it is probable that the two paintings are the same.

LITERATURE   Venturi 1932, 490-7; Suida 1933, 123, 126, 173, 190; Berenson 1957, 18; Pallucchini 1961, 290; Ballarin 1968, fig. 72; Pallucchini 1969, I, 169, 195, 196, 328, 333, II, fig. 537; Valcanover 1969, 127-28, no. 411; Wethey 1969, I, 135-36, no. 107; Meijer 1976, 17-19, fig. 9b; Pallucchini 1977, 60, pl. LIX; Fischer 1977, 78-9; Hope 1980, 155; Meijer 1981, 276-77; Pignatti 1981, II, 60, no. 463; Wethey 1987, 25, 86, 142, no. 16, 142.

G.B.

69

Judith

oil on canvas 112.8×94.5 cm
The Detroit Institute of Arts, Gift of Edsel B. Ford (35.10)

EXHIBITIONS New York 1939, New York 1956, Toronto 1960

This painting was probably first recorded in 1677 in the collection of Marchese Gerini (Bocchi and Cinelli 1677). In 1935 it was bought by Edsel B. Ford from a private collection in New York and presented to the Detroit Institute of Arts in the same year.

The only known depiction of *Judith with the Head of Holofernes* in Titian's work, the painting has been universally accepted as autograph since its publication in 1922 by Borenius, who was, however, unaware of the early provenance of the picture and of the engraving after the composition published in Florence in 1759, while in the collection of the Gerini family. Fredericksen found the mention of the picture in an earlier description of the Gerini collection published in 1677. While it seems logical that it is the same picture, it should be noted that the 1677 description mentions "una vecchia" as Judith's servant. This would conform to the traditional iconography of the subject, but in the Detroit picture only a black page boy serves as an attendant. Another related composition, representing *Salome with the Head of Saint John* (a version, deemed a "variant of a Titianesque original" by Wethey, was published as original by Morassi in 1968 who identified it with a painting formerly in the collection of Archduke Leopold Wilhelm, engraved by L. Vorsterman). It features an old woman next to the central figure, as well as a black page boy. The provenance of that picture was established by Morassi who traced it back to Bartolomeo della Nave in the early 1600s. It was in any case in the collection of Archduke Leopold Wilhelm in Brussels by 1660 when published by David Teniers in his *Theatrum Pictorium*. While this reinforces the hypothesis that the Detroit picture was indeed the one described in the 1677 publication, one should not exclude the possibility of another painting by Titian – perhaps another version of the ex-Leopold Wilhelm *Salome* – in the Gerini collection.

The most puzzling element in the Detroit picture is the discrepancy in style between the upper and lower parts of the composition, more particularly between the treatment of the facial features of the Judith and of the head of Holofernes. Borenius already noted it and credited the smooth texture of Judith's face to the "result of an attempt to remove the impression of a 'lack of finish.'"

Tietze (1936) and Valcanover (1960) followed by all other writers have recognized in this composition a late work by Titian, probably of the 1570s. The brushwork used in the fabrics, and even more emphatically in that of the head of Holofernes, can be compared to the loose and broken strokes Titian adopted in later compositions such as the *Flaying of Marsyas* (Státní Zámek, Kroměříž, Czechoslovakia).

Tietze believed that Titian had begun the composition in the 1550s, abandoned it, and finished it some twenty years later. Fredericksen theorized that this may not have been the case, basing his opinion on the publication by Morassi, of the above-mentioned *Salome*, which displays the same discrepancy of various styles on a single canvas. Since it seems improbable that both paintings could have shared the same history, both Morassi and Fredericksen concluded that Titian chose, in some cases, to paint some heads finely, while reserving a rougher execution for other parts of the same canvas. In both the Detroit picture and the *Salome* the painterly intensity of the severed heads not only contrasts with the sweetness of the female figures, but enhances the dramatic power of the pictures.

Tietze's opinion that parts of the picture were executed twenty years apart should however not be totally discounted. A recent x-ray analysis of the Detroit picture has revealed under the present paint surface an entirely different composition. Likewise the Washington *Venus with a Mirror* (c. 1552-55, see cat. no. 51) is painted over a double portrait (Shapley 1971-72). The habit, evidently not uncommon in Titian's studio, of painting over compositions abandoned for one reason or another could also explain how an early composition could be finished at a later date, and in a different style. The portrait under the Detroit *Judith* can be tentatively identified as a portrait of Charles V. He wears the closed crown, a privilege reserved for the Holy Roman Emperor, and holds both the orb and mace or scepter. If this identification is correct, it is an important addition to the corpus of portraits of the Emperor by Titian and the only one in which he wears his *insignia*.

LITERATURE Bocchi and Cinelli 1677, 497; *Raccolta di Stampe rappresentanti quadri più scelti dei Signori Marchesi Gerini*, 1, 1759; *Raccolta di ottanta stampe...*, 1786, pl. 22; Hume 1829, iii; Crowe and Cavalcaselle, II, 1878, 570; Borenius 1922, 88-89; Fischel 1924 (5th ed.), 325, no. 271; A. Venturi 1928, 367; Biermann 1929, 317-20; Suida 1933, 172; Valentiner 1935, 102-4; Valentiner 1935, 287-90; Tietze 1936, 286; Tietze 1937, 320, no. 275; Detroit Institute of Arts, *Catalogue...*, 1944, 134; Tietze 1950, 368-69; Pallucchini 1953-54, 122-23; Gronau 1955, 53; Dell'Acqua 1955, 132; Berenson 1957, I, 184; Valcanover 1960, II, pl. 117; Morassi 1968, 465, fig. 9; Pallucchini 1969, 176-77, 318; Valcanover 1969, no. 452; Wethey 1969, 95, no. 44, pl. 193; Shapley 1971-72, 93-105; Fredericksen and Zeri 1972, 202; Sterne 1980, 234; *One hundred masterpieces...* 1985, 15, fig. 6, Fredericksen 1990 (in press).

J.P.M.

70

The Entombment

oil on canvas, 130×168 cm
Madrid, Museo del Prado (inv. no. 441)

EXHIBITIONS   Ghent 1955, Los Angeles 1979
RESTORATION   1968

Signed on the side of the tomb: TITIANUS F.

The story of the entombment of Christ was told by all four Evangelists in the same way, although John (19: 38-42) and Luke (25: 50-6) gave the most details, the former signaling the presence of Nicodemus at the moment of burial, the latter lingering on other aspects. According to of them, the dead Christ was placed, according to Jewish ritual, in a cave, whose mouth was then covered by a stone. Nevertheless Titian, in keeping with Roman tradition, preferred to imagine the burial inside a marble sarcophagus, for greater dramatic effect.

In one version of this subject in the Louvre, the earliest we know of Titian eliminated the sarcophagus, faithful to the text of the Gospels, and because of this the Louvre version has been called 'preparations for the burial of Christ,' since the scene seems merely to be the sequel of the 'Descent from the Cross.' In 1556, Titian painted a second canvas for King Philip II, with figures in profile, which was stolen during transit to the Spanish court.

At the sovereign's insistence Titian painted a third version (Museo del Prado), which arrived in Madrid in 1559, and was undoubtedly of higher quality than the preceding version, which he had proudly signed 'cavaliere cesareo'.

Titian treated this theme for the last time c. 1565, and this was in all probability the canvas that Vasari saw in 1556 in the artist's studio. He retouched the painting, which in his late style, when it was acquired by the Republic in 1572, on the advice of the ambassador to Madrid, as a gift for the court secretary Antonio Perez.

The participants in this drama express intense suffering in an emotionally charged atmosphere reinforced by the pictorial technique of Titian's later years, described for us by Palma il Giovane. The canvas seems to be significantly cut down on the left side by comparison with the numerous copies in Spain, among them the one preserved in the Cathedral of Salamanca. The profound spirituality of the scene characterizes the last years of the artist's activity, and Titian himself is portrayed as Joseph of Arimathea. The rarefied general tonality of the painting, pervaded by the vibrant red of the sky, against which a fortress reminiscent of the Castel Sant'Angelo is silhouetted, takes on a tragic mood, assisted by the dissolution of the forms. The gestures of the mourners also convey Titian's dramatic intent.

The painting was acquired in 1585 for the royal collections, probably destined for the Alcázar of Madrid and later the chapel of the Aranjuez palace, where in 1626 it was seen by Cassiano del Pozzo. According to Father Santos, in 1657 it was in the Escorial Monastery and remained there until 1839 when it became part of the Museo del Prado.

LITERATURE   Madrazo 1843, 179, no. 822; Madrazo 1873, 91, no. 491; Crowe and Cavalcaselle 1877, II, 292; Beroqui 1927, 183; Rothschild 1931, 297; Beroqui 1946, 156-57; Valcanover 1960, II, fig. 124; *Catalogo Museo del Prado* 1963, no. 441; Pallucchini 1969, fig. 496; Valcanover 1969, no. 467; Lafuente Ferrari 1970, 162; Pallucchini 1967, fig. LIV; Pignatti 1979, 80, 163; Fasolo 1980, 76; Delaforce 1982, fig. 15.

J.U.

71

Christ Carrying the Cross

oil on canvas, 67×77 cm
Madrid, Museo del Prado (inv. no. 438)

Bears the signature on the cross: TITANUS AEQ.CAES.F
The painting constitutes Titian's interpretation of Matthew,
XXVII, 32-33; Mark XV, 21-22; and Luke XXIII, 26-27, in which
Simon the Cyrenian, father of Alexander and Rufus, was
compelled to bear the cross for Jesus. The figures are portrayed in profile, and the picture differs from the first version of
the theme (Museo del Prado, inv. no. 439), in which Christ is
overwhelmed by the weight of the cross and rests on his knees.
The vigor of Christ's face, observing us with a penetrating look
of recrimination or complicity, adds to the sense of His
determination to face martyrdom heroically. Simon the
Cyrenian is not depicted as a humble peasant. His noble face,
with thick hair and long beard gently touching the cross, and
the ring that decorates his right thumb, denote nobility. Even
if Ridolfi's theory (1648) that Francesco Zuccato was the
model for Simon the Cyrenian is unconvincing, nonetheless, as
in the Leningrad version of the same subject, Titian clearly
employed a live model.
The artist's signature is visible on the cross, inscribed in the
same direction as the grain of the wood. Despite its high
quality, the Leningrad painting is not signed, perhaps because
of the painter's desire to become one with the suffering of
Christ and to benefit from the redemption of the human race.
The glowing blue of the tunic, with scumbled brushstrokes of
luminous white, and the visage of Christ, stained with blood,
create a contrast to the austere and restless figure of Simon.
The rapid, broad strokes, characteristic of Titian's late work,
suggest a date between 1565 and 1570.
It is not known when this painting, which is in excellent
condition, entered the royal collections. It is first mentioned in
the Alcázar of Madrid in 1666. Following the fire in the old
palace, it was transferred to the Buen Retiro where it was in
1746. In 1794 it was inventoried in the new Palacio Real of
Madrid. In 1843 it was acquired by the Prado.

LITERATURE Madrazo 1843, 155, no. 725; Crowe and Cavalcaselle 1877, II, 405-06; Beroqui 1927, 197; Tietze 1936, II,
296; Beroqui 1946, 171; Berenson 1957, 188; Valcanover
1960, II, fig. 127; *Catalogo Museo del Prado* 1963, no. 438;
Pallucchini 1969, fig. 523; Wethey 1969, I, 36, 81, fig. 127;
Lafuente Ferrari 1970, 174; Valcanover 1969, no. 492; Angulo
Iñíguez 1979, 183; Fasolo 1980, 82.

J.U.

357

72

Boy with Dogs

oil on canvas, 96×115 cm
Rotterdam, Museum Boymans-van Beuningen (Inv. n. 2569)

EXHIBITIONS Amsterdam 1936, Rotterdam 1938, Rotterdam 1949, Paris 1952, Rotterdam 1955, London 1982-83, Leningrad 1986, Rotterdam 1989-90
RESTORATION 1982

The little boy has his left arm over the back of a white dog standing beside him. His left hand is raising the hem of his lilac tunic to reveal what looks like a bunch of grapes in the folds. Another dog, lying to his left, is suckling two pups. The scene is set in a landscape painted with broad brushstrokes, and what appears to be another bunch of grapes is visible among the leaves on the upper right-hand side. A few buildings appear on the slope of a steep mountain in the distance, one of which is a tall, brightly-lit tower. On the far left is a tree with its leaves sharply outlined against the sky.

Judging by the extremely sketchy manner, the work is generally believed to have been executed in the last years of Titian's life, around 1570-76. An some stage, the four sides of the canvas were out off rather crudely. Tietze took it to be a fragment of what had once been a far larger piece depicting a mythological theme. Panofsky, however, assumed that the original had not been much bigger and thought it might be related to Paolo Veronese's *Cupid with Two Dogs* at the Alte Pinakothek in Munich. Considering that the composition is more or less surrounded by the various elements, the painting is unlikely to have been part of a much larger canvas.

The significance of the representation is puzzling. The white dog, as was observed some time ago, is almost identical to the one in Titian's *Portrait of a Nobleman* in Kassel. The only difference is that the dog in the Rotterdam painting has a long-haired tail. The Rotterdam painting has always been thought originally to have come from the Serbelloni collection in Milan. According to early catalogues, it alludes to a fire that broke out at the Serbelloni's palace and the dogs portrayed in the picture are supposed to have rescued the little prince. Wethey *et al.* believed the original owner to be Agabrio or Gabriele Serbelloni (1509-80). Ost recently published a study of the Rotterdam and Kassel canvases that, taking account of the provenance of the Rotterdam painting, concludes that the nobleman in the Kassel painting would probably have been Gabriele Serbelloni. His theory was that the portrait had probably been lying in Titian's studio for some time and that the dog had at some point served as an example for the one in the Rotterdam painting. He also drew attention to the strong resemblance between the boy in the Rotterdam painting and Roman copies of Hellenistic sculptures representing Hermes or Bacchus as youths, and to the conceptual association

between the dog suckling its young in the painting and the wolf that suckled Romulus and Remus, the founders of Rome. The latter idea is unconvincing, however, as the animals depicted here are quite unmistakably dogs.

For the time being, we can only conclude that the boy, seen in conjunction with the bunches of grapes, seems to be a Bacchanalian figure. The significance of the dogs and the buildings in the background has yet to be ascertained.

The painting was restored in 1982, so that the colors and broad brushstrokes are now clearly visible. At the same time it was examined scientifically. X-ray photographs and infrared reflectrograms taken by J.R.J. van Asperen de Boer show that the tree was originally farther to the right and that there was a high mountain on the far left (see Giltaij 1982), while the boy had originally been higher up on the canvas. It is now plain to the naked eye that his feet were initially higher up and farther to the left.

The technique is characteristic of Titian, who tended to introduce radical changes while painting and to devote a great deal of time to it, as Marco Boschini so eloquently described in 1674. Charles Hope (1983) speculated that the sketchy technique might indicate that such paintings were unfinished. This particular piece, however, is unlikely to be an unfinished work. In spite of the broad brushstrokes – mainly in the landscape – there is nothing at all to suggest that is was not completed.

LITERATURE Venturi 1931, 388; Suida 1933, pl. 107, 113; Tietze 1936, I, 247-48, II, 308-09, pl. 263; Hannema 1949, no. 103; Tietze 1950, 392, pl. 260; Dell'Acqua 1955, 134, pl. 187; Berenson 1957, II, pl. 1020; *Catalogus ...*, 1962, 141; Pallucchini 1959, I, 328, II, pl. 541-44; Panofsky 1969, 171; Valcanover 1969, no. 500; *Old ...*, 1972, 223, 134; Wethey 1975, 129, no. 2; Roy Fischer 1977, 66, pl. 53; Giltaij 1982, Ost 1982, 49-55, pl. 28.

J.G.

73

Tarquin and Lucretia

oil on canvas, 114×100 cm
Vienna, Gemäldegalerie der Akademie der Bildenden Künste

EXHIBITIONS   Zurich 1946, Brussels 1947, Paris 1948, Stockholm 1948, Copenhagen 1948-49, London 1949, Washington, New York, Chicago, San Francisco, St. Louis, Toledo, Toronto, Boston, Philadelphia 1951-52, Oslo 1952, Innsbruck 1952, Vienna 1953
RESTORATION   1917, R. Eigenberger

The painting represents a scene from the story of Lucretia as narrated by Livy (*Ad Urbe Condita* I, 58) and by Ovid (*Fasti* II, 725-850): if the young wife of his friend and relative Collatino would not submit to his will, the Etruscan prince Sextus Tarquinius threatened to kill her together with a slave and pretend to her husband that the double assassination was punishment for committing adultery with the servant. Fearing this disgrace, Lucretia surrenders, but the following day, after revealing the truth to her father and husband, she takes her own life.
Three different versions of the same scene by Titian are extant, all late works. These are the version sent to Philip II, today in the Fitzwilliam Museum, Cambridge; the painting in the Musée des Beaux-Arts, Bordeaux, only slightly different from the Fitzwilliam version and most likely painted with workshop collaboration; and finally the Vienna version, which compared to the other two has its own peculiarities.
The Vienna painting first appeared in 1907, when the Pisko auction house put up for sale the Viennese collection of Jauner von Schroffenegg. The catalogue listed the work as *Othello* and attributed it to Veronese. It was purchased as such for the picture collection of the Akademie. Soon after, Gerish, director of the institution, exhibited it with the title *Tarquin and Lucretia*, identifying the artist as Titian. At this point controversy with the former owners forced the painting into storage, and only in 1915 was it exhibited publicly, on the initiative of Wilhelm Bode. Even today the earlier provenance of the painting is unknown. Several times (Popp 1921; Titian exhibition 1935; Bernard-Hours 1964) it has been suggested that the work is a fragment of a full-length version, which in 1622 was recorded in the collection of Lord Arundel, subsequently in Charles I's collection, and thence to the French Royal collections. But this hypothesis is contradicted by the fact that there is no evidence of cutting around the Viennese canvas. Apart from some stuccoing found mainly on the edges of the canvas, and apart from some retouches in the flesh and in the shadows between the two figures, the painting's state of conservation is generally sound.
With few exceptions, the attribution to Titian is universally accepted. Only Berenson omits it from his list of the painter's works (Berenson 1947), nor does Hope discuss it in his account of Titian's late work (Hope 1980, 1988). Wethey considered it to be by a follower of Titian, perhaps Palma il Giovane (Wethey 1975). Chronologically, the painting has always been placed in the context of Titian's last production, and indeed has repeatedly been assigned the role of "touchstone for the critical evaluation of the late style" (Walther 1978). Contrasting views diverge within this consensus. On the one hand, the painting is seen as one of the highest expressions of the last fifteen years of the artist's life. This style characterized his old age, in which form, through an ever more "open" brushstroke, dissolves into often purely tonal chromatic components, almost impressionistic in their effects: an "ultima maniera" considered analogous in its complexity and multiplicity to the drama of the human condition (Eigenberger 1927; Suida 1933; Dell'Acqua 1958; Valcanover 1960; Morassi 1964; Pallucchini 1969, 1980). In this case works that show a high degree of finish stand in contrast with the Vienna painting – the Fitzwilliam *Tarquin and Lucretia*, for example, which is carefully defined in every detail, or the *Temptation of Eve*, both works produced c. 1570 – constitute a "second late style," chronologically parallel to the first. Tietze (1950), Braunfels (1980) and Jaffé (1983, 1987) took a different position. For Tietze the Vienna painting was an oil sketch, preparatory to the Cambridge version. The other two scholars considered it autonomous but incomplete.
The weakness of the theory of two late styles is exposed by the *Flaying of Marsyas* in Kroměříž. Of all the works of the late period, this can be considered the product of the most slow and exacting gestation. Here the open brushstroke and the dissolution of form, taken to extremes, are coupled with detailed modeling in local color of closed surfaces, betraying great sensitivity to final detail.
Compared to this, with the exception of some missing glazes and lights, paintings such as the *Pietà* in Venice, the Leningrad *Saint Sebastian*, and even more the Munich *Crowning of Thorns* unquestionably leave the impression that they are unfinished.
Judged by these standards, the Vienna *Tarquin and Lucretia* appears as even less finished, in which the complex structure of different layers of color is clearly apparent, even if one certainly cannot speak of "dead color," as Jaffé does (1983, 1987). Certain elements, like the brushwork of thick and exuberant color on Tarquin's side, or the viscous sketches of drapery visible a little lower and on the side and sleeve of Lucretia's dress, seem unrelated to the paint underneath, as if indicating points where further details needed to be added. As for the degree of completeness, even if each individual form had not been perfected, we find ourselves before a composition that, step by step, had matured to the point of applying the first glazes prior to the final touches. The group of dogs

that attack Actaeon in *The Death of Actaeon*, begun 1559 (National Gallery, London) shows Titian's process at a similar moment. Indeed the Vienna *Tarquin and Lucretia* and the dogs of the *Actaeon* must surely have been contemporary. Titian's compositional method as he searched for definitive form can be clearly reconstructed on the basis of x-rays (soon to be published), which reveal the dense tangle of broad brushstrokes. Even in its incomplete state, the Viennese version is of particular interest in relation to the Fitzwilliam painting, which technically could hardly be more different. Two graphic works helped to determine the composition of both the Cambridge and Vienna versions, both of which, according to Titian himself, engaged the artist for several years. One of these is an engraving by Heinrich Aldegrever after Georg Pencz, dated 1539. In the first of these the Lucretia's gesture of repulsion with the arm nearest the observer, and the movement of Tarquin with his dagger raised in the act of stabbing, are taken up in both the Viennese and Bordeaux versions. Moreover, Tarquin's ancient armor and billowing cloak recur in the Bordeaux painting, as well as that of the Vienna Academy. From Aldegrever's 1539 engraving, the motif of Lucretia who, with her right arm raised is on the verge of fleeing, has been transformed into a twisting movement, giving an impression of frailty. The protracted evolution of the composition, that focused especially on Tarquin's stabbing gesture, becomes apparent in x-rays of the Bordeaux version. This initially replicated the Cambridge solution, but finally opted for the motif of stabbing from below (Barnaud-Hours 1964). Similar stages are visible in the x-ray of the Viennese painting, where the hand with the dagger at first lowered was in the end raised.

The analysis of these motifs would lead to the conclusion that the Vienna painting was preliminary to that in Cambridge, were it not for its affinity to Titian's later works – for example the *Nymph and Shepherd* of the Kunsthistorisches Museum, Vienna with its open brushwork and subdued chromatic range – and for its identity as an autonomous and separate work. Philip II's version is above all a history painting and, faithful to Livy's description, represents with technical perfection and high emotional intensity the tragedy of the heroic Roman woman of virtue. By contrast, the Viennese version is formally reductive and profoundly psychological in its revelation of meaning, analogous to other cases in which Titian returned to and revised earlier compositions (Panofsky 1969). In the full-length version the protagonists perform in a defined spatial setting, enriched by props and resembling a stage. Their movements seem inexorably to bind them to each other. Instead, in the Viennese painting Tarquin and Lucretia are confined in a more cramped space against a neutral and flat background. They clash one against the other as symbolic opposites.

Lucretia, who is dressed, as opposed to her semi-nakedness in most versions, especially those belonging to the Italian tradition, is painted in the act of twisting around, like a spindle. The heroine seems almost to spring from the lower margin of the painting, and gives the impression that she is about to stumble, an interesting comment on her innocence and chastity, which is implied in Ovid's poetic description of the young woman's nature, and the cause of Tarquin's infatuation. Titian's interpretation contrasts notably with the widespread tendency to emphasize the erotic content of the story. Examples of this are Enea Vico's engraving of 1524, influenced by Raphael (Bartsch 1978), and the very similar version executed on a majolica plate of 1540-50 from the workshop of Orazio and Flaminio Fontana (Museo Correr, Venice, collection Teodoro Correr).

LITERATURE Popp 1921, 9-13; Eigenberger 1927, 407; Suida 1933, 123, 145, 173; Tietze 1936, I, 244, II, 314; Berenson 1957, 184; Dell'Acqua 1958, 132; Valcanover 1960, II, 51; Barnaud and Hours 1964, 19-23, fig. 38; Pallucchini 1969, I, 189, 326; Panofsky 1969, 139; Wethey 1975, 220; *The Illustrated Bartsch* 1978, 207; Walther 1978, 70; Braunfels 1980, 410; Hope 1980, 144ff; Pallucchini 1980, 389; Jaffé and Groen 1987, 162-71, fig. 14, 16.

C.W.

74

Doge Antonio Grimani Kneeling before Faith

oil on canvas, 373×496 cm
Venice, Palazzo Ducale

EXHIBITION   Venice 1935
RESTORATION   1977-78, S. and F. Volpin

This official painting commemorating Doge Antonio Grimani (1521-23) was commissioned from Titian while Francesco Venier was doge, by act of the Council of Ten on March 22 1555 – a full thirty-two years after Grimani's death. Grimani, who was father of Cardinal Domenico, the famous collector who gave his name to the Grimani Breviary, had been disgraced (and only later publicly rehabilitated) for the defeat of the Venetian Navy by the Turks at Zonchio, 1499. The painting was intended to decorate a hall in the Palazzo Ducale (Lorenzi 1869), possibly the Sala del Collegio, which was destroyed by fire in 1574 (Sinding-Larson 1974).

Votive pictures such as these were usually commissioned by the doge shortly after his election. The exception in this case may be due to the brevity of Grimani's tenure. In 1555 fewer than 171 ducats were set aside for Titian's fee according to a procedure similiar to that used shortly earliers for the votive picture of Doge Marcantonio Trevisan (1553-54), likewise commissioned from Titian along with those of Andrea Gritti and Pietro Lando (Wolters 1987).

This was the last of Titian's votive pictures, and the only one to escape the fire in the Palazzo Ducale of 11 May 1574 (the others were replaced in 1581-84 by Jacopo Tintoretto and assistants), a circumstance that has been variously explained by historical findings and stylistic elements now in part confirmed as the result of the recent restoration (Nepi Scirè 1979).

It is quite possible that the number and scale of Titian's official commissions at this time – such as the *Battle of Cadore* for the Sala del Maggiore Consiglio – constitute an adequate explanation of why he failed to complete the Grimani painting and therefore why it survived, to be finished around 1600 by his relative Marco Vecellio (Boschini 1664).

The first mention of the huge canvas dates from 1604, in Giovanni Stringa's additions to Sansovino's *Venetia. Città Nobilissima*. Stringa attributed it to the master's own hand and described it in the Sala delle Quattro Porte where it remains today. This is confirmed in later sources (Ridolfi 1648, Boschini 1664, Zanetti 1771). The mention by Stringa is invaluable since, even if indirectly, it provides the *terminus ante quem* for the painting's completion, with the modifications and additions at the sides that Marco Vecellio carried out during the dogeship of Marino Grimani (1598-1605), great-grandson of the Antonio pictured here. These modifications were obviously necessitated by a different placement of the canvas from that was originally foreseen.

It has been argued therefore that the canvas either miraculously survived the fire of 1574 in the Sala del Collegio (Zanetti 1771) or remained unfinished in Titian's workshop at his death in 1576 (Sinding-Larsen 1974) and that the Grimani family, during Marino's tenure, obtained possession and entrusted Marco Vecellio with completing the work and making certain changes. The new Grimani doge would appear to have chosen a new location for the commemorative picture in the Sala delle Quattro Porte facing Andrea Vicentino's *Entry of Henri III into Venice* from c. 1593 (Zanotto 1858) and in the company of other paintings the same doge commissioned for the hall (Nepi Scirè 1979), specifically his own votive picture, and the *Battle of Verona* by Giovanni Contarini, the *Traditio legis* by Carletto and Gabrieli Caliari, and the latter's *Reception of the Persian Ambassadors.*

This hypothesis is supported also by the *terminus post quem* for Titian's painting. This can be deduced from certain deliberations of the Senate between 1588 and 1590 (Lorenzi 1868), which indicate that in those years Marino Grimani's predecessor, Doge Pasquale Cicogna, had not yet carried through the wall decoration of the hall in question, the canvases being "still unfinished" (Von Hadeln 1911).

Past and recent scholars have held differing opinions concerning both the relative dating of the individual parts of the large canvas, its complex iconography, and the role Titian's pupil played in completing it.

For Crowe and Cavalcaselle (1878), who proposed a symbolic and autobiographical interpretation of the military attributes and the Eucharistic and Trinitarian symbols so prominent in the painting, the work belonged to Titian's last period, with Marco Vecellio responsible only for completing it with the figures of the prophet and the standard bearer at either side. According to Hadeln (1911) the master's share was rather more limited, comprising only the group of figures to the right with the doge, while the rest would have been completed by Marco Vecellio before 1589. For Suida (1933), on the other hand, the general compositional conception was Titian's own, though the figure of Faith had remained merely sketched out by the master and was completed by his relative Cesare Vecellio. Tietze (1950) maintained that the major role was played by the workshop, while the date of 1566 proposed by Berenson (1957) – who insisted, on the contrary, that the work was from the master's hand – perhaps coincides rather too literally with the facts set down by Vasari, though he was followed in this by Bergstein (1987) who interpreted the Counter-Reformation and Tridentine iconographical elements in Titian's work in terms of overt political propaganda.

Pallucchini (1969) and Wethey (1969) both stress extensive collaboration on the part of the workshop along with completion by Marco Vecellio, while Valcanover (1969) proposes instead the name of Titian's pupil Cesare Vecellio. For Wolters

M. Vecellio, "A Prophet." Palazzo Ducale, Venice

(1987) the completing hand would have been that of Orazio Vecellio in 1589, although Titian's son had died as early as 1576.

X-ray analysis has confirmed the presence of Titian's own agitated manner of working his paint in the *pentimenti* of the doge's face and the figures of the halberdier and the soldier. At the same time it has revealed in the *repoussoir* hangings to the left and right (the latter draped differently by Titian) the limits of Marco Vecellio's contribution to the original image, as well as his own addition of the prophet and the standard bearer at the sides. Throughout the rest of the canvas, cleaning has demonstrated beyond doubt the full authorship. This includes the extraordinary figure of Faith – formerly believed to be a variant introduced into the painting after the fire of 1574 (Sinding-Larsen 1974) – and the view of Venice, now liberated from an inappropriate overpainting in the spirit of a *vedutista*, in which the Prisons (built considerably later) were added (Nepi Scirè 1979).

Analysis of the paint layers, in particular in the right-hand sector where Marco Vecellio's intervention overlays Titian's, has revealed the absence of pigmented glazes and of layers of dirt between the respective contributions of the older and younger painter, these having been realized, it now appears, with entirely similar technique and pigments (Lazzarini 1979). While this consideration does not exclude specific iconographical and stylistic links between the Grimani votive picture and works of the 1560s such as the *Transfiguration* and the *Annunciation* of the church of San Salvador in Venice, it nevertheless suggests that Titian's execution of a large part of the canvas, or at any rate the right-hand sector, may be datable as late as the first half of the 1570s.

Among various reproductions, following a not very felicitous print produced by Francesco Del Pedro at the end of the eighteenth century, the Grimani painting was engraved in 1837 by Giuseppe Bernasconi and later by F. Zanetti, the latter used in Zanotto's work of 1853-61 (Chiari Moretto Wiel 1988).

A copy on canvas, made in the early nineteenth century by Marianna Pascoli, was acquired by the Museo Civico of Padua from the Meneghetti collection.

LITERATURE Vasari 1568 (ed. Milanesi 1881), VII, 437; Stringa 1604, 225 v; Ridolfi 1648 (ed. 1914), I, 206; Boschini 1664, *San Marco*, 10; Zanetti 1771, 112; Zanotto 1858, II, and 1861; Lorenzi 1868, docs. 608, 619, 623, 981, 983, 1012; Crowe and Cavalcaselle 1878, II, 244-48; Von Hadeln 1911, XXXII, 19-20, 24; Suida 1933, 173; Fogolari 1935, 157; Tietze 1950, 49, 394; Berenson 1957, 191; Pallucchini 1969, 319-20; Valcanover 1969, 136; Wethey 1969, 93; Sinding-Larsen 1974, 14-15; Lazzarini 1979, 93-94; Nepi Scirè 1979, 83-91; Bergstein 1987, 29-37; Wolters 1987, 103-35; Chiari Moretto Wiel 1988, 154, 195, 230.   E.M.

M. Vecellio, "A Standard Bearer." Palazzo Ducale, Venice

75

Saint Sebastian

oil on canvas, 210×115.5 cm
Leningrad, State Hermitage Museum (inv. no. 191)

EXHIBITIONS   Venice 1935, Washington 1987
RESTORATION   1975, A. Colbassov

In 1648 Ridolfi noted among Titian's paintings in the Barbarigo Collection *Saint Sebastian* "...the generous martyr Sebastian standing." It was later acquired by Cristoforo Barbarigo as part of the contents of Titian's in the Biri Grande. Bevilacqua (1845) described the work thus: "...the preciousness of this painting surpasses that of all the others by this author, especially for students of painting and for amateurs." However when the painting went to the Hermitage in 1850 it seems to have been inadequately appreciated. In the appraisal of all the paintings of the Imperial Gallery ordered by Nicholas I in 1853, the *Saint Sebastian* was classified "Third Category" and placed in storage. In the MS catalogue by Ernest Lipgart (c. 1920-28) the history of the canvas was described as follows: "The merit for having taken this masterpiece out of the depot belongs to Charles de Lipgart. M. Ghedenov, Director of the Hermitage, gave my father access to the depot when he was passing through Saint Petersburg in 1866." The *Saint Sebastian* has only occupied the place it deserves since 1892. In the catalogues of the Hermitage up to 1912 the painting was judged a preparatory work or sketch. Crowe and Cavalcaselle (1877) believed it definitely ruined, with a great deal of repainting. This was not the case, however, given that the state of conservation instead is excellent.
The interest in Titian's late style has contributed to the reevaluation of the *Saint Sebastian*. Fischel (1904), Lipgart (1910), Venturi (1912) and later other scholars describe it as a masterpiece. It is dated in the 1570s by all authors except Fischel (1904) who placed it in 1545, later revising this (1907) to 1565. The documents make no mention of Titian being commissioned to paint this subject during his last years. Ridolfi remarked that Titian had painted a *Saint Sebastian* for Charles V, presumably in the 1540s or earlier, which is known from descriptions by Father Los Santos (1657) and Abbot Ponz (1788) and which cannot therefore be the Hermitage picture. Wethey (1969) believed the "Saint Sebastian" of the Harrack Collection, Vienna, to be a copy of the lost Escorial version. The pose of the Saint in the Viennese collection harks back to Titian's early work: the *Saint Mark Enthroned with Saints Cosmas and Damian* (Santa Maria della Salute, Venice, see cat. no. 38) and the *Madonna in Glory with Child and Six Saints* (Pinacoteca Vaticana, Rome). Unfortunately, a second *Sebastian* has also disappeared, which in 1655 may have belonged to the Earl of Arundel (Hervey 1941); "...Saint Sebastian standing as if alive" (Ridolfi). Fomiciova (1867) believed that the

Hermitage painting was a model, kept by the painter in his studio, whereas Pallucchini (1969) rejected this in view of the painting's large dimensions, an opinion shared by the present writer.
The *Saint Sebastian* is instructive for Titian's creative methods. Initially he conceived a half-length figure, but later resolved to paint the Saint full-length and enlarged the canvas with additions on the right side and at the bottom. The lower part of the picture is not finished. Even so, although Titian barely outlined Sebastian's calf and left foot, as a whole the painting presents itself as complete.
The exceptional pictorial fluency here approaches Titian's other late works, such as the *Nymph and Shepherd* (Kunsthistorisches Museum, Vienna), the *Crowing with Thorns* (Alte Pinakothek, Munich) and the *Tarquin and Lucretia* (Kunsthistorisches Museen, Vienna, see cat. no. 73). It is not easy to point to a picture of analogous strength and spiritual power. The heroic opposition of the man to the enmity that surrounds him reaches a high point of expression. Illuminated by the flicker of the embers and by the dusky evening light, the figure of Saint Sebastian emerges gradually from the shadows. Brendel (1955) suggested the Belvedere Apollo as a prototype, while the outlines of the face recall one of the sons of Laocoon. The palette that from a distance seems a brown monochrome hides within it a thousand shades of ochre, olive green and red, which spring now like sparks of fire, now like drops of blood, now disappearing in the shadows, now reverberating in the glow of the embers. In this vibrant diversity of color the contours of the real world almost disappear "as if earth, the water, and the air revert to primitive chaos" (Venturi 1912).

LITERATURE   Ridolfi 1648 (ed. Von Hadeln 1914), 200; Cochin 1769, 142; Bevilacqua 1845, no. 40; Crowe and Cavalcaselle 1877, II, Penther (1886), 32; Levi 1900, 287; Fischel 1904, 1907; Ricketts 1910; Lipgart 1910, 18; Venturi 1912, 140; Borenius 1922, 88; Suida 1933, 137; Serra 1934-35, 549; Tietze 1936, 291, 325; Laazarev 1939, 80; Pallucchini 1944, XXV; Brendel 1955, 123; Berenson 1957, I, 188; Bazin 1958, 62; Valcanover 1960, II, no. 132; Formiciova 1967, 68; Valcanover 1969, no. 502; Pallucchini 1969, I, 326; Wethey 1969, 155-56, 194, cat. 134; Fomiciova 1974, 469; Pignatti 1980, no. 472; Braunfels 1976-80, 410; Vsrevolozhskaya 1981, no. 276; Siebenhuner 1981, 29, 31.

I.A.

76

The Flaying of Marsyas

oil on canvas, 212×207 cm
Kroměříž, Státní Zámek (no. 102)

EXHIBITION London 1983
RESTORATION 1960/67

Signed on the rock in the foreground to the right: TITIANVS P Probably acquired by the Countess of Arundel during her voyage to Italy in 1620, perhaps from a Venetian collection, the painting later belonged to Thomas Howard, Earl of Arundel. It appeared subsequently as "Marsyas flayed," by Titian, in the 1655 inventory of the paintings which, at the death of the earl's wife Alethea (1654), were in Amsterdam whence the collection had been transferred (Cust-Cox 1911, 280-86). Around 1655 the Marsyas was acquired by Franz von Imstenraed of Cologne. From 1673 it passed to the collection of Karl von Lichtenstein, Bishop of Olmütz, and from there to the archbishop's palace in Kroměříž.

Although it had been attributed previously to Titian (Neumann 1962, Wethey 1975), the painting only came to the attention of modern critics following Neumann's fundamental studies (1961, 1962). While it is generally agreed that the painting belongs to Titian's late works, from as late as the 1570s, the iconography of a number of details is controversial. The scene depicted is that of a well-known episode in classical mythology, that of Marsyas, the Phrygian satyr flayed alive by Apollo, winner of the musical contest between them. The one plays pipes, the other the lyre. The pact was that the winner could do what he wished with the loser.

As Hartt (1958) – who was not convinced by the attribution to Titian – has pointed out, the source for the image, even if significantly varied, was a fresco of the same subject, today very badly damaged, by Giulio Romano in the Sala delle Metamorfosi, Palazzo del Te, which Titian could have known from his visits to Mantua. Wethey (1975) and Freedberg (1986) speculated that the preparatory drawing (now in the Louvre, no. 3487) may even have been given by Giulio to Titian, in view of the friendship between them.

Like Giulio, Titian included King Midas, with ass' ears, the sign of his punishment by Apollo for failing to achieve victory in his musical contest with Pan. Unlike Giulio, Titian added a faun and two dogs, and modified the figure on the left who in the Mantuan version holds Apollo's lyre. The young man in Titian's version, in the act of holding the *lira da braccio*, is one of the most elusive details in the picture. Neumann (1962) suggested that he is a second and symbolic image of Apollo, alluding to the moment before the flaying when Apollo's music triumphed over Marsyas'.

The theory of the double presence of Apollo was not taken up by Fehl (1968), Gentili (1980) nor Rapp (1987), all of whom suggested other possible explanations.

According to Fehl this represents Olympus, Marsyas' pupil. Gentili published x-radiography of the upper left part of the canvas, which "revealed that, where there is presently the musician, there had previously been a rather fully developed figure carrying a lyre, exactly as in Giulio's version." Further examining this figure, that of the faun, and the dog next to him, Gentili perceived a lower qualitative level than in the rest of the painting. He suggested that it had been left unfinished in the studio (including the now-overpainted carrier of the lyre), and was brought to its present state partly by Palma il Giovane who transformed the lyre bearer into a second Apollo figure, and partly by another less skilled artist who would have added the faun and the dog. On stylistic grounds, Mason Rinaldi (1984) considered Palma il Giovane's intervention "out of the question." All doubt is eliminated if one compares the lyre player's face to the Leningrad *Saint Sebastian* (see cat. no. 75). Gentili himself, returning to the problem in 1988, observed that among possible points of reference for the player, the most compelling was that of *Saint Sebastian*, posing an enigma to which he confessed he did not have the answer, of whether the *Saint Sebastian* was in truth a late masterpiece by Titian or rather an autonomous masterpiece by Palma il Giovane in Titian's style. Gentili's comparisons with genuine works by Palma, all of them it must be said from the seventeeth century, do not, according to this writer, hold up. Nor can we accept the hypothesis of yet a third, inferior hand, given the glaring similarity of the faun to the virtually contemporary *Boy with Dogs* in Rotterdam (see cat. no. 72). (Wethey's theory [1975], which has had no critical following, that part of the execution is that of Titian's workshop assistant Girolamo Dente, is not acceptable either.)

According to Rapp (1987), who more or less accepted Neumann's interpretation, the player can be identified as Orpheus whose presence becomes logical in relation to the Christian-Neoplatonic doctrine that attributed to the Orphic music of the lyre an important role in the process of liberating the spirit from the body. Neumann's proposal that the face of Midas is a self-portrait, on the basis of the *Self-Portrait* in the Prado – to which it does in fact bear some resemblance – has also played its part in the variety of interpretations advanced for this painting.

Neumann felt that several interpretive keys were interwoven in the painting – from the ancient tradition of the "artistic allegory" (the victory of Apollo representing the triumph of divine art, the stringed instrument, over natural art, the wind instrument), to "moral and cosmological allegories," relating to Neoplatonic thought (Apollo Victorious personifying also the state of divine harmony, the liberated soul freed from earthly bonds) and of the "escatological and messianic

allegory" (the flaying of Marsyas as an allusion to the redemption of the sufferer).

According once more to Neumann, Midas, as Titian, mediates on the "triumph of divine art," on the meaning of life and on the meaning of art. Gentili, offering a different reading, observed among other things that "Midas... is synonymous with human judgment, which places in doubt the superior reality of divine harmony." Freedberg's contribution (1986) emphasized a particular historical event, the horrendous fate of Marcantonio Bragadin who was flayed alive by the Turks in 1571, which would have provoked the artist's choice of this theme.

In the final count, the various interpretations of this painting pay tribute to the fascinating spell woven by this masterpiece, created in the painter's last phase of activity (c. 1570-76) in which, with a vital force peculiar to great men, the artist dominates his medium. He applied the paint with force, giving meaning to Longhi's phrase of "magic impressionism," achieving the summit of his career and creating a matchless legacy for later generations. As in the *Saint Sebastian* in Leningrad, to which one can add the *Tarquin and Lucretia* in the Vienna Academy, the *Crowning with Thorns* in Munich, and the *Nymph and Shepherd* in Vienna, the pictorial language of this last period opens new coloristic and expressive possibilities capable of profound emotion, allowing us glimpses of the tragedy of human suffering and evoking a world made tumultuous by the quivering touch of his brush.

LITERATURE   Hartt 1958, 111; Neumann 1961, 325-67; Pallucchini 1961, 294-5; Neumann 1962, 7ff (with preceding bibliography); Fehl 1968, 1387-1415; Pallucchini 1969, 197-98, 329; Valcanover 1969, 135, no. 496; Wethey 1975, 91-93, 153-54, no. 16 (with preceding bibliography); Gentili 1980, 147-58; Pallucchini 1983, 282; Robertson 1983, 231-3; Davis 1984, 48; Mason Rinaldi 1984, 77; Rearick 1984, 66; Rosenauer 1984, 305; Rosand 1985, 295-6; Freedberg 1986, 140-52; Rapp 1987, 70-89; Gentili 1988, 225-43; Oberhuber 1989, 138; Prohaska 1989, 286-88.

P.R.

Pietà

oil on canvas, 378×347 cm
Venice, Gallerie dell'Accademia (cat. no. 400)

EXHIBITION   Venice 1935
RESTORATION   1984-85, O. Nonfarmale

According to Ridolfi (1648) Titian planned this painting for the Cappella del Cristo at the Frari, in exchange for the concession to be buried there, "but either he took a long time or because, as other say, they didn't want to lose the ancient devotion to the Crucifix which can be seen there, it was not finished, but came after his death into the hands of Palma, who completed it with the addition of some little angels and this humble inscription.... 'QUOD TITIANUS INCHOATUM RELIQUIT/ PALMA REVERENTUR ABSOLVIT DEOQ. DICAVIT OPUS.'"
In 1664, Boschini described it for the first time in the church of Sant'Angelo, "on the left hand side," and stated: "this was begun by Titian and completed by Palma. The lights and darks are all by Titian, but the other figures are in many places retouched and covered by Palma." Ten years later he added: "the above mentioned painting was taken away and put in the *Cappella dal Santissimo* on the left side," a chapel that was at the *cornu evangelo* of the chancel.
Titian died on 27 August 1576 while the plague was raging in Venice. He was buried the next day at the Frari, "at the foot of the altar of the Crucifix," with a hurried ceremony given the circumstances, but evidently under the patronage of the Republic, since the canons of San Marco were present. Following his death and that of his son Orazio, Titian's lavish home in the Biri was looted. "Much property of great value... and things of gold, silver and gems and other furniture and innumerable paintings of great value," were the losses incurred by his son Pomponio and his son-in-law Carmelo Sarcinello, as described by the lawyer (*avogadore*) Nicolò Barbarigo of 24 July 1577.
The house was sold by Pomponio on 27 October 1581 to Cristoforo Barbarigo, presumably with some paintings by Titian himself, if in his will of 13 March 1600 Barbarigo left to his brother Domenico four paintings representing "the Christ who carries the Cross, the Magdalene, the Madonna framed in ebony, the Venus." There was no mention of the *Pietà*, but in 1675 Sandrart informed us further, while erroneously maintaining that its original destination was the church of San Pantalon: "Pro templo San Pantaleontis venetiis, Christi etiam de Cruci ablati in gremio Matris reposti imaginem pingere coepit, sed non absolvit, quod deinde sic volnete Titiano, a Jacopo Palma consummatum est, notatum tamen Titiani, ad mandatum Senatus nomine." Thus the *Pietà* was finished by Palma, but countersigned with the name of Titian, in accordance with the wishes of the Senate. Having been finished "at

the hands of Palma," it would have remained with him at least until his death in 1628, transferring to the church of Sant'Angelo most probably in 1631. Here the end of the plague of those years was celebrated with particular devotion and solemnity since, as Corner recorded, it officially ceased on the feast day of the Arcangel Michael, patron of Sant'Angelo. Thus Titian's "special panel," finished almost as an *ex voto* in similar circumstances, found a logical and worthy placement. The painting was not mentioned in Pastoral Visits to Sant'Angelo in the years 1581-1622, but it reappeared after a long interval before the next visit, that of Badoer, on 25 April 1690: "A large painting in the chapel of the SS.mo of the Madonna of the Pieta by Titian's hand" (Archivio Patriarcale, Venice, *Visite Pastorali*).
The theory that the *Pietà* was begun for the Marquis of Ayamonte (Hope 1980 and 1988) is unconvincing. Ayamonte, who lived in Milan, was delegated by Philip II to arrange for the payment of a pension to Titian, and on 27 January 1575 he expressed to Guzman de Silva the desire to possess a painting by the artist with "a dead Christ in a sheet and the mother standing" (Ferrarino 1975, no. 164). Nor is it likely that Titian initially intended to execute a painting of smaller dimensions, limited to the Virgin and Christ, enlarging it later to include the architecture, the Magdalene and the other figures. After the recent cleaning, during which seven canvas inserts were counted on the back, it became clear that the central zone was not large enough to contain even the Madonna group (Nepi Scirè 1987). However, Ayamonte's letter to Guzman de Silva of 27 April 1575 is of the greatest interest: "I have seen the dimensions of Titian's painting and, even if it will be large, being for so many years the official one, it will be better thus, because it cannot be as fine in style as he is accustomed to [if] work on small canvases, even if where there is the Mother and Son there is no need for additional effects, it is good that there is the Magdalene, because she is such a great example of the effect God has on sinners and such a great lesson of how those who have sinned should put themselves aright, and so she is welcome in the painting of the Mother and the Son...." The description, at that date, of a painting with the Mother, the Son and the Magdalene, of large dimensions, can only apply to The *Pietà*, and represents therefore our first notice of the painting.
It is conceivable that Titian, having failed in his negotiations with the monks of the Frari, for whom he had patched his votive painting from several canvases, could have hoped briefly in 1575 to send it to the Marquis of Ayamonte, transforming it, in the following year, during the fury of the plague, into an *ex voto* against the epidemic, and in any case into a most unusual autobiographical statement. After the suppression of the church of Sant'Angelo in 1810 (and its destruction in 1837), the painting was passed to the Gallerie dell'Accademia in 1814

and was included in 1829 in a project to exchange works for examples from Italian and foreign schools of painting, which fortunately came to nothing (Archivio Accademia, Venice, *carta* 251).

During its most recent restoration it became clear that Titian, in addition to having pieced the support from canvases of different types and weaves, and consequently of different thicknesses and textures, even used in the central section, where he may have wanted a more densely prepared ground, a fragment already-painted with a male face. The elimination of the heavily pigmented varnishes highlighted how Palma's intervention was limited to a few glazes tending to disguise the seams of the various inserts, to the angel with the torches (which was painted over a previous less traditional putto sketched and left unfinished by Titian, whose leg bent back can be seen in x-rays), to the inscription, and perhaps to the retouching of the pediment which reveals a high finish quite different from the rustication below and from the nine lamps above, rendered in thickly impastoed overlapping colors. Even so, it is not impossible that even this detail, the pediment, is by Titian from an earlier period of his career, comparable for example to the *Presentation of the Virgin in the Temple* also in the Accademia.

The compositional scheme is entirely his – the niche within which the iconic central group is presented is inspired by that blending of canonical and rustic architecture typical of Giulio Romano, and particularly of the doorframes of the Palazzo del Te, Mantua. Nor was this kind of architecture alien to Palladio (see for example his 'Study for a Palace,' London, RIBA, XVII/6,7), and it recurs in the portals of Sebastiano Serlio's *Extraordinario Libro* of 1551. Titian responded to other influences. The mosaic half-dome in which the pelican, symbol of the Resurrection, is portrayed, amounts to an homage, as does the entire central part of the composition, to Giovanni Bellini.

The *Pietà* includes three types of inscriptions: the most elegant are those in Latin on the socles of the statuary – Moses (MOYSES) and the Sibyl (ELLESPONTICAS). Those in Greek above the statues are virtually illegible. Several times reworked and altered by restoration, they can be partially deciphered by means of infrared reflectography:

ΔI...   ΘEO(Σ)
HO....N   over the Moses, and   ANO...

corresponding to the Sibyl. Finally the phrase in dialect, written in a contemporary hand appropriate to its popular nature, on the panel at the bottom right can also be deciphered with the help of reflectography: "Dona Katta venir nostra pecata bene pixt. Sig[navit?][natur?]...."

Much has been written about the iconography of the *Pietà*. It has tended to focus on themes of death, Eucharistic sacrifice and resurrection. The symbolism has been interpreted vari-

ously: from the lion's heads, which could allude to Titian's family or Saint Mark, or the resurrection or divine wisdom; to the spectral statuary, entirely autograph, of Moses the Hebrew legislator, representative of the Old Testament and precursor of Christ the Redeemer, and of the Hellespontic Sibyl who prophesied both the crucifixion and the resurrection. Like Michelangelo, Titian portrayed himself in a *Pietà* destined for his own tomb: the old half-naked man, variously identified as Joseph of Arimathea, Saint Jerome, and Nicodemus, but perhaps after all 'Saint' Job, prostrate in front of the Virgin who holds Christ, is a self-portrait.

The work is in the broadest sense a 'devotional' painting, insofar as it was originally destined for the tomb of the artist and later transformed into an immense *ex voto*, even before the 'Grace received,' in which Titian genuflects twice before Mary and her Son, asking intercession by the Father in this life and the next.

The drama of the image, equivalent to the artist's testament, is accentuated by the 'magical expressionism,' the outstanding 'chromatic alchemy' that destroys and recomposes the pictorial matter, sometimes approaching the threshhold of the inchoate. The votive panel, a painting within a painting, certainly not a later addition, in which Titian and his son Orazio beg the Virgin for immunity from the plague, draws us empathetically even further into the narrative. The tragic outstretched arm at the feet of the Sibyl has a similar protective effect. Perhaps it was the terrible threat of the plague that provoked Titian in the same period to return to the theme of *Saint Sebastian* (see cat. no. 75) for his miracle-working powers. These were fearful but futile attempts to assuage the Godhead. The plague, raging even as Titian daubed his final brushtrokes, would strike down both Titian and his favorite son, Orazio.

LITERATURE Ridolfi 1648 (Von Hadeln 1914) 206; Boschini 1664, 199 ff, 1674, 93; Von Sandrart 1675, 165; Moschini-Marconi 1962, 260-1, no. 453 (with preceding bibliography); Ferrarino 1975, nos.164, 171; Hope 1980, 165; Siebenhüner 1981, 28 ff; Mason Rinaldi 1984, 135-6 (with preceding bibliography); Niero 1984, 323-9; Nepi Scirè and Valcanover 1985, 180, no. 305; Goffen 1986, 151-54, 246-48; Huse 1986, 321-23; Nepi Scirè 1987, 30-41; Hope 1988, 72.

G.N.S.

TITIAN'S TECHNIQUE

Paolo Spezzani
NON-DESTRUCTIVE ANALYSIS

The laboratory for non-destructive analysis of the Soprintendenza in Venice has, since its foundation in 1967, dedicated considerable time to Titian's paintings, from the small Pieve di Cadore altarpiece to the *Assumption* in the Frari and the most recent conservation of the Titian in the Salute.

The first example of scientific analysis was conducted for the *Pesaro Madonna* in the Frari: this was the first time that a large painting had been examined with x-rays in such a way that the photographs could be recomposed to form a fullsize image of the picture. The challenge, since it was not possible to rely on any comparable previous experience, was rewarded with such a quantity of data (*pentimenti*, variant compositions, the revelation of lacunae and damage concealed by later restorations) that it is still considered one of the triumphs of our laboratory. Moreover, the infrared photographs that were taken of the same painting provided complementary information on the creative processes of this work of art.

Recent technological developments have enabled us to improve significantly the results obtained by infrared research. From simple infrared sensitive photographic plates, first came the infrared image converter and then the television camera with Infrared vidicon, linked in the 1980s to a computer. This enabled us to realize the first reflectographs and to begin working with infrared image elaboration to form a new method of research that we have called the computerized infrared reflectoscope.

For x-radiography, it is customary to arrange the painting flat, face up on a temporary frame, at a height of about two meters, on a scaffolding that allows the x-ray camera to pass freely through all parts of the canvas. Then a network of fine copper wire that is slightly smaller than the x-ray plates is placed over the paint surface to make it easier to match each photograph with the adjacent one and thus make for a more precise reproduction. Then the radiographs are taken, one by one, of the whole canvas. The values are usually 25-30 Kv., 4mA, for an exposure of 15-45 seconds with a camera specially adapted for works of art. Each radiograph, developed automatically, is reproduced in small format (6 x 7 cm) on black and white film; the prints are then cut along the lines left by the copper wire, and fitted together to form one panel that is then itself duplicated. A personal computer is used for the reflectography that is equipped with a program capable of collecting and displaying the images gathered by a multistandard television camera with an infrared sensitive vidicon tube. The light source is a normal electric light bulb, although filters should be used to eliminate any visible radiation. The use of the personal computer for image processing has made it possible to achiew results that would have been unthinkable a few years ago. As well as being capable of producing modifications that show borders, horizontal or vertical lines, and that improve the overall quality of the image, it is also possible to differentiate the infrared image from the visible one, in this way providing much more information than an infrared image on its own.

These techniques have been applied to the following paintings by Titian, as can be seen in the publications by the Soprintendenza ai Beni Artistici e Storici of Venice: the *Assumption* and the *Pesaro Madonna* in the Frari, the *Martyrdom of Saint Lawrence* in the Church of the Gesuiti, *Saint James* in the Church of San Lio, the *Pentecost, David and Goliath, Cain and Abel* and the *Sacrifice of Isaac* in the Salute, the *Doge Antonio Grimani before Faith* in the Palazzo Ducale, the *Annunciation* in the Church of San Salvador, *Saint John the Almsgiver* in the church of the same name, nineteen panels by the school of Titian from the ceiling of the Scuola di San Giovanni Evangelista, the *Presentation of the Virgin in the Temple, Saint John the Baptist*, the *Pietà* and the *Madonna and Child*, all in the Accademia.

Many of these paintings have been fully x-rayed and an overall recomposition of the photographs was made for all of the larger ones.

We would particularly like to thank Olivetti who, in addition to donating numerous computers, have helped our work considerably with their technical skills and the financing of an image elaborating program that was provided by the "Stylo" software house in Bologna specifically at our request, and which is periodically up-dated with new operating possibilities.

The x-rays:
Gilardoni Neodermo camera with a beryllium window, portable Gilardoni Art Gil camera, Agfa Gevaert Gevamatic 60 automatic developer, 3 mm film of the 2R type, Curix Agfa film.

For the Reflectography:
Olivetti M290 Personal Computer, portable personal computer, Matrox pip 640 graphic program for the collection and display of 512x512 images at 256 levels of gray, a matrox pg640 graph program for display at 256 colour and 256 gray levels, Grundig SN76 television camera equipped with American and European standard, Vidicon Hamamatsu tube no.214, standard 35mm Olympus camera lens, series 87 wratten filters, Oriel filters for the registration exclusively of visible images. The images are recorded and kept on standard DOS, using 3 1/2 and 5 1/4 disks and streamer tapes.

Lorenzo Lazzarini
A STUDY OF VARIOUS WORKS FROM THE
PERIOD 1510-1542

The physical and chemical study of Titian's paints and pigments is fundamental in shedding light on the techniques used by this artist, about which, unlike the art-history and iconography of Titian, very little has been written. This type of study, especially the micro examination of paint layers, is often the only method capable of revealing the phases of painting of many of Titian's works. The richness of the materials used and the structural complexity makes these paintings rather hard to understand, even when examined by techniques as effective as x-ray analysis and infra-red reflectography. For this reason we are presenting here a summary of the results of the examination of paint layers, with a number of samples from some of the most important paintings of Titian early and mature periods, from 1510 to 1542, and therefore from his pre-mannerist phase. The paintings, all in Venice are *Saint Mark Enthroned with Saints*

Cosmas and Damian, a panel in the sacristy of the Salute of c. 1510, the *Assumption*, the huge panel painted from 1516-18 and the *Pesaro Madonna*, a canvas painted from 1519-26, both in the Frari; the *Presentation of the Virgin in the Temple*, painted between 1534 and 1539 (Accademia); the *Annunciation*, a canvas painted toward the end of the 1530s, originally in the Scuola di San Rocco and now in the Accademia.

During the restoration of these works it was possible to carry out sampling with the objective not only of documenting the state of preservation of the pictures (the presence of over-painting, stucco, retouching etcetera) but also of studying materials and techniques.

This study sets out the results of the microscopic and microchemical analyses of the samples and the relative transverse paint-layer sections that were prepared from them.[1]

As has already been noted in other publications,[2] Titian's painting technique was extremely complex and even in his early paintings of "*La Schiavona*" and the "*Ariosto*" he used large quantities of color in many layers, often with thick brushwork to build up the chromatic tones that he desired.

In the works of his youth and early maturity, including works that are examined here, there is a constant intensification of the colors due to a skiful use of glazes, (virtually transparent layers of brushwork), mainly of intense greens, blues and reds that when applied over layers of paler hues intensify the colors without losing any of their brilliance, giving added depth to the zones where they were applied.

The panel in the Salute is no exception to this rule. The study of a number of sections revealed that there is not necessarily any relationship between the final color of the paint surface, that visible with the naked eye, and the deeper underlying layers.

It seems that in this painting Titian experimented as he proceeded; it is almost as if the tones of the paints while they were on his palette did not convince him and that he felt that he had to apply them directly onto the panel where the interaction with the primer or the color that had already been applied was different and thus called for continual adjustment. This was particularly apparent when the structure of the garments of Saints Rocco and

Sebastian were examined; it is too simple to say that they were painted over the sky and a column respectively, since they have been done with a number of different applications almost as if he intended that they should minutely influence the visible blue.

This fact also suggests that Titian did not make a drawing for the altarpiece (in fact no traces of drawing were discovered in the paint samples), which was constructed by the superimposition of the various figurative elements that were created according not only to the rules of perspective, but also according to the chromatic taste of the painter.

The fact that there is neither a single drawing nor a detailed work plan for the painting seems evident from the lack of painted backgrounds, or uniform base-colors, which would have been necessary in order to save time and pigments. For example the fabric on the throne could simply have been painted in the same way as any other seventeenth-century Tuscan or Venetian might have done by using two layers of brushwork: one green (background) and one red (decoration with vertical lines). Instead it is made up of four layers of pale gray, which correspond to the background sky, or more probably, with a rough sketch of the throne, with three layers that first create the green tones and then bring out the contrasts that we now see on the throne, and finally some red brushwork for the decorations (fig. 1).

The painter has therefore built up the work, often by experiment, from the background of the painting towards the observer, first painting the sky, then the architecture and finally the figures. This is also shown by a sample taken from the hair of Saint Sebastian (fig. 2) which is painted over the flesh of his face, which in turn is painted over the green of the column which itself is painted onto the cloudy sky.

Nor are Saints Cosmas and Damian, who are not superimposed on any architectural elements and could therefore have been done with a drawing separately from the rest of the composition, any exception to this Titianesque rule. The garment of Saint Cosmas is painted over the black one of Saint Damian which in turn is painted over the pale-gray background sky (or primer) (fig. 3).

In the *Assumption* the enormous dimensions of the panel dictated Titian's technique more in the number of layers that he used than in their thickness. In fact the presence of a charcoal drawing (fig. 4) allowed the artist to limit the quantity of paint that he used, and there is much less paint than in the Saint Mark altarpiece. Hence there are far fewer superimpositions; the figures are never painted over the sky, and even details such as the edges of flowing garments (fig. 5) and cloaks rarely overlap the apparently underlying color. This is perfectly comprehensible since if Titian had built up the *Assumption* in the same way that he had the *Saint Mark Enthroned*, he would have had to have used vast quantities of extremely expensive pigment for this commission (in some areas there are as many as seven different layers of brushwork). It is interesting to note the use of pure pigments in the *Assumption* that create large expanses of color (for example the ultramarine of the Virgin's cloak).

However, the structure of the color is not always simple and does not show any significant differences between the upper and lower parts of the panel. It is noticeable that some areas have been primed with lead white (*biacca*), applied as an undercoat for the cloaks (i.e. that of the Virgin) not only to intensify the color, but probably also for other reasons that are not yet clear. These primers have also been encountered in other works,[3] some of which are examined later in the article and that have another peculiarity; the presence of films of drying oils (fig. 6) that were very probably applied when there were interruptions in the execution of the work in order to keep the paint "fresh," and adhesive, ready for subsequent brushwork. Such interruptions, also apparent on the *Pesaro Madonna*, which was also worked on for a considerable length of time, possibly take the place of the continual chromatic adjustments that he made to the *Saint Mark Enthroned*, providing Titian with a much quicker technique in the second decade of the fifteenth century, and thus allowing the master to change his mind and to apply final touches to the areas that were affected by these pauses.

In the *Assumption* a particular technique appears for the first time that goes on to become a standard feature of Titian's use of color. Many pigments, such as ultramarine, cinnabar and charcoal black, but also lead white and ochre, were very finely ground, giving the painter a new tonal range that was made possible by playing with the grain-size of the particles of color in the paint layer, thus broadening an already vast range, given the richness of Titian's palette that included all the pigments in use in the sixteenth century, including the most precious ones.[4] The painting technique of the *Pesaro Madonna* also appears to be highly complicated, above all due to the numerous *pentimenti* and, as has already been pointed out, to the interruptions in the work, given that the canvas remained in the master's studio for a long period. As has already been noted in an earlier article,[5] the canvas was prepared and treated almost as if it were a panel. Indeed as with the *Assumption* there are traces in some areas (for example in the lower parts of the work), of charcoal drawing on lead white, which are understandable due to the complex and innovative architecture in the altarpiece.

The background elements of the painting were built up from the ground by continually superimposing the generally very fine brushstrokes, in order to create the various composite details. The lower parts of the painting are primed with lead white (fig. 7) over which is painted, with numerous intervals, the Pesaro family and Saint Peter's podium.

Titian first applied the color of the architectural structures and then that of the figures. For instance the Madonna and Child were painted over the plinth and left-hand column, and in the same way the clothes and cloak of Saint Peter (figs. 8, 9) also cover parts of the column. Therefore it can be concluded that the columns are original: the one on the right partially covers the architecture of the first composition, which otherwise is covered by the sky, an area notable for its complex layering. The structure of the color is always composite, made up of numerous fine layers, sometimes so thin as to be almost a glaze, but always opaque, since it contains lead white mixed with different colors, which are made up of a huge variety of various, often very fine grained sizes.

There is frequent use of lacquer and copper resinate glazes, and of complex mixtures of precious pigments such as realgar (red arsenic), orpiment and natural ultramarine.

The *Presentation of the Virgin in the Temple* was subjec-

ted to a limited sampling, in order to identify parts that had been repainted. However this has also allowed us to establish that Titian used a technique similar to that which has been described for the last two paintings. For example, the arcade on the left painting has been applied with very thick brushstrokes (fig. 10) over a whitish primer; the cloth that covers the child near the puppy and the white clothes of the woman in front of the stairs (figs. 11, 12) has a complicated layering made up of numerous brushstrokes of various tones of gray and gray brown, that in the first case corresponds with the dark dress of the woman who is holding the child by the arm, and in the second can be linked to the same woman's cloak.

In this painting (figs. 11, 12), as in the *Assumption* (figs. 4, 6), in the *Pesaro Madonna* (figs. 7-9), and also in the *Annunciation* (figs. 13, 14), there is a thin layer of drying oil (that gives off yellow/orange fluorescence under ultraviolet light) over the gypsum and glue primer that replaces the layer of glue that the more primitive and Quattrocento painters used as a primer and waterproofing agent.

The *Annunciation* has a simpler color structure than the other paintings, with only a few different layers of brushwork of varying thicknesses, that are usually rather fine. Only rarely do the brushstrokes get any thicker and this usually corresponds with background vegetation where many of the brown tones correspond with glazes based on copper resinates that have decomposed and as a result have turned completely brown.

This painting technique, both simple (fig. 15) (of the traditional type) and complex (more probably Titianesque) (fig. 13), perhaps testifies in favor of the theory put forward by many scholars that this painting was actually the work of the school of Titian. There are layers of lead white primer and also brown films of drying oils that correspond with the interruptions in his work, as well as the different chromatic tones that he managed to obtain with the same pigment, or with mixtures of pigment with varying grain-size, showing a remarkable continuity in the constructive technique maintained by Titian, at least until the 1540s.

[1] The chemical and physical research techniques are those described by J.R.J. Van Asperen De Boer in, "An introduction to the scientific examination of paintings," *Nederlands Kunsthistorisch Jaarboek*, 26, 1975, 146-55.

[2] L. Lazzarini, "Lo studio stratigrafico della Pala di Castelfranco e di altre opere contemporanee," *Giorgione, La Pala di Castelfranco Veneto*, Exhibition Catalog, Milan, 1978, 49-50 and L. Lazzarini, "Il colore nei pittori Veneziani tra il 1480 e il 1580," *Studi Veneziani*, Supplement n. 5, of *Bollettino d'Arte*, Rome, 1983, 137 ff. Some technical complexities are also covered in a painting later than those studied, see L: Lazzarini, "Il Doge Grimani inginocchiato di fronte alla Fede. Note tecniche," *Quaderni della Soprintendenza ai Beni Artistici e Storici di Venezia*, 8, 1979, 57 ff.

[3] S. Delburgo, J. P. Rioux, E. Martin, "Notes sur la technique picturale du Titien," *Annales du Laboratoire de recherche des Musées de France*, 1976, 31 and 34.

[4] J. Plesters, "Titian's 'Bacchus and Ariadne': the materials and technique," *National Gallery Technical Bulletin*, 2, 1978, 40 ff.

[5] L. Lazzarini, "La Pala Pesaro: note tecniche," *Quaderni della Soprintendenza ai Beni Artistici e Storici di Venezia*, 8, 1979, 68 ff.

1

2

The sections have all been photographed in reflected light and should be read from the base up. When they have been enlarged it is stated. Layers of varnish or overpainting are not described.

1. *Saint Mark Enthroned*, sample no. 7: from the red decorations on the green carpet (70× enlargement).
Preparatory layer of gypsum and glue; four layers of brushwork made up of lead white and carbon black: corresponding with the background sky; verdigris and massicot = the "half-tone" of the carpet; verdigris and lead white = "light" on the carpet; copper resinate glaze = "shade" on the carpet; red lacquer glaze.

2. *Saint Mark Enthroned*, sample no. 11: from the brown of the hair of Saint Sebastian (120× enlargement).
Preparatory layer of gypsum and glue; two layers of brushwork made up of lead white and carbon black; verdigris and a little lead white; lead white; lead white and a little carbon black and lead white and yellow ochre = flesh tones; carbon black with a little lead white and cinnabar.

3. *Saint Mark Enthroned*, sample no. 8: from the red of Saint Cosmas' garments (120× enlargement).
Preparatory layer of gypsum and glue; two layers of brushwork made up of lead white and carbon black = background sky and primer; layer of carbon black = the garment of St Damian; brushstrokes with cinnabar.

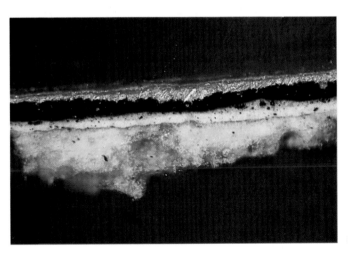

3

4. *Assumption*, sample no. 7: from the green of the third figure from the right (120× enlargement).
Preparatory layer of gypsum and glue; thin film of drying oil; lead white and a little verdigris; verdigris and lead white.
5. *Assumption*, sample no. 14: from a yellow highlight on the garment of the Virgin (120× enlargement).
Preparatory layer of gypsum and glue; thin layer of drying oil; lead white and a little carbon black and red lacquer; lead white and a little cinnabar; lead white and red ochre; lead white and carbon black with a little cinnabar; lead white and red-purple lacquer (two layers of brushwork); altered yellow lacquer.
6. *Assumption*, sample no. 17: from the blue-black in the fold in the Virgin's cloak (120× enlargement).
Preparatory layer of gypsum and glue; film of drying oil; lead white; lead white with a little natural ultramarine and a some red lacquer; natural ultramarine and a little lead white.

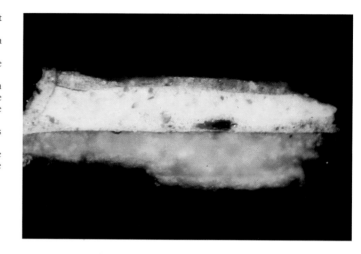

4

7. The *Pesaro Madonna*, sample no. 9: from the red light of the decoration on the cloak of the first Pesaro on the right (120× enlargement).
First preparatory layer of glue with only a little gypsum; second preparatory layer of gypsum and glue; film of drying oil; lead white; red earth and a little lamp black; red lacquer and a little lead white; lead white; red lacquer glaze.
8. The *Pesaro Madonna*, sample no. 25: from the pale blue light on the garment of Saint Peter (120× enlargement).
The preparation was not examined during the sampling; lead white; lead white and a little lamp black; burnt ochre and a little red ochre; lead white with a little lamp black and a little red lacquer; lead white; natural ultramarine and lead white.
9. The *Pesaro Madonna*, sample no. 18: from the dark brown shadow on the cloak of Saint Peter (120× enlargement).
Preparatory layer of gypsum and glue; film of drying oil; lead white; lamp black and a little lead white; lead white and a little lamp black; lead white and ivory black; burnt ochre and a little lead white (back of the cloak); burnt ochre and lead white and a little red ochre; brown lacquer and orpiment; glaze of brown lacquer.

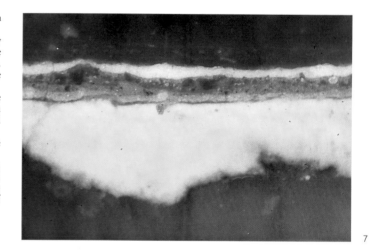

7

10. The *Presentation of the Virgin in the Temple*, sample no. 3: from the brown background over the figure on the left (enlargement).
Preparatory layer of gypsum and glue; lead white and a little carbon black; lead white and lamp black; lead white and bitumen with a little lamp black.
11. The *Presentation of the Virgin in the Temple*, sample no. 1: from the white of the sleeve of the child's garment (120× enlargement).
Preparatory layer of gypsum and glue; lead white and a little carbon black; lead white; lamp black and a little lead white; lead white and lamp black; lamp black and a little lead white and cinnabar; lamp black with a little lead white and a little cinnabar and red lacquer; lead white.
12. The *Presentation of the Virgin in the Temple*, sample no. 10: from the flesh of the hand of the last figure on the right (120× enlargement).
Preparatory layer of gypsum and glue; film of drying oil; lead white and a little carbon black; lead white; lead white and a little red ochre and a little lamp black; lead white and a little lamp black; lead white and lamp black with a little cinnabar; lead white and a little lamp black and a little red and yellow ochre.

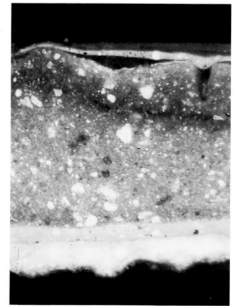

10

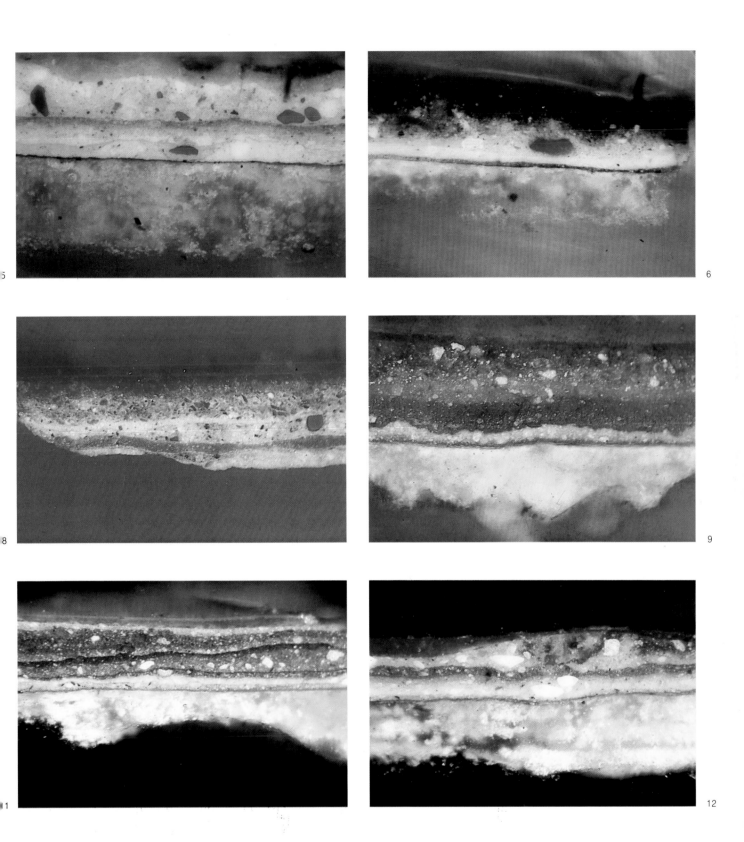

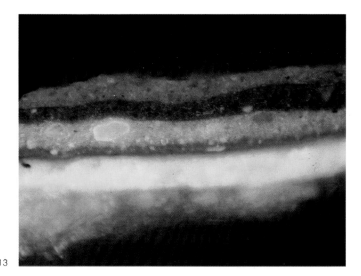

13

13. The *Annunciation*, sample no. 22: from the brown of the imitation marble of the lectern (240× enlargement).
First layer of yellow preparation and a lot of glue; second layer of white preparation of gypsum and a little glue; film of drying oil; layer of burnt ochre and a little red ochre; lead white and a little finely ground cinnabar; lamp black and a little lead white; burnt ochre and red ochre and a little cinnabar.
14. The *Annunciation*, sample no. 22, as in fig. 13, but in UV light (70 enlargement).
The yellow fluorescence of the glue in the preparation layers and the dark-orange fluorescence of the oil film should be noted.
15. The *Annunciation*, sample no. 4: from the right-hand side of the black background above the Madonna (120× enlargement).
Preparatory layer of gypsum and a lot of glue; film of drying oil; lead white and a little red lacquer; burnt ochre and cinnabar and a little lead white.

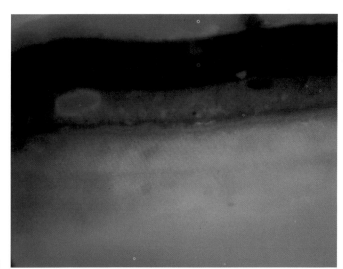

14

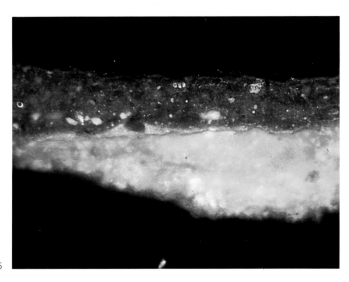

15

Giovanna Bortolaso
A STUDY OF VARIOUS WORKS FROM THE PERIOD 1542-1576

Six works from the period 1542 to Titian's death, representing the evolution of the master's technique in the last thirty years of his life, are examined here. These are, in chronological order: three canvases in the sacristy of the church of Santa Maria della Salute that portray the old testament scenes of *David and Goliath*, *Cain and Abel* and the *Sacrifice of Isaac*; the *Martyrdom of Saint Lawrence* in the church of the Gesuiti, *Doge Antonio Grimani before Faith* in the Palazzo Ducale and finally the *Pietà* in the Accademia. As was the case in the previous article, on the period 1510-42, the samples studied come from tests carried out on the paintings during restoration, and their analysis was conducted using the usual microscopic and microchemical tests that are carried out on transverse paint layer sections.

The huge canvases that were originally conceived for the church of Santo Spirito in Isola and painted between 1542 and 1544 had a number of common features. The *Cain and Abel* is an example of a painting technique that has been reduced to the essentials. Very few pigments were employed exclusively for their chromatic values, and little attempt was made to use the layering and glazing techniques that are typical of his early works. The reason for this sudden simplification of Titian's style was probably the destination of the works and the haste with which they were painted. For the other two works, portraying *David and Goliath* and the *Sacrifice of Isaac*, the sampling could not be as comprehensive owing principally to problems that arose during their restoration. In spite of this it is possible to reveal that for all of these paintings, now in the church of the Salute, Tiziano's palette was limited to only a few colors that he used very sparingly, and that were subsequently contaminated during later restorations. Only a few fragments of the azurite and the lead white that Titian used for the extensive backgrounds of sky and clouds have been saved from the previous restorations that almost completely changed the appearance of the painting.

There is consistent application of gypsum and glue, sometimes quite thick, while only in some areas is there any primer (fig. 1, sample 17). This based on red ochre and carbon black, is applied over the gypsum and glue preparation. The application of the color can be considered to be "direct," as in the flesh of *Cain and Abel*, in that it is done with a layer of vermilion and lead white directly onto the preparation. This is also true in the other paintings where, for example, the yellow of Abraham's garments, of orpiment, or that of Goliath's breastplate, based on lead-tin yellow, lie directly over the preparatory layers. It can be concluded that these works were supported by careful drawings (even though the tests did not find any traces of a charcoal drawing), and the preparatory study now in the Ecole des Beaux-Arts in Paris is evidence of this.

The information that emerges from the study of these works of the 1540s is not, however, completely true for the later *Martyrdom of Saint Lawrence* in the church of the Gesuiti where Titian returns to various techniques more typical of his early period.

As with the paintings studied above, the composition of the paint layer is still relatively restricted, as is shown in parts of the details in the foreground. The flames beneath the martyr's girdle are brought to life by a simple superimposition of two different layers of brushwork, the first made up of red and burnt ochre and the second, that of the half-tones of the fire, of a mixture of finely ground vermilion with lead white, yellow ochre, red lacquer and carbon black. This last paste, again painted directly onto the preparation, creates the disturbing light of the flames (fig. 2, sample 1). Nevertheless, Titian's tendency to construct the final layer with numerous superimpositions and the frequent use of glazes is also apparent in this canvas. The red cloak of the executioner of Saint Lawrence toward whom the martyr directs his last dying gaze exhibits shades and half-tones that are more characteristic of his early periods (fig. 3, sample 8). A layer of paint based on red lacquer is applied over a brown layer that probably belongs to part of the background architecture, using glazing and brushwork to create the transparent effect so dear to the artist in his early years.

The vast canvas that portrays *Doge Antonio Grimani*

before Faith bears witness to the last period of Titian's career,[1] and exhibits the painstaking techniques common to many of his early paintings. It is a work in which the artist roams freely through the entire range of colors used at this time.

Ultramarine is the pigment chosen for the bright blue of Saint Mark's cloak and for the final layers of the sky in the centre of the painting. In this last instance, as is the case with many old master paintings, the powdered lapis lazuli is applied to a base made up of the less precious azurite. The blue areas of the Venetian lagoon in the background, which were discovered during the most recent restoration, were obtained with a mixture of paint and lead white.

The yellows used were also made up of different pigments that varied depending on where they were to be applied: ochre for the more intense tones and lead-tin yellow for the colder more luminous tones of the rays around the figure of Faith (fig. 4, sample 14).

As well as a freer use of color in this canvas, Titian once again adopted his tactic of applying a layer of drying oil when he was obliged to discontinue his work on the painting for any length of time, as in the paintings of his early period. The final color rarely has anything to do with the initial one, and is often composed of numerous layers; in some areas lead white with traces of carbon black is found on top of the gypsum and glue preparation.

This study closes with an examination of the *Pietà* in the Accademia, the artist's last work, which was left unfinished and was then altered by Palma il Giovane ("*reverenter absolvit*"). It has therefore been extensively repainted[2]. The sampling was carried out on the flesh of Christ, the garments of the Magdalene and the cloak of Saint Jerome (or Joseph of Arimathea) who is kneeling on the right of the central group.[3] As with his early works there is no trace of a preparatory charcoal drawing, and the torso of Christ, in which the flesh tones are obtained using red ochre and lead white, is painted over the cloak of the Madonna, the red of which shows traces of lacquer. The superimposition of one layer over another is also evident in the cloak of Saint Jerome, where Titian reached the final pink of the drapery by building up the color with more than fifteen different layers. The final

half-tone is achieved using a finely ground red lacquer and cinnabar that is applied with only a few layers of brushwork, but below which are found superimposed layers of the flesh tones and then again below them appear the series of gray tones of the background architecture (figs. 5, 6, sample 7).

For other bibliography on Titian's technique, see Lorenzo Lazzarini's essay in this catalogue.

[1] L. Lazzarini, "La 'Fede' di Tiziano: note tecniche," *Quaderni della Soprintendenza ai Beni Artistici e Storici di Venezia*, 8, 1979, 57.
[2] S. Moschini Marconi, *Gallerie dell'Accademia di Venezia. Opere d'arte del sec. XVI*, Rome 1962, 260 pp.; and G. Nepi Scirè, "Tiziano, La Pietà," *Quaderni della Soprintendenza ai beni Artistici e Storici di Venezia*, 13, 1987, 30 - 9. The work was analyzed in 1971 by Joyce Plesters. Three of the paint sections (pls v, vi and vii) were published in the above-mentioned *Quaderno*, no. 13.
[3] Sampling and preparation of the samples carried out by Joyce Plesters.

1. *David and Goliath*, sample no. 17: from the blue of the sky near David's abdomen (120× enlargement).
Preparatory layer of gypsum and glue; primer made up of red ochre and carbon black; lead white and cinnabar (the flesh of David); azurite; overpainting based on lead white and colored glaze; second blue over-painting with lead white, cinnabar and yellow ochre.
2. The *Martyrdom of Saint Lawrence*, sample no. 1: from the red of the middle flame under the griddle (240× enlargement).
Preparatory layer of gypsum and glue; finely ground cinnabar with lead white, yellow ochre, red lacquer and carbon black.
3. The *Martyrdom of Saint Lawrence*, sample no. 8: from the dark red of the cloak of the figure behind Saint Lawrence (120× enlargement).
Carbon black, lead white, cinnabar and red lacquer; lead white and a little red lacquer; red lacquer glaze with a little carbon black and cinnabar; layer of brushwork of lead white and red lacquer; red-lacquer glaze with a little carbon black and cinnabar.
4. *Doge Antonio Grimani before Faith*, sample no. 14: from the yellow of the rays above the cross (120× enlargements).
Lead white with lead-tin yellow, cinnabar and carbon black; lead white with natural ultramarine and red-lacquer; lead white with lead-tin yellow, cinnabar, red lacquer and carbon black layer of brushwork of lead white and lead-tin yellow.
5-6. The *Pietà*, sample no. 7: from the red of the cloak of Saint Joseph of Arimathea (or Saint Jerome) (120× enlargement).
Architecture: traces of a preparatory layer of much glue with lead white; carbon black with lead white; carbon black, cinnabar and lead white; lead white and burnt ochre; layer of brushwork with lead white; carbon black with lead white and red ochre; carbon black; carbon black, red ochre and lead white.
Flesh: lead white and carbon black; cinnabar and lead white; lead white; a layer of brushwork of red lacquer glaze; lead white and red ochre with carbon black; varnish.
Cloak: lead white; red lacquer glaze; lead white with red lacquer; red lacquer with cinnabar; cinnabar with carbon black.

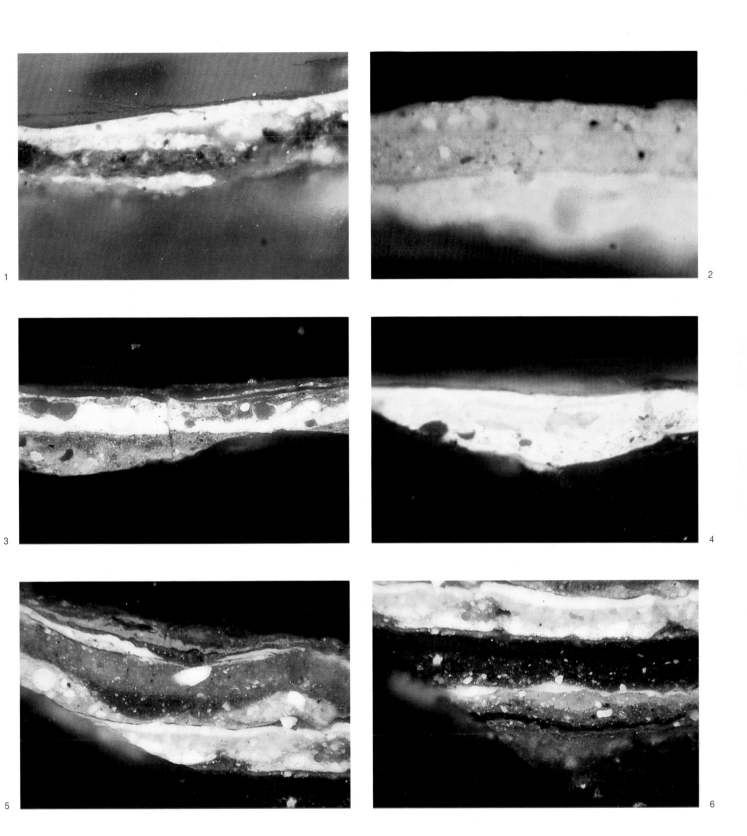

Vasco Fassina, Mauro Matteini, Arcangelo Moles
A STUDY OF THE BINDERS
IN SEVEN PAINTINGS BY TITIAN IN VENICE

The identification of the binders in paintings has always presented serious analytical problems with because of respect to the analysis of pigments. This is not only because of difficulties in distinguishing the different materials, but also because of alterations that occur as a result of natural aging or following preservative treatments.[1]

Improvements in analytical technique have made it possible to remedy this lack of information at least partially.[2] From a practical point of view the identification of the binders can help us to understand why some works of art are in a better state of preservation than others, and perhaps more important it can help the restorers to decide which are the most suitable solvents for the removal of varnishes or over-painting. It is the type of binder used that determines whether the technique used is tempera, oil, or mixed. It is well known that before the fifteenth century the materials most frequently used as binders were animal glues in the preparations and egg "tempera" for the paint layer. After the fifteenth century the traditional binders were replaced with drying oils, initially using mixed techniques where the oils were emulsified with egg, glue, casein, milk etcetera (fatty tempera) and gradually evolving until oils were used by themselves.

This article examines seven works: *Christ Carrying the Cross* in the Scuola di San Rocco, *Saint Mark Enthroned with Saints Cosmas and Damian*, from Santo Spirito; *the Presentation of the Virgin* in the Accademia; *the Annunciation* in the Scuola di San Rocco; *Saint John the Almsgiver* in San Giovanni Elemosinaro; *the Annunciation* in the church of San Salvador and the *Pietà* in the Accademia.

We have tried to identify any evolution or modification in the use of paint binders by Titian, examining a selection of paintings from the whole of Titian's career, since preliminary results made it clear that at some point he may have changed his technique to cope with the numerous commissions that he was receiving.

Titian's rich use of color and layering may have limited his use of oil because it tooks so long to dry. For this reason it was decided to broaden the research, so as to cover his later period as well. While the sampling may seem paltry in the face of the prolific activity of the artist, it is nevertheless a solid starting point. There is very little information available on the binders used by Titian in his paintings. However, data on three paintings examined in the laboratories of the National Gallery in London have been published. The binders used in the *Venus and Adonis*[3] and *Bacchus and Ariadne*[4] were identified as being oil-based, more specifically linseed oil-based, while in *The Vendramin Family* walnut oil was used as a binder (table 1).

A few years ago, during the exhibition *Giorgione a Venezia*, two of Titian's early paintings were analyzed and compared with works by other painters of the same

Tab. 1.

Artist	Picture	Date	Sample	Medium	P/S	Oil Type
Titian	*Venus and Adonis* NG 34	Mid 16th C.	1. Brown on bow	Oil	1.52	Linseed
			2. Adonis' leg	Oil	2.14	Linseed
	The Vendramin Family NG 4452	Mid 16th C.	1. Deep red glaze central profile figure	Oil	2.80	Walnut
			2. Blue sky	Oil	2.40	Walnut
			3. Boy's red stocking	Oil	2.60	Walnut
			4. Maroon robe, old man center	Oil	2.90	Walnut
			5. Black boy's robe L.H.S.	Oil	2.60	Walnut
			6. Ermine sleeve, old man	Oil	2.50	Walnut
	Bacchus and Ariadne NG 35	Mid 16th C.	1. White	Oil	1.95	Linseed

Tab. 2.

Ref. no.	Artist	Title	Sample	P/S	Binder
G B 2	G. Bellini	Pietà	The white if Christ's garments	1.25	Linseed oil
T C 5	Titian	Christ Carrying the Cross	From the gray-green of Christ's garments	1.1	Linseed oil
T S 10	Titian	Saint Mark Enthroned	From the white of St Sebastian's loincloth	1.2	Linseed oil
G T 4	Giorgione	La tempesta	From the purple-brown of the column	1.6	Linseed oil
G V 4	Giorgione	La Vecchia	From the gray-green of the fascia at the bottom of the picture	1.6	Linseed oil
S S 4	Sebastiano del Piombo	Sacra Conversazione	From the green background behind the Virgin	2.7	Walnut oil
S L 1	Sebastiano del Piombo	Saint Louis	From the red of the sleeve near the crosier	3	Walnut oil
B M 1	B. Montagna	Saint Peter	From the white of the arch on the right	1.33	Linseed oil

period. On that occasion only one sample was examined for each painting. The works examined revealed the presence of oil-based binders. In particular linseed oil was used as opposed to walnut oil (table 2). An examination of the painters working in this area between 1500 and 1600 showed that they immediately took advantage of the introduction of oil techniques. This is why the analysis carried out by the National Gallery in London discovered oil-based binders, and more specifically the prevalence of linseed oil, in the selection of paintings that they examined.[5]

1. The Procedure for the Identification of Binders

The first analyses were based on the determination of the composition of the fatty acids in a fragment of the painting after saponification and subsequent acidification and methylification, using gas chromatography.

High levels of azelaic acid indicate the presence of a drying oil, while smaller amounts of azelaic acid in relation to the proportions of palmitic and stearic acids are characteristic of fatty acids that are derived from eggs. Insignificant amounts of fatty acids imply the absence of both eggs and oil, and one must therefore assume that an exclusively proteic binder, such as animal glue, has been used. If medium amounts of azelaic acid are found, then it is likely that a mixed technique was used.

When dealing with oil-based binders, it is possible within certain limits to distinguish walnut, linseed and poppy oil, when the proportions of palmitic (P) and stearic (S) acids are known. The P/S correlation for walnut oil is not indicative because it gives exactly the same value as hemp oil. However it should be noted that hemp oil was hardly ever used in paintings, principally because it tends to turn greenish. When mixtures of these oils are used, medium values are registered, making the data involved in their identification highly ambiguous. Various events in the history of the painting can also cause uncertainty, particularly any preservative treatments and retouching that may have been carried out. As we have already pointed out, there has been very little analytical material published on Titian.

In the case of the five paintings under examination, a different technique was used, that of pyrolysis gas chromatography (P.G.C.). Using this technique, a carefully chosen sample of the paint layer weighing not more than a few milligrams, without any chemical treatment, and which has been separated from any layers of varnish or primer, is put into a quartz crucible and placed inside a platinum probe into which a high temperature thermic flash (900 °C) is induced. In this way the separation of

Tab. 3. Results of the analysis of the paint binders identified in seven paintings by Titian.

Painting	Date	Binder
Christ Carrying the Cross		Linseed oil
Saint Mark Enthroned		Linseed oil
Saint John the Almsgiver	1532-33	Linseed oil
Presentation in the Temple	1539	Linseed oil
San Rocco Annunciation	1540	Drying oil + egg
San Salvador Annunciation	1564-66	Drying oil + egg
Pietà	1576	Linseed oil

any organic substances is induced in the absence of oxygen.[6] The mixture of gaseous or gasifiable fragments are separated on a chromatographic column[7] and the chromatogram (pyrogram) obtained is compared with pyrograms of a paint medium whose composition is already known.

To complete the analysis carried out a series of microanalytical tests were performed. Principally an examination of the solubility differential of the sample and its behavior when it comes into contact with specific reactive solutions (various alkalis, organic solvents, coloring agents) and a series of observations with an optical microscope in reflected light, dark background, but above all under ultra-violet radiation so as to examine accurately the fluorescence of the various paint layers.

2. The Results of the Sampling

Firstly we will set out the results of the analysis carried out a few years ago using gas chromatography on the *Christ Carrying the Cross* and the *Saint Mark Enthroned with Saints Cosmas and Damian*.[8] The chromatograms obtained are shown in tables 1,2,3. As mentioned, in order to identify the type of oil-based binder it is necessary to examine the proportions of palmitic and stearic acid.

For the paintings *Christ Carrying the Cross* and *Saint Mark Enthroned with Saints Cosmas and Damian* the chromatograms show a P/S correlation of 1.1 and 1.2 respectively showing that the binder used in these two works is linseed oil as was found in the *Venus and Adonis* and the *Bacchus and Ariadne* by Mills and White at the National Gallery in London.

For the other five paintings that we analyzed using P.G.C., micro-analytical tests and microscopic study of the fluorescence of the stratigraphy under ultraviolet light, we will now give, individually, the results of the observations and the analyses carried out.

Presentation of the Virgin (Gallerie dell'Accademia)

Two samples from this painting were examined using microanalytical tests and microscopic examination of sections of the fragments under ultraviolet radiation (figs. 1, 2).

The sample TP2 (white) was also examined using pyrolysis gas chromatography (graph 4).

All the examinations carried out confirm that the paint binder is linseed oil, and some other (probably proteic) substances. A different form of the same oil is not possible.

Annunciation (Scuola Grande di San Rocco)

The stratigraphic analyses carried out with an optical microscope, particularly those done under ultraviolet radiation so as to examine the fluorescence, have revealed whites in the paint layer that, though of similar intensity to those produced by oil-based binders, have a less yellow appearance more characteristic of oil/protein mixtures.

The micro-analytical solubility tests confirm this supposition, revealing the presence not only of easily saponifiable substances, but also of typical proteic components that can only be increased in size with alkaline reactants. It is, however, unlikely that the proteic parts are made of animal glue, their behavior being much more compatible than that of egg protein.

The tests using pyrolysis gas chromatography, carried out on the white paint layer of the sample SRA2, show some anomalies when compared to pyrograms obtained from reference paint samples that only contain drying oils (graph 5).

However, it is possible at least partially to prove that these differences can be attributed to egg protein. When compared to a pyrogram of lead white and egg yolk paint, the peaks show some similarities.

In the case of complex mixtures (for example oil and egg) the pyrograms show patterns of fragmentation in substances that cannot necessarily be identified by a straightforward addition of the pyrograms of the pure components.

In conclusion, an examination of all the tests carried out shows that it is not unreasonable to assume that a mixed binder (the so-called fatty tempera) with a drying oil base (probably linseed oil) and egg was used for this picture.

Saint John the Evangelist (Church of San Giovanni Elemosinario)

Microscopic examination under ultraviolet radiation of the stratigraphic sections of various samples (SGE2, SGE3, SGE4, SGE5, SGE7) (figs. 4,5,6,7), did not encounter any intense yellow fluorescence in correspondence with the paint layers. This optical characteristic is typical of oil-based binders (linseed and other drying oils) and it is much easier to see where the pigment that has been mixed in is made up of lead white.

In the samples examined this was more evident in the whiter paint layers of SGE2 and SGE4 (respectively right margin and sky).

The micro-analytical solubility tests, made on samples SGE2, SGE3 and SGE5, confirmed the presence of a predominantly oilbased binder.

The tests using pyrolysis gas chromatography were only carried out on the white layer of SGE1 and show a clear analogy with the pyrogram of a sample consisting of boiled linseed oil and lead white (graph 6), which has been artificially prepared and aged. Reference pyrograms using walnut and poppy oil samples were less similar. An overall examination of the tests carried out lead us to conclude that the painting was done using a binder essentially based on linseed oil.

Annunciation (Church of San Salvador)

Seven samples taken from this painting, and examined using micro-analytical tests and observation with an optical microscope of the ultraviolet fluorescence of the fragments, show less evidence of an oil-based binder in the paint layers, in which, however there were significant quantities of non-saponifiable substances, which were probably proteic (fig. 8,9).

Checking with pyrolisis gaschromatography of sample no. 5, once the layers of varnish and primer had been removed (graph 7), confirms the presence of fragmentation substances that have the characteristics not only of drying oils, but also of egg yolk (graph 5).

We can therefore conclude that the paint binder, at least in some of the color layers, consists of a proteic tempera (egg) rich in oils.

In this the preparation is not of gypsum and animal glue as in the other paintings but mainly of lead white as opposed to gypsum and, while the first coats are bonded with the usual glue, the upper coats are enriched with drying oils.

Pietà (Gallerie dell'Accademia)

The available sample only analyzed using the techniques that have already been outlined (fig. 10) was made up of thick layers of paint consisting of lead white suspended in a binder that was very like boiled linseed oil, and this was confirmed by the pyrolysis gas chromatography (graph 8). The pattern of the fragmentation substances corresponded perfectly with those of the test sample. The other analyses also confirmed this result.

3. Observations on the Results

Reviewing the facts that have emerged from the analyses carried out on the two paintings of his early period, on the four of his mature period, and finally on the *Pietà* (data that we have summarized in table 3), it seems possible to conclude that, in the majority of the paintings that we have examined, the artist used an exclusively or at any rate predominantly oil-based binder. Exceptions to this are the two *Annunciations*, in which a proteic substance identified in our tests as egg, seems to have been added to the binder. A fatty tempera of this type is particularly predominant in the Annunciation in San Salvador. This painting is a particularly good example of what we consider to be a modification of the binder used by Titian, which seems to denote a change in his painting technique in order to adapt to requirements that we cannot now reconstruct. It is possible that this mixed technique might also be present in the last painting: the *Pietà*.

However only one sample from this painting was examined and for this reason it could be considered that the results obtained from this cannot be applied to the whole painting. The thick layers of color that had been used do not conform with the use of the exclusively oil-based binder that was identified by the analysis. Still it is not impossible that the painter had returned to the technique that he used the most. Both the gas chromatography tests and those using P.G.C. exclude the possibility of an oil other than linseed.

We would like to thank Giancarlo Lanterna and Carlo Lalli of the Opificio delle Pietre Dure for having the analysis by pyrolysis gas chromatography of the samples and the reference standards and for the analysis of the stratigraphic sections respectively.

We would also like to thank Paolo Fuga and Dino Zanella, from the laboratory of the Soprintendenza ai Beni Artistici e Storici, Venice, for elaborating of the graphics and photographs.

Finally we would like to thank the Superintendent Giorgio Bonsanti for the collaboration of the Opificio delle Pietre Dure.

[1] M. Matteini, A. Moles, *La chimica nel restauro. I materiali dell'arte pittorica*, 1989.
V. Fassina, "Note sull'identificazione dei leganti nei dipinti", in *Quaderno della Soprintendenza ai Beni Artistici e Storici di Venezia*, 7, 1978, 133-37.
V. Fassina, "Identificazione dei leganti del 'Convito in casa Levi' di Paolo Veronese," in *Quaderno della Sovrintendenza ai Beni Artistici Storici di Venezia*, 11, 1984, 73-81.
[2] M. Johnson, E. Packard, "Methods used for the identification of binding media in Italian paintings of the Fifteenth and Sixteenth centuries," *Studies in Conservation*, 16, 1971, 145-64.
J. S. Mills, "The gas chromatographic examination of paint media, part 1. Fatty acid composition and identification of dried oil films," *Studies in Conservation*, 11, 1966, 92-107.
J. S. Mills, "The identification of paint media, an introduction," *Conservation of Paintings and the Graphic Art, Papers of the Conference*, Lisbon 9-14 October 1972, 701-03.
J. S. Mills, R. White, "The gas chromatographic examinations of paint media, part II. Some examples of medium identification in paintings by fatty aid analysis," *Conservation of Paintings and the Graphic Arts, Papers of the Conference*, Lisbon, 9-14 October 1972, 721-28.
J. S. Mills, R. White, "Natural resins of art and archaeology. Their sources, chemistry and identification", *Studies in Conservation*, 22, 1977, 12-31.
J. S. Mills, R. White, "Organic analyses in the arts; some further paint medium analyses," *National Gallery Technical Bulletin*, 2, 1978, 71-76.
[3] J. S. Mills, R. White, "The gas chromatographic examination of paint media. Some examples of medium identification in painting by fatty acid analysis," *Conservation and Restoration of pictorial art*, edited by N. Bromelle and P. Smith, 1976, 72-77.
[4] J. S. Mills, R. White, "Analyses of paint media," *National Gallery Technical Bulletin*, 1, 1977, 57-59.
[5] J. S. Mills, R. White, "Analyses of paint media," *National Gallery Technical Bulletin*, 3, 1979, 66-67.
J. S. Mills, R. White, "Analyses of paint media," *National Gallery Technical Bulletin*, 5, 1981, 66-67.
J. S. Mills, R. White, "Analyses of paint media," *National Gallery Technical Bulletin*, 7, 1983, 65-67.
J. S. Mills, R. White, "Analyses of paint media," *National Gallery Technical Bulletin*, 12, 1988, 78-79.
R. White, "The application of gas chromatography to the analyses of waxes," *Studies in Conservation*, 23, 1978, 57-68.
[6] M. Matteini, A. Moles, A. Masala, V. Parrini, *Examination through pyrolysis gas chromatography of binders used in painting. Scientific methodologies applied to works of art*, Florence, 1984, 41-44.
[7] The conditions of pyrolysis gas chromatography.
The samples that are to be analyzed are ground up with Alumina, placed in a quartz test tube sealed with quartz wool, and placed inside a COIL Probe where they are heated to 900°C for 20 seconds
- RAMP = OFF
- Metal column 2m long with a diameter of 2mm
- Phase: FFAP at 10%
- Gas vehicle: Nitrogen with a flow of 15cc per minute
- FID detector and injector kept at 250°C
- Temperature programmed to rise from 50°c to 230°C with a rise rate of 5°C per minute
- Isotherm at 230°C for 20 minutes.
[8] The analyses were carried out using two types of column so as to be sure that the results obtained could be averaged out, even when different experimental conditions were used.
Firstly a series of analyses was conducted using an OV column at 3% with the temperature programmed to rise from 130°C to 210°C with a rise rate of 4°C

per minute. The following sequence of components was used: azelate, palmitate, stearate, oleate. In this case the separation of the components is based on rising boiling points, as long as the stationary phase of the column used is not polar.

Then a second series of analyses was conducted using a DEGS column (diethyleneglycol succinate) at a constant temperature of 190°C. The frequency of the components issuing forth was as follows: palmitate, azelate, stearate, oleate. As can be seen in the diagrams the palmitate and azelate have been inverted. The reason f or this lies in the use of the different stationary phase, that being polar separates the components on the basis of the polarity of the molecule.

GRAPHS

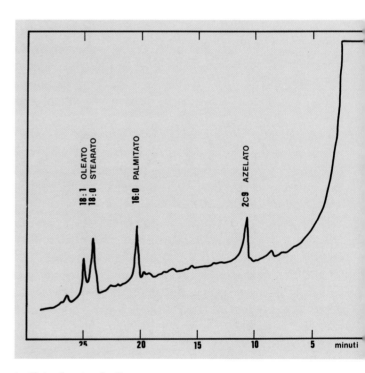

1. *Christ Carrying the Cross*
Analysis of the sample TC5 using pyrolysis gas chromatography (from the gray-green of Christ's garments.)
Operating conditions: OV1 column, 3% silicone; gas vehicle: nitrogen 25 ml/min; temperature programmed from 110-210°C.
Results: P/S correlation = 1.1 LINSEED OIL.

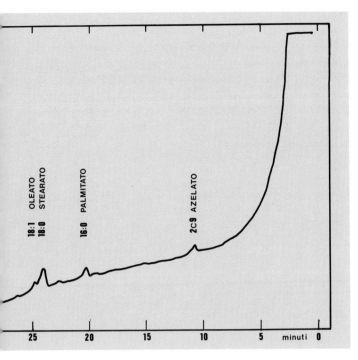

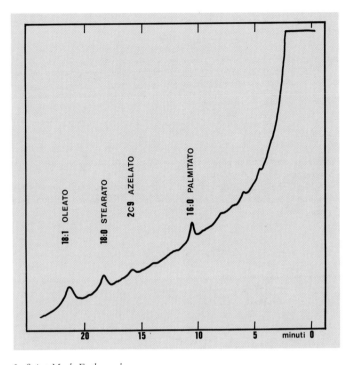

2. Saint Mark Enthroned
Analysis of sample TS10 using pyrolysis gas chromatography (from the white of the loincloth of St. Sebastian.)
Operating conditions: OV1 column, 3% silicone; gas vehicle: nitrogen 25 ml/min; temperature programmed from 110-210°C.
Results: P/S correlation = 1.2 LINSEED OIL.

3. Saint Mark Enthroned
Analysis of sample TS10 using pyrolysis gas chromatography (from the loincloth of St Sebastian).
Operating conditions: DEGS column; gas vehicle: nitrogen 25 ml/min; constant temperature at 190°C.
Results: P/S correlation = 1.2 LINSEED OIL.

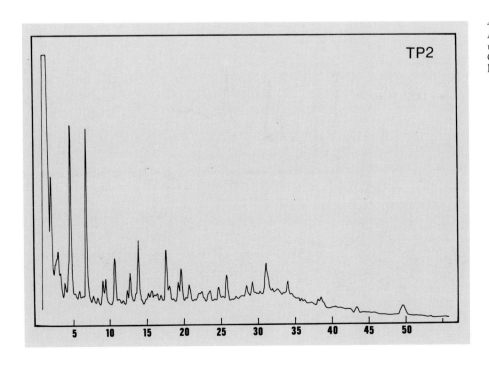

4. Presentation of the Virgin in the Temple
Analysis of the white paint layer of sample TP2 using pyrolysis gas chromatography.
Comparison with pyrograms of reference paint layers shows a marked similarity with linseed oil.

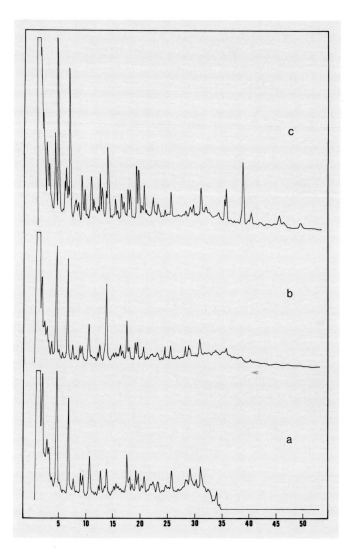

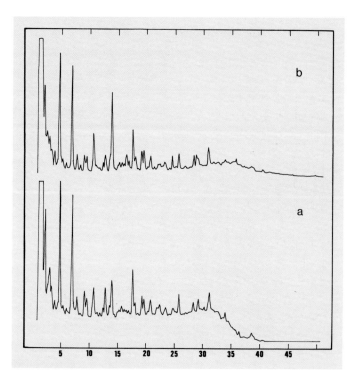

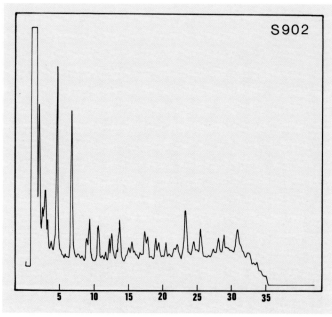

5. The Annunciation
Comparison of the pyrograms obtained from the paint layer of sample SRA2 (a), with a reference paint layer of lead white and linseed oil prepared and aged artificially and (b), another with lead white and egg yolk.

6. Saint John the Almsgiver
Comparison between the pyrograms obtained from the paint layer of sample SGE1 (a), and a reference paint layer of lead white and linseed oil artificially prepared and aged (b).
There is a notable similarity between the fragmentation substances of the two graphs.

7. Annunciation (San Salvador [Venice])
Analysis of the paint layer of samples using pyrolysis gas chromatography. As is shown by the comparison with reference pyrograms of graph 5 (linseed oil and egg yolk) the nature of the paint binder is assimilable with that of a fatty tempera (egg yolk with linseed oil).

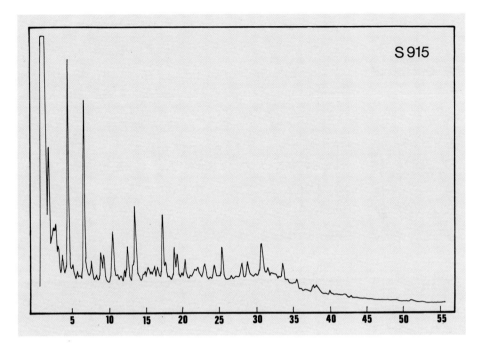

8. *Pietà*
Analysis using pyrolysis gas chromatography; comparison with the reference pyrogram shows that the binder in the sample examined is definitely linseed oil.

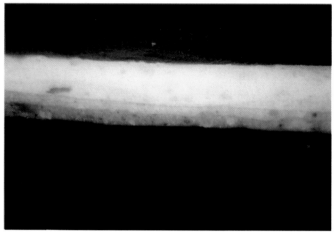

1a

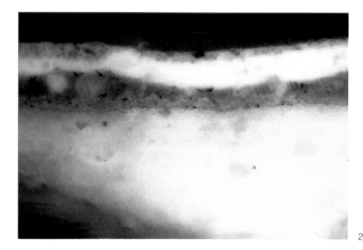

2a

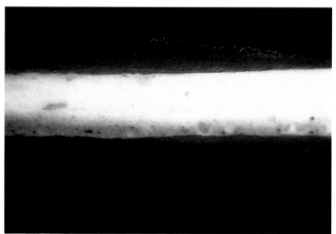

1b

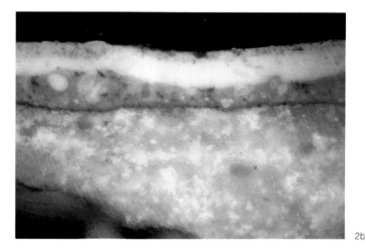

2b

STRATIGRAPHIC RESEARCH AND ULTRA-VIOLET FLUORESCENCE ANALYSIS

1. Presentation of the Virgin in the Temple
Stratigraphic test on a fragment of the sample TP2 taken from the white of the garment of the woman with her hand on her chest. In A the photograph was taken in reflected light (microscopic enlargement x65); in B the photograph of the UV fluorescence (see text). Sample TP2.
1. Regular paint layer and thin (15 microns) coat of beige based on lead white with charcoal black added, red lacquer or ochre in oily binder. Medium to slight UV fluorescence.
2. Thin (15 microns) layer with a similar tone and composition to the preceding one, though a little paler, with less pigments added.
3. Thick (60-70 microns) white paint layer almost entirely made up of lead white an oil-based binder. Two different applications can be made out of which the inner layer is the thinner.

2. Presentation of the Virgin in the Temple
Microphotograph A (microscopic enlargement x65) of a fragment in section of sample TP1, taken from the sky above the top of the mountain (blue). In B, the same section shows fluorescence produced by the materials when under UV radiation (see text). Sample TP1.
1. Pale yellow application based on gypsum and animal glue with some traces of resin that had penetrated through the cracks. Two applications can be clearly seen and there is also a very thin layer of animal glue on the surface.
2. Traces of carbon black in a thin (3-4 microns) layer between the preparation and paint layers (probably a preparatory drawing).
3. Thick (30-40 microns) and irregular paint layer of yellow-gray based on lead white, black and yellow ochre in an oil-based binder but with only slight fluorescence due to the presence of small quantities of verdigris.
4. White paint layer (30-40 microns) exclusively of lead white, an oil-based binder that gives off an intense light yellow fluorescence.
5. Thin blue paint layer (18-20 microns) of lead white in an oil-based binder.

3. Annunciation
Microphotograph A (microscopic enlargement x65) of a section of a fragment of sample SRA1 taken from the upper blue border (see text). B is a photograph of the same section after the colormetric test for the identification (in blue) of animal glues. C is a photograph of the same section after the colormetric test for the identification (in yellow) of the lead white SRA1.
1. Yellow/white paint preparation based on gypsum and animal glue with a thin film of glue on the surface.

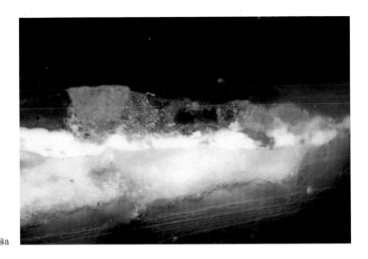

3a

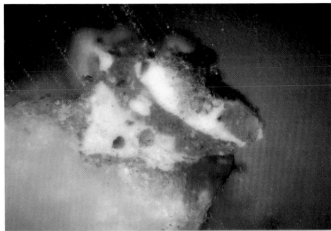

4a

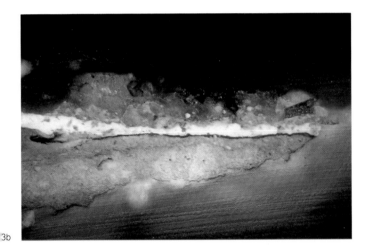

3b

4b

3c

4. Saint John the Almsgiver

Microphotograph (microscopic enlargement) of a section of a fragment of the sample SGE2 which was taken from the right margin at the height of the Saint's head. B a photograph of the UV fluorescence (see text). Sample SGE2.

1. Paint preparation based on gypsum and animal glue with a thin film of pure glue on the surface. White/gray fluorescence.

2. Brown paint layer made up of a mixture of pigments including lead white and transparent verdigris with small quantities of red lead and ochre etc. The brown color is the result of the alteration of the transparent verdigris.
An inner stratum of this layer is also shown in the stratigraphy with the original pale green tone. The yellow-orange fluorescence of the oil-based binder is obstructed by the presence of the non-fluorescent layer of copper pigment.

3. White paint layer (lead white with oil) with intense yellow UV fluorescence.

4. Traces of a light blue paint layer based on lead white and azzurite in which the binder gives off only slight fluorescence due to the interference of the copper pigment which has a very low fluorescence.

5. Fragmentary semi-transparent film made up of restoration varnishes mixed with animal glue.

2. Blue paint layer (lead white with azzurite). UV fluorescence similar to that of the oil-based binders but slightly less yellow (20-25 microns thick).

3. Irregular and worn blue paint layer based almost entirely of roughly ground azzurite with a little lead white, heavily impregnated with a coating, probably the result of a previous restoration, that is likely to be animal glue (60-90 microns thick).

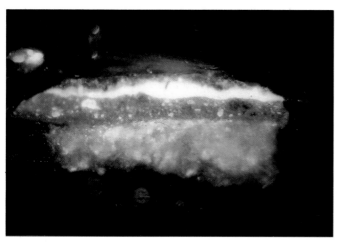

5a

6a

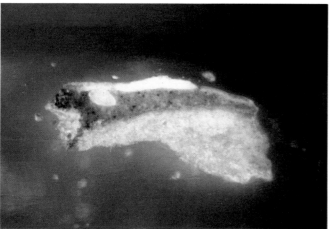

5b

6b

5. Saint John the Almsgiver
Microphotograph (enlargement x65) of a section of a fragment of the sample SGE5 taken from the sky in the indentation in the cloud. B the photograph of the UV fluorescence of another fragment of the same sample (see text). Sample SGE4.

1. Preparatory paint layer of the same type as the preceding samples, heavily impregnated with orange/brown varnishes that have penetrated through the cracks in the paint layers.
2. Brown paint layer the same as the one described for the sample SGE2.
3. White paint layer the same as layer 3 of sample SGE2.
4. Blue paint layer based on azzurite with a little lead white and a low fluorescence.
5. Traces of animal glue on the surface (probably from a restoration).

6. Saint John the Almsgiver
Microphotograph (enlargement x65) of a section of a fragment of sample SGE5 taken from the red cloak of the saint. B the photograph of the UV fluorescence (see text). Sample SGE5.

1. Preparatory paint layer the same as that described in the previous samples.
2. Brown paint layer similar to the one described for samples SGE2 and SGE4, applied in two coats with a thin nonflorescent separating layer, probably made up of verdigris. This film and the one mentioned above very probably correspond with interruption and resumption in the work.
3. Thick red-brown paint layer (a mixture of Carmine lacquer and azzurite suspended in an oil-based binder). The fluorescence of the binder is less than that of the pigments.

398

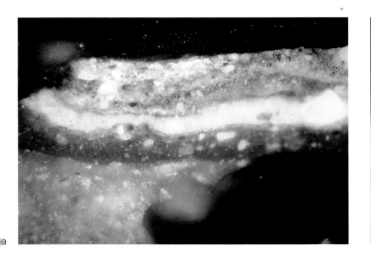

a

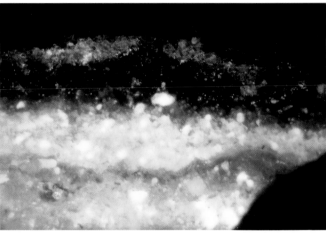

8a

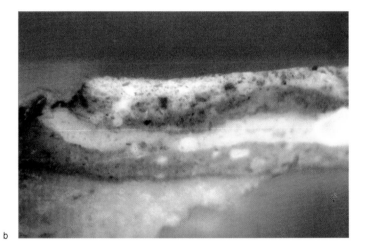

b

8b

7. Saint John the Almsgiver
Microscopic photograph (enlargement x65) of a section of a fragment of the sample SGE7 taken from the background below the book. B the photograph of the UV fluorescence (see text). Sample SGE7.
1. preparatory paint layer similar to the one described for sample SGE2.
2. Brown paint layer similar in appearance, composition and thickness to the one described for sample SGE2.
3. Paint layer similar in appearance, composition and thickness to those described for sample SGE2. At least two applications can be distinguished.
4. Irregular gray paint layer (18-20 microns thick), of lead white into which finely ground carbon black and what seems to be transparent verdigris in an oil-based binder have been added. The fluorescence of the binder is impeded by the presence of the copper pigment.
5. Paint layer of an undefinable color (20-25 microns thick) based on lead white with various other pigments added (mainly azzurite, red lacquer and transparent verdigris).
6. Blue paint layer (lead white and azzurite that saturates and evens out the underlying layer). Since there are no solutions that exist in both this and the preceding layer, the florescence of this layer appears pale and cold compared, for example, with layer 4 which is also made up of lead white. Therefore it is possible that this is material that was added later (retouch). The binder is oil-based.

8. Annunciation, Church of San Salvador
Microphotograph (enlargement x65) of a section of a fragment of sample 4, taken from the cloak of the Madonna. B a photograph of the fluorescence of the materials. Sample 4.
1. Primer based mainly on lead white with large quantities of added oil and animal glue that is applied in three distinct layers with varying quantities of the components. The lowest layer contains the least amount of glue.
2. Brown paint layer composed of natural ultramarine in a large amount of binder that has turned brown as a result of alteration.
3. Blue paint layer (20 microns) based mainly on natural ultramarine.
4. Minute traces of faintly fluorescent varnish (see layer 6 in sample 5).
5. Film of resinous varnish with the same pale-yellow fluorescence as layer 4 in sample 7.
Intense fluorescence in the paint layers with pale tones; these are yellower in the primer.

399

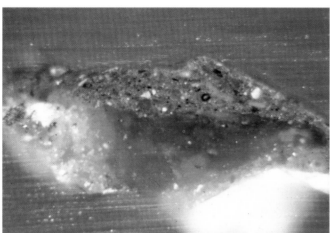

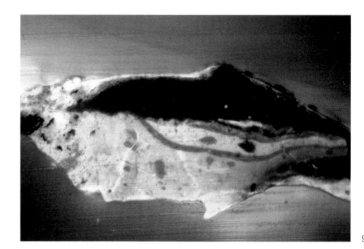

9a

9b

9. Annunciation, Church of San Salvador
Microphotograph (enlargement x65) of a section of a fragment of the sample 8, taken from the Madonna's bodice; the red in the shade. B the photograph of the fluorescence of the same sample. Sample 8.
1. Preparatory layers (in some areas that have been applied in two easily distinguishable layers) of lead white and vermilion with an oil-based binder and can be inferred from the yellowish fluorescence.
2. Thick and irregular semi-transparent red layer (120130 microns) of carmine lacquer rich in binder. On part of the fragment there are traces of red lead and vermilion instead of the lacquer.
3. Highly irregular red-purple layer based on carmine lacquer, ochre and carbon black with traces of vermilion and lead white (60 microns). Low fluorescence.

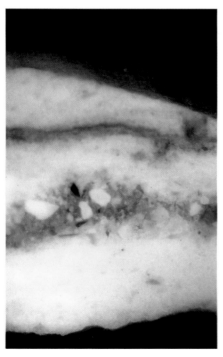

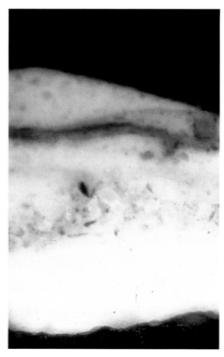

10. Pietà
Microphotograph (enlargement x65) of a fragment in section: of the amphora on the bottom left; white. B shows the UV fluorescence of the paint layers.
1. Traces of a thick white/yellow layer made up of lead white with small quantities of ochre in oil-based binder. Very intense UV fluorescence.
2. Thin and irregular gray layers (lead white and finely ground carbon black) 15-20 microns.
3. Thick layer (50-70 microns) of coarsely ground lead white in an oil-based binder. Intense yellow UV fluorescence.
4. Thick layer (100-130 microns) exclusively of lead white in oil-based binder. Intense fluorescence.

10a

10b

COMPARATIVE CHRONOLOGY
compiled by Francesco Valcanover

YEARS	HISTORICAL EVENTS	CULTURAL EVENTS	THE LIFE AND WORKS OF TITIAN
1488-1490			This was the period of Titian's birth in Pieve di Cadore, according to Dolce (1557) and Vasari (1568). Each date is more credible than the dates given by the artist himself (see below, 1571) and by the *Registro dei morti* of San Canciano (see below, 1576), which would have his birthdate go back respectively to 1476-77 and to 1473. These dates seem also to be ruled out by Aretino's letter of 1548 in which he sent to Lorenzo Lotto the best regards of Titian who was on his way to Augsburg.
1492	Discovery of America.		
1493	Emperor Maximilian I succeeds to Frederick II.	Marin Sanudo begins keeping his *Diaries*.	
1494	Invasion of Italy by Charles III of France.	Philippe de Commynes judges Venice to be the most beautiful, glorious and triumphant city of the Western world.	
1495	31 March: Venice allies with the Pope, the Duke of Milan and the King of Spain to defend the independence of the peninsula against France.		
1498	Vasco da Gama, after circumnavigating Africa, reaches the coast of India.		
1499	Venice allies with France, ambitious to conquer Lombardy, in exchange for the promise of Cremona and Ghiara d'Adda. The Turks devastate the Friuli as far as the Livenza River.	Aldus Manutius publishes the *Sogno di Polifilo* by Francesco Colonna.	
1500	23 February: Charles, future Emperor, is born in Ghent to Philip the Fair, Duke of Burgundy, and Juana the Mad. The Turks conquer Modon, Coron and almost all the Venetian strongholds in Greece.	Leonardo comes to Venice for a brief visit. Gentile Bellini signs and dates the *Miracle of the Cross at the Ponte San Lorenzo*. Jacopo de' Barbari draws his monumental perspective map of Venice, published by Antonio Kolb, merchant of Nuremberg.	
1501	13 May: Venice allies with the Pope and Hungary.	Michelangelo begins sculpting the *David*, which he finishes in 1504. 15 May: Ottaviano Petrucci, from the Marches, prints the first complete musical work. 17 October: privilege granted to Aldus Manutius for new typographical characters. Aldine editions of Virgil and Horace, followed in 1502 by Ovid and Catullus. Vittore Carpaccio paints in the Sala dei Pregadi in the Palazzo Ducale. Giovanni Bellini paints the portrait of Doge Loredan.	
1502	Battle of Santa Maura. Jacopo Pesaro commands the Papal Fleet; Benedetto Pesaro that of the Venetians.	The construction begins on a project by Mauro Codussi, Palazzo Vendramin-Calergi. From this year through c. 1507, Vittore Carpaccio is working on the canvases for the Scuola di San Giorgio degli Schiavoni. The "Neoacademia" of Aldus Manutius, which has hosted Erasmus of Rotterdam, is by this time the most important intellectual center for book production in Europe.	

YEARS	HISTORICAL EVENTS	CULTURAL EVENTS	THE LIFE AND WORKS OF TITIAN
1503	23 March: institution of baptismal registers in Venetian parishes. After the sack of the Friuli, Venice on 20 May signs a peace treaty with the Ottoman Turks, losing Lepanto, Modon, Croton and several cities in Albania. 7 December: Julius II Della Rovere, recently raised to the pontificate, denounces Venetian territorial accessions in the Romagna.	Leonardo is commissioned to paint the *Battle of Anghiari* for the Sala del Consiglio in Palazzo Vecchio, Florence. The second edition of *Supplementum chronicarum* by I.F. Foresti is published in Venice. Alvise Vivarini dies.	
1504	Venetian dominion spreads to Puglia and to the Romagna. 30 April: Girolamo Tron, who had surrendered Lepanto to the Turks, is beheaded. 24 May: the proposal to the Sultan to cut through the Suez isthmus is abandoned. 22 September: the Treaties of Blois between Louis XII of France and the Emperor Maximilian, against Venice. 15 October: the Venetian Senate prohibits long trains on women's clothing. This is one of the first of the numerous sumptuary laws in Venice in the 16th century against luxury in clothing and jewelry.	Raphael paints the *Marriage of the Virgin*. Michelangelo paints the *Doni Tondo*, and in October begins the cartton of the *Battle of Cascina* for the Sala del Consiglio of Palazzo Vecchio, Florence. The Church of San Giovanni Crisostomo, designed by Mauro Codussi, is completed. Luca Pacioli's treatise *De Divina Proportione* is published in Venice. From this year through 1507 (q.v.) Gentile Bellini is working on *Saint Mark Preaching in Alexandria* for the Scuola Grande di San Marco. Between this year and 1506 Giorgione paints the *Castelfranco Madonna*.	
1505	10 February: it is decided to return to the Pope territories conquered in the Romagna excepting Rimini and Faenza. 19 May: the Council of Ten institutes the *Collegio solenne delle Acque*. 4 November: the dowries of brides may not exceed 3,000 ducats.	Bramante designs the Belvedere Courtyard in the Vatican. Michelangelo begins his first project for the grandiose tomb monument of Julius II. Between 26 and 27 January, a fire destroys the Fondaco dei Tedeschi. Aldus Manutius publishes *Gli Asolani* by Pietro Bembo, dedicated to Lucretia Borgia. Giovanni Bellini paints the altarpiece for the church of San Zaccaria. Lorenzo Lotto signs and dates his *Landscape with an Allegorical Scene* (cover for the *Portrait of Bishop Bernardo de' Rossi*) and paints the altarpiece of the parish church of Santa Cristina di Quinto (Treviso).	
1506	6 June: Nuremberg requests from Venice a copy of its laws for the protection of orphans and wards. 6 October: Venice refuses a new alliance with France.	The *Laocöon*, discovered on the Esquiline Hill, enters the collections of the Vatican. 28 May: the Veronese Fra' Giovanni Giocondo, architect and engineer, is in the service of the Venetian government. Albrecht Dürer, in Venice from 1505, finishes in six months *The Madonna of the Rose Garlands* for the Vicaria of the Fondaco dei Tedeschi in San Bartolomeo, and writes in a letter to his friend Pirkheimer of Nuremburg that the only genial painter in Venice is Giovanni Bellini. Antonio Lombardo models the *Madonna and Child* for the Zen chapel in San Marco. Gentile Bellini dies.	

YEARS	HISTORICAL EVENTS	CULTURAL EVENTS	THE LIFE AND WORKS OF TITIAN
1507	9 February: Venice rejects proposals for alliance with Maximilian. 27 March: Venice proposes a general league against the Turks. 27 August: fears in Venice that the Pope is allying with Maximilian.	Raphael signs and dates the *Deposition* for San Francesco, Perugia. Giovanni Bellini commits himself to finishing the *Preaching of Saint Mark in Alexandria* left unfinished by his brother Gentile. On 18 September he takes Alvise Vivarini's place to complete three canvases in collaboration with Vittore Carpaccio and Vittore Belliniano, for the Sala del Maggior Consiglio of the Palazzo Ducale. 14 August: Giorgione receives the commission to paint a canvas for the Sala dell'Udienza in the Palazzo Ducale, which was still unpainted on 24 January 1508. Ottaviano Petrucci publishes in Venice the seventh book of *Frottole*.	
1508	4 February: with Julius II's approval, Maximilian I adopts in Trent the title of Holy Roman Emperor. 2 March: in Cadore, Venetian troops led by Count Vecellio, Titian's grandfather, rout the army of Maximilian I. 10 December: the League of Cambrai unites the Papacy, the Empire, Spain, France and some Italian states against Venice. 29 December: the Council of Ten prohibits theatricals.	At the wish of Julius II and on a project by Bramante, from this year to 1511, the urban restructuring of Rome is in part carried out. Michelangelo begins the frescoing of the vault of the Sistine Chapel in Rome, completing it in October 1512. Fra' Bartolomeo della Porta stays in Venice. Giorgione is at work on the frescoes of the Grand Canal façade of the Fondaco dei Tedeschi, recently rebuilt (see also 1505). 19 December: a copyright is granted to Luca Pacioli for mathematical works.	Titian paints the frescoes of the façade of the Fondaco dei Tedeschi that looks on to the calle del Buso (today the calle del Fondaco), probably finishing them the following year.
1509	Venetian population numbers 115,000 (see also under 1563). 15 June: of 300,000 people in the city, Sanudo counts 11,654 courtesans. 27 April: Julius II excommunicates Venice. The Council of Ten forbids publication of the Bull. 14 May: at Agnadello in the Ghiara d'Adda the Venetian army is defeated by French and Imperial troops, who then advance to the edges of the lagoon. 17 July: Andrea Gritti, Provveditore General of the army and future doge (see also under 1523) recaptures Padua and defends it from the siege of the Imperial army. In the following months Venice exploits the lack of coordination of the members of the League of Cambrai to ward off the danger of losing its liberty.	Between this year and 1511 Peruzzi builds the Villa Farnesina in Rome. Raphael begins the frescoes in the Stanza della Segnatura in Rome, finishing them in 1511. Sebastiano Luciani, later known as del Piombo, finishes the organ shutters of the church of San Bartolomeo, Venice.	
1510	24 February: Julius II solemnly lifts the excommunication of Venice, in Saint Peter's. The plague rages in Venice.	Sebastiano Luciani moves to Rome. Giorgione dies in the autumn. Vittore Carpaccio signs and dates the altarpiece of San Giobbe (Venice, Galleria dell'Accademia).	1 December: Titian's name appears in the account book of the Scuola del Santo, Padua, for the painting of three frescoes with *Miracles of Saint Anthony*.

YEARS	HISTORICAL EVENTS	CULTURAL EVENTS	THE LIFE AND WORKS OF TITIAN
1511	20 September: Antonio Savorgnan treacheriously hands the city of Udine to Maximilian. 4 October: Venice draws up an alliance with France and the Papacy.	Sebastiano del Piombo contributes to the fresco decoration of the Sala dei Pianeti of the Farnesina. Between this year and 1512, Raphael paints the *Madonna di Foligno*.	By 2 December, Titian completes the three frescoes for the Scuola del Santo.
1512	5 February: the Venetians recapture Brescia, but are almost immediately driven out by the French, commanded by Gaston de Foix. 6 April: truce with Maximilian is signed. 14 September: Crema is ceded to the Venetian Republic.	Raphael is commissioned to paint frescoes in the Stanza di Eliodoro in the Vatican, which he will complete in 1514, the year he begins the frescoes of the Stanza dell'Incendio. His portrait of *Julius II* is also of 1512.	
1513	Death of Pope Julius II, succeeded by Leo X. 23 March: Treaty of Blois between Venice and Francis I of France. 7 October: Venetian troops commanded by Alviano are defeated by the Imperial army.	Bramante dies. Michelangelo works on the *Rebellious Slave*, destined for the tomb of Julius II for which he has made a second project. Raphael paints the *Sistine Madonna*, and may already be at work on the fresco of the *Triumph of Galatea* in the Farnesina. Giovanni Bellini paints the *Altarpiece of San Giovanni Crisostomo* for the church of the same name in Venice. Girolamo Romanino is commissioned on April 30 to paint the large *Altarpiece of Santa Giustina*.	After being invited to Rome to the papal court by Pietro Bembo, in a letter of 31 May to the Council of Ten Titian chooses instead to offer his services to the Republic of Saint Mark saying that he was ready to paint in the Sala del Maggior Consiglio of the Palazzo Ducale, beginning with a battle. In exchange he asked that the first *sensaria* of the Fondaco dei Tedeschi to become vacant should be assigned to him with the same benefits enjoyed by Giovanni Bellini. In May his petition is granted. Titian opens a workshop at San Samuele and is assisted by Antonio Buxei and Ludovico di Giovanni, the latter a former assistant of Giovanni Bellini.
1514	10 January: a disastrous fire destroys many buildings in the area of the Rialto. In Venice the magistracy of the *Provveditore alle Pompe* is established.	Andrea del Sarto finishes the fresco of the *Birth of the Virgin* in the atrium of the Santissima Annunciata, Florence. At the Este Court of Ferrara, Giovanni di Nicolò Luteri, known as Dosso Dossi, begins his activity and will work for both Alfonso I and Ercole II. Giovanni Bellini signs and dates *The Feast of the Gods* for the *Camerino d'Alabastro* of Alfonso I d'Este. Palma Vecchio receives a payment for the *Assumption of the Virgin*.	20 March: at the instigation of some Venetian painters the Council of Ten retracts its concessions to Titian in 1513, only to concede to Titian once more in November of the same year.
1515	14 September: Venetian and French allies win at Marignano.	Marc'Antonio Michiel begins his *Notizie d'opere di disegno*. Giovanni Bellini signs and dates the *Nude Woman at a Mirror*. 8 February: Bernardino Benalio, in a request for a privilege for woodcuts, mentions a *Drowning of Pharoah* (see also 1549). Pietro Lombardo dies, leaving his workshop to Tullio and Antonio Lombardo. Aldus Manutius dies.	
1516	26 May: the Venetians reconquer Brescia, after allying with France against the pope and the King of Spain, extending in subsequent years, in alternate alliances with the European political leaders, Venetian dominion on the mainland to the Adda, Cadore, Friuli, Istria, Dalmatia, and the islands of Corfù, Cypress and Crete. The Treaty of Noyon between Charles I, King of Spain, future Emperor, and Francis I, King of France.	Raphael until 1520 is involved with Antonio da Sangallo and Giulio Romano in the construction of Villa Madama. 30 January: Andrea Navagero is named official historian, censor of prints and librarian of the Republic, succeeding Sabellico. 29 November: Giovanni Bellini dies.	Titian begins his relations with the Este court of Ferrara, where he stayed, with his assistants from 31 January to 22 March, certainly in connection with the planned decoration of the *camerino d'alabastro* of Alfonso I d'Este, for which Giovanni Bellini had painted *The Feast of the Gods* (see 1514). Dosso Dossi had also painted an episode, and Raphael and Fra' Bartolomeo were contacted without results. Titian is commissioned to paint *The Assumption* for the church of Santa Maria Gloriosa dei Frari.

YEARS	HISTORICAL EVENTS	CULTURAL EVENTS	THE LIFE AND WORKS OF TITIAN
1517	7 January: truce between Venice and Maximilian. 13 April: Maximilian renounces his claims to the Friuli.	Martin Luther publishes his protestant theses against the Roman Church on the door of the Cathedral of Wittenberg. Giovanni Battista di Jacopo, known as Rosso Fiorentino, frescoes *The Annunciation* in the Santissima Annunciata, Florence.	The concession of the *sensaria* of the Fondaco dei Tedeschi, formerly Giovanni Bellini's, signifies for Titian tax exemption, 100 ducats annually, and 25 ducats for each official portrait of the new doge. Titian is at work on a painting for Alfonso I d'Este, of a "bath," as well as on the design of a parapet, and the purchase of some antique objects. 27 May: Marin Sanudo recorded that among certain things that the Republic sent as gifts to the marshal of France Odet de Foix, Viscomte de Lautrec, was a triptych by Titian depicting *Saint Michael Archangel between Saints George and Theodore* "which is in the palace and people are not happy at it being sent" (fragment in the Ferraro collection, San Giorgio, Venice). 6 June: Titian receives 65 ducats for the fresco of the *Resurrected Christ and Prophets* over the stairway of the Scuola del Santissimo Sacramento, Treviso.
1518	23 July: at San Basilio factories polluting the air are forbidden.	Between this year and 1520, Raphael paints the *Portrait of Leo X between Cardinals Giulio de' Medici and Luigi de' Rossi* and the *Transfiguration*. Rosso Fiorentino paints the *Madonna and Saints* and Pontormo the *Madonna and Saints* at San Michele Visdomini, Florence. 21 June: In a document, Paris Bordone is noted as "pictor", living in Venice "in contrata sancti juliani" (San Giuliano). Jacopo Robusti, known as Tintoretto, is born in Venice.	19 May: the day before the feast of Saint Bernardine, the large altarpiece of *The Assumption* is inaugurated in the church of Santa Maria Gloriosa dei Frari. Titian is working on a painting for the *Camerino d'Alabastro* of Alfonso I d'Este (see 1514). This was most probably the first of the three mythologies, the *Venus Worship* (Madrid, Prado).
1519	The Emperor Maximilian dies and Charles V unites the Kingdom of Spain with the Hapsburg Empire. The balance of power between the great European states sanctioned by the Treat of Noyon in 1516, with regard to the partition of Italy, breaks down.	Between this year and 1524, Antonio Allegri, known as Correggio, frescoes the vault of the room of the Abbess in the convent of San Paolo, Parma. The making of the Riva delle Zattere, known previously as the Carbonaria.	24 April: Titian is commissioned to paint the altarpiece for the altar of the Immaculate Conception in Santa Maria Gloriosa dei Frari, ceded to the family of Jacopo Pesaro, Bishop of Paphos. 17 October: Titian is in Ferrara at the court of Alfonso d'Este with the painting commissioned from the previous year, after being peremptorily summoned by the Duke on 29 September through his agent in Venice Giacomo Tebaldi.
1520	26 August: The Pontifical Brief against Luther is presented in Venice. 20 October: Charles V is crowned Holy Roman Emperor at Aix-la-Chapelle. 15 December: Friar Andrea di Ferrara preaches in Venice in Campo Santo Stefano against the pope and the Curia.	6 April: Raphael dies in Rome. Correggio frescoes the cupola of San Giovanni Evangelista, Parma, with the *Vision of St John on Patmos*, finished in 1521. From this year Michelangelo is engaged in the construction of the Medici Chapel in San Lorenzo, Florence, and in its sculptural decoration which he will leave unfinished in 1534. Pordenone frescoes the Malchiostro Chapel in the Cathedral of Treviso. Around this time, Girolamo Savoldo moves to Venice (see also 1548).	Titian signs and dates the altarpiece commissioned from him by Alvise Gozzi for the church of San Francesco in Ancona. Titian is in Ferrara to repair the damage provoked by a bad varnish on one of his works. On Alfonso I d'Este's behalf he concerns himself with maiolica, glass vases and drinking glasses. Titian is engaged in painting the *Saint Sebastian* for the polyptych commissioned by the Papal Legate Altobello Averoldi for the church of Santi Nazzaro e Celso, Brescia, neglecting the paintings promised to Alfonso I d'Este. At the insistence of the duke *via* Tebaldi Titian proposes to send to Ferrara the *Saint Sebastian*. The offer is refused by Alfonso I, for fear of possible offence to the powerful Papal Legate.
1521	21 June: Doge Leonardo Loredan dies. He is succeeded on 6 July by Antonio Grimani. 19 November: French and Venetian troops leave Milan. 11 December: Treaty with Suleyman II.	The first translation into Italian of Vitruvius is published in Como edited by the architect Cesariano. Rosso Fiorentino paints the *Deposition* in Volterra. The cartoon of the *Conversion of Saint Paul* by Raphael, for one of the Sistine tapestries, is already in the possession of Cardinal Domenico Grimani.	Titian paints frescoes, including the *Judgment of Solomon* in the Loggia del Capitanio, Vicenza, destroyed during Palladio's reconstruction. Titian is in Brescia.

YEARS	HISTORICAL EVENTS	CULTURAL EVENTS	THE LIFE AND WORKS OF TITIAN
1522	21 April: The Venetian Senate votes that Francis I should invade Italy. 29 April: The Franco-Venetian Army is defeated at the Bicocca. 27 September: Sebastian Cabot offers his services to the Republic of Saint Mark.	Francesco Mazzola, called Parmigianino, is commissioned to decorate with frescoes the three chapels of San Giovanni Evangelista, Parma. In April, Giovanni da Udine is in Venice, and informs Michelangelo of the fame he enjoys in Venetian art circles.	Titian completes the Averoldi polyptych (see 1520). Titian is urged to complete the *Battle* for the Sala del Maggior Consiglio in the Palazzo Ducale on the threat of losing all his benefits (see 1513). Tebaldi assures Alfonso I d'Este that Titian is attending to the execution of the *Bacchus and Ariadne* (London, National Gallery) for the *Camerino d'Alabastro*.
1523	20 May: Andrea Gritti is elected Doge on the death of Antonio Grimani. 29 July: Venice allies with Charles V against France. 7 November: Antonio Pigafetta reports in the *Collegio* on the first voyage around the world.	The Bolognese singer and organist Marc' Antonio Cavazzoni publishes the *Ricercari* in Venice. 16 August: in his will, Cardinal Domenico Grimani leaves to the Republic his *Breviary* and other "anticaglie."	Titian goes to Ferrara in February, a few days after the arrival of one of his paintings, probably the *Bacchus and Ariadne*. Titian is in contact for the first time with Federico Gonzaga: his first painting is a portrait of the Marquis. Titian begins work again on the *Battle*. 3 June: payment to Titian is ordered for his portrait of Doge Antonio Grimani, who died 7 May. In the new chapel in the Palazzo Ducale commissioned by Andrea Gritti, Titian paints frescoes of the *Madonna and Child Adored by Doge Gritti* over the altar and *The Evangelists, Saints Mark and Alvise* on the other walls, which Marin Sanudo admired on 6 December, when they were already complete.
1524	3 July: The Duke of Urbino is feasted in Venice. 12 December: Peace treaty and alliance of Venice with France to resist the territorial appetites of the Hapsburgs.	Giulio Romano, established in Mantua, designs the Palazzo del Te, finished in 1535, including its frescoes in the Sala dei Giganti, Sala dei Cavalli, and Sala di Psiche. Decision to rebuild in stone the Rialto Bridge. This would only take place in 1591. Francesco Vecellio signs and dates the *Altarpiece of Bernardino Constantini* in the parish church of San Vito di Cadore (Belluno).	From November to the beginning of the following year, Titian is at the court of Ferrara.
1525	19 June: It is decided to appoint custodians at the edges of the lagoon.	Between this year and 1528, Pontormo frescoes the Capponi Chapel in Santa Felicita. 20 December: Lorenzo Lotto has a workshop in the monastery of Santi Giovanni e Paolo, Venice. Pietro Bembo publishes the *Prose della volgar lingua*.	Titian marries Cecilia, by whom he already has two sons Pomponio and Orazio. Titian's witness was his pupil Girolamo Dente. Doge Gritti nominates Titian's father, Gregorio Vecellio, Vicar of the Mines. The brother-in-law of the artist, Matteo Soldano, is named *Cancelliere* of Feltre.
1526	22 May: Formation of the League of Cognac 'for the liberty of Italy' against Charles V. The Venetians acquire Lodi and conquer Cremona.	From this year to 1530, Correggio is engaged in the fresco of the *Assumption of the Virgin* in the cupola of the Cathedral of Parma. Vittore Carpaccio dies. The first letter by Aretino with a reference to the figurative arts is dated 10 December of this year. The last will be December 1554. The *Letters* of the Tuscan writer constitute one of the principal episodes in Italian culture of the 16th century.	8 December: on the Feast of the Immaculate Conception, Titian's *Pesaro Madonna* is inaugurated in Santa Maria Gloriosa dei Frari, begun in 1519.
1527	26 April: The Florentines rise to the cry of 'France, Saint Mark, Liberty.' In May, the Sack of Rome on the part of the imperial troops. Ravenna and Cervia return to the dominion of the Republic of Saint Mark.	Jacopo Sansovino, Sebastiano del Piombo and Giovanni da Udine find refuge from Rome in Venice, where in April Aretino has already settled, coming from Mantua, which he left on 25 March. Doge Andrea Gritti invites the Fleming Adrian Willaert to Venice as Master of the Ducal Chapel of San Marco.	Aretino offers to duke Federico Gonzaga portraits painted by Titian of Aretino, and Girolamo Adorno, Charles V's ambassador in Venice.

YEARS	HISTORICAL EVENTS	CULTURAL EVENTS	THE LIFE AND WORKS OF TITIAN
1528	29 April: After Monopoli, Bari and Trani, Brindisi cedes itself to Venice. 18 May: Venice allies with France against Charles V.	Baldassare Castiglione's *Cortegiano* is sent to press, set in 1507 and written between 1513 and 1514. The ideas of Sebastiano Serlio spread in Venice, prior to the publication in 1537 of the fourth book of his treatise on architecture. The German synagogue is built in the Ghetto of Venice, followed in 1531 by the Scola Canton, in 1538 by the Levantine synagogue, in 1555 by the Spanish and in 1575 by the Italian.	Titian is staying in Ferrara. He is chosen over Palma Vecchio and Pordenone in the commission to paint the altarpiece of the *Death of Saint Peter Martyr* for the church of Santi Giovanni e Paolo, Venice. The work, finished in 1530, will be destroyed by fire in 1867.
1529	5 August: The Treaty of Cambrai between France and Charles V. The Venetians begin a policy of neutrality, abandoning any pretense to primacy in Italy. 23 December: The Peace of Bologna sanctions the Spanish domination of Italy. Venice keeps its dominion of the Gulf, as the Adriatic was known, but not Ravenna, Cervia, nor the cities of Puglia.	In the fall, between September and November, Michelangelo is staying in Venice. Jacopo Sansovino is nominated *Proto* (chief architect) of San Marco. Lorenzo Lotto receives his first public commission in Venice, the altarpiece with *San Nicolò of Bari and Saints* for the church of the Carmini. Bonifacio de' Pitati, called Veronese, begins a series of paintings for the Palazzo dei Camerlenghi at the Rialto, which will keep him and his workshop busy for two decades. Pordenone completes the shutters of a cupboard for the silverware of the church of San Rocco, depicting *Saints Martin and Christopher*.	In March Titian is at the court of Mantua. He goes with assistants to Ferrara between the end of January and the end of February and a second time between the end of April and 18 June, apparently to work on the paintings in the *Camerino d'Alabastro* and on the "modernization" of *The Feast of the Gods* by Giovanni Bellini (see 1514). In October Titian met for the first time, in Parma, Charles V, through Federico Gonzaga, Marquis of Mantua. The emperor discharges Titian with the offer of a gold ducat, to which Federico Gonzaga added 150 ducats more.
1530	22-4 February: Charles V is crowned in Bologna by Clement VII as King of Italy and Holy Roman Emperor.	The decoration of the Villa Imperiale begins for Francesco Maria della Rovere, Duke of Urbino, with the collaboration of, among others, Agnolo di Cosimo, known as Bronzino, and of Dosso Dossi. Rosso Fiorentino stays with Pietro Aretino in Venice. 26 September: Pietro Bembo is named official historian of the Republic.	5 February: Giacomo Malatesta informs Federico Gonzaga that the portrait of the duke himself is approaching completion, as well as a *Sacra Conversazione* and a "painting of a nude woman." The latter is described by Titian as "of the nude women" in a letter from him to the duke. 27 April: the *Death of Saint Peter Martyr* is placed on its altar in Santi Giovanni e Paolo, begun in 1528. 5 August: Titian's wife Cecilia dies, after giving birth to Lavinia. Before 6 August, Titian sends to Federico Gonzaga, now the Duke of Mantua, a version of the *Saint Sebastian* of the Averoldi polyptych (see 1522); he then sends him the *Portrait of Cornelia*, a lady-in-waiting of the Countess Isabella Pepoli, finished before 26 September.
1531		Poems by Lorenzo Venier, a follower and friend of Aretino, *La puttana errante* and *La Zaffetta*, are distributed in Venice. Parmigianino is commissioned to decorate the church of Santa Maria della Steccata, Parma. Jacopo Sansovino makes silver for the court of Mantua based on drawings by Titian.	For Federico Gonzaga Titian is working on a *Saint Jerome* and a *Magdalene*, and he sends to Mantua also a *Christ and the Adulteress*. Titian obtains from the duke of Mantua the benefice of Medole for his son Pomponio, launched on his ecclesiastical career. In September Titian leaves his studio in San Samuele and transfers to a house in the Biri Grande, in the parish of San Canciano on the edge of the lagoon, where works until his death. Not far away, in the same parish, lives Aretino. 6 October: Marin Sanudo noted the exhibition in the Palazzo Ducale of the votive painting of Doge Andrea Gritti by Titian, which will be destroyed in the fire of 1574. 8 October: Titian sends a *Saint John the Baptist* to Count Massimiano Stampa.
1532	1 August: a nocturnal festival on the Giudecca is organized in honor of Ranuccio Farnese by the Patriarch of Grado.	Ludovico Ariosto publishes the third and last edition of *Orlando Furioso*. Sansovino is entrusted with raising an additional floor over the Procuratie Vecchie. Pordenone has already painted the fresco decoration of the palace of Martino d'Anna on the Grand Canal.	Through Sebastiano Serlio Titian initiates relations with Francesco Maria I, Duke of Urbino and Captain General of the Republic of San Marco. Titian paints for him a *Nativity* (Florence, Palazzo Pitti), a *Hannibal* and a *Christ*. 22 June: Titian sends to Federico Gonzaga a painting of "an animal come to Venice from Alexandria which has never been seen in these parts."

YEARS	HISTORICAL EVENTS	CULTURAL EVENTS	THE LIFE AND WORKS OF TITIAN
1533		30 September: the *Diaries* of Marin Sanudo are completed (see also 1496). Jacopo Sansovino designs Palazzo Corner, finished in 1556. Ludovico Ariosto dies in Ferrara.	In January Titian paints Charles v in Bologna. Charles v pays Titian 500 ducats, and on returning to Spain on 10 May, names the artist Count of the Lateran Palace, of the Consiglio Aulico and of the Concistoro, with the title of Count Palatine, as well as Knight of the Golden Spur, with the right of access to the court. The Emperor concedes to Titian's sons the title of noble of the empire, with the privileges of those who have held such titles for four generations. Titian, while in Bologna, also portrays the Cardinal Ippolito de' Medici (Palazzo Pitti). 18 November: the Duke Francesco Maria della Rovere declares himself most satisfied with the *Nativity* which he has received (see 1532). From the correspondence between the ambassadors of Spain in Venice, Rodrigo Niño and Lope de Soria, and Francisco de Los Cobos, Secretary of State of Charles v, it emerges that Titian is working on some paintings for the Emperor and that, although invited to Madrid, he is prevented from going there by the Venetian government on account of his commitments in the Palazzo Ducale (see 1535).
1534	Henry VIII Tudor annnounces the independence of the Church of England from Rome. The Society of Jesuits is founded. Alfonso I d'Este, Duke of Ferrara, dies. His son Ercole II succeeds him. 7 March: the regulation of the Piave River and the construction of the *Argine* (lagoon bank) *di San Marco*.	5 March: Correggio dies. Jacopo da Ponte, known as Bassano, signs and dates the *Flight into Egypt*. In November Paris Bordone's *Consignment of the Fisherman's Ring to the Doge*, for the Scuola Grande di San Marco, is almost finished.	Working from an earlier portrait by Francesco Francia, Titian paints Isabella d'Este as a young girl. The painting reaches the patron in 1536. Gregorio Vecellio, Titian's father, dies.
1535	Venice does not participate with its fleet in the naval expedition of Charles v against the Turks. 2 September: two *Savi* are elected, charged with "the decoarion and arrangement of the city" ("*de ornar et commodar la città*").	Leone Ebreo's *Dialoghi d'Amore*, already known in manuscript, are published in Rome. F.P. Morato's *Del significato dei colori* is published in Venice. 21 January: Michele Sanmicheli presents a report on the state of the sandbanks and the lagoon entrances of Venice. On the basis of his projects, it is decided on 28 August to rebuild the fortifications on the Lido. 15 July: Aretino thanks Vasari for having sent him certain drawings after sculptures by Michelangelo for the New Sacristy, San Lorenzo, Florence. Pordenone moves definitively to Venice, where he lives with Andrea Meldolla, known as S-chiavone.	30 January: Lope de Soria alerts Francisco de Los Cobos that Titian does not want to leave Venice and go to Madrid (see 1533), because he was "so enamoured and in love with his city." In March, the two other works which Gian Giacomo Leonardi, Urbino's ambassador in Venice, had seen during execution in Titian's studio in 1532, arrive in Urbino. 1 April: Titian, with Sebastiano Serlio and Fortunio Spira, signed the memorandum prepared by Francesco Zorzi, on commission from Doge Andrea Gritti, on Jacopo Sansovino's model for the church of San Francesco della Vigna.
1536	24 January: the League with Charles v against Francis I is renewed. 29 May: a loan of 100,000 ducats is forced from the Clergy to expand the mercantile fleet. The plague rages in December.	Michelangelo begins the frescoing of the *Last Judgment* on the east wall of the Sistine chapel, which he will finish on 31 October 1541. On 9 July Scarpagnino's project for the façade of the Scuola Grande di San Rocco is approved.	Titian begins in Venice the *Portrait of Francesco Maria della Rovere, Duke of Urbino* (Florence, Uffizi) and probably also that of the *Duchess Eleonora* (Florence, Uffizi). The two portraits will be finished in 1537 and sent to Pesaro in 1538. Federico Gonzaga plans to decorate a room in the Castle of Mantua with *Twelve Caesars* commissioned from Titian. In Asti, Titian meets Charles v, in the presence of Federico Gonzaga. Charles v gives instructions to the Viceroy of Naples, Don Pedro di Toledo, that Titian should be given a payment of 300 wagons of grain from the Kingdom of Naples, defining him as his painter "primero." Titian never receives this pension.

YEARS	HISTORICAL EVENTS	CULTURAL EVENTS	THE LIFE AND WORKS OF TITIAN
1537	Aretino, writing on 26 November 1537 to Giovanni Agnello, reminds him that "any poltroon would live like the Pope and be like the Emperor living in this city [Venice] and away from the courts." ("...ogni poltrone starebbe da papa e la farebbe da imperatore vivendo dentro questa città e fuor de le corti".) The magistracy against blasphemy is instituted in Venice (*Esecutori contro la bestemmia*). 1 December: the Venetian government gives a house at Santa Fosca to Francesco Maria della Rovere Duke of Urbino.	Sebastiano Serlio publishes the *Quarto Libro* of his treatise on architecture. The Loggetta is under construction (see also 1549) and the Libreria Marciana (see also 1553) designed by Jacopo Sansovino. The imposing building forms part of the restructuring of the Piazza San Marco and of the Piazzetta urged by Gritti to give monumental decorum to the focal point of public ceremony in the city.	The *Annunciation*, commissioned from Titian for Santa Maria degli Angeli, Murano, is rejected by the nuns who prefer to place on the main altar a painting by Pordenone of the same subject. Titian gives his version to the Empress Isabella. The painting, highly praised by Aretino in a letter of 9 November to Titian, will be destroyed during the French Revolution. Ercole II, Duke of Ferrara, collects from Titian's studio in Venice a portrait of his father, Alfonso. Four of the *Twelve Caesars* (see 1536) reach Mantua. Titian in future years will be urged to send the others.
1538	8 February: Venice joins the league of the Papacy and the Empire for the Crusade. 27 September: as allies Charles V the Venetians are defeated by the Turks at Prevesa, and lose the Morea. 22 October: Francesco Maria della Rovere, Duke of Urbino, dies. 17 December: Andrea Gritti dies.	Pordenone works on the decoration of the ceiling of the Sala dello Scrutinio in the Palazzo Ducale in competition with Titian.	Titian, in August, finishes the *Battle* for the Sala del Maggior Consiglio of Palazzo Ducale (see 1513 and 1532). For his blatent shortcomings, the commission of the large canvas next to the *Battle* is transferred to Pordenone, and Titian's *sensaria* of the Fondaco dei Tedeschi is retracted. For the new Duke of Urbino, Guidobaldo II, Titian is working on the *Venus of Urbino* (Florence, Uffizi). From a medal by Benvenuto Cellini, Titian portrays Francis I King of France.
1539	19 January: Pietro Lando is elected Doge. 20 September: Institution of the three *Inquisitori di Stato*. 27 April: Decision taken to divert the mouth of the Brenta from Chioggia to Brondolo. 1 May: Queen Isabella of Portugal, wife of Charles I, dies in Toledo.	Between this year and 1550, 179 new buildings are put up in Venice. The Venice Arsenal is enlarged. Francesco Salviati and his pupil Giuseppe Porta called Salviati arrive in Venice. Pordenone dies in Ferrara.	Titian paints the portrait of Pietro Lando. 6 March: the large canvas of the *Presentation of the Virgin in the Temple* which the Scuola Grande di Santa Maria della Carità had planned to have painted as early as 21 August 1534, is completed "by the excellent *missier* Titian." 20 June: Leonardi communicates to Guidobaldi II of Urbino that Titian is finishing for him the portraits of Charles V, Francis I of France and of the "Gran Turco" Suleyman. 23 June: Titian is given back the *sensaria* of the Fondaco dei Tedeschi.
1540	27 April: The mouth of the Brenta must be diverted from Chioggia to Brondolo and a canal from Moranzano to Novissimo should be dug. 2 October: Treaty between the Venetians and Suleyman II, who takes possession of the Aegean dukedom of the Sanudo, signed by the Council of Ten without informing the Senate. Federico Gonzaga, Duke of Mantua, dies.	Andrea Calmo's *Rhodiana* is performed in Venice. Giovanni Girolamo Savoldo paints his *Nativity* in Brescia.	In a letter to his friends Ludovico Becci and Luigi del Riccio, the Latinist Francesco Priscianese remembers the evening spent on 15 August in the hospitable house of Titian in the company of Tuscan guests including Aretino, Jacopo Sansovino, and Jacopo Nardi. Titian paints the *Crowning with Thorns* (Paris, Louvre) for the Santa Corona Chapel in Santa Maria delle Grazie. In exchange for a harpsichord for his house in the Biri Grande, Titian paints the *Portrait of Alessandro Trasuntino degli Organi*. He also portrays Pietro Bembo and Pietro Cappello.
1541	23 July: The Papal Bull against Lutheranism is published in Venice. 5 August: The proposal of the Pope to convoke the Council in Vicenza is rejected.	M.A. Michiel's *Notizia d'opere del disegno*, end incomplete. Giorgio Vasari is in Venice. He is responsible for the setting up of a theater for the Compagnia della Calza dei "Sempiterni," where Aretino's *Talanta* is performed during the 1542 carnival.	In August Titian delivers *The Speech* (Madrid, Prado), begun in 1540, to the Marchese del Vasto e di Pescara, Alfonso d'Avalos, in Milan. On 25 August he obtains, in Milan, a pension of 100 ducats from Charles V. The first version of the *Pentecost*, for the church of Santo Spirito in Isola, dates from this year, as does the *Portrait of Don Diego Mendoza*, Ambassador of Charles V in Venice.

YEARS	HISTORICAL EVENTS	CULTURAL EVENTS	THE LIFE AND WORKS OF TITIAN
1542	2 October: Venice signs a peace with Suleyman the Magnificent, destined to last until 1570.	Lorenzo Lotto, during his last stay in Venice, paints *Sant'Antonino Distributing Alms* for the church of Santi Giovanni e Paolo. On commission from the Compagnia dei Sempiterni, Tiziano Minio designs a "machina del mondo." Giorgio Vasari paints the ceiling of a room in Palazzo Corner Spinelli. Andrea Palladio builds Villa Godi Valmarana, Lonedo (Vicenza).	Francesco, Titian's brother, who had for some time retired to Pieve di Cadore to look after the family interests, joins the *Magnifica Comunità*. Titian signs and dates the *Portrait of Clarice Strozzi* (Berlin, Staatliche Museen) and finishes the *Portrait of Ranuccio Farnese* (National Gallery, Washington), nephew of Pope Paul III. Titian begins the cycle of paintings for the ceiling of Santo Spirito in Isola (see 1544).
1543	The *Provveditori alle Pompe* forbids courtesans to wear silk dresses, jewels, gold and silver.	Michele Sanmicheli designs the Forte di Sant'Andrea. Alessandro Vittoria comes to Venice and joins the workshop of Jacopo Sansovino.	On the occasion of the meeting at Busseto of Charles V and Paul III Farnese, Titian paints the portrait of the pope, while the Emperor commissions a portrait of his wife Isabella, who had died in 1539. Titian signs and dates the *Ecce Homo* (Kunsthistorisches Museum, Vienna) for the Flemish merchant Giovanni D'Anna.
1544	The Republic of Saint Mark has in reserve or under construction in the Arsenal 155 galleys.	Gasparo Contarini publishes the *De Magistratibus et Republica Venetorum*. Anton Francesco Doni's *Dialogo della Musica* is published.	Payments to Titian cease from the Confraternita del Corpus Domini of Urbino for the processional standard (Urbino, Galleria Nazionale), begun 1542. Titian is painting the *Danäe* (Capodimonte, Naples) for Cardinal Alessandro Farnese. The ceiling paintings for the church of Santo Spirito in Isola are already finished by December, begun in 1542 (Venice, Sacristy of the Salute), after initially being commissioned from Giorgio Vasari. Titian is commissioned to decorate the ceiling of the *albergo* of the Scuola di San Giovanni Evangelista, which will be finished with the help of the workshop toward the end of the decade, before the artist's trip to Augsburg (National Gallery, Washington; Gallerie dell'Accademia, Venice).
1545	The Council of Trent opens. It will close in 1563. On 9 November, Doge Pietro Lando dies and on 24 November he is succeeded by Francesco Donà.	18 December: a part of the vault of the Libreria Marciana, designed by Jacopo Sansovino, falls.	In Venice Titian paints the portraits of Daniele Barbaro, Guidobaldo II of Urbino, Aretino, Ferdinand I, Alessandro Corvino, and Marcantonio Morosini. In September, with his son Orazio, guest of Guidobaldo II, Titian stays in Pesaro and in Urbino, traveling then by 9 October to Rome, where he is festively welcomed at the Papal Court. He paints several portraits for the Farnese, including that of *Paul III between His Nephews Alessandro and Ottavio* (Capodimonte, Naples) and also a *Magdalene* and an *Ecce Homo*. 9 November: Titian informs Charles V from Rome that he wishes to make a present to him of a *Sleeping Venus*. Still in Rome, Titian intercedes with the Venetian government on behalf of Jacopo Sansovino who is accused of causing the fall of the vault of the Libreria Marciana. Accompanied by Sebastiano del Piombo and Vasari, Titian calls on Michelangelo with whom he admires the ancient monuments, writing to Charles V "I go about learning, among these marvelous antique stones."
1546	2 June: the guilds ("*Fraglie*") of the ferrymen are regulated. 11 December: the game of the "pandolo" (tip-cat) is forbidden in public spaces for the protection of passersby.	Benedetto Varchi's *Lezione sulla maggioranza delle arti* is published.	19 March: Roman citizenship is conferred upon Titian. Titian leaves Rome, after having offered his services to Cosimo de' Medici Grand Duke of Tuscany without result, and returns to Venice.

YEARS	HISTORICAL EVENTS	CULTURAL EVENTS	THE LIFE AND WORKS OF TITIAN
1547	Charles V defeats the protestant princes at the Battle of Mühlberg. 18 January: the excavation of the Grand Canal and of many smaller canals. 3 December: unauthorized buildings must be demolished at the warehouses of Terra Nova.	Sebastiano del Piombo dies. Jacopo Tintoretto signs and dates the *Last Supper* for the church of San Marcuola. Leon Battista Alberti's *De Pictura* is reprinted.	In vain Titian asks Alessandro Farnese for the office of Keeper of the Papal Seals, formerly held by Sebastiano del Piombo. Titian completes, with the assistance of his workshop, the altarpiece for the Cathedral of Serravalle, begun in 1542. At Christmas he gives Aretino an *Ecce Homo*. Charles V sends Titian to Augsburg.
1548		Paolo Pino's *Dialogo della Pittura* is published in Venice. There is notice of Girolamo Savoldo in Venice in this year, living in Venice near Santa Croce. In a few months, and during the absence of Titian from Venice, Tintoretto completes in a few months only the *Miracle of the Slave* for the Scuola Grande di San Marco, receiving much praise from Pietro Aretino. Lambert Sustris dates the *Portrait of Wilhelm IV the Elder of Waldburg-Trenchburg*.	In January, Titian with his son Orazio, his nephew Cesare and Lambert Sustris, leave for Augsburg, taking with them "an *Ecce Homo* [Prado, Madrid] and a *Venus*." In the spring he is present at the festive opening of the Diet of Augsburg together with kings, princes, dukes and electors. He paints portraits of several of these, above all three of the Emperor of which only one is extant, *Charles V on Horseback* (Prado, Madrid) completed between April and September. Still in Augsburg, Mary Queen of Hungary commissions from Titian the series of paintings known as *The Furies* or *The Damned*. On his return journey, Titian stays at Innsbruck where he begins the portraits of King Ferdinand, brother of Charles V. In Venice at least by October, two months later he paints in Milan the portrait of Prince Philip, son of Charles V (Prado).
1549	Pope Paul III dies and is succeeded by Pope Julius III. A terrible famine in November fills Venice with beggars.	Anton Francesco Doni's *Disegno* and Michelangelo Biondo's *Della Nobilissima Pittura* are both published in Venice. Donato Giannotti's *Dialogo della Repubblica de' Veneziani* is published. Jacopo Gastaldi is commissioned to paint a new map of Africa in the Palazzo Ducale, updated with respect to recent geographical discoveries. Jacopo Sansovino completes the Loggetta. 15 May: Lorenzo Lotto abandons Venice definitively, leaving his paintings and cameos to Jacopo Sansovino "per deposito etiam farne dinari."	29 January: Prince Philip gives orders for the payment of a thousand *scudi d'oro* to Titian for certain portraits. Titian finishes with workshop assistance the polyptych for the parish church of Castello Roganzuolo, commissioned in 1543. Three of the paintings (Prado, Madrid) of the series commissioned from Titian the year before by Mary Queen of Hungary are already on the walls of the Palace of Binche in Flanders. Domenico dalle Greche publishes the woodcut of the *Drowning of Pharoah in the Red Sea*, based on a drawing by Titian (see 1515).
1550	Alvise Cornaro and Cristoforo Sabbadino campaign for the conservation of the Lagoon.	The first edition of Vasari's *Lives*. The cartographer C. Stadino publishes a treatise on the lagoon of Venice. Giovan Battista Ramusio publishes the *Navigationi et Viaggi*.	On the invitation of Philip Titian is again in Augsburg in November where Charles V had called the Diet in July to announce his imminent retirement from public life. For his friend Aretino Titian asks the Emperor for a Cardinalate. In Augsburg, Cranach paints Titian's portrait.
1551	23 March: it is decided that the dowries of brides cannot exceed 5,000 ducats.	Andrea Palladio designs the monastery of the Lateran Canons annexed to the church of Santa Maria della Carità. The dedication of the Giustiniani chapel in San Francesco della Vigna, for which Paolo Veronese paints the altarpiece.	6 February: Prince Philip agrees to pay the artist 200 *scudi* "for certain works in his service." These form part of the payments made by the Imperial Court to Titian for a total of 1630 *scudi*. By August Titian returns to Venice. Titian is invited to join the Scuola Grande di San Rocco.
1552		A. Catarino Politi's *Disputatio... de cultu et adoratione imaginum* is published in Rome. Paolo Veronese paints the *Temptation of Saint Anthony* for one of the altars of the Cathedral of Mantua, designed by Giulio Romano.	The beginning of the correspondence between Prince Philip and Titian. The august patron will ask for increasing numbers of new paintings; Titian will ask to be paid. Titian sends Philip a *Saint Margaret and the Dragon* (Escorial, Apartments of Philip II), and a *Landscape*, perhaps the *Pardo Venus* (Louvre, Paris). Titian signs and dates the *Portrait of Ludovico Beccadelli* (Uffizi, Florence). From 29 October Titian is again the beneficiary of the *sensaria* of the Ufficio del Sale. In the winter of 1552-53, Titian gives to Philip II a *Queen of Persia* and a *Self-portrait with a Miniature of Philip II in his Hand*.

YEARS	HISTORICAL EVENTS	CULTURAL EVENTS	THE LIFE AND WORKS OF TITIAN
1553	Prince Philip of Spain in London, through 1555, to marry Mary Tudor at the wish of his father Charles v. 31 May: doge Marc'Antonio Trevisan dies and is succeeded on 11 June by Francesco Venier.	Between this year and 1555 the church of San Zulian is rebuilt according to a design by Jacopo Sansovino with the collaboration of Alessandro Vittoria for the sculptural decoration. Sansovino finishes the 16th bay of the Libreria Marciana. Paolo Veronese, through 1556, is engaged with Ponchino and Zelotti in the decoration of the ceiling of the Hall of the Council of Ten in the Palazzo Ducale. Ludovico Dolce publishes his translation of the *Metamorphoses* of Ovid. 23 April: the poetess Gaspara Stampa dies in Venice.	Titian paints the portrait of Marcantonio Trevisan, the new doge. In September he declares himself ready to paint a large picture for the *albergo* of the Scuola Grande di San Rocco. He begins work on some *poesie* for Prince Philip, including *Venus and Adonis* and *Danäe* (Prado, Madrid). In Titian's studio Don Francisco de Vargas, Ambassador of Charles v to Venice, sees the *Noli Me Tangere* commissioned by Mary, Queen of Hungary (Prado, Madrid, fragment).
1554			On 1 April, through Vargas, Charles v, from Brussels, urges Titian to finish some paintings. On 11 October Titian sends to Flanders a *Mater Dolorosa* (Prado, Madrid), a *Venus* and the *Adoration of the Holy Trinity* (Prado, Madrid). In the latter painting, destined for the main altar of the monastery of Yuste in Spain, Titian portrays himself with Francisco de Vargas, Charles v and Isabella with their son Philip. In the autumn he sends to London a *Venus and Adonis* (see 1553) for Philip to whom he promises a *Perseus and Andromeda* (Wallace Collection, London), a *Medea and Jason* and a "most devout work." Certain mythologies together with previous ones (see 1553) were to decorate a *camerino* of Philip. Titian gives *The Appearance of the Resurrected Christ to His Mother* to the church of Santa Maria of Medole after his nephew has been granted the canonry of the small town near Mantua, which had been taken from Pomponio, who was ill-suited to the ecclesiastical life (see 1531).
1555	26 September: peace in the religious wars between Charles v and the Lutherans.	The Fabbriche Nuove at the Rialto are completed, designed by Sansovino. Paolo Veronese begins the decoration of the church of San Sebastiano, beginning with the sacristy. This will continue up to 1570.	Lavinia, Titian's daughter, marries Cornelio Sarcinelli of Serravalle, with a dowry of 1400 *scudi*. Girolamo Dente, Titian's assistant, is witness to the marriage. Before 6 March Titian completes the *Portrait of Doge Francesco Venier*. Even though this was to be Titian's last official portrait of a Doge he continued to benefit from the *sensaria* of the Ufficio del Sale. 22 March: Titian is commissioned to paint the large votive painting of Doge Antonio Grimani for the Palazzo Ducale. Seen by Vasari unfinished in 1566, this remained incomplete at Titian's death since it was not destroyed in the Palazzo Ducale fire of 1577. 5 September: Titian agrees to carry out the votive painting of Doge Marcantonio Trevisan, located in 1556 in the Sala dei Pregadi in the Palazzo Ducale.
1556	28 August: Charles v abdicates and withdraws to Yuste. The imperial crown passes to his brother Ferdinand i. His son Philip governs Spain, the New World possessions and the Italian dominions. 10 October: institution of the *Provveditori sopra i Beni Inculti*, to promote the reclamation of farmland. A serious plague strikes Venice in December.	21 October: Pietro Aretino dies. Between this year and 1561, Jacopo Sansovino erects the monument of Doge Francesco Venier in the church of San Salvador. The decoration of the ceiling of the Sala Grande of the Libreria Marciana begins.	

YEARS	HISTORICAL EVENTS	CULTURAL EVENTS	THE LIFE AND WORKS OF TITIAN
1557		Sansovino's church of San Geminiano in the Piazza San Marco is completed, and construction begins on the Palazzo Grimani on the Grand Canal designed by Michele Sanmicheli, which will be finished in 1571. Ludovico Dolce's *Dialogo della pittura* is sent to the press. In Venice, for the wedding of Doge Lorenzo Priuli, the Guild of Butchers erect in Piazza San Marco an arch for the parade of the nobles and members of the Guilds.	Orazio, in the name of his father, collects the pension from Milan. Pomponio, reconciled with his father, obtains the benefices of Sant'Andrea del Fabbio. *The Deposition* sent in November to Philip II by Titian is lost in Trent. Titian, with Jacopo Sansovino, is a jury member for judging the decoration of the ceiling of the large room of the Libreria Marciana painted in February by the leading exponents of mannerism in Venice and the Veneto: Giuseppe Salviati, Battista Franco, Giuseppe Demio, Giulio Licinio, Giambattista Zelotti, Andrea Schiavone, Paolo Veronese.
1558	The Spanish conquer the Low Countries. 21 September: Charles V dies in the monastery at Yuste.	In January, Federico Badoer founds the Accademia della Fama at San Canciano, which will be closed in 1561 accused of fraudulent bankruptcy. Scarpagnino finishes the Scala d'Oro in the Palazzo Ducale, begun in 1544 on Sansovino's design.	Titian signs and dates the *Portrait of Fabrizio Salvaresio* (Kunsthistorisches Museum, Vienna) and paints the *Standard* for the confraternity of San Bernardino, Venice, mentioned as already paid for on 11 June. On 22 July, Titian's *Crucifixion* is placed on the altar of the church of San Domenico Maggiore, Ancona.
1559	The end of the religious wars in Europe: the Treaty of Cateau-Cambrésis, and the dominion of Spain and Austria over a major part of Italian territory.	Alessandro Vittoria attends to the *stucchi* for the grand staircase of the Libreria Marciana, while Battista Franco and Battista del Moro carry out the frescoes. Pope Paul IV Carafa institutes the *Index* of forbidden books.	Francesco, Titian's older brother, dies. Titian's *Martyrdom of Saint Lawrence* (Chiesa dei Gesuiti, Venice) is by this time in place on the altar of the Crociferi. This had been commissioned from Titian by Lorenzo Massolo in 1548 and was still not delivered on 15 March 1557. 12 June: Titian informs Philip II of the attempt on the life of his son Orazio, in Milan, by Leone Leoni, engraver of the Imperial Mint. 27 September: Titian advises Philip II of the dispatch of a new *Deposition* (Prado, Madrid, see 1557), of two *poesies* of *Diana and Actaeon* and *Diana and Callisto* (National Gallery of Scotland, Edinburgh) and that he was working on a "*Christ in the Garden* and two other *poesies*: *The Rape of Europa* [Gardner Museum, Boston] and *Diana and Actaeon* [National Gallery, London]."
1560		Andrea Palladio begins work on the project for the monastery for the Lateran Canons at the church of Santa Maria della Carità.	22 April: Titian assures Philip II that he has almost finished the two paintings of the *Agony in the Garden* and the *Rape of Europa* and refers to some "glorious and immortal" *Victories of Caesar* in memory of Charles V. Titian is paid the shipping expenses to Spain for an *Adoration of the Kings* (Nuevos Museos, Escorial).
1561	It is ruled that new churches, hospitals, or monasteries cannot be built in Venice without the consent of the Council of Ten. 17 May: the prohibition of games in Piazza San Marco is reiterated.	Jacopo Bassano begins the *Crucifixion* of San Teonisto (Treviso), finishing it the following year.	Titian's daughter Lavinia dies. 22 October: Philip II urges Garcia Hernandez to take every precaution for the shipping of a *Magdalene* by Titian, which will be delivered to the Ambassador in November. Titian signs and dates the *Portrait of a Man* now in the Baltimore Art Museum and another in the Gemäldegalerie, Dresden.
1562	4 August: Venice lends 100,000 gold ducats to France.		26 April: Titian promises a *Madonna and Child* to Philip II (Alte Pinakothek, Munich). The *Agony in the Garden* (Nuevos Museos, Escorial) and the *Rape of Europa* arrive in Spain. Titian, through his son Orazio, delivers "a painting of Adonis" to Vecellio Vecelli in Cadore.

YEARS	HISTORICAL EVENTS	CULTURAL EVENTS	THE LIFE AND WORKS OF TITIAN
1563	The Council of Trent, which had opened in 1545, closes. The population of Venice is just under 169,000 (see also 1509).	Philip II commissions the building of the monastery of the Escorial, dedicated to Saint Lawrence. It is decided to build the Palazzo delle Prigioni (prisons) on a project by Giovanni Antonio Rusconi, which will be finished by Antonio da Ponte (1589) and Antonio and Tommaso Contino (1614). Cipriano de Roze is named master of the Ducal Chapel of San Marco, in place of Adrian Willaert, who died in 1562. Paolo Veronese finishes in little more than a year the enormous canvas of the *Marriage Feast at Cana* for the refectory of the Benedictine monastery of San Giorgio Maggiore, Venice. In addition to himself, he portrays Titian, Jacopo Bassano and Tintoretto.	On 28 July, Titian assures Philip II that he had almost finished the *Last Supper*, "seven *braccia* wide" and "more than four" high, begun in 1558.
1564	Maximilian II, King in Vienna. 22 July: Venice accepts the resolutions of the Council of Trent, published as *Professio Fidei Tridentinae*.	8 February: Michelangelo dies in Rome. 3 March: the Compagnia degli Accesi constructs a theater that will proceed on barges down the Grand Canal. The Arsenal of Venice is enlarged. Jacopo Tintoretto begins his decoration of the Scuola Grande di San Rocco, which he alone will carry out for over twenty more years.	Titian has to renounce the pension in grain from Naples conceded to him by Charles V in 1536 because, writes Garcia Hernandez, "he can't remember, being extremely old, where he put the receipt." Titian is dealing in timber, assisted by his son Orazio, and even acquires some for the Duke of Urbino for works in the Ducal Ports. 25 July: Philip II alerts Don Gabriel de la Cueva, Governor of Milan, of the imminent arrival of four works by Titian, three of religious subjects and a fourth of the *Portrait of the Queen of the Romans*. The paintings reached Spain in August. 31 August: Philip II expresses to García Hernandez, secretary of the Spanish embassy in Venice, his desire to have a *Martyrdom of Saint Lawrence* for the monastery of the Escorial (see 1565 and 1567). In October Titian is in Brescia, for a contract for three paintings for the ceiling of the Palazzo Pubblico, decorated with *trompe l'oeil* architecture by Cristoforo Rosa.
1565	The *Catalogo de tutte le principali e più honorate cortigiane di Venezia* is published.	Andrea Gabrieli publishes his book of *Motetti*. 28 February: the wooden theater by Andrea Palladio for the *Accesi* is inaugurated with the production of *Antigono* by the Vicentine Antonio Pigatti.	Accompanied by assistants, including Cesare Vecellio, Emanuele of Augsburg and Valerio Zuccato, Titian gives instructions in Pieve di Cadore for the painting of frescoes in the Archdeaconry on the basis of his drawings. The decoration will be finished in 1568. In December Philip II charges García Hernandez with urging Titian to complete the *Martyrdom of St Lawrence*, begun in 1564, and tells him that the *Last Supper* and other works have been shipped from Genoa to Barcelona.
1566	Selim II ascends the Ottoman throne and with arrogance informs the doge of it.	Andrea Gabrieli becomes the organist of San Marco. The construction of the church of San Giorgio Maggiore begins, on a design by Andrea Palladio. Jacopo Sansovino carves his monumental sculptures of *Neptune* and *Mars*, for the terrace of the Giant's Staircase at the Palazzo Ducale.	26 January: Agatone assures the Duke of Urbino that Titian has declared that the *Christ* and the *Magdalene* are "by his own hand." The Council of Ten gives Titian the copyright of the prints that Cornelis Cort and Niccolò Boldrini make after his paintings. 22 May: Giorgio Vasari, in Venice to update his *Lives*, makes a note of the unfinished works in Titian's studio in the Biri Grande: the *Martyrdom of Saint Lawrence*; the *Doge Antonio Grimani before Faith* (Palazzo Ducale, Venice); the three canvases for the Palazzo Pubblico, Brescia (see 1568); a large *Crucifixion*; an allegorical painting with Minerva and Neptune begun for Alfonso I d'Este; an *Appearance of Christ to the Magdalene* and a *Deposition* of the same dimensions and with life-sized figures; a *Madonna and Child*; a *Self-Portrait* (Berlin, Staatliche Museen); and a half-length *Saint Paul*. Titian is elected a member of the Accademia del Disegno, Florence, together with Andrea Palladio, Jacopo Tintoretto and other Venetian artists.

YEARS	HISTORICAL EVENTS	CULTURAL EVENTS	THE LIFE AND WORKS OF TITIAN
1567		19 May: Palma il Giovane, just over twenty years old, arrives in Rome, where according to the sources he will stay until 1573-74. Domenico Theotokopulos, known as El Greco, settles in Venice.	24 January: through Titian and in his presence the Turkish Ambassador in Venice, Albain Bej, meets García Hernandez, Ambassador of Philip II. Titian paints and sends as gifts to Rome some paintings for Pius V (*Death of Saint Peter Martyr*), Cardinal Alessandro Farnese (*Mary Magdalene*) and Cardinal Michele Bonelli (*St Catherine*). 2 December: Titian informs Philip II that he has finished the *Martyrdom of Saint Lawrence* (Escorial, Iglesia Vieja) begun in 1554 (see 1565) and that he will send along, with the larger painting, a *Nude Venus*.
1568	September: peace between the Emperor Maximilian II and Selim II.	Giorgio Vasari publishes the second edition of his *Lives*.	In Brescia the three paintings *The Furnace of the Cyclops, Brescia with Minerva and Mars*, and *Ceres and Bacchus*, finished in 1567 (see 1564) are put in place, and will be destroyed in the fire of 18 January 1575 in the Palazzo Pubblico. 28 November: Veit von Dornberg lets Maximilian II know that Titian has at his disposal seven "fables," versions of which had been sent to Philip II, judged well-suited to the collection of the Imperial Palace by the antique dealer Jacopo Strada. 8 December: Maximilian, while interested by the offer, expresses the fear that Titian in his advanced years can no longer paint as he used to. Titian dispatches the *Portrait of Jacopo Strada* (Vienna, Kunsthistorisches Museum) and, for Philip II, the *Tribute Money* (National Gallery, London).
1569	13 September: devastating fire at the Arsenal. Venice lends another 100,000 gold ducats to France.	Agostino Gallo's *Le vinti giornate dell'agricoltura et de' piaceri della villa* is published in Venice.	The *sensaria* of the Ufficio del Sale is transferred to Orazio, at the request of his father Titian.
1570	The Turks request the surrender of Cyprus. On 1 July they land on the island and capture first Limisso, then Nicosia (9 September). 16 August: the regulation of the Bacchiglione River. More than 4,600 workers are employed in the Venetian Arsenal. Notaries, dentists and itinerant salesmen are forbidden to frequent the porticos of the Palazzo Ducale.	Jacopo Sansovino dies in Venice. Andrea Palladio's *Quattro libri di Architettura* is published in Venice. In November El Greco is in Rome, where the miniaturist Giulio Clovio recommends him to Alessandro Farnese as the "young Cretan pupil of Titian."	At the end of this year, or at the beginning of 1571, Titian sends Philip II a *Tarquin and Lucretia* (Fitzwilliam Museum, Cambridge).
1571	25 May: Venice allies with Spain and the Papacy against the Turks. 5 August: the Turks conquer Famagosta, and after hanging Lorenzo Tiepolo, brutally slay Marc'Antonio Bragadin (17 August). 7 October: the Christian fleet, thanks above all to Doge Sebastiano Venier, defeats the Turkish fleet at Lepanto. 22-23 August: the Massacre of the Huguenots on the night of Saint Bartholomew.	Andrea Gabrieli publishes the *Giustiniane*.	18 June: the *Last Supper*, executed by Titian c. 1555, is destroyed in a fire in the refectory of Santi Giovanni e Paolo. 1 August: Titian claims to be 95 years old in a letter to Philip II. Philip II authorizes that the Milan pension should be transferred from Titian to his son Orazio.

YEARS	HISTORICAL EVENTS	CULTURAL EVENTS	THE LIFE AND WORKS OF TITIAN
1573	7 March: a separate peace with Selim II, with the definitive loss of Cyprus by the Venetians, who had received the island from Caterina Cornaro in 1489. 7 July: the decree of expulsion of the Jews is revoked and judged illegal.	Paolo Veronese replaces Titian's *Last Supper* in the refectory of the monastery of Santi Giovanni e Paolo, destroyed in a fire in 1571. Veronese's large painting, after the artist's trial of 18 July before the tribunal of the Inquisition, will bear the title of the *Feast in the House of Levi.*	Titian is working on *Philip II Offers to Victory the Infante Don Fernando*, commissioned by Philip II to commemorate the Battle of Lepanto of 1571. A dense correspondence between the Marquis of Ayamonte, Governor of Milan, and Diego Guzmán de Silva, Spanish Ambassador in Venice discusses obtaining religious paintings from Titian.
1574	Guidobaldo II Duke of Urbino dies.	11 May: in the devastating fire that destroys the Sala del Collegio and the Sala del Senato of the Palazzo Ducale several famous paintings in addition to those of Titian are destroyed. 12 May: it is decided to reconstruct and decorate those parts of the Palazzo Ducale destroyed by the fire. Andrea palladio designs a Triumphal Arch for the entry into Venice of Henry of Valois. Paolo Veronese begins and completes in 1577 the decoration of the ceiling of the Sala del Collegio in the Palazzo Ducale.	In order to be placed in the refectory of the Escorial, Titian's *Last Supper* (see 1563) must be cut down. In July Titian is visited by Henry of Valois, who, stopping briefly on his way from Poland to France to be crowned King, was festively received in Venice. 22 December: Titian sends to Antonio Perez, secretary of Philip II, the list of works that he could remember having sent to Spain, and urges payment for them.
1575	25 June: a new a terrible plague strikes Venice, which will last until the summer of the following year and which will claim about 50,000 victims from the population of 175,000.	Jacopo Bassano paints the *Deposition.*	Titian insists again on being paid by Philip II for the several paintings. 24 September: Titian sends to Philip II *Spain Succored by Religion* (Prado, Madrid, see 1573) and a *Saint Jerome* (Escorial, Nuevos Museos).
1576		El Greco leaves Italy for Toledo, Spain, where he is documented in July 1577.	27 February: Titian, in his last letter, presses Philip II to pay his many debts to him. 27 August: Titian dies in his house in the Biri Grande, a victim of the Plague, and is solemnly buried in the church of Santa Maria Gloriosa dei Frari on the following day. In the Registro dei Morti of San Canciano Titian's age is given as 103 years. Among other works Titian's large *Pietà* (Venice, Gallerie dell'Accademia) remains in Titian's studio. After Titian's death and that of his son Orazio, the house, full of precious objects and of paintings, is looted.
1577		20 December: in the devastating fire in the Palazzo Ducale, the famous cycle of paintings by Gentile and Giovanni Bellini, Alvise Vivarini, Vittore Carpaccio, Paolo Veronese, Jacopo Tintoretto and Titian are destroyed.	
1581			27 October: Titian's house, most probably still containing some paintings, is sold by Pomponio to Cristoforo Barbarigo.

Fundamental works for the reconstruction of Titian's life and works are: Sanudo 1496-1533 (ed. 1879-1902); Michiel 1521-43 (eds. 1800 and 1884); Aretino (ed. Camesasca 1957-60); Vasari 1550 and 1568; Dolce 1557; F. Sansovino 1581 and subsequent editions of 1604 and 1663; Lomazzo (1584); Verdizotti 1622; Ridolfi (1648); Boschini 1660, 1671, 1674; Sandrart 1683.

For archival sources pertinent to Titian see in particular: Bottari-Ticozzi 1822-25; Gaye 1840; Gualandi 1840; Cicogna 1853; Pinchart 1856; D'Arco 1857; Ronchini 1864; G. Campori 1866, 1870, 1874; Braghirolli 1881; von Schonherr 1884, 1890; Kreyczi 1887; Zarco del Valle 1888; Justi 1889, 1894,

1904; Luzio 1890, 1913; von Voltelini 1890, 1892; Campana 1908; Cox 1911; Ludwig 1911; Gliick 1933, 1934; Coulas 1967; Ferrarino 1975, 1977; Gandini 1977, 1988; Hope 1980, 1988.

Biographies on Titian by Neri Pozza (1976) and most recently by Flavio Caroli and Stefano Zuffi (1990) make fascinating reading, especially the latter, which is full of information and weighted on the philological and critical side. Alvise Zorzi has published his *La vita quotidiana a Venezia nel secolo di Tiziano* this year.

BIBLIOGRAPHY

compiled by Madile Gambier

1496-1533
Sanudo, M., *I diarii*. Eds. R. Fulin, F. Stefani, N. Barozzi, 1879-1902. 59 vols. Venice

1521-1543
Michiel, M., *Notizia d'opere di disegno*. Ed. J. Morelli, Bassano, 1800; Ed. G. Frizzoni, Bologna, 1884

1532
Ariosto, L., *Orlando Furioso*. Ferrara

1536
Dolce, L., *Horatius Quintus Flaccus. La poetica tradotta per Lodovico Dolce*. n.p.

1537
Serlio, S., *Regole generali di architettura sopra la cinque maniere de gli edifici*. Venice

1537-1538
Brucioli, A., *Dialogi della morale philosophia, libri cinque*. Venice

1537-1557
Aretino, P., *Lettere sull'arte*. Eds. F. Pertile & E. Camesasca, 1957-1960. 4 vols. Milan

1538
Dolce, L., *Paraphrasi della sesta satire di Giuvenale nella quale si ragiona delle miserie degli uomini maritati. Dialogo in cui si parla di che qualità si dee tor moglie, et che modo vi si ha a tenere. Lo Epithalamio di Catullo nelle nozze di Peleo et di Theti*. Venice

1540
Priscianese, F., "Lettera a Ludovico Becci e a Luigi Del Riccio," in *De primi principi della lingua romana*. Venice

1548
Vico, E., *Le Imagini con tutti i riversi trovati e le vite degli Imperatori*. Venice

1550
Apuleio, *Dell'Asino d'oro tradotto per Messer Agnolo Firenzuola Fiorentino*. Venice

Vasari, G., *Le vite de' più eccellenti Architetti, Pittori e Scultori italiani da Cimabue insino a tempi nostri*. Florence

1551
Sansovino, F., *Delle Cose più notabili che sono in Venetia*. Venice. Also Venice, 1561

1552
Lettere scritte al Signor Pietro Aretino. Venice

1557
Dolce, L., "Dialogo della pittura intitolato l'Aretino." Ed. P. Barocchi in *Trattati d'arte del Cinquecento - II*. Bari, 1960-1962

1568
Vasari, G., *Le vite de' più eccellenti Pittori Scultori e Architettori riviste e ampliate et con l'aggiunta delle vite de' vivi e de' morti, dall'anno 1550 insino al 1567*. 3 vols. Florence. G. Milanesi. 9 vols., 1878-1885, Florence; C.L. Ragghianti, 4 vols., 1942-1949, Milan.

1571
Cartari, V., *Le imagini de i dei degli Antichi raccolte dal sig. Vincenzo Cartari... nuovamente stampate*. Venice

1581
Sansovino, F., *Venetia città nobilissima et singolare descritta in XIII libri*. Venice

1584
Borghini, R., *Il Riposo*. Florence. Ed. Hildesheim, 1969

1590
Lomazzo, G.P., *L'idea del Tempio della pittura*. Milan (ed. Klein, Florence, 1974)

1604
Sansovino, F., *Venetia città nobilissima et singolare descritta già in XIII libri da Francesco Sansovino et hora con molta diligenza corretta emendata et ampliata dal M.R.D. Giovanni Stringa*. Venice

1605
Leoni, G.B., *Vita di Francesco Maria della Rovere quarto duca d' Urbino*. Venice

1609
Aretino, P., *Del primo libro dele lettere di M.Pietro Aretino*. 6 vols. Paris

1613
Francucci, S., *La Galleria dell'Illustrissimo e Reverendissimo Signor Scipione Cardinale Borghese cantata da Scipione Francucci*. Ed. 1647, Arezzo

1622
Verdizotti, G.M., *Breve compendio della vita del famoso Tiziano Vecellio di Cadore*. Ed. 1809, Venice

1630
Ripa, C., *La più che novissima iconologia*. Padua

1648
Ridolfi, C., *Le Maraviglie dell'arte ovvero le vite degli illustri pittori veneti e dello stato descritti da Carlo Ridolfi*. Venice. Ed. 1835, 2 vols., Padua; ed. D. von Hadeln, 1914-1924, 2 vols., Berlin

1650
Manilli, J., *Villa Borghese fuori di porta Pinciana*. Rome

1657
De Los Santos, F., "Descripción breve del Monasterio de San Lorenzo El real del Escorial," in *Fuentes literarias para la Historia del Arte Español*. Ed. F. Sanchez Canton. Madrid, 1933

Scannelli, F., *Il microcosmo della pittura*. Cesena

1660
Boschini, M., "La carta del navegar pitoresco, dialogo tra un senator venetian deletante e un professor de pitura, soto nome d'eccelenza e de compare, comparti in oto venti." Venice. Ed. A. Pallucchini con la *Breve Istruzione* premessa alle *Ricche Minere della pittura veneziana*. Venice-Rome, 1966

1663
Sansovino, F., *Venetia città nobilissima et singolare descritta dal Sansovino con nuove e copiose aggiunte di D. Giustinian Martinioni*. Venice

1664
Boschini, M., *Le minere della pittura. Compendiosa informazione di Marco Boschini, non solo delle pitture pubbliche di Venezia, ma delle isole ancora circonvicine*. Venice

1665
Chantelou (Fréart), *Journal du voyage du Cavalier Bernin en France*. n.p.

1666-1688
Felibien, A., *Entretiens su les vies et sur les ouvrages des plus excellens peintres anciens et modernes*. 2 vols. Paris

1672
Bellori, G.P., *Le vite de' pittori, scultori et architetti moderni*. Rome

1674
Boschini, M., *Le ricche Minere della pittura veneziana. Compendiosa informazione di Marco Boschini, non solo delle pitture pubbliche di Venezia, ma delle isole ancora circonvicine*. Venice

1675
Sandrart, von, J., *Teutsche Academie*. Nürnberg

1677
Bocchi, F., & Cinelli, G., *Le bellezze della città di Firenze*. Florence

1680
Sandrart, von, J., *Iconologia Deorum oder Abbildung der Gotter*. Nürnberg

1681
G.P. (G. Palazzi), *Le Virtù in Giocco, ovvero Dame Patrizie de Venetia*. Venice

1683
Sandrart, von, J., *Accademia Nobilissimae Artis pictoriae*. Nürnberg-Frankfurt

1684
Martinelli, D., *Il ritratto di Venezia, diviso in 2 parti*. Venice

1700
Montelatici, D., *Villa Borghese fuori di Porta Pinciana*. Rome

1705
Martinelli, D., Ganessa, L., *Il Ritratto di Venezia ovvero le cose più notabili di Venezia... ampliato*, Venice

1715
Milesio, G.B., *Descrizione del Fondaco dei Tedeschi*. Venice; ed. 1941, Venice

Coypel, A., *Inventaire des tableaux du Roy, placez dans les appartements de Mgr le duc d'Antin en son hotel à Paris en l'année 1715*

1724
Palomino, A., *El Parnaso español pintoresco, laureado con las vidas del los pintores y estatuarios eminentes españoles.* Ed. 1947, Madrid

1733
Zanetti, A.M., *Descrizione di tutte le pubbliche pitture della città di Venezia.* Venice

1751
Bailly, J., *Catalogue des tableaux du cabinet du Roi au Luxembourg.* Paris

1752
Aedes Walpolianae, or a Description of the Collection of Pictures at Houghton Hall in Norfolk, the seat of the Right Honourable Sir Robert Walpole. Oxford

Dezallier D'Argenville, A.J., *Voyage pittoresque de Paris ou Indication de tout ce qu'il y a de plus beau dans cette grande ville en Peinture, Sculpture, et Architecture.* Paris

1752-1754
Lepicie, F.B., *Catalogue raisonné des tableaux du Roy avec un abregé de la vie des peintures.* 2 vols. Paris

1758
Corner, F., *Notizie storiche delle chiese e monasteri di Venezia.* Padua

1759
Raccolta di stampe rappresentanti quadri più scelti dei Signori Marchesi Gerini 1. Florence

1760
Jeaurat, E., *Inventaire des tableaux du Cabinet du Roy placés à la Surintendance des Bastiments de sa Majesté à Versailles.*

Rossini, P., *Mercurio errante.* Rome

Zanetti, A.M., *Varie pitture a fresco de' principali maestri veneziani.* Venice

1761
Zatta, A., *L'augusta basilica dell'evangelista San Marco.* Venice

1764
Piganiol de La Force, J.A., *Nouvelle description des chateaux et parcs de Versailles et de Marly.* Paris

1769
Cochin, Ch. N., *Voyage d'Italie ou recueil de notes sur les ouvrages de Peinture et de Sculpture qu'on voit dans les principales villes d'Italie.* 3 vols. Paris

1771
Zanetti, A.M., *Della pittura veneziana e delle opere pubbliche de' veneziani maestri.* Venice

1772-1794
Ponz, A., *Viaje de España, en que se da noticia de las cosas más apreciables, y lignas de saberse que hay en ella.* 2 vols. Madrid

1775
Roma antica e moderna. Rome

1776
Papillon, J.M., *Traité historique et pratique de la gravure en bois.* 3 vols. Paris

1778-1790
Heinecken, *Dictionnaire des artistes dont nous avons des estampes.* 4 vols. Leipzig

1780
Ratti, C.G., *Istruzione de quanto può vedersi di più bello in Genova.* Genoa

1783
Mechel, von, C., *Verzeichnis der Gemälde der Kaiserlich Königlichen Bilder Galerie in Wien.* Vienna

1786
Raccolta di ottanta stampe del Marchese Gerini. Florence

1793
Catalogue des objets contenus dans la galérie du Musèum francais. Paris

1797
Boschini, M., & Zanetti, A.M., *Della pittura veneziana. Trattato.* Venice

1800
Cean Bermudez, J.A., *Diccionario histórico de los más ilustres profesores de las bellas artes en España.* 6 vols. Madrid

1804-1828
Lavellée, J., *Galérie du Musée Napoléon.* 11 vols. Paris

1808-1810
Bembo, P., "Opere del Cardinale Pietro Bembo." 12 vols. *Lettere*, 5-9, Milan

1815
Moschini, G.A., *Guida per la città di Venezia.* Venice

1816
Nota dei quadri che D. Camillo Borghese fece trasportare a Parigi nel 1809 ritornaron in Roma nel sett. 1816

1817
Ticozzi, S., *Vite de' pittori vecelli di Cadore.* Milan

1822-1825
Bottari, G., & Ticozzi, S., eds., *Raccolta di lettere sulla pittura, scultura ed architettura.* 8 vols. Milan

1827
Hand, F., *Kunst und Altertum in St Petersburg* 1. Weimar

1828
Schnitzler, J.H., *Notice sur les principaux tableaux du Musée Imperial de l'Ermitage à Saint-Petersboug.* Berlin

1829
Hume, A., *Notices of the Life and Works of Titian.* London

1830
Zanotto, F., *Pinacoteca della I.R. Accademia Veneta di belle Arti.* Venice

1833
Cadorin, G., *Dello Amore ai veneziani di Tiziano Vecellio.* Venice

1838
Waagen, G.F., *Works of Art and Artists in England.* London

1839
Waagen, G.F., *Kunstwerke und kunstler in England und Paris.* Berlin

1840
Gaye, G., *Carteggio inedito d'artisti.* Florence

1842
Gualandi, M., *Memorie originali di Belle Arti.* Bologna

1843
Madrazo, P., *Catálogo de los cuadros del Real Museo de Pintura.* Madrid

1845
Bevilacqua, G.C., *Insigne pinacoteca della veneta nobile famiglia Barbarigo della Terrazza.* Venice

1846
Alizeri, F., *Guida illustrativa per la città di Genova.* Genoa

1851-1860
Mariette, P.J., *Abecedario... et d'autres notes inédites.* Paris

1853
Cicogna, E., *Delle iscrizioni veneziane* VI. Venice

1853-1861
Zanotto, F., *Il Palazzo Ducale di Venezia.* Venice

1854
Waagen, G.F., *Life of Titian.* 3 vols. London

1854-1888
Le Blanc, Ch. M., *De l'amateur d'estampes.* 3 vols. Paris

1855
Burkhardt, J., *Der Cicerone.* Basel. Ed. Ital., 1952, Florence

1856
Pinchart, A., "Tableaux et Sculptures de Marie d'Autriche," in *Revue Universelle des Arts.*

Pinchart, A., "Tableaux et Sculptures de Charles-Quint," in *Revue Universelle des Arts.*

1857
D'Arco, C., *Delle Arti e degli artefici de Mantova, notizie - 2.* Mantua

1860-1864
Passavant, J.P., *Les Peintres graveurs.* Leipzig

1864
Cittadella, L.N., *Notizie relative a Ferrara.* Ferrara

Ronchini, A., "Delle relazioni di Tiziano coi Farnese," in *Atti e memorie delle R.R. Deputazioni di storia patria per le province modenesi e parmensi.*

Waagen, G.F., *Die Gemaldesammlung in der Kaiserliche Ermitage zu St Petersbourg nebst Bemerkungen über andere dortige Kunstsammlungen.* Munich

1868-1869
Lorenzi, G.B., *Monumenti per servire alla storia del Palazzo Ducale di Venezia.* Venice

1869-1874
Forcella, U., *Iscrizioni delle chiese e di altri edifici de Roma.* 16 vols. Rome

1869
Robinson, J.C., *Descriptive Catalogue of the Drawings by the Old Masters, forming the Collection of John Malcom of Poltalloch, Esq.* London

1870
Campori, G., *Raccolta di cataloghi ed inventari inediti.* Modena

1871-1876
Crowe, J.A., & Cavalcaselle, G.B., *Geschichte der italienischen Malerei.* Leipzig

1873
Duvaux, L., *Livre journal (1748-1758).* Paris

1874
Campori, G., "Tiziano e gli Estensi," in *Nuova Antologia.* (November)

Villot, F., *Notices des tableaux exposés dans les galéries du musée National du Louvre, 1ère partie, écoles d'Italie et d'Espagne.* 3d. Paris

1877
Crowe, J.A., & Cavalcaselle, G.B., *Titian, His Life and Times.* 2 vols. London

Thausing, M., "Tizian und die Herzogin Eleonora von Urbino," in *Zeitschrift für Bildende Kunst* 12

Wolf, A., "Tizian's Madonna der Familie Pesaro in der Kirche der Frari zu Venedig," in *Zeitschrift für Bildenden Kunst* 12

1877-1878
Cavalcaselle, G.B., & Crowe, J.A., *Tiziano, la sua vita, i suoi tempi.* Florence

1879
Heath, R.F., *Titian.* London

1880
(Lermolieff, I.), Morelli, G., *Die Werke italienischer Meister in den Galerien von Munchen, Dresden und Berlin.* Berlin

1881
Braghirolli, W., "Tiziano alla Corte dei Gonzaga di Mantova," in *Atti e Memorie dell'Accademia Virgiliana di Mantova.* Mantua

1882
Bode, W., *Kaiserliche Gemaldegalerie der Ermitage in St.Petersburg.* Berlin

Fulin, R., "Documenti per servire alla storia della tipografia veneziana," in *Archivio Veneto* 22

1883
Both de Tauzia, L., *Notice des tableaux exposés dans les galéries du Musée du Louvre, 1ère partie: écoles d'Italie et d'Espagne.* Paris

Jouin, H., *Conférences de l'académie royale de peinture et de sculpture recueillies, annotées et précédées d'une étude sur les artistes écrivains.* Paris

1884
Cosnac, de, G.J., *Les richesses du Palais Mazarin. Inventaire inédit dressé après la mort du Cardinal Mazarin en 1661.* Paris

Engerth, von, E.R., *Kunsthistorische Sammlungen des allerhochsten Kaiserhauses. Gemälde, I. Italianische, Spanische und Franzosische Schulln.* Vienna

Madrazo, P., *Viaje artístico de tres siglos por las colecciones de cuadros de los Reyes de España.* Barcelona

Schonherr, von, D., "Urkunden und Regesten aus dem Kaiserlichen u. Königlichen Staathalterei. Archive in Innsbruch," in *Jahrbuch der Kunsthistorisches Sammlungen in Wien.*

1885
Lalanne, L., *Journal du voyage du Cavalier Bernin en France par M. de Chantelon, manuscrit publié et annoté.* Paris

1885-1913
Champlin, Jr., J.D., & Perkins, C.C., *Encyclopedia of Painters and Paintings.* 4 vols. New York

1886
Frizzoni, G., *Collezione di quaranta disegni scelti dalla raccolta del senatore G. Morelli.* Milan

1886
Penther, O., *Kritische Besuch in der Ermitage zu St. Petersburg.* Vienna

Morelli, G. (Lermolieff, I.), *Le opere dei maestri italiani nelle Gallerie di Monaco, Dresda e Berlino.* Bologna

1887
Kreyczi, F., "Urkunden und Regesten aus dem Kaiserlichen und Königlichen Reichs-Finenz-Archiv," in *Jahrbuch der Kunsthistorisches Sammlungen in Wien.*

1888
Chiavacci, E., & Pieraccini, E., *Guide de la Galérie Royale du Palais Pitti.* Florence-Rome

Luzio, A., *Pietro Aretino nei primi suoi anni a Venezia e la Corte dei Gonzaga.* Turin

Malamani, V., *Memorie del conte Leopoldo Cicognara tratte dai documenti originali - II.* Venice

Zarco del Valle, M.R., "Unteroffentliche Beitrage zur Geschichte der Kunstbestrebungen Karls V und Philip II mit besonderer Beruchrichtigung Tizians," in *Jahrbuch der Kunsthistorisches Sammlungen in Wien.*

1889
Justi, K., "Verzeichnis der früher in Spanien befindlichen jetzt verschollenen oder in das Ausland gekommenen Gemälde Tizians," in *Jahrbuch der Kunsthistorischen Sammlungen des Allerhochsten Kaiserhauses* 10

Migliozzi, A., *Nuova guida generale del Museo Nazionale di Napoli.* Naples

1890
Ferri, P.N., *Catalogo riassuntivo della raccolta di disegni antichi e moderni posseduta dalla R. Galleria degli Uffizi di Firenze.*

Luzio, A., "Tre lettere di Tiziano al Cardinale Ercole Gonzaga," in *Archivio Storico dell'Arte*

Morelli, G., *Die Gallerien Borghese und Doria Pamphilij.* Berlin

Morelli, G., "La pinacoteca del Museo Nazionale," in *Napoli Oggi*

1890-1893
Schonherr, von, D., "Urkunden und Regesten aus dem Kaiserlichen u. Königlichen Staathalterei-Archiv in Innsbruck," in *Jahrbuch der Kunsthistorisches Sammlungen in Wien.*

Voltellini, von, H., "Urkunden und Regesten aus dem Kaiserlichen u. Königlichen Hans-Hof und Staats Archiv in Wien," in *Jahrbuch der Kunsthistorisches Sammlungen in Wien*

1892
Frizzoni, G., "Serie di capolavori dell'arte italiana nuovamente illustrati," in *Archivio Storico dell'Arte*

Morelli, G., *Italian Painters. Critical Studies.* London

1893-1895

Delacroix, E., *Journal*, 3 vols., Paris. Ital. ed. L. Vitali. Turin, 1954

Wickhoff, F., "Les écoles d'Italie Musée du Louvre," in *Gazette des Beaux-Arts* 25, no. 3

1894

Berenson, B., *The Venetian Painters of the Renaissance*. New York-London

Justi, C., "Das Tizian Bildnis der Galerie Kassel," in *Jahrbuch der Königlich Preussischen Kunstsammlungen*.

Justi C., "Tizian und Alfonso von Este," in *Jahrbuch der Königlich Preussischen Kunstsammlungen*

1895

Urbani de Gheltof, G.M., *Guida storico-artistica alla Scuola di S. Giovanni Evangelista in Venezia*. Venice

1896

Cavalcaselle, G.B., & Morelli, G., "Catalogo delle opere d'arte nelle Marche e nell'Umbria," in *Le gallerie nazionali Italiane. Documenti storico-artistici*. Rome

Harck, F., "Notizen über italienische Bilder in Petersburger Sammlungen," in *Repertorium für Kunstwissenschaft* 19

Saccardo, P., *Les mosaiques de Saint-Marc à Venise*. Venice

1897

Phillips, C., *The Earlier Work of Titian*. London

Tschudi, von, H., *Kaiserliche Gemäldegalerie der Ermitage*. Berlin

1898

Knackfuss, H., *Tizian*. Bielefeld-Leipzig

1900

Cook, H., "The Date of Birth of Titian," in *Nineteenth Century* 1

Cook, H., *Giorgione*. London

Gronau G., *Titian*, London

Levi, C.A., *Le collezioni veneziane d'Arte e d'Antichità dal secolo XIV ai giorni nostri*. Venice

Oberziner, O., *Il ritratto di Cristoforo Madruzzo*. Trent

1901

Hurll, E.M., *Titian: a collection of Fifteen Pictures*. Boston

1903

Hamel, M., *Titien*. Paris

1904

Fischel, O., *Tizian. Des Meister Gemälde*. Stuttgart-Leipzig

Gronau, G., "Die Kunstbestebrungen der Herzoge von Urbino," in *Jahrbuch der Königlich Preussischen Kunstsammlungen* 24

Justi, C., "Tizian und der Hof von Urbino," in *Jahrbuch der Königlich Preussischen Kunstsammlungen*

1905

Cook, H., "La Collection de Sir Frederick Cook, Visconde de Monserate à Richmond," in *Les Arts* 44

1906

Gronau, G., "Zwei Tizianische Bildnisse der Berliner Galerie," in *Jahrbuch der Königlich Preussischen Kunstsammlungen* 27

Kristeller, O., *Il Trionfo della Fede*. Berlin

Phillips, C., *The Earlier Work of Titian*. London

Justi, L., *Giorgione*. 2 vols. Berlin

1907

Fischel, O., *Tizian. Des Meisters Gemälde*. Stuttgart

Gronau, G., "Di due quadri di Tiziano poco conosciuti," in *Rassegna d'Arte*

1908

Malaguzzi Valeri, F., *Catalogo della R. Pinacoteca di Brera*. Bergamo

1909

Beckerath, von, A., "Über einige altitalienische Zeichnungen in der Kgl. Graphischen Sammlungen in Munchen," in *Repertorium für Kunstwissenschaft* 32

Dennistoun, J., *Memoirs of the Dukes of Urbino*. 3 vols. London

Guiffrey, J., & Tuetey, A., "La Commision du Museum et la création du Musée du Louvre (1792-1793)," in *Archives de l'art Français* 3. Paris

1910

Allende Salazar, J., & Sanchez Canton, F., *Retratos del Museo del Prado*. Madrid. Also Madrid, 1919

Lafenestre, G., & Richten Berger, E., *La peinture en Europe*. Paris

Lipgart, E., "L'Ermitage Imperiale: acquisizioni e riesposizioni," in *Starie godni* (January)

Ricketts, C., *Titian*. London

1908

Campana, L., "Monsignor Giovanni della Casa e i suoi tempi," in *Studi Storici*, XVII

1911

Catalogo dei ritratti eseguiti in disegno e in incisione da artisti italiani fioriti dal sec. XV alla prima metà del sec. XIX. esposti nella R. Galleria degli Uffizi. Florence

Cox, M.L., "Inventory of pictures," in *The Burlington Magazine* 29

De Rinaldis, A., *Guida illustrata del Museo Nazionale di Napoli*. Naples

Fischel, O., *Tizian*. Stuttgart

Hadeln, von, D., "Beitrage zur Geschichte das Dogenpalastes," in *Jahrbuch der Königlich Preussischen Kunstsammlungen* 32

Ludwig, H., "Archivalische Beitrage für Geschichte der venezianischen Kunst," in *Italienische Forschungen* 4

1912

Hourticq, L, "Promenade au Louvre. Titien," in *Revue de l'Art* (10 July)

Venturi, L., "Saggio sulle opere d'arte a Pietroburgo," in *L'Arte* 5

1912-1921

Loeser, C., "Disegni di Tiziano e Jacopo Robusti detto il Tintoretto," in *I disegni della R. Galleria degli Uffizi*, series 1, no. 2. Florence

Fröhlich-Bum, L., *Andrea Meldolla genamnt Schiavone*. Vienna

Hadeln, von, D., "Über zeichnungen der früheren zeit Tizians," in *Jahrbuch der Königlich Preussischen Kunstsammlungen* 34

Luzio, A., *La Galleria dei Gonzaga venduta all'Inghilterra nel 1627-1628*. Milan

Raffaelli, J.F., *Les Promenades au Musée du Louvre*. 2nd. ed. Paris

Ricci, de, S., *Description raisonée des peintures du Louvre. I. Ecoles étrangères. Italie et Espagne*. Paris

Venturi, L., *Giorgione e il giorgionismo*. Milan

1914

Longhi, R., "Piero dei Franceschi e lo sviluppo della pittura veneziana," in *L'Arte*

1914-1915

Coggiola, G., "Per l'iconografia di Pietro Bembo," in *Atti del reale Istituto veneto di Scienze, Lettere ed Arti* 74

1917

Friedberg, M., "Über 'das Konzert' im Palazzo Pitti," in *Zeitschrift für Bildende Kunst*

Lavallee, P., "Les dessins de l'Ecole des Beaux-Arts," in *Gazette des Beaux-Arts* 59

Hourticq, L., *La jeunesse de Titien*. Paris

1920

Hadeln, von, D., "Compte-rendu du livre de Theodor Hetzer. Die Frühen Gemälde Tizian," in *Kunstchronik* 31

Hetzer, Th., *Die frühen Gemälde des Tizian*. Basel

Hill, G.F., *Medals of the Renaissance*. Oxford

Lorenzetti G., "Per la storia del 'Cristo Portacroce' della chiesa di San Rocco di Venezia," in *Rivista di Venezia*

Scrinzi, A., "Un disegno inedito di Tiziano," in *Studi di Arti e di Storia* 1

1921

Gronau, G., *Titian*. London

Popp, A., "Tizians *Lucrezia und Tarquinus* in der Wiener Akademie," in *Zeitschrift für bildende Kunst* 56

1922
Borenius, T., "Some reflections on the last phase of Titian," in *The Burlington Magazine* 41

1924
Baumeister, E., "Eine studie Tizians für die *Schlacht von Cadore*, in *Munchener Jahrbuch der bildenden Kunst* 1

Fischel, O., *Tizian*. Stuttgart

Hadeln, von, D., "Some little-known works by Titian," in *The Burlington Magazine* 2 (October)

Hadeln, von, D., *Zeichnungen des Tizian*. Berlin. English ed., 1927, London

Pastor, von, L., *Storia dei Papi*. vol. 5. Rome

1925
Longhi, R., "Giunte a Tiziano," in *L'Arte* 28

1926
Beroqui, P., "Tiziano en el Museo del Prado," in *Boletín de la Sociedad Española de Excursiones* 33-35

Hetzer, Th., "Vecellio, Tiziano," in *Allgemeines Lexikon der bildenden Kunstler von der Antike bis zur Gegenwart*, eds. U. Thieme & F. Becker, vol. 26. Leipzig

Justi, L., *Giorgione*. Berlin

Hautecoeur, L., *Musée National du Louvre Catalogues des peintures exposées dans les galleries. II. Ecole italienne et école española*. Paris

Lorenzetti, G., *Venezia e il suo estuario. Guida storico-artistica*. Venice

Panofsky E., & Saxl, F., "A Late Antique Religious Symbol in Works by Holbein and Titian," in *The Burlington Magazine* 49

1927
Eigenberger, R., *Die Gemäldegalerie der Akademie in Wien*. Vienna

Hadeln, von, D., *Titian's drawings*. London

Suida, W., "Rivendicazione a Tiziano," in *Vita artistica* 2

1928
De Rinaldis, A., *Pinacoteca del Museo Nazionale di Napoli. Catalogo*. Naples

Fröhlich-Bum, L., "Studien zu Handzeichnungen der italienische Renaissance," in *Jahrbuch der Kunsthistorischen Sammlungen in Wien* 30

Venturi, A., *Storia dell'Arte italiana: la Pittura del Cinquecento*. pt. 9, vol. 3. Milan

Washburn Freund, F.F., "Paintings of Titian in America," in *The International Studio* 90, no. 372 (May)

1929
Biermann, G., "Tizians Judith mit dem Haupte des Holofernes," in *Cicerone* 21

Rouches, G., *La peinture au musée du Louvre, II, écoles étrangères*. Paris

1930
Catalogus des nouvelles acquisitions de la collection Goudstikker. Amsterdam

Catalogus van de Kersttentoonstelling in het Museum Boymans. Amsterdam

(Pivo) *Il tempio della Salute eretto per voto della Repubblica Veneta*. 26-10-1930. Venice

Hadeln, von, D., "Dogenbildnisse von Tizian," in *Pantheon* (November)

Hanfstaengl, E., "Castle Rohoncz Collection show in Munich," in *The Art News* (August)

Hourticq, L., *Le problème de Giorgione*. Paris

Italian Art 1200-1900. [Exh. cat.] London

Mayer, A.L., "The Jahrborough *Magdalena* by Titian," in *Apollo* 11

Panofsky, E., "Eine tizianische Allegorie," *Hercules am Scheidewege*. Hamburg

Steinmann, E., *Michelangelo im Spiegel seiner zeit*. Leipzig

Suida, W., "Die Ausstellung italienischer Kunst in London," in *Belvedere* 2

Suida, W., "Un second homme au gant de Titian au Louvre," in *Gazette des Beaux-Arts* 1

Valentiner, W.R., *Unknown Masterpieces in Public and Private Collections*. London

1930-1931
Popham, A.E., *Italian Drawings Exhibited at the Royal Academy, Burlington House*. [Exh. cat.] Oxford-London

1931
Rothschild, von, E., "Tizians Darstellungen des Laurentiusmarter," in *Belvedere* 10

Van Marle, R., *The Development of the Italian Schools of Painting*. The Hague

Venturi, L., *Pitture italiane in America*. Milan

Wittgens F., "The contributions of Italian private collections to the Exhibition at Burlington House," in *Apollo* 11 (February)

1932
Berenson, B., *Italian Pictures of the Renaissance*. Oxford

Venturi, L., "Contributi a Tiziano, a Tintoretto," in *L'Arte* 35 (November)

1933
Gluck, G., "Bildisse aus dem Hause Hapsburg. I. Kaiserin Isabella," in *Jahrbuch der Kunsthistorischen sammlungen in Wien*

Suida, W., *Tiziano*. Rome. German ed., 1933, Zurich-Leipzig; French ed., 1935, Paris

Venturi, L., *Italian Paintings in America*. 3 vols. New York-Milan

Wilde J., "Die Probleme um Domenico Mancini", in *Jahrbuch der Kunsthistorischen Sammlungen in Wien*

1934
Gluck, G., "Bildnisse aus dem Hause Hapsburg. Konigin Maria von Ungarn," in *Jahrbuch der Kunsthistorisches Sammlungen in Wien*

Italiaensche Kunst in Nederlandsch bezit. Amsterdam

Poglayen-Neuwall, S., "Titian's Pictures of the Toilet of Venus and their Copies," in *The Art Bulletin* 16, no. 4 (December)

1934-1935
Serra, L., "Una mostra di Tiziano a Venezia," in *Bollettino d'Arte* 28

1935
Buscaroli, R., *La pittura di paesaggio in Italia*. Bologna

Dussler, L., "Tizians Austellung in Venedig," in *Zeitschrift für Kunstgeschichte*

Fogolari, G., in *Mostra di Tiziano*. Venice

Foscari, L., *Iconografia di Tiziano*. Venice

Gallo, R., "Per il San Lorenzo Martire di Tiziano. I committenti, la datazione," in *Rivista di Venezia* (April)

Hetzer, Th., *Tizian: Geschichte seiner Farbe*. Frankfurt am Main

L'Art Italienne de Cimabue à Tiepolo. [Exh. cat.] Paris

Mostra di Tiziano. Catalogo. Venice

Norris, C., "Titian's Exhibition," in *The Burlington Magazine*.

Pallucchini, R., "La mostra di Tiziano a Venezia," in *Ateneo Veneto* 126

Valentiner, W.R., "Ein Alterswerk Tizians," in *Pantheon* 16

Valentiner, W.R., "Judith with the Head of Holofernes," in *Detroit Institute of Arts Bulletin* 14, no. 8

1935-1936
Tietze-Conrat, E., "Titian's *Cavalli*," in *Old Master Drawings* 10

1936
Catalogus van de tentoonstelling van oude kunst. Amsterdam

Gronau, G., *Documenti artistici urbinati*. Florence

Suida, W., "Correggio e Tiziano," in *Manifestazioni Parmensi nel IV centenario della morte del Correggio*. Parma

Suida W., "Epilog zur Tizian Ausstellung in Venedig," in *Pantheon* (March)

Tietze, H., & Tietze-Conrat, E., "Tizian-Studien," in *Jahrbuch der Kunsthistorischen Sammlungen in Wien* 10

Tietze, H., *Tizian. Gemalde und Zeichnungen*. Vienna

Tietze, H., *Tizian. Leben und Werk*. 2 vols. Vienna

1937

Mather, F.J., *Venetian Painters*. London

Mayer, A.L., "A propos d'un nouveau livre sur le Titien," in *Gazette des Beaux-Arts* 18, no. 892 (December)

Richter, G.M., *Giorgio da Castelfranco, called Giorgione*. Chicago

1938

Dussler, L., *Italienische Meister Zeichnungen*. Frankfurt am Main

Mather, F.J., "When was Titian born," in *The Art Bulletin* 20

Meesterwerken nit vier eeuwen 1400-1800. Rotterdam

Tietze-Conrat, E., "Titian's Woodcuts," in *Print Collectors Quarterly* 25

Tietze-Conrat, E., "Tizian Graphik. Ein Beitrag zur Geschichte von Tizians Erfindungen," in *Die Graphischen Kunste* 3

Wilde, J., *Katalog der Gemäldegalerie*. Vienna

Zarnowski, J., "L'atélier de Titien, Girolamo Dente," in *Dawna Sztuka*

1938-1939

Wittkower, R., "Transformations of Minerva in Renaissance Imagery," in *Journal of the Warburg and Courtauld Institute* 2

1939

Emert, G.B., *Fonti manoscritte inedite per la Storia dell'Arte nel Trentino*. Florence

Frankfurter, A., *Art News Annual*

Kelly, F.M., "Note on an Italian Portrait at Doughty House," in *The Burlington Magazine* 75, no. 437, (August)

Lazarev, V., *Il tardo periodo di Tiziano*. Iscusstvo

Masterworks of Five Centuries. San Francisco

Ozzola, L., *Studi sul Tiziano*. Strasbourg

Panofsky, E., *Studies in Iconology. Humanistic Themes in the Art of the Renaissance. Blind Cupid*. New York

1940

Adriani, G., *Anton van Dyck. Italienische Skizzenbuch*. Vienna

Bodmer, H., "Die Zeichnungen des Giacomo Cavedoni," in *Die Graphisches Kunste* 5

Gourvic, N.A., *Tiziano*. Leningrad

Hetzer, T.H., "Tizian," eds. U. Theime & F. Becker, in *Allgemeine Kunstler Lexikon* 34. Leipzig

Luzio, A., "Le *Maddalene* di Tiziano," in *La Lettura* 8

1941

Brunetti, M., *Il Fondaco nostro dei Tedeschi*. Venice

Fiocco, G., *Giorgione*. Bergamo

Hervey, M., *The life correspondence and collections of Thomas Howard Earl of Arundel*. Cambridge

Mauroner, F., *Le incisioni di Tiziano*. Venice

Wulff, O., "Color, Light and Shade in the Figure Compositions of Titian," in *Jahrbuch der Preussischen Kunstsammlungen* 62

1942

Modigliani, E., *La collezione di Luigi Albertini*. Rome

Morassi, A., "Il mio Giorgione," in *Arte Veneta*

1943

Pallucchini, R., *La critica d'arte a Venezia nel Cinquecento*. Venice

1944

Catalogue of Paintings. Detroit Institute of Arts. Detroit

Pallucchini, R., *La pittura veneziana del Cinquecento*. 2 vols. Novara

Tietze, H., & Tietze-Conrat, E., *The drawings of the Venetian painters in the 15th and 16th centuries*. New York

Tietze, H., & Tietze-Conrat, E., "Titian as Letter Writer," in *The Art Bulletin* 26, no. 2 (June)

1945

Cinque secoli di pittura veneziana. [Exh. cat.] Venice

1946

Beroqui, P., *Tiziano en el Museo del Prado*. Madrid

Capolavori dei musei del Veneto. [Exh. cat.] Venice

Fiocco, G., "Francesco Vecellio: note su Cesare Vecellio," in *Lettere ed Arti* 1

Longhi, R., *Viatico per cinque secoli di pittura veneziana*. Florence

Malajoli, B., *Musei ed opere d'arte di Napoli. Attraverso la guerra*. Naples

1947

Kunstschatten uit Wehen. [Exh. cat.] Amsterdam

Moschini, V., "Vicende di guerra delle opere d'arte venete," in *Arte Veneta*

1948

Douglas, R.L., "The Date of Titian's Birth," in *The Art Quarterly*

Dussler, L., *Italienische Meisterzeichnungen*. Munich

Hetzer, Th., *Tizian*. Frankfurt am Main

Kunstschatten fra Wien. [Exh. cat.] Amsterdam

Ortolani, S., "Restauro d'un Tiziano," in *Bollettino d'Arte* 33, no. 1

Wind, E., *Bellini's Feast of Gods*. Cambridge, Massachusetts

Paintings from Berlin Museums. [Exh. cat.] Washington

1948-1949

Masterpieces from Berlin Museums. [Exh. cat.] Detroit

1949

Arnolds, G., *Italienische Zeichnungen. Zeichnungen des Kupferstichkabinetts in Berlin*. Berlin

Art Treasures from Vienna. [Exh. cat.] London

Ferraton, C., "La collection du duc de Richelieu au musée du Louvre," in *Gazette des Beaux-Arts* (June)

Hannema, D., *Catalogue of D.G. van Beuningen Collection*. Rotterdam

Honderd jaar Museum Boymans Rotterdam. Meeter-werken uit de verzameling D.G. van Beuningen. Rotterdam

Zurückgekehrte Meisterwerke aus dem Besizt Berliner Museum. [Exh. cat.] Weisbaden

Tietze, H., *Tizian*. Innsbruck

Tietze, H., "Unknown Venetian Renaissance drawings in Swedish collections," in *Gazette des Beaux-Arts* (March)

1950

Delogu, G., *Tiziano*. Bergamo

Hours, M., *L'illustration* (December)

Tietze-Conrat, E., "La xilografia di Tiziano, Il Passaggio del Mar Rosso," in *Arte Veneta* 4

Tietze, H., *Tizian Gemalde und Zeichnungen*. Vienna (Engl. ed. *Titian the Paintings and Drawings*, London)

1950-1951

Meisterwerke aus dem Berliner Museen. [Exh. cat.] Berlin

1951

Fiocco, G., "La mostra dei Vecellio a Belluno," in *Emporium* 2

Valcanover, F., & Fabbro, C., *Mostra dei Vecellio*. [Exh. cat.] Belluno

1952

Arslan, E., "Titian's Magdalen," in *The Burlington Magazine* (November)

Chef d'oeuvre de la collection D.G. van Beuningen. Paris

Lauts, J., *Isabella d'Esta Furstin der Renaissance 1474-1539*. Hamburg

Lazzari, A., "Il ritratto dei Mosti di Tiziano nella Galleria Pitti," in *Arte Veneta* 6

Suida, W., "Miscellanea tizianesca," in *Arte Veneta* 6

1952-54
Pallucchini, R., *Tiziano* (Lezioni tenute all'Università di Bologna 1952-1954). Bologna

1953
Kunstschätze aus Wien-Österreichs. [Exh. cat.] Vienna

Meisterwerke Italienischer Kunst. [Exh. cat.] Weisbaden

Tietze-Conrat, E., "The Pesaro Madonna – a footnote on Titian," in *Gazette des Beaux-Arts* (October)

1953-1954
Fiocco, G., *Dispense universitarie*
Le peinture vénetienne. [Exh. cat.] Paris

1954
Phillips, J.G. & Raggio, O., "Ottavio Farnese," in *The Metropolitan Museum of Art Bulletin* 12

Morassi, A., "Esordi di Tiziano," in *Arte Veneta* 8

Tietze, H., "An early version of Titian's *Danae*: an analysis of Titian's Replicas," in *Arte Veneta* 8

Vicentini, U., "Francesco Zorzi," in *Le Venezie Francescane* 21

1955
Battisti, E., "Le arti figurative nella cultura di Venezia e de Firenze nel cinquecento," in *Commentari* 6

Brendel, J.O., "Borrowings from ancient art in Titian," in *The Art Bulletin* 38 (June)

Carlos V y su tiempo. [Exh. cat.] Gante

Coletti, L., *Tutta la pittura di Giorgione.* Milan

Della Pergola, P., *Galleria Borghese. I dipinti.* Rome

Dell'Acqua, G.A., *Tiziano.* Milan

Elia, R., "La Chiesa di S. Domenico in Ancona e gli artisti che vi operarono," in *Studia Picena* 23

Gnau, A., *Diabolis in musica. A dynamic view of Western music.* Detroit

Kunstschatten uit Nederlandse verzameligen. Rotterdam

Hulftegger, A., "Notes sur la formation des collections peinture de Louis XIV. L'entrée dans le Cabinet du Roi des tableaux provenant de Jabach, Mazarin, Foucquet, etc.," in *Bulletin de la Societé de l'Histoire de l'Art Francais*

Rousseau, Th., *Titian.* New York

Sartori, A., *L'Arciconfraternita del Santo.* Padua

Zampetti, P., ed., *Giorgione e i giorgioneschi.* [Exh. cat.] Venice

1956
Hill, J., "An Identification of Titian's *Allegory of Prudence* and some Medici-Stuart Affinities," in *Apollo* 43

Kennedy, R.W., "Tiziano in Roma," in *Il mondo antico nel Rinascimento.* Florence

Morassi, A., *Tiziano, gli affreschi della Scuola del Santo a Padova.* Milan

Parker, K.T., *Catalogue of the Collection of Drawings in the Ashmolean Museum.* vol. 2. Oxford

Richards, L.S., "Titian's Woodcut by Domenico Dalle Greche," in *Cleveland Museum of Art Bulletin* 43

Sartori, A., *Santa Maria Gloriosa dei Frari a Venezia.* Padua

Suida, W., "Miscellanea tizianesca - II", in *Arte Veneta* 10

Walker, J., *Bellini and Titian at Ferrara.* London

1957
Baldass, L., "Tizian in Banne Giorgiones," in *Jahrbuch der Kunsthistorisches Sammlungen in Wien* 17

Bazin, G., *Trésors de la peinture au Louvre.* Paris

Berenson B., *Italian Pictures of the Renaissance. The Venetian School.* 2 vols., London (Ital. ed. Florence, 1958)

Innamorati, G., *Tradizione e invenzione in Pietro Aretino.* Messina-Florence

Lettere sull'arte di Pietro Aretino. E. Camesasca, ed. 2 vols. Milan

Levi D'Ancona, M., "The Iconography of the Immaculate Conception," in *The Burlington Magazine* (April)

Moschini, V., "Nuovi ordinamenti e restauri alle Gallerie di Venezia," in *Bollettino d'Arte* 42
Popham, A.E., *Correggio's Drawings.* London

Saxl, F., "Titian and Pietro Aretino," in *Lectures.* London

Zeri, F., *Pittura e Controriforma. L'arte senza tempo di Scipione da Gaeta.* Turin

1958
Bazin, G., *Musée de l'Ermitage. Les grands maîtres del la peinture.* Paris

Bottineau, Y., "L'Alcazar de Madrid et l'inventaire de 1686," in *Bulletin Hispanique* 60

Degenhart, B., Halm, P., Wagner, W., *Hundert Meisterzeichnungen aus der staatlichen Graphischen Sammlung.* Munich

Hartt, F., *Giulio Romano.* New Haven

Kennedy, R.W., "Tiziano in Roma," in *Il mondo antico nel Rinascimento.* Florence, 1956 (published 1958)

Tea, E., "La *Pala Pesaro* e l'Immacolata," in *Ecclesia*

1959
Gioseffi, D., *Tiziano.* Bergamo

Gould, C., *National Gallery Catalogues. The Sixteenth Century Venetian School.* London

Oberhammer, V., *Die Gemäldegalerie des Kunsthistorisches Museum in Wien.* Vienna (Ital. ed. Milan, 1960)

Suida, W., "Miscellanea tizianesca - IV," in *Arte Veneta* 13

Wulfingen, von, B., *Ardenberg Tiziano Vecellio Danae.* Stuttgart

1960
Mostra di disegni dei grandi maestri. [Exh. cat.] Florence

Fomiciova, T., *Tiziano Vecellio.* Moscow

IV Mostra di Restauro. Ed. R. Causa. [Exh. cat.] Naples

Klauner, F., & Oberhammer, V., *Katalog der Gemaldegalerie* vol. 1. Vienna (2 ed. Vienna, 1965)

Molajoli, B., *Notizie su Capodimonte.* Naples

Richter, J.P., & Morelli, G., *Italienische Malerei der Renaissance in Briefwechsel (1876-1891).* Baden-Baden

Valcanover, F., *Tutta la pittura di Tiziano.* 2 vols. Milan. Also English ed. 4 vols., New York, 1960

Zampetti, P., *L'opera completa di Giorgione.* Milan

1961
Forlani, A., *Disegno italiano di cinque secoli.* [Exh. cat.] Florence

Ivanoff., N., "Il ciclo allegorico della Libreria sansoviniana," in *Arte antica e moderna* 13-16

Lotz, W., "La libreria di San Marco e l'urbanistica del Rinascimento," in *Bollettino del Centro Internazionale di Studi di Architettura A. Palladio*

Neumann, J., "Tizianuv Apèollo a Marsyas v Kromerizi Z umelcovy pozdni tvorby," in *Umeni* 10

Pallucchini, R., "Studi tizianeschi," in *Arte Veneta* 15

Puppi, L., "Une ancienne copie de *Cristo e il Manigoldo* au Musée des Beaux-Arts," in *Bulletin du Musée National Hongrois des Beaux-Arts* 12

Schulz, J., "Vasari at Venice," in *The Burlington Magazine* 103

1962
Ames, W., *Great Drawings of All Time* vol. 1. New York

Arslan, E., "Studi Belliniani," in *Bollettino d'Arte* 47, n. 1 (January-March)

Catalogus Schilderijen tot 1800, Museum Boymans-van Beuningen. Rotterdam

Gould, C., "Sebastiano Serlio and Venetian Paintings," in *Journal of the Warburg and Courtauld Institute* 25

Konstens Venedig. [Exh. cat.] Stockholm

Marconi Moschini, S., *Gallerie dell'Accademia di Venezia: opere d'arte del secolo XVI.* Rome

Neumann, J., *Le Titien Marsyas écorché vif.* Prague

Panofsky, E., *Il significato delle arti visive.* Turin

Sinding-Larsen, S., "Titian's *Madonna di Ca' Pesaro*," in *Acta ad Archeologiam et Artium Historia Pertinenta* 1

1963
Catalogo Museo del Prado. Madrid

Chastel, A., & Klein, R., *L'Age de l'humanisme*. Paris

Fabbro, C., "Notizie storiche sulla tomba dei Vecellio nell'antica chiesa Arcidiaconale di Pieve di Cadore e sul dipinto di Tiziano conservato nella nuova Chiesa," in *Archivio Storico di Belluno Feltre e Cadore* (January-March)

Kennedy, R.W., *Novelty and Tradition in Titian's Art*. Northampton, Mass.

1964

Baldass, L., & Heinz, G., *Giorgione*. Vienna

Barnaud, F. & Hours, M., "Etudes sur deux tableaux du Titien intitulés *Tarquin et Lucrèce*, in *Bulletin du Laboratoire du Louvre* 9

D'Onofrio, C., "Inventario dei dipinti del Cardinal Pietro Aldobrandini compilato da G.B. Agucci nel 1603," in *Palatino* 8

Della Pergola, P., "L'inventario Borghese del 1693 (II)," in *Arte antica e moderna* 28

Hours, M., *Les secrets des Chef-d'oeuvres*. Paris

Ivanoff, N., "Il ciclo dei filosofi della Libreria Marciana a Venezia," in *Emporium* 140, n. 2

Ivanoff, N., "Il coronamento statuario della Marciana," in *Ateneo Veneto* 2

Kennedy, R.W., "Apellis redivivus," in *Essays in Memory of Karl Lehmann*. New York

Mirimonde, de, A.P., "Le language secret des vieux tableaux," in *Journal de Genève* (21-22 March)

Morassi, A., *Tiziano*. Milan

Wittkower, R., *Principi architettonici nell'età dell'umanesimo*. Turin

1965

Adriani, G., *Anton van Dyck. Italienische Skizzenbuch*. Vienna

Friedländer, W., "Titian and Pordenone," in *The Art Bulletin* 47, n. 1

Mezzetti, A., "Le *Storie di Enea* del Dosso nel *Camerino d'Alabastro* di Alfonso I d'Este," in *Paragone* 16, n. 189 (November 1965)

Saxl, F., *La storia delle immagini*. Bari

1966

Bacci, M., *Piero di Cosimo*. Milan

Da Mosto, A., *I Dogi di Venezia nella vita privata*. Milan

Dionisotti, C., "Bembo, Pietro," in *Dizionario Biografico degli italiani*. vol. 8. Rome

Kahr, M., "Titian's Old Testament Cycle," in *Journal of the Warburg and Courtauld Institute* 29

Mills, J.S., "The gas chromatographic examination of paint media. Part I. Fatty acid composition and identification of dried oil films," in *Studies in Conservation* 2

Morassi, A., "Tiziano Vecellio," in *Enciclopedia dell'Arte*

Oberhammer, V. & Heinz, G., *Neuerworben*

1955-1966 Neugewohnen Gemäldegalerie. Vienna

Oberhuber, K., *Renaissance u. Italien XVI Jahrhundert (Die Kunst der Graphik II. Werke aus dem Besitz der Albertina)*. Vienna

Pope-Hennessy, J., *The Portrait in the Renaissance*. New York

Putelli, L., *Tiziano Vecellio da Cador*. Turin

Schulz, J., "Titian's Ceilings in the Scuola of San Giovanni Evangelista," in *The Art Bulletin* 48 (March)

Turner, R., *The Vision of Landscape in the Renaissance*. Princeton

1967

Bazin, G., *Les temps des musées*. Liège-Brussels

Claulas, A., "Documents concernant Titien conservés aux Archives de Simancas," in *Mélanges de la casa de Velasquez* 3

Fabbro, C., "Tiziano. I Farnese e l'Abbazia di San Pietro in Colle nel Cenedese." in *Archivio Storico di Belluno, Feltre e Cadore* (January-June)

Fomiciova, T., "I dipinti di Tiziano nelle Raccolte dell'Hermitage," in *Arte Veneta* 21

Forsmann, F., "Über Architekturen in der venezianischen Malerei des Cinquecento," in *Wallraf-Richartz Jahrbuch* 29

Friedländer, W., in *Studies in Renaissance and Baroque Art Presented to A. Blunt*. London-New York

Garas, K., "Die Entstehung der Galerie des Erzherzogs Leopold Wilhelm," in *Jahrbuch der Kunsthistorischen Sammlungen in Wien* 63

Garas, K.,[1] "The Ludovisi Collection of Pictures in 1633 - I," in *The Burlington Magazine* (May)

Garas, K.,[2] "The Ludovisi Collection of Pictures in 1633 - II," in *The Burlington Magazine* (June)

Holst, von, N., *Creators, Collectors and Connoisseurs*. New York

Ivanoff, N., "I cicli allegorici della Libreria e del Palazzo Ducale di Venezia," in *Rinascimento Europeo e Rinascimento Veneziano*. Ed. V. Branca. Florence

Longhi, R., "Cartella tizianesca. Vita artistica 2," in *Saggi e Ricerche 1925-1928*. Florence

Lotz, W., "Sansovino Bibliothek von San Marco und die Stadtbaukunst der Renaissance," in *Kunst des Mittelalters in Sachsen. Festschrift W. Schubert*. Weimar

Pallucchini, R., & Berence, F., *Titien*. Paris

Schmitt, A., *Italienische Zeichnungen 15-18 jahrundert Staatliche Graphische Sammlungen München*. [Exh. cat.] Munich

Valcanover, F., "Gli affreschi di Tiziano al Fondaco dei Tedeschi," in *Arte Veneta* 21

Wind, E., *Pagan Mysteries in the Renaissance*. London (Ital. ed. Milan, 1985)

1968

Ballarin, A., *Tiziano*. Florence

Branca, V., "Tiziana scrittore inedito," in *Corriere della Sera* (19 March)

Fehl, P., "Realism and Classicism in the Representation of a Painful Scene: Titian's *Flaying of Marsyas* in the Archiepiscopal Palace at Kromeriz," in *Czechoslovakia past and present. Essays on the Arts and Sciences*. vol. 2. The Hague

Garas, K., "Das Schikksal der Sammlung des Ertherzog Leopold Wilhelm," in *Jahrbuch der Kunsthistorischen Sammlungen in Wien* 64

Ivanoff, N., "La Libreria Marciana," in *Saggi e Memorie di Storia dell'Arte* 6

Longhi, R., "Tiziano: tre ritratti," in *Paragone* 215 (January)

Morassi, A., "Una Salome di Tiziano riscoperta," in *Pantheon* (November-December)

Puppi, L., "La Pala votiva Mocenigo del National Gallery di Londra," in *Antichità viva*, VIII

Robertson, G., *Giovanni Bellini*. Oxford

Roskill, M.W., *Dolce's "Aretino" and Venetian Art Theory of the Cinquecento*. New York

Shapley, F.R., *Paintings from the Samuel H. Kress Collection. Italian Schools. XV-XVI Century*. London

Schulz, J., *Venetian painted ceilings of the Renaissance*. Berkeley-Los Angeles

Stuffmann, M., "Les tableaux de la collection de Pierre Crozat," in *Gazette des Beaux-Arts* 72

Walther, A., in *Venezianische Malerei. 15 bis 18 Jahrundert*. [Exh. cat.] Dresden

Wolters, W., *Plastische Deckendekorationen des Cinquecento in Venedig und im Veneto*. Berlin

Zampetti, P., *L'opera completa di Giorgione*. Milan

1969

Gould, C., *The Studio of Alfonso d'Este and Titian's "Bacchus and Ariadne."* London

Konstskatter fran Dresden. Stockholm

Pallucchini, R., *Tiziano*. 2 vols. Florence

Panofsky, E., *Problems in Titian. Mostly Iconographic*. London

Pignatti, T., *Giorgione*. Venice (Engl. ed., 1971)

Pignatti, T., *L'opera completa di Giovanni Bellini*. Milan

Ramsden, E.H., "A 'lost' portrait and its identification," in *Apollo* (June)

Schefer, J.L., *Scénographie d'un tableau*. Paris

Schneider, L., "A Note on the Iconography of Titian's Last Painting." in *Arte Veneta*

Tafuri, M., *Jacopo Sansovino e l'architettura del '500 a Venezia*. Padua

Valcanover, F., "L'attività della Soprintendenza alle Gallerie ed opere d'arte del Veneto," in *Arte Veneta* 23

Valcanover, F., *Tiziano, l'opera completa* (preface by C. Cagli). Milan

Wethey, H.E., *The Paintings of Titian. I. The Religious Paintings.* London

Wind, E., *Giorgione's Tempesta with Comments on Giorgione's Poetic Allegories.* Oxford

Zampetti, P., ed., *Lorenzo Lotto. Libro di spese diverse.* Venice-Rome

1970

Calvesi, M., "La *Morte di Bacio. Saggio sull'Ermetismo di Giorgione,*" in *Storia dell'Arte* 2, n. 7-8

Gould, C., "On Dürer's Graphic and Italian Painting," in *Gazette des Beaux-Arts* (February)

Lafuente Ferrari, E., *El Prado: Escuela italiana y francesa.* Madrid

Pignatti, T., "La Scuola Veneta," in *I disegni dei maestri.* vol. 2. Ed. W. Vitzthum

Valcanover, F., & Beguin, S., *Tout l'oeuvre peinte de Titien.* Paris

1971

Cocke, R., "Titian's Santo Spirito Ceiling: An Alternative Reconstruction," in *The Burlington Magazine*

Dreyer, P., *Tizian und Sein Kreis: 50 venezianische Holzschnitte aus dem Berliner Kupferstichkabinett staatliche Museen Preussischer.* Berlin

Freedberg, S.J., *Painting in Italy 1500 to 1600.* Harmondsworth

Giovio, P., "Raphaelis Urbinatis vita-Fragmentorum trium dialogorum," in *Scritti d'arte del '500.* ed. P. Barocchi. Milan-Naples

Hope, C.[1], "The *Camerino d'Alabastro* of Alfonso d'Este - I," in *The Burlington Magazine* 113 (November)

Hope, C.[2], "The *Camerino d'Alabastro* of Alfonso d'Este - II," in *The Burlington Magazine* 113 (December)

Johnson, M., & Packard, E., "Methods used for the Identification of Binding Media in Italian Paintings of the Fifteenth and Sixteenth Centuries," in *Studies in Conservation* 16

Mariacher, G., *Arte a Venezia. Dal Medioevo al Settecento. Testimonianze e Recuperi.* [Exh. cat.] Venice

Meyer zur Capellen, J., "Überlesungen zur Pietà Titians," in *Munchen Jahrbuch der bildenchen Kunst* 22

Niero, A., *Chiesa di S. Maria della Salute.* Venice

Oberhammer, V., "Gendanken zur Werdegang und Schicksal von Titian's Grossbild," in *Studi in onore di Antonio Morassi.* Venice

Olivato, L., "Per il Serlio a Venezia. Documenti nuovi e documenti rivisitati," in *Arte Veneta*

Pignatti, T., *Giorgione.* London

Rosand, D., "Titian in the Frari," in *The Art Bulletin* (June)

Wethey, H.E., *The Paintings of Titian. II, The Portraits,* London

Shapley, F.R., "Titian's *Venus with a Mirror,*" in *Studies in the History of Art* 4-5

1971-1972

Pignatti, T., "Über die beziehungen zwischen Dürer und dem jungen Tizian," in *Anzeiger des germanischen Nazional-museums Nürnberg*

1972

Dorment, K., "Tomb and testament: architectural significance," in *The Art Quarterly* 25

Aguilera, E.M., *El desnudo en las artes.* Madrid

Old Paintings 1400-1700. Museum Boymans van Beuningen. Rotterdam

Fredericksen, B., & Zeri, F., *Census of Pre-Nineteenth-Century Italian Paintings in North American Public Collections.* Cambridge, Massachusetts

Gould, C., "The Cinquecento in Venice. IV. Pordenone versus Titian," in *Apollo* (August)

Mills, J.S., "The identification of paint media. An introduction," in *Conservation of Paintings and the Graphic Arts. Atti del Convegno.* Lisbon

Mills, J.S., & White, R., "The gas chromatographic examination of paint media, part II. Some examples of medium identification in paintings by fatty acid analysis," in *Conservation of Paintings and the Graphic Arts. Atti del Convegno.* Lisbon

Moussalli, U., *A la recherche de Georges de la Tour.* Paris

Muraro, M., "E. Panofsky. Problems in Titian: mostly iconografic. New York 1969" (review), in *The Art Bulletin* (September)

Perry, M., "The *Statuario Pubblico* of the Venetian Republic," in *Saggi e memorie* 8

Petrioli Tofani, A.M., *I grandi disegni italiani degli Uffizi.* Milan

Rosand, D., "Ut Pictor Poeta: Meaning in Titian's *Poesie,*" in *New Literary History* 3, no. 3

Yates, F., *L'arte della memoria.* Turin

1973

Bruyn, J., "Notes on Titian's Pietà," in *Album amicorum J.G. van Gelde.* The Hague

Forssman, E.. *Dorico, ionico, corinzio nell'architettura del Rinascimento.* Bari

Gilbert, F., "Venice in the crisis of the League of Cambrai," in *Renaissance Venice.* ed. J. Hale. London

Lane, F., *Venice. A Maritime Republic.* Baltimore

Nanni, M., *Restauri nelle Marche.* [Exh. cat.] Urbino

Pignatti, T., *Il Passaggio del Mar Rosso di Tiziano Vecellio.* Vicenza

Pignatti, T., "The relationship between German and Venetian Painting in the late quattrocento and early cinquecento," in *Renaissance Venice.* Ed. J. Hale. London

Sarfatti, M.G., *Tiziano.* Buenos Aires

Zeri, F., & Gardner, E., *Italian Paintings. The*

Metropolitan Museum of Art. Venetian School. New York

1974

Bermejo de La Rica, A., *La mitologia en el Museo del Prado.* Madrid

Fehl, P., "Saint, Donors and Columns in Titian's *Pesaro Madonna,*" in *Renaissance Papers*

Fehl, P., "The Worship of Bacchus and Venus in Bellini's and Titian's Bacchanals for Alfonso d'Este," in *Studies in the History of Art* 6

Fomiciova, T., "Venetian Painting of the Fifteenth to Eighteenth Centuries," in *Apollo* (December)

Gaston, R.W., "Vesta and the Martyrdom of St. Lawrence in the Sixteenth Century," in *Journal of the Warburg and Courtauld Institute*

Maschio, R., "Una data per l'*Annunciazione* di Tiziano a S. Salvador," in *Arte Veneta* 28

Meijer, B.H., "Early drawings by Titian: some attributions," in *Arte Veneta* 28

Pérez Sánchez, A.E., *Museo del Prado.* Madrid

Rossi, P., & Pallucchini, R., *Jacopo Tintoretto. I. I Ritratti.* Venice

Sinding-Larsen, S., *Christ in the Council Hall. Studies in the religious iconography of the Venetian Republic.* Rome

Wilde, H., *Venetian Art from Bellini to Titian.* Oxford

1975

Ferrarino, L., *Tiziano e la corte di Spagna nei documenti dell'Archivio Generale di Simancas,* Madrid

Howard, D., *Jacopo Sansovino. Architecture and Patronage in Renaissance Venice.* New Haven and London

Lavin, M.A., *Seventeenth Century Barberini Documents and Inventories of Art.* New York

Muraro, M., "The Political Interpretation of Giorgione's frescoes on the Fondaco dei Tedeschi," in *Gazette des Beaux-Arts* 86

Rosand, D., "Titian and the 'Bed of Polyclitus'," in *The Burlington Magazine* 117 (April)

Sinding-Larsen, S., "Titian's Triumph of Faith," in *Institutum Romanum Norvegiae Acta* 6

Van Asperen de Boer, "An introduction to the scientific examination of paintings," in *Nederlands Kunsthistorische Jaarboek* 26

Wethey, H.E., *The paintings of Titian. III. The Mythological and Historical Paintings.* London

1976

Benvenuti, F., "Tiziano incisore e i suoi tempi," in *Tiziano e la silografia veneziana del Cinquecento.* [Exh. cat.] eds M. Muraro & D. Rosand. Venice

Bernini Pezzini, G., *Tiziano per i Duchi d'Urbino.* [Exh. cat.] Urbino

Beschi, L., "Collezioni di antichità a Venezia al tempo di Tiziano," in *Aquileia nostra* 48

Brandi, C., "Le due Danae," in *Atti dei Convegni dei Lincei*. Rome

Chastel, A., "Titien et les humanistes," in *Atti dei Convegni dei Lincei*. Rome

Chastel, A., "Tiziano," in *Nuova Antologia* (February)

Delburgo, S., Rioux, J.P., & Martin, E., "Note sur la technique picturale du Titien," in *Annales de laboratoire de Recherche des Musées de France*

Dopo Mantegna. Arte a Padova e nel territorio nei secoli XV e XVI. [Exh. cat.] Milan

Gould, C., *The Paintings of Correggio.* Ithaca, New York

Gould, C., "Three Titian Exhibitions," in *Master Drawings* 15

Gould, C., *Titian as Portraitist.* London

Hornig, C., "Giorgione's Spatwerk," in *Annali della Scuola Normale Superiore di Pisa* 6

Hours, M., "Contribution à l'étude de quelques oeuvres de Titien," in *Laboratoire de Recherche des Musées de France.* Annales

Karpinski, C., "Some Woodcuts after Early Designs of Titian," in *Zeitschrift für Kunstgeschichte* 29

Maschio, R., in *Dopo Mantegna.* [Exh. cat.] Milan

Meijer, B.H., *Omaggio a Tiziano. Mostra di disegni, lettere e stampe di Tiziano e artisti nordici.* [Exh. cat.] Florence

Merkel, E., "Giorgio Vasari e gli artisti del Cinquecento a Venezia: limiti e aporie di un critico moderno," in *Vasari storiografo e artista. Atti del convegno internazionale di studi.* Florence

Mills, J.S., & White, R., "The gas chromatographic examination of paint media. Some examples of medium identification by fatty acid analysis," in *Conservation and Restoration of Pictorial Art.* eds. N. Brommelle & P. Smith. Butterworth

Muraro, M., "Titien: iconographie et politique," in *Symboles de la Renaissance.* Paris

Muraro, M., & Rosand, D., *Tiziano e la silografia veneziana del Cinquecento.* Venice

Niero, A., "Le tele del soffitto della Sagrestia Grande di Tiziano Vecellio," in *La Madonna della Salute e i suoi seminari* 52, no. 1 (March)

Oberhuber, K., *Disegni di Tiziano e della sua cerchia.* [Exh. cat.] Vicenza

Pallucchini, R., "Presentazione," in *Tiziano e la silografia veneziana del cinquecento.* Eds. M. Muraro & D. Rosand. Venezia

Pallucchini, R., "Tiziano e la problematica del Manierismo," in *Atti dei Convegni dei Lincei.* Rome

Perocco, G., "Tiziano e il mondo politico e sociale di Venezia," in *Atti dei Convegni dei Lincei.* Rome

Petrioli Tofani, A.M., *Omaggio a Leopoldo dei Medici.* [Exh. cat.] Florence

Pozza, N., *Tiziano.* Milan

Rearick, W.R., *Tiziano e il disegno veneziano del suo tempo.* [Exh. cat.] Florence

Rosand, D., *Titian and the Venetian Woodcut.* [Exh. cat.] Washington

Rosand, D., "Titian's *Presentation of the Virgin in the Temple* and the Scuola della Carità," in *The Art Bulletin* (March)

Speck, D., *The Authenticity of a Painting.* Minneapolis

Tassi, R., *Tiziano. Il Polittico Averoldi in San Nazaro.* Brescia

Tiziano per i duchi di Urbino. [Exh. cat.] Urbino

Zampetti, P., "Una lettera dell'Aretino e gli anni di Tiziano," in *Notizie da Palazzo Albani* 1

1976-1977
Catelli Isola, M., ed., *Immagini da Tiziano. Stampe dal sec. XVI al sec. XIX.* [Exh. cat.] Rome

Anderson, J., "*Christ carrying the cross* in San Rocco: its commission and miraculous history," in *Arte Veneta* 31

Barocchi, P., *Scritti d'arte del Cinquecento. I. Generalia. Arti e Scienze. Le Arti.* Turin

Bettini, S., "Il colore di Tiziano," in *Tiziano.* Venice

Cannon-Brooks, P., *The Cornbury Park Bellini. A Contribution towards the study of the Late Paintings of Giovanni Bellini.* Birmingham

Chastel, A., "Titien," in *Tiziano nel quarto centenario della sua morte, 1576-1976.* Venice

Dell'Acqua, G.A., "Tiziano e il Cavalcaselle," in *Tiziano nel quarto centenario della sua morte, 1576-1976.* Venice

Ferrarino, L., "Il caso Tiziano," in *Tiziano nel quarto centenario della sua morte, 1576-1976.* Venice

Ferrarino, L., ed., *Lettere di Artisti italiani ad Antonio Perrenot di Granville.* Madrid

Fisher, M.R., *Titian's Assistants during the Later Years.* New York

Fomiciova, T., "Lo sviluppo compositivo della *Venere allo specchio con due amorini* nell'opera di Tiziano e la copia dell'Ermitage," in *Arte Veneta* 31

Gandini, C., ed., *Tiziano. Le lettere.* Belluno

Garberi, M., "Tiziano: i ritratti," in *Omaggio a Tiziano.* [Exh. cat.] Milan

Harprath, R., *Italienische Zeichnungen des 16. Jahrhunderts aus eigenem Besitz. Staatliche Graphische Sammlung.* [Exh. cat.] Munich

Hood, W., & Hope, C., "Titian's Vatican Altarpiece and the Picture Underneath," in *The Art Bulletin* (December)

Hope, C., "A neglected document about Titian's *Danae* in Naples," in *Arte Veneta* 31

Hubala, E., "Titians Vier Evangelisten Bild in der Nikolaus Kapelle des Dogen-palastes," in *Festshrift Holfgang Braunfels.* Tübingen

Ivanoff, N., "Tiziano e la critica contenutistica," in *Tiziano nel quarto centenario della sua morte, 1576-1976.* Venice

Ivanoff, N., "Tiziano e la critica d'arte dal '500 ad oggi," in *Tiziano nel quarto centenario della sua morte, 1576-1976.* Venice

Meller, P., "Tiziano e la scultura," in *Tiziano nel quarto centenario della sua morte, 1576-1876.* Venice

Mills, J.S., & White, R., "Natural Resins of Art and Archaeology. Their Sources, Chemistry and Identification," in *Studies in Conservation*

Mills, J.S., "Analyses of Paint Media," in *National Gallery Technical Bulletin* 1

Mucchi, L., "Radiografie di opere di Tiziano," in *Arte Veneta* 31

Muraro, M., "Tiziano pittore ufficiale della serenissima," in *Tiziano nel quarto centenario della sua morte, 1576-1976.* Venezia

Pallucchini, R., *Profilo di Tiziano.* Florence

Pallucchini, R., "Tiziano e Filippo II," in *Tiziano nel quarto centenario della sua morte, 1576-1876.* Venice

Perocco, G., "Tiziano e alcuni committenti a Venezia," in *Tiziano nel quarto centenario della sua morte, 1576-1976.* Venice

Pignatti, T., *I grandi disegni italiani nelle collezioni di Oxford. Ashmolean Museum and Christ Church Picture Gallery.* Milan

Pozza, N., "Tiziano e il figlio Pomponio," in *Tiziano nel quarto centenario della sua morte, 1576-1976.* Venice

Puppi, L., "Michelangelo e Tiziano," in *Tiziano nel quarto centenario della sua morte, 1576-1976.* Venice

Puppi, L., "Mito e rappresentazione allegorica in un sogno del luogo di Utopia," in *Veneto.* Milan

Rearick, W.R., "Titian drawings, 1510-1512," in *Tiziano nel quarto centenario della sua morte, 1576-1976.* Venice

Robertson, G., "Titian. The Mythological and Historical Paintings. Vol. III. By H.E. Wethey" (review), in *The Burlington Magazine* (April)

Seymour, C., "A Note on Early Titians: The Circumcision Panel at Yale," in *Studies in Late Medieval and Renaissance Painting in Honor of Millard Meiss.* Eds. I. Lavin & J. Plummer. New York

Stella, A., "La società veneziana al tempo di Tiziano," in *Tiziano nel quarto centenario della sua morte, 1576-1976.* Venice

Valcanover, F., "Il restauro dell'Assunta," in *Tiziano nel quarto centenario della sua morte, 1576-1976.* Venice

Walker Art Gallery Liverpool. *Foreign Catalogue.* 2 vols. Liverpool

Zampetti, P., "Giorgione e Tiziano: considerazioni," in *Tiziano nel quarto centenario della sua morte, 1576-1976.* Venice

1978

Allegri, E., in *Tiziano nelle galerie fiorentine.* [Exh. cat.] Florence

Barocchi, P., *Scritti d'arte del Cinquecento. IV. Pittura.* Turin

Bernabei, F., "Tiziano e Lodovico Dolce," in *Tiziano e il Manierismo Europeo.* ed. R. Pallucchini. Florence

Brigstocke, H., *Italian and Spanish Paintings in the National Gallery of Scotland.* Glasgow

Chastel, A., "Titien et le néo-byzantinisme vénetien," in *Tiziano e il Manierismo Europeo.* ed. R. Pallucchini. Florence

Chastel, A., "Titien et les Humanistes," in *Tiziano e il Manierismo Europeo.* ed. R. Pallucchini. Florence

Chiarini, G., in *Tiziano nelle gallerie fiorentine.* [Exh. cat.] Florence

Dell'Acqua, G.A., "L'ultimo Tiziano," in *Tiziano e il Manierismo Europeo.* ed. R. Pallucchini. Florence

Dionisotti, C., "Tiziano e la letteratura," in *Tiziano e il Manierismo Europeo.* ed. R. Pallucchini. Florence

Fassina, V., "Note sull'identificazione dei leganti nei dipinti," in *Quaderni della Soprintendenza ai beni artistici e storici di Venezia* 7

Germann, G., *Pfaeffikon. Art Vénetien en Suisse et au Lichtenstein.* [Exh. cat.] Geneva

Ginzburg, C., "Tiziano. Ovidio e i codici della figurazione erotica nel Cinquecento," in *Paragone* (May)

Gregori, M., "Tiziano e l'Aretino," in *Tiziano e il Manierismo Europeo.* ed. R. Pallucchini. Florence

Harprath, R., *Italienische Zeichnungen des 16. Jahrunderts aus eigenem Besitz. Staatliche Graphische Sammlung.* [Exh. cat.] Munich

The Illustrated Bartsch. vol. 26. New York

Lazzarini, L., "Lo studio stratigrafico della Pala di Castelfranco e di altre opere contemporanee," in *Giorgione. La Pala di Castelfranco.* Milan

Mills, J.S., & White, R., "Organic analysis in the arts: some further paint media analyses," in *National Gallery Technical Bulletin* 2

Millner Kahr, M., "Danae: virtuous, voluptuous, venal woman," in *The Art Bulletin* (March)

Mucchi, L., *Caratteri radiografici della pittura di Giorgione.* Florence

Muraro, M., "Grafica tizianesca," in *Tiziano e il Manierismo Europeo.* ed. R. Pallucchini. Florence

Nepi Scirè, G., "Giorgione: Nuda," in *Giorgione a Venezia.* [Exh. cat.] Milan

Oberhuber, K., "Tiziano disegnatore di paesaggi," in *Tiziano e il manierismo Europeo.* ed. R. Pallucchini. Florence

Pallucchini, R., "I due *creati* di Giorgione: Sebastiano e Tiziano," in *Giorgione a Venezia.* [Exh. cat.] Milan

Pallucchini, R., "Prolusione," in *Tiziano e il Manierismo Europeo.* ed. R. Pallucchini. Florence

Pignatti, T., *Giorgione. l'opera completa.* Milan

Pignatti, T., "Giorgione e Tiziano," in *Tiziano e il Manierismo Europeo.* ed R. Pallucchini. Florence

Pignatti, T., "Tiziano e il Veronese," in *Tiziano e il Manierismo Europeo.* ed. R. Pallucchini. Florence

Plesters, J., "Titian's Bacchus and Ariadne: the materials and technique," in *National Gallery Technical Bulletin* 2

Puppi, L., "Tiziano e l'architettura," in *Tiziano e il Manierismo Europeo.* ed. R. Pallucchini. Florence

Rapp, J., "Das Tizian-Porträt in Kopenhagen: ein Bildnis des Giovanni Bellini," in *Zeitschrift für Kunstgeschichte* 50, n. 3

Rearick, W.R., *Maestri veneti del Cinquecento.* Florence

Rosand, D., *Titian.* New York

Rossi, P., "Tiziano e Jacopo Tintoretto," in *Tiziano e il Manierismo Europeo.* ed. R. Pallucchini. Florence

Settis, S., *La "Tempesta" interpretata.* Turin

Squellati, F.P., in *Tiziano nelle gallerie fiorentine.* [Exh. cat.] Florence

Sutton, D., "Charles Ricketts' Titian," in *Apollo*

Tenenti, A., "Le trasformazioni urbanistiche di Venezia al tempo di Tiziano c. 1470-c. 1580," in *Tiziano e il Manierismo Europeo.* ed. R. Pallucchini. Florence

Tiziano nelle gallerie fiorentine. [Exh. cat.] Florence

Ulivi, F., "Tiziano e la letteratura del Manierismo," in *Tiziano e il Manierismo Europeo.* ed. R. Pallucchini. Florence

Valcanover, F., "Tiziano Vecellio. Cristo portacroce," in *Giorgione a Venezia.* [Exh. cat.] Milan

Valcanover, F., "Il classicismo cromatico di Tiziano: I. Dagli Affreschi del Santo all'Assunta. II. Dall'Assunta al San Pietro Martire," in *Tiziano e il Manierismo Europeo.* ed. R. Pallucchini. Florence

Valcanover, F., "Tiziano Vecellio: la Giustizia," in *Giorgione a Venezia.* [Exh. cat.] Milan

Walther, A., *Tizian.* Leipzig

White, R., "The application of gas-chromatography to the analysis of Wares," in *Studies in Conservation* 23

Zampetti, P., "Qualche considerazione sul colore di Tiziano," in *Tiziano e il Manierismo Europeo.* ed. R. Pallucchini. Florence

Zampetti, P., "Tiziano e Lorenzo Lotto," in *Tiziano e il Manierismo Europeo.* ed. R. Pallucchini. Florence

Zecchini, M., in *Tiziano nelle gallerie fiorentine.* [Exh. cat.] Florence

1979

Angulo Iñiguez, D., *Museo del Prado. Pintura italiana anterior a 1600.* Madrid

Dreyer, P., *I grandi disegni italiani del Kupferstichkabinett di Berlino.* Milan

Einem, von, H., "Tizians Grabbild," in *Bayerische Akademie der Hissenscheften. Philosophische-Historische Klasse. Sitzungsberichte* 5

Ettlinger, H.S., "The iconography of the columns in Titian's Pesaro altarpiece," in *The Art Bulletin* (March)

Fahy, E., *The Legacy of Leonardo. Italian Renaissance Painting from Leningrad.* [Exh. cat.] New York

Giorgione. Atti del convegno di studio. Castelfranco Veneto

Gli Uffizi. Florence

Smith, C.H., "Michelangelo and Giorgione," in *Giorgione. Atti del Convegno di studio.* Castelfranco Veneto

Ivanoff, N., "Antonio Negretti detto Antonio Palma," in *I pittori bergamaschi dal XIII al XIX secolo. Il Cinquecento.* vol. 3. Bergamo

Lazzarini, L., "Il *Doge Grimani inginocchiato di fronte alla Fede.* note tecniche," in *Quaderni della Soprintendenza ai Beni Artistici e Storici di Venezia* 8

Lazzarini, L., "La *Pala Pesaro:* note tecniche," in *Quaderni della Soprintendenza ai Beni Artistici e Storici di Venezia* 8

Longhi, R., *Disegno della pittura italiana. II. Da Leonardo al Canaletto.* Florence

Meijer, B., "Tiziano nelle gallerie fiorentine," in *Prospettiva* 19

Merkel, E., "Il San Grisogono di San Trovaso, fiore tardivo di Michele Giambono," in *Quaderni della Soprintendenza di Beni Artistici e Storici di Venezia* 8

Mills, J.S., White, R., "Analyses of Paint Media," in *National Gallery Technical Bulletin* 3

Nepi Scirè, G., "La *Fede* di Tiziano," in *Quaderni della Soprintendenza ai Beni Artistici e Storici di Venezia* 8

Nepi Scirè, G., "Tiziano Vecellio. *San Marco in trono fra i Santi Cosma, Damiano, Rocco e Sebastiano,*" in *Venezia e la peste.* [Exh. cat.] Venice

Olivato, L., "Dal teatro della memoria al grande teatro dell'architettura: Giulio Camillo Delminio e Sebastiano Serlio," in *Bollettino del Centro internazionale di Studi A. Palladio* 21

Olivato, L., "Per l'epistolario di Tiziano: una novità e un recupero," in *Paragone* n. 249-351

Pellizzari, P., "Autobiografia nei dipinti di Giorgione," in *Giorgione. Atti del Convegno di studio.* Castelfranco Veneto

Pignatti, T., & Chiari, M.A., *Tiziano. Disegni.* Florence

Puppi, L., "Tiziano e l' 'epopea antoniana' della scoletta del Santa. Nota sui significati iconografici e sulla committenza," in *Il Santo* (May-December)

427

Rossi, P., "Tiziano nelle gallerie fiorentine," in *Arte Veneta* 33

Seracini, M., "La tecnologia al servizio dell'arte," in *Gazzetta Antiquaria* 17, no. 3/4

Shapley, F.R., *A Catalogue of the Italian Paintings. National Gallery of Art*. Washington

The Golden Century of Venetian Painting. ed. T. Pignatti. [Exh. cat.] Los Angeles

Tressider, H., *The Classicism of the early Work of Titian: its Sources and Character*. Ph. D. dissertation. Ann Arbor, 1979

Valcanover, F., "La Pala Pesaro," in *Quaderni della Soprintendenza ai Beni Artistici e Storici di Venezia* 8

1980

Anderson, J., "Giorgione, Titian and the Sleeping Venus," in *Tiziano e Venezia. Atti del Convegno*. Vicenza

Arasse, D., "La signification figurative chez Titien: remarques de theorie," in *Tiziano e Venezia. Atti del Convegno*. Vicenza

Ballarin, A., "Tiziano prima del Fondaco dei Tedeschi," in *Tiziano e Venezia. Atti del Convegno*. Vicenza

Battisti, E., "Di alcuni aspetti non veneti di Tiziano," in *Tiziano e Venezia. Atti del Convegno*. Vicenza

Beguin, S., "A propos de la Sainte Conversation et de la Vierge au lapin de Titien du Louvre," in *Tiziano e Venezia. Atti del Convegno*. Vicenza

Bettini, S., "Linguistica di Tiziano," in *Tiziano e Venezia. Atti del Convegno*. Vicenza

Bonicatti, M., "Tiziano e la cultura musicale del suo tempo," in *Tiziano e Venezia. Atti del Convegno*. Vicenza

Braunfels, W., "I quadri di Tiziano nello studio a Biri Grande (1530-1570)," in *Tiziano e Venezia. Atti del Convegno*. Vicenza

Bresciani Alvarez, G., "Bassorilievo in marmo," in *Alvise Cornaro e il suo tempo*. [Exh. cat.] ed. L. Puppi. Venice

Brown, D.A., "A drawing by Zanetti after a fresco on the Fondac dei Tedeschi," in *Tiziano e Venezia. Atti del Convegno*. Vicenza

Byam Shaw, J., "Titian's drawing: a summing-up," (review of T. Pignatti, *Tiziano Disegni*. Florence), in *Apollo* (December)

Chastel, A., "Titianus Cadorinus," in *Tiziano e Venezia. Atti del Convegno*. Vicenza

Chiarini, M., "Tre dipinti restaurati di Tiziano a Palatto Pitti," in *Tiziano e Venezia. Atti del Convegno*. Vicenza

Chojnacki, S., "La posizione della donna a Venezia nel Cinquecento," in *Tiziano e Venezia. Atti del Convegno*. Vicenza

Clark, K., *Feminine Beauty*. London

Cloulas, A., "Les peintures de Titien conservées a l'Escurial sous le regne de Philippe II," in *Tiziano e Venezia. Atti del Convegno*. Vicenza

Cozzi, G., "La donna, l'amore e Tiziano," in *Tiziano e Venezia. Atti del Convegno*. Vicenza

Creighton, E.G., "Some finding on early works of Titian," in *The Art Bulletin*

D'Argaville, B.T., "Titian's *Cenacolo* for the Refectory of SS. Giovanni e Paolo reconsidered," in *Tiziano e Venezia. Atti del Convegno*. Vicenza

Dreyer, P., "Sulle silografie di Tiziano," in *Tiziano e Venezia. Atti del Convegno*. Vicenza

Fallay-D'Este, L., "L'amour sacre et l'amour profane," in *Tiziano e Venezia. Atti del Convegno*. Vicenza

Fasolo, U., *Tiziano*. Florence

Fehl, P.P., "Titian and the Olympian Gods: the *Camerino* for Philip II," in *Tiziano e Venezia. Atti del Convegno*. Vicenza

Freedberg, S.J., "Disegno versus colore in Florentine and Venetian painting of the Cinquecento," in *Florence and Venice: Comparisons and Relations. II. Cinquecento*. Florence

Furlan, C., "Aspetti del disegno," in *Tiziano e Venezia. Atti del Convegno*. Vicenza

Garas, K., "Qualche ritratto di Tiziano," in *Tiziano e Venezia. Atti del Convegno*. Vicenza

Gentili, A., *Da Tiziano a Tiziano. Mito e allegoria nella cultura veneziana del Cinquecento*. Milan. 2nd ed. Milan 1988

Gentili, A., "Il significato allegorico della caccia nelle *poesie* di Tiziano," in *Tiziano e Venezia. Atti del Convegno*. Vicenza

Gilbert, C.E., "Some findings on early works of Titian," in *The Art Bulletin* 62, no. 1 (March)

Ginzburg, C., "Tiziano. Ovidio. e i codici della figurazione erotica nel '500," in *Tiziano e Venezia. Atti del Convegno*. Vicenza

Gioseffi, D., "Tiziano e il Manierismo," in *Tiziano e Venezia. Atti del Convegno*. Vicenza

Gould, C., "The oriental element in Titian," in *Tiziano e Venezia. Atti del Convegno*. Vicenza

Haskell, F., "Titian-A new approach?," in *Tiziano e Venezia. Atti del Convegno*. Vicenza

Herlihy, D., "Popolazione e strutture sociali dal XV al XVI secolo," in *Tiziano e Venezia. Atti del Convegno*. Vicenza

Hope, C., "Problems of interpretation in Titian's erotic paintings," in *Tiziano e Venezia. Atti del Convegno*. Vicenza

Hope, C., "Titian's role as official painter to the Venetian Republic," in *Tiziano e Venezia. Atti del Convegno*. Vicenza

Hope, C., *Titian*. London

Hope, C., "Tiziano nelle Gallerie fiorentine" (review), in *The Burlington Magazine* 72

The Illustrated Bartsch 24, pt. 1. New York

Lazzarini, L., "Microfotografie," in *Quaderni della Soprintendenza ai beni Artistici e Storici di Venezia* 8

Lehmann, J.M., *Italienische, franzosische und spa-nische Gemälde des 16. bis 18. Jahrunderts. Staatliche Kunstsammlungen Kassel. Katalog I*. Fridingen

Lucco, M., *L'opera completa di Sebastiano del Piombo*. Milan

Magagnato, L., "Tiziano e il teatro," in *Tiziano e Venezia. Atti del Convegno*. Vicenza

Maschio, R., "La sinopia di Tiziano alla Scuola del Santo a Padova," in *Tiziano e Venezia. Atti del Convegno*. Vicenza

Meijer, B., "Titian en het Breriarum Grimani," in *Relations Artistiques entre les Pays-Bas et l'Italie à la Renaissance*

Melcer, W., "L'Aretino' del Dolce e l'estetica veneta del secondo Cinquecento," in *Tiziano e Venezia. Atti del Convegno*. Vicenza

Meller, P., "Il lessico ritrattistico di Tiziano," in *Tiziano e Venezia. Atti del Convegno*. Vicenza

Merkel, E., "Tiziano e i mosaicisti a San Marco," in *Tiziano e Venezia. Atti del Convegno*. Vicenza

Meyer zur Capellen, J., "Beobachtungen zu Jacopo Pesaros Ex Voto in Antwerpen," in *Pantheon* 38, n. 2 (April-May-June)

Muraro, M., "Tiziano e le anatomie del Vesalio," in *Tiziano e Venezia. Atti del Convegno*. Vicenza

Nepi Scirè, G., with technical notes by L. Lazzarini, "La *Fede* di Tiziano," in *Quaderni della Soprintendenza ai Beni Artistici e i Storici di Venezia* 8

Oberhuber, K., "Titian woodcuts and drawings: some problems," in *Tiziano e Venezia. Atti del Convegno*. Vicenza

Olivato, L., "La submersione di Pharaone," in *Tiziano e Venezia. Atti del Convegno*. Vicenza

Padoan, G., "*Ut pictura poesis*: le pitture di Ariosto, le *poesie* di Tiziano," in *Tiziano e Venezia. Atti del convegno*. Vicenza

Padoan, G., "A casa di Tiziano, una sera d'agosto," in *Tiziano e Venezia. Atti del Convegno*. Vicenza

Pallucchini, R., "Tiziano e la problematica del Manierismo," in *Tiziano e Venezia. Atti del convegno*. Vicenza

Passavant, G., "Tizians Darstellungen der Dornenkronung Christi," in *Tiziano e Venezia. Atti del Convegno*. Vicenza

Pedretti C., "Tiziano e il Serlio," in *Tiziano e Venezia. Atti del Convegno*. Vicenza

Pellizzari, P., "I significati di *Amor Sacro e Profano*," in *Tiziano e Venezia. Atti del Convegno*. Vicenza

Perocco, G., "Tiziano e alcuni aspetti della società del tempo a Venezia," in *Tiziano e Venezia. Atti del Convegno*. Vicenza

Perry, M., "On Titian's 'Borrowings' from Ancient Art: a cautionary case," in *Tiziano e Venezia. Atti del convegno*. Vicenza

Petrelli, F., in *Capolavori del Rinascimento italiano*. [Exh. cat.] Tokyo

Petrocchi, G., "Scrittori e poeti nella bottega di

Tiziano," in *Tiziano e Venezia. Atti del Convegno*. Vicenza

Pignatti, T., "Tiziano e le figure della 'Lingua Romana' del Priscianese," in *Tiziano e Venezia. Atti del Convegno*. Vicenza

Pignatti, T., *Tizian. Das Gesamtwerk*. Frankfurt am Main

Pirrotta, N., "Musiche intorno a Tiziano," in *Tiziano e Venezia. Atti del Convegno*. Vicenza

Poirier, M., "*Disegno* in Titian: Dolce's critical challenge to Michelangelo," in *Tiziano e Venezia. Atti del Convegno*. Vicenza

Pozza, N., "La casa di Tiziano a Biri Grande," in *Tiziano e Venezia. Atti del Convegno*. Vicenza

Prijatelj, K., "Tiziano e la Dalmazia," in *Tiziano e Venezia. Atti del Convegno*. Vicenza

Puppi, L., "Tiziano tra Padova e Vicenza," in *Tiziano e Venezia. Atti del Convegno*. Vicenza

Puppi, L., "L'immagine della città," in *Tiziano e Venezia. Atti del Convegno*. Vicenza

Rearick, W.R., "Tiziano e Jacopo Bassano," in *Tiziano e Venezia. Atti del Convegno*. Vicenza

Rosand, D., "Ermeneutica amorosa: observations on the interpretation of Titian's Venuses," in *Tiziano e Venezia. Atti del Convegno*. Vicenza

Rudel, J., "Quelques remarques sur la technique de la composition chez Titien. Schemes et structures plastiques," in *Tiziano e Venezia. Atti del Convegno*. Vicenza

Ruhmer, E., "Tiziano e l'Ottocento," in *Tiziano e Venezia. Atti del Convegno*. Vicenza

Sambo, A., "Tiziano davanti ai giudici ecclesiastici," in *Tiziano e Venezia. Atti del Convegno*. Vicenza

Siebenhuner, H., "Il San Giorgio-Cini," in *Tiziano e Venezia. Atti del Convegno*. Vicenza

Sinding-Larsen, S., "La Pala dei Pesaro e la tradizione dell'immagine liturgica," in *Tiziano e Venezia. Atti del Convegno*. Vicenza

Sinding-Larsen, S., "The columns in Titian's Pesaro Altarpiece," in *The Art Bulletin* (June)

Sterne, M., *The passionate Eye. The life of William R. Valentiner*. Detroit

Sunderland-Wethey, A., & Wethey, H.E., "Titian: Two Portraits of Nobelmen in Armor and their Heraldry," in *The Art Bulletin* 62 (March)

Sunderland-Wethey, A., & Wethey, H.E., "Two portraits of noblemen in Armor and their heraldry, II: Giovanni Francesco Acquaviva d'Aragona, Duke of Atri," in *The Art Bulletin* 62

Tafuri, M., " 'Sapienza di Stato' e 'altri mancati': architettura e tecnica urbana nella Venezia del '500," in *Architettura e Utopia nella Venezia del Cinquecento*. [Exh. cat.] ed. L. Puppi. Milan

Tucci, U., "Venezia industriale e l'Arsenale," in *Tiziano e Venezia. Atti del Convegno*. Vicenza

Valcanover F., with technical notes by L. Lazzari-

ni, "La pala Pesaro," *Quaderni della Soprintendenza ai Beni Artistici e Storici di Venezia* 8

Wazbinski, Z., "Tiziano Vecellio e la 'tragedia della sepoltura'," in *Tiziano e Venezia. Atti del Convegno*. Vicenza

Welliver, W., "The buried treasure of Titian's perspective: the architecture in the *Pala Pesaro*," in *Tiziano e Venezia. Atti del Convegno*. Vicenza

Wethey, H.E., "Tiziano e i ritratti di Carlo V," in *Tiziano e Venezia. Atti del Convegno*. Vicenza

Wolters, W., "Qualche ipotesi sui quadri votivi di Tiziano in Palazzo Ducale," in *Tiziano e Venezia. Atti del Convegno*. Vicenza

Zampetti, P., "Celebrazioni tizianesche, ad Urbino," in *Tiziano e Venezia. Atti del Convegno*. Vicenza

1980-1981
Marchini, G.P., "Il collezionismo d'arte a Verona nel Settecento: la Pinacoteca Mosconi," in *Studi Storici Veronesi Luigi Simeoni*. Verona

1981
Bardi, P.M., *L'opera completa di Velasquez*. Milan

Brejon de Lavergnee, A., & Thiebaut, D., *Catalogue sommaire illustré des peintures du musée du Louvre*. II. *Italie. Espagne. Allemagne. Grande Bretagne et divers*. Paris

Briganti, G., "Signori, il Manierismo non esiste," in *La Repubblica* (29 September)

Coltellacci, S., Reho, I., Lattanzi, M., "Problemi di iconologia nelle immagini sacre, Venezia c. 1490-1510," in *Giorgione e la cultura veneta tra Quattrocento e Cinquecento. Atti del Convegno*. Rome

Dell'Acqua, G., "Il Manierismo a Venezia," in *Arte Veneta* 35

Furlan, C., "G.A. Pordenone," in *Da Tiziano a El Greco. per una storia del Manierismo nel Veneto*. [Exh. cat.] ed. R. Pallucchini. Milan

Hope, C., in *Splendours of the Gonzaga*. [Exh. cat.] London

Lewis, D., "Jacopo Sansovino, Sculptor of Venice," in *Titian. His World and His Legacy*. New York

Mascherpa, G., "L'apparizione di Tiziano fa sbiadire i suoi vicini," in *L'Avvenire* (September 29)

Meijer, B.H., "Titian sketches on canvas and panel," in *Master Drawings* 3

Meyer zur Capellen, J., "Zum Venetianischen Dögenbildnis in der Zweiten Hälfte des Quattrocento," in *Kunsthistorisk Tidskrift* 42

Mills, J.S., & White, R., "Analyses of paint media," in *National Gallery Technical Bulletin*

Pallucchini, R., ed., *Da Tiziano a El Greco. Per una storia del Manierismo nel Veneto*. [Exh. cat.] Milan

Paolucci, A., "La sala della Libreria e il ciclo pittorico," in *Da Tiziano a El Greco. Per una storia*

del Manierismo nel Veneto. [Exh. cat.] ed. R. Pallucchini. Milan

Rearick, W.R., "Venice. Palazzo Ducale e Libreria Marciana" in *The Burlington Magazine* (November)

Romanelli, G., "Il progetto di Sansovino e lo scalone," in *Da Tiziano a El Greco. Per una storia del Manierismo nel Veneto*. [Exh. cat.] ed. R. Pallucchini. Milan

Romano, S., "La vetrata dei Santi Giovanni e Paolo: esercizi di attribuzione," in *Arte Veneta* 35

Rosand, D., "Titian drawings: a crisis of connoisseurship?," in *Master Drawings* 3

Siebenhuner, H., *Der Palazzo Barbarigo della Terrazza in Venedig und seine Tizian sammlung*. Centro Tedesco di studi Veneziani. Studien 5. Munich-Berlin

Sponza, S., "San Giacomo Maggiore," in *Da Tiziano a El Greco. Per una storia del Manierismo nel Veneto*. [Exh. cat.] ed. R. Pallucchini. Milan

Testori, G., "La critica propone. Tiziano dispone," in *Il Corriere della Sera* (16 September)

Valcanover, F., "Tiziano Vecellio," in *Da Tiziano a El Greco. Per una storia del Manierismo nel Veneto*. [Exh. cat.] R. Pallucchini. Milan

Vsevolozhskaya, S., *Italian Painting from the Hermitage Museum 13th to 18th Century*. New York-Leningrad

1982
Benvenuti, F., "Il *Sacrificio del Patriarca Abramo* di Tiziano," in *Titianus Cadorinus*. Vicenza

Birr, F., & Y Diez, J., *Autoportraits*. Paris

Causa, R., ed., *Le collezioni del Museo di Capodimonte*. Milan

Chastel, A., "Titianus Cadorinus," in *Titianus Cadorinus*. Vicenza

Chiappini di Sorio, I., "La donna nell'arte di Tiziano," in *Titianus Cadorinus*. Vicenza

Chiari, M.A., *Incisioni da Tiziano*. catalogue of the Museo Correr. Venice

Concina, E., "Il Cadore al tempo di Tiziano: territori e cultura," in *Titianus Cadorinus*. Vicenza

Delaforce, A., "The Collection of Antonio Pérez Secretary of State to Philippe II," in *The Burlington Magazine*

Fallani, G., "La forza della sua arte," in *Titianus Cadorinus*. Vicenza

Fasolo, U., "Introduzione all'anno tizianesco," in *Titianus Cadorinus*. Vicenza

Giltaij, J., *Titiaan, Jongen met honden in een land schap*. Rotterdam

Hornig, C., "Hans Ost. Tizians Kasseler Kavalier. Ein Beitrag zum hofischen Portrat unter Karl V" (review), in *Pantheon* (October-November-December)

Laclotte, M., & Cuzin, J.P., *Le Louvre. La peinture européenne*. Paris

Lopez Torrijos, R., *La Mitología en La Pintura espanola del siglo XVII*. Madrid

Lowinsky, E., "Music in Titian's *Bacchanal of the Andrians*: Origin and History of the *canon per tonos*," in *Titian. His World and His Legacy*. New York

Mazzorana, G., "Il paesaggio bellunese," in *Titianus Cadorinus*. Vicenza

Mazzotti, G., "Itinerario tizianesco da Venezia a Pieve di Cadore," in *Titianus Cadorinus*. Vicenza

Mendelsohn, L., *Paragoni. Benedetto Varchi's due lezioni and Cinquecento Art Theory*. Ph. D. Dissertation. Ann Arbor, Michigan

Muraro, M., "Tiziano e il Cadore. Aggiornamenti critici," in *Titianus Cadorinus*. Vicenza

Ost., H., *Tizians Kasseler Kavalier. Ein Betrag zum hofischen Portrat unter Karl v.* Cologne

Pallucchini, R., "Tiziano e Filippo II," in *Titianus Cadorinus*. Vicenza

Pignatti, T., "Gli inizi di Tiziano (1505-1511)," in *Titianus Cadorinus*. Vicenza

Pozza, N., "Tiziano fra letterati e committenti," in *Titianus Cadorinus*. Vicenza

Romanelli, G., "Ritrattistica dogale: ombre, immagini, volti," in *I Dogi*. Milan

Rosand, D., *Painting in Cinquecento Venice: Titian, Veronese, Tintoretto*. New Haven and London

Rosand, D., "Titian and the Critical Tradition,". in *Titian. His World and His Legacy*. New York

Rossi Bortolatto, L., "Emblema e allegoria nell'opera di Tiziano," in *Titianus Cadorinus*. Vicenza

Schulz, J., "The Houses of Titian, Aretino and Sansovino," in *Titian. His World and His Legacy*. New York

Semenzato, C., "Tiziano e il Cadore," in *Titianus Cadorinus*. Vicenza

Tieri, M., "Presenze musicali nelle opere di Tiziano Vecellio," in *Titianus Cadorinus*. Vicenza

Titianus Cadorinus. Celebrazioni in onore di Tiziano. Pieve di Cadore 1576-1976. Vicenza

Valcanover, F., "L'anno tizianesco in Pieve di Cadore," in *Titianus Cadorinus*. Vicenza

Zampetti, P., "Omaggio a Tiziano," in *Titianus Cadorinus*. Vicenza

1983

Chastel, A., *Giorgione und Tizian: Landliches Konzert*, in *Bilder vom Irdischen Gluck*, Berlin

Folena, G., "La scrittura di Tiziano e la terminologia pittorica rinascimentale," in *Miscellanea di studi in onore di Vittore Branca*. vol. 3, pt. 2. Florence

Foscari, A., & Tafuri, N., *L'armonia e i conflitti*. Turin

Freedberg, S.J., *Painting in Italy 1500-1600*. 2nd ed. Harmondsworth

Goodman, E., "Petrarchism in Titian. The Lady and the Musician," in *Storia dell'Arte*

Goodman-Soellner, E.L., "Poetic Interpretations of the *Lady and her toilette* theme in Sixteenth Century Painting," in *The Sixteenth-Century Journal* 14, no. 4

Harprath, R., in *Zeichnungen aus der Sammlung des Karfursten Carltheodor. Staatliche Graphische Sammlung*. Munich

Jaffe, M., "Tarquin and Lucretia," in *The Genius of Venice. 1500-1600*. [Exh. cat.] eds. J. Martineau & C. Hope. London

Lazzarini, L., "Il colore nei pittori veneziani tra il 1480 e il 1580," in *Bollettino d'Arte* 5

Lucco, M., "Venezia fra Quattro e Cinquecento," in *Storia dell'arte italiana. Dal Medioevo al Quattrocento*. pt. 2, vol. 1. Turin

Merkel, E., "Giovanni Bellini: 1480-1490," in *Quaderni della Soprintendenza i beni artistici e storici di Venezia* 3

Mezzetti, A., & Mattaliano, E., *Indice ragionato della "Vite de' pittori e scultori ferraresi" di Gerolamo Baruffaldi. Artisti - Opere - Luoghi*. vol. 3. Bergamo

Mills, J.S., "Analyses of Paint Media," in *The National Gallery Technical Bulletin* 7

Nepi Scirè, G., "Il restauro della *Presentazione di Maria al Tempio* di Tiziano," in *Bollettino d'Arte* 5

Nepi Scirè, G., "La Pittura su tela," in *Dal Museo alla Città* 4

Pallucchini, R., "*The Genius of Venice: 1500-1600* alla Royal Academy of Arts di Londra," in *Arte Veneta* 37

Petrioli Tofani, A.M., *Restauro e conservazione delle opere d'arte su carta*. [Exh. cat.] Florence

Ramsden, E.H., "*Come, take this lute.*" *A quest for identities in Italian portraiture*. Salisbury

Richardson, F., in *The Genius of Venice 1500-1600*. ed. J. Martineau & C. Hope

Robertson, G., "Jacopo Pesaro Presented to St. Peter by Pope Alexander VI," in *The Genius of Venice. 1500-1600*. [Exh. cat.] eds. J. Martineau & C. Hope. London

Rosand, D., *Tiziano*. Milan

Scrase D., "Catalogue of the Drawings," in *The Genius of Venice. 1500-1600*. [Exh. cat.] eds. J. Martineau & C. Hope. London

Sesti, E., & Baldi, P., in *Urbino e le Marche prima e dopo Raffaello*. Florence

Sheard, W.S., "Giorgione's Tempesta: External vs. Internal Texts," in *Italian Culture* 4

Shearman, J., *The Early Italian Pictures in the Collection of Her Majesty the Queen*. Cambridge

Spezzani, P., "La *Presentazione di Maria al Tempio* di Tiziano ai raggi X," in *Bollettino d'Arte* 5

Steer, J., "Titian and Venetian colour," in *The Genius of Venice. 1550-1600*. [Exh. cat.] eds. J. Martineau & C. Hope. London

Tanner, M.C., *Titian: the "Poesie" for Philip II*. Ph.D. dissertation. Ann Arbor

Venezia nell'Ottocento. Immagini e mito. [Exh. cat.] eds. G. Pavanello & G. Romanelli. Milan

1984

Argan, G.C., "Il Manierismo nell'arte veneta," in *Cultura e società nel Rinascimento tra riforme e manierismi*. eds. Branca & C. Ossola. Florence

Bolzoni, L., *Il teatro della memoria*. Padua

Cocke, R., *Veronese's Drawings. A catalogue raisonné*. London

Davis, C., "La grande 'Venezia' a Londra," in *Antichità Viva* 2

Fassina, V., "Identificazione dei leganti del Convito in Casa Levi di Paolo Veronese," in *Quaderni della Soprintendenza ai Beni Artistici e Storici di Venezia* 11

Fortini Brown, P., "Painting and History in Renaissance Venice," in *Art History* 7 (September)

Gentili, A., "Due paragrafi per Tiziano e i della Rovere," in *Studi in onore di Giulio Carlo Argan*. 2 vols. Rome

Goldfarb, H.T., "An early masterpiece by Titian rediscovered, and its stylistic implications," in *The Burlington Magazine* 126 (July)

Hoffman, J., "Giorgione's *Three Ages of Man*," in *Pantheon* (July-September)

Ingenhoff-Danhäuser, M., *Maria Magdalena. Heilige und Sünderin in der Italienischen Renaissance. Studien zur Iconographie der Heiligen von Leonardo bis Tizian*. Tübingen

Mason Rinaldi, S., *Palma il Giovane. L'opera completa*. Milan

Matteini, M., Moles, A., Masala, A., & Parrini, V., *Examination through pyrolisis gas chromatography of binders used in painting. Scientific methodologies applied to works of art*. Florence

Niero, A., "Pietà liturgica e pietà popolare nel Vesperbild di Tiziano," in *Studi di storia dell'arte in onore di Michelangelo Muraro*. Venice

Niero, A., "Riforma cattolica e Concilio di Trento," in *Cultura e società nel Rinascimento tra riforme e manierismi*. eds. V. Branca & C. Ossola. Florence

Puppi, L., "Iconografia di Andrea Gritti," in *"Renovatio urbis." Venezia nell'età di Andrea Gritti (1523-1538)*. ed. M. Tafuri. Rome

Rearick, W.R., "Observations on the Venetian Cinquecento in the light of the Royal Academy Exhibition," in *Artibus et Historiae* 9

"Riflettoscopia all'infrarosso computerizzata," in *Quaderni della Soprintendenza ai Beni Artistici e Storici di Venezia* 6

Rosenauer, A., "London. Venice at the Royal Academy," in *The Burlington Magazine* 126 (May)

Ruggeri, V., "La decorazione pittorica della Libreria Marciana," in *Cultura e Società nel Rinascimento tra riforma e manierismi*. eds. V. Branca & C. Ossola. Florence

Sgarbi, V., *Fondazione Magnani-Rocca. Capolavori della pittura antica.* Milan

Tafuri, M., "Politico, scienza e architettura nella Venezia del '500," in *Cultura e Società nel Rinascimento tra riforme e manierismi.* Florence

Trevisani, F., *Restauri nel Polesine. Dipinti: documentazione e conservazione.* Milan

Valcanover, F., "Tiziano e la crisi manieristica," in *Cultura e società nel Rinascimento tra riforme e manierismi.* eds. V. Branca & C. Ossola. Florence

Zampetti, P., "Due mostre e la pala di S. Lio: Lorenzo Lotto, Tiziano, il Manierismo a Venezia," in *Scritti di Storia dell'arte in onore di Roberto Salvini.* Florence

Zampetti, P., "La scuola del Santo," in *Le pitture del Santo di Padova.* ed. C. Semenzato. Vicenza

Zecchini, M., in *Raffaello a Firenze.* Florence

1985

Boehm, G., *Bildnis und Individuum. Über den Ursprung der Porträtemalerei in der Italienische Renaissance.* Munich

Bosque, de, A., *Mithologie et maniérisme: Italia, Baviera, Fontainebleau.* Prague

Brown, B.L., "Giorgione. Michelangelo and *the maniera moderna*," in *Renaissance Studies in honour of C.H. Smyth.* Florence

Howard, D., "Giorgione's *Tempesta* and Titian's *Assunta* in the context of the Cambrai Wars," in *Art History* 3

Humfrey, P., "The Bellinesque Life of St. Mark Cycle for the Scuola Grande di San Marco in Venice in its Original Arrangement," in *Zeitschrift für Kunstgeschichte* 48

Maltese, C., "Il *San Marco in trono* di Tiziano: un approccio sematometrico", in *Prospettiva* 33-36

Marek, M.J., *Ekphrasis und Herrscherallegorie. Antike Bildeschreibungen bei Tizian und Leonardo.* 3. Worms

Meyer zur Capellen, J., *Gentile Bellini.* Stuttgart

Nepi Scirè, G., Valcanover, F., *Gallerie dell'Accademia di Venezia.* Milan

One hundred masterpieces from the Detroit Institute of Arts. New York

Ost, H., "Tizian: Paul III und die Nipoten," in *Wallraf Richartz-Jahrbuch*

Rosand, D., "Exhibition Review: the Genius of Venice," in *Renaissance Quarterly* 38, no. 2

Rosand, D., *Painting in Cinquecento Venice: Titian, Veronese, Tintoretto.* New Haven-London

Schleier, Z., "J. Lehmann. Italienische Franzosische und Spanische Gemälde des 16. bis 18. Jahrunderts. Staatlichen Kunst Sammlungen Kassel. Gemäldegalerie Alte Meister," (review), in *The Burlington Magazine*

Tafuri, M., *Venezia e il Rinascimento.* Turin

Walther, A., *Weltschatze der Kunstder Menscheit bewart.* Berlin

Zampetti, P., "Due Mostre e la pala di S. Lio:

Lorenzo Lotto, Tiziano e il Manierismo a Venezia," in *Notizie da Palazzo Albani* 1

1986

Borghero, G., *Thyssen-Bornemisza Collection. Catalogue Raisonné of the Exhibited Works of Art.* Milan

Chiari, M.A., "Per un catalogo dell'incisione a Venezia (1500-1515)," Doctoral Thesis. Università degli Studi di Venezia

Freedberg, S.J., "Il musicista punito. Il supplizio di Marsia," in *FMR* 45

Ginzburg, C., "Tiziano. Ovidio e i codici della figurazione erotica nel Cinquecento," in C. Ginzburg, ed., *Miti, emblemi, Spie. Morfologia e storia.* Turin

Goffen, R., *Piety and Patronage in Renaissance Venice. Bellini, Titian and the Franciscans.* New Haven-London

Gould, C., "The earliest dated Titian?," in *Artibus et Historiae* 13

Hirthe, T., "Die Libreria des Jacopo Sansovino. Studien zur Architektur und Ausstattung eines Öffentlichen Gebäudes in Venedig," in *Munchner Jahrbuch der Bildenden Kunste*

Hirthe, T., "Le 'Foro all'antica' di Venezia. La trasformazione di Piazza San Marco nel Cinquecento," in *Centro Tedesco di Studi Veneziani* 35

Lehmann, J.M., *Italienische, franzosische und spanische Meister in der Kasseler Gemäldegalerie.* Kassel

Levinson-Lessing, V., *La storia della Galleria della Pittura dell'Ermitage.* Leningrad

Meesterwerken van Westeuropese shilderkunst van de XVI-XIXe eeuw uit de collectie van het Museum Boymans-van Beuningen. Leningrad

Orso, S.N. *Philip IV and the decoration of the Alcázar of Madrid.* Princeton

Petrioli Tofani, A.M., ed., *Gabinetto disegni e stampe degli Uffizi. Inventario 1. Disegni esposti.* Florence

Praz, M., *Mnemosyne Paralléle entre Litterature et Arts Plastiques.* Paris

Puppi, L., "Raffaello e Venezia," in *Studi su Raffaello. Atti del Congresso Internazionale di Studi.* eds. M. Sambucco Hamoud & M.L. Strocchi. Florence

"Restauri a Venezia," in *Quaderni della Soprintendenza ai Beni Artistici e Storici di Venezia* 14

Ricciardi, M.L., "L'Amor sacro e profano. Un ulteriore tentativo di sciogliere l'enigma," in *Notizie da Palazzo Albani*

Sponza, S., "S. Giacomo Maggiore," in *Tesori d'arte nei musei diocesani.* [Exh. cat.] ed. P. Amato. Rome

Walther, A., in *Rinascimento a Venezia.* [Exh. cat.] Moscow

1987

Bergstein, M., "*La fede*: Titian's votive Painting for Antonio Grimani," in *Arte Veneta* 40

Brejon de Lavergnée, A., "L'inventaire Le Brun de 1683. La collection des tableaux des Louis XIV," in *Notes et documents des Musées de France* 17

Camesasca, E., "Il Cardinale Cristoforo Madruzzo," in *Da Raffaello a Goya... da Van Gogh a Picasso. 50 Dipinti del Museu de Arte di Sao Paulo.* Milan

Christiansen, K., "Titianus (per)fecit," in *Apollo* (March)

Hope, C., "The Camerino d'Alabastro. A Reconsideration of the Evidence," in *Bacchanals by Titian and Rubens*, ed. G. Cavalli-Bjorkman. Stockholm

Jaffé, M., *Old Master Drawings from Chatsworth.* [Exh. cat.] Alexandria, Virginia

Jaffé, M., & Groen, K., "Titian's *Tarquin and Lucretia* in the Fitzwilliam," in *The Burlington Magazine* 129 (March)

Nepi Scirè, G., "Tiziano. *La Pietà*," in *Quaderni della Soprintendenza ai Beni Artistici e Storici di Venezia* 13

Rapp, J., "Das Titian-Porträt in Kopenhagen: ein Bildnis des Giovanni Bellini," in *Zeitschrift für Kunstgeschichte* 3

Rapp, J., "Tizians Marsyas in Kremsier. Ein neuplatonischorphisches Mysterium vom leiden des Menschen und seiner Erlosung," in *Pantheon* 45

Scalini, M., *Armature all'eroica dei Negroli.* Florence

Shearman, J., "Alfonso d'Este's Camerino," in *Il se vendit en Italie. Etudes offertes à André Chastel.* Rome

Space in European Art. [Exh. cat.] Tokyo

Studdert-Kennedy, G., "Titian: metaphors of love and renewal," in *World Image* 3, no. 1

Wethey, H.E., *Titian and his Drawings with Reference to Giorgione and some Close Contemporaries.* Princeton

Wolters, W., *Storia e politica nei dipinti di Palazzo Ducale.* Venice

Zeri, F., *Dietro l'immagine.* Milan

Zorzi, M., *La Libreria di San Marco. Libri, lettere, società nella venezia dei Dogi.* Milan

1988

Berce, F., & Boubli, L., *Le Palais Royal de Richelieu aux Orléans.* [Exh. cat.] Paris

Bertini, G., *La Galleria del Duca di Parma. Storia di una collezione.* Bologna

Bora, G., *I disegni della collezione Morelli.* Bergamo

Chiari Moretto Wiel, M.A., "Per un catalogo ragionato dei disegni di Tiziano," in *Saggi e memorie di storia dell'arte* 16

Chiarini, M., *Palazzo Pitti.* Florence

Fortini Brown, P. *Venetian Narrative Painting in the Age of Carpaccio*. New Haven-London

Freedberg, S.J., *Le pitture in Italia dal 1500 al 1600*. 5th ed. Bologna

Hope, C., "La produzione pittorica di Tiziano per gli Asburgo," in *Venezia e la Spagna*. Milan

I Mestieri della moda. [Exh. cat.] Venice

Lawner, L., *Le cortigiane. Ritratti del Rinascimento*. Milan

Lucco, M., "La pittura a Venezia nel primo Cinquecento," in *La pittura in Italia. Il Cinquecento*. ed. G. Briganti. Milan

Maderna, V. "Restauri. La Predica di S. Marco d'Alessandria di Gentile e Giovanni Bellini," in *Brera. Notizie della Pinacoteca* 17

Mason Rinaldi, S., "La pittura a Venezia nel secondo Cinquecento," in *La pittura in Italia. Il Cinquecento*. ed. G. Briganti. Milan

Mills, J.S., & White, R., "Analyses of Paint Media," in *National Gallery Technical Bulletin* 12

Nepi Scirè, G., ed., *Renaissance in Venice* [Exh. cat. Sydney, Brisbane] Rome

Rosand, D., *The Meaning of the Mark: Leonardo and Titian*. The Franklin D. Murphy Lectures 8. Lawrence, Kansas

Rosand, D., "Tiziano: *l'Assunta*," in *Eidos* 3

Rylands, P., *Palma il Vecchio. L'opera completa*. Milan

Valcanover, F., "Profilo artistico," in *La Biblioteca Marciana di Venezia*. ed. M. Zorzi. Florence

Wiedmann, G., "Gaspare Diciani da Belluno. Note su un disegno sconosciuto," in *Arte Documento* 2

Zampetti, P., "Tiziano fino al 1520," in *Tiziano. La Pala Gozzi di Ancona. Il restauro e il nuovo allestimento espositivo*. [Exh. cat.] Ancona

1989
Binaghi Olivari, M.T., "Partita doppia milanese per Tiziano," in *Arte Veneta*. in press

Bull, D., "The *Feast of the Gods*: conservation, treatment and interpretation," in *Studies in the History of Art* 40

Bury, M., "The *Triumph of Christ* after Titian," in *The Burlington Magazine* (March)

Chiari Moretto Wiel, M.A., *Tiziano. Corpus dei disegni autografi*. Milan

Ekserdjian, D., "Piranesi and Titian," in *The Burlington Magazine* (October)

Goffen, R., *Giovanni Bellini*. New Haven-London

Oberhuber, K., "Giulio und die figurilichen Künste," in *Fürstenhöfe der Renaissance. Giulio Romano und die Klassische Tradition*, Vienna

Huse, N., & Wolters, W., *Venezia. Arte del Rinascimento*. Venice

Larivaille, P., ed., *Lettere di Pietro Aretino nel fondo Bongi dell'Archivio di stato di Lucca*. Nanterre

Lucco, M., "*Le tre età dell'uomo* nella Galleria Palatina," Florence

Matteini, M., & Moles, A., "La chimica del restauro. I. Materiali dell'arte pittorica," Florence

Parronchi, A., *Giorgione e Raffaello*. Florence

Pignatti, T., *Venezia. Mille anni d'arte*. Venice

Plesters, J., "The *Feast of the Gods*: Investigation of Materials and Techniques," in *Studies in the History of Art* 40

Prohaska, W., "Concetti anticamente moderni e modernamente antichi. Giulio und die Folgen," in *Fürstenhöfe der Renaissance. Giulio Romano und die Klassische Tradition*, Vienna

Scalini, M., in *Arti del Medioevo e del Rinascimento omaggio ai Carrand 1889-1989*. Florence

Van Titiaan tot Tiepolo. Italiaanse schilderkunst in Nederlands bezit. [Exh. cat.] Rotterdam

Zeri, F., *La percezione visiva degli italiani*. Turin

1990
Caroli, F., & Zuffi, S., *Tiziano*. Milan

Fredericksen, B., *Catalogue of the Early Italian paintings in the Detroit Institute of Art* (in press)

Gentili, A., "Savoldo, il ritratto e l'allegoria musicale," in *Savoldo*. [Exh. cat.] Milan

Pedrocco, F., "Iconografia delle cortigiane di Venezia," in *Le cortigiane di Venezia dal Trecento al Settecento*. [Exh. cat.] Milan

Pilo, G.M., "Rubens e le 'poesie' di Tiziano," in *Scritti in ricordo di Giovanni Previtali. Prospettiva*, 57-60

Pilo, G.M., "Rubens e l'eredità del Rinascimento Italiano," in *Rubens* [Exh. cat.] Rome

Pilo, G.M., & Others, "Rubens e l'eredità veneta," in *Liber Extra I di Arte Documento*

Polverari, M., *Tiziano. La Crocefissione di Ancona*. Falconara

Raffaelli, J.F., *Les promenades au musée du Louvre*. Paris

Zorzi, A., *La vita quotidiana a Venezia nel secolo di Tiziano*. Milan

PHOTOGRAPHIC REFERENCES

Special Exhibition Photography for MODONESI STUDI FOTOGRAFICI S.R.L. BERGAMO by Lodovico Saita and Paolo Stroppa: pp. 7, 11, 13, 15, 19, 21, 58, 69, 73, 74, 76, 91, 95, 97, 115, 136, 137, 139, 143, 153, 171, 173, 174, 185, 186, 195, 197, 215, 216, 217, 221, 223, 229, 241, 243, 247, 259, 260, 261, 262, 263, 264, 265, 268, 271, 277, 279, 281, 283, 287, 289, 309, 313, 315, 319, 321, 325, 333, 337, 365, 366, 367, 375

ARCHIVIO FOTOGRAFICO SOPRINTENDENZA AI BENI ARTISTICI E STORICI, VENICE: pp. 110, 111, 112, 113, 114, 116, 117, 118, 119, 120, 121, 122, 124, 125, 126, 127, 128, 138, 202, 214, 257, 273, 342, 381, 382, 383, 384, 387, 396, 397, 398, 399, 400

ARCHIVIO FOTOGRAFICO SOPRINTENDENZA AI BENI ARTISTICI E STORICI DEL VENETO, VENICE: p. 341

GABINETTO FOTOGRAFICO SOPRINTENDENZA AI BENI ARTISTICI E STORICI, FLORENCE: pp. 145, 147, 189, 249

GABINETTO DISEGNI E STAMPE DEGLI UFFIZI, FLORENCE: pp. 205, 225, 234, 306, 317, 322, 323

ARCHIVIO FOTOGRAFICO PINACOTECA DI BRERA, MILAN: p. 237

ARCHIVIO FOTOGRAFICO MUSEO CORRER, VENICE: pp. 34, 36, 37, 38, 39, 40, 41, 58, 78, 89, 156, 157, 158, 159, 176, 235, 270, 310

VENERANDA ARCA DEL SANTO, PADUA: pp. 9, 155

ARCHIVIO BÖHM, VENICE: pp. 70, 77, 81, 89

ARCHIVIO SCALA, FLORENCE: pp. 56, 86, 88, 96, 98, 344, 345

CAMERAPHOTO, VENICE: p. 103

FOTO TARGHETTA, VENICE: pp. 168, 169

MUSEO CIVICO, ANCONA: pp. 87, 90

FONDAZIONE MAGNANI ROCCA, PARMA: pp. 162, 165

ASHMOLEAN MUSEUM, OXFORD: p. 233

BRITISH MUSEUM, DEPARTMENT OF PRINTS AND DRAWINGS, LONDON: pp. 175, 177

NATIONAL GALLERY, LONDON: pp. 17, 59, 61, 63, 70, 71, 79, 102, 206, 349

THYSSEN BORNEMISZA COLLECTION, LUGANO: pp. 301, 351

GEMÄLDEGALERIE DER AKADEMIE DER BILDENDEN KÜNSTE, VIENNA: p. 362

KUNSTHISTORISCHES MUSEUM, VIENNA: pp. 64, 107, 179, 219, 251

STAATLICHE KUNSTSAMMLUNGEN, KASSEL: p. 291

STAATLICHE MUSEEN, GEMÄLDEGALERIE, BERLIN: p. 237

STAATLICHE MUSEEN, KUPFERSTICHKABINETT, BERLIN: p. 183

STAATLICHE GRAPHISCHE SAMMLUNG, MUNICH: p. 231

MUSÉE DU LOUVRE, PARIS: pp. 191, 193, 211

NATIONAL GALLERY OF ART, WASHINGTON: pp. 75, 199, 200, 201, 239, 245, 253, 275, 303, 304, 305

STATE HERMITAGE MUSEUM, LENINGRAD: pp. 335, 369

THE MARQUESS OF BATH, LONGLEAT HOUSE, WARMINSTER: p. 161

MUSEO DEL PRADO, MADRID: pp. 83, 92, 103, 104, 105, 285, 295, 297, 299, 339, 355, 357

METROPOLITAN MUSEUM OF ART, NEW YORK: p. 329

THE INSTITUTE OF ARTS, DETROIT: pp. 65, 353

MUSEU DE ARTE DE SÃO PAULO (BRAZIL): p. 293

YALE UNIVERSITY ART GALLERY, NEW HAVEN: p. 62

KONINKLIJK MUSEUM VOOR SCHONE KUNSTEN, ANTWERP: pp. 60, 61, 149, 150

MUSEUM BOYMANS-VAN BEUNINGEN, ROTTERDAM: pp. 359, 360

BIRMINGHAM MUSEUMS AND ART GALLERY: p. 60

ART MUSEUM, SAN DIEGO: p. 72

STÁTNÍ ZÁMEK, KROMĚŘÍŽ: p. 371

Color Separations by	AMILCARE PIZZI ARTI GRAFICHE *Cinisello B.* (MI)
Typeset by	CENTRO FOTOCOMPOSIZIONE DORIGO *Padua*
Designed by	T. ZARAMELLA REALIZZAZIONE GRAFICA *Padua*
Printed by	AMILCARE PIZZI ARTI GRAFICHE *Cinisello B.* (MI)
Bound by	LEGATORIA ZANARDI *Padua*

PRINTED IN MAY 1990
FOR MARSILIO EDITORI®, VENICE